WOODROW WILSON

II: World Prophet

WOODROW WILSON

From the portrait by Seymour Thomas hanging in the office of the Governor of New Jersey

WOODROW WILSON

II: *World Prophet*

by

ARTHUR WALWORTH

LONGMANS, GREEN AND CO.

NEW YORK · LONDON · TORONTO

1958

LONGMANS, GREEN AND CO., INC.
55 FIFTH AVENUE, NEW YORK 3

LONGMANS, GREEN AND CO., Ltd.
6 & 7 CLIFFORD STREET, LONDON W 1

LONGMANS, GREEN AND CO.
20 CRANFIELD ROAD, TORONTO 16

WOODROW WILSON

II: WORLD PROPHET

PUBLISHED SIMULTANEOUSLY IN THE DOMINION OF CANADA BY
LONGMANS, GREEN AND CO., TORONTO

FIRST EDITION

LIBRARY OF CONGRESS CATALOG CARD NUMBER 56-12569

Printed in the United States of America

To

Betsy Ross

and

a little "Miss Ellie Lou"

CONTENTS

CHAPTER I

The War Strikes Home

DURING THE MONTHS in which he mourned Ellen Wilson and wooed Edith Galt, the war in Europe haunted the President as "a nightmare" to which he could see no finish.

His first and most immediate responsibility—that of defending neutral rights against the pressures of the belligerents—put him in the position of an arbiter who was challenged to make judgments without benefit of either reliable evidence or a binding code of law. Such precedents as existed had grown out of international conferences at The Hague, the American Civil War, and the Congress of Paris that met in the year of Wilson's birth. But these antecedents seemed vague or definitely obsolete.[1] The President confessed that he saw no shore lights to a channel in which he might sail safely.

His own people were bombarding him with denunciation of atrocities said to have been committed by the contending armies. Lurid stories were given jingoistic play in the press of the United States, and taken up by citizens whose European ancestry made them susceptible to emotional reaction. But the President did not act hastily. When a niece spoke of one of the horrible tales that were in circulation, he said sternly: "The facts are bad enough. Don't repeat such a story."[2] Second thought, he found, often shaded the blacks and whites of morality into grays. It was cruel torture that his will inflicted on his heart; but the very same scholarly sensibility that was wounded deeply by the burning of the Louvain library by Germans restrained him from delivering verdicts on the basis of incomplete and partisan testimony. It would be unwise, premature, and unneutral, he said, for any single nation, no matter how remote, to form a final judgment.

He felt that war could be kept at ocean's length only by hard thinking, not by wishing. Keeping his eye intently on all vital dispatches of the State Department, he took foreign affairs upon his own conscience

[1] Counselor Robert Lansing, preparing to answer possible questions from Congress about the attitude of the State Department toward violations of The Hague Conventions, drew up for the President, on Nov. 23, 1914, three reasons for inaction: (1) that evidence was purely *ex parte* and impartial investigation was impracticable; (2) that a neutral government was not bound to interfere in the actions of belligerents which did not affect its own citizens; (3) that The Hague Conventions did not bind the parties to joint action in enforcing their observance. Wilson's comment on these observations was "sound and wise."

[2] Alice Wilson McElroy to the writer, April 30, 1950.

more closely than ever. He intended to uphold neutrality as rigidly as he had once kept classroom discipline—by immediate action against disturbances and deviations.

It was soon apparent that the Entente looked to the United States for large supplies of munitions, and Germany would need food, copper, and cotton. Wilson must deal, therefore, with commercial impulses that were as great a threat to neutrality as the emotions of moralists.

Before long, it became clear that the credit balances outstanding in America would not be sufficient to pay for the volume of goods needed by the hard-pressed belligerents, and Americans were tempted to stake money on the outcome of the fighting.

At the very outbreak of the war, Bryan had frowned on a proposal of French financiers for getting credits in the United States. Feeling that money was "the worst of contrabands" because it commanded all other things, the secretary of state argued that dollars committed to the service of a belligerent were no more entitled to protection by the nation of their origin than were citizens who enlisted in a foreign army. Moved by this argument during the days when he was distraught by bereavement, Wilson ruled that loans by American bankers to any foreign government that was at war were "inconsistent with the true spirit of neutrality." For a time New York bankers curbed their anxiety to aid France.

Early in October, however, officials of the National City Bank of New York sought a definition of government policy. They proposed to Counselor Robert Lansing of the State Department, who as a New York lawyer had learned to talk the language of the financiers, that to make it possible for foreign buyers to purchase from the United States rather than elsewhere American bankers should grant short-term credits to European governments, both belligerent and neutral, under certain conditions.

Adopting the views of the financiers as his own, Lansing took their statement to the President. Bryan was out of town, and Wilson's confidence in the counselor was sufficient to make it seem unnecessary to consult other advisers. The arrangement set forth by Lansing would neither draw gold from the American people nor result in the commitment of the savings of individual citizens to the financing of foreign war. It seemed to Wilson merely a means of facilitating trade by a system of credits that would avoid the clumsy and impracticable method of cash payments. Also, it offered hope of lifting the nation's foreign trade from the doldrums into which it had fallen. On October 30 the National City Bank announced that arrangements were being completed for a special credit to the French government, setting a precedent for a subsequent series of accommodations to the Allies that reached a total value of $1,900,000,000.

Not only credits, but munitions of war as well, were allowed to flow freely to belligerents. Wilson confirmed as "absolutely right" the contention of those who asserted that it would be unneutral to resort to a ban that might in practice hurt one belligerent more than another. Moreover, he told House that it would be "foolish" to check the trade in munitions because this would discourage American preparedness for the possibility of war. It would be neither practical nor constitutional, he explained, for him to do more than "exercise influence." Thus the way was left open for economic interest to complicate the problem of maintaining political neutrality.

Each armed camp was ready to strain any point of law and usage to check commerce that was suspected of aiding the enemy. To interrupt shipments that might conceivably strengthen their opponents, the British Navy was willing to adopt any measures short of provoking the United States to shut off the flow of supplies essential to the war machinery of the Allies. The Foreign Office was on very insecure ground but held its footing adroitly. Replying evasively to an American attempt to commit all belligerents to the code set forth in 1909 in the Declaration of London,[3] the British government extended its list of commodities that were to be subject to seizure at sea until even foodstuffs were included as "conditional contraband." Furthermore, British Orders in Council proclaimed that conditional contraband was liable to capture even if shipped to a neutral port, unless the shipper could prove that there was no intent that it should reach the enemy.

Britain's interferences with cargoes were obnoxious to Yankees who felt that under the Declaration of London no one had a right to meddle with shipments of staple commodities to the Germans, or with any kind of cargo consigned to European neutrals. American shippers, outraged particularly by Britain's assertion of a right to seize vessels on suspicion and take them into port for search, charged that British interests intended to kill American commercial competition.

[3] The Declaration of London, drafted at an international conference that closed on Feb. 26, 1909, divided marine shipments in time of war into absolute contraband (military goods), conditional contraband (commodities useful to civilians as well as to the military and destined for a belligerent port), and noncontraband (goods not essential for war, such as cotton, rubber, and metallic ores). Though passed by the House of Commons, the Declaration was not approved by the House of Lords and therefore never became binding on Britain.

With Wilson's approval, the State Department urged the belligerents to accept the Declaration of London immediately after the outbreak of war. Germany and Austria acceded, but only on condition that Britain also agreed. Since Britain stipulated conditions that she thought essential to efficient conduct of her naval operations, the understanding never became an instrument of international law. The American government hoped nevertheless that it might serve as a basis of practice; but it was soon apparent that new techniques of warfare were outmoding the Declaration's classifications of contraband.

Wilson did not take British departures from the Declaration of London lightly. The new Orders in Council offended him, and he instructed the State Department to prepare a "vigorous protest—one with teeth in it." The note that was drafted was dispatched on September 26. It directed Page to tell Sir Edward Grey of the "grave concern" of the American government and to suggest that public discussion of Britain's announced policy might "awaken memories of controversies which it is the earnest desire of the United States to forget or to pass over in silence." (Explaining to House that present circumstances and those of the War of 1812 ran parallel, he deplored Madison's folly and said: "I only hope I shall be wiser.")[4]

Meanwhile Page, on his own responsibility, was diluting the force of his government's representations. When pressed by Lansing to make representations to Sir Edward Grey that seemed disingenuous, the ambassador protested frankly and heatedly to his friend in the White House. They were "getting into deep water uselessly," Page complained to Wilson, and the argument seemed "academic" to one close to the life-and-death struggle for the existence of "English-speaking civilization." To ask Sir Edward Grey to accept a code of neutrality that Parliament had rejected even in time of peace, Page explained, was to weaken the foreign secretary's defense of the rights of neutral commerce against the attacks of the Admiralty.[5]

Energetic, magnetic, and wholly charming, Page was a powerful force in guiding public opinion both abroad and at home. Thinking that his envoy was overworked and overwrought, and unduly prejudiced by his immediate environment, the President acted to strengthen Page's loyalty in a way that would not wound his generous heart. Not wishing to reprove him directly, Wilson left it to House to steady and guide him. And then, on the 28th, he wrote, himself, to comfort Page:

[4] Foreseeing that the tone of this dispatch would offend Page and Sir Edward Grey, the Colonel persuaded Wilson that before official action was taken the matter should be explored further in private talks. House conferred with Ambassador Spring Rice, showed him a copy of the offending note, and observed that the British envoy was thoroughly alarmed and felt that one paragraph amounted almost to a declaration of war, and that once the message became public, both nations would be committed to positions that it would be difficult to reconcile and embarrassing to abandon. They prevented official presentation of the stern note and substituted a more tactful statement of the case of the United States.

[5] To make sure that his plaint would be heard sympathetically at the White House, Page sent a message secretly, through his son, to the Colonel: "God deliver us, or can you deliver us, from library lawyers. They often lose chestnuts while they argue about burns. See our friend and come here immediately if the case be not already settled. Of utmost importance . . ." House immediately sent the ambassador's feverish communication to the White House with a cooling statement: "I hardly know to what he refers, but perhaps you do. It may be the Declaration of London matter . . . Page is evidently disturbed."

House received another message from Page, dated Oct. 22, which warned that the ambassador had reached the end of his patience. "The Foreign Office doubts our wisdom and prudence since Lansing came into action," the ambassador reported. "If Lansing again brings up the Declaration of London—after four flat and reasonable rejections—I shall resign."

"You need not doubt, my dear friend, that we comprehend and look into the murky darkness of the whole thing with the same thoughts that you have, though, of course, on this side of the water our own life is, at any rate, still free, and I fancy we can manage a little more perspective than it is conceivable should be obtainable from any point of view on your side of the water. I have been distressed to have to maintain our recent debate with Sir Edward Grey, but it was absolutely necessary . . . if we are to remain neutral and to afford Europe the legitimate assistance possible in such circumstances. . . ." This letter was "not a sermon," Wilson assured Page, but "a message of friendship and sympathy and of sincere appreciation" for the ambassador's vivid letters.[6]

The diplomats were constantly embarrassed by the Admiralty's insistence on detaining, in British ports, American goods that were destined apparently for neutral cities but sometimes, actually, for Germany. Legislators, chambers of commerce, and trade associations badgered the State Department and demanded relief from interferences with cargoes and mails. Americans who sympathized with Germany contended that their government was not being strictly impartial in its protests. Tumulty frankly told his chief that he was being criticized for "letting up on Great Britain"; but looking his secretary squarely in the eye, Wilson replied: "I have gone to the very limit in pressing our claims upon England . . . War with England would result in a German triumph. No matter what may happen to me personally in the next election, I will not take any action to embarrass England when she is fighting for her life and the life of the world."

Unfortunately, salt was rubbed in the wounds when, near the end of October, the British added such commodities as petroleum and rubber to their list of absolute contraband. Moreover, retaliating against alleged planting of mines in the North Sea by Germany, they announced that they themselves would mine certain zones; and at the beginning of November they proclaimed the North Sea a military area into which neutral ships would go at their own risk except in accord with directions from the Admiralty. Protest rose to so high a pitch that

---

[6] W.W. to Page, Oct 28, 1914, Page Papers. Meanwhile Lansing, doubtless influenced by the softening that the flinty contentions of the State Department's lawyers had undergone at the White House, had sent the correspondence on the controversy to the President with a letter of capitulation. "In view of the rigid attitude of the British government," he wrote on Oct. 20, "further attempts to obtain an agreement on the Declaration of London would be useless." Accepting this position, Wilson approved a dispatch that was sent to Page on Oct. 22, bidding him inform his British friends of the concession, and asserting at the same time that the United States would insist upon "the existing rules of international law and the treaties of the United States." The ambassador responded by reporting that within twenty-four hours of the change in American policy every detained ship and cargo but one were released by the British authorities; and he and Sir Edward soon made progress in devising a "working arrangement."

Wilson was forced to take notice. It was now apparent that he must go to the length of issuing a public protest against the vexations that Page had not been able to end by private talks.

Bryan brought a draft of a formal note of remonstrance to the President's desk; but Wilson perceived that it was "in an entirely rough and unliterary form, threatening too." Deleting passages that might give offense, he handed the draft to the secretary of state and suggested that it be rewritten. A few days later, however, Bryan returned with the same text, without changes except those that his chief had indicated. But Wilson swallowed his disappointment and said nothing—"What was there to say?" he remarked in telling a friend of the incident.[7] After he polished the phrasing, the message was cabled to Page on December 26.

This public protest served to demonstrate to neutral shippers that action was being taken to protect their rights. Sir Edward Grey's reply was conciliatory; and the President was content to rest upon the "substantial agreement" on principles that was reached. He felt that it was not worth-while to debate details and he was not unaware that some of the neutral rights now claimed by Americans had been denied by their own government to British traders during the Civil War. Furthermore, he knew that some shippers had made dishonest manifestoes and had concealed contraband goods.

Unfortunately, however, Wilson did not escape detailed litigation with the Foreign Office. Early in January a citizen of the United States named Edward N. Breitung, acting for the German government, availed himself of the American Ship Purchase Act and bought an interned freighter, the *Dacia,* from the Hamburg-American Line with the intention of making shipments to Germany under the American flag. The British government quickly got wind of this transaction. ("Their spy system—'intelligence bureau,' they called it—discovers absolutely everything," Page informed Wilson.) Perceiving that, if the plan was carried out without challenge, it would set a precedent that would perhaps break the blockade, the Foreign Office warned the State

[7] Going over a dispatch written at the State Department at this time, Wilson threw down his pencil and exclaimed: "It's not right to impose such a task upon me." Asked whether he wished another term in the Presidency, Wilson said: "I wish with all my heart that it wouldn't be necessary. I should be much happier doing anything else. If I run again for the Presidency, it will be only to keep Bryan out. I feel like a pig when I sit in my chair and look at him and think, I mustn't let *him* be President; he would be ruinous to the country, ruinous to his own reputation . . . he's the worst judge of character I ever knew, a spoilsman to the core and a determined enemy to civil service reform." House's diary records that when Bryan telephoned to Wilson to discuss patronage and the best means of putting an independent senator "in the hole," the President was amused by the absurdity of the secretary of state's concern with so petty a matter when the world was on fire. When he hung up the receiver he uttered a forceful "damn." Wilson seldom swore, but there were two irritants that could drive him to it—Bryan, and a refractory golf ball.

Department that the ship would be seized if she sailed for a German port.

When the *Dacia* set out on the Atlantic, therefore, the diplomats were thrown into dismay. To be sure, the immediate dilemma was solved when, thanks to a canny suggestion by Page, the French Navy seized and purchased the ship and its cargo. But the President was convinced that the storm aroused was no passing cyclone when he received from Sir Edward Grey a protest so severe that it was designated for his eyes only and those of House.

Woodrow Wilson could say hardly anything now without being accused of favoring one warring alliance or the other. After hours of meditation he sent off to Page, on January 23, one of the longest telegrams that he ever wrote, explaining that the registration of the *Dacia* was no indulgence of German interests, but an affirmation of the constitutional rights of American citizens of German blood. "The great majority of our people," he insisted, "are sensitive about nothing more than about their legitimate trade."

Page was instructed to transmit this message to Sir Edward when a favorable opportunity came and to assure him that the government of the United States would adhere conscientiously to its course of neutrality. The ambassador, however, tucked the note in a pigeonhole and left it there.

There seemed to be only one way to escape the tentacles of controversy that were violating the veil of neutrality, and that was to stop the fight by finding a formula that would satisfy the contending powers. Woodrow Wilson therefore urged his ruling elder to explore the path of mediation.

Colonel House already had put himself on a friendly footing with the foreign offices and with the ambassadors at Washington as well as those at Berlin and at London, and he was ambitious that his great friend should win world-wide renown as a peacemaker. His political instinct told him that discussions might be carried on in private that, if made public or official, would run afoul of jingoism. During the first week of the war House prophesied that Germany was "riding for a fall." He saw that, if a political vacuum developed in Central Europe, it would be exploited fully by Czarist Russia—a view in which Wilson concurred and which he asked House to put before Sir Edward Grey as an argument for immediate peace talks.

Dining with the ambassador of Austria-Hungary, Count Dumba, and listening very well, the Colonel elicited information that Wilson thought "little less than amazing" and "immensely useful as a cross light." The envoy admitted that Germany, dreading that a long war might bring famine, would be ready to consider overtures for peace if only she could first win a decisive victory in France. And at the same time Wilson learned that Ambassador Bernstorff had just told German-American friends that in his opinion Berlin would accept an offer of mediation.

Unfortunately, Bernstorff's informal overture was not guarded so closely as Dumba's frank remark; and when it was reported in the press it lost whatever weight it might have had. For, while neither warring camp could afford to deny that it would cease fighting on what it considered "reasonable terms," yet neither was willing to appear to sue for peace for fear that the world would interpret this as a confession of weakness. Spring Rice hinted that a direct challenge to mediation might be considered by Britain to be an "unfriendly act." Wilson was forced to conclude, therefore, that there was little hope of fashioning a peace out of nothing more substantial than American good will.

Yet he told House that there would be "no harm" in going on with his negotiations; and the Colonel continued the tentative talks. The President agreed that House should keep the secret negotiations in his own hands and concurred in the Colonel's recommendation that "all outside efforts" be discouraged. He was unresponsive to Bryan's plea that the United States, as the leading exponent of Christianity and the foremost advocate of universal peace, should try to fix responsibility for continuing the war and, assuming leadership of world opinion, should urge the warring nations to confer.[8] Bryan's ideals were shared by Wilson and the Colonel; but the President preferred the methods of House. He knew that the Colonel could accomplish more than any official because he could talk and be talked to without commitment.

The envoys of the Central Powers, believing that their fatherlands should consolidate their gains and avoid possible destruction, continued to speak of peace, and Bernstorff fostered House's ambitions. Moreover, the Colonel had an encouraging note from Undersecretary Zimmermann of the Foreign Office at Berlin, intimating that Germany would be glad to listen to any overture that House might elicit from the enemy. This presented an opening, the Colonel suggested to Wilson on December 27: it would be easy now, he thought, to test the reliability of Bernstorff.

[8] Supporting a suggestion by Wilson that munitions be manufactured by a government monopoly, Bryan proposed reduction of armaments, an agreement among nations to respect present boundaries, and compulsory investigation of disputes before hostilities began. His argument was given force by a threat of South American neutrals to act on their own account if the United States did not lead—a challenge in which Wilson saw "dynamite" and which was first parried at a session of the Pan American Union by reference to a commission headed by Bryan, and then met by the proposal of a Pan-American Pact. *See* Vol. I, p. 384 ff.

During January the Colonel made two visits to the White House. On the first of these it was decided that he should prepare to sail for Europe at the end of the month. The friends confessed that their neutrality no longer commanded the respect necessary to keep them out of war and enable them to serve as peacemakers. Wilson was so sure that the Texan wizard would know what to do to restore American prestige that he did not attempt to bind his hands by instructions.

Instead he strengthened the personal bond between them by taking the Colonel into the bosom of the family, reading to him from essays on contemporary great men from the pen of the English liberal, A. G. Gardiner, and diverting him by the sort of high jinks that the clan was accustomed to enjoy when they were alone. McAdoo, sharing in the hilarity, pranced up the marble stairway with legs bowed; and outdoing him, the President followed, not only bowlegged but pigeontoed. Cousin John Wilson said it made his legs ache, they all laughed immoderately, and the President was for a few moments the playboy who did not care whether or not school kept.

The sedulous Colonel recorded every detail in his diary for posterity, and did not fail to note that he was urged to remain another day at the White House, that the President said to him: "You are the only one in the world to whom I can open my mind freely, and it does me good to say even foolish things and get them out of my system."

On January 24 the friends had their last evening together before the Colonel sailed. The President approved what his agent intended to say to the Germans and to Sir Edward Grey, with whom Wilson instructed House to be entirely frank; and when the Colonel asked whether, if a peace conference could be arranged and the President were asked to preside, he would go to Europe, Wilson replied that the American people would desire that he do so. The next day, after House conversed with members of the Cabinet to see whether there were domestic matters that needed his attention before his departure, the friends practiced the use of a secret code that they had worked out; and the Colonel, for the first time, agreed to accept a credit for expenses that Wilson insisted he should have.

When the hour of parting came, they rode to the station and the President walked along the platform to the train, refusing to leave until the agent who carried the best hope for peace disappeared into a car.

The Colonel went first to London. There he took care to explain that he was en route to Berlin, but not as a tool of German diplomats who wished to embarrass Britain by a peace challenge. On February 15 he received from Wilson a report, sent by Ambassador Gerard, that an immediate and tactful proposal to Berlin might yield results. "If peace does not come immediately," the President warned, "a new and pro- tracted phase of war will commence." However, when House told Sir Edward Grey of Gerard's suggestion of haste, the foreign secretary thought it absurd.

Wilson wondered whether the Colonel, like Page, was not falling too deeply under the spell of the English leaders. He suspected that the British were deliberately delaying until they might be in a position to drive a better bargain at the peace table.[9]

When Sir Edward was finally persuaded that the time had come for House to go, the Colonel made his way via Paris into Germany, arriv- ing at Berlin on March 20. It was more than a month since Gerard had reported that the possibility of successful peace talks was "a matter of hours." Now Germany was committed to submarine warfare and hope- ful that this would bring Britain to her knees; and it was the turn of the statesmen at Berlin to discourage immediate talk of peace. Only when the Colonel explained what benefits Germany might expect from an international understanding—and particularly when he outlined conditions for freedom of the seas—did Zimmermann show interest.

Sorrowfully, the enterprising Texan had to conclude that his second mission to Europe was as barren of immediate results as the first had been. "The trouble with Germany," he concluded in a letter to Wilson on April 11, "is that it is antiquated in some of its ideas. They started upon the rule of force at a time when the most advanced nations were going in the opposite direction." And in other letters he reported that some way must be thought out "to let the Governments down easy with their people." The Colonel detected in each of the belligerent camps the feeling that it would be worth-while to hold on for a few months longer in the hope that better terms could be gained.

House's work in Europe, however, was of value both to the cause of peace and to his friend's leadership in that cause. He made friendly contacts not only with statesmen and diplomats, but with other leaders of opinion who shared the ideals of international cooperation that Wilson and the Colonel had been urging upon Pan-American diplo- mats. The Colonel had impressed hardheaded Europeans by his argu- ment for giving the sanction of law to usages that were at the mercy of national whims. However, he saw that the best-laid plans for peace

[9] The Colonel did not deny this possibility; but he had to inform the President that, if he left for Germany immediately, British statesmen would cease to consider Wilson as a mediator. House feared that his friend in the White House could not understand the popular psychoses that were bedeviling the diplomats: the hatred of the United States that existed at Berlin, and the suspicions at London.

might be scuttled by the intransigence of France concerning her eastern frontier, that of the British Empire regarding the right of blockade and the annexation of German colonies, and that of Germany vis-à-vis Belgium.

Thus it became apparent to Wilson that European governments, by and large, were as shortsighted as in the days when his ancestors had sought freedom in the New World. He again rejected a plea from fervent William Jennings Bryan for a public appeal to the belligerents. "I wish I could see it as you do," Wilson confessed to his secretary of state on April 28. "But in view of what House writes me I cannot. It is known to every government concerned that we believe the war should be ended and that we speak for all neutral nations in that wish . . . They are at present most appreciative and cordial,—ready to accept help when they can accept it. We know their minds and we know their difficulties. They are dependent upon their own public opinion (even Germany) and we know what that opinion is. To insist now would be futile and probably would be offensive. We would lose such influence as we have for peace . . . God knows I have searched my mind and my conscience both to get the best, the nearest approach to wisdom, there is in them."

And so the possibility of a cessation of hostilities through American mediation evaporated, if indeed it had existed; and even while House was abroad Woodrow Wilson was forced to wrestle, catch-as-catch-can, with a series of sinister challenges to the peace and security of his own people.

When the President had warned House that "a new and protracted phase of war" would commence if peace was not made immediately, he was responding to a challenge that Berlin had just issued to neutrals. Noting that the Allies had been able to follow the dictate of what they called "imperative necessity" without provoking the United States to war,[10] the German government decided that it too would take a step

---

[10] Wilson listened patiently to arguments that the United States was unjust in feeding Allied guns while permitting Britain to stop a flow of foodstuffs to German civilians. He wrote to Page early in 1915: "The protests made by German-Americans and by a portion of the Irish-Americans, while entirely without justification, are not unnatural. It is difficult for people to think logically when their sympathies are aroused." No one knew how difficult better than he, for he had constantly to guard himself against the tugging of his own personal ties with Great Britain. Nevertheless, the dismal picture of food shortages that was painted by German propagandists was not wholly convincing. He was not disposed to alter the legalistic policy that was based on neutral rights. It did not seem to devolve upon him to compensate Germany for the disadvantages that resulted from her geographical position and inferior naval power.

Ambassador Gerard, who was packing up to be prepared for a diplomatic break, reported that America was the object of a "veritable campaign of hate" in Berlin and that Zimmermann had warned that "in case of trouble" a half-million trained German-Americans would join with Irish-Americans and start a revolution in the United States. This, and subversive activ-

that was beyond the purview of nineteenth-century law. On February 4 it proclaimed that the waters surrounding the British Isles would be considered a war zone in which enemy merchant vessels would be destroyed without any guaranty of safety to crews and passengers; and it added that, in view of the misuse of neutral flags by the British government, ships of noncombatants that entered the forbidden zone would risk torpedoing through mistakes in identity. Though her submarines were ordered to avoid violence to neutral ships in so far as they were recognizable, Germany would give no guaranty against errors.

Already the Germans had offended American opinion by making air raids that killed civilians; and now they proposed an invasion of humane rights on the sea that seemed more reprehensible than the interferences of the British Navy. Yet when Lansing drafted a bitter note of protest to Berlin, the President gave to it the same judicious treatment that he and House had administered to the first drafts of earlier complaints to London. He agreed with the counselor in holding the German government to "strict accountability" for any act that caused the destruction of an American merchant ship or the death of United States citizens. But he added to the text an explanation that the United States was holding all belligerents responsible "for any untoward effects upon American shipping which the principles of international law do not justify," and that representations were being made to London regarding the unwarranted use of the American flag for the protection of British ships.

When Germany responded with an appeal for equalization of her trading position with that of Britain, Wilson sent identical notes to Great Britain and Germany, suggesting that the belligerents reach agreement on the proper use of mines, submarines, and neutral flags, and provide at the same time for the entry of food into Germany under American supervision.

This proposal was rebuffed quickly, however. The Germans demanded imports of raw materials in addition to food, as compensation for giving up their submarine warfare. On the other hand, the British and French let it be known that they were thinking not of relaxing their blockade of Germany, but of making it total; and on March 11 an Order in Council directed that the British Navy intercept and search all neutral ships presumed to be carrying commodities of any kind to or from Germany.

Another note went from Washington to London, protesting against

---

ities by professional German propagandists in New York, made the President even less inclined to cut off the flow of munitions to Britain, or to take other stern measures to reinforce his protests to London.

this severe measure. But two days before, Germany's first overt atrocity against the United States was committed. Several British merchantmen had been sunk previously, but on March 28 the *Falaba* went down with a citizen of the United States aboard.

The American press printed stories of the sinking that lacked extenuating facts and damned the act as "barbarism run mad," a "triumph of horror," "an atrocity against which the civilized world should protest with one voice." The fire of righteous indignation blazed through the land. Counselor Robert Lansing, like Wilson responsive to Presbyterian moral law, allowed emotion to ruffle his legalistic patience. He agreed with the journalists in thinking Germany's act "indefensible both legally and morally." Convinced that certain German officials thought it advantageous to their country to provoke war with the United States, he wished to instruct Ambassador Gerard to protest promptly and vigorously and to demand that Germany disavow the "wanton act" and punish the officer responsible for it.

William Jennings Bryan, however, was bound to question any public policy that threatened the peace of his people. He tempered Lansing's fiery denunciations with a series of questions. Was there not some force in the argument of contributory negligence? he asked. Was there, after all, some inconsistency in the position of a government that had warned its citizens to flee trouble in Mexico but failed to discourage travel on ships liable to torpedoing? Could the American people be asked to risk war in behalf of an individual whose action might be considered reckless? The secretary of state wrote repeatedly to keep his doubts before the President, and suggested that the victim of the *Falaba* sinking was not "differently situated from those who by remaining in a belligerent country assume the risk of injury."

Wilson himself was inclined to temporize. He thought it best to "compound policy with legal right in wise proportion." Professing the "greatest anxiety" about the case, he expressed to Bryan a desire for further details and for an opportunity to give his thoughts "time to settle" before taking action. He raised, too, a very pertinent and vital question: in view of the fact that the British government had advised merchantmen to arm themselves against submarines and ram them whenever possible, was the German commander who sank the *Falaba* perhaps justified in assuming that this ship was an armed adversary that could not safely be visited and searched? The peculiar vulnerability of submarines to ramming and small-gun fire was a factor not yet taken into account by international law.

Many courses were considered, and notes were drafted and not sent. Wishing to uphold the right of his people to trade and travel in peace, and at the same time fearful of giving offense unnecessarily to any belligerent, Wilson shrank from decisive action and took refuge in spiritual prophecy. Convinced that the root of the evil was in the human soul, he said to Southern Methodists on March 25: "Wars will never have any ending until men cease to hate one another, cease to be jealous of one another, get that feeling of reality in the brotherhood of mankind which is the only bond that can make us think justly of one another and act righteously before God himself."

Persisting on his exalted plane of aspiration, Wilson spoke prophetically to members of the Associated Press. "My interest in the neutrality of the United States," he declared, "is not the petty desire to keep out of trouble . . . I am interested in neutrality because there is something so much greater to do than fight; there is a distinction waiting for this Nation that no nation has ever yet got. That is the distinction of absolute self-control and self-mastery." He was no more ready than Bryan to risk war because of the death of one American citizen; nor would he allow himself to be drawn into a controversy over the manner in which it had happened.

As the President pondered over the phraseology of a note of protest that Lansing had drafted at his suggestion, news came of violence done to two American vessels by Germany. One was attacked by a seaplane; the other was torpedoed by a submarine and three lives were lost.

Lansing was now ready to go to the limit in moral fulmination. He was the more outraged because on May 1, under a newspaper advertisement of the sailing of the Cunard liner *Lusitania,* appeared a notice from the German embassy that concluded with this warning: "Travellers sailing in the war zone on ships of Great Britain or her allies do so at their own risk." The counselor considered the release of such an announcement, without approval by the State Department, to be not only "highly improper" but even "insolent." But Bryan, in forwarding Lansing's ideas to the President, continued to question the right of individual travelers to involve their country in war and accepted the German warning as evidence of a friendly desire to avoid trouble.

Wilson could not escape the force of Lansing's contention. And yet he listened carefully to Bryan, for he was impressed by the sincerity of the man's convictions and by the vitality of the popular roots from which they stemmed. After a long talk with the secretary of state on May 4, Wilson hoped to satisfy public opinion and at the same time avoid war by making a strong protest to Germany, and then, if it were ineffective, deferring his claims until the end of the war.

On May 7 occurred the calamity that Wilson had dreaded—a deed that turned American sentiment against Germany with a violence that could never be overcome. Soon after the close of the Cabinet meeting on that day, and before he could start on his afternoon automobile ride, the President was handed a terse cablegram reporting that the *Lusitania* had been sunk by a submarine. One hundred and twenty-eight Americans were lost, among them thirty-seven women and twenty-one children. The ship was unarmed and was unprotected by a convoy, carried no troops, but had thousands of cases of ammunition in her hold.

When news of the disaster reached Wall Street, stock prices fell abruptly. In the view of the American press the act was palpably a slaughter of innocents, a barbarity without precedent in modern times. The mail sacks coming to the executive offices bulged with protests and resolutions from the citizens. Would the President hold Germany to the "strict accountability" that he had proclaimed?

Woodrow Wilson was stunned. He did not trust himself to express his thoughts, but left the White House quickly and walked a long way, alone, until his wrath was under control. Later he accepted Dr. Grayson's prescription of golf as usual.

When Tumulty tried to give "the Governor" a lurid account of the tragedy, Wilson silenced him, explaining that if he gave too much heed to heart-rending news stories he would "see red in everything" and could not act justly. He was not afraid to lead the nation to fight, he said, but he must not do it hastily or prematurely. If he went to the Congress the next day and asked for a declaration of war, he would be supported; but when the casualty lists came and people read them, might they not wonder why their President had rushed into war with Germany after he had been so indulgent of Great Britain, why he did not first exhaust every possibility of peaceful settlement? When he moved against Germany—and he now felt that he might eventually be forced to move—he wanted his people to be united and enthusiastic for a crusade. Moreover, he was governed by a sense of trusteeship not only to his own people, but to the whole civilized world. He foresaw that if the United States, the only mighty nation still standing aloof, were to join in the fight, civilization might be bankrupt in every respect.

He left his desk on the evening of May 10 to fulfill a promise to speak at Philadelphia to several thousand citizens who had just been naturalized. These immigrants before him were men whom Congress wished to exclude unless they could prove themselves literate; but by an executive veto Wilson had redeemed a political pledge and had kept the door open to the educational opportunities that his nation offered.

He began nervously, rocking back and forth on his heels, and his hands plucked at his lapels and his pockets. ". . . A man who thinks of himself as belonging to a particular national group in America has not yet become an American," he said, "and the man who goes among you to trade upon your nationality is no worthy son to live under the Stars and Stripes. . . . America was created to unite mankind by those passions which lift and not by the passions which separate and debase . . ."

Then he made one of his rare platform errors. He used a sentence against which Tumulty had warned him: "There is such a thing as a man being too proud to fight." And he went on to say: "There is such a thing as a nation being so right that it does not need to convince others by force that it is right."

The speech at Philadelphia was acclaimed by peace-loving citizens, and particularly by the press of the South and West. But political opponents and partisans of Britain cited the words "too proud to fight" as evidence of poltroonery. On the day after his *faux pas* the President, wishing that he had either avoided the offensive phrase or developed it more fully, let it be known that his address was not a declaration of policy in regard to the *Lusitania* case. It was merely an expression of "a personal attitude," he explained in his news conference.

Tumulty had never seen "the Governor" more serious than when he sat down alone to write a note of protest to Berlin. This was a charge too solemn to be delegated to another conscience.

By the time Wilson was ready to bring his draft before the Cabinet, on the morning of May 11, he had received an expression of regret from Bernstorff for the loss of American lives; and a dispatch from Berlin gave assurance that submarine attacks on neutral ships were contrary to orders and that regrets and compensation for mistakes would be tendered when justified.

Accepting the German assurances, repeating the argument of his February note of protest against the submarine blockade, and enumerating the grievances of his people, Wilson did not break diplomatic relations or deliver an ultimatum with a time limit, as bellicose citizens thought that he should. Rather he asserted that his government confidently expected that Germany would disavow the acts of which the United States complained, that she would "make reparation as far as reparation is possible for injuries which are without measure," and that she would take immediate steps to prevent the recurrence of "anything so obviously subversive of the principles of warfare for which the Imperial German Government have in the past so wisely and so firmly contended."

After the Cabinet deliberated for three hours, and Lansing and Bryan made suggestions that were accepted, Wilson was finally ready to release the protest. Bryan, however, wrote twice to the President of his qualms. "With a heavy heart," and in order to give direction to public opinion, he agreed that they should immediately send the note prepared. But he wanted to issue a supplementary statement that would call attention to the fact that Germany had conditionally endorsed the principle of the Bryan "cooling-off" treaties and consequently that there would be a year's time for investigation of the current dispute.

Wilson concluded that it might be wise, when the note of protest was released from the State Department, to give out at the same time from his office an interpretive "tip" such as Bryan had proposed. He even went so far as to compose a draft of such a statement and send it to the secretary of state.

However, Lansing and Tumulty saw dire perils in this scheme. Lansing warned that his own position was "becoming difficult," which might have been taken as an intimation that he would resign if the "tip" were released; and Secretary of War Garrison also opposed any qualification of the note. Tumulty was thoroughly alarmed, feeling that if Bryan's scheme were carried out, Wilson would be accused by his own people of double-dealing and Germany would infer that the United States would not fight for her rights. In what he described afterward as "the worst half hour of my life," Tumulty persuaded the President to reverse his decision, though Wilson at first insisted that Bryan could be trusted as a judge of public opinion.[11]

The *Lusitania* note was effective both at home and in Britain, and restored to a degree whatever prestige the President had lost by use of the phrase "too proud to fight." By and large, the public men of the nation stood behind him, and the press exulted.

Wilson acknowledged the response to his leadership in a letter to Nancy Toy: "I am deeply touched and rewarded above my desert by the extraordinary and generous support the whole country has given me. . . ." But with his gratitude he felt a "sense of overwhelming responsibility" and he was haunted again by the oft-recurring dread that someday he might have to sacrifice popularity, if his conscience should lead one way and the will of the people another.

When the reply from Berlin disputed the contention that the *Lusitania* had been unarmed, and claimed that the liner was in fact an auxiliary cruiser of the British Navy, the press of America immediately lashed out at the tone of this response. After making a Memorial Day address at Arlington, Wilson went to work at once on the drafting of

---

[11] For further information about the abortive supplement to the first *Lusitania* note and Lodge's use of the incident in the 1916 election campaign, *see* Blum, *Tumulty*, p. 97 and n.; Garraty, *Lodge*, pp. 329–32; Baker, V, 340–41 and n.; and p. 63n. below.

a second protest. He labored late into the evening; and the next morning, after a news conference in which he calmly refused to discuss the German reply, he met his Cabinet and read his draft to them.

Bryan came late to the meeting, and sat back in his chair and let his eyelids droop. He seemed to be straining to control himself; but when his colleagues turned down his suggestion of a counterprotest to London, he charged that they were not neutral.

Wilson resented this. His eyes turned to steel as he said: "Mr. Bryan, you are not warranted in making such an assertion. We all doubtless have our opinions in this matter, but there are none of us who can justly be accused of being unfair."

When the dissenter asked heatedly whether they were prepared to bend the knee to England, members of the Cabinet buttressed their chief's position by explaining that exports of cotton and foodstuffs to Europe had not been stopped, but had increased during the past months. But William Jennings Bryan was not a man to be convinced by economic statistics. At the end of the session he told the President that he could not bring himself to sign the second note, that it was unfair for him to remain in the Cabinet. He was convinced now that he was being asked to give to Germany the power to plunge his people into war. And so he denounced the proposed protest as a reversal of established policy. During the days that followed he persisted in bringing his arguments to bear upon the President. Wilson continued to listen respectfully, but had less and less sympathy for the Great Commoner's efforts to cooperate with Ambassador Bernstorff in giving the German Foreign Office "a way out."

The day after the grueling session of the Cabinet, he received Bernstorff. Though willing to negotiate, the President was determined not to give any hint of compromise. But he made it clear that, if Germany would voluntarily give up her inhumane tactics, he would try again to persuade the British to relax their blockade.

Two days later, on June 4, when he met his Cabinet again, the discussion was confused and tiresome. Wilson gave evidence that his patience was sorely tried and he seemed too weary to give leadership. He had no heart, either, to argue with Bryan. It had always been difficult for him to beg a man whom he respected to change a decision that was arrived at prayerfully.

The next day McAdoo came to his father-in-law to report that Bryan, haggard and nervous from lack of sleep, had confided that he proposed to resign and that he wanted to do it in a way that would embarrass the Administration as little as possible. He had just received support for his position from Democratic leaders in Congress, and hoped that their letters and the threat of his own resignation might move the President.

McAdoo had sought the aid of Mrs. Bryan. From her he had learned that, while the President wrote the most important notes and directly consulted the counselor of the State Department, while House negotiated with ambassadors who got no satisfaction from the secretary of state, Bryan had felt neglected and had tired of playing the role of a figurehead.

Wilson was not surprised. Actually, he had been embarrassed by Bryan's ineptness for some months and had been careful not to reveal the extent of his dependence on House, fearing that the secretary of state's feelings would be hurt. The President had intimated to the Colonel, near the end of 1914, that if his "elder son" ever wished to leave his office because of a disagreement on policy, it might be wise to let him go. And now, when he spoke to Edith Galt of the disaffection of Bryan—a man whom Ellen Wilson had worked to bind in loyalty to the Chief—Mrs. Galt begged him to accept a resignation if it were offered, "and thank God for the chance." But the crisis with Germany was so acute that the President feared the effect on the opinion of the world, and especially that of Germany, if Bryan were to step out immediately.

The Great Commoner came to the White House for one last effort at conversion, and the Presbyterian prophets confronted each other for the last time with their most persuasive arguments. Wilson said again that Bryan's fears were exaggerated, that his resignation would complicate the perils that did exist. Asking for a glass of water, the Great Commoner raised it to his lips with a hand so unsteady that it spilled. "Colonel House has been Secretary of State, not I," Bryan said, "and I have never had your full confidence. I know you are busy, and I will not detain you longer." They rose and clasped hands, and each said a "God bless you." [12] The secretary of state went home and wrote out a courteous but formal letter of resignation. On June 8 the President received it and announced its import to his Cabinet. Bryan came to the meeting and, taking his colleagues to lunch afterward, evoked their pity. Though Wilson did not attend this party, he contributed a felicitous letter to the send-off of the dissenting brother.

That evening, as newsboys were crying the resignation of the secretary of state, Wilson gave his attention to the note that Bryan would

[12] As recorded by W. C. Williams in *William Jennings Bryan*, p. 387; House Diary, June 24, 1915. During the summer of 1915 Bryan called at the White House; but he and, particularly, Mrs. Bryan were so hurt by the coolness of their reception that the Great Commoner vowed never to darken the doors of the mansion again while Wilson was there. House Diary, Sept. 14, 1915.

not sign. It was released on June 9 over the signature of Robert Lansing, secretary of state *ad interim*. Its tone indicated that the nation's policy was to be dictated neither by jingoes nor by those who sought peace at any price. Public opinion, except that tinged by German sympathies, back the President as solidly as had the Cabinet.

In this message Wilson showed his genius for extracting from a legalistic dispute those elements that could give it historic significance for humanity. He served notice to the world that the United States would expect the new weapons of the age to be used with the same regard for fair play and civilian rights that the usages of civilization had stipulated in nineteenth-century warfare. Brushing aside the assertions about the status of the *Lusitania* that Germany had made and that he did not accept, Wilson asserted that he was setting forth principles that lifted the case "out of the class of ordinary subjects of diplomatic discussion or of international controversy." There was an intimation that an ultimatum might follow if Germany did not give certain assurances.

This note reached Berlin at a time when there was a controversy between the naval authorities and the Foreign Office. Finally the Emperor was persuaded that submarine commanders should spare all large passenger ships and that no vessel should be attacked unless it was positively identified as hostile. Orders to this effect were given during the first week of June, but they were kept secret for fear that the world might interpret them as a sign of German weakness.[13]

When Germany's reply to the second *Lusitania* note arrived on July 8 it was analyzed by Lansing, who had become secretary of state. A quiet, philosophic gentleman, Lansing was to be—in the words of Secretary Houston—merely "the President's Private Secretary for Foreign Affairs." Wilson explained to his new appointee that experience and training were far more vital than political background, especially under present conditions; and, moreover, Lansing seemed to him young enough to adapt his thinking to changing conditions.

The President was not satisfied by Berlin's reply to the second *Lusitania* note. The imperial government still held that its duty "to protect and save the lives of German subjects" took precedence of its obligation to "the interests of neutrals." The old plaints against the British blockade and the "starvation" of Germans were repeated. The note explained that Germany would not allow American citizens to protect British

---

[13] Ambassador Gerard, who found the Kaiser "rabid" on the subject of shipments of American arms to the Allies, transmitted to Lansing, on June 24, a German suggestion that the Admiralty might be persuaded to agree to offer security to merchant vessels carrying passengers if the President would favor a guaranty that such ships would not carry arms and ammunition; but Wilson replied that this was "entirely unwise, or, at the least, impossible of acceptance."

vessels by their presence as passengers, but it offered to cooperate in safe-guarding American ships under certain conditions.

Wilson warned Gerard that the question was entirely one of principle and would not admit of compromise. Lansing advised that it was "well nigh impossible" to avoid war and at the same time force Germany to yield; and public sentiment plainly was growing more hostile to Germany. Yet Wilson persisted in hoping that firmness might bring peace. He felt that the Germans were modifying their methods, but should be made to feel that they must continue in their new way unless they deliberately wanted to provoke war.

At the same time Gerard, at Berlin, was finding it difficult to present a bold front to German officials who made light of America's will and power to fight. "They feel that our 'New Freedom' is against their ideas and ideals," he wrote on July 20, "and they hate President Wilson because he embodies peace and learning rather than caste and war."

With the aid of Lansing, the President drafted a third *Lusitania* note that was calculated to put an end to the correspondence that critics had begun to ridicule for its length and inconclusiveness. Calling the most recent communication from Berlin "very unsatisfactory," Wilson pointed out that the German government regarded itself as in large degree exempt from observing principles to which it subscribed. In conclusion, he warned that his government would feel impelled to insist very solemnly on the scrupulous observance of neutral rights; and he served notice that further sinkings in contravention of those rights "must be regarded, when they affect American citizens, as deliberately unfriendly."

The third *Lusitania* note, sent off to Berlin on July 21, was, if not an ultimatum, at least the last word of the United States on the subject. If the message left any doubt about the finality of the American position, Lansing removed it with blunt remarks to Ambassador Bernstorff. The secretary of state warned that war could not be avoided if American lives were lost in another torpedoing of a merchant ship.

Just before this, Wilson had urged House to work with Bernstorff and "to make him feel not only that some way should be found, but that some way *must* be found," that his government owed it to itself and the rest of the world to help find it. Persuaded by House that Wilson did not want war and was not swayed by pro-British opinion, Bernstorff reported this to his Foreign Office, at the same time giving assurance that if Germany met America's demands Wilson would then prosecute his case against England strenuously.

But at this very time McAdoo, having been instructed by the President to put the Secret Service on the trail of violators of neutrality, and

hoping to frighten foreign spies and propagandists operating in the
United States, revealed hostile activities on the part of Germans at New
York. Wilson himself was sure that his country was "honeycombed
with German intrigue and infested with German spies." When the
telephone wires of the German and Austro-Hungarian embassies were
tapped and conversations were found to contain unflattering references
to high officials, Wilson found it hard to cling to the measure of faith
that he still retained in the good will of Germany.

Gerard reported that Wilson's latest *Lusitania* note was received with
hostility by the German press and by a government now dominated by
the party of frightfulness. On the other hand, immoderate persecution
of American citizens of German blood made it difficult for Bernstorff to
feel that the United States was impartial.

On August 19 occurred the inevitable accident for which diplomats
were waiting. The *Arabic,* a British merchantman bound for New
York and therefore carrying no contraband, was sunk without warning
by a submarine. Two Americans were lost. This seemed to be the overt
act that the third *Lusitania* note had warned against; and it was regarded by Bernstorff and the American press as cause for at least a
diplomatic break.

At this juncture there was a turn toward moderation in German
policy. The American government was informed at last of the orders
issued secretly at Berlin in June against ruthless sinkings; public assurance was given that just compensation would be forthcoming; and the
State Department was urged to refrain from drastic steps until particulars of the *Arabic* case could be ascertained.

Again Wilson was the target of contending voices. He looked askance
at the "extraordinary stuff" that was coming in dispatches from his
somewhat bumptious ambassador at Berlin.[14] At the same time he suspected that Berlin's apparent yielding was merely a sparring for time;
and he informed House that he trusted neither the accuracy nor the
sincerity of Bernstorff. Finally, he told Lansing that they must demand
satisfaction at once.

---

14 Wilson's irritation at the tactlessness of Gerard mounted after the sinking of the *Arabic*.
When his ambassador suggested that the President retaliate against Bernstorff for indignities
suffered by Gerard at Berlin, Wilson wrote on a slip: "Ordinarily an ambassador ought to be
backed up as a matter of course, but—this ass? It is hard to take it seriously." On another
dispatch from Gerard regarding German politics, Wilson jotted: "Who can fathom this? I
wish they would hand this idiot his passports!" His comment on still another message was a
large black exclamation mark.

At the same time the President was dissatisfied with Page's attitude. On Sept. 10, 1915,
almost a year since the ambassador at London had sent his protest about "library lawyers"
who allowed chestnuts to burn, Wilson pinned this handwritten comment to a dispatch from
Page: "I wish Page could feel a little more strongly that we are acting upon our own convictions and not upon English opinion. Of course they want us to pull their chestnuts out of the
fire."

On his own responsibility the secretary of state delivered an oral ultimatum to Bernstorff on August 27, telling the ambassador that the time for debating the question of submarine warfare had passed, that unless the German government frankly declared that there would be no more surprise attacks on vessels carrying passengers, and lived up to that declaration, the United States would certainly declare war. Lansing had not told the President of his intention to say this; for he wished to be able, if his bluff was called, to withdraw gracefully from his threat by revealing that the President had not sanctioned it.

Fortified by Bernstorff's reports of the severity of the crisis at Washington, the German Foreign Office was able to persuade the Kaiser to overrule the Admiralty and stop the tactics to which the United States objected. Moreover, under pressure from Lansing, Bernstorff exceeded his orders. On September 1 he gave this assurance to the secretary of state in writing: "Liners will not be sunk by our submarines without warning and without safety to the lives of non-combatants, provided that the liners do not try to escape or offer resistance . . ."

Still Wilson was not satisfied. Feeling that the German government was deliberately moving with exasperating slowness, Wilson let Bernstorff know that he would not be content with anything less than an explicit disavowal of the attack on the *Arabic*. "Shall we ever get out of the labyrinth made for us by all this German 'frightfulness'?" he asked House. And on September 17 he wrote: "The country is undoubtedly back of me in the whole matter, and I feel myself under bonds to it to show patience to the utmost. My chief puzzle is to determine when patience ceases to be a virtue."

Meanwhile the circumstances of the sinking of the *Arabic* were established by the German government. Willing to concede that their submarine commander had acted "unfortunately not in accordance with instructions," they agreed to reprove him and indemnify the United States. Their pride, however, held them back from a frank admission of responsibility.

Lansing and Wilson agreed that the statement from Berlin was inadequate and were inclined to send Bernstorff home. But the secretary of state again raised the bludgeon of war over the envoy's head; and Bernstorff, convinced that only by a precise disavowal could a break be avoided, took it upon himself again to stretch his authority in the interest of peace. The Kaiser's orders to submarine commanders, he wrote to the State Department on October 5, had been "made so stringent that the recurrence of incidents similar to the Arabic case is considered out of the question. . . . The Imperial Government regrets and disavows this act . . ." Though there was still no disavowal of the sinking of the *Lusitania,* Woodrow Wilson had fought his long battle with the German Admiralty to a state of suspension.

By the end of 1915 Woodrow Wilson knew that a world at war had no comfortable place for a self-respecting neutral. The greater his restraint toward one contender, the greater the indignation shown by the other. The Germans repeatedly had tried to divert attention from their own offenses by pointing a finger at Britain's maritime policy; and while the *Lusitania* notes were being exchanged, the mood of the British public had been resentful of the President's patience.

It was plain by the end of 1915 that Wilson's notes of protest to Germany and the remonstrances to Britain were inconclusive in enforcing neutral rights. And the longer American complaints went unsatisfied the less seriously the belligerents took them. They could see that the United States was becoming for the first time a creditor nation, that the rewards of peace were sufficient to restrain America from taking part in European quarrels after keeping clear of them for a century.

During his honeymoon at Hot Springs, in the first week of 1916, Woodrow Wilson took time to think deeply, and with long perspective. Called back suddenly to Washington by the torpedoing of the British liner *Persia,* he found Tumulty panicky.

"I have made up my mind," the President said to his secretary, "that I am more interested in the opinion that the country will have of me ten years from now than the opinion it may be willing to express today. Of course, I understand that the country wants action, and I intend to stand by the record I have made in all these cases, and take whatever action may be necessary, but I will not be rushed into war, no matter if every last Congressman stands up on his hind legs and calls me a coward. . . . I believe that the sober-minded people of this country will applaud any efforts I may make without the loss of our honour to keep this country out of war."

His tough-fibered patience had endured the arrogance and espionage of Prussians, the gibes of English and French nationalists and their American friends, the quibbles of legalists, the pious protestations of pacifists, the indiscretions of ambassadors, and, what was perhaps most trying of all, the indignant surges of his own blood. But the succession of crises pressed him hard to reconcile himself to the necessity of preparing his people for war, both morally and materially, in case it should be forced upon him.

CHAPTER II

The Prophet Hears the Voice of the Lord

DURING THE YEAR 1915 it became clear that in the twentieth century America might not be able to remain a hemisphere unto itself. The hope that economic depletion would end the fighting faded; and a policy of legalistic neutrality, lacking a firm base in international law, was invalidated when each of the warring camps reverted to the law of necessity. Diplomats found no recourse in history on which they could depend to stop the martial madness. The President perceived that, if the United States were publicly to start a neutral movement for peace and fail in it, her influence in the future would be nil.

Yet it was in 1915 that the vision of a world order of which he had caught a glimpse in earlier years gradually became fixed in his mind as a necessity for the salvation of mankind. With Europe destroying itself, he embraced the cause of international organization as an essential article of his faith.

Colonel House wished to keep alive the President's impulse to build a new world. If Wilson were ever to get out of the "labyrinth" that he conceived to have been created by "German frightfulness," it seemed to the Colonel that he could do so only by taking initiative. After his return from London in June of 1915, House received strong support from Sir Edward Grey. The foreign secretary wished to bring the United States into the war, but realized that any public expression of his desire would militate against its fulfillment. He ventured, however, to appeal to America to lead in making peace. "The pearl of great price," Grey wrote to House on August 10, ". . . would be some League of Nations that could be relied on to insist that disputes between any two nations must be settled by the arbitration, mediation, or conference of others. International law has hitherto had no sanction. The lesson of this war is that the Powers must bind themselves to give it a sanction. If that can be secured, freedom of the seas and many other things will become easy. . . ."[1]

---

[1] Charles Seymour has pointed out (*American Diplomacy during the World War*, p. 174 n.) that Grey's proposal reflected ideas from letters that the latter had received from Theodore Roosevelt. Moreover, British Liberals and Laborites, impressed by the domestic reforms that had been achieved under Wilson's leadership, looked to him to further the postwar objectives to which they were pledged and toward which imperialists at London were unsympathetic. Believing that a punitive peace would be unwise, and that by saying so they might stimulate

On September 22 the foreign secretary wrote again, to ask the Colonel how far the United States would go to get security against aggressive war. "Would the President," he queried, "propose that there should be a League of Nations binding themselves to side against any power which broke a treaty; which broke certain rules of warfare on sea or land . . . ; or which refused, in case of dispute, to adopt some other method of settlement than that of war? Only in some such agreement do I see a prospect of diminishing militarism and navalism in future, so that no nation will build up armies or navies for aggressive purposes. I cannot say which Government would be prepared to accept such a proposal, but I am sure that the Government of the United States is the only Government that could make it with effect . . ."

Wilson was receptive when House put a bold plan before him. The Colonel's idea was to ask the British first whether it would be agreeable to them if the United States demanded that hostilities cease; and then, if they gave the assent that was to be expected, House would go to Berlin and present the American demand without saying that he had discussed the matter first at London. He would even try to delude the Germans into believing that the British would reject the plan, hoping thus to make it the more tempting to Germany. If the Central Powers turned him down, House had it in mind to break diplomatic relations and marshal the force of all neutrals against them.

Such a scheme involved the hazard of eventual involvement in the fight; but if that came to pass, at least the United States would stand in a moral position that would command the respect of the world. Consequently it seemed better to take the risk than to let human nature take its course, and to slip into war on terms that had been familiar to mankind ever since its progenitors fought in trees and caves.

Wilson suggested, therefore, that the Colonel put his plan in writing for Grey; and House discussed with him a draft of a letter that explained that the United States stood ready to intervene and "demand that peace parleys begin upon the broad basis of the elimination of militarism and navalism." Furthermore, it suggested that when Grey

---

liberal opinion in Germany, Ramsay MacDonald and other leaders had organized a Union of Democratic Control a few days after the war's outbreak, with these principles:

1. No transfer of territory without consent of the populace.
2. No treaty-making without consent of Parliament.
3. Guarantee of peace by a concert, rather than a balance, of powers.
4. Drastic reduction and national control of armaments.

On May 2, 1916, a fifth point was added: Economic warfare should not go on after military operations ceased. By 1918 the U.D.C. had some 650,000 members.

In April of 1915 English intellectuals formed a League of Nations Society. *See* Lawrence W. Martin, "Anglo-American Liberalism and the Wilson Peace Program of 1918," a dissertation at the Yale University Library, 1955.

thought the hour propitious, House might go to London, and then on to Berlin, to notify Germany that, if she insisted on continuing the fight, "it would be necessary" for the United States to join the Allies and force the issue.

A vital word was inserted by the President, so that the clause read: "it would *probably* be necessary." He was not willing, he explained to House the next day, "to make it inevitable that the United States would be a party to forcing terms on Germany," for the exact circumstances of a future crisis seemed impossible to determine. In general, though, he thought the Colonel's draft altogether right. "I pray to God it may bring results," he wrote.[2]

On October 19 House sent off the letter to Grey; and during the next few weeks he devoted himself to furthering the project. He listened patiently to the chimerical pleas of American pacifists and cultivated the sympathy of journalists for the cause of peace, assuring them that no one was more eager than the President to serve that cause, no one more competent to decide what steps could be taken with hope of success.

The British foreign secretary, in his first reply to House's exploratory letter, merely asked whether the scheme proposed was to be considered in conjunction with Grey's own suggestion of a League of Nations. The President agreed that they should tell the foreign secretary that they found "the necessary programme" for the future in Grey's suggestion of a League of Nations. Thus was Woodrow Wilson committed, as early as November of 1915, to the greatest cause of the twentieth century. It was the beginning of the end of American isolation.

Meanwhile, Wilson had become alarmed by the prospect of a break with Germany. In September of 1915 House found his friend thinking more of preventing a German victory than of building a new world order. Wilson confessed that he had never been sure that the United States ought not to enter the war and, if it became evident that Germany would win, the obligation of America to act would be the greater. While the *Lusitania* case was still unsettled, violations of American law by Germans with diplomatic immunity made it seem necessary to send the attachés von Papen and Boy-Ed home to Berlin. On August 19 the *Arabic* was sunk, with loss of American lives. In

[2] House discussed his grand scheme with Lansing in the President's study while Wilson was out calling on Edith Galt. He won the approval of the secretary of state, who despite the sharpness of his legal protests to London was personally partial to the Allies. The Colonel wrote gleefully in his diary: "I now have the matter in my own hands. The President's only questions were when and how."

October Nurse Cavell faced German executioners with her immortal
cry: "Patriotism is not enough"; and her martyrdom impressed American hearts once more with the frightfulness of Prussian militarism.
In November sentiment in the United States was further aroused by
the torpedoing of the Italian liner *Ancona,* with the loss of a score of
American lives. Moreover, Lansing had become more aggressive and
agreed with Tumulty that there should be more "punch" in the American policy.[3]

As the righteous wrath of Americans had turned against those whom
they glibly called "Huns" and a hue and cry against German sympathizers had risen, the pacifists also had become still more alarmed and
importunate. Twenty thousand telegrams urging a peace movement
reached the White House in one day, and delegates paraded in to see
the President. Henry Ford came to tell Wilson of an impractical plan
of dramatizing the cause of conciliation by a "peace ship," only to find
the Chief Executive in a prophetic mood, ready to make war in order
to put an end to wars.

The conflict within Wilson's soul was becoming unbearable. His
desire to enforce justice wrestled with his determination not to allow
his people to use the barbaric instrument of war as a means of enforcement. By mid-December, just before his wedding, he was ready to spur
the Colonel to undertake the mission that they had planned in October but for which, in the view of House and Grey, the time was not
yet ripe.

Since Wilson thought it futile for the Colonel to go to Berlin unless
he was invited,[4] House put the President's views before Bernstorff; and
within a week word came from the German government that they
would like to have the Colonel go directly to their capital to discuss
general terms of military and naval disarmament.

When House asked for written instructions for his mission, the President at first told him that he needed none. "You know what is in my
mind and how to interpret it . . ." Wilson wrote. "Your own letters
exactly echo my own views and purposes." But he decided to make the
Colonel a "special agent" in order to forestall possible Congressional
criticism of him as a man acting for the government without authority.

---

[3] The secretary of state feared that Spain, which had been asking Cuba whether Latin-
American countries would approve mediation by its king, would wrest leadership of peace sentiment from Wilson. Informed of this, the President advised Lansing to avoid direct comment
and to tell the Cuban minister that the United States hoped that all the Americas would work
in union.

[4] Conversing with Lansing and House, the President went to his safe and took out a
message from Gerard that reported an interview with the Kaiser in which the German ruler
had threatened "to attend to America when this war was over" and had spoken slightingly of
Wilson as one ineligible to mediate because of his attitude toward Germany. On Oct. 1 Gerard
had written to House: "Germany seems to be winning this war . . ."

In a note written during his honeymoon the President outlined his ideas very succinctly. The United States, he wrote, was to have nothing to do with local settlements. Lansing had given warning of complicated questions of boundary and indemnity that would have to be settled after the war; but Wilson wanted House to concern himself only with international undertakings essential to future peace. "The only guarantees that any rational man could accept," the President wrote on December 24, "are (a) military and naval disarmament and (b) a league of nations to secure each nation against aggression and maintain absolute freedom of the seas. If either party to the present war will let us say to the other that they are willing to discuss peace on such terms, it will clearly be our duty to use our utmost moral force to oblige the other to parley, and I do not see how they could stand in the opinion of the world if they refused."

Armed with this psychological weapon, the Colonel sailed for Europe on his third quest for the Grail of peace. He reached London on January 6 and reported to Wilson that the foreign secretary favored "freedom of the seas" provided the Germans granted "freedom of the land," and that Grey stipulated also that the United States should join in a general covenant of guarantee. They were to talk again soon, the Colonel said, and it would help if Wilson would cable some assurance of his willingness "to cooperate in a policy of seeking to bring about and maintain permanent peace among civilized nations."

This appeal elicited from the President a message promising to do exactly what his agent suggested. It was not enough, however, to sway the British statesmen from their will to fight until German militarism was crushed beyond hope of revival. The government at London was unmoved when House warned that Russia might be knocked out of the war and Germany might acquire a military position from which she could dictate terms far less palatable than those that could be secured through President Wilson. The British leaders felt that they must await the outcome of promising plans for spring campaigns on the battlefield.[5] House was discouraged by the attitude of the British statesmen.

[5] As for Page, the Colonel found him deeper than ever in sympathy with his English friends, critical now of the President as well as of the State Department, and opposed to any negotiations that might prevent the smashing of Germany. The "fatal moral weakness" of House's scheme, Page thought, was that the United States should "plunge into war, not on the merits of the cause, but by a carefully sprung trick." The ambassador had taken no effective steps to explain in London that "the freedom of the seas" was not a subversive slogan invented by German propagandists, but rather an ideal conceived at Washington. Page recorded in his diary that people were laughing at "the empty House" and were offended by his vanity for Wilson's "prestige." British opinion thought that, if the United States truly wished to help to kill the root of war, she could best do so by acquiescing in the blockade by which German militarism could be strangled.

Circumstances at Washington, however, were pushing the President in the opposite direction. On Jan. 12 he cabled to House that an adjustment of controversies with Germany was in prospect and that, if it came, American opinion and the Senate would demand that London

"I was never more impressed by their slowness and lack of initiative," he wrote to Wilson on February 9.

Going to Berlin, he learned that the naval officials were still at odds with the Foreign Office over submarine policy. The contention within the government was much the same as that at London. At each capital the men of the Admiralty felt that the protests of the United States had pulled the teeth of their blockade.

The President's agent left Germany convinced that, if the Foreign Office were forced to admit that deeds of German submarines were illegal, the Admiralty would gain supremacy and would force a break with Washington. On January 30 House cabled this conclusion to the President. Four days later he wrote that he doubted whether the German people would rise against their rulers, as many Americans hoped.

Believing more firmly than ever that the fighting had reached a stalemate and that the United States was the only nation able to break the deadlock, House worked at Paris to cultivate appreciation of this fact. But the statesmen of France were responsible to a public that put faith in military dominance and abhorred any gesture that smacked of pacifism. They feared that moves toward conciliation would be regarded by the world as signs of weakness. Sickened by the incompetent statesmanship that he had observed in Europe, House was more than ever convinced, as he wrote Wilson, that the President's opportunity was "the greatest, perhaps, that has ever come to any man." [6]

Returning to London, House hastened to resume conversations with Sir Edward Grey—the statesman who had given him the best hope of a humane peace in which the United States could play a leading part. After assuring Grey of the ability of the enemy to fight on, House thought that he had persuaded the foreign secretary [7]—at least for the

---

concede as much as Berlin to neutral rights. Page sensed in this message, when House showed it to him, "a certain fierce, blue-bellied Presbyterian tone." The Colonel informed Wilson that, if the United States pressed its case too strongly, it might force the resignation of Sir Edward Grey and thus lose its best friend.

[6] "In each government I have visited," the Colonel reported, "I have found stubbornness, determination, selfishness, cant. One continually hears self-glorification . . ." Observing the Kaiser playing at war as if it were the prerogative of royalty and never doubting that God was on his side, and noting the befuddlement of Chancellor Bethmann, House observed in disgust: "In such hands are the destinies of the people placed."

[7] "One of the Colonel's defects," comments Charles Seymour, "was that he was so irresistible in his quiet manner that he persuaded many persons out of their real beliefs."

Regarding House's persuasiveness in this instance, the *New Statesman* commented on March 13, 1926: "Sir Edward Grey seems to have been a better diplomat than most of us knew, for all talk of intervention was at that moment sheer nonsense, but Colonel House was allowed to suppose that he had made a deep impression and had even carried his point." Grey was not converted permanently—if at all—to a view that Wilson expressed to House; that is, that the war would last longer if the United States were a belligerent rather than a neutral. *See* E. H. Buehrig, *W.W. and the Balance of Power*, pp. 222–28.

moment—that rather than make the submarine issue a *casus belli* it would be best for the President to demand that all belligerents sanction the calling of a peace conference. Grey explained that every window in his house would be broken by mobs if it were known that he was discussing peace; but with a courage that the Colonel thought admirable, the foreign minister consented that the American proposal should be considered with his colleagues at a dinner to be given by Lord Reading.

On this occasion, after hearing his hosts cheerfully divide up the territory of Turkey, the Colonel observed the President's injunction against involvement in selfish war aims and went only so far as to commit Wilson to attend a European peace conference if one should be called at The Hague. When the gathering broke up, at midnight, it was with agreement that Grey and House should draft a memorandum setting forth a presidential offer of mediation that would be discussed with France, if Wilson approved it. There were conflicting opinions in the British Cabinet that made a decision as to timing difficult. Certain ministers doubted the nation's ability to withstand many more months of economic attrition. On the other hand, the men at Reading's dinner felt, and made House admit, that if the Allies could gain military victories, Germany would then be the more likely to accept mediation. Finally, it was decided that the choice of an opportune moment for the making of the American offer should rest with the Allies.

The memorandum resulting from this conference was taken to the President by House, whose name had now become a symbol in twentieth-century diplomacy.[8] Returning to Washington on March 6, the Colonel went riding with the Wilsons and gave them a full account of his stewardship. Before the ruling elder left the White House the President put a hand on his shoulder and said: "It would be hard to imagine a more difficult task than the one placed in your hands, but you have accomplished it in a way beyond my expectations." The next day Wilson typed a telegram for Sir Edward Grey, approving the memorandum that House had brought, in so far as he could speak for the

[8] During his visits to London, House discovered that English radicals against whom Spring Rice had warned him as "copperheads," were sane and able men who held views similar to his own and were potential allies in efforts to convert the British government to the new diplomacy. Moreover, influential journalists with whom the Colonel had cultivated friendships now came to him freely for information and guidance. His handling of newsmen elicited the admiration of Lloyd George—himself a master of the art. Fancying his talent in this regard, the Colonel wanted the President to appreciate it and suggested, after dinner at the White House on March 29, that Wilson read an article by A. G. Gardiner in the London *News*. The President responded with the appreciation that was called for. "I seem to see," he said with a smile, "something of the Colonel's fine Italian hand in this article." However, when Mark Sullivan wrote, in *Collier's*, "there are a good many thoughtful folk who think that the best thing about President Wilson is Colonel House," the Colonel recorded in his diary that this was the sort of thing that he feared most.

future action of the United States. To make doubly sure that it would be understood that he could not act without Senate approval, and also to make the memorandum completely consistent, he added one word— "probably." [9] House signed the message that the President had written and sent if off to Grey. Thus Woodrow Wilson was committed secretly to throw the moral force of his nation on the side of those statesmen who would accept a peace that would strike neutral opinion as humane and just.

On March 10, citing a Wilson victory over the pacifists in Congress [10] as evidence of his mastery of affairs at Washington, House wrote to Grey thus: "It is now squarely up to you to make the next move." Leaders of belligerent nations, however, could not accept the challenge if they would. They were now the victims of those popular passions that they had allowed to run unchecked and had even fanned, in their desperation. The French were fighting for their lives at Verdun, and the British did not dare to suggest anything that might weaken their resistance. Therefore, London failed to respond to reminders from the White House that Wilson's offer might at any time be withdrawn, and the United States revert to a policy of prosecuting its own interests, including that of unrestricted commerce on the seas.

On March 24 the French steamer *Sussex* was torpedoed, with loss of lives, and several Americans were wounded. Wilson's diplomatic battle with Berlin broke out anew, and for a time it seemed that his patience was strained to the breaking point.

Lansing, venting his wrath against the person of Bernstorff, wanted to send a protest to Germany that would be virtually an ultimatum. House thought a rupture inevitable and, looking forward to a peace conference at which Wilson, reinforced by technical experts and persuasive lobbyists, would represent his country alone and would preside, argued that this prospect justified a strong stand at the risk of war.

[9] With this change the "Memorandum of Sir Edward Grey" read, in part: "Colonel House told me that President Wilson was ready, on hearing from France and England that the moment was opportune, to propose that a Conference should be summoned to put an end to the war. Should the Allies accept the proposal, and should Germany refuse it, the United States would probably enter the war against Germany. Colonel House expressed the opinion that, if such a conference met, it would secure peace on terms not unfavorable to the Allies; and, if it failed to secure peace, the United States would *probably* leave the conference as a belligerent on the side of the Allies, if Germany was unreasonable. Colonel House expressed an opinion decidedly favorable to the restoration of Belgium, the transfer of Alsace and Lorraine to France, and the acquisition by Russia of an outlet to the sea, though he thought that the loss of territory incurred by Germany in one place would have to be compensated to her by concessions in other places outside Europe. If the Allies delayed accepting the offer of President Wilson, and if, later on, the course of the war was so unfavorable to them that the intervention of the United States would not be effective, the United States would probably disinterest themselves in Europe and look to their own protection in their own way."

[10] *See* pp. 47–49.

The President asked the Colonel to tell Bernstorff that they were at the breaking point and the United States would surely go to war unless a decisive change were made in Germany's submarine policy.[11] The dilemma upset his digestion and made him seem intractable. For weeks he had not been able to go to bed free from fear that he might be awakened by news that would mean war for his people. Dr. Grayson reported to House that the President was giving his entourage, from the secretary of state down, an unhappy time and was showing intolerance of any who dared to give advice that countered his convictions. Nevertheless, the Colonel ventured to speak his mind. On April 11, when he went to the White House to volunteer counsel on the note that Wilson had drafted to deal with the *Sussex* case, the President's voice seemed weak. But when the Colonel and Mrs. Wilson argued that the text needed strengthening, he held to his views. He said that he was not inclined to consult the Cabinet, for he did not want their ideas; and, moreover, he feared that the document would leak out through them and appear in the afternoon papers. He did decide finally, however, to present it to his colleagues—as an argument that ran in his own mind rather than as a note about to be sent. Mainly he trusted his intuition and his God, though he made a few concessions to pleas of Lansing and House for strengthening of his message.[12]

The note went off to Berlin on April 18, and the next day the President went before the Congress and reviewed the situation. He looked forward with unaffected reluctance, he said, to the possibility of a diplomatic break; but, he went on, "we owe it to a due regard for our own rights as a nation, to a sense of duty as a representative of the rights of neutrals the world over, and to a just conception of the rights of mankind to take this stand now with the utmost solemnity and firmness." On May 3, the day before the German reply arrived, he surprised House in a private talk by the virulence of his feeling against German leaders.

---

[11] Informed by both House and Lansing that the situation was very grave, Bernstorff pressed his government for concessions that might placate American opinion. But all that was vouchsafed by the officials at Berlin, who were incensed at Washington's failure to force Britain to moderate her blockade and who seemed utterly unable to control the submarine commanders, was a note that asserted that the *Sussex* was not torpedoed but rather the victim of a floating mine.

Wilson had been convinced by a study of affidavits that a German submarine sank the *Sussex*. He saw both falsehood and clumsiness in the message from Berlin, and the American press thought it filled with ludicrous evasions.

[12] The draft that was finally sent gave Germany a chance to avoid a break by disavowing the tactics used by her submarines. It served notice that "unless the Imperial German Government should now immediately declare and effect an abandonment of its present methods of warfare against passenger and freight-carrying vessels, the Government of the United States can have no choice but to sever diplomatic relations." Since no time limit was fixed, the note was not an ultimatum; and three days later the President indicated, in a letter to House, that it would be right to discuss with the Germans any plan that they suggested, provided that submarine warfare was stopped entirely during the talks.

He considered them responsible for the war and thought they should be punished personally, like erring directors of corporations.

Realizing that there were only two alternatives, the German Foreign Office on May 4 gave the pledge that was demanded. No more merchant ships would be torpedoed without warning and without regard to loss of lives, unless they offered resistance or tried to escape. But Germany made a reservation. Attacking America's plea for humanity by accusing her of acquiescence in the starvation of Germany, she reserved "complete liberty of decision" in case the United States did not succeed in inducing the Allies to lift their blockade.

Learning of the substance of the German message during a Cabinet meeting the President discussed it immediately with his men. He perceived that at last Germany had accepted his main contention. He therefore acted immediately to seize upon this vital concession, stating at the same time that he could not "for a moment entertain, much less discuss," the German reservation.[13]

Thus Woodrow Wilson again demonstrated the great truth that he had taught—that it took more courage to keep out of a fight than to mix in. As he wrestled with chauvinistic forces, like Antaeus, he sought strength from contact with the solid ground on which his people lived. The birth of his first granddaughter brought him joy, and on Easter Monday he was cheered by the traditional egg rolling on the lawn of the White House. Even more avid than usual for escape and anonymity, he said, "I seriously think of renting a pair of whiskers . . . because I am sorry to find out that the cut of my jib is unmistakable and that I must sail under false colors if I am going to sail incognito." He took weekend voyages down the Potomac and up the James for a few hours, substituting history for politics under the spell of infinite calm that he had always found in the sites along these rivers. He liked to study charts and explore back waters, to pass the time with fisherfolk and buy their catch for his luncheon.

Even on vacations, however, his trusty typewriter was taken along, and a packet of papers to study. He digested editorials in influential journals, and predicted that it was going to be "increasingly difficult to keep off the insistent demand" that he act. "It is much better," he wrote, "that we should initiate the final movement [for peace] than that the Pope should."

---

[13] "Responsibility in such matters is single, not joint; absolute, not relative," the President wrote in his best academic manner in a paragraph that he added to a legalistic text drafted by Lansing.

On May 8, the day on which this final message on the *Sussex* case was sent to Berlin, the air was further cleared by an admission from the Foreign Office of liability for the attack upon the vessel and an offer of indemnification.

The Colonel thought it a bit too early to force mediation; but it seemed to him none too soon for the President to demand some action looking toward permanent peace. The nominating conventions were only a month away, and the canny Texan wanted Wilson to announce a strong, positive policy before the Republicans could steal his thunder. He found the President keen for this strategy.

House cast about for an occasion on which Wilson could publicly assert America's determination to lead in the making of a just and enduring peace. It occurred to him that the First National Assembly of the League to Enforce Peace, to be held in Washington on May 26 and 27, gave opportunity for an epochal declaration; and so he arranged that William Howard Taft, president of the League, should urge Wilson to make the main speech on that occasion.

Though in the midst of the *Sussex* crisis the President had declined an invitation to speak at the League's meeting, he reconsidered when Germany met his demands with its pledge of May 4. For a week or so he pondered, feeling his way to a momentous decision. On May 12 he opened his mind completely to Ray Stannard Baker, a man of letters whose instincts and discretion he trusted. Baker saw the rise and fall of the prophet's intellectual passions expressed in his eyes. Wilson's face seemed "singularly living." He pounced deftly upon things half-said, to consume them and add them to his own view, and thus carry along his auditor and make him feel that their minds had met and been enriched by the experience. The first need of a leader, he told Baker, was enthusiasm. He must have a definite program and a direction in which he could believe strongly, and then must stir people to respond, either emotionally or intellectually. He was seeking, more than anything else, a program for action by America to help to bring about peace. Speaking confidently of his plan for a Pan-American Pact, he expressed hope that such an idea might be applied to the rest of the world. He cautioned Baker to breathe no word of this, and asked whether he should tentatively outline his ideas at this time before the League to Enforce Peace; and the journalist replied that, though the hour had not come for calling a peace conference, the President could help to prepare opinion by making guarded statements in his coming speech.

Thinking aloud at a meeting of the National Press Club on May 15, the President sent up a trial balloon. Speaking of the strain that he was under in trying to interpret the spirit of his country, he confessed that he had only the most imperfect means of knowing what his people were thinking about. He particularly needed, he said, the support of "men who will divest themselves of party passion and of personal preference and will try to think in terms of America." Such citizens, he declared, "will take the right leadership if they believe that the leader is also a man who thinks first of America." As for himself, he was convinced that his land could not afford to withdraw from responsibility toward the European war and, when it had passed, "have the reckonings." Like his elders who had left their cloisters in South Carolina to wrestle with the chaos of Reconstruction, Woodrow Wilson felt that moral men could not ignore the threat of anarchy in Europe. If the United States was to have the part that he coveted for her—that of leader in the peacemaking—her President thought it necessary that she should "act more or less from the point of view of the rest of the world."

At one point his words became sinister and Cromwellian: "If I cannot retain my moral influence over a man except by occasionally knocking him down, if that is the only basis upon which he will respect me, then for the sake of his soul I have got occasionally to knock him down . . . If a man will not listen to you quietly in a seat, sit on his neck and make him listen." This point of view had seemed ridiculous to Lord Grey, when Page had advocated the shooting of Mexicans into political morality. Fortunately for the repute of the United States in European diplomatic circles, these brash sentences were not reported to the public.

The day after his frank talk to the Press Club, Wilson's yearning for positive action had become so strong that he wrote to House: "It seems to me that we should get down to hard pan." The situation had altered since the Colonel's visit to Europe, he observed. Indeed, it had reached a decisive "turning point." The bettering of relations with Germany by the *Sussex* pledge had concentrated attention on "the altogether indefensible course" that Great Britain was pursuing. Wilson's eye was still fixed upon a league of nations—Lord Grey's "pearl of great price."

The prophet's zeal was now fully aroused, and he decided to reveal the American vision to all the world. "To do nothing is now, for us, impossible," he wrote to House on May 16. Two days later he accepted the second invitation of the League to Enforce Peace, and on the same day he informed House that the speech in prospect might be the most important he would ever be called to make. He asked the Colonel to give him the benefit of his insight into the minds of the leaders of the Allies. He studied parliamentary addresses and winnowed editorial wisdom from American journals that he respected. Clippings and shorthand notes were kept in a folder that no one was allowed to touch.

The final text put forth the principles that the President had advocated already in his enunciation of Latin-American policy at Mobile in 1913. But, going further now, the President of the United States became the first chief of state of his era to commit his people to support a permanent international organization to enforce these principles. His pronouncement on this occasion was the most significant of its kind since James Monroe set forth his doctrine.

On May 27, in the new Willard Hotel, facing some two thousand influential members of the League to Enforce Peace, the American prophet embarked publicly on his crusade for humanity. The occasion was the climax of a two-day session at which peace policy had been discussed and almost a half million dollars raised. Though the leadership of the organization was largely Republican, the meeting gave promise of a nonpartisan approach to the great problem of collective security. William Howard Taft and A. Lawrence Lowell sat on the platform; and Henry Cabot Lodge spoke before Wilson and deferred to the intellects of the League to the extent of recognizing the necessity for putting force behind international peace. "The difficulties cannot be overcome unless we try to overcome them," the senator said. Asserting that the founding fathers would not have discouraged an alliance that could diminish war and encourage peace, Lodge spoke of the aspirations of his audience as "beautiful and good and beneficent to humanity," and he quoted Matthew Arnold:

> Charge once more, then, and be dumb!
> Let the victors, when they come,
> When the forts of folly fall,
> Find your body by the wall.

At this time, however, Lodge's faith in the practicality of a League to Enforce Peace was already waning, particularly as he contemplated its effect upon American sovereignty. He suggested to his audience that they might not achieve their end and the outcome might be disappointing. He was willing to accept the benefits of an association of nations, but wary of the sacrifices that would make it effective. The learned man from Boston lacked the greatness of soul and the unshakable faith that were needed to force constructive action in this crisis in human history.[14]

If mankind was to be saved from the ravages of international an-

---

[14] A year earlier, at Union College, Lodge had spoken more confidently of international action for peace. A letter from Theodore Roosevelt to Lodge commended the Union College speech as "admirable." Moreover, Roosevelt, in a speech delivered upon receiving the Nobel Peace Prize in 1912, had declared that it would be "a master stroke" for the great powers to form a league that would use force, if necessary, to prevent breaches of world peace. And in a magazine article entitled "Utopia or Hell" he had proposed "a world league bound by a solemn covenant" to "act with the combined military strength of all of them against any recalcitrant nation." But on June 7, 1916, he wrote to Arthur Lee: "Wilson and Taft are now bleating for leagues to enforce peace." Morison (ed.), *Letters*, VIII, 1056. In 1912 the Republican Congress had passed a resolution calling for arbitration and disarmament and even for constituting the combined navies of the world an international police force for the preservation of peace.

archy, it would require the perspective of Olympus and the faith of the Apostles. A prophet who had been bred on Scripture and had regenerated institutions by the power of spiritual truth scarcely could fail to respond to this supreme call. Woodrow Wilson was ready to lead his people over the edge of a world that was, politically speaking, still thought to be flat. He was as eager as ever to explore new dimensions of government. When the critical, poetasting senator sat down, after telling the audience that the supreme vision of the age might fail, Wilson rose and proclaimed that it must prevail.

He played masterfully upon the creative impulses that he felt throbbing in the hearts of his national congregation. Beginning with assertions of inescapable fact, he spoke of the profound effect of the European war on American liberties and property, and the resulting conviction that the prevention of war had become a primary concern to Americans, as to Europeans. Pointing out that the current war would not have begun if there had been a period of open discussion of its causes, he concluded that peace must henceforth depend upon "a new and more wholesome diplomacy." He reasserted a familiar doctrine of Anglo-Saxon liberalism: nations should follow the same high code of honor that is demanded of individuals. Moreover, they must agree on the things that are fundamental to their common interests and concur on a way of acting in concert against any threat to those essentials.

We believe these fundamental things: First, that every people has a right to choose the sovereignty under which they shall live. . . . Second, that the small states of the world have a right to enjoy the same respect for their sovereignty and for their territorial integrity that great and powerful nations expect and insist upon. And, third, that the world has a right to be free from every disturbance of its peace that has its origin in aggression and disregard of the rights of peoples and nations.

So sincerely do we believe in these things that I am sure that I speak the mind and wish of the people of America when I say that the United States is willing to become a partner in any feasible association of nations formed in order to realize these objects and make them secure against violation.

There is nothing that the United States wants for itself that any other nation has. We are willing, on the contrary, to limit ourselves along with them to a prescribed course of duty and respect for the rights of others which will check any selfish passion of our own, as it will check any aggressive impulse of theirs.

If it should ever be our privilege to suggest or initiate a movement for peace among the nations now at war, I am sure that the people of the United States would wish their Government to move along these lines: First, such a settlement with regard to their own immediate interests as the belligerents may agree upon. We have nothing material of any kind to ask for ourselves, and are quite aware that we are in no sense or degree parties to the present quarrel. Our interest is only in peace and its future guarantees. Second, an universal association of the nations to maintain the inviolate security of the highway of the seas for the common and unhindered use of all the nations of the world, and to prevent any war begun either contrary to treaty covenants or without warning and full submission of the causes to the opinion of the world—a virtual guarantee of territorial integrity and political independence.

But I did not come here, let me repeat, to discuss a programme. I came only to avow a creed and give expression to the confidence I feel that the world is even now upon the eve of a great consummation, when some common force will be brought into existence which shall safeguard right as the first and most fundamental interest of all peoples and all governments, when coercion shall be summoned . . . to the service of a common order, a common justice, and a common peace. God grant that the dawn of that day of frank dealing and of settled peace, concord, and cooperation may be near at hand!

The response of Wilson's countrymen to this challenge was warm enough to convince him that he was moving in the right direction, and by the end of May his course was so firmly set that it never would be altered. To be sure, many contemporary observers failed to grasp the epochal portent of this speech, and Secretary Lansing questioned from a sickbed the wisdom of subjecting the nation's independence of action to the will of powers outside the Western Hemisphere. But the *Independent* called the address a "declaration of interdependence," to be set beside the nation's Declaration of Independence.

The pioneering prophet had found another Great Cause—greater than "Princeton in the Nation's Service," greater even than "The New Freedom." On Memorial Day he declared: "America is roused, roused to a self-consciousness such as she has not had in a generation." Addressing himself to critics who were still under the spell of the injunction of the founding fathers against "entangling alliances," he said: "I shall never myself consent to an entangling alliance, but I would gladly assent to a disentangling alliance—an alliance which would disentangle the peoples of the world from those combinations in which they seek their own separate and private interests and unite the people of the world to preserve the peace of the world upon a basis of common right and justice. There is liberty there, not limitation. There is freedom, not entanglement."

Unfortunately, Philistines in Europe fell upon a few phrases in the speech of May 27 that were infelicitous, and by harping on them obscured the great central purpose of the President. Nationalistic editors

at London were apprehensive of a league that would try to make the
seas secure "for the common and unhindered use of all nations" and
the publicists of the Allies thought Wilson unsympathetic because he
said of the war: "with its causes and its objects we are not concerned."
It seemed as if he were placing France and England on a moral level
with Germany. Page reported that the British people were "skittish
about the President" because he seemed to speak only to "the gallery
filled with peace cranks." Wilson learned, moreover, that by asserting
the right of small peoples to self-determination he had angered the
rulers of Austria-Hungary and had raised embarrassing questions about
the status of minorities in the British Empire. Furthermore, France's
ambassador hinted to House that the United States might find herself
without sympathizers in a future war with aggressors unless she took
the side of the Allies in their hour of trial. At the same time reports
of an economic conference held at Paris suggested that the Allies intended to encroach on the commerce of neutrals and set up industrial
monopolies if Germany were vanquished.

The prophet was exasperated by these rebuffs. Wilson had committed his emotions so completely that he would never be satisfied,
from this day forth, until he realized his aspiration for American
leadership in organizing the world for a peace based on reason. He
knew that a longing for such a peace lay deep in the hearts of the
French and British peoples. His stern sense of mission projected jagged
edges in a note written to House on June 22: "The letters and the
glimpses of opinion [official opinion] from the other side of the
water are not encouraging, to say the least, and indicate a constant
narrowing, instead of a broad and comprehending view of the situation. They are in danger of forgetting the rest of the world, and of
waking up some surprising morning to discover that it has a positive
right to be heard about the peace of the world. I conclude that it will
be up to us to judge for ourselves when the time has arrived for us
to make an imperative suggestion."

And then, as if conscious of the inconsistency of this hint of compulsion with his policy of free self-determination, he added a qualification: "I mean a suggestion which they will have no choice but to
heed, because the opinion of the non-official world and the desire of
all peoples will be behind it." And if they were not behind it? In-
fatuated by the new concept of manifest destiny that the elders among
his people were shaping, the prophet did not raise this question.

CHAPTER III

Keeping His Powder Dry

With an election in prospect, Woodrow Wilson realized that 1916 was "a year of political accounting" and that Americans were good accountants. If his own stewardship could not stand the glare of pitiless publicity, it seemed to him that it ought to be terminated. "I hope that every public man will get what is coming to him," he said to a New York audience on January 27. He intended to re-establish the rapport with his people that he had enjoyed in his first year in the Presidency.

Wilson's firm mastery of the party men had relaxed during his preoccupation, in 1915, with foreign affairs and with the winning of Edith Galt. Indeed, he had suffered a legislative defeat when his shipping bill was filibustered to death in the Senate. And when the Congress met again in December the members reflected misgivings that had become rife among their constituents. At one extreme, Bryan's friends wished to reduce the risk of war by refusing passports to citizens intending to sail on belligerent ships; and at the other end of the arc of opinion, jingoes proposed measures that would promote war with Mexico or a break with Britain or Germany.

Many citizens feared that the United States would be attacked if Germany triumphed. The people—particularly those in the East—had been thoroughly frightened by the propaganda of organizations promoting preparedness, as well as by books and moving pictures that dramatized the force of Prussian militarism. Experts of the Army and Navy had been warning the public for many months that they lacked means to defend the nation. Theodore Roosevelt bellowed about the President's incapacity to face the world that he had to live in. And Franklin D. Roosevelt and Secretary of War Garrison gave comfort to those who championed preparedness.

The President, however, felt that the dogs of war, no less than the pacifists, must be held firmly in leash. Many citizens, he sensed, mistrusted the motives of professional soldiers who advocated expansion of their own business. Likewise many suspected sinister self-interest behind journalistic clamor for purchase of war materials. Yet early in 1915, under the pressure of public agitation, the President had signed a bill increasing the Navy. Furthermore, he had talked with Garrison about a plan for a military system that would have many of the features of the Swiss and would provide what was known as a "continental army." His interest in defense was stimulated by the defiant attitude of Germany in the *Lusitania* case and the embarrassment that American diplomats suffered in Europe because of the scorn of the belligerents for the inability of the United States to put military force behind her diplomatic notes.

On July 21 the President had asked Daniels and Garrison to draw up a preparedness program; and ten days later he had begun to prepare the doubting minds of Congressional leaders—Republican as well as Democratic—for nonpartisan discussions that might lead to "a single judgment in the matter and a single programme of action."

By November Wilson had final recommendations from Daniels and Garrison. He was ready to fulfill what he conceived to be the duty of going before the people and, at the same time, to satisfy those Democratic politicians who had been urging him to seize leadership of the growing sentiment for preparedness. It went against the grain to do this. He intended to prepare "not for war but for defense," he explained, and it was made clear to the generals of the Army—and particularly to Leonard Wood—that they were to refrain from any talk or acts that might be construed as "political." The President conceived that self-defense did not require the building of a military machine, for it seemed to him that even if Germany won, she would not be able to menace America for some years. He thought that labor leaders would balk and that his people expected him to lead in extending pacific idealism to the world rather than to expose America to such fears and jealousies as had followed military buildups in Europe. He had just had a letter from Oswald Garrison Villard that denounced the preparedness program as "a waste of the nation's resources" and "anti-moral, anti-social, and anti-democratic."

Wilson ventured to plot a path between the extremists by speaking at a dinner at the Manhattan Club in New York on November 4. He was glum and silent during the meal, and when he rose to speak his face was solemn, his voice strained. It seemed to an observer that he was "taking his medicine without licking the spoon." With war ablaze in the world, he asked, how far were Americans prepared to go to maintain themselves against any interference with their national action and development? Asserting again that there was no question of the willful use of force against any nation or any people, he declared: "We feel justified in preparing ourselves to vindicate our right to independent and unmolested action by making the force that is in us ready for assertion." The speech elicited only perfunctory applause, extremists on all sides being irritated by its moderation.

A fortnight before the date set for his marriage the President was immersed in contemplation of his third annual address to Congress. Delivering it on December 7, he talked first about Pan-Americanism and asserted that his nation's purpose was to make a common cause of national independence and political liberty. Then he said: "If our citizens are ever to fight effectively upon a sudden summons, they must know how modern fighting is done, and what to do when the summons comes to render themselves immediately available and immediately effective. . . . They must be fitted to play the great role in the world, and particularly in this hemisphere, which they are qualified by principle and by chastened ambition to play." With these ideals in the forefront, the President went on to recommend "essential first steps" that seemed to him "for the present sufficient." [1]

A gentle persuasiveness shone from the soul of the bridegroom as he pleaded with his men—"the sweetness of conscious strength," Secretary Redfield called it. The President was convinced, however, that he must use weapons more eloquent than courtesy. The essential responsibility of a real leader, he perceived, was to proclaim the preparedness program as a gospel, out in the West where many of his Congressional opponents had their roots and where vast rural areas were slumbering in ostrichlike isolation from the perils of the world. He could not permit vital divisions in the party as he led it toward the verdict of the voters. He must hammer home the truths that gave unity, eschew particulars that provoked debate. And so the prophet went forth, at the end of January, to tell his people that they must keep their powder dry and to lead them to a Lord whom they could trust—a God of peace and good will, but one jealous of his honor and his character. This was the only time during his first term that he appealed to the people in order to whip the Congress.

In twelve addresses, at New York and in the Middle West, he gave voice to the growing apprehension of danger from abroad. "All the rest of the world is on fire, and our own house is not fireproof," he said. He confessed that he had been awakened to many things that he had not realized a year earlier. "I cannot tell twenty-four hours at a time," he remarked, "whether there is going to be trouble or not. And whether there is or not does not depend upon what I say, or upon what any man in the United States does or says. It depends upon what foreign govern-

[1] Wilson proposed an increase in the tiny regular Army, and a supplementing force of 400,000 disciplined citizens who would volunteer for three short annual training periods and for service at call at any time during the ensuing three years. He then commended the five-year building program prepared by the Navy Department and went on to demand revival of the campaign for strengthening the merchant fleet that had been defeated by filibuster in the last Congress. As a part of his program for security, moreover, he asked for sedition laws adequate for the prosecution of "creatures of passion, disloyalty, and anarchy."

ments do; what the commanders of ships at sea do; what those in charge of submarines do; what those who are conducting blockades do."

The prophet told off fanatical critics on both sides. There were actually men in America who were preaching war, he declared. On the other hand, some of those who counseled peace went much further than he could go or his people could follow. America could not pay the price of losing her character, her self-respect. She must maintain the right of her citizens to travel unmolested, and to buy and sell in the markets of the world. He brought his people face to face with the dismal realities of the European scene. Modern wars were not won by mere numbers, or by sheer enthusiasm and patriotism. "They are won by the scientific application of irresistible force." In view of these considerations, it seemed "almost ridiculous" to state how little the administration was asking. The President had hardly troops enough to patrol the Mexican border. He was not seeking an army to command, but a trained citizenship. He did not aspire to be the "ruler on horseback" of which Americans were so deeply suspicious, but wanted rather to command the confidence and support of fellow citizens.

Near the end of his tour he invited his people to apply their "hard business sense" to the proposition, dismissing as "preposterous" the popular suspicion that agitation for preparedness had come chiefly from profiteers. But much of the President's philosophical argument went over their heads, and they could not be sure, from his veiled statements, just how imminent war with Germany was. The people found it hard to believe that this compassionate man could become the tool of irresponsible militarism. There was one phrase, however, that gave them pause: at St. Louis he spoke carelessly of a navy that would be "incomparably the greatest in the world." Opponents cited this as evidence of megalomania.[2] War-shy Democratic legislators perceived contradictions in the President's speeches and were perturbed at their ominous hints of fighting to come; and it became clear that the secretary of war was still unable to negotiate effectively with congressmen for a compromise plan of military training for civilians.

On February 4, the day on which Wilson returned to Washington full of cheer and confident that he carried with him the good will of an awakening majority of his people, the Senate passed the Clarke Amendment, which provided for Philippine independence in two years under

---

[2] When Wilson was told of the criticism, he confessed to the fault attributed to Gladstone—"intoxication by the eloquence of his own verbosity." The printed version of the St. Louis speech was changed to read "incomparably the most adequate navy in the world"; but when he returned to Washington and the Cabinet asked him whether he had been correctly quoted, he said: "Yes, and it is one thing that I said in my swing around the circuit that I actually believe." Daniels, *Years of War*, p. 41.

certain conditions. Garrison's ire was aroused by this. Believing that the Filipinos were not ready to rule and defend themselves, fearing that Japan would seize and exploit them, the secretary of war protested against the action of the Senate. "I cannot accept it or acquiesce in its acceptance," he wrote to the President.[3] If the War Department could not have its way immediately in this matter and in its plan for a strong standing army, he was through. He decided, for the fifth time, to resign.

This time the President did not try to dissuade him. As early as the summer of 1915 he had decided to let Garrison go. He wrote a gracious letter accepting the resignation, with "very warm appreciation" of distinguished service. Thus the departure of the militant Garrison followed that of the ultrapacific Bryan.

Fortunately the Middle West, the very region that had been most suspicious of Garrison's military program, raised up a man who could carry out its essentials. Mayor Newton D. Baker of Cleveland, whom Wilson had hoped to bring into his Cabinet in 1913, had risen higher in the President's esteem when he declined that honor in order to finish the job of reform to which the people of his city had committed him.[4] Now his second term as mayor had ended and he was looking forward to private practice of law.

"Would you accept the secretaryship of War?" Wilson telegraphed to him on March 5, 1916. "Earnestly hope that you can see your way to do so. It would greatly strengthen my hand."

Receiving a tentative acceptance, the President announced the appointment forthwith. When the appointee came to the White House three days later and explained that his association with peace societies made it inappropriate for him to serve in the War Department, Wilson merely asked: "Are you ready to take the oath?" At last he had found the perfect servant, a man who would feed his mind with the pith of fact and logic, never waste his time, and always accept the Chief's

---

[3] Wilson, for his part, had been opposed to the acquisition of the Philippines by the United States after the Spanish-American War; and when he became president he thought of these islands as a trust that must never be appropriated by the trustees. He had suggested that the Filipinos be given assurance of independence, to be conferred as soon as they were ready for self-government. The question of timing was difficult, however. Feeling that the hour for cutting the islands loose had not yet come, he had decided to move toward independence a step at a time. His first act was to give native citizens a majority in the governing commission, and he had done this in the hope that the Filipino leaders would prove their political capacity.

In the summer of 1914, Chairman Jones of the House Committee of Insular Affairs introduced a bill providing for independence as soon as a stable government should be established. On Nov. 4, 1915 Wilson told House that he thought it necessary to go through with the Jones Bill. On Feb. 4, 1916, the Senate passed the measure with the Clarke Amendment. Though the House passed the Jones Bill in 1914, it defeated the amendment in 1916.

[4] After the 1914 election Baker had written to Secretary Redfield about his city's vote, asserting that Cleveland was "the brightest spot" in the "general back-sliding . . ." and that there was no area in the nation where the President's policies were so keenly appreciated and so devotedly followed. Wilson had been delighted by this letter when it was shown to him.

decision on matters of general policy and strive to carry it out loyally and effectively.

Because of statements that he had made recently against preparedness, his slight stature, his glasses—he had been rejected as a volunteer for the Spanish-American War because of bad eyesight—Baker was nicknamed "Violet" by journalists in Washington. But they came to respect his ability and devotion. When they asked him whether it was true that he was a pacifist, his reply was: "So much so that I would fight for peace."

Avowing innocence of "obsessions or prejudices," Baker appreciated the value of political confidences better than his predecessor had. He established cordial relations with the legislators with whom the department had been at loggerheads. Moreover, he tactfully prevented the President from interfering unwisely with the work of the War College.

The day before Baker took office, Congressman Hay introduced a National Defense Bill in the House with the President's approval. This measure, which conceded more responsibility to the National Guard than Garrison would permit and more than Wilson himself desired, was passed on March 23 with only two contrary votes. Though the pacifism of rural progressives had not been overcome by the President's speaking tour, the enthusiasm of his city audiences had its effect on congressmen. Moreover, the need for troops had been highlighted when two outrages by Francisco Villa resulted in the death of thirty-five American citizens and the subsequent crossing of the Mexican border, on March 15, by a punitive expedition under General John J. Pershing.[5] In the same month further impetus was given to the drive for preparedness by the

---

[5] Though overshadowed by the European war, the Mexican situation had continued to plague the President after Huerta's retirement and the submission of the matter to Latin-American arbitration in the summer of 1914. In the autumn of that year, Wilson and Bryan persisted in their efforts to reconcile the contending factions and at the same time to protect American rights without using force. By Nov. 23 the administration felt that the situation was stable enough so that troops could be withdrawn from Veracruz. But in 1915 civil war continued. On Oct. 19 Carranza's government was recognized.

By January of 1916 the situation had become so chaotic that Wilson wrote to Cleveland Dodge that his heart was "pretty sad" about it. On the 11th Villa, whom Wilson and Bryan had made the mistake of supporting because of his amenability to Yankee advice and his pretensions of land reform, went berserk in northern Mexico and seized and massacred sixteen citizens of the United States. Moreover, on Mar. 9 the bandit general crossed the border and raided Columbus, New Mexico, burning towns and killing nineteen persons. Thereupon, popular demand for military action became irresistible; and after negotiating a diplomatic agreement with President Carranza that sanctioned temporary police action, the President sent a punitive expedition into Mexico on March 15, 1916, under Pershing. The decision caused mental anguish. The night before it was made Wilson walked out alone and paced the portico pensively, fearful of falling into war in the manner of President Polk. In a message to the press Wilson explained that the "single object" of the intervention was to stop Villa's forays by capturing him, "in entirely friendly aid of the constituted authorities in Mexico and with scrupulous respect for the sovereignty of the Republic." Inevitably there were clashes with Carranza's troops in which blood was shed and by May there was serious danger of full-scale war. *See* pp. 50 and 61.

outbreak of a rash of German submarine outrages, particularly by the torpedoing of the French steamer *Sussex.*

Advocates of a large regular army made the most of these immediate threats to the nation's safety. It seemed to them that Wilson had capitulated to the National Guard lobby as a political expedient. His policy frightened Republicans, who conceived that their party had saved the Union, won the Spanish-American War, and projected their country to material eminence in the world. They feared that the United States would fade from the first rank of the nations. Moderates now attacked Wilson openly. Democratic Senator Chamberlain and his Military Affairs Committee persuaded the Senate to adopt a bill, on April 18, that would almost double the Regular Army approved by the House, "federalize" the National Guard, and establish a "continental army"—a volunteer reserve force of a quarter million men. Thus the President was challenged to mediate between the two houses of Congress to get a reasonable measure of protection for the nation.

Wilson's position was the more difficult because, after his return from the Middle West, he had been engaged in a battle within his own party over the question of the status of armed liners. This issue had come to the front again with the torpedoing in early January of the British ship *Persia,* with appalling loss of passengers, including an American consul. To remove the provocation of armaments, which Germany cited as justification for such acts, Wilson and Lansing had urged the Allies not to arm their merchantmen. But when Germany gave warning on February 8 that armed vessels would be dealt with as ships of war, the State Department had been forced to give up its hope of persuading the Allies to let their vessels go unarmed. The statesmen at London felt that by removing armament they would merely make their ships easier prey.

When American diplomats abroad were notified that merchant shipping had a right to defensive armament and that the killing of American passengers would be regarded as "a breach of international law and the formal assurances given by the German government," Congressional leaders, unaware of the ill-fated effort that had been made to placate Germany, began to suspect that the Administration wanted to maneuver the nation into war. Their fear increased when the President, asked on February 21 by three legislative leaders what would happen if Americans traveling on an armed ship were drowned as a result of a submarine attack, told them that he would hold Germany strictly accountable. He asserted that the Allies, though unwise, were within their rights in arming their merchantmen. Furthermore, he made it clear that he did not wish to forbid Americans to travel on armed ships.

Replying to a warning of Congressional opposition, Wilson wrote on February 24 to Chairman Stone of the Senate's Committee on Foreign Relations: "I cannot consent to any abridgement of the rights of American citizens in any respect . . . Once accept a single abatement of right and many other humiliations would certainly follow, and the whole fine fabric of international law might crumble under our hands piece by piece. What we are contending for in this matter is of the very essence of the things that have made America a sovereign nation. She cannot yield them without conceding her own impotency as a nation and making virtual surrender of her independent position among the nations of the world."

Early on the morning of the 25th influential congressmen called at the White House and Speaker Champ Clark, whom many Democrats hoped to nominate for the Presidency in 1916, told Wilson that two-thirds of his colleagues were ready to approve a resolution offered by McLemore of Texas, warning Americans against traveling on armed ships of belligerents. But the President stood firmly on what he had written to Stone.

Fortunately Wilson was physically in good fighting trim and fortified politically by the sentiment that he had built on his speaking trip. The excess of energy that he had brought back from his honeymoon vacation at the first of the year had been lavished in talks with congressmen of both parties and letters to publicists. On January 20 he had seen Senator Lodge, thanked him for advice, and agreed with him in opposing an embargo and deploring investigation of pending foreign negotiations by Congressional committees. He tried to hold the ruling elders to the patriotic, nonpartisan creed that he preached to the national congregation. But the task strained his patience when revolt was seething. His temper flared up on February 25 and he told a visitor what he really thought about Congress: "It is with such a ——— outfit as that that I am supposed to act and achieve nationally for America!"

Legislators who feared to offend pacifistic and hyphenated constituents were shamed by the prophetic lash. They began to shift ground and talk of delaying a vote on the McLemore resolution and a similar one introduced by Gore in the Senate. But Wilson, advised by Cabinet members that his scepter as leader of the party would pass to Bryan if he did not demand a showdown, insisted that his position be made crystal clear in the eyes of the world, and immediately. He took the unprecedented step of writing to the ranking member of the House Committee on Rules. Asking for a prompt vote on the Gore and McLemore resolutions, he wrote: "The report that there are divided counsels in Congress in regard to the foreign policy of the Government is being made industrious use of in foreign capitals. I believe that report to be false, but so long as it is anywhere credited it cannot fail to do the greatest harm and expose the country to the most serious risks."

This brought the legislators quickly to balloting on the question of tabling the controversial resolutions. In both chambers the President's supporters, responding to the popular feeling that Wilson had evoked, won an impressive victory. Senator Lodge and other Republicans took a nonpartisan position behind the President.

After this rift in the party, Wilson found it difficult to get the leaders to unite on a compromise between the plans for preparedness that were approved by the House and the Senate. He had to plead time and again for cooperation in the interest of national unity, asking for an act that would provide the large number of units that the Senate desired but would keep them at the skeleton size that the House recommended; and he requested "unmistakable authority" to fill up the ranks at any time that the public safety might require it.

Early in June the National Defense Act became law.[6] Moderate progressives and pacifists felt that it provided reasonable protection for the nation, but the act fell far short of the ambitions of ardent military men. There were mass meetings and parades under the slogan "America First," and those who dissented were stigmatized as "subversives" and became objects of derivision.

The President gave repute to the clamor by issuing a Flag Day proclamation calling for rededication to the nation, "one and inseparable." He himself joined in a huge parade at Washington and, to the dismay of the secret service guards, led the procession carrying a small flag over his shoulder. He came through the ordeal unharmed, though

[6] A compromise, this measure authorized a federal army of nearly a quarter million and, dropping the plan of the military experts for a continental reserve force, it provided that the National Guard be increased to nearly a half million within five years and integrated into the federal defense structure. Moreover, the War Department was empowered to conduct summer training camps for volunteers and to build and operate a nitrate plant. In the new act there was a clause authorizing the President to draft, in time of war and after authorization by Congress, enough militia to keep the Army's reserve battalions up to battle strength—a provision that came to be variously interpreted but paved the way for the acceptance of conscription a year later.

The National Defense Act was but the first of several measures to enable the nation to defend its rights in an anarchic world. To secure adequate appropriations for naval construction, the President found it necessary again to mediate between the houses of Congress. Moved by fear of the navies of Germany and Japan and, more immediately, by a desire to be independent of Britain, Wilson persuaded an antipreparedness block in the House to go along with the larger program voted by the Senate, after it was altered by provisions for reorganization of the service and for the erection of a government armor-plate factory that would check profiteering. The naval appropriation bill was signed by the President on Aug. 29, along with a measure making allotments for the Army and creating a Council of National Defense for the coordination of industries and resources for national security. In August of 1916, also, the long running battle to strengthen the nation's shipping came to an end, with the Senate following party lines to adopt a bill that laid the foundation for a twentieth-century merchant marine.

a week later a similar demonstration at San Francisco was broken up by a death-dealing bomb.

On June 18, when Villa was still at large, Carranza was accusing Washington of bad faith in keeping Pershing's punitive expedition in Mexico, and the War College was drawing up plans for full-scale invasion, Wilson took advantage of the National Defense Act to call out about a hundred thousand National Guardsmen to protect the Mexican border. And yet at the same time he used his eloquence to warn his people against chauvinism.

The conscience of the prophet was not satisfied by the discharge of obvious duties that were forced upon him by threats from abroad. Amid the controversies stirred by his program for preparedness, and to hold the loyalty of progressives who distrusted that program and thought it inspired by influences militaristic and venal, he carried forward the cause of the New Freedom.

The most telling impetus given to the progressive movement by the emergency of 1916 was in the field of taxation. Unprecedented appropriations for the armed services made it necessary, in this election year, to issue bonds or to levy higher taxes. Conservative legislators wished to raise new funds by inflating the public debt; but Wilson made it clear that he regarded borrowing as a shortsighted policy.

The Congress, with uneasy eyes on the 1916 election, began to debate a plan advanced by McAdoo for additional excises and a schedule of income taxes that bore heavily upon citizens of moderate and low incomes. The Ways and Means Committee of the House was overwhelmed by protests from labor leaders and from Eastern progressives; and Democratic congressmen gave notice that they would not support McAdoo's plan even if a party caucus commanded them. They insisted that funds for preparedness should be taken from large incomes, inheritances, and the profits of arms-makers.

Immediately there were countercharges that irresponsible demagogues were trying to "soak the rich"; but for the first time Wilson's administration lost control of the rebellious Ways and Means Committee, and the House approved imposts more revolutionary than any sponsored by the President.[7] Though the leveling effect of the legislation went far beyond Wilson's intention, he signed the bill.

Moreover, in this election year, he consented to a measure designed to

---

[7] The new measure did not lower exemptions, but raised the surtax above the limit imposed by the law of 1913, levied a tax on large estates, repealed excises of the emergency law of 1914, and placed a tax on the gross receipts of manufacturers showing a net profit of 10 per cent and over. Moreover, under the influence of such men as Robert M. LaFollette and George W. Norris, the Senate increased several of the rates and placed a levy on corporation capital, surplus, and undivided profits.

mitigate the problems of agricultural credit. Up to this time, provisions for the peculiar needs of the farmer had lagged and Wilson himself had given very little study to this matter. The President had commended to the Congress a proposal for a system of land banks that would be privately controlled under federal charter; but he had been unwilling that the government supply the funds that would be necessary to subsidize this "single class of the community."

In January of 1916, with the secretary of the Rural Credits Association stating publicly that the Democratic party could command the support of Midwestern farmers by providing special credits, Wilson listened sympathetically to Secretary Houston and Congressman Lever. He not only agreed that the government would buy the minimum of farm bonds that these men specified, but doubled their figure. The Administration put its full power behind a rural credits bill, and Congress passed it almost unanimously. As Wilson had feared, it was denounced by conservatives as "class legislation"; and agrarian radicals felt that it was inadequate. But the President signed it, on July 17. Like the Federal Reserve, the new system was to be regulated by a board appointed by the President. Wilson was able to say to his people that never before in their lifetime was credit so available to individuals. Farmers responded. Many Republicans shifted their allegiance; and the Nonpartisan League, mushrooming in the Middle West, became Wilson's partisans.

The imminence of an election also gave impetus to legislation that had long been urged by independent advocates of better working conditions. On February 2 the House passed a bill forbidding interstate commerce in goods produced by children under fourteen; but Wilson, feeling that such a measure invaded the police power of the states and hence was unconstitutional, made no effort for months to overcome the apathy that the Senate showed. In mid-July, however, he was warned that progressives were restive and considered this bill a test of the sincerity of his progressivism; and on the 18th he went to the Capitol to tell Democratic senators that the fortunes of the party demanded that they let the measure come to a vote. As a result, Southerners who like himself were jealous of states' rights yielded; and the opposition of the National Association of Manufacturers, who regarded the law as a forerunner of less justifiable interferences with industry, was overcome. The President signed this humanitarian act on September 1 [8] with great satisfaction, and he gave further comfort to advocates of labor by approving a model compensation bill for federal employees.

[8] The Child Labor Act of 1916 was declared unconstitutional two years later and thus Wilson's first opinion of the measure was sustained.

Meanwhile Wilson had been committed by his party to stand for re-election. Prominent Democrats were depending on him to keep them politically solvent, and he had said to his bride that he would respond if his people called him. But he had made it clear at a Gridiron dinner, on February 26, that he had no personal craving for a second term.[9]

In the early months of 1916, the leaders had lost their easy confidence in the re-election of the Chief. Wilson's New Freedom was still regarded by financiers with suspicion. Ambassador Morgenthau, undertaking the task of raising a campaign fund and finding wealthy New Yorkers cool and Tammany bitter, got no comfort from the President's entourage. Not one of the high officials with whom he talked thought that Wilson could be re-elected. Even House was dubious; for the minority triumph in 1912, when the opposition was split, could not be repeated unless the President made a strong appeal to independent voters.

Entertaining the National Committee at the White House, the President said: "The facilities of publicity are not on our side. We have to do something very dramatic and very striking to be talked about at all . . . It is absolutely necessary that the impression we make on the country should be one of momentum . . . We are not partisans of men, we are partisans of ideas." He touched upon ideas as delicately as if they were explosive.

As the day of the nominating convention drew near, he became absorbed in planning for it. He dramatized his intention when, going to the circus and passing a show ring, he pretended to throw his hat in. He took into his own hands the shaping of the party's platform, adding a plank advocating woman suffrage and, conscious that independent voters would swing the coming election, stressing the progressive legislation that had been enacted.

Urged by House to seize leadership of peace sentiment before the

[9] A month before entering the Presidency, asked for his opinion of a Congressional resolution that would prohibit a second term, Wilson had argued that to impose a constitutional ban against a second term would be to suggest that the people could not be trusted to choose wisely at the polls. "Four years is too long a term," Wilson had written to A. Mitchell Palmer on Feb. 3, 1913, "for a President who is not the true spokesman of the people, who is imposed upon and does not lead. It is too short a term for a President who is doing or attempting a great work of reform, and who has not had time to finish it. . . . I am not speaking for my own re-election; I am speaking to redeem my promise that I would say what I really think on every public question and take my chances in the court of public opinion." There was no doubt, in 1915, that Wilson's party was depending on his leadership for another victory at the polls, in spite of a Bryan-inspired plank in its 1912 platform that had favored limitation of each president to a single term.

Newton D. Baker, surprised at finding the President more of a party man than he himself was, remarked upon it, and Wilson replied: "But not stronger than you will be. You will discover that in a government like ours, progress is possible only through parties, and parties are possible only when men are willing to concede minor matters for great policies." N. D. Baker to Frederick Palmer, Jan. 5 and July 18, 1931.

Republicans, whose convention would precede the Democratic, could pre-empt this channel of appeal to the voters, the President wrote the great vision of the twentieth century into the party's platform. He asserted that the circumstances of the past two years had revealed necessities of international action that no former generation could have foreseen. Repeating three fundamental principles that he set forth on May 27, in his address to the League to Enforce Peace, he wrote:

The time has come when it is the duty of the United States to join with the other nations of the world in any feasible association that will effectively serve those principles, to maintain inviolate the complete security of the highway of the seas for the common and unhindered use of all nations, and to prevent any war begun either contrary to treaty covenants or without warning and frank submission of the provocation and causes to the opinion of mankind.

The platform committee of the party, reviewing this far-reaching statement, disapproved the last proposition. They accepted the rest, along with statements of other foreign policies of the Administration—respect for human and political rights above material interests, Pan-American concord, and nonintervention in Mexico.[10]

It was the intention of the President that his Indians should vent their war whoops in a patriotic demonstration to which no voter could take exception. He conceived that, while he paraded in Washington with a flag upon his shoulder, the nominating convention would celebrate Flag Day at St. Louis, subordinating the traditional strains of "Dixie" to "The Star-Spangled Banner." He telegraphed to the convention to urge adoption of a strong plank on Americanism that he had written.

The President's plank was accepted unanimously; but when the hubbub on the floor of the convention hall subsided and Martin H. Glynn, former governor of New York, rose to deliver a keynote speech that had been approved in part by Wilson and House, the delegates responded with no more than due respect to patriotic hyperbole. However, when the speaker came to what he called "the paramount issue"—the avoidance of war—pulses beat faster. Democrats felt that, because of Germany's disavowal of ruthless submarine tactics early in May, the party could claim credit for saving the nation from armed conflict.

Glynn quickly detected the note that made the sweetest music in the ears of the party men. When he cited cases in which the nation had not gone to war though her rights were violated, his audience roared for

---

[10] Wilson was not confident enough of his Mexican policy to wish to have it stated in detail, but the platform committee overruled him.

more. And so he alluded to instances in the administrations of five presidents, and after each he repeated a line that became a slogan: "But we didn't go to war."

Leaders who had hoped to unite the party under Wilson's program of Americanism were aghast at the demonstration of pacifist feelings. A slip of paper was passed to Glynn, to suggest that Democrats were willing to fight if necessary. But his Celtic spirits were roused, and he went on to strengthen the bond that was being woven. "Do Republicans realize," he said, "that when they arraign the policy of the President of the United States today, they arraign the policy of Harrison, of Blaine, of Lincoln, and of Grant?" There was no staying the tide of sentiment.

The next day Senator Ollie James, the permanent chairman, attributed the people's blessings to their chief. "Four years ago they sneeringly called Woodrow Wilson the school teacher. . . . Today . . . the confines of his schoolroom circle the world. His subject is the protection of American life and American rights under international law, the saving of neutral life, the freedom of the seas. . . ."

When he finished, every delegate was on his feet, cheering spontaneously in a bedlam that lasted for twenty-one minutes. They called for William Jennings Bryan, who was moved to tears by the apotheosis of peace; and the Great Commoner soon added his tribute. A few hours later Woodrow Wilson was nominated by acclamation.

The President was far from happy over the inclination of the party men to make political capital out of his avoidance of war. When the Resolutions Committee drafted a platform plank that commended "the splendid diplomatic victories of our great President, who has preserved the vital interests of our Government and its citizens, and kept us out of war," [11] and the last five words were picked out of context, used as a slogan, and flaunted on billboards, Wilson feared that his people were gloating over their blessings and forgetting their duty to prepare to defend their way of life by arms if it became necessary.

Though he gave eloquent notice that he was standing for the Presidency as a free moral agent, not responsible to any faction or party, Wilson's interest in a Democratic victory mounted during the summer. A series of speeches—three were given on a single July day—and conferences held almost daily with party leaders were imposed upon a docket of executive duties that in itself was staggering. Finding even the summer days too short, the President said that he would "steal up

[11] *Democratic Textbook,* 1916, p. 25. For comment on the origin of the controversial phrase "kept us out of war," *see* Baker, VI, 257 n. Robert W. Woolley, director of publicity, was careful in all campaign releases to use the wording: "With honor he has kept us out of war." It is Mr. Woolley's recollection that this wording was approved by both Wilson and Vance McCormick. R. W. Woolley to the writer, Dec. 6, 1955.

on them in the dark," and he and Edith Wilson made a practice of breakfasting at five or six o'clock.

House and Vance McCormick—new chairman of the National Committee—busied themselves in rebuilding party machinery. Funds were scraped together, and the managers allotted these and the party's speakers to a few states that were critical. They felt that the best hope for victory lay in running the President as if he were a candidate for justice of the peace. On July 25 House wrote cockily to the Chief: "I feel satisfied that we will have the only efficient organization that has ever been constructed in a Democratic national campaign." Noting that "the skein was getting tangled," Wilson decided to concentrate discussion of party policy in the hands of McCormick, who came to his study regularly on Monday evenings. "He brings the suggestions to me," Wilson wrote on Aug. 8, "and I know by experience what confusion will result if we do not coordinate and use a single channel."

Realizing the importance of capturing the independent vote, the Republican Old Guard felt that their best hope for victory lay in nominating Charles Evans Hughes, who had won popular acclaim by disclosures of questionable practices on the part of New York utilities and insurance companies. Hughes, who since 1910 had been a justice of the United States Supreme Court, was nominated easily and stood on a platform that differed from that of Wilson chiefly in its planks on Mexico, the Philippines, and the tariff.

Wilson respected this opponent as one who would have to be met with sound argument, and he discouraged politicians who wished to condemn Hughes publicly for "dragging the Supreme Court into the mire of politics." Members of the President's family were friendly to Hughes, but Wilson was disappointed when he received from his opponent a note of resignation so curt that he was advised not to dignify it by acknowledging it. Insisting, however, that the President of the United States must always do "the gentlemanly thing," he replied to Hughes's single sentence with two that were scarcely more gracious.

The son of a clergyman, Hughes had none of the love of polemics that was in the Wilson blood. His speeches were without color and warmth. His progressive pronouncements lacked the confirmation that the public found in the President's record. Independent journals in the East that welcomed his nomination were discouraged when he spoke to Western audiences in a way that left them cold. Roosevelt, struck by the similarity of background and aims, spoke of Hughes as "the whiskered Wilson."

Noting the feebleness of Hughes's campaign, Wilson was the more disposed to refrain from making speeches. On August 19 he wrote to

B. M. Baruch: "I am inclined to follow the course suggested by a friend of mine who says that he always has followed the rule never to murder a man who is committing suicide, and clearly this misguided gentleman is committing suicide slowly but surely." He was content, he said, to let the Republican nominee "blow himself off." He was more concerned about being worthy of re-election than about asserting his own claims for votes.

Immediately after his nomination, in July, he made a determined effort to commit representatives of special interests to a national covenant. To government workers, to labor leaders, to businessmen, his message was essentially the same: service to one's fellows above service to self.

In the summer of 1916 he was forced to act to protect the public against the consequences of a serious strike. The railroad brotherhoods demanded shorter hours without loss of pay and with time-and-a-half for overtime work. The United States Board of Mediation failed to settle the matter by arbitration; a strike was approved almost unanimously by the workers; and the Clayton Act made it impossible to prevent it by court injunction. Perceiving the seriousness of the threat, Wilson invited the spokesmen of management and labor to the White House on August 13. He reminded them that a strike would bring hardships to the public, perhaps even starvation, and that it would impede the preparedness program. He appealed for compromise in the national interest. But when both sides were unmoved, he resolved to end the impasse by imposing a settlement that seemed to him fair, and depending on public sentiment to enforce it.

Wilson went before the Congress on August 29, after the railroad presidents had finally refused to accept his verdict and the unions had called a strike for the midnight before Labor Day. The atmosphere in the Capitol was tense as the President proposed six measures that would facilitate the settlement of similar controversies in the future. Calling attention to the demands of national defense, the lawgiver made one last plea for judiciousness: "We should make all arbitral awards judgments by record of a court of law in order that their interpretation and enforcement may lie, not with one of the parties to the arbitration, but with an impartial and authoritative tribunal."

For a few days the outcome hung in the balance, while the President, fearing that he had failed, called 15,000 men from the Mexican border to preserve order in case of a strike. However, the Congress responded to his leadership and passed the Adamson Act on September 3, the day before the walkout was to begin. This measure decreed an eight-hour day and set up a commission to study the problem, and Wilson redeemed a promise to the executives by urging the Interstate Commerce Commission to grant the increases in freight rates that would be necessary. The Adamson Act became a model law governing labor relations.[12]

In his sympathy for farmers and laborers the President did not lose sight of the importance of healthy growth in industry. He threw his weight behind the Webb Bill, which would amend the antitrust laws to permit American manufacturers to combine in selling goods abroad. In order to give his people confidence that economic facts were considered in the fixing of tariffs, he overcame his earlier aversion to commissions, from which he feared that special interests might get favors more easily than from Congress. Yielding to the opinion of members of his Cabinet and to an overwhelming vote by the nation's Chambers of Commerce, he persuaded the Congress to provide a tariff commission. He responded to a plea from McAdoo for prompt appointment of commissioners as a means of nullifying the tariff platform of the Republicans, and sought "nonpartisan" rather than "bipartisan" members. Professor Taussig of Harvard, a low-tariff economist, was named chairman, and soon the new body won the admiration of both the President and his people.

Wilson's impulse toward another progressive goal was less productive of obvious gains. Personally, he was deeply interested in plans for conserving the natural resources of the nation. There were diverse opinions among senators, however, as to how his ideals could best be realized; and none of the measures proposed seemed to Wilson acceptable. Not until June of 1920 did the President have an opportunity to

---

[12] Wilson's enterprising spirit was responsible not only for the passage of the model Adamson Act, but also for its acceptance by a single vote in the Supreme Court on March 19, 1917; for he had the temerity to appoint a justice who was a champion of liberal interpretation of the law. On Jan. 28, 1916, after asking McAdoo whether Congress would approve the nominee and getting assurance that it would after a stiff fight, he had sent to the Capitol the name of Louis D. Brandeis, whom Attorney General Gregory endorsed as "the greatest lawyer in the United States." (This choice was in keeping with Wilson's long-standing concept of the nation's courts as not "strait jackets," but "instruments of the nation's growth." In his academic days he had likened the Supreme Court to "a constitutional convention in continuous session.")

Wilson was not insensitive to the political returns that would accrue in this election year from the honoring of a progressive such as Brandeis. He could afford to risk offending Southern conservatives who were congenital Democrats and would support the party ticket in any event.

When a storm of protest rose from private interests that Brandeis had tried to bring within federal regulation, Wilson sent an eloquent personal plea to the Senate's Committee on the Judiciary. He had not depended on "endorsements," he said, but named Brandeis only because he knew him to be singularly qualified by learning, by gifts, and by character. When the Senate acted favorably, Wilson could honestly say: "I am indeed relieved and delighted. I never signed any commission with such satisfaction."

On July 14, 1916, Wilson made his third and last appointment to the Supreme Court, that of John H. Clarke. "I dare say you are surprised by the nomination of Clarke . . ." he wrote to House on July 23, 1916. "He is a close friend of Newton Baker's and Gregory (whom I love and trust more than ever) picked him out."

sign a water-power bill; but on August 25, 1916, he approved an act establishing a National Park Service.[13]

Thus, before beginning to campaign for re-election, Wilson had made further progress toward the objectives of his New Freedom. By exerting both the power of persuasion and the persuasion of power, he had achieved results during his first term that could justly be compared with the first administration of his parliamentary hero, William E. Gladstone.

August of 1916 was a harrowing month. At the end, after the President had sat up part of a night working on his railroad labor message to Congress and had been called at six in the morning to face a full docket of appointments, his eyes were bloodshot, his face drawn and haggard. Finally, when the danger of a railroad strike was averted at the beginning of September, he was induced to go to his own state of New Jersey for the formal notification of his nomination. He consented to leave his desk only because it semed unfitting to use the White House for a purpose so partisan.

The Wilsons rented Shadow Lawn, an estate near Asbury Park. Its pretentious and ornate interior was offensive—it looked "like a gambling hell," the President thought—but he and his family enjoyed the privacy of the grounds and an out-of-doors dining room.

On September 2 hundreds of party men came for luncheon and performed the rite of notification. Independent voters listened attentively when Wilson, disclaiming any desire to "boast," declared: "The Republican party is just the party that *cannot* meet the new conditions of a new age." Not content merely to review his accomplishment, the prophet looked toward the future. Apologizing for lack of progress in developing natural resources, he called on advocates of conservation and capitalists "to get together in a spirit of genuine accommodation

[13] One phase of the conservation movement was so controversial and so complicated by technicalities that Wilson did not venture to discuss it openly with his people. The question of the leasing of the public oil reserves provoked a sharp division of opinion within the Cabinet. Franklin K. Lane wished to use his prerogative as secretary of the interior in ruling on the claims of private interests for patents to oil lands in the midst of California territory that had been set apart for the Navy by Taft's administration. Secretary Daniels, however, protested against Lane's leasing policy, feeling that the latter's California friends were being favored and that the Navy would be forced to pay exorbitant prices for oil. When Daniels explained his views to the President, Wilson asked him to put them before the Cabinet, so that Lane also could be heard and the attorney general could make a ruling. After the pros and cons had been frankly stated in the official family, the President was not willing to make a final decision.

Early in 1916 the problem was intensified by the drive for preparedness. Wilson therefore pleaded for enactment of a General Leasing Bill that had been worked out by Lane with experts in oil production and conservation. The legislators, however, took no conclusive action; and Wilson, hesitating, asked Lane to sign no leases until they could have another conference. Time and again he refused to sign documents that the secretary sent to him.

and agreement . . ." He asked for "justice to the labourer, not only by paying a living wage but also by making all the conditions that surround labor what they ought to be." He proposed coordination of the railway systems for national use and "their better adaptation as a whole to the life and trade and defense of the Nation." Recalling the measures taken to facilitate foreign trade, he proclaimed an end of "the day of Little Americanism with its narrow horizons."

In defense of his Mexican policy he said: "Test is now being made of us whether we be sincere lovers of popular liberty or not and are indeed to be trusted to respect national sovereignty among our weaker neighbours . . . Upon the outcome of that test (its outcome in their minds, not in ours) depends every relationship of the United States with Latin America, whether in politics or in commerce and enterprise." This was the great issue, he declared, and it was "a barren and provincial statesmanship" that lost sight of it.

In his survey of past and future, Wilson did not say whether or not he would continue to keep his people out of war, for he did not know. But he said: "If you elect my opponent, you elect a war." And he declared that, though property rights could be vindicated by claims for damages at the war's end, loss of human life and direct violations of sovereignty could not be brooked without resistance. The prophet was chiefly interested in something more fundamental and far-reaching —the prevention of a recurrence of the present catastrophe.

When the President returned to Washington, where the Congress was ending its session, the pressure of work became so intense that Dr. Grayson warned him that he must take time out for golf.

In mid-September, as he was laboring to clear his desk of an accumulation of papers, news of his sister's death reached him. He journeyed to old Columbia for the funeral, and visited once more the church of his father, the grave for which he had written the loving inscription, the house that his mother had designed, and the Woodrow relatives who shared memories of beloved Uncle James.

Returning from sleepy Columbia to the arena of political combat, Wilson found that the Republicans, desperate for an issue that would give vitality to their campaign, had seized upon the Adamson Law, on which his signature was hardly dry. Hughes challenged it as an abanment of principle. As governor of New York he himself had signed a bill prescribing an eight-hour day for certain railway workers, but he asserted that Wilson had surrendered to dictation without adequate study of the facts and without resort to arbitration. Conservative sentiment joined exultantly in this criticism, and it seemed in September that the vote of the North and the East might go so solidly to Hughes that he would be elected.

When House and McCormick told the President of the wrath of employers, Wilson felt that at last he must take the warpath. Warming up to battle, he talked about "Labor and Capital" from a platform on the estate at Shadow Lawn. He spoke of the distress that had come to him when he spoke frankly with managers and employees of the railways. The nation could not compel citizens to work, he held, but the government could say to organizations: "You must not interrupt the national life without consulting us."

As in earlier campaigns, the President became combative in the face of unfair criticism. People who disliked him were repeating charges that he failed to pat public officials on the back, was not a good mixer, and was neglectful of the newsmen, to whom he no longer granted regular conferences. Wilson was accustomed to these reproaches; but he suffered when enemies descended to new depths of scurrility and pandered to the shallow minds of voters who had taken a personal dislike to him. Some said that Wilson was a megalomaniac whose object was to outdo Lincoln and sit at a table with czars and princes. It was bruited, by word of mouth, that he had left the tomb of Ellen Wilson unmarked and that corn was growing on it: actually, war conditions had delayed the shipment of a headstone of Carrara marble, and during the prolonged illness of an old friend who had taken care of the grave on Myrtle Hill, corn had sprouted from manure that had been put on the roses. It was gossiped that a pregnant young lady had demanded to see the President at the executive offices and had walked out with a check in her hand; actually, kindly Woodrow Wilson had been generous to a relative who was about to bear a child and lacked security.[14] Then, too, the old canards about Mary Hulbert and the letters were revived. Colonel House countered this by explaining, "We Southerners like to write mush notes." But the Colonel could reach only a few. Others close to the President were so outraged by the imputations that they refused to discuss them, and thus the roots of scandal spread in the shadow of secrecy. Wilson himself felt helpless. To deny the insinuations publicly would be merely to give them greater currency among the prurient. The more abusive the attacks the more impenetrable was his silence.

He suggested an antidote for poisonous gossip, however, in a letter to the Reverend Sylvester W. Beach, who had been his pastor at Prince-

---

[14] These sentences are based upon statements made to the writer by Mrs. Hallie Alexander Rounseville and Mrs. Will Harbin of Rome, Ga., and by Woodrow cousins of Woodrow Wilson: Helen Woodrow Bones, Katharine Woodrow Kirkland, James Woodrow, and Fitz-William McMaster Woodrow.

ton: "I do not know how to deal with the fiendish lies that are being invented and circulated about my personal character other than to invite those who repeat them to consult anybody who has known me for any length of time . . ." The campaign managers persuaded Stockton Axson to come immediately to Washington and write an article on "The Private Life of Woodrow Wilson." It was edited by Colonel House,[15] published in the Sunday supplement of the *New York Times,* and printed for distribution far and wide.

Easier to counter were the criticisms of policy offered in public by Republicans. Hughes continued to point to errors of the past rather than appealing to progressive hopes for the future. He pointed particularly to the inconclusiveness of Wilson's Mexican policy, even though it had resulted in negotiations by a Joint High Commission that gave hope of settlement.[16] The President, annoyed by criticism that seemed to him pettifogging, told newsmen that his opponent, while closeted in the Supreme Court, had lost touch with the spirit of the people.

Wilson was given an opportunity to show his independence when an importunate telegram came from the Irish president of an anti-British organization that had German support. The President read it calmly and penciled a reply on the same sheet, to be sent off at once. It said: "I would feel deeply mortified to have you or anybody like you vote for me. Since you have access to many disloyal Americans and I have not I will ask you to convey this message to them."

To a delegation that waited upon him, he said: "Politics must be left out because, don't you see, to put it plainly, that is a form of blackmail. I would resent it from one set of men as from another. You can vote as

15 "I edited Dr. Axson's article on the President, cutting out what the newspaper boys term 'sob stuff.' It was too intimate and I was afraid the President would not like it." House Diary, Sept. 30, 1916. Mrs. Malcolm Forbes of Boston endowed the printing of a million copies for free distribution.

16 Relations with Mexico had so deteriorated that House suggested to the President in mid-June that war was "inevitable." On the 20th Lansing gave notice that United States troops would not be withdrawn, and warned that Mexican attacks on them would "lead to the gravest consequences." Only a few hours after this stern note reached Mexico City, a skirmish near Carrizal resulted in the killing of twelve soldiers of the United States and the capture of twenty-three by Mexican troops.

Wilson demanded the immediate release of the prisoners, while at the same time insisting that he was not willing to determine for the Mexican people—unless they asked him—what the form and personnel of their government should be. He countered agitation for intervention that was coming from jingoes and investors by a fervent plea for tolerance. "The easiest thing is to strike," he said to the Press Club of New York on June 20. "The brutal thing is the impulsive thing . . . Do you think the glory of America would be enhanced by a war of conquest in Mexico?"

On July 4, Carranza suggested negotiations, and a Joint High Commission, with three members from each nation, met from Sept. 6, 1916, into January of 1917. Grievances of the United States and Mexico were discussed, and thus partisan attacks on Wilson lost force and Carranza was given an opportunity to hold elections.

you please. It matters little to me provided I am sure that I am doing the right thing at the right time." Sometimes, by sheer indifference to political consequences, he achieved effects that politicians strove for in vain. When most natural, he seemed most forceful.

Yet he was too canny to say anything to deflate Democratic orations that won voters by asserting that he had kept them out of war with honor and implying that he would continue to do so. It was obvious, too, that in catering to special interests of farmers, laborers, and industrialists he had used the national resources to benefit organized minorities. His devotion to a classless society and the common good had yielded to the exigencies of an election in which many citizens would cast ballots not as disinterested individuals but as members of groups seeking favored treatment. An impression of opportunism grew out of his recital of things done "for business," "for agriculture," and "for labor." There were sundry measures that he labeled "for general service," but "for mankind" only the premature child labor law. The necessity of rallying all factions and interests for defense against foreign aggression had made it the more difficult to resist pleas for special consideration.

The campaign theme that most clearly set apart Wilson the statesman from the politicians of the day was one that, though it was suggested by many, he was making peculiarly his own. In the last weeks of the campaign, he summoned his people repeatedly to sublimate their thought in a vision of united service to the cause of world peace. He said at Omaha: "For the next decade, at any rate—after that it will be a matter of our own choice whether it continues or not— . . . we have got to serve the world. That alters every commercial question, it alters every political question, it alters every question of domestic development."

The Wilsons jumped through the hoops of political publicity at Omaha. The President reviewed a pageant and his wife was introduced to Indian participants as a descendant of Pocahontas. They even went to a swine show, and afterward jested with newsmen about the size of the prize swine. Edith Wilson was proving herself a durable campaigner and took pains to write personal notes of appreciation to those who were kind to them. Her husband was proud of her. In one rear platform appearance he said: "I want you to see Mrs. Wilson. She is much better worth looking at than I am."

Liberal spokesmen and journals rallied to the President during October. Though the betting ran 20 to 17 in favor of Hughes, Wilson thought in the middle of the month that the outcome of the election was incalculable because of the large independent vote that would be cast.[17] In the closing days of the campaign he was not at all certain that his speeches were hitting the mark. Responding to House's urging he made a final assault, on November 2, on New York City, the metropolis that seemed to him "rotten to the core" and deserving to be wiped off the map.

The Colonel put on a good show at Madison Square Garden, intent that the meeting should be the greatest in the history of New York and should result in Wilson's carrying the state. Sheriff Alfred E. Smith led a parade of 30,000 of the faithful. The Garden was packed to the roof, and a crowd of 25,000 milled around outside and made it impossible for the Wilsons to approach the door. Going to the other end of the building, the President and his party crept up a fire escape, entered a window, and made their appearance on the platform. When he rose to speak, he was blasted for a half hour by brassy music and roars of the warriors. But for all its enthusiasm, the affair did not swing New York State away from Hughes.

In his last campaign speech, delivered at Shadow Lawn on November 4, Wilson made a personal confession, wistful and very humble: "To me has fallen the unspeakable good fortune of happening to be the spokesman of the American people at this critical and fateful time. . . . I cannot be sure that I judge right, but I am sure that my heart speaks the same thing that they wish their hearts to speak. It is only in this impulse, in this sympathetic connection which I am sure that I have with them, that I am worthy to speak for them at all."

The next day he acted to square his position with the gospel that he had been preaching. It seemed to him that if he was to be truly the servant of the people he should resign immediately if they voted against him. Thus he could give his country, in this instance, one benefit of the

---

17 Wilson was plagued by a charge put forward by Henry Cabot Lodge, to the effect that after sending a *Lusitania* note to Berlin, the President had added a postscript that suggested that the Germans should not take his protest too seriously. Wilson had indeed considered tempering the first *Lusitania* note by releasing a qualifying statement to the press and had been dissuaded from that course by advisers; but he asserted that Lodge's statement was "untrue," that "no postscript or amendment" was secretly sent to Berlin. *Cf.* p. 17 above. This adroit denial satisfied citizens who were pestering Wilson for the truth; and Lodge, still incredulous, had to accept it.

On Dec. 29, 1916, Wilson declined to attend a church anniversary celebration when it was announced that Lodge was to be one of the speakers. He explained that the senator's conduct during the campaign made it impossible "with self-respect to join in any exercise in which he takes part." One of Wilson's favorite stories was about Colonel Pettigrew, a Southern lawyer who lost a civil suit and was called a cheat and a liar by his client but did not take offense until he was denounced as a Federalist. Asked why this accusation enraged him, he replied: "Damn him. It was the only true thing he said." There was just enough truth in Lodge's accusation to draw blood.

parliamentary system that he had long advocated. Discussing the idea with House and Burleson, he worked out a plan that would be both constitutional and effective. He wanted to put himself on record before the election, so that if he was defeated he could resign with no appearance of petulance or pique. But he did not attempt to make political capital of this decision by publicizing it, as some of his colleagues wished him to do. Two days before the election he set forth his intention in a letter that he addressed to Secretary Lansing, put in a wax-sealed envelope, and marked "most confidential."

Pointing out that if he were defeated he would be without authority to speak for the nation during his remaining months in office, he asserted that it would be his duty to relieve the country of the perils of such a situation. If he could gain the consent of the vice-president, he would ask Lansing's permission to invite Hughes to become secretary of state, and would then join the vice-president in resigning, thus opening to Hughes the immediate succession to the Presidency.

Having thus set his conscience at rest, Woodrow Wilson waited patiently at Shadow Lawn for the outcome of a campaign that had been waged by both candidates with a dignity unusual in American politics. The President's hope for victory was strong, and he made a little speech to his wife, outlining a program for his second term. When she spoke of a day to come when they could live their own lives, he said: "What a delightful pessimist you are! One must never court defeat. If it comes, accept it like a soldier; but don't anticipate it, for that destroys your fighting spirit."

He applied himself to his work, pausing once to telephone to the executive office nearby to ask for the early returns. At dinner he listed the states that seemed reasonably sure to support him, but they gave him only 217 of the 266 electoral votes that were needed. In the evening he threw himself wholeheartedly into a game of twenty questions with the family.

Finally bad news penetrated his seclusion: Hughes had won almost all the Northeastern states and his election had been conceded by New York newspapers. Over the phone Tumulty's voice sounded so dismal that Wilson chuckled and said: "Well, it begins to look as if we have been badly licked. . . . The only thing I am sorry for, and that cuts me to the quick, is that the people apparently misunderstood us. But I have no regrets. We have tried to do our duty." His chief concern seemed to be that his wife might not be so happy as he in retirement. Oppressed by the gloom of those around him, he took a glass of milk, went to bed, and slept soundly.

It was not until Friday morning that the Wilsons were sure that they would serve another term in the White House.[18] Hughes did not send his congratulations until November 22, when at last the official count of California ballots was virtually complete. By that time the electoral vote was 277 to 254 in Wilson's favor. His popular vote exceeded that of Hughes by more than a half-million, though it was a little less than half of the total.

While Wilson succeeded in his quest for the confidence of his people, serious rifts opened in his official family. In the spring of 1916 Dr. Grayson had whispered to House that Tumulty was responsible for most of the President's misfortunes and that the secretary was even trying to discredit the Colonel. Then, too, there were complaints from Protestant citizens against communicating with the President through a Catholic secretary.

Appreciative of his secretary's good intentions and abilities and reluctant, as always, to dispense with a man to whom he had grown accustomed, Wilson resisted for months the voices raised against Tumulty. He did not wish to risk dissension in the ranks until the election was over. In November, however, he yielded, and told his secretary, with concern for his financial welfare, that he would appoint him to the Board of General Appraisers if he would resign.

Tumulty was brokenhearted. He wanted neither money nor glory, but only the privilege of continuing to serve a great man. He told four intimate friends what had transpired. One of them was David Lawrence, the journalist, who had known Wilson since Princeton days. Lawrence's indignation was so great that he ventured to intrude upon the Presbyterian in the White House on a Sabbath afternoon. He told Wilson bluntly that the release of Tumulty would be the worst case of ingratitude ever known in politics and that the press would not stand for it. Woodrow Wilson had learned in the case of George Harvey, to his sorrow, what damage could be done to political repute by allegations of ingratitude; and he decided not to compel his faithful secretary to take another position. The President also stood firm against superficial—and often ill-founded—criticism of Secretary Daniels. He would not accept suggestions from House and Edith Wilson that these men be dismissed.

In addition to Tumulty and Daniels, McAdoo was giving concern to

18 Wilson's deep satisfaction in the victory was revealed when he congratulated George Creel, a campaign speaker, on winning bets. When Creel remarked that he had supposed Presbyterians frowned on wagers, Wilson replied with a laugh: "Yes, but in this case it has the sanctification of a good cause. Spoiling the Egyptians has biblical approval." Creel, *Rebel at Large*, p. 156.

the President; and this was the more painful because in dealing with him Wilson was touching upon one of his dearest loves—that for his daughter Nellie. To House, in August of 1916, McAdoo seemed piqued because the President did not take him more closely into his confidence, and as ambitious as ever to occupy the White House. In fact there were indications at the end of 1916 that there might be contention among Cabinet members for the succession four years hence.[19]

But despite the jealousies and ambitions that were gnawing at the hearts of men close to him, the Chief still commanded their fealty. Moreover, during 1916 he had enlisted new associates who were serving with the undivided loyalty that would be required in surmounting the tasks ahead.

[19] Jesting about the competition for succession, House wrote to Wilson thus on Dec. 5: "Burleson . . . is grooming Josephus Daniels for the place with prohibition and woman suffrage to be the issues. With Lansing, McAdoo, Baker, and Burleson with their lightning-rods erect and with Crane grooming Houston and Bryan grooming Josephus, you have a Cabinet with a single-hearted purpose. Lane and [W. B.] Wilson were unfortunately born in British possessions."

CHAPTER IV

Caught in the Web of War

In the election year of 1916, while Wilson satisfied the yearnings of idealists by his vision of American leadership toward an international order, he was careful to refrain from public comment on issues that might involve the nation in war overnight. Indeed, he did his best to quiet diplomatic controversy and to hold himself aloof from it. Nevertheless, he could not escape for a moment from the pressures from London and Berlin.

Britain's will to fight to a finish was impressed upon him by Walter Hines Page, who was called home to get what Wilson called "a bath of American opinion." Twice in August the President invited his old friend to a family luncheon at the White House. The talk was light and jocular; but Page got an inkling of the sternness of his chief's concept of neutrality when one of the Wilson girls asked, in all seriousness, whether she was unneutral in speaking of her admiration for the French. Unable to inject a word of business into the conversation, the ambassador was told to go off for a rest and come back for a serious discussion after the President had relieved his mind of the railroad labor crisis. Page left the White House distressed by what he called the "college professor's habit" of aloofness. He thought that Wilson was proving a vast failure as a leader.

Wilson wished to give Page time to feel the strength of anti-British sentiment at Washington before undertaking to argue with him. But finally he received a direct plea from the ambassador that he could not ignore. Inviting his friend to Shadow Lawn, Wilson devoted a morning to a thorough airing of the differences of view that had been developing for two years. The ambassador argued the British case fervently, and gave the President certain ideas that Grey had asked him to convey when the foreign secretary had bidden him farewell in July.

Wilson replied bluntly that when the war began he had been heartily in sympathy with the Allies, but that now he saw no one who was not vexed by Britain's acts. "Tell those gentlemen for me," he charged Page, that damage to any American citizen was in effect damage to himself, personally. When Page spoke of Germany's desire for an armistice and intimated that Britain would not grant it and would indeed be offended if the President fell in with any such scheme, Wilson replied that he would have nothing to do with promoting a military armistice; but he added, "If they propose an armistice looking toward peace—yes, I shall be glad."

The men parted friends, Page putting his hand on the President's shoulder and Wilson's eyes filling with tears. The ambassador thought him the loneliest man he had ever seen and quite out of touch with the pro-British sentiment that the popular envoy met as he went about in the South and the Northeast. And once again Wilson had to torture his heart by shutting it against the heresies of a friend whom he wanted to love. They never met again. When Page sent a note of resignation, in November, Wilson questioned its sincerity and could not bring himself to accept it at once. Soon thereafter American involvement in the war became so imminent that Page could not leave his post immediately without a consciousness of disloyalty; and the President, failing to persuade House or Cleveland Dodge to serve at London, concluded that he could find no wartime envoy more effective than Page.[1]

Wilson gave close attention to the dossier of reports that Page left with him on September 23, and the next day he read them to House in the Colonel's apartment. His friend suggested that the greatest irritant to English pride was the rapid expansion of the American Navy; but Wilson, who had just approved the largest naval appropriation ever passed by Congress, was not inclined to remove this source of friction.

Meanwhile sentiment at London turned still more emphatically against Wilson and the pacifism that was associated with his name. To be sure, there was agitation for peace among British radicals; and Wilson, kept informed of this by letters that House forwarded to him from British leaders as well as from W. H. Buckler, a special agent at the London embassy, was pleased by what he called "a strong drift of opinion towards reasoned calculation." Yet despite the appalling attrition of the warfare, and in spite of the failure of their armies to win the conclusive victories that were hoped for, the British people, by and large, were still not ready to take the reasonable, long-range view that House had commended to them. Laborers had lost patience with the American President, and men in the trenches referred to shells that failed to explode as "Wilsons." David Lloyd George, soon to succeed Asquith as

[1] On Nov. 14, House told Wilson of Page's opinion of the President—an able man, like Jefferson, who would not fight in any circumstances. The Colonel observed that his friend was "not pleased" but did not resent this. When the President calmly discussed possible remedies and declared that no man should stand in the way, House said that the whole staff of the London embassy should be removed. A few months earlier, House had passed along to Wilson the opinion that the embassy was "a nest of disloyalty to the President." Wilson told House on Jan. 12, 1917, that he was determined to accept Page's resignation, though fearful that the ambassador would come home disgruntled and write embarrassing articles for the *World's Work*. But when, on March 5, Mrs. Wilson asked House to take the London post, the President said that he had written Page that he would make no change for the moment.

prime minister, put himself *en rapport* with this sentiment. On September 28 he publicly challenged what he characterized as "a defeatist spirit working from foreign quarters to bring about an inconclusive peace."

When House told the President of the ugliness of the feeling at London, Wilson replied on October 10: "These are indeed deep waters. . . . I can only say that if our friendly relations with England should be imperilled . . . it would be only another illustration of how difficult it is to be friends with Great Britain without doing whatever she wants us to do." Moreover, his discouragement deepened a few days later when London sent unsatisfactory replies to a protest that he had made on July 26 against seizure of mails and the blacklisting of American firms that had dealt with the enemy.

Though annoyed by the British to the point of assigning them motives scarcely higher than those of Germany, Wilson could see no advantage in making war upon the Allies. Moreover, reports from Berlin suggested that, while England had closed the door to efforts to make peace, the German Foreign Office was being hard pressed by the Admiralty, as well as by desperation among the people, to sanction a renewal of offenses that Wilson already had designated as a cause for war.

Toward the end of October, Wilson received this memorandum, sent by the Kaiser to Ambassador Gerard:

Your Excellency hinted to his Majesty in your last conversation at Charleville in April that President Wilson possibly would try towards the end of the summer to offer his good services to the belligerents for the promotion of peace. The German Government has no information as to whether the President adheres to this idea and as to the eventual date at which this step would take place. Meanwhile the constellation of war has taken such a form that the German Government foresees the time at which it will be forced to regain the freedom of action that it has reserved to itself in the note of May 4th last and thus the President's steps may be jeopardized. The German Government thinks it its duty to communicate this fact to Your Excellency in case you should find that the date of the intended action of the President should be far advanced towards the end of this year.

"The German memorandum," House warned the President in forwarding this message on October 20, "is clearly a threat to resume submarine warfare, their idea being to force you before election to act, knowing that if you are defeated nothing can be done by anyone for months to come. They do not want to take the chance."

House's diagnosis made the President even more reluctant to act before the election. Nevertheless, Wilson received Gerard at Shadow

Lawn on October 24. Both he and his wife asked penetrating questions. Their ambassador told them bluntly that the United States faced war unless it made peace, that to gain the respect of German officials who did not understand the ideal of peaceful coexistence America must make a show of strength. There was nothing to suggest that the German government would listen to terms that the Allies would accept, or even the general principles that the President had laid down in his address of May 27 to the League to Enforce Peace and had repeated in his campaign speeches. And doubtless the German militarists were not endeared to Wilson's heart when Gerard said that they believed their atrocities might frighten Americans out of going to war. Nevertheless, when a cake presented by a German-American was served at luncheon, the Wilsons ate freely of it while their envoy abstained.[2]

The grim alternative mentioned in the Kaiser's memorandum became more menacing when submarine activity was stepped up. Three ships with Americans aboard had been sunk in September; on October 12 it was reported from Berlin that naval officers had petitioned the Kaiser for immediate resumption of submarine warfare; citizens of the United States were killed when the British merchantman *Marina* was sunk without warning on October 28; and ten days later the liner *Arabia* met the same fate.

Hesitating to take any step that might affect the voting of his people, Wilson tried to make light of the *Marina* disaster in talking with House and McCormick on November 2. "I do not believe," he said, "the American people would wish to go to war no matter how many lives were lost at sea." He and House had been doing all that they could, he thought, to persuade both warring alliances to take a long-range view of peacemaking. His essential duty, as he saw it, was to maintain faith with a people who rejoiced because he had kept them out of war and at the same time to rescue humanity from the scourge of international conflict. It seemed clearer than ever that security could be attained only by stopping the war and arranging a concert of nations to keep peace. "The minute the campaign is over," he wrote on November 4, "I shall be obliged to prepare some of the most interesting papers I have yet had to prepare."

Finally the voters made what Wilson called their "fundamental, final choice with regard to our foreign relationships." He had his mandate,

---

[2] When Gerard returned to Berlin, on Dec. 21, he told Joseph Grew that the President had given him two injunctions: he must "jolly the Germans" and must support the American stand against attacks on armed merchant ships without warning. Gerard also reported that, when he had agreed, Wilson banged his desk and said: "I don't want you merely to support my view; I want you to *agree* with it." Grew, *Turbulent Era*, I, 300–301.

and he could at last act boldly. The burden of responsibility was "heavier than ever," he confessed to his old friend Edith Reid. "If we can escape entering the war and bring about a rational peace, it is something worth living and dying for, and I believe the country feels that way or it would not have re-elected me."

The prophet found it hard to command time to concentrate on his ultimate objective, in the midst of pressures that had built up during the campaign. Faithful warriors of the party wanted to shake his hand, to congratulate him, and to keep their own interests before him. Executive decisions delayed by the election must be made in both domestic and foreign affairs. But on November 13 he demanded time to think, and penciled a note to Tumulty instructing him to say to everyone that he was engrossed with "business of the most pressing sort."

The next day he told House that he wanted to address to all belligerents a demand that the fighting cease. Unless he did so, he argued, the United States would inevitably drift into war with Germany on the submarine issue. It seemed to him that Berlin already had violated the pledge given on May 4 after the sinking of the *Sussex*; and if the United States was to maintain her position she would have to break diplomatic relations, unless he could move Britain to discuss peace.

The Colonel felt sure that the Allies would be offended by any venture of this sort and would interpret it as an effort to "pull Germany's chestnuts out of the fire." When his opinion was asked, he gave it with more directness than he was accustomed to use.

The President, in his zeal for a great purpose, seemed unable to understand that his friend, sincerely sharing in the enthusiasm, could not agree with the method that he had set his heart on using. He did not sleep well that night; and the next morning the Colonel noted his host's distress and was remorseful because he knew that he had caused it. But neither man yielded his opinion. Wilson told the Colonel that he would compose a first draft of an appeal and that then they could go over the matter with more intelligence. After House left, he felt so wretched that he went back to bed. He ate little lunch, and slept all afternoon; but after supper his spirits revived and he and Edith Wilson had one of their delightful evenings of companionship. For a fortnight he was not well, and Dr. Grayson made him give up the Army-Navy football game. His wife helped him to keep up with the torrent of papers, and after supper, too fagged to converse or play games, they would sit in the firelight and listen to opera music played by an electric piano.

But all the while he kept his mind on the great state paper that he had conceived. In a bulky folder he collected documents that revealed public opinion on questions of war and peace, at home and abroad. There were clippings from journals, tissues of diplomatic dispatches, quotations from speeches of foreign statesmen, reports from House of confidential talks with Bernstorff and with English observers. He set down his ideas first in shorthand, then in typing on small sheets. Brackets and parentheses were inserted, and shorthand notes in the margins.

Meanwhile House, closer than the President to the thinking of those liberals in Britain who held out the best hope for international concord, was eager to save his friend from giving unnecessary offense to London opinion. On the whole, the people of the United States seemed ready to accept the view of House that, if they were to have a war, it had best be with Germany. Americans who had at first condoned some manifestations of German frightfulness or had balanced it against suffering inflicted by the armed forces of the Entente, were inclined by an accumulation of misdemeanors to condemn the morality of the Central Powers. Furthermore, blood ties with Britain were stronger than those with other belligerents, and Americans had warm memories of French aid during their Revolution. To be sure, they were out of sympathy with Russian despotism, but the menace of czarism was far more remote than that of the Hohenzollerns. American youths were so partial to the cause of the Allies that they were enlisting in the British and French armies and auxiliary services.

It was not only ties of morality, blood, and historical sentiment that tugged the American people toward the Allies. During the war years their economic resources had been to a large extent pooled with those of England and France; and as a result of the need of the Allies for funds for the purchase of war goods in America, the extension of credit was reaching alarming proportions. Wilson thought that it would be most unwise to risk a loan to certain German cities, and he was skeptical also about a plan of the house of Morgan for accepting renewable notes of the British and French treasuries. The Federal Reserve Board, responding to his wishes, announced publicly that it did not regard it "in the interest of the country" that they invest in foreign notes of this character, that American banks must stand ready to meet domestic requirements that could not be foreseen, and that the British should arrange to get credit by pledging the collateral that remained in their hands or by stimulating trade "in other directions."

This warning was a jolt to Americans who were riding the crest of a wave of wartime prosperity. There was danger, on the one hand, that the nation's abnormal export trade would suddenly be curtailed; and, on the other, that the Allies, not allowed to purchase with treasury notes, would be forced to sustain the war commerce by pledging so much gold and collateral to the United States that inflation and instability would result. New York bankers were frightened, and the prices of foreign bonds dropped. Wall Street threatened to accept the proposed treasury notes anyway; but the British grudgingly decided not to provoke a crisis by issuing them.[3]

On November 24 Colonel House, having informed Bernstorff that the next submarine crisis could result only in a diplomatic breach, reported to the President that Germany was willing to evacuate Belgium and France under certain conditions. House already had sent intimations of support from British radicals for an American peace move at this juncture. Wilson felt that the moment was near, if not already at hand, for him to act. He wrote, therefore, to inform House that he hoped to make his peace note "the strongest and most convincing thing" that he had ever penned. Four days later he reported that he had finished his labor and had recovered partly from a severe cold. "I think things are thickening," his letter to the Colonel said, "and we should choose our course at once, if we have data enough to form a judgment on . . . I hope that I had a clear head for the draft."

Visiting the White House on November 27, House perceived that Wilson's text contained moralizing that might offend the Allies. He persuaded his friend to delete certain clauses and induced him to insert a specific renunciation of any desire to demand or force peace through his mediation. The Colonel advised also that the President delay release of his manifesto until public opinion in France and England was prepared to receive it favorably.

Appreciating the force of the Colonel's remarks, Wilson repeated a proposal that he had made before: he insisted that House go abroad in advance of his appeal for peace and, like a minor prophet, prepare the way. The Colonel, preferring "Hades for the moment" to such a mission, thought of many reasons why it was best for him to remain at home. He feared, for one thing, that his appearance at London would precipitate Page's resignation,[4] an eventuality that he viewed with more concern than the President. But, fearing that his friend might think

[3] Actually, Wilson feared that his people would think that the nation already had been partial to Britain in extending credit. When he was informed, on Dec. 6, that the comptroller of the currency was about to divulge the amounts invested by national banks in foreign securities, he questioned the wisdom of this, fearful of "the indirect effect the publication might have on some of our foreign relations."

[4] That House had reason for this apprehension is suggested by a draft of a letter to Wilson found among Page's papers, saying that House's visits had been "a mistake" that had provoked endless gossip about Page's position and about the intentions of the United States, and that the mistake should not be repeated. By advice of Irwin Laughlin, first secretary of the embassy, Page's letter was not sent. The Ambassador had written in his diary, after House's last visit to London: "He cannot come again or—I go." But Page realized that he must not appear to be moved by personal pique.

him giving way to selfish considerations, the Colonel asked Lansing to exert his influence to dissuade Wilson. Four days later he recorded in his diary, with relief, that he had learned from Counselor Polk that the President would not insist further.

On December 3 Wilson pressed ahead on his peace note. "One of the reasons why early action is necessary," he confessed to House, "is W.J.B." He had learned that Bryan was intent on going abroad "to fix the whole matter up himself" and would publicly oppose Wilson if the President showed any inclination to break relations with Germany.

The President's obligations to Congress diverted his thought for a day or two. He gave his annual address in the Capitol on December 4, calmly ignoring the flaunting of a yellow banner from a balcony by suffragettes. On the 8th he wrote to House: "Members of Congress have been sucking the life out of me, about appointments and other matters affecting the destiny of the world, and I have been prevented from perfecting the document."

While the President was polishing his masterpiece, the Foreign Office tired of waiting for Wilson to act and made a gesture of peace of its own. If this failed, Germany was to unleash its submarines in January. On December 12 the chancellor announced to the Reichstag those items of German policy that would bear the scrutiny of mankind. The imperial government, he said, was ready to act with its enemies to end the war. He informed Washington that he hoped that Germany's "formal and solemn offer" would "coincide with the wishes of the President of the United States"; and Wilson was asked to forward the overture to the capitals of the enemy.

Though complying with the German request, the President held to his resolve to go ahead on the single track to which his conscience had guided him. American liberals saw that it was too late, that Wilson was "fishing behind the net." But he released his paper to the State Department on December 18. It was delivered to the press and to all belligerent governments, and its text became known to the world on the 20th.

The manifesto that the President had finally arrived at, after many more changes than he was accustomed to make in his papers of state, stands as a landmark in the diplomacy of the century. The Colonel immediately recognized its immortality. "There are some sentences in it," House wrote in his diary, "that will live as long as human history." The message proclaimed:

Each side desires to make the rights and privileges of weak peoples and small States as secure against aggression or denial in the future as the rights and privileges of the great and powerful States now at war. Each wishes itself to be made secure in the future, along with all other nations and peoples, against the recurrence of wars like this and against aggression or selfish interference of any kind. Each would be jealous of the formation of any more rival leagues to preserve an unbalance of power amidst multiplying suspicions; but each is ready to consider the formation of a league of nations to insure peace and justice throughout the world.

To be effective, a move for peace at this juncture would have to satisfy the lusts of the creature man, as well as his aspirations. Before the final step in international organization could be taken, Wilson recognized that it was necessary to fix terms of peace that would guarantee to every belligerent its independence, territorial integrity, and political and commercial freedom. And so the President's appeal went on in a more practical vein. His own government did not wish to propose terms: he was not even offering to mediate; but he did feel "altogether justified," in view of the interest of his people in arrangements for the peace of the world, in "suggesting an immediate opportunity for a comparison of views as to the terms which must precede those ultimate arrangements." Though statesmen had set forth their war aims in general terms, none had "avowed the precise objects which would, if attained, satisfy them and their people that the war had been fought out." An interchange of views on this matter, he suggested, would clear the way at least for conference and make the permanent concord of the nations a hope of the immediate future, a concert of nations immediately practicable.

On December 18, the day on which this manifesto was given to the State Department, the President reverted to his old custom of calling a press conference. Fearing that his statement might be thought an endorsement of the German overture of the 12th, he made it clear that he merely had acted as a messenger in forwarding Germany's proposal.[5] He refused flatly to be drawn out on the significance of his own appeal, and insisted that anyone who spread false rumors regarding his intentions would be guilty of a very serious crime.

Unfortunately the secretary of state admitted to newsmen on December 21 that the nation was "drawing near the verge of war" and that the release of Wilson's statement indicated the possibility of her being forced in.[6] Thus Lansing raised British hopes, and German fears, that the

[5] Advised by Page that the German peace move was merely an offer "to buy a pig in a poke," the Allies indignantly rebuffed it on Dec. 30, 1916.

[6] Contemporary notes and manuscript of Arthur Sweetser, who was present. Also Sweetser to the writer. At his press conference on the morning of the 20th Lansing merely said that in the afternoon a note would be released that did not suggest peace and was not connected with the German proposal of the 12th. The secretary asked that the content be kept secret until the hour set for release—3:30 P.M. However, the tenor of the note was revealed by indiscreet newsmen and was reported by the Dow-Jones ticker at 2:05 P.M. The news aggra-

United States would join the Allies. This, coming after the long struggle of the President to draft a manifesto that would be genuinely conciliatory, vexed him greatly. It seemed to him that the secretary of state was not in sympathy with his purpose to keep out of war.

He summoned the offender to the White House on the afternoon of the 21st and once again stretched his patience to save an indiscreet servant. Though Lansing was impenitent, and argued that his remarks revealed nothing but the stark truth, Wilson did not force him to make a public retraction. He merely instructed Lansing to say that he had been misinterpreted.

Six days after he released his manifesto Wilson, the champion of "pitiless publicity," showed that he now fully understood the importance of deepest secrecy in discussions of a matter so delicate as the making of peace. On December 23 he instructed Lansing to suggest to the belligerents that they reply to his message "in strict confidence; it being understood that the Government of the United States may in its turn convey it in like confidence to the governments of the other group of belligerents, in order that it may in that way be ascertained without publicity whether there is any present ground or basis to hope for negotiations or conferences of any kind."

However, on January 12, when the British replied unfavorably to Wilson's appeal and made it clear that they intended to destroy German militarism and to exact huge indemnities, their reply did not take the private channels that Wilson suggested. British leaders, believing that they fought for principles that Americans were too timid to champion in battle, had been infuriated when Wilson stated in his appeal that the objects of European statesmen on both sides of the conflict were "virtually the same."

Germany's formal reply to Wilson also was made public. It repeated the suggestion of direct negotiations that had been made from Berlin on the 12th and made it clear that the Germans intended to use conquered lands as bargaining pawns over the peace table. A complete rebuff, it raised Wilson's temper so high that he almost demanded Bernstorff's resignation.

Baffled by the wilderness in which he could find no path to an honorable peace, Wilson found release in holiday festivities at the White House. On Christmas Eve, after walking over to the Treasury Building

---

vated a slump in security prices that had followed the German peace overture of the 12th. Men close to the administration were suspected of using inside information to speculate profitably; but in an investigation conducted by the Rules Committee of the House of Representatives they were exonerated. *See* Blum, "The 'Leak' Investigation of 1917," *American Historical Review*, LIV, No. 3 (April, 1949).

to hear children sing carols to the Prince of Peace, the family trimmed a tree in the oval room. The next morning they gathered around it, with a crackling fire on the hearth; and after a day of receiving callers, twenty-two relatives gathered for dinner and took part in charades, using the hall upstairs for a stage. For a moment Woodrow Wilson and his three daughters lived again in the rapture of the early years at Princeton. Three days after Christmas his sixtieth birthday was celebrated.

It was a time when Wilson needed the warmth of human sympathy as never before. For, though Democratic congressmen applauded his peace note, Bryan telegraphed congratulations, and the *New Republic* asserted that at last the liberals had "a leadership expressive of American idealism," General Leonard Wood proclaimed to advocates of preparedness that there was no leadership at Washington and partisans of the Allies were vociferous in condemnation of the President. On the day after Christmas, Wilson vented his annoyance in a letter to sympathetic Secretary Baker: "I wish every day that there were more mere Americans in this country. Almost all our fellow citizens this side of the Mississippi seem to think in terms set by the thinking or prepossessions of one side or the other across the water." On January 2 he wrote in discouragement: "Neither side in the war is pleased by anything I write unless it can be construed as favorable in feeling to them."

Yet Wilson continued to breast the tide that was floating his nation into the maelstrom. He refused to take part in plans for the relief of peoples persecuted by the Central Powers, though his friend Cleveland Dodge was one of the sponsors; for he felt that this would be unneutral. The Colonel repeated a warning that he had given often before, telling his friend, on January 4, that the nation should not be so totally unprepared in the event of war. But the lonely prophet replied: "There will be no war. This country does not intend to become involved in this war. We are the only one of the great white nations that is free from war today, and it would be a crime against civilization for us to go in." It seemed to House that Wilson was carefully avoiding any conference of advisers in which he might be outvoted overwhelmingly.

The President's manifesto of December 18 was the object of a furious debate in the Senate. The conservatives were as alarmed as Princeton's trustees had been by Wilson's soaring aspirations. His Republican adversaries were not slow to criticize Wilson's advocacy of a league of nations "to insure peace and justice throughout the world" and his commitment of the people of the United States as "ready to lend their every resource, whether of men or money or substance, to such a combination, so proposed and organized." A characteristic bellow came from Roosevelt; and Lodge attacked the President publicly and privately.[7] Other senators, resentful that the Chief Executive had taken so momentous a step without consulting them, raised doubts.

When Hitchcock of Nebraska submitted a resolution endorsing Wilson's action, a debate began that was to last for three years and to be recognized as one of the most portentous in the history of the century. Borah of Idaho argued that Wilson's proposal, committing American armed forces to protect the integrity of every little country, would plunge the nation into the storm center of European politics, and that the advice of the founding fathers would be renounced and the Monroe Doctrine destroyed. Weakening under the force of nationalistic oratory and tradition, Hitchcock accepted a substitute for his resolution. Only that part of Wilson's note was endorsed that requested terms of peace from the belligerents; and even on this basis seventeen senators were opposed and thirty-one abstained from voting.

Nevertheless, the prophet was so confident of the receptiveness of the plain people of the world that he resolved to speak to them over the heads of their rulers. On January 11 the Colonel came again to the White House. A week before, the friends had outlined an American plan to make the world secure from future wars and had decided that it should be revealed in a speech before the Senate. Now Wilson, closing the door of his study, read his first draft. House recognized that this, like the peace note of December 18, was a noble document that was imperishable. When he emerged from the room, after a talk of an hour or more in which the President agreed to strike out a word and a phrase that might give offense, the Colonel was glowing with praise. A few days later Wilson wrote to inform House that he had shown his masterpiece to the secretary of state and also Chairman Stone of the Senate Foreign Relations Committee, and that the latter seemed slightly stunned. The secret was shared only with these three advisers, and Edith Wilson.

On January 22, after an early round of golf in Virginia, Woodrow Wilson went before the Senate. Believing that he spoke for "liberals and friends of humanity in every nation," he stood as pastor to the whole human race, with compassion for all peoples and condemnation

---

[7] On Jan. 9, 1917, Lodge wrote to his cousin, John T. Morse, Jr.: "He [Wilson] has been working in combination with Germany, not that he sympathizes with Germany but because Bernstorff is willing to make deals, and also, I fear, has some sort of hold on him arising from other sources. Wilson thinks only of himself. The motives of his note were, I think, two: one, which you point out, to get into the position of peacemaker and be the saviour of civilization; and, the other, intense fear that if the war continued the Germans would press the submarine warfare so as to create a situation here which he might find difficult. I am inclined to think that in the back of his mind lurks the desire for a third term, and if he was not hopelessly cowardly at heart our damage would be greater than it is." Morse Papers.

for none. Reviewing the discouraging replies to his December request for the peace terms of the belligerents, he asserted optimistically that the world was "that much nearer a definite discussion of the peace which shall end the present war." When the settlement did come, he said, it must be followed by "some definite concert of power which will make it virtually impossible that any such catastrophe should ever overwhelm us again." This was taken for granted by "every lover of mankind, every sane and thoughtful man."

He then probed more deeply into the causes of war than many of the hot-minded patriots of the several nations could follow. He said:

The question upon which the whole future peace and policy of the world depends is this: Is the present war a struggle for a just and secure peace, or only for a new balance of power? If it be only a struggle for a new balance of power, who will guarantee, who can guarantee the stable equilibrium of the new arrangement? Only a tranquil Europe can be a stable Europe. There must be, not a balance of power, but a community of power: not organized rivalries, but an organized common peace.

. . . first of all . . . it must be a peace without victory. It is not pleasant to say this. I beg that I may be permitted to put my own interpretation upon it and that it may be understood that no other interpretion was in my thought. I am seeking only to face realities and to face them without soft concealments. Victory would mean peace forced upon the loser, a victor's terms imposed upon the vanquished. It would be accepted in humiliation, under duress, at an intolerable sacrifice, and would leave a sting, a resentment, a bitter memory upon which terms of peace would rest, not permanently, but only as upon quicksand. Only a peace between equals can last. Only a peace the very principle of which is equality and a common participation in a common benefit. The right state of mind, the right feeling between nations, is as necessary for a lasting peace as is the just settlement of vexed questions of territory or of racial and national allegiance.

The equality of nations upon which peace must be founded if it is to last must be an equality of rights; the guarantees exchanged must neither recognize nor imply a difference between big nations and small, between those that are powerful and those that are weak. Right must be based upon the common strength, not upon the individual strength, of the nations upon whose concert peace will depend . . . Mankind is looking now for freedom of life, not for equipoises of power . . . the nations should with one accord adopt the doctrine of President Monroe as the doctrine of the world . . .

Summarizing the three conditions that he had stated in earlier messages and explained fully in this one, he declared:

I am proposing government by the consent of the governed; that freedom of the seas which in international conference after conference representatives of the United States have urged with the eloquence of those who are the convinced disciples of liberty; and that moderation of armaments which makes of armies and navies a power for order merely, not an instrument of aggression or of selfish violence.

These are American principles, American policies. We could stand for no others. And they are also the principles and policies of forward-looking men and women everywhere, of every modern nation, of every enlightened community. They are the principles of mankind and must prevail.

Thus was the great manifesto of Anglo-Saxon liberalism delivered. It was cabled in advance to the European capitals. Humanitarian critics in both the United States and England rallied to the crusading leader. Never was Wilson's genius displayed more brilliantly. He had reflected the feeling of the peoples of the world, had given expression to thoughts pent up and perplexing. Eighty-nine Socialists in the French Chamber of Deputies characterized the speech as "the charter of the civilized universe." Even the Czar's Foreign Office commended Wilson's "broad humanitarian principles."

However, minor prophets in America found much to criticize in the President's broad commitment. The dissent was ominous, and the President did not miss its import. He wrote about it to Cleveland Dodge: "I must admit that I have been a little low in my mind the last forty-eight hours because of the absolute lack of any power to see what I am driving at which has been exhibited by the men who are looked upon as the leading Republican members of the Senate. After all, it is upon the Senate that I depend for the kind of support which will make acts possible, and there are sometimes hours of discouragement connected with trying to lift things into a better air. But discouragement is weakness and I do not succumb to it long. I firmly believe that I have said the right thing, and I have an invincible confidence in the prevalence of the right if it is fearlessly set forth."

At the same time Wilson, having kept his speech free from any specific plan for world organization that opponents might attack effectively, resolved to avoid any act that would give the Senate cause for irritation. Replying to a suggestion from Edward Bok that a part of his past writing on the Presidency be printed at this juncture, he wrote: "My feeling is that I better not seem to be talking too much just now about the functions of the Presidency. Those functions have their irritating sides to some of my colleagues in the Senate in particular, and I can do as much without talking about it."

As for the warring chieftains of Europe, they regarded the American President as wolves might look upon an interloper who would take away their meat after a kill. The idea of "government by consent of the governed" was not acceptable in empires that, like Austria-Hungary and Turkey, were honeycombed with unwilling subjects; nor could the Allies conceive of a lasting "peace without victory" [8] over German militarism.

Wilson had expected no enthusiasm from London for his appeal. Writing to House on January 24, he expressed interest primarily in discovering what was in the minds of the German officials. "If Germany wants peace," he wrote, "she can get it soon, *if she will but confide in me and let me have a chance.*" Under the sort of world order that the American President envisioned, Germany could afford to moderate the demands that had made it impossible that her enemies would negotiate with her.

Feeling that he had put himself in a position to help without favor to either side, Wilson asked the Colonel to see Bernstorff again, secretly, and to tell him that there was "a terrible likelihood" that relations between the United States and Germany might come to the breaking point. He added a personal word to enhearten the faithful agent who was so eager to have a hand in any deal that might bring peace and glorify the name of Woodrow Wilson. "God bless you for the encouragement and support you so constantly give me. I feel very lonely sometimes, and sometimes very low in my mind, in spite of myself."

The Colonel's response was prompt and cooperative. He found the ambassador discouraging, however. Though Bernstorff was restrained by his instructions from revealing Berlin's decision to unleash its submarines at the end of the month (a decision that the ambassador had learned on January 19), he confided to House that the situation was getting out of hand.

In desperate last-minute appeals Bernstorff warned his government of the inevitable effect of their new policy on relations with Washington, and begged for delay. But already twenty-one submarines had set out on their deadly missions under the new instructions and the Admiralty was intoxicated by the prospect of success.[9]

---

8 The phrase "peace without victory," taken from context by critics unfriendly to Wilson and used to denote the sense of the speech, was perhaps suggested to the President by an editorial in the *New Republic* that developed an argument different from that of Wilson's address. *See* Baker, VI, 425. Wilson later explained to the French ambassador that "a scientific peace" would be a better term to describe his ideal.

9 The German General Staff had promised that their large fleet of submarines would paralyze Great Britain before the United States could exert enough force to succor the Allies; and the Crown Council, meeting at Spa on Jan. 9, decided to unleash the sea dogs upon neutral and defenseless prey on Feb. 1 and meanwhile to keep the world in ignorance of their design.

Though in mid-January Bernstorff, acting on instructions, signified Germany's willingness to sign the Bryan treaty of arbitration, to enter a league of nations, and to approve a Wilsonian program for a peace conference, he qualified his statement when the President, burdened with the ultimate responsibility and more suspicious than House of Berlin's protestations, asked for

Wilson's inclination to exert economic pressure upon the Allies was increasing and the British treasury was close to bankruptcy. The President was still eager to cooperate with Berlin to end the fighting, and convinced that the opposing alliances were almost equally responsible for its perpetuation. Nevertheless, in spite of these considerations working in their favor, the Germans gave Wilson the only provocation that could have induced him to throw the power of the United States on the side of the Allies. On the last day of January they notified the American government of the withdrawal of their pledge of May 4, 1916. Henceforth all merchant ships that were met in certain zones around France, Italy, and the British Isles, whether belonging to neutrals or to belligerents, would be sunk—except for one ship that would be permitted to sail from America to Falmouth weekly, under strict regulations.

On the afternoon of January 31 Tumulty brought in a news bulletin announcing the German threat. Wilson read it and reread it. He was amazed at first, then incredulous. Color left his face as he took in the full meaning. His lips tightened and his jaw locked. Then he said with quiet grimness: "The break that we have tried so hard to prevent now seems inevitable." At eight in the evening he received official documents that Bernstorff had been holding in secret for twelve days and that he had just given to Lansing. Reaching for the telephone, Wilson called his secretary of state to the White House. He was ready now to break diplomatic relations with Berlin; but he was not so inclined as Lansing to go to war. His indignation at British policy had not abated. He said that, if he concluded that it was best for the world for the United States to remain at peace in the circumstances, he would be willing to bear the abuse of critics, which seemed negligible unless it impaired his usefulness. He must have more time to think; but he directed the secretary of state to draw up formal papers for a breach.

When Lansing brought them to the White House the next morning, Wilson was in conference with Colonel House, whom the crisis moved to hasten to Washington and give to the President certain hypothetical peace terms that Bernstorff had presented confidentially at the last moment. Wilson read the curious document aloud; and when he came

---

assurance regarding Germany's conduct while arbitration was in progress. "I do not want to walk into a trap and give them immunity for the next year," the President wrote to House on Jan. 17. His caution seemed justified when Bernstorff answered his queries by repeating an earlier proposal, that the general peace conference would take place only after the belligerents had bartered for peace in the time-honored European tradition. On Jan. 24 the President wrote to House: "What Bernstorff said to you the other day as trimmed and qualified by what he wrote afterward amounts to nothing." Wilson's confidence in House's judgment doubtless was shaken by the fact that Bernstorff's proposal, which proved to be so disappointing, had been naïvely commended to him by the Colonel on Jan. 12 as "the most important communication since the war began."

to a sentence that begged him to continue his efforts to bring about peace, the irony became cutting. In the light of the grim official announcement from Berlin, the protestations seemed shallow, almost mocking. When a cable came from Gerard with news that Zimmermann wanted the President to keep silent for two months to give the submarines time to bring England to her knees, it seemed clear that the Germans hoped to stall the United States until they would be in a position to disregard her.[10] While talking peace, they had been plotting a kind of war that would respect neither neutral nor humane rights.

The President's disillusionment was as intense as his hopes had been extravagant. He felt, he said, as if the world had reversed the direction of its rotation and he could not get his balance. He spoke of Germany as "a madman that should be curbed." When House asked whether it seemed fair to ask the Allies to do the curbing alone, he winced, but nevertheless held to his determination to keep clear of hostilities if he could.

They waited listlessly through the morning for Lansing's arrival. House could not lift his friend's spirits. Wilson paced the floor and nervously fingered his books. His wife suggested a game of golf, but the Colonel doubted that the President should do anything that might seem to his people like fiddling during a holocaust. At last Wilson suggested pool, and they were finishing their second game when the secretary of state was announced. It was agreed that Bernstorff be given his passports at once, in the faint hope that the Germans might be brought to their senses before the commission of an overt act that would make war unavoidable.

On the next day the President consulted his Cabinet and received the reactions that he expected. Reflecting the anxiety of the whole nation, the men rose to their feet when their chief entered the conference room. Wilson read aloud the offensive German declaration and called it an "astounding surprise." The faces around him showed sardonic wrath; and in the discussion that followed their voices were low. In so solemn a moment they hesitated to give advice, and the President drew it out with questions. "Shall I break off diplomatic relations with Germany?" he asked, repeating what he had said before about his willingness to bear imputations of weakness, even of cowardice, in order to keep the white race strong.

10 The chief of the Admiralty staff was less eager than the German diplomats to immobilize the United States. On Dec. 22, 1916, Holtzendorff wrote to Hindenburg thus: "By entering into the war the United States Government will give up by a single move the sources of that commercial prosperity which has given it the towering political prominence which it now occupies. It stands face to face with the Japanese peril; it can neither inflict material damage upon us, nor can it be of material benefit to our enemies . . ." *Official German Documents*, II, 1269–70.

Most of the men answered his query with an impulsive affirmative. McAdoo's blood boiled at what he regarded as an attempt to order the United States off the Atlantic. If the nation meekly accepted Germany's colossal insult, said Houston, she would not be worth saving if she were attacked. Which side would the President like to be the winner, one of the men asked; and Wilson maintained that he still believed in a "peace without victory." Both sides had been callous to the rights of neutrals, he said, though Germany had been brutal in taking life and England only in taking property. Lansing asserted that all nations must have liberal governments before peace could be permanent, and that democracies were never aggressive or unjust; and Wilson, saying "I am not so sure of that," argued that probably a draw would bring a more just settlement than a victory. Still another official mentioned the possibility of a combination of Germany, Japan, and Russia, and at this point the President observed that "the Russian peasant might save the world this misfortune."

After two hours with the Cabinet he went to the Hill. "I wonder what you are thinking I should do?" he said to the several legislators who gathered about him. One suggested addressing a note of remonstrance, but at that he drew himself erect and declared sternly: "Let us be done with diplomatic notes. The hour to act has come."

Returning to the quiet of his own chamber, he faced up to the decision forced upon him. The charge that Presbyterianism set upon its leaders oppressed him. His brother, realizing the strain that the family conscience put upon him, sent a "God be with you," and he thanked Josie for this "from the bottom of a very troubled heart."

His conclusion was not to declare war, but to go before the Congress and announce a break with the rulers of Germany, in the hope that they would be jolted into sanity. Thus, once more, he would put upon Berlin the responsibility for final decision for war or peace. He labored until midnight to compose an appropriate address, and the next day, after conferring with Lansing, he addressed the legislators at two o'clock. Three minutes before, Bernstorff had been given his passports.

The people came by the thousands, overflowing from the corridors of the Capitol into the streets. Those who could hear applauded when, after reviewing the diplomatic correspondence with Berlin that had followed the *Sussex* incident, the President announced that the United States must now take the measure that it had declared it would take to meet unrestricted submarine warfare: that is, sever relations with Germany. He followed this with an appeal to the better nature of the Germans. Drawing the distinction between people and government that he was later to exploit adroitly, he asserted:

We are the sincere friends of the German people and earnestly desire to remain at peace with the Government which speaks for them. We shall not believe that they are hostile to us unless and until we are obliged to believe it; and we purpose nothing more than the reasonable defense of the un-doubted rights of our people. We wish to serve no selfish ends. We seek merely to stand true alike in thought and in action to the immemorial principles of our people which I sought to express in my address to the Senate only two weeks ago,—seek merely to vindicate our right to liberty and justice and an unmolested life. These are the bases of peace, not war. God grant that we may not be challenged to defend them by acts of wilful injus-tice on the part of the Government of Germany!

CHAPTER V

Leading a United People into Conflict

THE PRESIDENT HARDLY had finished speaking before he could sense that his people were uniting in support of him. The Senate passed a resolution of approval with only five contrary votes. Immediately American life began to move with a martial tempo. Ten thousand men were withdrawn from Mexico and the mustering out of National Guardsmen was delayed. Youths lined up to enlist while the War College began work on a plan for conscription. Warships were ordered to be prepared for action and the Congress was asked for a huge naval appropriation. Executive offices at Washington were closed to the public, and soldiers appeared to guard areas that might be targets of sabotage. A Shipping Board that the President had nominated to carry out the Shipping Act of 1916 was beginning to function; and men chosen to form a Council of National Defense were organizing for action. Even Christian ministers were preaching a gospel of hate that made the President wonder whether they were "going crazy."

Wilson did his best to check the trend of opinion that he had been forced to accelerate by breaking with Germany. In his message to Congress he had neither damned German "barbarism," as some advisers wished, nor had he appealed to his people to prepare for inevitable war. He continued to complain to his advisers of Britain's maritime policy. He cautioned the War Department against any extraordinary activity that would give Berlin reason to believe that the United States was expecting hostilities.

Wilson was alarmed by the virulence of popular feelings. He was embarrassed when advocates of preparedness tried to stampede him into a headlong rush to arms. Industrial and financial magnates besieged Washington with offers of cooperation in which Wilson thought that he saw patriotic motive not untainted by hope for profit. Realizing that dictatorship could feed upon national emergency, he feared for democratic processes and shied away from agitation by conservative Republicans for a coalition government that might become totalitarian. "It is the *Junkerthum* trying to creep in under cover of the patriotic feeling of the moment," he wrote to House. "They will not get in. They have now no examples of happy or successful coalitions to point

86

to. The nominal coalition in England is nothing but a Tory cabinet such as they are eager to get a foothold for here. I know them too well, and will hit them straight between the eyes, if necessary, with plain words."

His diplomatic resources were not yet exhausted. There was a glimmer of hope in the possibility of collective action with other nations. In informing neutral governments of his decision to break with Germany, Wilson had suggested that they could contribute to the making of peace by taking similar action. Receiving a favorable report from the Swiss minister, he was encouraged to set down four "Bases of Peace," rephrasing the essential principles that he had already proposed as a foundation for a league of nations, and adding a prohibition against "any joint economic effort to throttle the industrial life of any nation." On February 10, however, the Swiss envoy forwarded a German proposal that any point might be negotiated except one that might break her blockade of England. Obviously talks on this basis would get nowhere. Moreover, only one other neutral, China, responded favorably. By February 12 Wilson had given up hope of effective joint action.

Austria-Hungary now remained the only agency that might help to thwart the will of her ally. Regarded by American opinion as a luckless pawn of Germany, that nation echoed the provocative German declaration of submarine warfare, while at the same time she sent an envoy, Count Tarnowski, to replace Dumba, who had made himself *non grata* at Washington. Moreover, the minister of foreign affairs at Vienna explicitly notified the United States of his nation's desire to maintain friendly relations.

Seizing this twig of olive, Wilson directed Page to discuss the matter with British statesmen. But the divergence in the aims of the two great English-speaking nations was too great to permit joint action. The State Department undertook to negotiate with Vienna and received a conclusive refusal to enter into discussions without Germany's participation. Tarnowski was not received, Ambassador Penfield was recalled to Washington, and on Easter Sunday, April 8, Chargé Joseph C. Grew was given his passports.

While the negotiations with Vienna were in process, Wilson acted vigorously to meet the emergencies that had been created by the break with Germany. He did not want Berlin to be goaded to a quick declaration of war by fear of growing military power in America; yet neither did he want the Germans to underestimate the force that the United States could muster if driven to it. On February 5 he told the secretaries of war and the navy that the diplomatic breach took the nation so close to war that they must prepare for anything. "Each of you must surround himself with the ablest men you have," he said, asking them whether their advisers were all worthy of being retained. "Get and keep the best" was his last word to them.

When sailings of American ships were canceled as a result of the menace of German submarines, and cargoes piled up on the docks, outraged citizens implored their government to give protection. Their pleas were ardently supported by members of the Cabinet, and Secretary Baker explained that unless American vessels were armed they would be kept off the seas by the German threat. After discussion, the President accepted the contention of the Navy that the supplying of convoys would merely double the risk. He allowed his officials to tell inquiring shipowners that they might take any measures against unlawful acts; but he resisted Lansing's contention that guns and gunners should be furnished to merchant vessels by the government. He felt that this should not be done without the approval of Congress. And about the interned German ships Wilson was most punctilious: he would seize neither the vessels nor the crews who had disabled them. On February 15 he said at a Cabinet dinner that he was not in sympathy with a high degree of preparedness, for by the end of the war European nations would be destitute of manpower and wealth and would not menace America.

Finally, on February 23, the Cabinet pierced the academic shell behind which Wilson had sought detachment as his mind went "around the clock." Although Germany's threat had so far proved worse than her performance and American shippers had recovered somewhat from their fright, sailings had been cut almost in half during the month of February. McAdoo, whose confidence in his own executive ability had led him to propose to House that he take the Navy portfolio and let Houston replace him in the Treasury, argued that the President should act immediately, Congress or no Congress. He and Lane were so aggressive that Wilson turned on them bitterly, letting them know that he thought them guilty of fomenting hatred and jingoism. When he reproached the group for appealing to the code duello, and for urging him to unseemly and dictatorial action, they were inclined to revolt. Yet for all their impatience, they knew their Chief well enough to contain themselves a little longer. It seemed to Houston that the President agreed with what they said but, awed by his responsibility, was determined to make them prove their points beyond any doubt. And Lane, who thought Wilson "slower than a glacier," reminded his impetuous brethren that, though in the past they had had to press the Chief hard to bring him to the point of action, he had always responded in the end, when convinced that something had to be done.

To Wilson's family his equanimity was amazing.[1] Nevertheless his indignation had flared when he learned that Gerard was being detained at Berlin, apparently as a hostage to bring pressure on Washington to make concessions to German vessels in American ports. But on February 25 a far greater strain was placed upon his patience. On this day he received evidence that German intrigue was threatening the territorial integrity of the United States. The President learned that Zimmermann, now foreign secretary at Berlin, had instructed his minister at Mexico City to tempt the Mexican government to join with Germany if she should become involved in war with the United States. Offering "the lost territory of Texas, New Mexico, and Arizona," Zimmermann had suggested also that Mexico seek the cooperation of Japan.

This revelation was the more shocking to the President because Zimmermann's message had been transmitted by the American Department of State, under an arrangement that had been made by House with Bernstorff in order to facilitate communications with Berlin that might promote the cause of mediation and peace.[2] Intercepted by British agents, the text was sent to the President through Page. Wilson was flabbergasted at this evidence of German plotting at the very time when he had been earnestly trying to reach an understanding through Bernstorff.

The President checked his first impulse to make the Zimmermann message public, for he realized that the reaction of his people might force him to go to war immediately. He had it sent to Mexico City— "to give Carranza a chance to say what he will about it," he explained. However, he was impelled at last to take the action that his Cabinet had been urging and that he had warned the Congress, in his speech of February 3, it might be necessary for him to take. Going again to the Capitol to address a joint session, he read a message to hushed expectant legislators. Because the term of the Congress was about to expire and time would be required for its successor to assemble and organize, he wanted assurance of an authority that he thought his under the Constitution and that he might be forced to exercise.

"There may be no recourse," he warned, "but to *armed* neutrality, which we shall know how to maintain and for which there is abundant American precedent." He asked authorization to supply merchant ships with defensive arms, should that become necessary, and with the means

[1] Letter shown to the writer by Margaret Flinn (Mrs. George) Howe.

[2] As early as Jan. 24 Wilson had written to House of his suspicion of the use to which Bernstorff might be putting his privilege. Informing the Colonel that the German ambassador had sent a long message to his government and that he did not know its content, the President wrote: "By the way, if we are to continue to send messages for him, we should know that he is working in this cause [that of peace] and should in each case receive his official assurance . . ."

of using them, "and to employ any other instrumentalities or methods that may be necessary and adequate to protect our ships and our people in their legitimate and peaceful pursuits on the seas." He asked also for a grant of sufficient credit, including insurance against war risks.

But certain legislators did not go along with the prophet. Senator LaFollette, sitting with hands folded across his breast, saw in the President's request merely a long step toward war. And at the opposite pole of opinion, but equally resistant, was Henry Cabot Lodge, regarding the speaker critically, with hands clasped just under his chin. He could agree with Wilson's specific request for authority to arm merchant ships; but when the President came to his second point, and asked for power "to employ any other instrumentalities or methods that may be necessary and adequate," Lodge unclasped his fingers and tapped their tips together tentatively. LaFollette, despairing of keeping the peace, threw up both hands.

The President reviewed damages inflicted by German submarines since the breaking of relations, and told the legislators that an "overt act" had not yet occurred; but even as he was speaking, news came to the State Department of the sinking of the Cunard liner *Laconia,* with the loss of two American passengers. This atrocity, which occurred on the 25th, shared the front pages with the President's address on the 27th; and the American people now had dramatic, convincing proof that Germany intended to take the law into her own hands, as she had threatened.[3]

Wilson already had drafted the ship-arming bill that he wanted, and it was introduced in the House. The President consulted his politically minded advisers, McAdoo and Burleson, to decide on the best way of using the Zimmermann telegram to influence Congress to act favorably. He approved a canny suggestion from the State Department that they allow the document to be published as one that had leaked out rather than as an official release, for thus they might avoid exciting suspicion of their real motive. When questioned in the Senate about the authenticity of the document, Wilson affirmed it; and on March 4 Zimmermann himself acknowledged that it was genuine. The impact of the revelation and of the reaction of citizens stampeded the House to pass an armed-ship bill on March 1 by the overwhelming vote of 403 to 14.

In the Senate, the Republicans marshaled their forces to defer action and thus force the President to call a special session of the Congress.

[3] After the Cabinet meeting of the 27th it was made known "semiofficially" that the sinking of the *Laconia* was the dreaded "overt act." For a discussion of this event, and also of the Zimmermann message, *see* S. R. Spencer, Jr., *Decision for War.* When a newsman asked Wilson to define "overt act," the President said that he could not, but would know one if he saw one.

(Plans already had been laid at a party caucus for obstructive tactics that would prevent the passage of essential legislation before March 4, the date set for adjournment.) The filibuster that finally developed, however, was led by fanatical devotees of peace from both parties. "Gumshoe Bill" Stone of Missouri, who as chairman of the Foreign Relations Committee had had to lay the armed-ship bill before the Senate, joined with LaFollette and ten others in continuous talk that prevented action on the measure. Wilson's disappointment vented itself in rage against Stone. He was through with this man. "I'll not even shake hands with him again," he told Tumulty.[4]

It rankled Wilson that a few stubborn men could so effectively controvert the will of the people, and he was incensed because they did not accept his protestations of peaceful intent. He denounced them bitterly to House, and when the Colonel begged him to release something in the newspapers the next morning, he said that he would try. Shutting himself in his study almost all afternoon, he prepared a blast; and discussing it after dinner with McAdoo, Burleson, and Tumulty, he let it go. On Monday, March 5—the day of the formal inauguration ceremonies— the Jovian thunderbolt fell: "A little group of willful men, representing no opinion but their own, have rendered the great Government of the United States helpless and contemptible."

A vast exaggeration, but a timely and effective one! It rallied his people to protect and defend him as the symbol of patriotism. When he rode to the Capitol for the inauguration ceremony on March 5 he was hedged about by force and vigilance. Threatening letters had come to the White House in greater volume than ever, and the President's family were alarmed for his safety.

Giving only a brief paragraph of his second inaugural speech to the record of his first term, the President said: "Perhaps no equal period in our history has been so fruitful of important reforms in our economic

[4] Brahany Diary, March 4, 1917, in the possession of Thomas W. Brahany.

The Republican regulars, once they were sure that a special session would have to be summoned, were ready to express the sympathy that they felt for the President's policy. Senator Hitchcock of the Foreign Relations Committee, who had taken over promotion of the bill from the dissenting Stone, was able to get seventy-five senators to sign a manifesto of approval. Emboldened by this, the President, who had consulted the Congress merely out of courtesy and a desire for a show of unanimity, proceeded to act on the authority that the attorney general assured him was his under the Constitution. Supported by a press that denounced the filibuster with such phrases as "dastardly moral treason" and assured by legalists that the arming of merchantmen would not contravene the piracy law of 1819, the President, confined to his room by a cold, discussed the matter with naval advisers. He bade his wife tell Daniels that the Navy was to arm ships; and on March 9 he gave instructions that any officer who failed to keep these orders secret should be court-martialed. On March 12, Lansing released the news that the government would provide armed guards for American merchantmen sailing in war zones. Thus the United States came a long step closer to open hostilities. Wilson would be able to engage in war without exposing defenseless American vessels at sea.

and industrial life or so full of significant changes in the spirit and purpose of our political action. . . . It is a record of singular variety and singular distinction. But I shall not attempt to review it. It speaks for itself and will be of increasing influence as the years go by." He claimed no credit for person or party.

Reviewing the effect of the war on national life, he came to the immediate present. "We stand firm in armed neutrality," he declared, "since it seems that in no other way can we demonstrate what it is we insist upon and cannot forego." But it was of the future that he spoke most eloquently. "We are provincials no longer," he said. "The tragical events of the thirty months of vital turmoil through which we have just passed have made us citizens of the world. There can be no turning back. Our own fortunes as a nation are involved, whether we would have it so or not."

After the ceremony the President returned to the White House to greet two or three hundred guests at a buffet luncheon, and afterward he stood in the biting air to review the traditional parade. In the evening the family and Colonel House went upstairs to the oval sitting room to look out upon the fireworks. The Wilsons took seats by a side window, curtained off, and the President held his wife's hand and leaned with his face against hers. They asked the Colonel to join them; and House, rising to the occasion, spoke of his joy that it was they, and not the Hughes family, who were there. He was achieving the great ambition of his life. Not only had he captivated the heart of a great man, but he had won the confidence of his hero's wife. She confided to him that McAdoo irritated the President and seemed to her thoroughly selfish; and she asked House what chance such a man would have for the next nomination for the Presidency.

The excitement of inauguration day, coming after the strain of the battle for the armed-ship bill, was too much for the President's endurance. Dr. Grayson put his patient to bed, and for a fortnight he was almost constantly in his own room, seeing few visitors and, with his wife's help, writing only essential letters. Nevertheless, in his illness Wilson discussed the disposition of the fleet with Franklin D. Roosevelt and House, and the Colonel noted that he was "pushing Daniels to an activity that did not seem possible." Propped up in bed, the President tried to find diversion in consulting the ouija board, but the spirit of Admiral Nelson presented itself and discussed submarine warfare.

The first weeks of his second term brought no slackening of the tensions that were racking Wilson's soul. With the backing of labor interests that feared the competition of immigrants, Congress re-enacted the Burnett Bill, which restricted immigration by means of a literacy test and discriminated against Orientals. Wilson repeated the veto that he had imposed two years earlier, but now the measure was passed over his opposition. Organized labor consolidated the victory that it had won in September of 1916. Railroad managers were testing the constitutionality of the Adamson Law, and the impatient brotherhoods issued a general strike order on March 15. The President appealed to both sides to seek a settlement "in this time of national peril." Finally, on March 16, it was decided in Cabinet meeting that Secretaries Lane and Wilson should go at once to confer at New York with representatives of labor and management. A settlement was negotiated and a tie-up averted.

Meanwhile, the Czar of Russia abdicated on March 15 and a constitutional government was established; and thus the Allies were relieved of an association that had embarrassed them in appealing for American sympathy. Woodrow Wilson was in a serious mood as he read an official report of the upheaval from his ambassador at Petrograd, David R. Francis, who naïvely pictured the revolution as the "practical realization" of the American principle of government by consent of the governed and argued that it was desirable from every point of view that the United States be the first to recognize the new regime.

Wilson was now to pay dearly for the tendency that he and House had shown to give more weight to political expediency than to efficiency, in choosing envoys to Russia. The President was too learned to accept unquestioningly the views of Francis, a former governor of Missouri. In his academic years Wilson had thought and written much about revolutions, particularly those of his own nation and of France. At Princeton he had scorned revolution as a "puerile doctrine," socially expensive and yet apparently necessary in eighteenth-century France as a path to freedom. Talking with a young colleague, one evening, about "liberty" as it applied to Russian peasants, he suggested that they were like birds in a cage—not conscious of their confinement and therefore free. In an undergraduate essay he had written: "The most despotic of governments under the control of wise statesmen is preferable to the freest ruled by demagogues."

It was clear, however, that the generous impulses of Wilson's people, like those of their genial ambassador, were stirred by the overthrow of a despotic regime. Americans wished the new government well and, in their ignorance of the true nature of the political processes at work in Russia, even ventured to hope that a democratized government might fight German autocracy with a zeal that the czarist armies lacked. Few Americans realized that at that very time Leon Trotsky, a political exile living on New York's East Side, was proclaiming that the revolution reflected a hunger for peace among the masses of Russia.

Colonel House, inspired by the Russian Revolution to see "more hope for democracy and human liberty than ever before," wrote thus to Wilson on March 17: "I want to urge that you recognize the new Russian government as soon as England and France do . . . you stand easily as the great liberal of modern times." Half-sick and despondent, Wilson put aside his intellectual doubts and made the United States the first nation to recognize the new Russian government.[5]

Meanwhile the offenses of the U-boats were increasing. Ships were being sunk at the rate of almost 600,000 tons a month. Even vessels carrying supplies for Belgian relief were sent down. American ships, which in February suffered little damage, were now being attacked; and on the 18th three were sunk without warning and with loss of American lives.

The press reacted violently to these outrages. Committees of Defense sprouted like the minutemen of 1776 all through the land. Yet peace sentiment was still strong at the grass roots. Many of the plain people were lethargic, or positively hostile to a declaration of war. But it was daily becoming clearer that Germany was making war on the American people, that to refuse the challenge now would be both shameful and dangerous. Responsible labor leaders pledged their loyalty in case of war; and a group of influential Socialists broke with the pacifistic policy of their national committee.

On March 19 the President was well enough to talk with the secretary of state about the three sinkings of American ships. The next day, having almost entirely regained his strength, he came face to face with his impetuous Cabinet. Walking through the swarm of newsmen, he entered the room smiling genially and shook hands with each official as if nothing exceptional was to take place. Recounting the measures taken to protect American ships, he asked questions that seemed to take it for granted that further action would be necessary. He asked whether he should summon Congress before April 16, the date he had already set, and what he should say to the legislators. He said he understood that the liberal element in the Prussian Diet was grumbling against its rulers, and he spoke of the warlike temper of his own people in the East and their apathy in the Midwest.

His deliberate manner sobered the men at the table. McAdoo spoke in a low, earnest voice, favoring an immediate call to the Congress and

[5] When the Russian Revolution was discussed by the Cabinet on March 23, Wilson, expressing pleasure at the speedy recognition of the new government, said: "It ought to be good, because it has a professor at the head." The next day the President told Daniels the story of the life of Foreign Minister Milyukov.

support for the ebbing credit of the Allies.[6] Baker spoke out for universal military training and the raising of a large army, believing that the people would demand it. The secretary of state thought war the best course, especially in view of the liberalizing of the Russian government, and he hoped that Wilson would publicly indict Prussian autocracy. Lansing spoke loud and vehemently; and the President asked him please to lower his voice so that no one in the corridor would hear.

As a whole, the Cabinet desired to clash with the Germans at once and with all the nation's power, though Daniels, the last to give in to martial sentiment, had tears in his eyes. Burleson, who wanted Congress to convene at the earliest moment, read telegrams typical of sheafs that were coming from the people, demanding war.

To this Wilson replied solemnly: "We are not governed by public opinion in our conclusion. I want to do right whether it is popular or not." He agreed that there would be added justification for entering the war if that act would strengthen the liberal forces in Russia and Germany; but he could not offer this motive as a reason for calling the Congress immediately, and he was not sure that he could influence the Russian people by yielding to a plea by Lansing for a public denunciation of German autocracy. The *casus belli* would have to be Germany's offenses and the obvious need of protecting American rights and safeguarding civilization against Prussian militarism.

After two and a half hours he felt that he had thoroughly canvassed the thought of the Cabinet. "Well, gentlemen," he said, "I think there is no doubt as to what your advice is. Thank you." He did not tell them what he would do, but he asked Lansing and Burleson to remain after the others went, and inquired how long it would take to prepare legislation by which Congress could declare war. More than a week, they replied. Encouraged by his question, Lansing ventured to ask whether the President would issue a call to Congress that afternoon. "Oh, I think I will sleep on it," Wilson replied.

He did not sleep well, however. In fact, he had been lying awake night after night, agitated by the doubts that he kept submerged under a cool exterior. The vital question, to him, was not the immediate cause

---

[6] Wilson gave no evidence that he was influenced by a desire to secure the credit of the Allies and help them to honor their commitments to American citizens. He made no reply to a plea from Page for support of British credit. The Federal Reserve Board had followed up its action of November, 1916, against accepting short-term notes from abroad by issuing a statement on March 8 that warned against unsound methods while encouraging foreign loans. There was no assurance that the Allies would not be bankrupt by the war and that by excessive loans and credits to them the United States herself would not, in the long run, suffer severe economic loss. In his speeches in 1916 Wilson had given expression to a hope that the surplus of economic strength that his nation was accumulating might be used "for the benefit of the world"; and he still hoped for a peace settlement that would make this possible. But economic interest was to him a consideration secondary to "the rights of humanity."

of war, but rather the larger problem that he had recognized as early as May, 1916, when he had said: "The danger of our time is nothing less than the unsettlement of the foundations of civilization." And so he asked himself: What would be the probable consequences to humanity if the United States entered the fight?

During the night of March 20 the prophet made his great decision. He was convinced that the hour that he had long dreaded had struck, that he could no longer "preserve both the honor and the peace of the United States." He issued a special proclamation the next morning, calling the new Congress to convene in special session on April 2.

Wilson and his colleagues acted henceforth as if they thought war inevitable. On the 23rd the Cabinet urged that the attorney general draft drastic security laws. On the 24th a plan for voluntary censorship was announced; and the President approved an increase in naval personnel and told Daniels that Marines should be placed aboard interned ships to prevent sabotage. House, to whom a member of the Council of National Defense had complained about inefficiencies, recommended that Daniels and Newton D. Baker be replaced,[7] and warned that the President would be held responsible by his people for their mistakes. But Wilson clung to these loyal, cooperative associates. Daniels's genius for public relations was compensating, in the view of many publicists, for the uncommunicativeness of Wilson and Baker. People liked his flamboyant speeches, filled with worn jokes, poetry, and biblical quotations. And he could be depended on to fight hard against graft and profiteering. Early in 1915, when the President had been told of derogatory gossip about Daniels, he had brought down his fist on a table and exclaimed: "His enemies are determined to ruin him. I can't be sure who they are, but when I do get them—God help them!"

Wilson pondered whether he should ask for a declaration of war or merely say that a state of war existed and that he needed means to carry it on. House advised the latter, fearing that an acrimonious debate might develop if the decision were left to the legislators. Mulling over this counsel, which coincided in the main with the sentiments of his Cabinet, Wilson jotted down the substance of an address; and House was as pleased as if he had written the memorandum himself.

---

[7] This recommendation by House reflected the feeling of Counselor Frank L. Polk of the State Department. House and Polk agreed that the Colonel's son-in-law, Gordon Auchincloss, should represent the department in New York in matters of security, finance, and trade.

For a while the Colonel wondered whether he himself should not take an official position on the President's staff in the event of war and organize, with Auchincloss, a confidential bureau. When he made this suggestion to Wilson twice in early February, the President replied: "I will with the deepest pleasure and alacrity place you wherever you are willing to be placed—as I am sure you know. But just what have you in mind?" To this confining question the tentative, roving mind of the ruling elder had no answer.

The President did not discuss the text of his address with the Cabinet when he met them on March 30. He feared that his work might be picked to pieces if he invited criticism of it. When the men raised the bogie of sabotage and recommended that protective measures already taken should be followed up, Wilson recounted absurd rumors that had come to him. Mentioning the fear of the White House staff of a German who tended the furnace, he said: "I'd rather the blamed place should be blown up rather than persecute inoffensive people." In this hour of crisis he deliberately tried to be casual and relaxed. At one point he stood up and did setting-up exercises, explaining that he had been sitting at a desk all morning and was stiff.

After two days of soul-searching, he felt the need of a confessor other than House; and so he sent for Frank I. Cobb, editor of the *World*, a man who was in sympathy with his policy. Entering the little study at one o'clock in the morning of April 2, Cobb had never seen him so worn down. Wilson confessed that he had not been so uncertain about anything in his life. He felt that he could honestly say that he had considered every loophole of escape and Germany had blocked each with a new outrage.

The consequences that he envisioned from American intervention were terrifying. The society that his people knew would be overturned. There would no longer be a preponderance of neutral nations and the whole world would be on a war basis. He predicted: "Once lead this people into war, and they'll forget there ever was such a thing as tolerance. To fight you must be brutal and ruthless, and the spirit of ruthless brutality will enter into the very fibre of our national life, infecting Congress, the courts, the policeman on the beat, the man in the street . . ." He thought the Constitution would not survive, that free speech and the right of assembly would go. Legal and moral restraints would be relaxed, industry would be demoralized, and profiteering run rampant. After the coming of peace it would require a generation to restore normal conditions. He said a nation couldn't put its strength into a war and keep its head level; it had never been done. "If there is any alternative," he cried out to Cobb, "for God's sake, let's take it."

On April 2 he was determined not to appear to be importunate; and House urged him to meet the convenience of the legislators. Learning that they would be ready for him at eight-thirty, he dined at six-thirty and talked of everything except the grave issue of the day. At eight-twenty the Wilsons left the White House, accompanied by Grayson and Tumulty. Heavily guarded, they drove through rain along the brilliant avenue, past thousands of citizens who waved little flags.

Edith Wilson left him in the room reserved for him at the Capitol.

He was alone for a few moments except for a secret service man—
Ellery Sedgwick, editor of the *Atlantic Monthly,* who had allowed himself to be sworn in so that he might enter the House chamber and hear
his hero deliver the decision that he had been advocating editorially for
two years. Unaware of the editor's observing eye the President walked
toward a large mirror. Sedgwick saw in the glass a face that was suffering the tortures of inferno. The features were twisted in spiritual agony,
the chin awry, the flesh deeply drawn and flushed. The President placed
his left elbow on a mantel and looked steadfastly at his distorted countenance. "A stroke!" the editor whispered to himself. But no; the tortured figure put his left hand to his brow to smooth the corrugations,
the right to his chin to set it straight and firm; and gradually the
features fell into a physiognomy as rigid as Calvin's. His "make-up"
completed, Woodrow Wilson was resolved to play out the tragedy that
had been forced upon him.

The President strode into the corridor and through the swinging
doors of the House chamber, ten minutes late. Champ Clark, re-elected
speaker, did his duty though he loathed both the occasion and the man.
"Gentlemen," he announced as the echo of his gavel died out, "the
President of the United States." The members of the Supreme Court
arose, and after them the other dignitaries who packed the room—legislators, Cabinet, and diplomatic corps. Woodrow Wilson was now, more
than ever, the symbol of security for the nation, and this feeling was
conveyed by the heartiness of the applause—the greatest ever given to
this President at the Capitol.

Wilson had never faced a more curious audience. No one, except
House and Edith Wilson, knew exactly what would be said. Waiting
for the clamor to die out, the President stood nervously on the rostrum,
fingering the cards on which his address was typed. Even from the
rear benches his face looked gaunt. As soon as the air was still, he rested
his arm on the green lectern and began to read in a voice that was at
first husky and low. But there was no gesture of voice or hand that
might rouse feeling in his audience; only an occasional raising of his
eyes. He dramatized the "absolute self-control and absolute self-mastery"
that he had bespoken for his nation.

His prophetic dignity made the cold indictment the more cutting.
Asserting that Germany had swept aside such international usages as
had been built up with great travail by humanity, that their submarine
policy was a menace to all mankind, he came to the essential that had
made his people ready to fight the Germans while they bore the insults
of the Allies. "Property can be paid for," he said; "the lives of peaceful
and innocent people cannot." Explaining why armed neutrality was

both impractical as a means of defense and ineffectual as a guarantee of peace, he made a ringing declaration: "There is one choice we cannot make, we are incapable of making; we will not choose the path of submission . . ."

At this point a tall figure rose in the audience. The secret service men fingered their guns; but it was Chief Justice White, an ex-Confederate soldier, raising his hands high and bringing them together with a clap. The galleries took the cue and roared their applause. They were obviously ready for what was to come, and the President came immediately to his grave pronouncement:

With a profound sense of the solemn and even tragical character of the step I am taking and of the grave responsibilities which it involves, but in unhesitating obedience to what I deem my constitutional duty, I advise that the Congress declare the recent course of the Imperial German Government to be in fact nothing less than war against the government and people of the United States; that it formally accept the status of belligerent which has thus been thrust upon it; and that it take immediate steps not only to put the country in a more thorough state of defense but also to exert all its power and employ all its resources to bring the Government of the German Empire to terms and end the war.

As for Austria-Hungary, a government that despite its adherence to German submarine tactics had not "actually engaged in warfare against citizens of the United States on the seas," Wilson took the liberty of postponing a discussion of relations. He spoke of the practical measures that must be taken immediately to prosecute the war in cooperation with the Western Allies. He made it clear that Americans were the sincere friends of the German people, and indeed had put up with the Berlin government through bitter months because of that friendship. Alluding to "the wonderful and heartening things" that had happened in Russia, he said: "The great, generous Russian people have been added in all their naïve majesty and might to the forces that are fighting for freedom in the world, for justice, and for peace. Here is a fit partner for a League of Honor."

He concluded with his great commitment of America to the service of humanity:

The world must be made safe for democracy. Its peace must be planted upon the tested foundations of political liberty. We have no selfish ends to serve. We desire no conquest, no dominion. We seek no indemnities for ourselves, no material compensation for the sacrifices we shall freely make. We are but one of the champions of the rights of mankind. We shall be satisfied when those rights have been made as secure as the faith and the freedom of nations can make them. . . . It is a distressing and oppressive duty, Gentlemen of the Congress, which I have performed in thus addressing you. There are, it may be, many months of fiery trial and sacrifice ahead of us. It is a fearful thing to lead this great peaceful people into war, into the most terrible and disastrous of all wars, civilization itself seeming to be in the balance. But the right is more precious than peace, and we shall fight for the things which we have always carried nearest our hearts,—for democracy, for the right of those who submit to authority to have a voice in their own Governments, for the rights and liberties of small nations, for a universal dominion of right by such a concert of free peoples as shall bring peace and safety to all nations and make the world itself at last free. To such a task we can dedicate our lives and our fortunes, everything that we are and everything that we have, with the pride of those who know that the day has come when America is privileged to spend her blood and her might for the principles that gave her birth and happiness and the peace which she has treasured. God helping her, she can do no other.

In thirty-two minutes he had finished speaking. For a few seconds there was stillness, save for the patter of rain on the glass roof, then a deafening roar in which Republicans and Democrats—Americans alike —gave voice to the feelings of a preponderance of the people. Henry Cabot Lodge, his face slightly puffed as a result of fisticuffs with a pacifist, shook the hand of the President warmly. At last the time had come for which Wilson had waited so patiently, the time when, as he explained later, his people were willing not merely to follow him, but to do so "with a whoop." In no previous crisis in American history had feeling been so unanimous.

War resolutions were quickly passed, with few dissenting votes. At one-eighteen on the afternoon of April 7 Wilson left his luncheon and with his wife stepped into the head usher's office. He was given the proclamation that formally declared the state of war that had "been thrust upon the United States." He read it with rigid jaw and grim countenance, then signed with a gold pen that he had given to Edith Wilson and that she asked him to use. The occasion was too solemn, he thought, to be witnessed by newsmen or photographed.

CHAPTER VI

CALL TO ARMS

A COUSIN, Fitz William McMaster Woodrow, accompanied Wilson from the Hill to the White House, and as they rode up in the elevator, the President said suddenly, with deep feeling: "Fitz, thank God for Abraham Lincoln."

"Why do you say that, Cousin Woodrow?" the astonished young man asked.

"I won't make the mistakes that he made" was the response.[1]

The circumstances of geography gave the President time to follow the rational process by which he was accustomed to attack new problems. The Atlantic Ocean, which had served so well to insulate the New World from the turbulence of the Old, made it impossible for the enemy to attack in force at once. The immediate need was to stiffen the morale of the Western Allies; and it seemed at first that this could be done best by providing ships and munitions, and the credits necessary, rather than by sending an American army to Europe.

Actually, there was no army to send. German military experts ranked the force of the United States on a level with those of tiny nations. Even had the President called up hundreds of thousands of volunteers, in the manner of "Father Abraham" a half-century before, there would not have been enough officers to train them. If he sent all of the little Regular Army abroad and it was decimated, as Britain's "First Hundred Thousand" had been in 1914, there would have been no training officers left. Americans must now do what Ambassador Gerard had told the Kaiser they would do: they must "invent something."

Given ample time to think, the President and his secretary of war applied themselves to building a foundation on which a large military machine might be erected if it should become necessary. While Wilson kept in mind the mistakes of Lincoln, Baker resolved to avoid such quarrels as Secretary of War Stanton had with Civil War generals. History taught that the fighting of a war demands unified control, that decentralization breeds delay, confusion, and error; and in the mechanized warfare of the twentieth century, good planning was more imperative than ever. Wilson realized that democracy could be saved

[1] F. W. McM. Woodrow to the writer, April 12, 1948. MS checked by Mr. Woodrow, May, 1956.

only if the people abdicated their power temporarily in favor of the experts.

At the beginning he used the soundest professional instrument available—the General Staff that had been created in 1903 as a result of the blunders of the Spanish-American War.[2] To the officers of this body was entrusted the shaping of military policy and its execution.

The problem of manpower, however, was one that could not be left entirely to military experts, for it affected a people who loathed the principle of conscription and whose grandfathers had rioted in protest against the Civil War draft. Many citizens felt that a knockout blow could be delivered if untrained volunteers rushed to France and communicated their enthusiasm to Allied armies that had become bogged in trench warfare. The President was besieged by petitions from Indian fighters, Texas Rangers, and Southern "Colonels" who had more zeal for vigilante raids than for subordination to military authority. Even close associates of Wilson were affected by a red-blooded urge to volunteer for combat, and he had to persuade them that they could serve best at their desks in Washington. The most embarrassing plea came from Colonel Theodore Roosevelt, who had served on his own terms in the Spanish-American War and wanted to do so again. Already he had rounded up some of his comrades of the "Rough Riders"; and even before the declaration of war he had offered to assemble a division and to put it into the trenches in France after six weeks of training. The enterprise would be financed from private sources, but the War Department would have to provide arms and supplies and some of the best officers.

The idea caught the imagination of the public; but Secretary Baker analyzed it carefully and immediately sent a courageous reply. Meeting with the Colonel face to face, Baker explained the technical difficulties. But Roosevelt sent another blast, and the secretary of war forwarded it to the President. On March 27 Wilson replied: "This is one of the most extraordinary documents I have ever read! Thank you for letting me undergo the discipline of temper involved in reading it in silence!"

When war was declared, Roosevelt determined to take his case directly to the White House. He called on April 10, and Wilson talked patiently with him, explaining that he had had for a long time the feelings that he had expressed in his war message, but had bided his time

---

[2] "In April, 1917, the General Staff consisted of fifty-one officers, only nineteen of whom were on duty at Washington. Of these, eight were occupied with routine business, leaving but eleven free for the real purpose for which the staff had been created—'the study of military problems, the preparation of plans for national defense, and utilization of the military forces in time of war.'" Seymour, *Woodrow Wilson and the World War*, p. 120. General Tasker H. Bliss supplanted General Scott, who was near retirement, as chief of staff.

until the people shared his sentiments. He said that he had been misunderstood by many people, and added that of course he did not refer to his guest as one of them.

It seemed to Roosevelt that this polite absolution was delivered "with obvious uncertainty." The Colonel was confident that he could still inspire youth, though he himself might "crack" after three months at the front; and he said that if his petition was granted and he went abroad to fight, he would promise not to come back. He suggested that, as good patriots, they let past hostilities be "as dust on a windy street."

Wilson was so charmed by the spirit of the petitioner that he almost gave way. For the moment he could forget that Roosevelt, now almost sixty years old, was blind in one eye and intermittently plagued by poisoning that had resulted from equatorial fever. The gallantry that had made Wilson speak of the battlefield as a glorious place to die responded to the exalted emotion of his rival. It would have been so easy and pleasant to give the old fellow his head. The President hated to burst the bubbles by asking penetrating questions. But to be true to his trust and his comrades he must.

Roosevelt failed to overcome the main obstacle—the President's fear that if he sanctioned a volunteer division, the Congress would be influenced against the essential principle of compulsory universal service. Nevertheless, the old warrior left with ardor undampened, slapped Tumulty on the back, and promised him a place in his division—it was not to be near headquarters, he later confided to a friend, for Wilson's secretary must be given no chance to act as a watchdog. Roosevelt had emotionally identified his own leadership with the salvation of the nation that he dearly loved. His mind was not disposed toward judicial review, nor his conscience toward shame. He continued to fulminate—constructively as long as there was a chance of realizing his martial dream, destructively when there was not.

If Wilson suspected political motives behind the fervor of Roosevelt, he made no allegations even to those closest to him. When he told his family that he could not release General Wood, Roosevelt's comrade-in-arms, from training duties in a Southern camp to which Wood had been assigned, they asked him why he did not give his people the reason for his decision. "In the first place, no one would believe me," he replied. "In the second place, they'd think they were getting under my skin. And in the third place, I'd see 'em in Hell first." [3]

[3] Letter, F. W. McM. Woodrow to the writer, May 6, 1956.
Roosevelt's argument was not ingenuous, according to an account that he himself wrote of his conversation with Wilson: "Of course, strictly for your private information, I had to choose my words rather carefully, in private and in public." T.R. to John C. O'Laughlin, April 13, 1917. *The Letters of T.R.*, VIII, 1173.

Asked for a press statement of his attitude toward Roosevelt's plea, Wilson wrote to Tumulty: ". . . I really think the best way to treat Mr. Roosevelt is to take no notice of him. That breaks his heart and is the best punishment that can be administered. After all, while what he says is outrageous in every particular, he does, I am afraid, keep within the law, for he is as careful as he is unscrupulous."

Finally, on May 17, Wilson's restraint gave way before an insult delivered in person by John M. Parker, one of Roosevelt's Rough Riders who came to the White House to plead for his comrade. "I feel I have the right to criticize," Parker said, "because you are my hired man, just as you are the hired man of the people." Moreover, he told Wilson to his face that the civilized world held "no more arbitrary ruler" than he.

In the position that he occupied, the President could not retaliate as man to man. Curbing his rage, he replied civilly but with complete frankness: "Sir, I am not playing politics . . . General Wood is needed here. Colonel Roosevelt is an admirable man and a patriotic citizen, but he is not a military leader . . . It is not I but the Republicans who have been playing politics and consciously embarrassing the Administration. I do not propose to have politics in any manner, shape, or form influence me in my judgment." [4]

Long before Roosevelt made his dramatic appeals, Wilson had been committed to a plan that would not only raise men for the armed forces

---

Roosevelt appealed to the British and French ambassadors for the intercession of their governments, and he sent them copies of voluminous arguments that he wrote to Secretary Baker. Encouraged by messages from thousands of sympathizers who felt that he was being martyred for his politics, Roosevelt proposed to influential legislators a device that he had suggested to Wilson—a rider to the draft bill that would provide for his division. But Baker, to whom General Bridges of the visiting British military mission had protested against the dispatch of amateur units from the United States, was adamant. On May 19th, the day after the choice of Pershing to command an expeditionary force was announced, Wilson telegraphed to Roosevelt that he could not permit him to raise a volunteer division; and on the same day he gave his reasons to the public. He had handled his adversary in the way that he had recommended to a new police commissioner of the District of Columbia. "When a man comes to you seeking special favors," he said, "be sure to control the conversation yourself and take high moral ground. Often he will be ashamed to mention his self-interested errand." Louis Brownlow to the writer.

Roosevelt thought of the Administration as "those Y.M.C.A. banditti at Washington," and in his office at the *Outlook* he was heard to squeak over the phone about the restraints put upon his freedom of action by "that skunk in the White House." Kerney, p. 248, and T. H. Watkins to Charles Seymour to the writer. Wilson was "an utterly selfish, utterly treacherous, utterly insincere hypocrite," Roosevelt wrote to William Allen White on May 28, 1917. *The Letters of T.R.,* VIII, 1198–99. Again and again, during the ensuing year, Roosevelt wrote to his friends in this vein, and in the columns of journals bitterly criticized the Administration's war policies.

Finally reacting against this persistent villification, Wilson said almost two years later, at Paris, that if he had published his interchanges with Roosevelt, the latter probably would have denied what he said. The President asserted that Roosevelt's object was personal publicity, that he had admitted a lack of necessary qualifications and wanted to use the Army's best officers to make up for his own shortcomings. Edith Benham Helm's "Letters," *Cosmopolitan*, August, 1930.

[4] Hagedorn, *Wood,* II, 219–22. Actually, some of Wilson's advisers thought it would be politically expedient to send his Republican adversaries as close to the front line as possible.

but would bring home to every citizen his obligation to serve the nation in its hour of crisis. In the autumn of 1916 he had agreed to the publication of an opinion submitted by the chief of staff, General Hugh L. Scott, a son of an old Princeton family who had shown himself an able general and had served without political ambition or prejudice. The report of the staff held that the volunteer system, "in view of the highly organized, trained, and disciplined armies in Europe," should be abandoned, that "the only democratic method is for every man in his youth to become trained in order that he may render efficient service." The military experts had observed the failure of the people to volunteer for service in Mexico in large numbers; and the necessity for compulsion became even more evident when enlistments in the spring of 1917 fell far short of the need for soldiers. Moreover, it was noted that Britain's efforts at voluntary recruiting had been neither adequate nor just and had, after eighteen months, given away to a systematic plan of conscription.

Soon after the diplomatic breach with Germany, Secretary Baker had brought these considerations before the President and found him open-minded. Wilson's instincts revolted against the idea; but he was convinced that the War Department's plan offered a democratic way to meet a universal obligation. He said that he wanted to have a conscription bill ready so that, if he had to read a war message, he could refer to it.

The recommendation that the President made to the Congress on April 2 called for a half-million more men for the armed forces, as provided by the National Defense Act that he had sponsored in 1916. In his opinion, he said, they "should be chosen upon the principle of universal liability to service." The day after the declaration of war, the President insisted publicly that "the safety of the nation" required conscription, and he reassured zealous democrats by explaining that the system would be in force only for the duration of the conflict.

A bill was ready for the Congress. It provided that men of draft age should present themselves on registration day to local civil authorities, as if they were going to the polls to vote. Thus they would submit their lives to their neighbors, not to an autocrat at Washington. There would be civil appeal boards, and sitting above them would be the provost marshal general, then the secretary of war, and finally the President. The system would be called "selective service," not "conscription"—ever a harsh word to American ears.

The President gave wholehearted support to the measure, declaring that the Administration would not "yield an inch of any essential parts of the programme." Selective service bills were passed by the two cham-

bers on April 28 over opposition that was bitter.[5] The system took effect
smoothly under the direction of General Crowder. Thus Wilson's administration proved itself as ingenious in solving a critical problem of
twentieth-century warfare as it had been in dealing with the new
economic forces of the era.[6]

In the proclamation that Secretary Baker had asked him to issue to
explain the new law to the public, Wilson again showed his genius in
summoning his national congregation to service in the Lord's work. He
made his people see a far wider vision than that of drafting privates.
"In the sense in which we have been wont to think of armies," he wrote,
"there are no armies in this struggle. There are entire nations armed
. . . The whole nation must be a team in which each man shall play
the part for which he is best fitted . . . It is in no sense a conscription
of the unwilling; it is, rather, selection from a nation which has volun-
teered in mass."

He was not willing to yield to political agitation for the forming of
a coalition war cabinet, like that adopted in Britain. He was held back
not only by mistrust of the capacity of certain Republican leaders for
nonpartisan thinking, but also by his preference for working with
familiar associates whom he knew thoroughly. As members of the
Cabinet filed into the regular meetings in the summer of 1917, all clad
in white, the Chief had a personal word for each one. He would go
around the table and give each a chance to speak, beginning one day
with the first, the next time with the second, and so on. As in an old-time
prayer meeting, there were no minutes, no votes, and no interruptions.
Discussion of politics was barred, though sometimes the President asked
Burleson to remain afterward to consider party matters. The President
listened with an inner ear to the best advice he could find at home and
abroad and tried to put himself and his authority at the disposal of
those who would use his powers wisely. "The business now in hand,"

[5] Though Wilson's party held a clear majority in the Senate, it was able to organize the
House only with the help of independent representatives. "This was a good thing from the
standpoint of efficient leadership from the White House," William E. Dodd has pointed out.
"It compelled the party in power to remain at its task and pay close attention to Mr. Wilson
for whom there was little love in either house." *W.W. and His Work*, p. 221.

[6] The Selective Service Act was one of the greatest legislative achievements of the Wilson
administration. It made it possible for all members of the National Guard to be taken into
federal service, and for adequate forces to be raised by selective draft without using men who
were essential to the normal functioning of civil life and war production. The act was accepted
by the people in the spirit in which it was conceived; and on June 5 some ten million men
between twenty-one and thirty, inclusive, peacefully registered with local civilian boards.
Later the age limits were extended and still more manpower became available.

The President was sympathetic to those who resisted military service on principle. Forwarding to Tumulty a letter from Villard about the conscientious objectors, he clipped a
note commending Villard's views as containing a great deal that was "interesting and sensible"
and predicting that they would be received by Secretary Baker with as much sympathy as by
himself.

he explained to his people, "is undramatic, practical, and of scientific definiteness and precision."

The Administration thought at first that the contribution of the United States should be chiefly in material. However, this view was changed by military missions that were sent to Washington by the Allies. When "Papa" Joffre, hero of the Battle of the Marne, paraded past cheering crowds in American cities, Wilson was impressed both by the man and by his plea for American aid. The marshal said that American troops should be seen in France at once, for moral effect,[7] and he promised that, if they knew the manual of arms and the rudiments of discipline, he could fit them for the front in five weeks. At the same time Balfour asked that men be sent immediately to the field of operations for training there; and his military adviser suggested that it would be best for American troops to cooperate with the British, rather than the French, because of their common language.

Adhering to a plan to send no large American army abroad until a million conscripts could be trained, Wilson and Baker made a concession to the pleas for a token force. On May 2 the President allowed Joffre to take it for granted that the troops that he wanted would be sent. On the 18th, the day on which Wilson signed the Selective Service Act, Baker announced that an expeditionary force of about one division would go to France as soon as practical, under the leadership of Major General John J. Pershing.

To select a commander for the first army that ever had gone from the New World to fight in the Old, the secretary of war had studied the records of all his senior generals. He resolved that he would choose the one who had shown himself most able and most devoted to duty, and then uphold his authority to the utmost. In the record of Pershing he found evidence of imagination, daring, and sound common sense. Moreover, this man had the rugged physique that would be essential. There was no hesitation, therefore, in selecting him in preference to five active major generals who outranked him.

Wilson was pleased by the choice. Pershing had handled the policing expedition in Mexico with restraint and fidelity. Moreover, he had shown himself an advocate of the principle of conscription. The President had read a letter from Pershing that interested him because of the light it threw on the man's loyalty to government policy, and he had suggested

[7] At this time the revolution in Russia had shaken the morale of the fighting men of Britain and France. British workers openly questioned the objectives for which their brethren had been conscripted to fight. At the same time French regiments, defeated in the Chemin des Dames and made restive by the emergence of "soldiers' councils" in Russia, were mutinous; and their leaders were fearful that the opposing German forces would be strengthened by troops released from the collapsing Eastern front.

to the secretary of war that they send this officer to France at once "to study the ground." When Pershing had been appointed and was about to sail, Wilson received him at the White House and said: "General, we are giving you some very difficult tasks these days."

When Pershing replied that he was "trained to expect this" and thanked the Commander in Chief for his appointment, Wilson said: "You were chosen entirely upon your record and I have every confidence that you will succeed." Thus was established a relationship of professional regard that was to withstand the strains of the hugest war in which the nation ever had been engaged.[8]

The President himself took little part in the shaping of military plans. Though he sometimes strolled over to the War Department and dropped in unannounced for a chat with Baker, he did not bother him about details and never overruled a decision made. Neither political expediency nor sentiment could induce Wilson to dispute disciplinary sentences. When Paderewski, Poland's patriot-pianist, proposed that a unit of Poles be organized within the American Army, Wilson felt that it would be unwise to do anything that might accentuate racial differences among his people.

Realizing that he was no military strategist, he still could follow the debates of the experts with keen attention. He spent his limited strength thriftily, disposing rapidly of minds that lacked balance and juice. "He knew a dry sponge on sight," Baker said of him. ". . . He sorted things out in the order of importance. Things never got lost in his mind, but lay there until it was time to act. . . . I deliberately thought a thing into its most compact form, and when he wanted details he asked for them."

It was soon clear that before the army could function on a large scale in France, the Navy had a challenging task to perform. Neither men nor supplies could be sent to the Western Allies in significant quantity if Germany's submarines were not checked. Their monthly toll had risen above a half-million tons and was still climbing. The Navy must gird itself to protect the transatlantic life line.

Wilson took a deeper interest in naval affairs than in those of the Army. He had once cherished an ambition to go to Annapolis, and ever since boyhood he had had a sentimental love for the sea and ships. Moreover, Secretary Daniels needed the stimulus of his mind, and his

[8] Sailing inconspicuously on the liner *Baltic* on May 28, Pershing took a few score of officers and men to London and Paris to pioneer the way. Soon after reaching France he advised Washington that the war must be won on the Western battlefront and that this required the use of a big American army as quickly as possible. With a large pool of manpower to draw upon, the General Staff already was making plans in this direction, developing a program for training junior officers and preparing to remedy a bad deficiency in guns.

support against the ridicule of critics. The secretary had made himself unpopular with industrial interests. After giving fair warning to American steel companies that made uniform bids, he had bought armor plate in England at lower prices; and he had attempted to reserve oil deposits for development by the government. Daniels had angered conservative naval officers by attempts to democratize the service. He had opened the door at Annapolis to qualified enlisted men and he had promoted able Captain Benson over the heads of admirals to be chief of naval operations. Furthermore, he had brought sophisticated ridicule on himself by prohibiting the use of alcoholic drinks in ships and installations of the Navy and by entertaining the French mission with nothing stronger than grape juice. Franklin D. Roosevelt's opinion of his superior had sunk so low that even House, who had urged the replacement of the secretary of the navy, was shocked.

Wilson had come to love Daniels for his geniality, his humor, his family life, and his long devotion to peace and to the public welfare. In basic matters they saw eye to eye. Contrary to the admirals who had wished to flaunt naval power in the Pacific, Wilson and Daniels had conceived that the proper function of the Navy was to defend American territory. The President now impressed upon the secretary the necessity of checking the undersea depredations of the enemy. He insisted that American enterprise find a defense against submarines that would be effective even if untraditional. Complaining that the Allies had not given enough attention to this and that they had not closed the English Channel with mines, he wrote to Daniels: "Can we not set this afoot at once and save all the time possible?"

After the declaration of war Wilson gave hearty approval to a message to Admiral Sims, who already had been sent abroad to make liaison with the British Navy, asking whether it was not practicable to blockade the German coast. Franklin D. Roosevelt had drafted a plan for a barrier of mines from Scotland to Norway and across the Straits of Dover, and Wilson had interested himself in this in 1916. However, Sims found no enthusiasm for the proposal in the tradition-bound British Admiralty and had to inform his chief that it was considered "wholly impractical."

When Page cabled that submarine warfare had created the most serious situation since the threat to Paris in the first month of the war, the President lost patience. Thinking that Sims, like Ambassador Page, was unduly awed by British prestige, he cabled very confidentially on July 4 to say that he expected Sims to send such advice as the admiral would give if handling an independent navy of his own. Observing that in the face of the emergency the Admiralty was "helpless to the point of panic," he asserted: "Every plan we suggest, they reject for some reason of prudence. In my view this is not a time for prudence but for boldness even at the cost of great losses." [9]

As early as February of 1917 the President had told his Cabinet that, in his view, merchant vessels should be gathered into groups and heavily protected by convoying warships. Though he suggested to the Cabinet that ships might dodge the enemy by constantly shifting their routes and ports of call, he thought the British policy of dispersion inadequate. The convoy system was tried out, and on May 20 the first group of ships arrived safely. Toward the end of June, Admiral Sims sent a series of messages to Washington to reinforce earlier pleas for destroyers, for convoying required the use of more small naval craft than the Allies could or would assign. Naval building plans were therefore revised. Franklin D. Roosevelt urged the use of small motorboats to patrol American harbors. Many private craft were purchased and armed, 110-foot submarine-chasers were built, and keels were laid for hundreds of destroyers.

The emphasis on small vessels would delay the construction of capital ships that had been authorized, and Colonel House feared that after the war the United States might find itself without adequate protection from battleships and cruisers. He raised the question with the British government and found them not unwilling to consider a postwar guaranty that would compensate the United States in some measure for unbalancing her naval strength by building destroyers.

Wilson was not impressed. He felt that his navy was already relatively strong in capital ships, and in this he was supported by British experts. Moreover, he observed that the submarine's success required that the traditional evaluation of capital ships be altered. He preferred to preserve America's freedom of action rather than bind her by naval treaties that might be as pregnant with future trouble as secret undertakings into which the Allies had entered under the stress of war. There

[9] In the summer of 1917 Admiral Mayo was ordered to England to tell the Admiralty of American plans for a mine barrier. The matter was considered at an Inter-Allied Naval Conference that met at London early in September, and finally the British gave their consent. On Oct. 29, Franklin D. Roosevelt wrote a letter to remind Wilson that the mine barrier had been approved by the naval authorities at Washington and London and definite orders should be given immediately for its execution. The next day Wilson replied that he was interesting himself in the plan. It was approved by him and by the Cabinet, but the project was not completed for a year.

In pressing his plan upon the President, Franklin D. Roosevelt had the aid of Winston Spencer Churchill, who as first lord of the admiralty had been largely responsible for the preparedness of the British fleet in 1914. The President received Churchill on July 25, 1917; and on the next day Roosevelt, who admired Churchill's grasp of naval affairs, wrote to his wife Eleanor: "The more I think over the talk with the President the more I am encouraged to think that he has begun to catch on, but then it will take lots more of the Churchill type of attack." *F.D.R.: His Personal Letters*, II, 356–57.

seemed to be no way of binding the British short of a treaty, and that would have to go to the Senate, which did not seem to be in a mood to welcome such a measure. When he visited House at Magnolia in September, and the Colonel argued his point with more persistence than he was accustomed to risk, Wilson replied that he did not choose to discuss the question further. He approved the Navy's program for turning out light antisubmarine craft in quantity.

At Magnolia he told House of a talk that he had made on August 11 to the officers of the Atlantic fleet. He had refrained from making extemporaneous speeches on policy during the early months of the war because he felt that every word must be weighed carefully when the life of a nation was at stake, and he lacked time for this. But on the deck of the battleship *Pennsylvania,* which he boarded from the *Mayflower* in the course of a weekend cruise, he spoke to the naval officers as he might once have talked to Princeton's football team. Reminding them that they were all novices in the new methods of twentieth-century war, he spoke very confidentially, urging them to "throw tradition to the winds" and criticizing the British Admiralty for its sluggishness.

To pessimistic journalists who wrote of the wonderful efficiency of German arms, he said his reply was "Rats!" The United States was to him "the prize amateur nation of the world," Germany the prize professional. He asserted:

When it comes to doing new things and doing them well, I will back the amateur against the professional every time because the professional does it out of the book and the amateur does it with his eyes open upon a new world and with a new set of circumstances. He knows so little about it that he is fool enough to try the right thing. . . . Do the thing that is audacious to the utmost point of risk and daring, because that is exactly the thing that the other side does not understand, and you will win by the audacity of method when you cannot win by circumspection and prudence.

"Somebody has got to think this war out," he declared. "Somebody has got to think out the way not only to fight the submarine, but to do something different from what we are doing. We are hunting the hornets all over the farm and letting the nest alone." He invited "the youngest and most modest youngster in the service" to tell his superiors what they ought to do if he knew what it was. He was willing to sacrifice half the navies of the United States and Britain to crush the hornets' nest, he said, because if they could do that the war would be won.

In mobilizing the armed strength of the nation in other fields than that of naval operations, the President was confronted by problems on which the precedents of history gave little guidance.

Communications had become so complex, in the age of electricity, that the safeguarding of military secrets was an operation far more difficult than in previous wars. Remembering that Lincoln had felt it necessary to suppress newspapers and imprison citizens without due process of law, Wilson hoped that he would not have to go to this extreme. He was on guard against unnecessary offenses to the civil rights of American citizens. But the attorney general ordered the seizure of some two thousand enemy aliens whose loyalty to the United States was questionable; Wilson issued, on April 28, an order for government censorship of cables and of telephone and telegraph lines; and he approved the operation of all wireless stations by the Navy for the war's duration. He gave approval to an espionage bill that was before Congress, and he made it clear that he would not permit the measure to be used to stifle criticism of himself or his official acts.[10]

The espionage bill that the House passed included a provision for censorship of the press that aroused protests from newspapermen. Tumulty warned his chief that there was growing resentment against the very idea of censorship. Nevertheless, on May 23 Wilson told conferees from the Senate, which supported his position, that the measure was "an imperative necessity," that though most journals would observe "a patriotic reticence," something more than moral obligation must be imposed on any newspaper that printed information by which the enemy might profit.

The final act, which he signed on June 15, did not give the President all the powers that he sought. It did, however, set forth a new definition of crimes against the public interest in time of war. It empowered the government to regulate the export of goods.[11] Furthermore, the act

[10] Daniels Diary, April 6, 1917. One of the conflicts of departmental interests that made the President's burden the heavier broke out when the seizing of wireless stations was discussed. When Daniels made the proposition that the Navy take them, Burleson said: "I serve notice that when communication becomes governmental, it must be under the Post Office Department." The President asked: "Is that a threat or a prophecy?" And Daniels put in: "It is a bluff or a boast." Daniels, *Years of War*, p. 28.

When newspaper stories reported an indiscreetly frank speech about maritime losses made by Secretary Lane, who hoped to strengthen morale by making citizens feel that they were told the whole truth, Wilson showed his displeasure. He did not want American shippers to be thrown into a panic, or war insurance rates to go up, and he became more careful than ever to withhold confidential information from the Cabinet.

When Cabinet members took petty grievances to House, he did not annoy the President with them in these critical days. Nevertheless, he noted in his diary that Wilson was holding "a tighter rein" over his Cabinet and was impatient with the taking of initiative on their part, that the President was "as usual doing things too casually" and not getting enough information from all sides before acting.

[11] The constitutionality of the Espionage Act was upheld by the Supreme Court, but only for times when "a clear and present danger" existed.

Under the new act an Exports Council was created and Vance McCormick, as its agent, undertook to organize a Bureau of Export Licenses. When neutral nations were disturbed by this move, Wilson explained it in a public statement.

A Trading-with-the-Enemy Act, signed by the President on Oct. 6, gave Wilson sufficient

made it possible for postal officials to prevent the circulation of periodicals that some citizens thought seditious and others, merely critical. More stringent censorship laws were enacted within the year, and overzealous officials and juries of panicky citizens did not always draw the line wisely between prosecution and persecution. To one of the prominent liberals who protested against acts that they thought violations of civil freedom, Wilson replied: "I think that a time of war must be regarded as wholly exceptional and that it is legitimate to regard things which would in ordinary circumstances be innocent as very dangerous to the public welfare, but the line is manifestly exceedingly hard to draw and I cannot say that I have any confidence that I know how to draw it. I can only say that a line must be drawn and that we are trying, it may be clumsily but genuinely, to draw it without fear or favor or prejudice." [12]

On April 14 George Creel, a Western journalist who had crusaded for many a liberal cause, became chairman of a Committee on Public Information that the Congress had quickly authorized. His colleagues were the secretaries of war and navy, who were cooperative and permitted him to attach trained reporters to their departments, and also the secretary of state, who resented the intrusion of the journalist and hesitated to confide secrets of state to a man whose leanings he thought "socialistic." [13] Creel's work was as difficult as it was untraditional. He had to hunt down and kill untruths as well as dispense and nourish truth. Although not always diplomatic, he carried through his mission with

---

authority so that he appointed on Oct. 12 a Board of Censorship, an Alien Property Custodian, and a War Trade Board of which McCormick was chairman and which, in cooperation with other agencies, conserved ocean tonnage, encouraged the import of war necessities, and blacklisted firms that traded with the enemy.

[12] W.W. to Max Eastman, Sept. 18, 1917.

One instance in which the President himself "drew the line" is related by Norman Thomas in his record in the Columbia Oral History Project. Asked to read an article by Thomas in the *World Tomorrow* of August, 1918, entitled "Russia, the Acid Test," Wilson saw no cause to indict the author, who had been told by Burleson that he should be in Leavenworth Prison for life and who opposed armed intervention in Russia. However, Wilson said to Nevin Sayre, who showed him the article: "Go and tell Norman Thomas [once a student of Wilson's at Princeton] that there is such a thing as the indecent exposure of private opinions in public."

[13] Finally, on June 29, Wilson wrote to Lansing to ask him to cooperate with Creel in the release of all information. When Lansing wrote to the President, weeks later, to suggest that a few representative and trustworthy newsmen be organized into a council to advise Creel, Wilson replied that this proposal, which he had heard from other sources, was based upon a complex of misunderstandings and of jealousies. "The net result of my impressions," he wrote on Sept. 4, "is that it would be safest not to call them into systematic conference. They are a difficult lot to live with. They do not agree among themselves."

Creel noted: "Lansing, a dull, small man, made himself so unpleasant at the first meeting of the Committee that I never called another." Creel felt that the "persisted antagonism" of the State Department was due to jealousies and conflicts of authority between officials of the department and agents of the CPI in foreign capitals. Professional diplomatists were unsympathetic to propagandists who addressed peoples without reference to embassies and foreign offices.

industry, thrift, and loyalty to a chief who was genuinely fond of him. Mobilizing hundreds of patriotic speakers, issuing pamphlets and news stories, posters, moving pictures, and advertisements that were given free display, the news bureau stimulated enthusiasm among the people and awakened in American minds an appreciation of the causes and stakes of the war.

Professional newsmen muttered about "censorship" and "repression" and resented what seemed to many to be an arrogant assumption of their function. They asked that the President's press conferences be resumed; but Wilson was adamant when Creel urged this upon him. He wanted only essential and productive interviews. In the war emergency, personal approaches had given way to memoranda.

Requesting secrecy on certain vital matters, Creel announced that any censorship that might result would be purely voluntary. Nevertheless, the protests of the press, fed by indiscreet remarks by Creel himself and fanned by the chronic adversaries of the Administration, led to a request by the Congress for the young man's resignation. Wilson took up the cudgels for his appointee. But he could not prevent the House from cutting the funds of Creel's committee.

Like House and Newton D. Baker, Creel had won Wilson's loyalty by understanding the processes of his brain and coordinating his own work with them. Before every interview at the White House he drew up a pithy, well-organized brief. Ten seconds after shaking hands he plunged into it, and he followed it through logically. Creel found the President's mind the most receptive of those that he met in official circles. He noted that Wilson reached conclusions too carefully to give them up quickly and that he resented assertions not supported by fact; but once his facts were shaken, he surrendered.

Though the Congress balked at appropriating all funds that Creel requested, it acted with alacrity to provide the billions needed for military and naval operations. Before war was declared, the President had approved the expenditure of nearly three billions for the Army and a half-billion for the Navy; but when a distinguished economist suggested that the government would have to spend ten billions in 1917, there were smiles of incredulity. In the three preceding years the annual federal budget had not reached a level of one billion dollars, and yet only the new income tax law had enabled Secretary McAdoo to avoid deficit financing.

The task facing the Treasury seemed to McAdoo prodigious. After frequent conferences with the President, it was decided that the government should be empowered to lend up to three billion dollars to the Allies [14]; and to finance this operation and America's own mobilization, Treasury issues of five billions of bonds and two billions of short-term certificates were to be authorized. The President had said that "the industry of this generation should pay the bills of this generation." But he felt that to raise even half the cost of war by taxation would be excessive, and perhaps destructive of "the capital energy that keeps the wheels turning." In September the Congress completed its work on a war revenue bill that increased existing taxes sharply and levied many new excises. Approximately a third of the war costs were met by current taxation.

On May 14 the secretary of the treasury announced that a bond issue of two billions would be offered to the public, to be known as the Liberty Loan of 1917. McAdoo proved himself a master salesman and enlisted ardent help from volunteers. The loan was oversubscribed by more than a billion dollars. Save for taking up $10,000 of bonds from his own small income (after America entered the war he invested in nothing but government bonds), Wilson had little to do with the First Liberty Loan. Noting the excellent publicity that was given to the drive, and the predictions of success, he explained that he would "reserve his fire" for later issues of Liberty bonds. The total subscribed in five loans, running over a period of two years, was more than twenty-one billions.

The spending of the funds in the war chest was more troublesome than the raising of them. Control of costs was a consideration that grew upon the inherently thrifty President, as the average price of metals almost doubled within three months. He knew that he would have to deal with the same interests that had fought his banking, tariff, and antitrust programs. But now he could exert a stronger compulsion than before, for patriotism had become a matter of life and death. On April 16, appealing to citizens in all walks of life, he said: "The industrial forces of the country, men and women alike, will be a great national, a great international, Service Army." Middlemen would be expected "to forego unusual profits," merchants to adopt the motto: "small profits and quick service." In a Cabinet meeting, when copper prices were

---

[14] McAdoo has recorded (in *Crowded Years*, p. 376) that he reached the decision to lend to the Allies with great reluctance, reminding himself of the old adage: "To make an enemy of a friend, lend him money." Nevertheless, he argued before the Ways and Means Committee that to the extent that the United States sent dollars abroad, they would be able to save the lives of their young men.

On June 28, Page sent a message marked "Greatest Urgency" that informed the President that "the British agents in the United States now have enough money to keep the exchange up for only one day more," that unless America came to the rescue Great Britain would have to abandon the gold standard. And the chancellor of the exchequer reported that unless the government of the United States could fully meet British expenses in America "the entire financial fabric" would collapse in a matter of days.

under discussion, the President advocated a uniform rate for American and Allied purchases. He would offer a price that seemed fair, and then appeal to the country if it were declined. Once, at least, he suggested that the government take over plants of manufacturers who would not accept prices that seemed to the government reasonable. Thanking Daniels for a letter about "steel" prices, he said that he hardly knew how he should spell the word. Daniels, a stubborn bargainer, suggested that before merchants grew as rich as they had in England, the government should set fair prices for fuel, metals, and similar raw materials; and the President provided funds for a study of ways to do this. There were many opinions within the official family on this vexing question, and in June an altercation over the price of coal almost resulted in the resignation of Lane; but all agreed that prices should be high enough to maintain good production and low enough to prevent profiteering. Wilson insisted, too, that whatever his own government bought for its war effort should be available to the Allies at the same prices.

By summer the Administration's purchasing policy had taken shape sufficiently so that the President could explain it to his people. Announcing that the government was about to try to set fair prices on war supplies, he asserted on July 12: "We must make the prices to the public the same as the prices to the Government. Prices mean the same thing everywhere now; they mean the efficiency or the inefficiency of the Nation, whether it is the Government that pays them or not. They mean victory or defeat."

Military necessity threatened industrial freedom, and the Administration was forced toward a conservative position. As Wilson had foreseen, many of the monopolies that were being prosecuted by the Department of Justice were essential to the supplying of the armed forces. As a result, five or six pending cases were dropped for the duration of the war. The President and the attorney general agreed that they should relax pressure temporarily on certain corporations so that there would be no excuses for not contributing unreservedly to the prosecution of the war, and the chief justice confirmed this course as "patriotic and proper."

The prophet who had preached self-discipline in politics now applied his lesson to industry. "Beyond all question," he said, "the highest and best form of efficiency is the spontaneous cooperation of a free people." He told state defense officials that he conceived that his function was not to give advice, but to coordinate activity so that there would not be lost motion. He hoped to avoid duplication of work and to keep the state bodies constructively active in bringing the war program home to the people.

By and large, the men of his Cabinet were not figures whose knowledge of industry could impress industrial magnates. In August of 1916 Wilson had assigned six of them to a Council of National Defense that was charged with the coordination of industries and resources for the national security and welfare.[15] But actually the work was done by seven civilian advisers and experts who served with them. These men concentrated not only on recommending fair prices, but on conserving resources, controlling distribution, and stabilizing labor relations. Trained and competent executives served for a dollar a year to provide sinews of war with the least possible dislocation of civil life.

Soon, however, the volunteers were working at cross-purposes and without over-all direction. Moreover, it was difficult to persuade some corporations—often those without representation at Washington—to sacrifice competitive positions to the demands of the general welfare. On July 8 the Council of National Defense established a coordinating War Industries Board of seven members; but, though this body gradually established valid principles of industrial mobilization, it lacked power to enforce its rulings.

In no field was the need for firm control more obvious than in that of food production and distribution. The ravages of war had increased the dependence of Western Europe on imports, and, realizing that their people could not fight on empty stomachs, the leaders of the Allies looked to the New World for bread. Unfortunately, at that time the United States had little surplus wheat to send. Food prices rose sharply between March and July. It was estimated that Great Britain's grain supply would last but eight weeks. Recognizing the emergency, the President conferred with Secretary Houston and the Congressional committee on agriculture and declared that they must act promptly to impose controls. "It would be difficult to express in parliamentary language," he said, "what should be done with anyone who would speculate in food products in a situation like the present."

Fortune had provided a man of great stature to meet the emergency, Herbert Clark Hoover had won the respect of the humanitarians of the world by a ministry of mercy to the people of invaded Belgium; and his work had elicited sympathy, confidence, and financial support from the American people. He had proved himself a genius in choosing able subordinates and inspiring and organizing them, and a man of vision

---

[15] The six Cabinet members were the secretaries of war, navy, interior, agriculture, commerce, and labor. Serving under the chairmanship of Newton D. Baker, these executives worked through an Advisory Commission of seven civilian volunteers. Most of the civilian volunteers were Republicans. Earlier bodies that contributed to the work of the council were the Committee on Industrial Preparedness, the Naval Consulting Board, and the National Research Council.

and reliability. Page wrote to Wilson about him: "a simple, modest, energetic little man who began his career in California and will end it in Heaven; and he doesn't want anybody's thanks."

The President was inclined to have the food supply regulated in the same way in which other commodities were—by a coordinating board without any power but that of patriotic opinion. Wilson feared that a grant of extraordinary authority to a single man might offend the secretary of agriculture and give substance to news stories picturing Hoover as a "food dictator." And so it was as the unpaid chairman of a committee of the Council of National Defense that Hoover set up an office at Washington and chose volunteers. Continuing the flow of supplies to Belgian civilians, he endeavored at the same time to devise plans for squeezing, from a country that suffered crop failures in 1916 and 1917, enough surplus food to make up serious shortages in other friendly nations of Europe.

The ingenious engineer was not content to operate merely in an advisory capacity. He pointed out to the President that in Europe division of authority had bred friction, indecision, and delay. He suggested that the tradition of American business required a single responsible executive who would use boards only for advice and adjudication. To allay doubts that were being expressed in the Congress, Hoover thought that he might be given the title of "administrator"—a term that would connote coordination and executive leadership rather than dictatorship.

On May 19 Wilson made a public announcement that was intended to dispel the misgivings that had been reflected in the press and in the Congress. Drawing a distinction between the normal activities of the Department of Agriculture and the emergency needs of the war, he set forth the specific powers that he wanted to confer on Hoover: fixing of prices; full inquiry into stocks, costs, and practices; prevention of hoarding; requisitioning and licensing; and prohibition of waste. These powers were to be exercised only as long as the war lasted, and with the voluntary cooperation of the nation's women.

The Congress was slow to confer absolute power on any individual, even on a temporary and volunteer basis. Not until June did the House take up a bill proposed by Chairman Lever of its Committee on Agriculture, providing for "a governmental control of necessaries . . . which shall be exercised and administered by the President." This was a grant of power without precedent in American history, and immediately it was assailed by legislators who feared dictatorship. But Wilson insisted that the bill was one of the most imperative of the war measures, that its object was not so much to control food as to release it from the control of speculators and profiteers, and to protect the people against extortions. When the measure came to a vote, only five representatives dared oppose it.

The Senate, however, debated the Lever Bill for more than a month. Senator Reed called it "vicious and unconstitutional," and Hoover was attacked as a man more alien than American. The measure was encumbered with provisions for a food committee of three and for a joint Congressional committee on the conduct of the war. These embarrassments were approved by a majority of the Senate.

The President protested hotly against the proposed creation of what he called "an espionage committee." Pointing out that such a body had harassed Lincoln constantly and had made his task all but impossible, Wilson asserted that the idea was not only entirely foreign to the subject matter of the food bill, but impinged on the responsibility of the Administration. Abundant means of investigation already existed, he said, and though he was ready to "cooperate" in practical ways he could interpret such a measure only as arising from lack of confidence in the President. The objectionable Senate amendments were eliminated when the bill went to a conference; and on August 10 Wilson was able to sign the Lever Act, giving himself power to control foods, fuel, fertilizer, and the machinery and equipment to produce them. The President now could name Hoover as food administrator with the specific Congressional authorization that others of his dollar-a-year men lacked. Moreover, he appointed President Harry A. Garfield of Williams College to be fuel administrator. The Food Administration proceeded to set a price on wheat, to meet what Wilson regarded as "a very serious crisis," and later on other commodities. By the time Hoover was ready to try to stabilize the price of sugar and brought his plan to the President, a relation of such understanding had been established that Wilson merely initialed the paper set before him and, when asked whether the White House shouldn't have a duplicate copy, grinned and replied: "Would that get any more sugar?" By 1918, as a result of "Hooverizing," the United States was able to export approximately three times the usual quantities of sugar, as well as of meats and breadstuffs, and the President had learned to have great confidence in Hoover's "practical judgment."

Hoover called on patriots to observe meatless days and wheatless days, preached a "gospel of the clean dinner plate," and distributed stickers that every citizen could display in his window. The White House set an example to the nation by cooperating with this program. One of the red-white-and-blue stickers appeared in a window of the executive mansion, and out-of-season delicacies disappeared from the table. A war garden was planted and, later, sheep were brought to graze

on the lawn and their wool was auctioned to benefit the Red Cross. The
ladies of the household knitted interminably; and in the evening the
President sometimes held their yarn on his hands while they rolled
it into balls. Edith Wilson got out her sewing machine and made
bandages.

When Wilson went riding and saw food stickers or Red Cross em-
blems [16] displayed in humble homes, his heart filled with gratitude to
the citizens who were responding so nobly to his leadership. "I wish I
could stop and know the people who live here," he would sometimes say
to his wife, "for it is from them that I draw inspiration and strength."

Not such good fortune attended American efforts to supply Western
Europe with a commodity that was needed as badly as food and munitions. The Allies were crying for ships. American men and supplies
would be useless without vessels to transport them.

As soon as war had broken out in Europe, Wilson had seen that the
United States must put an end to its dependence on the merchant tonnage of other nations; and after long legislative battles he had induced
the Congress to pass a Shipping Act in September of 1916. Under this
law the President appointed a Shipping Board of five men, with
William Denman of San Francisco as chairman. The board set up an
Emergency Fleet Corporation, which was to operate with businesslike
efficiency and without the restrictive red tape that hampers government
bureaus.[17] General Goethals of Panama Canal fame was made general
manager. But Goethals and Denman failed to work in harmony. Finding the general critical and "a most difficult person to deal with,"
Wilson accepted his resignation and thought it best to ask Denman to
withdraw also.

The President reached the conclusion that in creating shipping, as in
meeting other challenges thrown at him by the emergency, it was best
to depend on one man and to give him full authority. Edward N.
Hurley, a loyal Democrat from Chicago who had headed the Federal
Trade Commission and had been drafted into Red Cross work, was
asked to direct both the Shipping Board, which remained as a policy-

16 Wilson and House gave much thought to the promotion of the American Red Cross
under Henry P. Davison. The President issued public appeals, contributed $500 himself,
conferred with ex-President Taft, who remained chairman of the Executive Committee at
Wilson's request, and took an interest in the operations of the organization in Russia and
other countries of Europe. Stockton Axson became secretary of the American Red Cross in
December, 1917.

17 In June of 1917 an act of Congress gave the President authority to requisition, con-
struct, or operate ships without limits except those imposed by the availability of funds. On
July 11 Wilson delegated his powers to the Emergency Fleet Corporation. On July 27, Wilson
at last satisfied a long-standing desire to bring Thomas D. Jones, who had supported him
steadfastly in Princeton controversies, into the government. Jones was offered a seat on the
Shipping Board and accepted.

making, regulative body, and the Emergency Fleet Corporation. When Hurley protested to Tumulty that he was not a shipbuilder and hence was unqualified for the position, he was told that the President had said: "You tell Hurley that this is personal." Regarding this as an order from the Commander in Chief, the appointee acceded.

At the end of June Wilson seized the interned enemy vessels that he had not allowed his Cabinet to take before a state of war existed but that he had directed Denman, at the end of April, "to put in repair." These were made ready to go to sea under the American flag. The government also contemplated the requisitioning of American ships abuilding; and on August 3 Hurley commandeered all large hulls that were under construction. On October 12 he took over the American steel cargo vessels and passenger liners of more than twenty-five hundred deadweight tons. Eventually the Emergency Fleet Corporation succeeded in increasing available tonnage about tenfold, and laid down two ships for every one sunk by submarines.

Thus Woodrow Wilson accepted and met the challenge of twentieth-century war. In the hour of crisis he proved himself quick to perceive essentials in new conditions and wise to choose men who could aid in defining policies and could be trusted to execute them with zeal and intelligence. He initiated little, but rather selected and coordinated. When finally the war Congress adjourned, on October 6, he commended it for the accomplishments of a remarkable session.

By persuasion, by legislation, and by applying the pressure of a public opinion that had reached crusading fervor, Wilson had led the ruggedest of individuals to defer to necessity and share in the common sacrifice of the nation. Using sometimes his own power as commander in chief, sometimes the emergency powers that the Congress granted, the war President took measures that resulted in socializing many of the processes of the nation's economic and intellectual life. But he did this without losing his respect for the institutions to which he had to do violence, and with a resolve to restore them to full vigor after the madness had passed. Having noticed a reluctance on the part of government departments to relinquish any powers granted them, he had avoided giving them any extraordinary powers that it might be difficult to withdraw after the war.

Though he reserved his own strength for essentials and could encompass a vast volume of work, there was not enough energy left in him to meet all the demands of duty. However, his efforts did not seem to him excessive when he measured them by the contribution of those who put their lives in jeopardy. Occasionally he issued little homilies to his soldier boys. He kept in close touch with Raymond Fosdick, a former student at Princeton who was chairman of a committee working to sustain morale in the training camps. Often, just before dinner, he called for his wife at a Red Cross canteen and shook hands with as many boys as time permitted. On Sundays, when his church was crowded, he insisted on sharing his pew with soldiers. He signed the membership pledge of the Pocket Testament League, committing himself "to read at least one chapter in the Bible each day"; and he kept his pledge faithfully, using a Bible bound in khaki. When a White House guard mentioned the fact that his son was one of the first to be drafted, the President grasped the man's hand and said in a muffled voice: "God grant he may come back to you!"

Realizing that violence might be done to fair labor standards in the drive of industry for better production, Wilson spoke on May 15 to the labor committee of the Council of National Defense. "I have been very much alarmed," he said, "at one or two things that have happened: at the apparent inclination of the legislature of one or two of our states to set aside even temporarily the laws which have safeguarded the standards of labor and life." Promising to exert his influence against any lowering of standards that generations of Americans had brought to their present level, he went on:

. . . we are fighting for democracy in a larger sense than can be expressed in any political terms. There are many forms of democratic government and we are not fighting for any particular form; but we are fighting for the essential part of it all, namely, that we are all equally interested in our social and political life and all have a right to a voice in the Government under which we live; and that when men and women are equally admitted to those rights we have the best safeguard of justice and of peace that the world affords. . . . We are just now feeling as we have never felt before our sense of comradeship. We shall feel it even more, because we have not yet made the sacrifices that we are going to make, we have not yet felt the terrible pressure of suffering and pain of war, and we are going presently to feel it, and I have every confidence that as its pressure comes upon us our spirits will not falter, but rise and be strengthened, and that in the last we shall have a national feeling and a national unity such as never gladdened our hearts before.

And so he brought his national congregation into the shadow of the Cross and consecrated the sacrifice that each would be required to make, whether it was the laying down of a life or merely the temporary abnegation of luxury and profits and the civil rights and privileges that a democracy could not afford in time of war.

CHAPTER VII

"WE ARE NO LONGER PROVINCIALS"

As HE IMPARTED spiritual strength to his American congregation, Woodrow Wilson did not neglect the sources from which his own morale stemmed. Cruising down the Potomac with a classmate, on a Sunday in June, he suggested that they sing a hymn that had been a favorite at Princeton in undergraduate days:

> When peace like a river attendeth my way,
> When sorrows like sea billows roll;
> Whatever my lot, thou hast taught me to say
> It is well, it is well, with my soul.

He found refuge and restoration, too, in the atmosphere of love and understanding that his family and close friends had created. To his intimates he was still a charming, humorous gentleman, considerate of each one of them. The traditional family evenings persisted, though now the President often had to step out of the firelit circle to talk on the telephone or sign papers in his study. A cousin of Ellen Wilson, visiting the White House in May, found him "strong and ruddy, the embodiment of calm and cheerfulness—the kind that you can *tie* to."

No wish of his wife seemed too trifling for him to be attentive to it. When she was ill, he read to her. When she confessed that she could not ride a bicycle and therefore could not accompany him in the cycling tour of England that he dreamed of taking when released from public duty, he bought a bicycle and took her to the basement of the White House to give her lessons. When she fell off, they laughed hilariously.

He still went frequently to vaudeville and especially enjoyed tap dancing. It refreshed him, he said, to consort with people who "took on no more at their hearts than they could kick off at their heels." He liked to start a phonograph record after dinner and show how a jig step was done; and after official receptions that required hours of smirks and polite nothings, he would escape upstairs and rest the muscles of his face by exercising them as an actor might.

When the summer of 1917 scorched Washington, the President set the pace for his warring people by announcing that he would take no summer vacation. But he looked to the sea for relief. "Edith and I are on the *Mayflower*," he wrote to Jessie Sayre on July 21, "to get away from the madness (it is scarcely less) of Washington for a day or two, not to stop work (that *cannot* stop nowadays) . . . but to escape *people* and their intolerable excitements and demands." He was never sure that the next day would not bring him to the breaking point. Once he said to Creel, who noted that at times his face was gray as ashes: "I'm getting to be like Dickens's fat boy. I could go to sleep at an angle of ninety degrees."

Wilson spent two days with House at Magnolia and talked as intimately with this adviser as he had been wont to do. He had not seen House for more than three months, and newspapers were speculating again about a breach between the friends. In their conversation on the North Shore, Wilson made many confessions. When he found it hard to pick up a thread of conversation that the Colonel interrupted, he smiled plaintively and said: "You see I am getting tired. That is the way it indicates itself . . ." He spoke of the nervousness that still beset him before speaking in public. Describing himself as "a democrat like Jefferson, with aristocratic tastes," he explained that this was unfortunate because his mind led him where his tastes rebelled. He spoke more kindly of Lincoln than he had to his cousin at the war's beginning, said that though Lincoln's outlook was limited by his lack of education his judgment was equal to the situations confronting him.

A major reason for coming to see House was to discuss the shortcomings of Lansing, whose resignation the President was thinking of requesting. Every time he wrote a note or released a statement, he said, the secretary of state, who seemed to consort too much with society folk and reactionaries, would dilute it by putting a conservative construction on it. To be sure, he would correct it when the President objected, but nevertheless confusion was bred and the effect of the original was almost nullified. It seemed to him that Lansing was not well, and was leading a life that would tax a strong man, dining out every night, returning home to work until two in the morning, and reaching his desk regularly at nine. Moreover, he was consuming cigarettes and black coffee immoderately. The President thought that Baker might be a more serviceable secretary of state, though he did not see how this official could be spared from the War Department.

House was not surprised, for Polk had told him only three weeks before that Wilson did not appreciate Lansing and felt that the secretary of state did not write clearly and that he had to do too much rewriting. The Colonel suggested to his friend that he have a frank talk with the secretary and persuade him to delegate news conferences to Counselor Polk. If a change must be made, Lansing might be sent to replace Page; and then, too, at the war's end they might make him a peace commissioner. Wilson agreed tentatively that the London post might be suitable, but said that if Lansing were made peace commissioner he would nullify American efforts by indiscreet utterances.

While the President concentrated on the vital business of raising men, money, and supplies for a military establishment that would make the United States secure in a war-racked world, House pursued his special interest in foreign relations. He had many misgivings about the President's allocation of time and energy. Unable to persuade Wilson to act on more than one thing at a time, the Colonel thought him too dependent on his own individual efforts. It seemed as if diplomatic relations with South America, Japan, and Europe were being allowed to take care of themselves.

Actually, Wilson and Lansing were paying close attention to affairs in Latin America and the Far East and, in many instances, to good effect.

Immediately after Ambassador Bernstorff had been given his passports, the President ordered Lansing, contrary to that cautious official's inclination,[1] to send identical notes to the other American republics, inviting them to follow the course of the United States. Eight declared war on Germany and six broke relations. Yet reports coming to the State Department indicated that Germans were intriguing in Latin America along the lines suggested in the Zimmermann telegram.

In the early months of 1917 Mexico, the Latin-American nation that had been most troublesome, was reaching political equilibrium. The United States withdrew her troops, a Mexican election chose a new Congress and elected Carranza to the presidency, and Washington granted recognition. To a man who suggested that a shortage of petroleum for military purposes might be relieved by seizing the Tampico oil fields, Wilson replied: "You say this oil in Mexico is necessary for us. When they invaded Belgium, the Germans said it was 'necessary' to get to France. Gentlemen," he concluded, "you will have to fight the war with what oil you have."[2]

The importance of the Panama Canal in time of war, and rumors of

[1] Wilson and Lansing differed not only in general policy but in a specific Latin-American crisis in February of 1917. Federico A. Tinoco, a military man, seized power in Costa Rica by a personal coup that lacked popular support. Wilson told Lansing that the case was similar to that of Huerta, that he would "never recognize Tinoco," and that he intended to put a stop to revolutions of this sort in Latin-American countries.

Lansing obeyed orders, but with reservations in his own mind. He felt that if the people of Costa Rica accepted the man who had forced himself upon them, it was not "proper" for the United States to interfere.

[2] Wilson's sensitivity to the neutral rights for which he himself had until recently been contending led him to object on July 28 to a recommendation that no licenses be issued by the Exports Council for the shipment of foodstuff to Denmark. He had stood up for the rights

German plotting in that area and in Cuba, made it seem necessary for the United States to take emergency action. John Foster Dulles was sent to Panama, and warships and Marines to Cuba, where violence broke out in protest against a fraudulent presidential election. These republics were only one day later than the United States in declaring war on Germany. The proximity of Colombia to the canal made the friendship of this nation vital, and Wilson expressed to the Senate the hope that they might be moved to ratify the treaty that he had been at pains to negotiate. But there was no action on this important measure until the war was over, and Theodore Roosevelt dead.

No better success attended the efforts of Wilson and Lansing to clarify diplomatic relations with the chief countries of the Far East. For the better part of two decades, Americans had spasmodically challenged Japanese imperialism in China; and their distrust had increased when Japan declared war on Germany. Wilson, assured by both Britain and Japan that the integrity of China would be respected, accepted the assurances publicly; and the Japanese promises, given orally to the American ambassador, were set down in a note to Tokyo so that the interest of the United States in their fulfillment would be thoroughly understood.

However, in January of 1915 Japan secretly presented twenty-one demands to China that menaced American policy for that nation and threatened to reduce the country to vassalage. Though the most offensive of the demands was withdrawn as a result of protests from London and Washington, the substance of them had been forced upon the weak Chinese government. The United States had refused to recognize the conditions imposed, and reserved its right to discuss the matter in the future. But Japan saw no moral obloquy in playing an imperialistic game in which European rivals had taken the lead.

Wilson had regarded the course of Japan with anxiety but had seen no way in which he could intervene effectively without stirring a hostility in that nation that would be directed against China immediately.

Standing upon the traditional American policy of an "open door" in China for all nations, Wilson took a pastoral view of that distraught country. At a meeting of the Potomac Presbytery, in April of 1915, he pictured China as "cried awake by the voice of Christ," and a month later he spoke to newsmen of his joy in China's adoption of "a form of

---

of neutrals in the past, and he was not going to forbid them to trade with Germany. On Nov. 13, though willing to accept a policy of supplying Norway with only those goods in which she was deficient, he would not insist that that nation cut off all exporting to Germany. Such a policy, he pointed out, would be inconsistent with the rights on which the United States always had insisted.

government which seems to us the best vehicle of progress, the republican." Allowing his proselyting impulse to leap ahead of actuality, he dared to hope that China might share with the United States "a common conception of liberty for the progress of mankind." International misunderstanding, he felt, was often the result of lack of personal contact. He put faith in the Christian missions to which his father's parishioners had sent their mites even during the dark days of the Civil War. When he bade farewell to an envoy to Siam, his last words were: "Remember to be good to my missionaries." [3]

Whether or not China made war on Germany was of secondary importance to an American government that was chiefly interested in the long-range stability of the Chinese people. However, reactionaries in China, moved by internal politics, the diplomacy of the Allies, and urging from Minister Reinsch that exceeded Washington's intentions, declared war on Germany and Austria on August 14, 1917. On the 21st the President, who was kept posted constantly by Lansing, wrote to a cousin who was a missionary in China: "You may be sure we are watching developments in China, so well as we can from this distance, with the greatest solicitude. I hope with all my heart that in the providence of God some permanent and beneficent result may be worked out."

Britain and France, however, paid no more than lip service to Wilson's aspirations for the Chinese people. Indeed, they secretly negotiated deals with Japan whereby her active participation in the war against German submarines was encouraged by recognition of her claims to Shantung and certain Pacific islands. The prospect for a free, unified China was further clouded by the vulnerability of Chinese minds to foreign propaganda as well as by the venality of self-seeking war lords.

Washington's relations with Toyko already were strained as a result of the restrictions that the Pacific states had imposed on Orientals in 1913. As they deferred to the peculiarities of American law in this matter, the Japanese government pressed vigorously for some indication of American approval of the expansionist policy that overpopulation had forced upon the country. Apprehensive that the encroachment on Shantung that had begun so promisingly for them in 1915 might be checked, and fearful that the military force abuilding in the United States might be used in the Far East, Tokyo sent a special ambassador to Washington to try to secure clarification of a policy that the Japanese mind found difficult to understand. Viscount Ishii arrived at the American capital in the summer of 1917.

Wilson did not reciprocate the Japanese fear of a martial foray across

[3] Letter, F. C. MacDonald to the writer, June 19, 1950.

the vast distance of the Pacific Ocean, though he once admitted, confidentially, that the possibility of an attack on the Philippines "presented a possibility which could not be overlooked." Welcoming Ishii's mission cordially, he made it clear to his guest that the United States regretted the spheres of foreign influence that threatened the open door in China.

The task of concluding an understanding was delegated to the secretary of state. In thirteen conversations that extended over several weeks, Lansing and Ishii thoroughly canvassed, first, the war efforts of their nations, and then their policies vis-à-vis China. Finally they outlined, in identical notes exchanged on November 2, what became known as the Lansing-Ishii Agreement.

Wilson followed each step of the negotiations carefully and conferred at least twice with Ishii. He was gratified by Japan's assent to an agreement that declared not only that she herself had no purpose to infringe in any way upon the integrity of China or the rights of other foreigners in China, but also that she was opposed to infringement by other powers. There is no indication that Wilson was greatly disturbed by the fact that the protocol in which this pledge was stated had to be kept secret, in deference to Japanese opinion. The principle of the open door seemed to be completely upheld and Japan's ambition to develop a "Monroe Doctrine" for the Far East denied.

However, the Lansing-Ishii Agreement proved to be a formula that did not represent a true meeting of minds. The studied ambiguity of the document made it susceptible to many interpretations. It was publicized by Japanese spokesmen in a way that suggested to Chinese that Tokyo had won a great diplomatic victory at their expense and that traditional American policy had been reversed. The Chinese Foreign Office, indignant that, after they had joined the United States in the war, their territory should be considered a "special interest" of Japan, asked embarrassing questions.[4] Disturbed by the Chinese reaction, Wilson wrote on his own typewriter to Lansing, on November 9: "There has not only been no change of policy but there has been a distinct gain for China, of course, and I hope that you will be kind enough to send Reinsch such a message as will serve to put the whole thing in the right light at Peking and throughout China."[5]

[4] The ink was hardly dry on the Lansing-Ishii Agreement before Japanese officials in Asia were claiming "paramount interests," instead of the "special interests" agreed upon. In a note written to Lansing on July 3, Wilson had made it explicit that "Japan's *political* influence over China" was "the thing we have *not* assented to in the sense she evidently has in mind."

[5] Actually, two days before, Lansing had sent to Reinsch a statement for the Chinese Foreign Office, pointing out that the Lansing-Ishii Agreement introduced "a principle of noninterference with the sovereignty and territorial integrity of China, which, generally applied, is essential to perpetual international peace, as has been so clearly declared by President Wilson."

China's need for credit became desperate during 1917, as American bankers continued to

At the same time the President made efforts to improve relations with Japan. On October 19 he received a trade commission that was introduced to him by Ambassador Sato; and he sent one of his old Princeton boys, Roland Morris, as envoy to Tokyo. Saying an affectionate farewell to Morris, he cautioned him against falling into Page's irritating habit of writing notes that were too discursive. Soon Morris was giving his chief valuable summaries of the opinion of the Japanese people and press. When the President was told that it was remarkable that an untrained diplomat could do so well, he retorted: "Untrained? Why, I trained him myself."

The services of Colonel House were not solicited in 1917 in the delicate negotiations with Latin America and Japan. But Wilson considered that Europe, the third area that House felt was being allowed "to take care of itself," was a province in which the Colonel could operate most effectively. He agreed with House that their essential responsibilities were coordination of war effort with the Western Allies and leadership in a peace offensive that would erode enemy morale and appeal to the basic political impulses of the peoples of the world.

House insisted that the first duty was the more urgent in the spring of 1917. Most vital, in his view, was better rapport with London. By virtue of the personal relationships that he had cultivated the Colonel was prepared to guard and strengthen the diplomatic life lines that spanned the Atlantic. Despairing of any constructive action toward peace on the part of Lloyd George's coalition cabinet, House found in Sir William Wiseman a kindred spirit who, invalided from the front and attached to the Washington embassy as chief of intelligence, worked faithfully to seek better cooperation between Washington and London, and an early peace that would give immunity from militarism.[6]

---

hesitate to accept risks without guarantees by the State Department, and all the resources of large European powers were devoted to the needs of war. Britain and France, fearing that Japanese capital might secure monopolies in China, urged Wilson to set aside his objections to the sort of consortium loan on which he had frowned in 1913. On Nov. 9, 1917, the President permitted Lansing to announce that the government was thinking of forming a new four-power consortium. On July 4, 1918, the President approved a plan for a China consortium that, in his view, would bring no monopoly or commitment that might embarrass the government. Wilson had at last come to the view that bankers might be enlisted as agents of diplomacy. After nearly three years of negotiations as to shares and spheres of operations, the participating powers finally signed a new consortium agreement in 1920. *See* Whitney Griswold, *Far Eastern Policy of the United States,* pp. 208 ff.

6 Thinking Wiseman a reliable interpreter of British opinion, a resourceful diplomat, and a valuable liaison man, House arranged to have him introduced to the President in a way that would not arouse the jealousy of diplomatic functionaries. The meeting was brought about at a reception in the Pan American Building, late in the evening of June 26. Wilson found the young man so interesting that he talked with him until his entourage took him away, and Wiseman was invited to dine at the White House with the family. The President found him a sympathetic listener, more eager to get Wilson's ideas than to advance his own.

In the autumn of 1917 Wiseman occupied an apartment under that of Colonel House in

The Colonel and his British friends found the President at first fearful to offend a current of American thought that suspected that the United States had been lured into the war to fight the battles of England and France—a view as biased as that of British patriots who insisted that they were doing America's fighting for her. Wishing to appear independent, Wilson used the phrase "associated power" to indicate the position of his country and suggested that his people be led to think that the coordinating commissions that came from Europe in the spring of 1917 were merely symbols of unity. The President could not allow it to be thought that the United States was committed to fight for the glory of foreign empires; nor, while war raged, could he appear to differ with England and France.

Private talks of the realities of peacemaking went on in the friendly atmosphere that House was adept at creating. The President saw no harm in informal discussion of war aims with Balfour. He himself lunched with the distinguished Briton, with the secretary of state present, but felt that their talk was unsatisfactory—"Lansing has a wooden mind," he told House afterwards, "and continually blocked what I was trying to convey." He asked the Colonel to bring Balfour to a "family dinner," and first to sound out their guest about secret treaties in which Britain and France were said to have won allies by promising territorial rewards at the peace table. These agreements had been negotiated under the compulsion of necessity; and their spirit—distasteful to Sir Edward Grey and other British Liberals—was inconsistent with the war aims that the Allies professed in public and contradictory to Wilson's ideals of peacemaking.

On April 30, after House had talked with Balfour and had ventured the opinion that the diplomacy represented by the secret treaties was "all bad," the two men came to the White House. The President was at his genial best. He had been resting most of the afternoon and seemed keyed up for the occasion. He talked of the value of a liberal education, protested against the binding of men's minds by material fact, and pleaded for flights into spiritual realms.

When they turned to business, House tried to guide the talk so that it would cover the points that he had discussed previously with each of

---

New York and kept in touch with the Foreign Office by special code. Through him and House, the President could communicate with the foreign secretary more swiftly and more secretly than through formal diplomatic channels.

On June 23, Wiseman visited House at Magnolia and they planned a trip to London on the part of Wiseman, so that he might talk with Lloyd George to make sure that no important Anglo-American negotiations would be attempted except through the House-Wiseman channel. By Aug. 10 the Colonel was able to advise Wilson that word had come from Wiseman, at London, that a plan had been worked out with the British government whereby the President would be kept "fully informed about what is going on in the Allied countries and armies."

the statesmen. The Colonel had told the President of the Treaty of London, under which Italy's ambitions in the Adriatic region would be satisfied and had urged both Wilson and Balfour to refrain from discussion of war aims for fear that they might provoke controversies that would obscure the prime necessity—the defeat of German military power. Nevertheless, House asked Balfour about a plan that they had formed to have copies of certain secret treaties sent to Wilson, and the foreign secretary indicated that this would be done.[7] After the conference Balfour, a philosopher, praised the President's idealism and political sagacity; and Wilson rejoiced in his visitor's responsiveness to his own ideas of a peace settlement. Quizzed by Senator Knox about his talks with Balfour, the President said that it had been thought best to make no definite commitments to the British statesman. "But of course he knew that we should never go back on them," he added, "and that binds us in honor."

Nevertheless, the skein of Anglo-American relations often became tangled in the critical year of 1917. For one thing, the British had crushed the Sinn Fein movement for Irish independence in 1916 and had executed the leaders, and there were fiery denunciations by Irish-Americans and protests on the floor of the United States Senate. Wilson followed a policy of avoiding action that would endanger Anglo-American war effort, while at the same time intimating that public opinion in the United States would never be satisfied until the aspirations of Irish nationalists were realized to some degree.

Another strain was imposed on transatlantic relations when Lloyd George decided to send his overimportunate backer, Lord Northcliffe, on a special diplomatic mission to Washington. Because Ambassador Spring Rice deemed this dynamic journalist "a bounder" and because Wilson thought both the idea of another mission and the choice of agent "most unusual," House and Wiseman considered it inadvisable for Northcliffe to come. But when he arrived they made the best of the situation.

With inexhaustible energy, Northcliffe worked to stimulate America's production of war supplies; and he reported directly to the British

[7] Copies of certain secret pacts were sent to the President by Balfour, with a confidential statement about them that the foreign secretary had made to the Imperial War Council. See E. L. Woodward and Rohan Butler (eds.), *Documents on British Foreign Policy,* 1st Series, V (1919), 1015–17. No indication has been found that Wilson answered Balfour's covering letter or referred to the texts at this time. It is probable that, agreeing with House's view that the treaties were a dangerous source of potential friction and feeling powerless to do anything about them until the war was over, he thought it of no use to spend any of his precious time in studying them.

"I was absolutely open in 1917 with President Wilson about the secret treaties," Balfour wrote to House on July 17, 1922. See House Papers, IV, 364–65. Certain omissions in the papers sent to the President by Balfour, notably the agreements concluded with Japan in February of 1917 regarding Shantung and the Pacific Islands, are noted in Baker, VII, 74–75.

War Cabinet on the importance of the United States to the success of Allied arms. Pointing out that Sir William Wiseman was the only Englishman who could talk intimately with Wilson and House at all times, Northcliffe cabled thus to Winston Churchill: "The Administration is entirely run by these two men. Wilson's power is absolute and House is a wise assistant. Both are pro-English." On June 16 the President received the visitor, and the next day he was informed by House that he had "charmed Northcliffe."

By September the British Cabinet had been so well advised by its experts in the United States that it realized that America's heart was in the war and that she must be treated as the most important ally, and frankly and fully informed about everything. However, political hazards that menaced the flow of credit to the Allies had not yet been entirely overcome. McAdoo was apprehensive, not only that the war aims of the Allies would be questioned by legislators who held the strings of the public purse, but that Bryan's faction would object to the assumption by the government of loans that private bankers had made to the Allies before the United States entered the war. Responsible to American taxpayers, the secretary of the treasury wished to be certain that their money was expended wisely by those to whom it was advanced; and he proposed to the Cabinet that inter-Allied bodies be created at Washington and in Europe to coordinate the requisitions of the various armies and navies and to rule on matters of priority.

While tactfully refraining from making any one Cabinet officer so privy to his counsel that the others might take offense,[8] Wilson gave his son-in-law his head in so far as he could do so without interfering with the functions of other departments. When the chief Allied powers finally consented, in August, to the creation of a purchasing commission at Washington, McAdoo urged that Bernard M. Baruch be made the chairman of the body, and the President tried to bring this about. Secretary Baker objected because people said that Baruch was a Wall Street speculator. Moreover, House was opposed. Nevertheless, the President appointed Baruch.

---

[8] It seemed to McAdoo that the President was too slow to make executive decisions on matters such as this, and remiss in facing differences of opinion and settling them. He confessed to Colonel House, early in May, that the pace at which he was driving himself had affected his heart, and he never felt so much "the need of a complete deflection of thought." He had not been in the White House for six months except at large functions, he said, and he would resign if the President did not remove restrictions with which he felt himself hedged in. On the other hand, to fellow members of the Cabinet he seemed more than ever a man ambitious to extend his power and dominion.

McAdoo thought it necessary for himself to see all State Department dispatches, be represented on the embargo board, and control the shipping board and the purchase and the transport of supplies, so that he would know how to apportion loans to the Allies. "If given all this," House wrote in his diary on Aug. 7, "he would become arbiter of both the United States and Europe."

This upstanding, forthright Southerner had been active in the 1916 election campaign, and Wilson had invited him to come with his parents to tea at Shadow Lawn. The Wilsons were fond of old Dr. Simon, who had served as a surgeon in the Civil War, and of his wife Miss Belle; and they observed with approval that young Bernard's world revolved around these revered elders. As the nation was drawn into war, the man's keen, purposeful mind seemed hungry for jobs to be done efficiently. He did not presume to offer unsolicited advice. Wilson called him "Dr. Facts" and learned to admire his reluctance to seek power or profit in public service and his comprehensive grasp of the problems of resources and production. At the same time Baruch's respect for the President's qualities of leadership and statesmanship grew into veneration.

Though Wilson acted to coordinate Allied purchasing at Washington, he did not appoint an American delegate when representatives of the Allies met at Paris and drafted a plan for cooperation. Fearing that it might be inferred that the United States was discussing "ultimate purposes" and peace terms with imperialists, he suggested that American participation should be deferred until she had a larger force in Europe and took over a portion of the battle front.

During the summer credits were sustained mainly by the personal intervention of Colonel House, who simultaneously urged Washington to save the Allies from bankruptcy and London and Paris to coordinate their purchasing. Moreover, with Wilson's approval, Wiseman was sent to London to insist on the creation of an inter-Allied council and also to urge that a financial expert of high official rank be sent to Washington. Northcliffe reported to Viscount Reading, lord chief justice, that American pride demanded that someone of his eminence come as a special envoy. And House added his word in a cable to the Foreign Office, explaining: "What is needed is someone who can dominate the situation and who would have the entire confidence of the President."

Reading presented himself at the White House on September 20. This distinguished envoy brought to the President a long confidential letter from Lloyd George. Suggesting that the attacks of the Allies should be directed at the associates of Germany, who seemed weak both politically and militarily, the prime minister's note advised Wilson that soon it would be necessary to make far-reaching decisions that might be vital. He urged that at future conferences of the Allies the United States contribute "independent minds, bringing fresh views, unbiased by previous methods and previous opinions." Moreover, the Foreign Office wrote, in response to an inquiry from Wilson as to what was expected from the United States in the way of embargoing shipments to neutrals, that the difficulties arising in the policy of blockade could be resolved only by a conference at London in which American representatives would take part.

Finally, on October 9, Wilson summoned House to Washington to discuss the vital question of coordination of war effort. He was at first inclined to put the Colonel in charge of this matter and to appoint an American commission to function in Europe. Talking to his Cabinet on October 12, he revealed his concept of America's role in the postwar world. He felt that she would be so wealthy that by her power to give or withhold credit she could impose her views upon Europe for the common welfare and the preservation of peace.

House was advising that Lloyd George's methods and purposes, unlike those of Grey and Balfour, were not always the highest. "I find myself not altogether trusting Lloyd George's plan . . ." the Colonel wrote to Wilson on September 18. "The English naturally want the road to Egypt blocked, and Lloyd George is not above using us to further this plan." When Wiseman suggested that there was danger of shifting the center of gravity of the war from Washington to London or Paris, the President drew back. Wilson wished to guard his policy of independence of action and to keep a firm hand on the situation.[9] Therefore, instead of taking the risk of putting an American commission at the disposal of the Allies for the duration of the war, he decided to send House abroad with representatives of the American war services who could discuss their technical problems in conferences with their opposite numbers in England and France. He felt that such a delicate task could be entrusted to no diplomat but the Colonel. He was confident that this friend would not betray him and would keep free from entanglements and antagonisms. Moreover, he knew that the sending of House would please Lloyd George.

After a talk with Reading, the Colonel accepted the charge. Soon the ruling elder, drawn out from backstage and given a mission more vital than any that he had undertaken before, was showing the same jealousy of responsibility that he had marked in Wilson and McAdoo and other strong executives. "I am glad I am going alone," he wrote in his diary

[9] "He told me distinctly," House recorded in his diary on Oct. 13, "that he preferred everything to go to him rather than to the State Department, and he would refer to the State Department what he thought necessary. Later I got him to agree, since I am going to Europe, for Mezes to keep in touch with Lansing, but the President added, 'and also with me.' I shall arrange this and shall endeavor to give Lansing a larger and larger part." (Page wrote in his diary, on Nov. 24: "In a very important sense, there is no State Department.")

Immediately after the country went to war, the President had all letters from House and from the State, War, and Navy Departments go to him unopened. Brahany Diary, April 14, 1917. On Sept. 3, House wrote in his diary that Wilson was "something of an autocrat by nature" and desired no interference from commissions going or coming. Charles Swem noted that, under war conditions, the Chief seemed obsessed by the need for secrecy.

on October 19, "for I can do better work when the responsibility is entirely on my shoulders."

The House mission arrived in Europe at the moment when the Italian front had been pierced, the Bolsheviki were seizing power by violence, and the French Cabinet was facing dissolution. Moreover, the position of the British coalition government was shaken by insistent demands for what a respected elder statesman, Lord Lansdowne, called a "covenanted peace" and by protests against subordinating British military policy to an over-all grand strategy. The Colonel applied his peculiar talents to the vital issue of unity. After he had been at London for four days he reported to Wilson that the lack of organization was driving him "around in circles," but that the Foreign Office offered him access to any of their confidential papers that he wished to see. On November 15 he telegraphed that the military situation was critical.

When the Italian front broke and French reserves were obliged to walk over the Alps to reinforce their ally, the lack of coordinated planning became scandalous. Lloyd George, whose war cabinet had demonstrated the value of unified direction at the summit, hastened to Rapallo to press for a unifying command of all Allied armies. A Supreme War Council was formed, to act politically through monthly conference of the chiefs of state at Versailles and militarily through a permanent professional staff.

Lloyd George, back at London, explained his views to House and asked that the United States send a representative. That very night the Colonel, who felt that the prime minister was indiscreet in making such a positive proposal without consulting Washington, cabled to the President thus: "France, England and Italy have agreed to form a Supreme War Council and believe that we should be represented in it because of the moral effect that it will have here . . . I would advise not having a representative on the civil end . . . but would strongly urge having General Bliss on the military end . . . It is important that an immediate decision be made as to this . . ."

Wilson replied promptly and vigorously. He wanted House to take "the whip hand." His message directed: "Please take the position that we not only accede to the plan for a single war council but insist on it, but I think it does not go far enough . . . The war council will, I assume, eventually take the place of such conferences as you went over to take part in and I hope that you will consider remaining to take part in at any rate the first deliberations and formulations of plans. Baker and I are agreed that Bliss should be our military member. I am happy the conference is to be postponed until the recalcitrant parliaments have settled to their senses . . ."

Wilson's decisive support saved Lloyd George's government and the Supreme War Council. On November 20 opposition in Parliament was finally overcome, and on that day and the next House had frank conversations on war aims with Lloyd George, Reading, and Balfour. Going on to Paris on the 22nd, House's mission engaged in informal talks with Georges Clemenceau, who had just formed a government in which he was minister of war as well as premier and who was summoning French resistance to a heroic pitch. With General Pétain they revised Lloyd George's plan, so that the Supreme War Council would have an executive officer who would be in effect a commander in chief. However, when the prime minister arrived on the scene he made it clear that because of the prevailing feeling in England he would have to go back to London if his plan was not accepted as he had conceived it. House and Clemenceau were persuaded that they must give up their scheme for military efficiency; and when the council met at Versailles on December 1, under the presidency of Clemenceau, it took on the aspect of an academic body for the study of vital military problems, rather than that of an executive agency.

Though the new council had a strong military committee on which General Bliss served effectively—albeit handicapped by lack of liaison with the State Department—House was disappointed and thought that the armies of the enemy had superior organization.[10] He was distressed, too, because the conference had not provided intelligent diplomatic leadership at a moment when the morale of the Allies was dangerously low. It had failed to frame a "world-appealing policy" that would satisfy liberals and radicals throughout Europe. House felt that faith was not being kept with those who were fighting and dying. Nevertheless, when compelled to address the second plenary session, on December 3, he confined his talk to harmless amenities. He would wait until he returned to Washington, he resolved, and then would urge the President to say what should be said about war aims.

In mid-December House came home and gave an account of his mission, and he spoke also of his impatience with the unregenerate ideology of the Allies.

---

[10] House used the fortnight at Paris to good purpose, sitting with Clemenceau, Bliss, and Pétain to determine how many American soldiers should go to France, and when, and how, and the possibility of brigading them with French troops for training. He sensed the grandeur of Clemenceau—the "Tiger of France"—and Pétain's lack of vision; and he impressed upon Pershing the necessity of making good, so that people would not say that the President should have sent Roosevelt and Wood. The United States would be judged for a century or more by the conduct of its army in France, the Colonel said. House thought the progress made toward coordinating economic resources very great. "Heretofore," he wrote at Paris, "everything has been going pretty much at sixes and sevens. From now there will be less duplication of effort . . . This conference may therefore well be considered the turning point in the war even though the fortunes of the Allies have never seemed so low as now."

CHAPTER VIII

The War of Ideas and Words

In december of 1917—the month in which Colonel House returned to Washington to report on his mission to coordinate American policy with that of the Allies—two of the enemies of Germany stopped fighting. On the 3rd leaders of the Russian Bolsheviki met German representatives at Brest-Litovsk to discuss peace, and twelve days later an armistice was signed. On the 6th Rumania agreed to a truce.

The Western Allies, stunned by the collapse of Russian resistance, could conceive of no way of establishing relations with the new rulers at Petrograd, who were denouncing them as imperialistic robbers and proclaiming a strange code of personal and political morality. In this crisis Woodrow Wilson, driven by the commitment that he had made to his people to win the war, ventured to act to prevent a complete collapse of resistance to Germany on the Eastern front.

American policy toward Russia after the Czar's downfall had been based on the unwarranted faith that Ambassador Francis had put in the provisional government and had maintained with undiplomatic partisanship. In recognizing the new regime, Wilson had felt that the only practical course was to cultivate relations with the faction that was amicably disposed toward the United States and, for the present at least, in the seat of power. He had been encouraged when Russia's leaders recognized the independence of Poland and suggested the repudiation of aggressive war aims. In May the provisional government had renounced the idea of making a separate peace and had sent a commission to Washington. The President expressed "the greatest sympathy" with the revolution and welcomed the new ambassador, Boris A. Bakhmeteff, with the remark that now the United States had a partner in the fight for democracy. Wilson had consented to send a commission under Elihu Root to Russia,[1] and had written a message of "friendship of the

---

[1] Fearing that Root, a New York lawyer, would be regarded with suspicion by the revolutionaries in Russia, Wilson appointed a representative of labor and a moderate Socialist to the commission. He was so unsure of the wisdom of the venture that when a friend of labor declined to join it, he treated the man with great respect. The purpose of the mission, he informed Ambassador Francis, was to show sympathy for the "adherence of Russia to the principle of democracy" and to consider "the best ways and means to bring about effective cooperation between the two governments in the prosecution of the war."

When the mission returned, in August, Wilson paid little attention to Root's report, which events of the subsequent months showed to be illusory.

American People for the People of Russia." The President warned the Russians against professions of liberality and justice on the part of the ruling classes of Germany.

While asserting the purity of American motives, Wilson refrained from opposing the lust for the Bosporus that kept Russian patriots fighting. Credits totaling $325,000,000 were extended to the provisional government at low interest; and Root bluntly advanced the formula "no fight, no loans." Commissions of Red Cross workers and railway engineers were sent. At Wilson's insistence, a secret Anglo-American effort was organized to counter German propaganda in Russia. But in the strange assortment of American adventurers who pioneered on the new social-political frontier, Wilson saw risks of confusion and frustration.[2] The ambassador found himself without power to regulate the movements of his compatriots or to coordinate their work with official policy. Wilson and House talked so sympathetically with some of them before their departure from America that they considered themselves the personal agents of the President. Observing only a small segment of Russia, often without benefit of knowledge of the language, these men exuded the good will that Americans bore toward "the Russian people"; but some failed to sense that the Russians, by and large, conceived of the war as a creation of czardom and were as weary of battle as of despotism. Though a sort of democracy was practiced locally, there was no prevailing concept of disciplined freedom on which a national republic could be built. In fact a bitter contest for political power was raging among revolutionary factions. Of these actualities Wilson drew from the Americans in Russia no deeper understanding than came from his bemused ambassador. Fortunately House was able to supply somewhat more reliable reports from British agents at Petrograd.

Liberal sentiment among democratic peoples everywhere had been quickened by the Russian Revolution. In Britain the influential Union of Democratic Control, which even before the downfall of the Czar had enthusiastically endorsed Wilson's demand for statements of peace terms, now urged him to persuade the belligerents to renounce their aggressive war aims. Europeans who were familiar with the progressive achievement of the American prophet in his own country had begun to look to him to free the Old World, not only from political despotism, but even from the sort of economic aggression that had provoked war.

[2] By November, Wilson was so bothered by disorganized and unofficial American efforts in Russia that he wrote to Charles Edward Russell, the Socialist member of Root's mission: ". . . all sorts of work in Russia now is rendered extremely difficult because no one channel connects with any other, apparently."

For a colorful and compassionate account of Americans in Russia in 1917, see George F. Kennan, *Russia Leaves the War*, pp. 32 ff.

Tribunes of the people in many lands were trying to organize an international gathering of laborites and socialists, to be held at Stockholm; and the Kaiser's government was depending on the German delegates to that conference to fight the Fatherland's ideological battle.[3]

In his concentration on the prime necessity of overthrowing the Junkers, Wilson could not ignore the challenges to the war aims of the Allies that were rising from the forces of unrest all through Europe. For weeks he hesitated, fearing to weaken the military effort of the Allies and contradict policies announced by their statesmen. But when House informed him that sincere liberals, both in England and in Russia, wanted him to define the aims of the Allies, the President decided to speak out.

The Flag Day celebration at the Washington Monument was the occasion chosen for his pronouncement. A downpour of rain and hail had driven most of the crowd to seek shelter; but thousands remained under dripping umbrellas to hear an impassioned challenge to battle for the right as God gave their leader to see the right.

The prophet singled out the enemy and laid a curse upon him. "The war was begun by the military masters of Germany, who proved also to be the masters of Austria-Hungary," he said. Hurling charge after charge against the Kaiser's government, he repeated the assertion that he had made in his war speech of April 2: that Americans were not the enemies of the German people, who were themselves "in the grip of the same sinister power that has now at last stretched its ugly talons out and drawn blood" from the United States. In words reminiscent of his attacks on the bosses of New Jersey, he called the hosts of the Lord to the fray. "The military masters under whom Germany is bleeding see very clearly to what point Fate has brought them. If they fall back or are forced back an inch, their power both abroad and at home will fall to pieces like a house of cards . . . deep fear has entered their hearts." Their only hope, he asserted, was to secure an immediate peace with immense advantages still in their hands. They were trying to deceive and make use of liberal Germans whom formerly they despised. "Let

[3] Warned by Lansing that a gathering of Socialists near to Petrograd might undermine the mission of conservative Elihu Root, Wilson agreed that the Stockholm conference was "likely to make a deal of mischief, especially in connection with affairs in Russia," and the State Department ruled against the issue of passports to American delegates who made what the President considered "almost treasonable utterances."

The decision against issuing passports to Stockholm was made in spite of the intention of the Socialist minority in the French Chamber to send a representative and Balfour's view that it was inadvisable to try to keep British Socialists away from the conference. Considerations influencing the American decision, which was made orally by Wilson, are suggested in a footnote on page 84 of Baker, VII.

The conference convened on Sept. 5–7, 1917, and issued a manifesto of which the last lines were: "Long live the international mass struggle against the war! Long live the Socialist peace!"

them once succeed," he warned, "and these men, now their tools, will be ground to powder beneath the weight of the great military empire they will have set up; the revolutionists in Russia will be cut off from all succor or cooperation in Western Europe and a counterrevolution fostered and supported; Germany herself will lose her chance of freedom; and all Europe will arm for the next, the final struggle."

Despite this eloquent denunciation of the enemy, popular suspicion of the war aims of the Allies persisted. The German chancellor alleged to newsmen, on July 29, that Western powers were greedy for conquest and had concluded imperialistic secret treaties.

Wilson knew that his people felt themselves to be arbitrators who wished to stand apart from the Allies, that they were determined to crush Prussian autocracy, and longed to arrive at a peace settlement that would make future wars impossible. He wished to know what his allies meant by "security against German aggression," an aim with which he sympathized in general. He hoped that House would help him to understand the feelings that moved all European nations—friends, enemies, and neutrals—so that he might shape his policies wisely and pitch his public utterances in harmonious tones. Wilson wanted the Colonel to take steps to prepare the American case for a peace conference "with full knowledge of the position of all the litigants." Discussing the idea with Lansing, he decided to give his ruling elder a free hand to form a research organization.

House, whose attention already had been drawn by his English correspondents to the importance of such a step, envisioned a peace conference at which the President would be the only representative of the United States and the serious problems would be settled by a few qualified experts. "If good fortune follows," he wrote in his diary on September 4, "he has a chance to leave a record in history second to no man that has yet lived." [4]

In midsummer the President received another challenge to make peace on an idealistic basis. On August 1, Pope Benedict XV, probably prompted by Cardinal Pacelli, who as nuncio to Bavaria had been in touch with war-weary German Catholics, appealed for an ending of conflict on a basis of restoration of occupied territory, disarmament, and international arbitration. Wilson at first felt that appreciation of the Pope's motive and purpose should be expressed, but objected that his

---

[4] House brought together a group of experts that came to be known as "The Inquiry." Dr. Sidney Mezes, Mrs. House's brother-in-law, was named director; Walter Lippmann, who as editor of the *New Republic* had been in touch with many influential British Liberals, served as secretary; Dr. Isaiah Bowman, director of the American Geographical Society at New York, became executive officer.

terms constituted no settlement, that to discuss them would be "a blind adventure." He called Lodge and other senators into conference and said that he was "adrift and troubled" and ready to listen to all views. He thought that he ought to say publicly that they could not negotiate until there was a government of good faith in Germany; but he feared that if he did this he would be accused of renouncing the principle that every people was entitled to determine its own form of government.

American diplomats in the capitals of the Allies reported that sentiment was more or less favorable to the Pope's proposal. While Lloyd George steered an erratic middle course, British radicals were insisting on a frank statement of Allied war aims and were disappointed that Wilson had not forced his European associates to speak out. House felt that the President might lose a great opportunity to lead the pacifist opinion of the world, and to strengthen whatever liberal sentiment might exist in Russia. He wrote to Wilson more than once about this, and his persistence was as effective as it was unusual.[5] The President drafted a reply to the Pope and asked House for a frank opinion of it.

"You have again written a declaration of human liberty," the Colonel responded. "I endorse every word of it. I am sure it is the wise, the statesmanlike and the right way to answer . . ." Suggesting only slight changes of words that might offend the Allies, House thought it advisable to get their cooperation by giving advance copies of the note to them. But the President felt that if the Allies were informed they would ask for changes that the writer could not make in good faith, and he would be embarrassed.

Wilson sent off his note on August 27. Reasserting the disinterestedness of the United States, but insisting that the intolerable wrongs done by "the furious and brutal power" of the Kaiser's government should be repaired, he wrote: "We cannot take the word of the present rulers of Germany as a guarantee of anything that is to endure, unless explicitly supported by such conclusive evidences of the will and purpose of the German people themselves as the other peoples of the world would be justified in accepting."

[5] The Colonel realized that he was dissenting from the advice of the State Department and all those who suspected that the Pope's offer was designed to save the Germans from the consequences of their brutality, but he was confident that his sources of European opinion were superior to those of the State Department.

Influenced by reports of British radical opinion that came from his agent in the London embassy, W. H. Buckler, the Colonel urged the President not to frighten the German people with threats of dismemberment and economic discrimination.

The British government was embarrassed by the resignation from the Cabinet of Labor leader Arthur Henderson, who wished to sponsor British representation at the Stockholm conference, and Ambassador Page ordered Buckler to cease reporting the views of such men to House without telling the Colonel why he stopped. But House arranged to continue to receive information from Buckler through the latter's half brother, Henry White. *See* Lawrence W. Martin thesis.

The declaration was applauded alike by Anglo-Saxon liberals and by certain journals in France and Italy; and Americans of German ancestry took heart in the prospect of rapport with liberal opinion in the Fatherland. In Germany, where Bethmann-Hollweg had been forced out of office and his successor had yielded to the determination of the military men to disregard a peace resolution passed by the Reichstag, Wilson's statement was dismissed as "a trick." Nevertheless, the document was an effective part of the long-range campaign that Wilson had undertaken, with House's encouragement, to make war relentlessly on the German government and at the same time woo the German people. The President's position as a leader in peacemaking was strengthened when the Allies did not respond to Benedict XV, and Germany, replying on September 21, failed to mention the restoration of Belgium.

Affairs in Russia, as well as in Germany, challenged Wilson toward the end of 1917 to make specific applications of the creed of peace that he had been proclaiming in generalities for a year. After the Bolshevik revolution, it was futile to think of wooing Russia further with loans and technical aid. The Treasury Department was inclined to continue to extend credit as long as Russia remained in the war, but Ambassador Francis advised against this, and House telegraphed from Paris: ". . . the Russian situation is considered at the moment hopeless. There is no responsible government within sight. I would advise making no more advances at present or permitting any further contracts for purchases . . ."

Of all the leaders of the nations at war with Germany, the American President was in the best position to try to convince the Russians that the success of their revolution was imperiled by Germany's designs. Compared with the peoples of the Allied nations, Americans were remote and uninfluenced by socialistic propaganda, by financial stakes in the old Russia, or by ambitions to exploit the new. Their President could talk with them confidently about their attitude toward the Bolsheviki in Russia as well as toward fellow travelers in America.

Six days after the Bolshevik coup at Petrograd, Wilson left Washington to address labor delegates at a convention at Buffalo. As he took the train he received a report that he had requested, describing adjustments that had been made in certain war labor disputes. To his audience he said, on November 12: "Nobody has a right to stop the processes of labor until all the methods of conciliation and settlement have been exhausted." Speaking of "a body of free men" that he imagined to exist in Russia and misinterpreting the minds of the German leaders, who actually were more interested in breaking Russian resistance and making material gains than in any ideological campaign, Wilson said that, though his heart was with the pacifists in Russia, his mind held them in contempt. Then, alluding to efforts that had been made by agitators to stir American laborers to class hatred and mob violence, he gave this counsel: "Let us show ourselves Americans by showing that we do not want to go off in separate camps or groups by ourselves, but that we want to cooperate with all other classes and all other groups in the common enterprise which is to release the spirits of the world from bondage . . . There are some organizations in this country whose object is anarchy and the destruction of law, but I would not meet their efforts by making myself partner in destroying the law . . . I would be too proud not to see them done justice, however wrong they are." [6]

The President waited cautiously, unwilling to shape American policy until he had a clearer picture of events in Russia. On the 13th he indicated that he had not lost faith in the outcome by any means. "Russia," he wrote to a friend, "like France in a past century, will no doubt have to go through deep waters but she will come out upon firm land on the other side, and her great people, for they are a great people, will in my opinion take their proper place in the world."

But he was not led to hope for a quick restoration of good relations by the tactics of Trotsky, who had installed himself as foreign minister. On November 21 this leader publicly renounced any desire for the Bosporus and proposed to the United States and the Allies that there be no delay in arranging an armistice on all fronts and opening peace negotiations. Expressing profound respect for "the people" of the United States, he did not mention their government; and on November 24 it was reported in the American press that he had told a newsman that, if Wilson's government did not support his peace policy, the American people would. Thus he loosed against the United States the same kind of subversive argument that Wilson was aiming at Germany.

Moreover, Trotsky published the secret treaties among the Allies and delivered a speech before Soviet delegates that ascribed sordid war aims

---

[6] Wilson applied this principle to the case of Tom Mooney, a California labor leader who was under sentence of death and whose plight was publicized in Russia as an example of capitalistic oppression. Accepting a suggestion from House, he asked Attorney General Gregory to have a thorough investigation made of the Mooney case. Later he acted on a report of a mediation commission—which he permitted to be made public for its "effect on the people as a whole in this country and the effect in connection with our foreign relations"—by suggesting to the governor of California that the execution of Mooney be postponed until a new trial could be held that would give full weight to important changes in evidence. "I urge this very respectfully indeed but very earnestly," he wrote, on Jan. 22, 1918, "because the case has assumed international importance." (On Jan. 19 it had been announced that the Bolsheviki were holding Ambassador Francis responsible for the lives of Mooney and others who were being prosecuted in the United States.) When Senator Poindexter attacked Mooney and the I.W.W. in the Senate, two months later, this letter was read aloud to the senators, with Wilson's permission.

to America and asserted that Wilson had entered the conflict at the insistence of "finance capitalists" in order to create a boom in war industry.

This was more than a man could take who had striven to the limit of his strength to keep his people out of war. Reading the Russian's vitriolic sentences to his Cabinet, Wilson said that he would make no direct answer for fear that it might imply recognition. Ambassador Francis was told that there was no reply, was left at Petrograd with no clear directive, and was threatened with violence by Trotsky.

Nevertheless, Trotsky's attack spurred Wilson to try to purify the purposes of the nations still fighting Germany. On December 1, replying to a cable in which House proposed a mild joint manifesto of war aims, the President commended his agent's efforts and suggested that it would be "unfortunate" if the Inter-Allied Conference discussed peace terms in a spirit antagonistic to his own program. The Colonel had to conclude that it would be useless to press American purposes upon what he set down as "the reactionary crowd" at the Paris conference. It was left to each nation to notify the Bolsheviki of its willingness to discuss war aims with any stable Russian government.

Alarmed because the Bolsheviki were regarded at Paris as outcasts, and also because American jingoes were advocating that Russia be treated as an enemy, fearing that the President might state his case "piecemeal" and fail to cover all the ground that talks with the Allies had shown to be essential, the Colonel cabled from Paris to ask his friend to make no statement on foreign relations until they could confer. But Wilson replied: "Sorry impossible to omit foreign affairs from address to Congress. Reticence on my part at this juncture would be misunderstood and resented and do much harm."

In his annual message on December 4—the day after armistice negotions between the Bolsheviki and Germany began at Brest-Litovsk—the President called for "very grave scrutiny" of the war's objectives and of ways to attain them. He warned that the peace settlement must not impose "such covenants of selfishness and compromise as were entered into at the Congress of Vienna." Efforts to win must not slacken, he said, "but it is worth while asking the question, When shall we consider the war won?" Peace could be discussed, he asserted, only "when the German people have spokesmen whose word we can believe and when those spokesmen are ready in the name of their people to accept the common judgment of the nations as to what shall henceforth be the bases of law and of covenant for the life of the world." He declared that "the masters of German intrigue" were using a crude formula—"no annexations, no contributions, no punitive indemnities"—to lead the people of Russia astray. He prescribed "truth" as "the only possible anti-dote," asserting that it could not be uttered too plainly or too often. And he avowed that, though America had become a combatant, her idealistic attitude toward a peace settlement had not changed.

"Let there be no misunderstanding," he declared. "Our present and immediate task is to win the war, and nothing shall turn us aside from it until it is accomplished . . . One very embarrassing obstacle that stands in our way is that we are at war with Germany but not with her allies." Characterizing Austria-Hungary as "simply the vassal of the German government," he recommended an immediate declaration of war against that nation, with whom relations had been broken eight months earlier.

At this the applause that had punctuated the President's speech became a great shout. Ladies waved handkerchiefs, Southerners pierced the bedlam with the yip-yip-yip of the rebel yell. Wilson stepped aside until the hubbub was over, and his countenance masked whatever emotion he felt. This address, which many thought his greatest presidential speech so far, was sent to all the world by wireless and gave him the largest audience that an American president ever had reached. Within three days of its delivery, a resolution for war with Austria-Hungary was passed and was signed by Wilson.

As the Bolsheviki carried on peace negotiations with Germany at Brest-Litovsk in December, Wilson continued to express good will toward them. But on the 21st, commenting on the plan of Trotsky for propaganda abroad, he said to his Cabinet: "The impudence of it!"

While he waited in indecision, Boris A. Bakhmeteff, the lingering envoy of the overthrown provisional government, helped him to settle one immediate problem. Unable to get an appointment with Lansing, the ambassador of the fallen regime persuaded George Creel to put in the President's ear the idea that, extending the doctrine that Wilson had applied to Germany, he differentiate between the Russian people and the misguided Bolshevik government. Accepting the suggestion, Wilson allowed Bakhmeteff to remain at Washington as the agent of "the Russian people." This envoy, who was aided by Colonel House in maintaining his titular position, induced the United States government not to cancel contracts that had been made under the provisional government, and soon an official ban was placed on American trade with Bolshevik Russia.[7]

When an armistice was concluded at Brest-Litovsk, on December 15, the crisis in both arms and morale, already severe, threatened to become

[7] Boris A. Bakhmeteff's record in the Oral History Project, Columbia University.

extreme. Germany was free to transfer vast forces to the Western battle front, and now that the Bolsheviki had revealed secret treaties among the Allies and had denounced them,[8] the Germans could pose before the liberals of the world as a people no more imperialistic than their adversaries.

Colonel House reached Washington on the 17th, carrying discouraging reports about his efforts to persuade the Allies to announce liberal war aims. Wilson listened to him attentively. The next day the Colonel urged his friend to speak out. He found the President's mind receptive, and in a very few minutes Wilson decided that he might soon make an address that could prove to be a turning point in the psychological war. Before the Colonel left the White House, Wilson asked him to get a memorandum from The Inquiry on the various points that a peace conference should consider; and the President was persuaded that Wiseman should be allowed to check his draft for this address so that it would give no offense and would harmonize with British policy.

Wilson remarked that his first purpose in planning a statement on war aims was to persuade the Russian people that they would be trampled underfoot by a victorious Germany but could count on the Allies for a peace that would uphold democratic and liberal principles. At the same time he hoped to "knock the Kaiser off his perch" by feeding the suspicions of German Socialists that their government was waging a war of conquest rather than one of defense. And, thirdly, he wanted to stimulate the Allies to consent to a liberalization of their war aims.

Wilson had just had a report from Edgar Sisson, who had been dispatched to Russia in October to start an aggressive [9] publicity campaign.

[8] In January of 1918, Wiseman informed Balfour of the President's concern about the secret treaties, and especially the Treaty of London, concluded with Italy. According to the *New York Times* of Nov. 25, Dec. 1 and 2, 1917, Trotsky made public at that time the terms of the treaties negotiated by the Allies with the Czar's government as well as the terms of the Treaty of London. These pacts were published in full in the *Manchester Guardian* on Dec. 13, 1917, and in the New York *Evening Post* serially beginning Jan. 25, 1918. They were transmitted to the State Department by its representatives at Petrograd and Stockholm. *F.R., 1917,* Suppl. 2, I, 447, 493–507.

Boris A. Bakhmeteff recorded that in 1917, when he told Lansing that Russians were apprehensive about the secret treaties and suggested that, since the United States was financing the Allies she could ask them to clear the air, Lansing protested that it was better for him to be ignorant of the treaties, since he could not ask Europeans to wipe them out without danger of embarrassing the conduct of the war. Bakhmeteff's record.

Now that the terms of most of the secret treaties had been made public, Wilson could no longer afford to ignore them, as he had when the texts of most of them had been sent to him in May of 1917 by Balfour. Cf. p. 131n. above.

For an illuminating discussion of the "new diplomacy" that was developed by Wilson and the Russian leaders, see a dissertation by Arno Mayer entitled "The Politics of Allied War Aims," Yale University, 1954.

[9] "We want nothing for ourselves," the President wrote to Sisson in a personal note, "and this very unselfishness carries with it an obligation of open dealing. Wherever the fundamental principles of Russian freedom are at stake, we stand ready to render such aid as lies in our power, but I want this helpfulness based upon request and not upon offer. Guard particularly

Sisson promised that if the President would restate his warm aims and requisites for peace in "short almost placard paragraphs," such a declaration would be translated, fed into Germany in great quantities, and circulated in Russia. Wilson was amused at the prospect of such blatant propaganda. He told Creel, dryly, that he had never tried his hand at composing slogans or advertising copy. Nevertheless, the importunities of the publicists, coming simultaneously with similar pleas from other agents in Russia and with a blast from Trotsky assailing the Allies for refusal to talk peace or give their reasons, helped to induce the prophet to move swiftly from contemplation to action.

When Wilson and House buckled down to the drafting of a speech on war aims, during the first week of the year 1918, they considered particularly what they should say about Russia. The first half of the address was devoted to the significance of the peace parleys at Brest-Litovsk. Wilson asserted that the negotiations there had been broken off because the Russian representatives, lured to the peace table by German professions of liberalism, had discovered that the terms actually were to be dictated by "the military leaders who have no thought but to keep what they have got." Having made this charge, the address went on to ask whether the German delegates at Brest-Litovsk expressed "the spirit and intention of the liberal leaders and parties in Germany." Commending Russia's insistence on open peace negotiations—"in the true spirit of modern democracy"—and her challenge to adversaries to define their purposes,[10] Wilson's text asserted:

There is no good reason why that challenge should not be responded to . . . with the utmost candor. We did not wait for it. Not once, but again and again, we have laid our whole thought and purpose before the world, not in general terms only, but each time with sufficient definition to make it clear

---

against any effect of officious intrusion or meddling, and try to express the disinterested friendship that is our sole impulse."

As a result of this note and an interview with the President that Creel arranged, Sisson felt that he was Wilson's "special representative in Russia." But he was given no specific instructions regarding his relations with other Americans in Russia and was introduced to Ambassador Francis by the State Department as representing only Creel. Sisson exceeded his instructions by sending to Creel a recommendation that Francis be recalled and informal contacts with Bolshevik officials be established. The State Department intercepted his message and Lansing conferred with Wilson, who telegraphed to Sisson thus: "President insists that you avoid political entanglements and personal matters." See Kennan, op. cit., pp. 124–29. This was but one instance of the tangled relations that developed among Americans in Russia and that might have been prevented by adequate and precise instructions from Washington.

[10] In his wishful efforts to win Russia's military support, Wilson was able to overlook the undemocratic challenge that Trotsky had made on Dec. 29 in behalf of "the working class" and to accept unverified and false rumors to the effect that the negotiations at Brest-Litovsk had been broken off by Russian delegates who refused to be deceived.

Kennan (op. cit., pp. 255–57) has cited respects in which Wilson's eloquent passages on Russia in the Fourteen Points Speech were "inaccurate and unrealistic."

what sort of definitive terms of settlement must necessarily spring out of them . . . There is no confusion of counsel among the adversaries of the Central Powers, no uncertainty of principle, no vagueness of detail. The only secrecy of counsel, the only lack of fearless frankness, the only failure to make definite statement of the objects of the war, lies with Germany and her Allies. The issues of life and death hang upon these definitions . . .

There is, moreover, a voice calling for these definitions of principle and of purpose which is, it seems to me, more thrilling and more compelling than any of the many moving voices with which the troubled air of the world is filled. It is the voice of the Russian people. They are prostrate and all but helpless, it would seem, before the grim power of Germany, which has hitherto known no relenting and no pity. Their power, apparently, is shattered. And yet their soul is not subservient. They will not yield either in principle or in action. Their conception of what is right, of what is humane and honorable for them to accept, has been stated with a frankness, a largeness of view, a generosity of spirit, and a universal human sympathy which must challenge the admiration of every friend of mankind; and they have refused to compound their ideals or desert others that they themselves may be safe. They call to us to say what it is that we desire, in what, if in anything, our purpose and our spirit differ from theirs; and I believe that the people of the United States would wish me to respond, with utter simplicity and frankness. Whether their present leaders believe it or not, it is our heartfelt desire and hope that some way may be opened whereby we may be privileged to assist the people of Russia to attain their utmost hope of liberty and ordered peace . . .

Denouncing "secret covenants entered into in the interest of particular governments and likely at some unlooked-for moment to upset the peace of the world," the argument moved to the first of fourteen specific aims:

open covenants of peace, openly arrived at, after which there shall be no private international understandings of any kind but diplomacy shall proceed always frankly and in the public view.

The second point—freedom of the seas—had been forecast by statements that the President had made earlier. He knew that this point would meet opposition in England, and yet House had found some approbation for it in the minds of influential British Liberals. Wilson realized, too, that there would be criticism—in this case in the Congress —of his third proposal, calling for "the removal, so far as possible, of all economic barriers and the establishment of an equality of trade conditions among all the nations . . ." The fourth point called for disarmament "to the lowest point consistent with domestic safety"—a proposal with which the Bolsheviki were to show little sympathy. The fifth advocated "a free, open-minded, and absolutely impartial adjust-ment of all colonial claims," with due regard to the interests of the inhabitants and the claims of other governments.

It was in the sixth point that Wilson came to grips with the colossal problem that was the chief reason for his statement:

The evacuation of all Russian territory and such a settlement of all ques-tions affecting Russia as will secure the best and freest cooperation of the other nations of the world in obtaining for her an unhampered and unem-barrassed opportunity for the independent determination of her own political development and national policy and assure her of a sincere welcome into the society of free nations under institutions of her own choosing; and, more than a welcome, assistance also of every kind that she may need and may herself desire. The treatment accorded Russia by her sister nations in the months to come will be the acid test of their good will, of their comprehen-sion of her needs as distinguished from their own interests, and of their intelligent and unselfish sympathy.

In the points that followed, Wilson dealt with the specific problems of national territories and sovereignties. The phrasing of a statement about the future of Alsace-Lorraine perplexed him. In rewriting it he evolved the general principle that he would use the word "must" when there was no difference of opinion and "should" in setting down solu-tions of controversial questions. His final version read: "The wrong done to France by Prussia in 1871 . . . should be righted."

Only in shaping a settlement of the problem of the disposition of Austria-Hungary and the Balkans did he seek counsel beyond his circle of American advisers. He sent House, against the latter's judgment, to consult the head of the Serbian mission at Washington and was de-pressed when the Colonel returned with a report that Serbia insisted there could be no lasting peace in Europe without a breakup of the Austro-Hungarian Empire. He was aware that the freeing of subject nationalities, though in some cases to be desired, might, if pushed to an extreme, lead to the disruption of existing governments to an inde-finable extent. Disregarding the Serbian view, he stated in Point Ten merely that "the peoples of Austria-Hungary, whose place among the nations we wish to see safeguarded and secured, should be accorded the freest opportunity of autonomous development."

Wilson would have liked to limit his conditions of peace to thirteen, his favorite number. The Fourteenth Point, however, was the most significant of all, and the one that gave hope that the others might be given practical application. Though he had not talked much in the early months of the war about a "league of nations," he had not forgotten his oft-repeated commitment to the development of a world-wide political organism. A committee under Lord Bryce had drawn up a British plan for a League to Enforce Peace; and the American organization of that name was still active. Though he had endorsed its purposes, Wilson had been careful not to subscribe to its program, which he thought "very much too definite," or to any other program that might arouse jealousies or provoke differences of opinion. To a congressman who had come on August 3, 1917, to the White House to propose adapting the federal Constitution to the purposes of international organization, Wilson said that they must first win the war. "I quite agree with your general purposes," he went on, "but I fear that no accomplishment so great as our own Constitution can be hoped for. A most happy combination of historical conditions alone made that achievement possible. What I do hope to accomplish is to establish a structure containing the tendencies which will lead irresistibly to the great end we in common with all other rightly constituted persons desire. But there are going to be difficulties even with this modest desire. I have in mind the ridiculous importance which some persons assign to the official who will be charged with such conspicuous work —but, friends and enemies both will admit that my 'jaw' has proved adequate in past struggles!"

When finally he decided to draft a league-of-nations plank for his platform for world peace, he phrased it in this way:

A general association of nations must be formed under specific covenants for the purpose of affording mutual guarantees of political independence and territorial integrity to great and small states alike.

The timing of the release of the most far-reaching of all Woodrow Wilson's speeches gave anxiety to its author. He was eager to put out his manifesto before Lloyd George and Clemenceau could forestall him.[11] He typed a cable for the prime minister, stating the intention of speaking more specifically about war aims than he had before, and expressing the hope that no utterance was contemplated across the Atlantic that "would be likely to sound a different note or suggest claims inconsistent with" the objects of the United States.

---

11 The Colonel was disturbed by this and also because Taft, asked by Balfour to go to England and accepting, talked it over with the President and then told newsmen what Wilson said: viz., that the United States did not desire closer relations with England, and there was great anti-British feeling in the country. Citing the Treaty of London as an instance of British self-interest, Wilson said that there were too many Englishmen carrying on propaganda in the United States and he had asked House to have some of them go home. He told Wiseman that, to be permanent, Anglo-American understanding must rest on a surer basis than artificial propaganda.

But suddenly, on January 5, as the President was discussing his own address with the Colonel, Lloyd George, who was as sensitive as Wilson to the trends of opinion in Russia and Germany and the response of British radicals to them, restated Britain's war aims in a speech to trade-union delegates at London. Balfour telegraphed to Wilson to explain that there had been no time to consult allies about this move, that the prime minister had been forced to speak out immediately to facilitate negotiations with the union men, that a further statement along the same lines would receive an equally warm welcome.[12]

When Wilson learned that Lloyd George had spoken without consulting him, both his morality and his pride were offended. Not only had the prime minister differed in principle by insisting that Germany pay reparations, but by proposing almost all of the President's Fourteen Points he seemed to have pirated the ideas that Wilson had set down with great pains. Wilson, the man of literary property, seemed to forget the biblical truth that his father had preached but had often overlooked—that no servant of the Lord had light of his own, but merely bore witness to the "heavenly light." The ambition to seize the pulpit of peace for himself and to give leadership to his own people in serving the world still burned strongly in the prophet in the White House. He was no more inclined than he had been at the age of thirty to be any man's follower in a matter on which he felt that he had qualified himself to speak.

For a moment he thought that it would be impossible for him to make the address that he had been preparing. However, House insisted that Lloyd George had cleared the air and made it the more necessary to act, that the prime minister had not himself written the speech that he had delivered, that it would be so smothered by Wilson's own effort that the President would be recognized as spokesman for all the enemies of Germany.

Taking heart, Wilson set to work again on his momentous utterance. He and House were most anxious about the reaction of their own people to their declaration of territorial aims for Europe. Wilson was not so much concerned about a criticism that he expected from the Germans: that since the Monroe Doctrine forbade interference by Europeans in the Americas, the Old World should insist that there be no intrusion from the New into their affairs. He was prepared to reply that he was willing to have the same principles applied to the Western Hemisphere that he prescribed for the whole world. He was wary of

[12] House doubted that the political necessity for a pronouncement by Lloyd George was as dire as Balfour suggested. A letter from Sir William Wiseman, written to House on March 20, 1933, expressed the opinion that Lloyd George's speech was probably made to forestall the Wilsonian pronouncement, of which the Colonel had warned the prime minister.

provoking argument and spoke to House of the wisdom of avoiding assertions that might stir controversy. But he insisted that by and large their proposals were just, and he showed no hesitation in adhering to them. On January 8 he proclaimed his gospel before the Congress.

Once the epochal speech was uttered, the whole world gave heed. Washington circles and American newspapers, even some that were usually in opposition, were laudatory. Even in the uttermost parts of the world the words of the prophet stirred a worshipful response in hearts that were yearning for the American gospel of which missionaries and traders were telling them. Human beings everywhere felt the magic of the tug on sensibilities that are deep in all men. Here was a creed that was free from the class bitterness that was associated with the Stockholm conference and from the institutional origin of the Pope's appeal. The doctrine of self-determination appealed to traditionalists in Europe as a line by which radical opposition could be short-circuited.

Sophisticated foreign observers, however, were more reserved in their reception of this bold projection of American philosophy into world affairs. The Western Allies readily applauded Wilson's strictures on German militarism; and liberals welcomed his statement of general principles of peacemaking. But conservatives thought his ideals almost utopian and questioned their validity as a practical basis for peace. Queries arose about his proposals for territorial settlements. It seemed to some nations that they themselves would receive too small a share of the spoils of war, that their enemies would get off too lightly. Not only did the Fourteen Points speech fail to persuade the governments of the Allies to renounce the terms of the secret treaties; but by creating suspicion among the peoples that they might not get what they were fighting for, it made it the more difficult for statesmen to maintain resistance to Germany at a high pitch.

In Russia, Wilson's words were given the wide circulation that had been promised. When Sisson took a translation of them to Lenin, the commissar grabbed it and sprinted for a telegraph office to send it to Trotsky at Brest-Litovsk. According to Sisson, Lenin thought the speech a tolerant one for a "class opponent" to write and accepted it as "a great step ahead" toward world-wide peace. Its prescriptions for territorial settlements were similar to his own. But he criticized the clause dealing with colonial claims and pointed out that Marxist ideals transcended the right of peoples to self-determination. He continued to ask that the United States give substance to her professed friendship by recognizing the Soviet government. As for Trotsky, he read Wilson's speech and continued to speak cynically of America's motives. Composed without regard to the effect in Russian translation, and ambiguous as to Wilson's view of Bolshevik power, the address left many questions unanswered. While the government press followed Lenin's thinking, *Pravda,* speaking for the party dictatorship, raved against Wilson, calling him "the representative of the American dictatorship, chastising its own workers and poor people with prisons, forced labor, and death sentences . . ." One propagandist referred to the address as a "very deliquescent program of political rascality." Whatever effect Wilson's speech, translated and displayed on hundreds of thousands of posters, may have had on the plain people of Russia, it doubtless dulled their hope for immediate peace. By contrast, it highlighted the pacific prospect that Trotsky was offering.

However, Wilson did not entirely lose faith in the Russian Revolution as a manifestation of democratic potential, not even when, on January 18, the Bolsheviki dissolved the elected Constituent Assembly and served notice that they would rule by decree.[13] At one time he considered establishing *de facto* relations with Petrograd as a practical step toward combating German intrigue. The changes taking place in Russia were so kaleidoscopic that all information and advice seemed futile; but his conscience kept his mind working on the dilemma. On February 6 he wrote to John Sharp Williams: ". . . I do not know that I have ever had a more tiresome struggle with quicksand than I am having in trying to do the right thing in respect of our dealings with Russia."

Trotsky pursued a policy of making neither war nor peace with Germany, and the German Army lost patience, ended the armistice, and dispersed the remaining fragments of Russian forces. Finally at the end of February, when German seizure of Petrograd seemed imminent and Lenin's regime was tottering, Ambassador Francis, despairing of maintaining resistance to the enemy, left the city with his staff and the Red Cross mission. When the Bolsheviki decreed the repudiation of Russia's state debts, France became implacably hostile to the new regime and Lansing and McAdoo thought recognition impossible.

In a last desperate effort to prevent ratification of the Brest-Litovsk treaty, the President sent a greeting on March 11 to the Congress of Soviets that was convoked at Moscow to supplant the prorogued Constituent Assembly. He expressed sympathy with their efforts to free themselves forever from autocracy, and the hope that this body might be persuaded not to approve the peace with Germany. But the applause

---

[13] As Kennan has observed (*op. cit.,* pp. 362–63), the dissolution of the Constituent Assembly, which was not featured in the American press, overweighted any inclination that the Allies may have had to recognize the Soviet government and turned them toward a policy of aiding anti-Bolshevik factions in Russia. On Jan. 21 Wilson wrote to Samuel Gompers thus regarding the Assembly: ". . . apparently the reckless Bolsheviki have already broken it up because they did not control it. It is distressing to see things so repeatedly go to pieces."

that greeted his overture was scattered and thin.[14] The Bolshevik leaders replied with rant, and expressed concern for "all peoples suffering from the horrors of imperialistic war." A happy time was not far distant, the Soviet note predicted, "when the laboring masses of all countries will throw off the yoke of capitalism and will establish a socialistic state of society which is alone capable of securing just and lasting peace, as well as the culture and well-being of all laboring people."[15]

In view of this brash rejection of his sympathy and the violent methods that the Bolsheviki had to use to hold their power, and when reports came from both Ambassador Francis and Sisson that seemed to prove that the leaders of the Bolsheviki were in German pay,[16] the President abandoned efforts to establish cordial relations between the great revolutionary peoples of the New World and those of the Old. His government perpetuated the fallacy that had embarrassed the provisional government and that precluded diplomatic understanding between Washington and the Bolsheviki. The State Department took the position that the United States persisted in regarding the Russian people as comrades-in-arms and in refusing to recognize that there was any government to speak for them.

Wilson was frustrated, then, in two of the purposes that had been foremost in his mind when he prepared his Fourteen Points speech. He did not persuade the self-constituted rulers of the Russian people to stand with the Allies against Germany; nor did he shake the determination of Britain and France to honor the agreements that had been set down in secret treaties.

However, he realized to some degree his intent of jarring the confidence of the peoples of Germany and Austria in their military masters. Wilson had hurled words of peace so effectively that officials at Berlin and Vienna felt it necessary to parry them. There was talk of revolt, and strikes broke out. On January 24 legislative committees at both

[14] DeWitt C. Poole's record in the Oral History Project, Columbia University. Poole, who gave Wilson's message to the chairman of the Soviet Congress, confirms the account printed in *F.R., 1919, Russia*, I, 395 and 399, except as to the volume of the applause. According to Lawrence Martin, Wilson's communication was "really intended to caution Japan." Martin thesis.

[15] According to Ambassador Francis, a Soviet minister boasted: "With these words we slapped President Wilson in the face." House thought this "a tough one to answer" and concluded that formal correspondence had best be discontinued.

After Wilson's greeting of March 11 had been sent, the State Department received from Francis a message that Trotsky had given to Raymond Robins of the Red Cross on March 5. Trotsky asked what aid the United States would give if the war against Germany were renewed and also asked what could be done to get British help through Murmansk and to prevent a Japanese landing in Siberia. On March 19 the State Department replied that Wilson's message of March 11 was an adequate answer. When the British also failed to give definite assurances, the Congress of Soviets ratified the Treaty of Brest-Litovsk, in mid-March.

[16] *See* p. 263 below.

capitals were told that the governments tentatively agreed with Wilson's general points, though differing from most of the territorial proposals. Chancellor Hertling criticized the tone of the speeches of Lloyd George and Wilson, but expressed sympathy with the concept of a league of nations. Count Czernin, Austria's minister of foreign affairs, showing more sincerity and warmth than his ally at Berlin, remarked that "Austria-Hungary and the United States of America are the two great powers among the two groups of enemy states whose interests least conflict."

Encouraged by the mere fact that his adversaries took public notice of his attack, by a report from House that it looked "as if things were at last beginning to crack in Germany," and by a resolution of British Laborites calling for a joint declaration of peace terms, the President was disturbed by the disinclination of the leaders of the Allies to follow him in a peace offensive. He resented suggestions from abroad that this was not his business and wished to try to make it plain that "each item of a general peace is everybody's business." His irritation was inflamed in the first week of February when the Supreme War Council, which had been constituted to deal with military affairs, stepped into the political field and declared that the enemy's responses to Wilson's speech offered no basis for peace. He protested strongly. "I am afraid of *any* expression of policy framed jointly at Paris," he wrote to Lansing. "There has been none yet that seemed to me even touched with wisdom."

Wilson determined to reply to Hertling and Czernin. When he discussed his plan on January 29 with House he seemed to be feeling his way, without confidence that he was on the right track; but the Colonel reassured him by praising the first draft.

Addressing a joint session of the Congress on February 11 he reviewed the proposals of Hertling and Czernin and condemned their method of peacemaking as that of the Congress of Vienna. "We cannot and will not return to that," he proclaimed. "What is at stake now is the peace of the world. What we are striving for is a new international order based upon broad and universal principles of right and justice— no mere peace of shreds and patches." He threw in an economic threat that he and House had discussed at some length: if the making of a settlement in Eastern Europe was none of the business of the Allies, perhaps tariff barriers in Western Europe were none of Germany's business! [17] He felt that German citizens would not be indifferent to the

---

[17] In January, Wilson told Wiseman that control of raw materials would be a weapon of enormous value to England and America at the peace conference and he was prepared to use it fully, if necessary, to bring the German militarists to reason.

threat of a tariff war after the shooting was over. Then, in conclusion, he presented four generalizations that he thought essential to a just peace:

First, that each part of the final settlement must be based upon the essential justice of that particular case and upon such adjustments as are most likely to bring a peace that will be permanent;

Second, that peoples and provinces are not to be bartered about from sovereignty to sovereignty as if they were mere chattels and pawns in a game, even the great game, now forever discredited, of the balance of power; but that

Third, every territorial settlement involved in this war must be made in the interest and for the benefit of the populations concerned, and not as a part of any mere adjustment or compromise of claims amongst rival states; and

Fourth, that all well-defined national aspirations shall be accorded the utmost satisfaction that can be accorded them without introducing new or perpetuating old elements of discord and antagonism that would be likely in time to break the peace of Europe and consequently of the world.

Although the address was well received, it did not stir enthusiasm to the pitch that had been reached on similar occasions before. It seemed to House that few members of Congress understood the President's intention to "build a fire back of Ludendorff" and that fewer still sympathized with Wilson's strategy. Returning to the White House, the prophet himself appeared to be "only scantily hopeful" that his effort would be considered an immediate success. But he was cheered when the Colonel waxed enthusiastic and brought glowing praise from Reading and Wiseman—"I would have given a year of my life to have made the last half of the President's speech," the British ambassador said. It was gratifying, too, that his four principles were adopted by an Inter-Allied Labor-Socialist Conference that met at London.

Slight as was the immediate effect of the manifestoes that Woodrow Wilson delivered in the first months of 1918, their historical significance was immense. The Allied governments were unwilling to accept Wilsonian "points" that impinged upon their special interests and therefore held back from quick adherence to his program. But it had become evident, during America's first year of war and Russia's months of freedom from czarism, that in Washington there was a formidable rival to the Soviet commissars for leadership in the new diplomacy of propaganda.

CHAPTER IX

"FORCE WITHOUT STINT OR LIMIT . . . RIGHTEOUS AND TRIUMPHANT"

THE FAILURE OF Woodrow Wilson to maintain Russian resistance to Germany hardened his conviction that the immediate necessity was to smash his enemies in Central Europe.

The winter of 1917–18 was one of the coldest ever. On January 11 snow, sleet, and rain were falling as the President walked late one afternoon from the executive offices to the White House. "Well," he observed in a gloomy voice to his secret service guard, "this means stalled freight trains and more suffering because of lack of coal."

In this month in which he was concentrating on psychological warfare, the problem of mobilizing manpower and munitions of war became acute. During 1917 few of his people had dared openly to criticize his military program for fear of seeming unpatriotic; and save for outbursts of invective from the Roosevelt-Wood clique, the President had been relatively immune from obstruction by the Republicans and other factions.[1] When the Russian front collapsed, however, and the United States had hardly made its power felt in France, dissatisfaction that had been long seething erupted. A great wave of protest rolled up with the assembling of the Congress.

Sensing this, Wilson concluded that there must be a tightening of controls all along the line. In his annual address to the legislators, on December 4, he proposed an extension of measures already enacted to

[1] In August of 1917 General Leonard Wood, to whom Wilson had sent "a word of very warm and genuine congratulation" on his "admirable services" when Wood had left the post of chief of staff in 1914, was transferred to Camp Funston in Kansas. On Oct. 4 Pershing, in a letter to Secretary Baker, included Wood in a list of generals whom he considered "unavailable for overseas service." Wood was considered physically unfit because of a limp and an old injury to his skull.

However, Secretary Baker sent Wood abroad to study the training methods of the Allies. While overseas, the general embarrassed both Ambassador Page and Pershing by talking freely and indiscreetly in criticism of the President and America's war effort. Pershing wrote a "personal and very confidential memorandum" to Secretary Baker, on Feb. 24, 1918, saying that not only was Wood "seriously and permanently crippled," but was a "political general" who went about discrediting the Army and the Administration. Pershing ordered him home.

Democratic Senator Thomas tried to persuade Wilson to call Wood to the White House and hear his story, and the press asked whether the President could refuse to do this. But though this controversy hampered the efforts of the Administration to secure greater powers from the Congress, Wilson stood aside from it. On Jan. 30 he told House, who now had lost patience completely with Wood, that he had not known that the general had been sent abroad and that when he had asked Baker about it the secretary of war explained that it had seemed better to let Wood go than to have people feel that he was being martyred by being kept in the United States.

deal with enemy aliens. He said, too, that the government must be authorized to set price limits, for the law of supply and demand seemed to have been "replaced by the law of unrestricted selfishness." The Congress would be able to suggest other action, he declared, but he insisted that in the present session attention should be concentrated on the vigorous, rapid, and successful prosecution of the great task of winning the war.

On one recommendation that he made he was ready to act forthwith. It had become clear that the railroads of the country, handicapped by problems that were aggravated by the impact of war, were not able to move food and munitions expeditiously. In the autumn of 1917 their plight had disturbed Wilson more than any other domestic problem. He wished to avoid the responsibility of administering them if it was possible, shrank from adding this burden to those that were already overwhelming him. It was essential that he delegate the job to a man who would not bungle it. On a Sunday afternoon he said to Stockton Axson: "I know only one man who can handle the tangled, abortive situation—Mac—but unfortunately he is my son-in-law, and I can't reverse my position on nepotism." It seemed natural to turn to the secretary of the treasury because the problems of the railroads were largely financial. Canny advisers, perceiving that action was imperative, suggested that the President seek the advice of Brandeis. Wilson accepted this counsel, went to call on the justice, and was convinced that scruples should not interfere with the appointment of the man who seemed most suitable.

On December 26 the President issued a proclamation by which he took possession of the railroads, acting through the secretary of war. McAdoo was designated director general and took vigorous steps to accelerate the flow of war materials over the rails.

Another bold stroke for the general welfare was less pleasing to the American people. On the very day of the railroad proclamation, Fuel Administrator Garfield was testifying before a committee of the Senate that he would like to have the mines, as well as the railroads, operated by the government. Wilson did not endorse this idea; but when it became apparent that the fuel supplies were not adequate to meet the unprecedented needs of wartime industry as well as the heating requirements of civilians in a winter of abnormal cold, he conferred secretly with Garfield and the secretaries of war and navy. They told him that it would be necessary to limit civilian consumption of coal; there must be "heatless days," and closings of offices and factories for certain periods. Garfield thought that an executive order should go out immediately, before the press guessed their intention.

Wilson saw instantly that such a measure would raise a whirlwind of protest, and the storm was as furious as he expected. A Senate resolution requested that the order be suspended for five days until it could be investigated. Even Wilson's friends were shocked.

The President stood stanchly behind his administrator. On January 18—the same day on which he notified his people that they might have to tighten their belts further to conserve food—he explained to the nation that not only had he fully approved the fuel order, but that it was necessary, much as he regretted it. "It is extraordinary," he wrote to Baruch, "how some people wince and cry out when they are a little bit hurt." He expressed confidence that his people were willing to endure the same discipline that was involved in the actual fighting of the war. When Garfield telephoned to offer to supply fuel to country clubs at which the President played golf, Wilson asked Tumulty to say that he "would not for anything" have an exception of this sort made.

The President had no convincing rejoinder for the critics of his organization of the nation for war. Willing to discuss the criticisms with his confidants, he would not permit public replies. Asked to explain his policies, he said that he would not "exploit" them. He was determined not to forget the dignity and responsibility of his position, as he felt that Roosevelt had done. He feared that a brazen assertion of growing military power might be construed abroad as a note of defiance, calculated to operate as a rebuff of all peace offers.

Yet he was far from satisfied by the progress that was being made. Both politicians and businessmen worried him by their manipulations. He told his Cabinet that they should be cautious in guarding against a popular impression that rich men's sons were getting soft berths at Washington. And he said at a Gridiron dinner: "My troubles with the war are slight compared with the difficulties of satisfying my distinguished dollar-a-year associates . . . I am like an opera impresario, every member of whose troupe wants to be recognized and applauded as the prima donna." Sometimes it seemed as if everything that went well took care of itself, and only problems reached his desk.

The lid of patriotic restraint blew off completely in January of 1918. The Senate's Committee on Military Affairs, which for some time had been studying the munitions program, unanimously approved introduction of a bill providing for a director of munitions. The chairman, Democratic Senator Chamberlain, had commanded attention the month before when he spoke on the Senate floor of the lag that all knew to exist between production plans and actual output. Going to New York to address the National Security League on January 19, the senator declared that the military establishment of the nation had fallen down, that it had stopped functioning because of "inefficiency in every bureau and every department of the Government of the United States." As the speaker sat down, Theodore Roosevelt jumped to his feet and applauded loudly. Soon the old Rough Rider went to Washington to support a revival of the public demand for administrative reorganization that had risen spasmodically, in one form or another, ever since the beginning of hostilities.

The President's liberal friends, noting that the hotels of Washington were filled with businessmen from all parts of the country who were not getting what they wanted, insisted on attributing the attacks to political motives. They charged that Wilson was the target again of reactionary interests that feared government encroachment on their prerogatives, under the compulsion of national emergency. The President felt that he could not trust the Congress to act impersonally. On September 1 he had explained to Senator Williams that a supervising Congressional committee, if it was created, would introduce "very great added difficulty and burden," that fortunately the many consultative bodies that already existed were under his own authority, where he could hope to keep a coordinating eye on all at the same time.

Yet friendly newspapers suggested that there was some truth in the allegations of Chamberlain. House called on Baker to try to convince him that reorganization was desirable; and, though feeling that the criticism reflected political bias, the secretary was not unwilling to admit deficiencies in the Ordnance Department and to consider changes.

The President, however, was enraged by the immoderate onslaught and rose to defend the secretary of war. Ascertaining first that Chamberlain had been quoted accurately, Wilson publicly declared that the criticism was "an astonishing and unjustifiable distortion of the truth." As a matter of fact, he asserted, despite "delays and disappointments and miscarriage of plans" the War Department had "performed a task of unparalleled magnitude with extraordinary promptness and efficiency." His affection and admiration for Baker was such that he found it hard to restrain himself from more intemperate words.

Actually the attacks of January, coming while the President was wining prestige by his peace offensive, served to enlist support for the strengthening of controls that he wished to achieve as soon as popular opinion was ready. He could see that the criticism was advantageous in so far as it enabled the Administration to rebut reckless attacks. He felt the need of a law that would free his hands, rather than bind them in red tape wound up by political adversaries.

On January 24 he asked his associates to take up a remedial bill that

Secretary Baker had sent to him in a tentative draft. Burleson persuaded Senator Overman, known as a defender of states' rights, to introduce the measure in the Senate on February 6. It gave the President broad power to "coordinate and consolidate" the activities of the government, to win the war. The bill was worked over at White House conferences; after a month of vitriolic debate, in which the measure was denounced as a step toward absolute monarchy, it was passed by the Congress; and on May 20 Wilson signed it.[2] Authorized now to "make such redistribution of functions among executive agencies" as he thought necessary, he issued an executive order, on May 28, making the War Industries Board independent of the cumbersome Council of National Defense and delegating extraordinary powers to it. He had long been seeking a "superman" to direct this board—someone who could stand above tradition and special interests in making and carrying through decisions. In anticipation of the action of the Congress, and under the authority of a section of the National Defense Act, he had announced on March 5 that Baruch would head the board. The chairman was empowered to appoint committees at his own discretion and to control them absolutely, except the one that set prices. The price-fixing committee reported directly to the President and he passed upon its decisions.

Baruch already had won voluntary cuts in the prices of several metals; and Wilson directed him now "to guide and assist wherever the need . . . may be revealed" and to "act as the general eye of all supply departments, in the field of industry." This South Carolinian had shown a vast and detailed knowledge of the sources of strategic raw materials and the prevailing price scales; he knew the people who were in key positions; and he had a master plan, a vision of voluntary cooperation within industry to put the nation's need above profits. (As early as October of 1915 he had given the President an outline of a plan for industrial mobilization for defense.) But best of all, Baruch had a faith in the integrity of business that Wilson lacked. He did not share the President's feeling that industrialists would take advantage of the emergency raised by war to seize political power. Though Baruch, like the President, fancied lovely ladies—he had celebrated Wilson's sixty-first birthday by presenting a copy of Merrick's *Whispers*

---

[2] Of the Overman Act, Frederic L. Paxson has written (in *America at War*, pp. 224–25): "Few statutes have in so few words surrendered so much; and none has vested more discretion in the President. . . . The Overman Act authorized him to redistribute the functions of executive agencies as he saw fit; 'to utilize, co-ordinate, or consolidate any executive or administrative commissions, bureaus, agencies, offices, or officers now existing by law'; to create new agencies; to transfer, redistribute, or abolish the functions of others; and to utilize funds voted for any purpose for the accomplishment of that purpose by whatever means might to him seem good."

about Women—it was said of him that "his love of country exceeded that for any woman." Here was a man who seemed as gallant and patriotic as he was competent.

This lieutenant was both facile and persuasive in talk with everyone —colleagues, industrialists, and newsmen. Radiating love of work and achievement, and assuming sole responsibility while delegating authority, he got "jobs" done with dispatch and with the least friction possible.

Gradually the War Industries Board developed an authority over production and supplies that was almost as absolute as that of the War and Navy Departments over military affairs. "Let the manufacturer see the club behind your door," the President advised Baruch.

When his cooperation was sought, Woodrow Wilson directed the same close personal attention to Baruch's problems that he had been giving to those of Secretaries Baker and Daniels.[3] He formally notified all agencies and departments that the War Industries Board had become a separate administrative arm to act for him and under his direction. When Baruch and Baker had differences, and personal feelings were hurt, Wilson was able to mediate without losing the services of either man.

As the merciless grip of winter relaxed and the armies of Germany began to slog relentlessly forward into the mud of France, the President was convinced that it was no time for party considerations to govern appointments. His Council of National Defense was almost solidly Republican. Brushing aside protests that were based on political grounds, he allowed Baker to appoint Edward R. Stettinius, partner of J. P. Morgan & Company, to be surveyor general of army purchases. When aircraft production failed to match the rosy forecast that had been made by civilian promoters, and citizens in whom Wilson had confidence were insisting that the matter be probed, the President chose as investigator his rival of the 1916 campaign. Hughes's report, published October 31, 1918, found inefficiency, confusion, and minor violations of law.

When labor agitation slowed production that was essential to the war

---

[3] Grosvenor B. Clarkson, director of the Council of National Defense, wrote thus in *Industrial America in the World War*, p. 102: "The writer . . . interviewed some twoscore of the executives of the War Industries Board and the Council of National Defense, and . . . all of them, regardless of party affiliation, who had any personal contact with President Wilson, united in expressing appreciation of his quick grasp of the fundamentals of the most abtruse and technical problems that were laid before him. It is possibly true that the President did too long defer a determination of the problems of industrial centralization for war purposes; but, on the other hand, once he had decided his course and mapped it, in the lucid and comprehensive letter of authority to Mr. Baruch [March 4, 1918], the supporting decisions were always prompt and clear-cut."

effort, Wilson acted positively, but with regard for decent standards. To
the president of a carpenters' union that was striking in the shipyards he
wrote a tart note, ending with the question: "Will you cooperate or will
you obstruct?" [4] Relying in many instances only upon his power as commander in chief, Wilson invoked administrative sanctions that projected
the wartime power of the Presidency into new dimensions. Yet when a
strict court-martial bill was proposed he denounced it as no better than
Prussianism, and he warned against infringements of civil liberties that
were based on "a suspicious attitude."

On Wednesdays he conferred regularly with his war council—men of
action and achievement, lieutenants who could be given responsibility
with the knowledge that they would accept it conscientiously, function
within its limits, and soon report solid accomplishment. The value of
his Cabinet had been impaired by personal ambitions and animosities
and by indiscreet talking after meetings, so that the sessions of that
body, on Tuesdays and Fridays, were devoted to storytelling and trivial
matters. But in the war council the atmosphere was more nearly that
of a corporate executive committee.

McAdoo was the only member of the Cabinet who sat regularly in
the emergency body. To avoid hurting the feelings of the secretaries
who were not invited, the President said little about the meetings of the
new group and held them in his own study upstairs in the White
House.[5] He would stand near the door and greet each man with a
cheery, informal word. Before sitting down at his flat-top desk he took

---

[4] Daniels's diary reports discussions of labor problems in the Cabinet in July of 1917 during
which Wilson concurred when Baker stated that union labor should be recognized and union
wages paid everywhere. But when the President received a telegram from Hayward of the
I.W.W., threatening strikes, he said indignantly: "What Hayward desires is to be a martyr.
What shall I do?"

Secretary Baker pioneered in labor negotiations with unions. An adjustment commission
was set up, and the procedure developed was extended to the Navy, with Daniels's approval.
At Wilson's request, an attempt was made to extend this service to the shipbuilding industry;
and when Hurley insisted on reviewing the decisions of the adjustment board, Wilson upheld
the authority of the board. In the autumn of 1917, mediation of labor relations in other war
industries was placed by the President in the hands of a commission headed by the secretary of
labor, and the government did not enter into agreements.

On April 18, 1918, Wilson created a National War Labor Board "to promote and carry on
mediation and adjustment in the field of production necessary for the effective conduct of the
war" except "where there is by agreement or by Federal law a means of settlement which has
not been invoked." Ex-President Taft was made a member of this board. In one particularly
troublesome strike at Bridgeport, Conn., the President used what one observer has described as
"improvised compulsion," issuing a threat of outlawry similar to the medieval threat of
attainder. See Louis B. Wehle, *Hidden Threads of History*.

[5] Apparently the President's efforts to avoid hurt feelings were not altogether successful.
Resentment was shown by Lane, Redfield, and others, according to testimony given by Vance
McCormick to Ray Stannard Baker on July 15, 1928.

The men invited to the first meeting of the war council were McAdoo, Baruch, Hoover,
Hurley, McCormick, and Garfield.

away a vase of flowers so that he might see the faces of his visitors. He offered cigars, asked whether the extra chairs brought in from outside were comfortable, and told a story or two. Then, getting down to business, he would listen intently as specific problems were presented for solution. He surprised his men by his grasp of practical affairs; and at least one, Hurley of the Shipping Board, felt that he had never met a business executive who was Wilson's equal.

The President felt it his duty not only to listen patiently, but to reach constructive decisions. His mind did not shirk. He would give his opinion, sometimes jotting it on a slip of paper and passing it to the man on whom the responsibility would rest. When they left the room, each man knew what his duty was and that his chief would back him to the limit as long as he did not stray from its path. They knew, too, that they were not expected to make suggestions about the work of a department other than their own, and that they should not speak in public unless the President requested it.

Wilson took comfort in the loyalty and ability of this inner council, as he became increasingly suspicious of men's motives. He came to suspect disaffection in places in which there was no proof that it existed. Going with House on February 24 to the unfinished National Cathedral, it seemed to him that the rector was about to preach about deficiencies in the War Department but had changed his mind when the President entered. Wilson noted that whenever legislators battled with him there was a backwash of scurrilous letters and gossip. The newspapers and their owners still drew his ire.

Colonel House, who had been warned by Frazier, at Paris, that "everybody is feeling the working-class volcano under his feet," thought his friend was outdoing him in leaning toward the left, despite Wilson's insistence that labor should not obstruct the war program. House found him impressed by a labor conference that met at Nottingham, England, and challenged statesmen to set forth their war aims so that the people would know for what they were suffering. Wilson, believing that the Democratic party never could serve liberal causes because of the influence of Southern reactionaries, said that a new party might be needed to pursue the ends that they had in view; but then, turning to his friend, he said pathetically: "That is a big program for a tired man to think of undertaking." The Colonel noted that his weariness was genuine. "He does not remember names so well," House recorded on February 27, "and he does not do the things we decide upon." And yet the President seemed to do more work in the eight-hour day that Dr. Grayson permitted than any other man of the Colonel's acquaintance.

There were no official functions at the White House now. Wilson enjoyed the theater more than once a week, sometimes going backstage afterward, and often humming over the tunes that he heard and retelling the jokes. He had fun in going to the circus and sharing a bag of peanuts; and he was still a rabid baseball fan. After a benefit game for the Red Cross, he greeted his problem-weighted fuel administrator breezily: "Hang it all, Garfield, I have just been to a ball game and I wish I could say three strikes and out to this job." His artistic sensibilities were still alive, too: visiting the office of a war official, he protested that he had no time to sit down, and then, attracted by a piece of sculpture, dropped into a chair and talked at length about beauty and art and its place in a world at war. Sometimes he allowed himself to think of retirement. When his fighting days were over, he confided to House, he would follow warm weather. He spoke of Bermuda as a "lotus land" where he would like to live out his days if only it belonged to the United States.

Inspecting an English tank one afternoon in April, he burned his right hand painfully on a hot exhaust pipe. He had to keep his arm in a sling, but treated the wound cavalierly and managed to play golf with one hand and to do his desk work—"Woodrow is becoming the greatest one-arm champion in the world," Edith Wilson wrote to the Colonel. The injury made him lean more than ever upon his wife's competence. Four days after the accident she reviewed a parade in his behalf. It was the first time that she stood in his place before the people.

At the Inter-Allied Conference in December it had been agreed that the United States would have about a million men in Europe in 1918, and another million ready to go. All through the winter British and French officials had been asking that American forces might be consolidated with theirs, by regiments and companies. They wished to fill up their ranks, and felt that the newcomers would be seasoned most quickly by serving in battle alongside European veterans.

In December, after House's return from abroad, Wilson had discussed the matter with the Colonel and drafted instructions to Pershing. Cautioning the general against any loss of identity of American units, the message explained that this political consideration was "secondary to the meeting of any critical situation by the most helpful use possible" of the expeditionary force.

Later he informed Baker that they must continue to trust Pershing's judgment, but should advise the general that "nothing except sudden and manifest emergency should be suffered to interfere with the building up of a great distinct American force at the front, active under its own flag and its own officers." [6] When he sat on March 1 with his Cabinet for what seemed to Secretary Lane to be "the first real talk on the war in weeks, yes, in months," he still refused to speak of his European associates as "allies."

Before the end of the month a military catastrophe gave the impetus needed to break the bonds of national tradition and to create the international high command for which House had striven at Paris at the end of 1917. On March 21 Ludendorff's armies attacked at a point that already had been pronounced vulnerable by an Executive War Board of the Supreme War Council but had not been made secure. Severance of the British and French armies seemed imminent. Unity of command was immediately imperative.

On March 27 Wilson was relieved to learn from Secretary Baker, who had gone abroad for a firsthand view of affairs, that the line of defense had been restored, that Pershing was temporarily placing all American resources at the disposal of the British and French commanders, and that the Allies had agreed that General Foch, acting under Clemenceau, should be coordinator of the armies on the Western front. On the 29th he cabled his congratulations. By this time he had before him a resolution for the use of American infantry that the Supreme War Council had adopted and that Secretary Baker endorsed.[7]

Calling in Hurley on March 30 to ask for a survey of cargo ships available for army use, Wilson spoke of his concern. He said: "Unless we send over every man possible to support the Allies in their present desperate condition, a situation may develop which would require us to pay for the entire cost of the war to the Central Powers." With pale face and drawn features he went on, calmly but firmly: "Hurley, we must go the limit." Though hesitant to commit himself until Secretary Baker returned from Europe, Wilson agreed that 120,000 troops would be sent in each of the subsequent months, subject only to the limits of

---

[6] Wilson felt that, if the American government bargained for British transports by placing its troops at the disposal of foreign commanders, his people would resent it and would suspect that their national military machine had broken down. But the President thought that the effect on the public would not be so bad if Pershing, as American commander in chief, decided after the men arrived in France that it was necessary to place some of them at the disposal of the British. Nevertheless, he made it very clear that he had not delegated to Pershing the right to interpret the will of the American people as that commander ventured to do. Sir William Wiseman to the writer, April 22, 1957.

[7] In March, Lloyd George tried to force the President's hand through a message that was made public. Wilson was indignant at this breach of diplomatic decorum and thought it cause for sending the British ambassador home; but House urged him not to complain, and Reading called at the White House to present the prime minister's pleas. Wilson heard his story and responded fervently: "Mr. Ambassador, you need say no more. I will do my damnedest." But when Reading persisted in pleading the British point of view, Wilson thought the ambassador too much the advocate. In June, Wilson's irritation was so great that he refused to see Reading.

shipping facilities. By the middle of April the flow of Americans across the Atlantic was increasing and Wilson confirmed Pershing's approval of Foch's position as commander in chief of the Allied armies.

Occasions arose that required the President to intervene to preserve the chain of command that Baker had forged. General March, who as chief of staff showed an extraordinary capacity to get things done, sometimes phrased dispatches in a manner that his associates thought "very curt." Pershing and other generals were irritated to the point of protesting to the secretary of war. Moreover, Leonard Wood, acting under House's advice, again sought an interview with the President.

Wilson felt that as commander in chief he must now listen judicially to the protest of so able an officer. He received Wood on May 28, and in a half-hour interview he heard his protestations of loyalty and his objections to a last-minute order that forbade his going abroad in command of a division that he had trained.[8] But the President did not retreat from the position that had been taken by Baker and March and Pershing. They talked for an hour. Wilson praised his visitor's ability as a training officer and agreed that the nation must accept a program of universal military service. He promised nothing.[9]

Wood went back to Fort Houston under a halo of martyrdom. His case was aired in the Congress by partisans and in the *New York Times*. Taft intimated that the hero was still being disciplined for talking too frankly to the Senate's Committee on Military Affairs about the Army's shortcomings. The President was forced to defend his position even to such a sympathetic critic as Richard Hooker of the Springfield *Republican*. "In the first place," Wilson wrote, "I am not sending him because

[8] Wood's departure for Europe in command of an American division that he had trained was prevented by a belated order from the War Department. In a letter written to Pershing on June 6, 1918, Secretary Baker explained that March had delayed the Wood transfer order for a few days. Baker later blamed himself for not realizing that Wood and his division were heading abroad until the division had entrained for New York. James W. Wadsworth MS, pp. 188 ff., Oral History Project, Columbia University.

[9] Actually the President, warned by House that frustrating Wood might be a costly political mistake, asked Baker casually whether any harm would be done by giving Wood a command in Europe apart from Pershing. On June 1, therefore, Baker cabled to Pershing that the Wood incident had led to considerable newspaper agitation and much speculation. While assuring the American commander that Wood would not be sent to France without his assent, the secretary remarked: "I am strongly inclined to think it would be wiser to let him go to Italy when our first contingent goes there."

Asked for his opinion of this idea, Pershing replied on June 10 that Wood was not only physically unqualified, but politically ambitious, unscrupulous, superficial in his military knowledge, and inclined toward the spectacular, that General Bliss felt that Wood's presence would disturb relations with the Allies. Suggesting that Wood might well be sent to Russia as a military representative or retained in the important role of training officer, Pershing urgently requested that the man not be sent to France or Italy in any capacity. "This is no place for political generals," the message said.

Near the end of the war Wilson, advising a cousin to obey military orders without complaint, confessed he was "sick and tired" of army officers who wanted to be shifted. F. W. McM. Woodrow to the writer.

General Pershing has said that he does not want him, and in the second place, General Pershing's disinclination to have General Wood sent over is only too well grounded. Wherever General Wood goes there is controversy and conflict of judgment. On this side of the water we can take care of that sort of thing, because the fighting is not being done here, but it would be fatal to let it go on anywhere near the front . . . He is a man of unusual ability but apparently absolutely unable to submit his judgment to those who are superior to him in command. I am sorry that his great ability cannot be made use of in France."

His own proper function, Wilson conceived, was to exert his influence on the home front and the psychological front rather than in the councils of battle. He reacted to the military crisis of the spring of 1918 in the same way in which the political leaders of the Allies had responded to earlier crises.

On April 6, in a speech opening the campaign for a Third Liberty Loan, he delivered his most caustic indictment of German militarism and accepted without cavil the gage of battle. The prophet wished, in a brief, striking talk, to leave the door of peace open but at the same time to burn the fear of his God into the hearts of his adversaries. Only one response to the obduracy of the Philistines seemed to him possible; this was, he said, "Force, Force, to the utmost, Force without stint or limit, the righteous and triumphant Force which shall make Right the law of the world, and cast every selfish dominion down in the dust."

In this, again, he reflected the mood of his people, as their soldiers were getting into battle and casualty lists grew longer. In the middle of May they let their prophet know that they were harkening to his word. Visiting the Houses at New York, the Wilsons went to see Fred Stone perform in *Jack O'Lantern*; and when the President was impersonated on the stage the audience went into a frenzy of applause. But the object of their enthusiasm was not elated. Forced to respond, he rose and said: "Ladies and gentlemen, you are laboring under a delusion. You think you see the President of the United States. You are mistaken. Really you see a tired man having a good time!"

The next day he was to review a Red Cross parade; but he insisted, against the protests of his family, on marching. Walking for two miles at the head of the procession, he laughed like a Princeton boy when the multitude hailed him. In the evening Cleveland Dodge introduced him to a throng at the Metropolitan Opera House, and he delivered a powerful appeal for national unity and international amity. He warned against peace talk by the enemy, deprecated it as a ruse to get a free hand in carrying out their purposes of "conquest and exploitation" in the East. "So far as I am concerned," he said, "I intend to stand by Russia as well as France." Wilson was surprised when this bold assertion, injected as an afterthought, brought his New York audience to their feet cheering.

Though he had been harsh toward German militarism, Wilson had not lost his scholarly perspective. "I would be ashamed to use knockdown and drag-out language," he said to a group of foreign correspondents two days later. "That is not the language of liberty." Quoting Burke, he went on: " 'A government which those living under it will guard' . . . is the only possible definition of a free government. . . . There isn't any one kind of government which we have the right to impose upon any nation. . . . I am not fighting for democracy except for the peoples that want democracy . . . the people have the right to make any kind of government they please."

In shaping a policy for restoring the shattered Eastern front, the President found himself dealing with forces remote and enigmatic. As early as January of 1918 British officials had suggested that Japan send troops to occupy the trans-Siberian Railway and the port of Vladivostok, where a small British contingent was already stationed. The War Cabinet at London hoped that the United States would send a small force to cooperate. Moreover, at the end of February Wilson received a report from the American engineering mission in Siberia to the effect that the German menace was "imminent and increasing" and Japan would go in whether America joined or not.

Balfour pressed the proposition upon House at the end of January as one that the British Cabinet regarded as "of great military importance" and "of immediate urgency." But the Colonel advised Wilson that it would be a great political mistake to let Japanese troops enter Siberia. It seemed to House, who discussed the matter with Ambassador Boris A. Bakhmeteff, that such a venture would rouse ill will among the Bolsheviki and stir up Slavic resentment throughout Europe "because of the race question if for nothing else." The State Department, too, regarding the Japanese as the prime promoters of an occupation of Siberia, thought that it would be unwise for the United States to take part.

After discussing the arguments pro and con with House, the President drafted, and then redrafted, a note for the Allied ambassadors. In the first version, of which the State Department gave the substance to the envoys, Wilson explained that it seemed unwise to join in a Siberian expedition, while at the same time giving assurance that he had no objection to such an enterprise on the part of Japan.[10]

After the treaty of Brest-Litovsk was signed and ratified, French and Italian statesmen demanded immediate action in Siberia; and the British government renewed pressure upon Wilson. Six times, in the early months of 1918, the United States government rejected proposals of the Allies for intervention, and it warned its officials repeatedly to stay aloof from Russia's internal affairs. But the moral indignation of the Western world was castigating the revolutionaries in a torrent of messages to the State Department. It was asserted that, if the flags of the Allies appeared in Russia, the people would rally to them and throw out the leaders who had collaborated with their German enemy.

For months the President resisted the pleas that came to him from many quarters.[11] The reconstruction of an Eastern front seemed to him impractical. He did some very lonely thinking about Russia. Refusing the offer of a summer place that would take him away from the sweltering heat of the capital, he told House that he had been "sweating blood" and that the puzzle seemed to go to pieces like quicksilver under his touch. He found it hard to fix a policy, in his desire to leave the Russian people free to work out their own salvation and his fear of driving the terror to still greater extremes, as the French Revolution had been driven by external pressure.

In the first week of July he reached a decision. On July 3 he learned

[10] In a redraft of this paper, after further caveats from House, Wilson wrote on March 5: "If it were undertaken the Government of the United States assumes that the most explicit assurances would be given that it was undertaken by Japan as an ally of Russia, in Russia's interest, and with the sole view of holding it safe against Germany and at the absolute disposal of the final peace conference . . . it is the judgment of the Government of the United States, uttered with the utmost respect, that even with such assurances given, they could . . . be discredited by those whose interest it was to discredit them; that a hot resentment would be generated in Russia itself, and that the whole action might play into the hands of the enemies of Russia, and particularly of the enemies of the Russian revolution, for which the Government of the United States entertains the greatest sympathy, in spite of all the unhappiness and misfortune which has for the time being sprung out of it."

[11] French officials were especially vehement. Noting that philosophic Lord Balfour had succeeded in his mission to Washington, they drafted Professor Henri Bergson to go to the White House and plead with the prophet whom he admired and from whom his praise drew tears. Ambassador Reading, citing an inquiry from Trotsky about the aid that the Allies now could offer, persistently urged that the United States send many divisions to help to re-establish the Eastern front against Germany. Boris A. Bakhmeteff, too, now recommended the creation of a "political beachhead" in Russia at which all anti-Bolshevik forces could gather. On May 2, Ambassador Francis telegraphed that the hour for intervention had come ("The longer we wait," he wired, "the stronger foothold Germany will secure"); and on June 5, Minister Reinsch wired from China that all American agents in that country agreed that the Allied action in Siberia was "absolutely demanded" to save the region from German control, and that joint action was desirable because of Russian distrust of Japan.

The President was moved also by deep sympathy for Masaryk, the crusading Czech statesman who had come to Washington on May 9 to plead the cause of the army of his compatriots that had migrated eastward into Siberia. On June 19, Masaryk called at the White House and found the President to be "the most intensely human man" he had ever met—a man "actually incandescent with feeling!" *See* Kennan, *The Decision to Intervene.*

that migrating Czech units had entered Vladivostok and that more British and Japanese forces had landed there. Simultaneously a message came from the Supreme War Council, reporting a unanimous feeling that military intervention in Siberia was essential to an Allied victory. They sought Wilson's approval "before it is too late."

Jotting on a pad of paper an outline of American policy, the President read his notes to his chief military and civil advisers on the 6th. Though he would not sanction the participation of American troops in Russia's civil strife, and argued that intervention would not help to win the war against Germany, he did consent to the dispatch of two policing expeditions: one to support a British venture at Murmansk; [12] another to aid— and control—a Japanese force at Vladivostok. In each case the intention was to prevent the Bolsheviki from seizing supplies shipped to czarist armies; and it was hoped too that the expeditions would re-establish rallying points for anti-German factions and especially for beleaguered Czech troops. The forces dispatched to Vladivostok had the additional mission of protecting American railway engineers.

In July Wilson's determination to maintain his faith in the Russian Revolution was undermined by shocks to his emotions from the brutality of the new regime. While dining at the home of Secretary Lane he learned of the murder of the Czar and the royal family; and he rose from the table and broke up the party, saying that a great menace to the world had taken shape and he was sure that all would share his feeling that it was no time for gaiety.

Wilson had been urged, both by Soviet leaders and by his associates at Washington, to embark on a constructive policy of economic relations with Russia. Offering to permit American participation in the de-

[12] In May of 1918 Wilson had been ready to share in "any practical military effort" in North Russia as a part of the war effort against Germany, but only if the venture had the approval of Foch and would proceed "on the sure sympathy of the Russian people . . ." The President had approved, in April, the dispatch of an American warship to Murmansk; and as of June 11, after Washington had been warned that Germans planned to capture Murmansk and operate their submarines from arctic ports, a hundred and fifty American Marines landed.

When Foch cabled to the President on June 27 that since no appreciable diminution of the forces to be sent to France would result, the sending of a few American troops to Russia would be justified, and when Bliss reported on July 12 that there would be "undercurrents of resentment" and a greater possibility of failure if the United States refused to participate in Russia, and that the nation should be represented by her "fair part," Wilson gave his decision reluctantly to the secretary of war. Baker suspected that "other considerations" than the winning of the war moved those on the Supreme War Council who favored the expedition, and he had his first serious disagreement with Wilson over this policy. "Baker," the President said, "I wholly agree with all you say from a military point of view, but we are fighting this war with Allies and I have felt obliged to refuse to do so many things they have asked me to do that I really feel obliged to fall in with their wishes here. I have, however, stipulated that the American contingent in both cases is to be small."

When Wilson noted, at the conference on the 6th, that General March opposed the expedition to Siberia, for military reasons and because of a fear of Japanese expansion, the President replied: "Well, we will have to take that chance." See March, *The Nation at War*, pp. 123 ff.

velopment of railroads, mines, waterways, and agricultural tracts, Lenin had sent an overture to Washington in May through Raymond Robins, an American Red Cross man who maintained a precarious contact with the leaders at Moscow. Wilson considered the proposal and wrote thus to Lansing on July 3: "The suggestions are certainly much more sensible than I thought the author of them capable of. I differ from them only in practical details." In an *aide-mémoire* written on his own typewriter and given to the ambassadors of the Allies on July 17, the President asserted that it was the hope and purpose of the United States to send an economic mission to Siberia at the earliest opportunity; but when the British government approved his general plan he showed no eagerness to proceed, and remarked that the mission that he had in mind would be concerned much more with relief and education than with economic development.[13]

In giving priority to military intervention and the restoration of order, Wilson insisted that the expeditions should not fall into the paths of nineteenth-century imperialism. His *aide-mémoire* explained that the United States, feeling that military intervention would "injure rather than help" Russia, would not "take part in such intervention or sanction it in principle." It yielded, however, to the Supreme Command in establishing a small force at Murmansk to guard military stores, and it stated there was "immediate necessity for helping the Czecho-Slovaks at Vladivostok." However, Wilson proposed "to ask all . . . to unite in assuring the people of Russia in the most public and solemn manner that none of the governments uniting in action either in Siberia or in northern Russia contemplates any interference of any kind with the political sovereignty of Russia, any intervention in her internal affairs, or any impairment of her territorial integrity either now or hereafter, but that each of the associated powers has the single object of affording such aid as shall be acceptable, and only such aid as shall be acceptable,

[13] Lansing had warned the President on June 13 that the American people were demanding a constructive policy, and had favored putting off Allied demands for military intervention until an economic commission could report on the situation. But Wilson had not acted.

When House raised the question several weeks later, the President replied that Secretary of Commerce Redfield had "messed the matter up." Wilson felt that an economic mission to Russia, to be successful, must be unofficial and financed by private funds; but Redfield had objected that under private sponsorship a mission would be open to suspicion as a profit-seeking enterprise.

Agreeing with Wilson's purposes toward Russia, House—like Secretary Baker and Brandeis —disapproved of the President's temporizing. House, hoping that Hoover might undertake a mission of relief and economic aid and take along Leonard Wood and hold him "in subjection," had discussed the matter with Hoover in June and with Wilson. Lansing and Baruch also suggested Hoover as head of an economic commission; but Wilson felt that he could not get along without his food administrator at that time.

Finally, on Oct. 10, 1918, Wilson approved the sending of an *aide-mémoire* to the Allies regarding American plans for economic aid to Russia. In the spring of 1919 this idea was brought forward again, with emphasis on relief. See p. 292n. below.

to the Russian people in their endeavor to regain control of their own affairs, their own territory and their own destiny." Thus, while failing to provide liaison with the Allied forces in Russia, Wilson by an ambiguous and straddling pronouncement made his nation vulnerable to the charge of unauthorized meddling in the affairs of Russia.

However, Wilson pressed Tokyo, in particular, for assurance that the expedition to Siberia would not be used for imperialistic purposes. The elusiveness of Japanese statesmen fretted him, and he sent an impatient message to Ambassador Morris, suggesting that, unless the Japanese limited their force to seven thousand men, he could not approve the expedition. Finally, after several parleys between diplomats, Counselor Polk informed the President on August 3 that, though the Japanese government still felt that more than the stipulated number would be needed to maintain order in Siberia, they would yield to the necessity for immediate action and the pleas of the United States, while reserving the question of sending additional forces until circumstances should arise that might make this necessary.[14] Taking this as the best assurance that could be gotten from Tokyo, the President prepared a statement for the press that followed the argument of his *aide-mémoire* of July 17.

Thus Wilson accepted the view that military victory was the first essential and that the United States should do her share in the fighting on the Western front and the policing of the borders of Russia. But he resisted temptations to seek aggrandizement for self or nation. Refusing to buy British bonds that would yield 6 per cent, he invested every penny that he could save in American Liberty Bonds at lower rates of interest. Some of his people hoped that their commercial position in China and Latin America might be improved by the war's outcome, but he convinced Sir William Wiseman that he did not share this feeling.

In the months when the fighting in France ebbed and flowed precariously, the prophet kept his concept of a just peace clear and vibrant. It was the more important that he do this because, as a war leader, he now found himself obliged by the necessity for victory to pursue stern policies that he had criticized when he had been neutral, measures such as a bill extending the age limits of the manpower draft, an amendment to the espionage act that gave the government absolute powers, and the adoption of British strictures on neutrals in regard to contraband and trading with the enemy.

[14] Polk reported his conversation with the Japanese ambassador to the President thus: "I asked him two or three times whether it was his understanding that the Japanese forces would be limited to ten or twelve thousand men, and he said that . . . he felt there was no question on that point." Polk reported that the ambassador said that Japan had no intention of sending more men than were needed to assist the Czechs.

On July 4, when the United States had more than a million men overseas and they were helping to turn back the crest of a German wave, he reopened the moral battle that he had waged months earlier without immediate gain. On this day on which his people celebrated their own emancipation he reinforced the appeal to humanity that he had made in his epochal addresses of January and February.

Often Woodrow Wilson required an impresario to cast him in a compelling role. The spur for the Fourth-of-July address came from George Creel. The Committee on Public Information decided to celebate the holiday by asking every foreign-language group in the country to take part in a pilgrimage to Mount Vernon, and Creel begged the President to be the speaker of the occasion.

At first Wilson shrank from the idea as if it were grossly improper. "At the grave of Washington on the Fourth of July!" he exclaimed. "Why, my dear fellow, I would be crushed under a weight of presumption." It was a week before he surrendered, Creel tells us, but then he entered into the affair with enthusiasm and invited the foreign-language delegates to go downriver with him on the *Mayflower*. Waves of heat were shimmering over the Potomac; and Wilson, noticing the discomfort of guests who wore dress clothes, insisted that everyone "peel off the funeral wrappings." He set an example by taking off his own coat. Happy and laughing, he looked upon this cosmopolitan gathering as a living demonstration of the possibility of a league of nations.

The President's yacht anchored in midstream, the company went ashore and climbed the slope, and the prophet took his place beside the tomb. He said:

It is significant . . . that Washington and his associates . . . spoke and acted, not for a class, but for a people. It has been left to us to see to it that it shall be understood that they spoke and acted, not for a single people only, but for all mankind. . . . These are the ends for which the associated peoples of the world are fighting and which must be conceded them before there can be peace:

I. The destruction of every arbitrary power anywhere that can separately, secretly, and of its single choice disturb the peace of the world; or, if it cannot presently be destroyed, at least its reduction to virtual impotence.

II. The settlement of every question, whether of territory, of sovereignty, of economic arrangement, or of political relationship, upon the basis of the free acceptance of that settlement by the people immediately concerned, and not upon the basis of the material interest or advantage of any other nation or people which may desire a different settlement for the sake of its own exterior influence or mastery.

III. The consent of all nations to be governed in their conduct towards each other by the same principles of honor and of respect for the common law of civilized society that govern the individual citizens of all modern states in their relations with one another; to the end that all promises and covenants may be sacredly observed, no private plots or conspiracies hatched, no selfish injuries wrought with impunity, and a mutual trust established upon the handsome foundation of a mutual respect for right.

IV. The establishment of an organization of peace which shall make it certain that the combined power of free nations will check every invasion of right and serve to make peace and justice the more secure by affording a definite tribunal of opinion to which all must submit and by which every international readjustment that cannot be amicably agreed upon by the peoples directly concerned shall be sanctioned.

These great objects can be put into a single sentence. What we seek is the reign of law, based upon the consent of the governed and sustained by the organized opinion of mankind.

Again Anglo-Saxon liberals took heart. The American prophet could feel now that he stood pre-eminent before the peoples of the world as their champion in the human cause that he sensed to be the greatest of the century. The age was indeed writing its "political autobiography" through him.

But on the day after the speech at Mount Vernon a report from abroad revealed that Lloyd George had laughed at the proposed league and Clemenceau had sneered at it.

The prophet received this news with eyes unblinking and flashing. "Yes," he said, "I know that Europe is still governed by the same reactionary forces which controlled this country until a few years ago. But I am satisfied that if necessary I can reach the people of Europe over the heads of their rulers."

CHAPTER X

BUILDING FOR A WILSONIAN PEACE

IN THE SPRING OF 1918, while the warmaking agencies at Washington were being strengthened by centralization of authority, the President was embarrassed by the strong ego of a lieutenant very close to him. McAdoo, who wished to drive down the price that his railroads had to pay for coal, seemed to the fuel administration to be "butting in." Ill with tonsillitis and frustrated because his own conscience was overruled by his father-in-law's sense of right, he asked Colonel House whether he could hope to enforce his will by threatening to resign.

When the Colonel warned Wilson that McAdoo might resign over the issue of the price of coal, the President replied: "He may resign if he wants to, but I am determined that he shall not have his way because he is wrong in this instance." Complaining that his son-in-law had drawn up revenue bills and other important papers without consulting him, he felt that McAdoo had grown too arbitrary, that sooner or later their relationship must come to a crisis. "Son-in-law or no son-in-law," he declared, "if he wants to resign he can do so. The country will probably blame me, but I am ready to stand it." He feared that the people would think that he had turned McAdoo out because he himself was ambitious for a third term in the White House and regarded his son-in-law as a rival.

The Colonel, understanding and sympathizing with the complex emotions of kinship, public duty, and ambition that intertwined in the hearts of these Scots, brought about a reconciliation with the aid of Dr. Grayson. McAdoo satisfied his conscience by airing his views in an eleven-page letter to the President, without a suggestion of resignation. He then conferred with his father-in-law thrice during the next two days; and on May 24 the controversy over the coal price was settled and the railroads were required to pay the government rate.

House was active also in healing fissures in executive-legislative understanding. More cautious than ever about volunteering counsel that might be offensive, he never allowed himself to appear perturbed when his friend ignored him or differed with him, never complained if Wilson forgot to give him a share of credit for what they achieved together. In conversation with an English journalist, the Colonel confessed his method: "Never begin by arguing. Discover a common hate,

exploit it, get the President warmed up, and then start your business."
Fearing that a book published under the title *The Real Colonel House*
was too complimentary, he confessed to Wilson that he felt like soap
being advertised. His friend replied: "I have known in reading certain
passages that you would squirm. . . . We just have to grin and bear it."

If the President sensed that House was sometimes disingenuous, he
did not let this perception outweigh his appreciation of the Colonel's
good intentions and effectiveness. But it was not so easy as it had been
for the counselor to hold the confidence of the man through whom he
hoped to make his mark in history. Often Edith Wilson was present
when they met, and the tactics to which the President was responsive
were not equally appealing to her. Nevertheless, she sent House a confidential report on her husband's attitude toward McAdoo and assured
him that, though some people got on her nerves, it was always fun to
talk to someone as understanding as the Colonel. "Please remember we
need and want you always," she wrote to House on May 6.[1]

In mid-May the Wilsons and the Houses dined together at the
Waldorf Hotel, with no one else present but Dr. Grayson. It seemed to
the Colonel that the President talked most indiscreetly in the presence
of waiters. After the meal, when Wilson complained of acute indigestion, House urged him to get some rest by visiting at Magnolia during
the summer. The President promised to do this.

On August 14 the Wilsons arrived by special train at the North Shore
resort. The President showed a desire to be with his friend as much as
possible, and suggested that Mrs. Wilson chat with Mrs. House in the
evenings. Some of those present thought that his wife resented this
separation. She did not seem happy, either, when House ventured to
advise her that her husband did not delegate enough of his work, and
she protested that when it had been delegated it had not been done well.

Early in this summer of 1918 the enemies of Germany, striking back
from the verge of disaster, had been gaining on the battlefield. But at
last, under the impact of a threat to survival, the Western democracies
conferred upon capable men the authority that was required to check
the military machine of the Kaiser. Under Lloyd George and Clemenceau, divisive interests in Britain and France were channeled to the
common cause of victory. Ferdinand Foch directed the smashing of the

[1] Mrs. Wilson's own recollection of her feelings toward Colonel House at this time, as set
forth in *My Memoir*, pp. 155 and 237, does not agree with the documentary evidence. Either
her memory was faulty or, deferring to her husband, she did not reveal her true feeling to
House in 1918. In her book she testifies that as early as January of 1918 she thought the
Colonel a trimmer who changed his mind too quickly and that she questioned his ability as
an adviser.

last great German drive and took an initiative that he was never to relinquish. In the spearhead of his counterattack he used the fresh vigor of two American divisions. The United States had sent more than a million men across the Atlantic, and their generals were injecting a spirit of enterprise and selfless service into the councils of weary and cynical commanders.

In August it seemed that the military situation had improved enough so that a peace conference was not too remote for serious contemplation. A month earlier Wilson had felt that at last the time had come to put on paper the ideas for organizing the world for peace that he had repeatedly presented in general terms; and now he had with him a constitution for a league of nations that House had drafted at his request and had called a "Covenant"—to appeal to his friend's Scottish nature.

The President could not forget what he had taught his students: that the political constitution that had best withstood the buffets of fortune had been one that grew out of custom—that of England. He thought that, if the executive council of a world league commended itself to the public opinion of the world, it would get authority as it needed it. He still held the view that he had set before House in a letter of March 22, 1918:

My own conviction, as you know, is that the administrative *constitution* of the league must *grow* and not be made; that we must *begin* with solemn covenants, covering mutual guarantees of political independence and territorial integrity (if the final territorial agreements of the peace conference are fair and satisfactory and *ought* to be perpetuated), but that the method of carrying those mutual pledges out should be left to develop of itself, case by case, Any attempt to begin by putting executive authority in the hands of any particular group of powers would be to sow a harvest of jealousy and distrust which would spring up at once and choke the whole thing. To take one thing, and only one, but quite sufficient in itself: the United States Senate would never ratify any treaty which put the force of the United States at the disposal of any such group or body. Why begin at the impossible end when there is a possible end and it is feasible to plant a system which will slowly ripen into fruition?[2]

[2] On Sept. 3, 1917, Lord Robert Cecil had written to House to suggest that able men in Britain and America begin to consider peace machinery for the postwar world. He had warned against the danger of setting up another "Holy Alliance," which at its beginning, he said, was actually a "League to Enforce Peace." House had taken this letter to Wilson, and the President had suggested that the scholars of The Inquiry follow Cecil's suggestion. He dreaded premature discussion of a league of nations constitution by reformers whom he characterized as "woolgatherers."

House consulted many oracles—foreign as well as American, Republican as well as Democratic. After preparing his draft of a covenant, he had checked it with plans drawn up by a French government committee under the chairmanship of Léon Bourgeois and also with a constitution drafted by a committee of British experts under Lord Phillimore. He adopted several articles from the latter. Notified by Cecil that the British government proposed to

When the friends conferred at Magnolia, Wilson took the Colonel aside one morning and criticized the draft covenant that House had prepared. To put the author of the document in good humor, he told of once writing a platform for the Indiana Democratic Convention and receiving this comment: "We put it through just as you wrote it except we cut your six pages down to three." In comparison, the treatment that he had given to the Colonel's masterpiece seemed gentle. He had merely eliminated five of the twenty-three articles and rephrased some of the remaining text. Provisions that he struck out called for an international court and the use of national courts by members of the league.

As the friends talked at the seaside they had before them a long, scholarly letter from Elihu Root, who agreed with House and disagreed with Wilson, in thinking that legal institutions should be set up to which members of an international league could be directed to submit their differences for "consideration." Root raised a perplexity that had beset the President already. To what extent would the people of the United States stand back of world government? Would they agree to go to war at the command of a supranational organization? "Nothing can be worse in international affairs than to make agreements and break them," Root cautioned. Yet, in revising the Colonel's draft of a covenant, Wilson boldly strengthened the sanctions against offending nations by providing for the use of military force in addition to economic measures that House had proposed.

He differed, too, with the Colonel's reluctance to give small states an equal share with the large in a league of nations. To fail to insist on such a policy would contradict all his protestations, Wilson asserted, deeply concerned. To this criticism House tactfully replied that he believed in his friend's ideal, but had practical reservations: the little nations, voting as a majority, might overrule the few large nations that would bear the burdens of policing the world.

Protecting his views cannily from both journalists and politicians who might exploit them for selfish purposes, Wilson treasured the draft that was discussed at Magnolia, and later took it to Paris and used it as the basis of the final Covenant of the League of Nations.

Carrying out the President's wishes, House and Wiseman drafted a message to London that explained Wilson's views in detail. Not only did they inform the British government of his desire to postpone discussion of the nature of the league that might be set up to preserve peace; but in a separate cable they reported the President's adverse reaction to

---

publish the Phillimore report but first would welcome American views, the Colonel had warned Wilson that Britain and France might seize postwar leadership from America by publicly making a proposal around which opinion would crystallize.

the ambition of British and French citizens to divide the spoils of war and monopolize postwar trade.[3]

Six days after this cable was sent the Colonel recorded in his diary: "Both Sir William and I scent trouble between our governments and it will take considerable vigilance to ward it off. I think the main trouble comes from Lloyd George's inability to act in any but a thoroughly selfish way—a way, indeed, which approaches discourtesy . . . Both he and Clemenceau dislike the President and the President dislikes them. . . ." In September a letter from Lord Robert Cecil warned Wilson that the establishment of a league of nations would be opposed by the bureaucracies of Europe, who were past masters of threats and obstruction and resistance, by the militarists, of whom there were many outside Germany, and by people who thought that the Germans would join and make use of the league, "lulling us and others to sleep, and then falling on us when we have disarmed."

Old World statesmen were not ready to jettison the policy of preserving peace by balancing powers; for, after all, Europe had been free of major wars for almost half a century before the system had broken down in 1914. Traditionalists were skeptical of the prophet who was rising like a young Lochinvar in the West. To be sure, he had to be respected as leader of a nation that was swinging the military tide against Germany and that now possessed the most powerful economic force on earth. His words were glamorous and made hearts beat faster. But might not his prescription of a concert of powers take the world back to the war-breeding system of the Congress of Vienna? It was no easy task to achieve what Colonel House set down in his diary to be the prime essential to the creation of a league of nations—"get Great Britain and France committed first."

On August 14 the German General Staff confessed to their Kaiser that the Fatherland's hope of crushing victory must be abandoned; and with this prospect removed, the Austrians were theatening to sue for peace. Civilian morale in Germany drooped, so undermining the spirit

---

[3] The message, signed by Wiseman, said: "The President thinks we ought to adopt the line that we have no desire to deny Germany her fair share of the world's commerce, and that it is her own militarists who are ruining her trade by prolonging the war and obliging us to maintain a blockade. . . . For your own private information, I may tell you that the President will try to get Congress to give powers to the Executive to control American raw-material exports for a period of years after peace. While this would not be openly aimed at Germany, it would be a formidable weapon for the United States to bring to the Peace Conference."

While protesting against the British government's inclination to discriminate in favor of her own merchants—in a letter to Lansing on Aug. 29 he had asked that Britain be urged to reciprocate American policy of allowing the Allies to make purchases in the United States on the same terms as those applied to the American government and civilians—Wilson warned Hurley to make no plan for postwar shipping that might be taken to mean "that we, like the English, are planning to dominate everything and to oust everybody we can oust."

of the Army that by September 10 General Hindenburg thought the need for negotiation was "immediate."

Wilson continued to avoid argument that might threaten the unanimity of efforts to win the war. By the middle of the month, however, American troops were completing the pinching out of the St. Mihiel salient. Bulgars and Germans fled headlong north of Salonika. On the 16th an Austro-Hungarian note, reaching Washington through Swedish channels, proposed a "confidential non-binding conversation" on peace terms, to be held on neutral soil.

Wilson rejected the Austrian offer immediately and bluntly. "The United States," he declared, "will entertain no proposal for a conference upon a matter concerning which it has made its position and purpose so plain." His reply was approved heartily by the Congress. And his faith in democratic public opinion was stiffened when, on September 19, an inter-Allied labor conference unanimously endorsed his Fourteen Points as a basis for peace.

Further to strengthen the unity of his own people, and to sway the Allied governments to his kind of peace, he carefully wrote out a new pronouncement of his war aims. Calling House to Washington for a weekend visit, he said that he had decided to speak out publicly, rather than undertake secret negotiations with London as the Colonel had recommended.

The text of this address settled, the talk of the friends strayed to other subjects: world sentiment for an association of nations and the French concept of the ideal league, which Wilson now saw for the first time as House set it before him; a new stamp for imprinting "Woodrow Wilson" on the flyleaf of books, a device of which the President seemed as proud as he had once been of the ornate signatures that he had inscribed in the books of his boyhood. The Colonel found his friend pensive about his place in history, conscious that his fame depended largely on the result of the war.

The *éminence grise* put in a word for his own profession. When Wilson spoke of criticisms of George Washington, House repeated an opinion that he had expressed before, that Washington's greatness grew from his ability to know good advice from bad. This was a virtue that the Colonel did not attribute to the President. It seemed to House that in rejecting the Austrian peace overture, out of hand, the President had offended against the spirit of team play that he preached. The Colonel sometimes grew restive under his responsibilities, a little resentful of the exacting will of his master and of his secretiveness.

That evening at dinner the President was reminded again of his dependence on good counsel. Edith Wilson's sister told House of the compliments that she had heard paid to him. "You are a maker of men," she said to the Colonel.

The "made" man at the head of the table took the remark with a wry smile. "He ought to change his pattern," the President jested.

On September 27 Wilson went to New York to deliver the speech that he had prepared. On the train he explained to Tumulty that the time had come to proclaim America's opposition to a backsliding peace, a reversion to the old days of alliances, competing armaments, and land-grabbing. Reading his address at the Metropolitan Opera House before five thousand sellers of war bonds, he devoted only a few sentences to the finance drive and then went on to strike another strong blow for his peace aims.

Plainly the Allies could not "come to terms" with the Central Empires, he said; there could be no peace obtained by any kind of bargain or compromise with governments that were without honor and a standard of justice. His audience, fearful above all that America might be caught in a "peace-trap," understood this and applauded. But as the prophet lifted his thought from the jungle toward Heaven, the blood of the bond sellers responded less warmly. The price that must be paid for genuine peace, he insisted, was "impartial justice in every item of the settlement, no matter whose interest is crossed; and not only impartial justice, but also the satisfaction of the several peoples whose fortunes are dealt with."

Here Wilson's thinking ran into a fundamental dichotomy that was to rend him apart and prostrate him before the making of peace was achieved. Devotion to "justice" was nothing new among peacemakers. The delegates to the Congress of Vienna had professed it a century before. But nineteenth-century diplomats had been accustomed to accept the concepts of justice that grew out of their own nation's "sacred egoism" and special interests; and sitting down with the statesmen of other nations who took an equally practical view, they had tried to work out a reconciliation of purposes that they recognized to be conflicting.

At the end of this war, however, Wilson conceived that the United States had no selfish interests except those that she shared with all civilized nations—to prevent a recrudescence of chauvinistic despotism, trade wars, and other phenomena that might disturb the peace. Therefore, the prophet sensed a rare opportunity to build a great rainbow arch of what he called "impartial" justice far above the limited concepts of justice that were worshiped in the temples of the nations. He said: "No special or separate interest of any single nation or any group of nations can be made the basis of any part of the settlement which is not consistent with the common interest of all." National interests would be expendable for the good of all humanity. If only he could make the peoples see that all would be better off if each would sacrifice something! His sympathies forked out toward mankind where he found them, and at the same time to the exalted New Jerusalem to which he wished to lift them. He was expressing at once the palliative instincts of an Irish heart and the prophetic impulses of a Scottish soul.

A paralyzing fission was prevented by faith in an ideal plan of action. If he could set in motion a force that might in time lift all mankind to an estate a little below the angels, the motives that surged within him would be no longer irreconcilable. And so, after promising "impartial justice" and then "the satisfaction of the several peoples," he went on immediately to say: "[The] indispensable instrumentality is a League of Nations formed under Covenants that will be efficacious . . . And as I see it, the constitution of that League of Nations and the clear definition of its objects must be a part, is in a sense the most essential part, of the peace settlement itself." Within the league there were to be no "special covenants and understandings," economic or political; for such things, he was convinced, were "the prolific source in the modern world of the plans and passions that produce war."

Having put forth his platform for the peacemaking, Wilson then challenged the leaders of the Allies to "speak as they have occasion" as plainly as he had tried to speak. He invited them to criticize both his interpretation of the issues and the means that he recommended for settling them. He was giving them due notice of what they might expect from him at a peace conference.

After the address at the Opera House, still flushed with the fervor of his pleading, the President went to his hotel sitting room with the Colonel and speculated on the effect of the speech. The next day, returning to Washington in his private car and resting his mind by holding a skein of yarn for Edith Wilson to wind, he learned that the reactions of the American press were those of the five thousand who had heard him. Applauding his firmness toward the enemy and approving his general intent, they seemed to ignore his challenge to constructive peacemaking. To be sure, certain liberals at home and abroad endorsed the President's views: from England, Lord Grey cabled congratulations and Lord Robert Cecil called the speech "the finest description of our war aims yet uttered." But Clemenceau and Lloyd George were unconvinced.

Meanwhile events in Europe were speeding the approach of peacemaking. On the very day on which Wilson spoke out, General Bliss was writing to General Pershing: "It looks as if you are going to get the damned Germans out of France this year." Two days later Bulgaria, on whom the United States had never declared war, stopped fighting. The next day Allenby's British army took Damascus and Turkey was in an agony of collapse.

From Berlin, where already there had been efforts toward mediation by a neutral, the President's speech drew a positive response. On September 30 the Kaiser granted parliamentary government to his people; and on the same day General Ludendorff concluded that a proposal of peace should be sent forthwith to Washington through Switzerland, that the Army could not wait forty-eight hours longer for a move that would save it from disaster.

Prince Max of Baden, becoming chancellor on October 4 with an endorsement from the Reichstag, wished to delay. He sensed that the Army was trying to shift the onus for defeat to civilian shoulders. However, pressed by Hindenburg, he sent a note to Washington asking the President to take steps for the restoration of peace, to notify all belligerents of this request, and to invite them to send delegates to begin negotiations. Accepting the program laid down by the President, the Germans asked that further bloodshed be avoided by the immediate conclusion of a general armistice.

News of the coming of the German note reached Woodrow Wilson on Sunday, October 6. It was a day of uncommon quiet in Washington. While a lethal epidemic of influenza raged through the city and kept people from congregating in churches, dispatches from France reported the bitterest fighting in which Americans had taken part. As had been his habit since he had proclaimed the observance of "gasless Sundays," the President went riding in an old surrey with fringed top, drawn by a pair of bay horses and escorted by secret service men on bicycles. The German message dropped like a bomb into the doldrums in the capital.

The military leaders of the Allies, not daring to expect an end of hostilities before 1919, still were calling for men and munitions. Moreover, General March was insisting that shipments of troops proceed on schedule despite the urging of medical men that no more soldiers be sent to France until the influenza epidemic was checked. Pressed by March for assent to his plans at the very time when the enemy were asking for peace, the President turned in his chair and gazed through the window in a way that had become habitual. He found relief, as he made the life-and-death decisions that were required of him, in watching the antics of the birds and the squirrels outside. On this occasion, after a moment of relaxation, he sighed faintly and gave March a slow nod that might add hundreds of deaths by disease to America's lengthening casualty list.

Though Wilson was not ready to take the risk of curtailing military plans for a continuing war, he nevertheless took the German overture with the deepest seriousness. It was clear now that at last his gospel was penetrating the minds of the German people; and he did not feel it necessary to inquire too closely whether they were converted, or merely seeking a convenient sanctuary. He telephoned immediately to House and asked for advice. Responding with both a telegram and a letter, the Colonel recommended that the President make no direct reply to the German note. It seemed to House that the Allies should share the responsibility of replying to the enemy's overture.

The next day Wilson wrote a trial draft of a reply; and in the evening, going to his study as the clock was striking nine, he read from his script to House and Lansing.[4] The Colonel objected that the nation would think Wilson's tone too mild, that stronger guarantees were needed to assure acceptance of the President's terms by his own people, who had become "war-mad."

The President did not leave his study until after midnight; and the next morning he gave up his game of golf and again went into conference with the Colonel, each opening his mind to the point of view of the other. House reported opinions from European liberals that went along with the President's thought; and Wilson in turn read from bloodthirsty speeches that had just been delivered in the Senate. Their minds met finally on a version that satisfied neither, completely. Finally, suffering under the realization that thousands of lives hung upon their words, they allowed the text to be released as "not a reply, but an inquiry" into Germany's true intentions.

Would the Germans agree to base negotiations on the principles already set forth by the President? the message asked. Would they consent immediately to withdraw their forces everywhere from invaded territory? Was the chancellor speaking "merely for the constituted authorities of the Empire who have so far conducted the war"? The last of the three questions were an unheard-of intrusion into Germany's domestic politics and was resented as such.

In spite of the firm tone that House had injected into the note, the three queries did not satisfy the war-weathered premiers of the Allies. Conferring at Versailles on October 9, they addressed themselves to the President, recognizing the "elevated sentiments" that had inspired his reply to Germany but drawing his attention to the importance of basing conditions of armistice on the advice of the military men at Versailles.

---

[4] There is no evidence that Lansing played a part in shaping policy at this juncture. House's diary (Sept. 27, 1918) contains this note: "He [Wilson] remarked that Lansing was so stupid that he was constantly afraid that he would commit some serious blunder. I could not but confess that he was stupid. He seems less alert than when he first became secretary of state, and I wonder whether his health has not made this difference."

Lloyd George intimated that he would like a definition of the phrase "freedom of the seas"; and the President was asked to send a representative to Paris to explain the policy of the United States. Foch expressed to Pershing the fear that the President might get himself involved in a long correspondence and be duped.

Though there was no public display of pique by the Allied leaders, though the press by and large commended the President's note of inquiry, an undercurrent of feeling convinced American diplomats that French pride had been hurt by the addressing of the first German message directly to Washington. When a report of this reached the White House, however, it found Wilson perplexed over what General March denounced to him as the "astounding proceedings" of the premiers in suggesting conditions for an armistice. Realizing that immediate discussions with vindictive Allied generals might shake the confidence of the German people in his avowed purpose of making a just peace, Wilson resented any voice that might put the enemy in fear of extermination and give them the courage of despair.[5]

The peoples of Western Europe were appreciative of Wilson's efforts. Reports to the State Department told of peace demonstrations in Italian cities and strong sentiment for peace at Paris and among English laborers. It was a delicate game of psychological warfare that the President was playing, in his effort to bring peace before exhaustion exposed Europe to the virus of anarchy. The prophet again had "heaped all his winnings" on a single toss, against the advice of his most trusted counselor and without consulting his allies. He had risked a hard-won military ascendancy upon the promptings of his own intuitive sense of public opinion in Germany. Actually he thought his note of inquiry "dangerous," in view of the uncertainty of conditions in Central Europe.

Having placed his bet, Wilson could only let the wheel of German politics spin. Going to New York for Columbus Day, he marched for almost seventy blocks at the head of a parade, smiling broadly and doffing his tall hat frequently. He passed shop windows filled with paintings of German atrocities; and downtown, mounted police were carrying bedraggled effigies of the Kaiser.

Attending a benefit performance at the Metropolitan Opera House, in the evening, he learned that his number had come up. Word was brought that Germany had replied favorably to the three questions in his "inquiry." At his hotel that night he asked Tumulty to come to his

[5] On the evening of Oct. 10, Ambassador Jusserand delivered the premiers' note of Oct. 9 to the President and left the White House with the feeling that the misunderstanding had been cleared up. Later, however, House found that Wilson still failed to understand that the premiers were not attempting to dictate, as March had suggested, but only to propose a conference. Polk Diary, Oct. 11, 1918.

rooms and assured him that—as he was accustomed to say in considering the gravest problems of state—his mind was "open and to let" on the question of the next step toward peace. The ebullient Irishman gave him a sample of public feeling, vehemently denouncing traffic with "the Kaiser and his brood." It was two o'clock before the secretary had talked himself out; and the next day, traveling to Washington, the President had what he called another "dose of Tumulty." It was a medicine that helped him to keep his ear close to grass roots, to hear what was being said in the ward clubs and the country stores of the land. This was the primitive emotion that he was striving to channel from hate to constructive ends.

Never in all their association had Tumulty been more fearful that "the Governor" would disregard political realities in his zeal for ultimate truth. He found Wilson obsessed with determination to do the right thing, convinced that it would be foolish to go on to Berlin at a cost that he set at a million lives, confident that the notes from Germany set forth, by and large, the will of the people, regardless of the repute of the government that had written them. When Tumulty reminded him that he would disappoint his own people if he accepted less than unconditional surrender, Wilson recalled that John Jay had been burned in effigy and Hamilton stoned for defending Jay's treaty with Great Britain. "If I think it is right to accept the German note," Wilson insisted, "I shall do so regardless of consequences. As for myself, I can go down in a cyclone cellar and write poetry the rest of my days, if necessary."

Late on October 14th, the second note to Germany was made public. It bore down so hard upon the enemy that press comment was favorable and Senator Lodge expressed himself as "genuinely pleased." Before armistice terms could be discussed, the President wrote, atrocities must cease on land and sea, and the Allies and Americans must know with what sort of government they were dealing. Moreover, the military supremacy of the armies opposing Germany must be safeguarded absolutely. Bulletins went out from the White House emphasizing that there would be no letup in the military effort of the United States.

The prospect of peace was clear enough now so that it seemed time to try to reach an understanding with the Allied statesmen. General Bliss had reported that his English colleagues on the Supreme War Council had been advocating that the Allies agree on peace policies while they were still held together by military necessity.

From his friend House counsel came more soothingly. The Colonel had never seen "the Governor" more distraught than he was after breakfast on October 14. A maze of possibilities confronted him, Wilson said. If he went in at the right entrance, he would reach the heart of the matter, there would be no more note-writing, and the loss of human life would stop; but if he took a single false turn, he would have to begin all over again. Repeatedly he said that, if Germany was beaten, she would accept any terms; if she were not defeated, he did not wish to deal with her. He did not trust the sincerity of the German overtures, yet he felt that he must not give to the war-weary peoples of Europe any reason to feel that he was slamming a door against peace.

Giving the morning to the drafting of a tentative text, the President tried it out on his advisers in the afternoon. A senator reported that his colleagues were bewildered, and fearful that the President would commit the country to peace prematurely. Hurt by this lack of confidence, Wilson asked: "Do they think I am a damned fool?" He looked around at Lansing with the impish expression that he assumed when he made one of his occasional ventures in profanity; and the secretary of state was reminded of a little boy uttering his first "Gosh!" or a man learning to smoke with a cigarette holder.

Lansing spoke of expediency, suggesting that they keep in mind the coming Congressional elections. But Wilson and House already had heard too much from the pleaders for expediency; and the Colonel bristled a bit and asserted that they could not do their work "properly or worthily" if they thought of party politics.

Wilson therefore asked House to go to Europe at once, as the personal representative of the President for whom the Allied statesmen had asked. The Colonel had shied at the prospect of serving alongside the President as a delegate at the Peace Conference, as Wilson had suggested at Magnolia. He foresaw the risk that as equals in rank they might cease to be friends. But the place that was offered now was on the very summit of fame and alluring even to an ambition that, as the Colonel had himself confessed in 1916, was so great that it seemed futile to try to satisfy it. He had abjured officeholding because nothing short of the top position would satisfy him, and because he was not physically strong enough to fill such a post. Now he had the great chance of his lifetime—to go down in history as one of the illustrious statesmen of his century. And so he accepted the President's commission.

On the evening of the 14th, giving to his friend a letter of credence and a secret code-book, the President said as they parted: "I have not given you any instructions because I feel you will know what to do." There was no word of direction, advice, or discussion, no prescription of a program for peacemaking to be placed before the statesmen of the Allies.

The Colonel left for Paris on the 18th, and Wiseman went to London to serve his government as adviser on American affairs during the peacemaking. While they were on the high seas, the President fixed his mind on dealing with Austria-Hungary. A month earlier that empire had proposed discussion of a compromise peace and Wilson had replied tersely. In October the Hapsburg government tried again, suggesting this time that an armistice be concluded and peace negotiations begun on the basis of Wilson's principles.

This proposal had reached the White House on October 7. Ten days later it still lay on Wilson's desk, unanswered. Moreover, on October 14 he had a request from Turkey, against whom the United States had never declared war, asking that he take upon himself the task of re-establishing peace and invite all belligerents to appoint plenipotentiaries.[6] Wilson was intrigued by a vivid phrase from Senator John Sharp Williams, to whom he wrote on October 17: "Your idea about letting the populations of Germany, Austria-Hungary, and Turkey 'wobble on the gudgeon' has been in my own mind, and it has been partly for that reason that I have not replied to either the Austrian or the Turkish note yet. I shall presently have to do so, but the conditions of our dealing with Austria-Hungary have been radically altered by our recognition of the Czecho-Slovaks and our official encouragement of the national aspirations of the Jugo-Slavs."

For five months Thomas G. Masaryk, leader of the Czechoslovak nationalists, had been at Washington pleading the cause of the subject peoples of the Hapsburg Empire. This patriot-scholar had received recognition of his people as an Allied belligerent under the *de facto* government that he represented. Appealing to Wilson's political creed by quoting pertinent passages from one of the President's own books, Masaryk persuaded the President that the Hapsburgs were not merely the tools of the Hohenzollerns, but in their own right quite as wicked, and that protestations of reform that now came from Vienna under pressure of military collapse should be given little credence. In October this political adventurer drew up a Czechoslovak Declaration of Independence that was calculated to appeal to the pride that Americans took in their own Declaration.

No American felt more flattered than Woodrow Wilson at this emulation of a political gospel that he had honored all his life. When an

---

[6] Turkey accepted the principles of peace laid down by Wilson and asked an immediate armistice. The President intended to communicate this news to his allies and to urge them to hasten the collapse of Germany by making a separate peace with Turkey. But Lloyd George sent a hint that, since Turkey was about to collapse, it was necessary only to refer her to any Allied commander whom she might choose to approach. Word reached Washington on Oct. 22 that armistice discussions between Turkish and British representatives had been arranged, and on Oct. 30 an armistice was signed by Turkish delegates with a British general.

advance copy of the Czechoslovak document was given to him, he confessed to Masaryk that he was deeply moved, as would be seen when his reply to the Hapsburg Empire was published.

On October 19, the day after the publication of Masaryk's Declaration, Wilson sent off a message to Vienna that recalled that among the Fourteen Points was one that guaranteed to the peoples of the Hapsburg Empire "the freest opportunity for autonomous development." The President insisted that the liberated peoples, rather than an outside authority, should decide what the Hapsburg government must do to satisfy their aspirations. Wilson's verdict was received at Vienna as the death sentence of the old regime.

Meanwhile the German leaders were facing up to the clear and unpleasant choice that Wilson's second note put before them. Seeing no hope of stopping fresh armies that were advancing fast in Belgium and were poised to attack in Lorraine, the German ministers yielded to all of the President's conditions.

With the German capitulation in hand, Wilson was ready to take his Cabinet into his confidence. At their regular meeting on October 22 they found their chief plainly disturbed. For some weeks their sessions had been given over to storytelling and to trivial affairs. But now the President was all business, and said solemnly: "I do not know what to do. I must ask your advice. I may have made a mistake in not properly safeguarding what I said before. What do you think should be done?"

It was as if he had given to them a charge of pastoral responsibility. For a moment these ministers of state were as silent as praying elders. Then, one by one, they spoke. Their feelings ran with those of their fellow citizens; and they assured their leader that the people of the West, like the press of the East, were demanding drastic terms. It was agreed that armistice conditions should be dictated and not discussed, and that they be given only to a government that truly represented the German people. But when Secretary Lane declared that the Allies should not treat for peace "until Germany was across the Rhine," the President ventured to dissent.

Wilson felt that he must warn his men that threats to the world's future peace could now be expected from the Allies as well as from the enemy. The governments of Western Europe, the President explained, were "getting to a point where they were reaching out for more than they should have in justice." When it was objected that the publishing of peace notes without the consent of the Allies might seem to America's partners a form of coercion, Wilson replied that they needed to be coerced in the matter of peace aims and could attain their military objectives when they dictated armistice terms. He seemed fearful of bolshevism in Germany, but confident that a peace based on his Fourteen Points would do everything possible without crushing Germany and wiping her out—"everything except to gratify revenge."

After his war council was given a chance to make suggestions, the note went off to Germany almost as Wilson had drafted it. Copies of it and of the previous correspondence with Germany were transmitted to the Allies on the same day; and the President, having turned the negotions into the traditional channels, had only to await the outcome of events in Europe. Doubt crept into his mind. He clutched at words of moral support, uttered by men whom he trusted. To an old comrade who sent verses entitled "Fight and Hold Fast," he wrote: ". . . do you think, my dear fellow, that we are on the verge of yielding to the sort of hate which we are fighting in the Germans? I am beginning to be fearful lest we go too far to be in a mood to make an absolutely and rigorously impartial peace, and God knows the disposition to make a peace of that sort is growing less and less on the other side of the water." He was oppressed by a miasma of "unwholesome purposes" that seemed to be in the air at home and abroad.[7]

The first full breath of the acrid controversies of the Allies came to him in a cipher cable from House, who, reaching Paris on October 26, found the premiers inclined to shift responsibility for peace negotiations to the shoulders of the President, and at the same time frankly jealous of the role that he had assumed without consulting them. On the day of his arrival the Colonel received from Clemenceau, in deep secrecy, terms that Foch and his generals recommended for the Armistice. Taking the precious document to bed with him and posting a guard at the door, House tucked it under his pillow and the next day cabled its text to the President.

On the Sunday on which the armistice terms reached Wilson he already had before him a long report from Pershing that made seven recommendations about this matter. The coming of House perplexed the American military men. They were not sure that he had full authority to represent the President; nor did they have instruction regarding their own proper part in the deliberation on an armistice in the Supreme War Council.[8]

[7] Republican reaction is described by Alice Roosevelt Longworth in *Crowded Hours,* p. 273: "His note of the twenty-third we all at first professed to think good, but after a second reading we found flaws; we never failed to find them. We were ingenious in our criticisms—when it was not of content it was of presentation. 'Deliberately involved,' we would say ominously."

[8] Foch felt that the terms agreed upon were as severe as any that might have been imposed if Berlin were taken, and feared that if the conditions were hardened, Germany would not sign and would retreat to a strong position, and French opinion would be outraged by prolongation of the war. He complained to Clemenceau that it was "like going against granite" to get Pershing to accept advice.

General Bliss, who insisted that humane feeling required that an armistice be granted just

Encouraged by Wilson to take to House any consideration that might have been overlooked, Pershing handed to the Colonel, at their first meeting on October 30, a letter advocating a dictated peace and the winning of a complete victory through unconditional surrender.

House showed this paper to his colleagues, and they bristled. "Theatrical!" said Clemenceau. And Lloyd George: "Politics!" House let the general know that the statesmen favored granting an armistice, which they thought a political matter; and Wilson advised Secretary Baker not to send a proposed letter of reproof to Pershing, but to leave the matter in House's hands. Otherwise, he explained, the Colonel might be embarrassed.

In the meantime the President had under consideration a note from Austria-Hungary that claimed that all of the American conditions had been accepted and urged that Wilson take steps to bring about an armistice immediately. This appeal was laid before the Cabinet on October 29. The Hapsburg Empire, which the President had been content to let "wobble on the gudgeon," was breaking up so rapidly that Wilson hardly knew to whom he should reply. On the very next day Austria-Hungary made a military surrender to Italy. Terms were drafted at Versailles very swiftly—conditions so severe that Clemenceau remarked: "We have left the breeches of the Emperor, and nothing else." On November 3 Vienna accepted what was offered. Thus the matter was taken out of Wilson's hands and Austria-Hungary could come to the peace table without definite commitment to the President's principles.

At Berlin militarists now had lost the confidence of the civil government; Ludendorff had been dismissed; liberal amendments to the German constitution had been adopted by the Reichstag; and on October 27 the German government had reported to Washington that the people were in control of the nation, actually and constitutionally. Public opinion was responding to the threat in Wilson's last note that, if the United States must deal with "monarchical autocrats," it must demand not negotiations, but surrender. There were suggestions that the Kaiser resign. German leaders were telling their people that civil violence would play into the hands of vindictive Allied statesmen and make it difficult for Wilson to effect a humane peace.

Now that the time had come for each nation to demand its pound of flesh, Wilson and House thought it their duty to hold the Philistines to

---

as soon as complete victory was assured, felt that if complete disarmament and demobilization were accomplished, no other armistice terms would be necessary. He was not supported in this view by Pershing.

Cabling to Pershing on Oct. 27, the President approved all of his seven recommendations except those calling for occupation of Alsace-Lorraine, the east bank of the Rhine, and German submarine bases. This, he felt, would be an unjustified invasion of the enemy's land.

the law of the prophet. The President had pledged to "make the world safe for democracy"; and the United States could not afford to risk the danger of having to undertake another military crusade. This must be a peace that would breed no lust for revenge, a "peace without victory," one that would impose Wilsonian principles on the enemy without humiliating him. Woodrow Wilson had not forgotten the visitation of utter hopelessness that he had known as a boy in war-ravaged Columbia; House remembered post-Civil War days in Houston. The President might even have to become the advocate of the Germans "against American Prussianism," he said to Daniels. "We must never do the things that we condemn."

From the very beginning of his negotiations at Paris, House asked for endorsement of the President's principles. Wishing to offer a definite program to European statesmen who thought Wilson a visionary without capacity for decision, the Colonel seized upon the only specific statement of peace terms that the President had made—the Fourteen Points, which had been formulated as propaganda to influence public opinion in Germany and Russia rather than a scientific basis for peace. Men of The Inquiry who already were questioning the viability of some of Wilson's Points—particularly the doctrine of self-determination—were now asked by House to prepare an interpretive commentary of the American doctrine. They did so, and the Colonel set it before the leaders of the Allies and at the same time its text was cabled to the President. On the very next day Wilson replied. The document was "a satisfactory interpretation of the principles involved," he cabled, "though the details specified could be regarded only as suggestions, subject to further consideration at the Peace Conference." The next day the President made it clear to his agent that he considered Points I, II, III, and XIV to be "the essentially American terms in the programme."

One by one, the European premiers gave voice to their doubts and set forth national interests in the time-honored manner. Journalists at Paris and London sensed that the only definite policy of the Allies, individually and collectively, was to take control of peace negotiations out of the hands of President Wilson. The politicians, they reported, were showing "Junker tendencies," but the masses supported Wilson so overwhelmingly that the leaders dared not oppose him openly.

To the prophet in the White House, the fractious Europeans were like the Southern Secessionists whom he had set down as "legally right" but "historically wrong." They must be mastered and made to acknowledge the voice of the Lord as it spoke to free consciences that were consecrated to the common good. Philistines and Pharisees were always the same to a minister of a congregation, whether at Princeton, at Trenton, at Washington, or at Paris. They were heathen to be converted—by persuasion if possible; by force of public opinion if necessary.

Fortunately, in the greatest of all of Wilson's crusades for the common good he had an ideal ruling elder, a man loyal to gospel and yet one who knew how to fight Satan with his own wiles. Colonel House had learned the political language of the Allies and had found it not much different from that of his old friends in Texas. He made it his business, before going into conference at Versailles, to know exactly what each man was thinking and what he would say. Distilling the essential points into as few words as possible, he spoke scarcely above a whisper—"down where I come from," he explained, "if a man doesn't speak soft he may never speak again. . . ."

In so far as he could, House used persuasion and a frank appeal to national interests to achieve his ends. When the President cabled, menacingly, that, if the Allied statesmen intended to nullify his influence, the Colonel should "force the purpose boldly to the surface" and let him speak of it to all the world, House realized that if he read this intemperate message to his colleagues it might lead to serious trouble. He replied to his fervent friend thus: "I hope you will not insist upon my using your cable except as I may think best. If you will give me a free hand in dealing with these immediate negotiations, I can assure you that nothing will be done to embarrass you or to compromise any of your peace principles." Wilson replied on October 31 that he could not recede from his principles, but that he depended on House "to insist at the right time and in the right way."

And so the Colonel went about making personal friends, soothing suspicions, persuading Lloyd George that it was not America's intent to forbid naval blockade under certain conditions, explaining the strength of sentiment in the United States for revision of maritime law, arguing that reservations proposed by Italy impinged upon the Fourteen Points, enlisting the support of Lord Northcliffe's press for Wilson's principles, and encouraging Wiseman to stand up to Lloyd George when the Welshman tried to play a lone hand. Shrewdly this Texan statesman-elder sensed currents of jealousy and ambition that ran among the Allies. He appreciated the strength of what had been cabled to him by the President: "England cannot dispense with our friendship in the future and the other Allies cannot without our assistance get their rights as against England." House was alert also to the motives that prompted the tactics of the premiers. Reporting to the President that Lloyd George wished the United States to become trustee for German East Africa, the Colonel remarked that the British "would like to have us accept something so they might more freely take what they desire."

It soon became apparent, when House laid the Fourteen Points before the premiers for discussion, that diplomatic bargaining would not suffice to accomplish the President's purposes. Therefore, when Lloyd George opened the floodgates of reservation by attaching conditions to two of the Fourteen Points and Clemenceau was preparing to elaborate the objections of France, House decided that the time had come to make a stand, before Sonnino of Italy joined in a nullifying deluge and made the breach in the Wilsonian front irreparable. The Colonel resorted to a bluntness that he rarely exercised. He told his French friend that, if the Allies objected extensively to Wilsonian principles, he would advise the President to lay the facts before Congress and ask the American people whether they wished to fight on for such terms as the Allies were suggesting, or to make a separate peace with Germany.

The effect was magical. Delighted by House's reports of progress, the President cabled: "I am proud of the way you are handling things." [9]

The most perplexing difference of opinion, however—that between Britain and the United States regarding "freedom of the seas"—was still to be resolved. Because of Britain's alliance with Japan and the prospect that warships from the German Navy might be added to the British fleet, Americans feared that they would be at the mercy of an overwhelming naval force. A huge building program was under consideration in Congress, and the President authorized House to say that, if the Allies persisted in opposing "freedom of the seas" in principle, they could count upon the development of the strongest Navy that American resources permitted. Wilson felt that the problem of maritime blockade, so vexing during the years of America's neutrality, could be most satisfactorily solved by a league of nations that would eliminate all neutrals. He wished assurance against a repetition of the sort of blockade that the British had imposed in 1915. But to the average Englishman "freedom of the seas" meant an end to all blockades. Seeming not to realize that insular Britain was of all nations the most vulnerable to this form of attack, the English knew only that blockades of the Continent had helped them to win two great wars.

Seeing that the impasse could not be broken by threats and realizing that the British would not accept the President's position, nor the President the irrational attitude that had sprung from British pride and fears, House and Lloyd George finally faced realities and a formula for agree-

[9] Auchincloss, House's son-in-law and his secretary, wrote thus to Frank L. Polk on Nov. 19, 1918: "You have no idea how skillfully the Colonel conducted himself during the ten days of the negotiations . . . George and Clemenceau scrapped like wild cats at one meeting while we looked on and cheered inaudibly. . . . As usual the Colonel is the confidant of each of the Prime Ministers; each plays just as close to the Colonel as it suits his purpose at the time and go closer."

ment was found by Sir William Wiseman, who before leaving Washington had been told by Wilson that the latter had no desire to weaken British sea power and that the submarine had introduced a new element that must modify existing maritime law. At the Colonel's suggestion, the prime minister wrote a letter stating that the British were "quite willing to discuss the Freedom of the Seas in the light of the new conditions which have arisen in the course of the present war." Thus a basis was laid for the elimination of a bogie that had long haunted Anglo-American relations.

However, the naval terms did not please Admiral Benson, who felt that the German warships should be destroyed at once, and not added to the fleets of the victors. House relied implicitly on this officer. When the question was referred to Wilson, he felt that the naval terms proposed by the British were unduly severe. He struck out several conditions that appeared to cut German pride too deeply. It was enough, it was agreed, to require the enemy to surrender her submarines and submit most of her other vessels to internment. In leaving open the eventual disposition of these ships, the council handed down a thorny problem to the peace conference that was to come.

On another ground, also, seeds of future discord were allowed to fall and take root. Clemenceau insisted doggedly that his people would not accept armistice terms that did not specify "reparation for damages"; and to this the French minister of finance added a clause that reserved the right of the Allies to make financial claims in the future. Having concentrated his fire on getting recognition for Wilson's peace conditions, which covered the problem of reparations, House acceded to this demand, as a sop to French feelings.

The President did not challenge this French exception, nor did he resist the British reservation on "freedom of the seas." When House forwarded the conclusions of the council and outlined the action that the President was expected to take, Wilson proceeded accordingly. On November 5 he sent to the Germans the memoranda from Paris agreeing to accept his Fourteen Points as the basis for peace, with the two qualifications. At the same time the President wrote that Marshal Foch was authorized to receive German representatives and give them terms for an armistice. The next day the enemy delegates left Berlin, and on the 8th they were received by Foch on a train in the forest of Compiègne and given the actual military conditions. They had no defense, except to conjure up the specters of famine, anarchy, and bolshevism.

A mutiny of the German navy was spreading. Revolution broke out in Munich. On November 9 the abdication of the Kaiser was announced, red flags went up, and the next day a provisional government was proclaimed. The President's barrage of eloquence, beginning in May of 1916 and ending in September of 1918, had brought fighting to an end even before the armies of the enemy were completely broken; and not only the enemy but the Allies as well were committed to write such a peace as the world had never before known. The principles that the prophet had conceived first as a battle cry for his own people, and then as a softener of enemy morale, were now blithely accepted by Western liberals as omens of successful peacemaking. Germans depended on them for protection against vindictiveness; and Americans, by and large, were proud of them as something "made in America" that brought kudos to their President. Their shortcomings as a basis for a rational peace settlement were not yet generally apparent.

On the morning of November 7, responding to a false press report of the signing of the Armistice, throngs milled about in the streets of Washington. Bands blared and sirens cut loose. Nell McAdoo, crossing the street from the Treasury, was caught in a rush of dancing, singing citizens. Edith Wilson, loving the stir and good spirit of the people, begged the President to appear on the portico and, in the afternoon, to ride out into the streets. But he shook his head. "No," he said, "what a pity all this is going on, when it's not true." [10]

At breakfast on the 11th he got word of the end of hostilities. He telephoned right away to direct Lansing not to reveal the terms of the Armistice until he could address Congress. Then he took up a pencil and wrote out a little message to his people: "The armistice was signed this morning. Everything for which America fought has been accomplished. It will now be our fortunate duty to assist by example, by sober, friendly counsel and material aid in the establishment of just democracy throughout the world."

Going to the Capitol shortly after noon to address the Congress, he waited for a few moments in the anteroom of the House. There he spoke of his forebodings. The problems of policy that now confronted America, he said, were even more perplexing than those of the past. A tremendous duty rested upon the nation, he felt, to prevent chaos in the rest of the world. America had done well, militarily; and now she must prove herself, politically, to be worthy of the world's respect.

He spoke huskily at first. Reading the terms of the Armistice, he said: "The war thus comes to an end. . . . Armed imperialism such as the men conceived who were but yesterday the masters of Germany is at an end, its illicit ambitions engulfed in black disaster. Who will now seek to revive it?"

[10] E. W. McAdoo to the writer, March 12, 1952.

The representatives of the people could cheer this. But when their leader went on to preach and to teach, the House became quiet.

With a perspective that stemmed from his academic days, he analyzed the politics of Europe. The revolutions that had come to Russia and to Central Europe, he pointed out, seemed "to run from one fluid change to another, until thoughtful men are forced to ask themselves, With what Governments, and of what sort, are we about to deal in the making of covenants of peace? . . . When peace is made, upon whose promises and engagements besides our own is it to rest?" For their own best interest, he said, the victors would do well to help the vanquished to their feet and, if they chose the way of self-control and peaceful accommodation, put aid at their disposal in every way possible. "Hunger does not breed reform," he warned; "it breeds madness and all the ugly distempers that make an ordered life impossible."

For Woodrow Wilson it was a day of vindication rather than of triumph. His principles seemed to have conquered the legions of evil.

But once during the historic day he allowed himself to speak as the harassed, weary mortal that he was, beneath his cloak of ministerial responsibility. "Well," he said to Tumulty, "the war's over, and I feel like the Confederate soldier that General Gordon used to tell of, soliloquizing on a long, hard march: 'I love my country and I am fightin' for my country, but if this war ever ends, I'll be dad-burned if I ever love another country.'"

Radiantly happy in spite of weariness of mind and nerve, he reviewed a parade of war workers in the afternoon and in the evening he drove out with his wife to share the jubilation of his people. The whole Western world was rioting in joy. In New York, Paris, London, Rome, celebrations went on all day and all night, with gun salutes, snowstorms of paper, bells, sirens, searchlights, fireworks, and *Te Deums*. Crowds surged around the automobile of the Wilsons, overwhelming the secret service men and stopping their progress until soldiers locked arms and escorted the car back to the White House.

Too exhilarated for sleep, Wilson proposed going to a reception at the Italian embassy in honor of the King's birthday. There, on this day on which thrones were shaking in Central Europe, he drank the health of Victor Emmanuel.

When they returned to the White House they still were not ready for sleep. Kindling the fire in Edith Wilson's room, they sat on the big couch and talked far beyond midnight. Finally the President was ready for bed. But not until he had read a chapter of the Bible, and thus kept his covenant with the men who had done the fighting.

CHAPTER XI

PARTY BATTLES

THOUGH Wilson had refused to allow armistice negotiations to be influenced by considerations of domestic politics, he had not been unaware of the importance of retaining control of both houses in the Congressional election of 1918. He knew that, if the Republicans gained a majority in the Senate, Lodge would become chairman of the powerful Foreign Relations Committee and there might be subversion in his rear while he fought to represent America before the world as champion of an idealistic peace.

An opportunity had arisen for the Administration to strengthen itself at the polls. Suffragists were agitating for action by the Senate on a woman-suffrage amendment that already had been approved by the House. On September 16 the President told a delegation of them that he was heartily in sympathy and repeated an earlier pledge to help in every way possible; but militant women burned his words that afternoon in Lafayette Square, and he was periodically heckled until the suffragists won the right to vote.

Wilson had not forgotten that in the 1916 election he had carried most of the states where women had full suffrage. At the President's request, therefore, Secretary McAdoo had put in a hard week in the lobbies of the Senate, grubbing for votes; but he fell two short of the number required.

Fear of losing the chance to take the lead in the suffrage crusade drove McAdoo to call at the White House to talk business on a Sabbath morning, before church. The Senate would vote on the next day and no time could be lost in urging the President to go before the body and plead for the amendment.

On several occasions Wilson had been irritated because his son-in-law had presumed to invade his privacy to discuss matters that other officials would have reserved for more formal occasions. On this Sunday morning, however, Wilson listened patiently. But he hesitated to address the Senate, doubting that he could influence any votes. It was unprecedented for the President to address either house of Congress in behalf of any bill pending, and Wilson was afraid that senators would resent a breach of custom in a cause that had little relation to the war effort.

He still believed, however, what he had written in "Leaders of Men" thirty years before: that a President must "throw his bait" among the

majority and perform a minister's duty of translating the popular will
into law. He had often remarked that "a man who never changes his
mind is dead." Persuaded by his daughters to overcome his personal
distaste for emancipated women, he had become convinced that woman
suffrage was part of the "firm and progressive popular thought" that
a statesman must heed. And so on this Sunday afternoon he wrote a
message hastily; and on the next day, September 30, he appeared in the
Senate chamber and read it. As he expected, the air was chilly with
suspicion and resentment; but the frigidity merely stimulated his
powers. Speaking for only a quarter of an hour, he associated women's
voting so aggressively with the war and the peace that public opinion
was responsive, though none of the opposing Southerners was converted
then and there and the measure was not approved and submitted to the
states for ratification until June 4, 1919.

Woodrow Wilson needed all the votes that he could muster for his
Democrats as the Republicans laid plans to avenge their defeat of 1916,
perfecting their organization and raising the pitch of their criticism and
their protestations of devotion to the smashing of Germany. They had
offered nonpartisan cooperation in prosecuting the war; and they blazed
with indignation when Democratic leaders accused them of lack of
patriotism and even the President seemed to spurn their support. Theodore Roosevelt and George Harvey, meeting with Senator Beveridge at
Beverly Farms, arranged for the publication of a journal to be called
Harvey's Weekly, with a guaranteed circulation, and plotted a campaign to win the Presidency in 1920.[1]

Wilson was now staking the validity of his leadership on his exalted
concept of peacemaking. Though he thought it politically dangerous
for him to give "even so much as the appearance of an effort to pick
and prefer a candidate," he did not fail to act when his advisers told him

---

[1] William E. Dodd to Edith B. Wilson, May 29, 1921. This information was given to Dodd
on Nov. 12, 1918, at a dinner with Beveridge, to whom Dodd had given criticism on his biography of John Marshall. Beveridge also informed Dodd at that time that Roosevelt was to be the
Republican nominee for the Presidency in 1920 and he, Beveridge, the nominee for the Vice-
Presidency. Beveridge said, further, that Wilson was the ablest man they had ever had to do
with and must be destroyed.

According to a letter written by Dodd to Wilson on Nov. 19, 1918, Beveridge said that it
was planned to bring on serious industrial disturbances, even a financial panic. That, Beveridge
is alleged to have said, was "one thing that the President cannot escape the responsibility for if
it comes." Dodd wrote further: "He said in so many words that England was to be attacked
because she is making us take up this league of nations in her own interest. She must be
attacked because it would be snobbish submission to her lords if we kept close to her. I said
because the German and Irish votes were at stake? That was not denied or acknowledged. But
the real reason for the fight on the league of nations is the purpose of having a free hand in
Spanish America. He said no man who knows history will deny that we must some day annex
Mexico. Why then tie our hands in any league of nations? . . . He was not an extremist in
1916 and he says he has never spoken disrespectfully of you. Only now he must 'go down the
line with T.R.' "

that control of the Senate in the next Congress might hang upon the single vote of the senator to be elected from Michigan. He listened when Josephus Daniels reported that the only hope of electing a Democrat in Michigan lay in Henry Ford, and that the only man who could persuade the manufacturer to run was Woodrow Wilson, whom Ford admired heartily and had aided financially in the campaign of 1916. Advised by Daniels to apply the "selective draft" to this manufacturer who had shown himself a zealous advocate of peace, Wilson had asked his secretary of the navy to try his own hand at persuasion. "If you fail," the President said, "bring him over and I'll have a try at him."

Unable to persuade the manufacturer, Daniels had taken him to the White House, where the President came straight to the point. He would give anything to lay down his own job, he told Ford, but he could not expect to enjoy the quiet of private life until two great battles were won: that of the war and that of the peace. It was a challenge to the deepest consecration. The undemonstrative manufacturer was stirred and, returning to Michigan, he was nominated by the Democrats; but the Republicans raised a campaign fund of about a half-million dollars to support Truman Newberry, who had been Roosevelt's secretary of the navy.

As early as June, the President had asked Tumulty to work out a tactful plan for appealing to the country for a sympathetic Congress without arousing party rancor. In response his secretary had advised him to keep silent and to give the Republicans time to hoist themselves with a petard of rash allegations. When Wilson told the Colonel in September that he had decided to make an appeal in a speech or a letter, House indicated disapproval by saying nothing.

Undeterred by this, Wilson informed Vice-President Marshall that shortly before the election he would issue a call to his people for a Democratic Congress. "I have no doubt that they will give it to me," he said. "They have refused me nothing so far."

Finally, in mid-October, his conscience drove him to act in the direct way that was dearest to him. Resolving to lay his case frankly before his entire constituency, he concluded that he must risk a public appeal that to opponents doubtless would seem partisan and immodest. He explained that the Constitution made him "the greatest autocrat in the world." There were honorable precedents: Lincoln and McKinley had spoken out in time of crisis against divided councils and changing leadership.

So he drafted and redrafted an appeal to his people and discussed it with the party's chairman, Vance McCormick, and the temporary chairman, Homer Cummings. To them it was a life-and-death matter.

Conferring with the President, they found him disposed to accept their suggestions.

The final text of the message read: "Unity of command is as necessary now in civil action as it is upon the field of battle. If the control of the House and Senate should be taken away from the party now in power, an opposing majority could assume control of legislation and oblige all action to be taken amidst contest and obstruction. . . . Spokesmen of the Republican party are urging you to elect a Republican Congress in order to back up and support the President, but even if they should in this way impose upon some credulous voters on this side of the water, they would impose on no one on the other side." A Republican victory, he said with a frankness that he might come to rue, "would certainly be interpreted on the other side of the water as a repudiation of my leadership."

And in conclusion, to forestall criticism: "I need not tell you, my fellow-countrymen, that I am asking your support not for my own sake or for the sake of a political party, but for the sake of the Nation itself, in order that its inward unity of purpose may be evident to all the world. In ordinary times I would not feel at liberty to make such an appeal to you. . . . But these are not ordinary times . . . I submit my difficulties and my hopes to you."

The President did not show the appeal to his Cabinet before releasing it, but on the evening of October 24 he read it to Edith Wilson. "I would not send it out," she advised. "It is not a dignified thing to do."

"That is what I thought at first," was his reply, "but it is too late now. I have told them I would do it." He must do this for his loyal party men, as well as for the great cause that he was serving. Ringing for the head usher, he gave him the text for release.

The appeal was made public on October 25. It solidified party support behind some of the Democratic candidates; but, as certain advisers immediately sensed when they saw the message in cold print and as Wilson himself soon admitted, it opened him to a volley of blows from his archenemy.

Theodore Roosevelt fell upon the appeal with glee. Suffering from an ailment that was to carry him off within three months, the ex-President allowed his emotions to run riot. Deterred not at all by the fact that, without the existence of a war emergency, he himself in 1906 had written a letter [2] stressing the urgent need of keeping his Republican Congress in power, he called Wilson's appeal an insult to the patriotic honor of those Republicans who had supported the prosecution of the war. He telegraphed influential senators to urge that the Senate declare itself

[2] To James E. Watson, Aug. 18, 1906.

against adopting the Fourteen Points. "I am glad Wilson has come out in the open," he wrote to Lodge. "I fear Judas most when he can cloak his activities behind treacherous make-believe of nonpartisanship." It was the sort of message, he said, that could have been expected from a pro-German, unprincipled, cold-blooded, selfish, tricky, cowardly, unscrupulous, shameless, hypocritical, double-crossing President. Throwing away a paper that he had prepared for delivery at Carnegie Hall, Roosevelt sat down at his desk and drafted instead a denunciation of Wilson, his conduct of the war, and his peace proposals. Waving his manuscript in the packed auditorium, clicking his teeth, the old warrior charged that the President was placing support for himself above loyalty to the nation.[3]

Wilson's appeal united Taft and Roosevelt in a public statement to "all Americans who are Americans first," and some independents were goaded into the Republican party. "This is not the President's personal war," said opposition leaders in Congress who recalled that only five months earlier Wilson had proclaimed that politics was "adjourned." Torches of criticism that had seared Woodrow Wilson's good name so many times were rekindled. Already, in the year 1918, efforts had been made in Congress to pass emergency legislation that would give him a dictator's power; and his peace correspondence with Germany and his dependence on House to represent him at Paris had been held up by his foes as examples of personal, secretive diplomacy. And now this appeal for political support made it easy for his adversaries to stir dissension among legislators and journalists whose pride had been wounded because the prophet had ignored them.

While an epidemic of fatal influenza afflicted nearly a quarter of the people of the nation, killed a half-million, crippled the executive offices at Washington, and everywhere prevented the gathering of crowds to hear Democratic orators proclaim the achievements of their administration, newspapers printed Roosevelt's diatribes to good effect. Professional politicians dragged the campaign ever lower. At the end of October the restraints imposed by the Liberty Loan drive were gone, and there were protests against a pending revenue bill that would impose higher taxes to support the Administration's pay-as-you-go policy. Only an immediate announcement that Germany had surrendered unconditionally could have stampeded public sentiment toward the President.

[3] Letters from T.R. to S. P. Spencer, Oct. 15, 1918; A. Reaveley, Oct. 31, 1918; Senator Hinman, Nov. 6, 1918; and G. W. Maxcy, Nov. 4, 1918, Roosevelt Papers. Longworth, *Crowded Hours*, p. 274. Republican Chairman Will H. Hays, whose policy of nonpartisanship in foreign affairs was given luster by contrast with Wilson's effusion, spoke out indignantly: "A more ungracious, more unjust, more wanton, more mendacious accusation was never made by the most reckless stump orator, much less by a President of the United States, for partisan purposes." *New York Times*, Oct. 28, 1918.

But Woodrow Wilson was not a man to let this consideration influence his resolve to deal patiently with the enemy.

Election returns came in on November 5, the day on which the President was rejoicing with his Cabinet over the acceptance by the Supreme War Council of his Fourteen Points and the fixing of armistice terms that he felt would be accepted by Germany. He was confident of winning at home as well as abroad, and his advisers found him jocose and high-spirited. Asked whether he would resign if the vote went against the Democrats, he explained that the world's need for American leadership prevented this. "I cannot do it . . ." he said to William E. Dodd the historian. "It happens to be a case where, even if defeated by the people, I shall have to try to obtain the objects for which we went to war." [4]

And then the blow fell. Great blocks of German and Irish votes went against him; and the Republican electorate in the North was augmented by Negroes who had migrated for war work. Women voters in states that had enfranchised them, blaming Southern Democrats in the Senate for the blocking of the Suffrage Amendment, favored the Republican candidates. Added to the expected defection of farmers in the West who felt that the Democratic regime had supported the price of cotton better than that of wheat and the opposition of business interests that had been hurt by war restrictions and by the New Freedom, these forces gave the Republicans their innings. In Michigan, despite the delivery of labor support to Henry Ford by Gompers, Newberry won by about two thousand votes. When all the returns were in, the Republicans were in control of the upper chamber by a margin of one vote and of the House of Representatives by forty-five. The United States, for the aftermath of the greatest war that it had ever fought, was to have the sort of Congressional government that had prevailed after the Civil War and that Woodrow Wilson had criticized in his first book.

The President's appeal to the voters had stated plainly that defeat at the polls would be interpreted abroad as a "repudiation" of his leadership, and he knew that he now stood politically bankrupt in the eyes of the world. The last act of the tragedy of Woodrow Wilson had begun.

"You may be sure that the stubborn Scotch-Irish in me will be rendered no less stubborn and aggressive by the results of the election," he promised with a grimness reminiscent of his reaction to opposition to other great movements that he had championed.

There was no word of reproach for those who had helped to draft the fateful message. He would sink or swim with the loyal men of the party. But of those defeated Democratic congressmen who had been faithless

[4] Samuel F. Bemis, *The United States as a World Power*, p. 161.

he said to members of the National Committee: "Some of them got exactly what was coming to them and I haven't any bowels of compassion for them. They did not support the things they pretended to support. And the country knew they didn't." He believed what Tumulty and others told him, that his people simply did not understand the momentous problems of the peace. Someday he would have to tour the country to educate them. Assuring his daughter Jessie that he was very tired, but not too tired, and not at all dismayed or disheartened by the election, he wrote: "I think the Republicans will find the responsibility which they must now assume more onerous than joyful, and my expectation is that they will exercise it with some circumspection. I shall see to it that they are put in a position to realize their full responsibility, and the reckoning in 1920 may hold disappointing results for them."

Yet his conscience would not yield the categorical responsibility that he had assumed during the war—the personal obligation to make a peace that would be both durable and consistent with American concepts of justice. Weary and aging though he was, the prophet felt that he could effect another bloodless revolution. There was one more blow to be struck for rational political adjustment. In asking for an armistice the Germans had surrendered completely, in a military sense; but in committing both the Germans and the Allies to the Fourteen Points as a basis for peace, Wilson and House had deferred the political reckoning. His Americans had played a part in winning the fight by "inventing something." Now, by going to Paris himself, the President hoped to carry American political enterprise into the peace settlement. Once a neutral who wished to stand aside, he had turned belligerent in a world that would not respect American neutrality. As a belligerent, he had not only espoused such chauvinistic measures as had repelled him in the days of neutrality but, to shorten the conflict, had developed a new diplomacy of propaganda. Now, finding himself in a position to lead the world in reconciliation, he was to seek to prevent a recurrence of war by establishing those principles that he had proclaimed to soften the morale of the enemy. The greatest of his crusades against evil circumstances was yet to come.

Woodrow Wilson could not sit at his desk in the White House while lawyers and politicians, over in Europe, patched up an old fabric of diplomacy that he thought rotten. The Protestant pressures within him would not permit his taking sanctuary in a high pulpit in a hierarchical tabernacle. Wilson saw that there was still spiritual pioneering to be done, back at the hearths of Europe from which his own venturesome grandparents had set forth for the western frontier. Like the "saving remnant" of his ancestors in old Columbia after the Civil War, he could not hide out in a manse or a pulpit while civil chaos threatened the whole community. He knew what the historians of posterity would expect of him.

Six months earlier he had said emphatically to Stockton Axson that when peace came he would not go himself to the peace table, that House would be there to keep him informed; but as the lines of the diplomatic battle were drawn and the Colonel cabled his accounts of the pre-Armistice deliberations, Wilson felt that he must be present himself, to catch every word of the negotiations and the very tones in which they were spoken, and, most particularly, to look into the faces of the European leaders and see what purposes moved them. "I want to tell Lloyd George certain things I can't write to him," he said. Already he was spending almost half his time in decoding secret messages from Paris and answering them. A Scot who made it a principle never to give proxies could hardly be expected to delegate power in a matter in which he had committed himself so deeply and so personally. Ever since, as a lad, he had organized the Lightfoot Club in his father's hayloft, nothing had given him so much pleasure as to lead men in the drafting of laws and constitutions. Even had moral compulsions not forced him to go to Paris, his love for participation in great affairs hardly would have permitted him to stay away. On October 28 he had cabled to House: "I assume that you cannot honorably turn the present feverish meeting into a peace conference without me."

A few counselors, daring to stand in the way of the prophetic impulse that possessed the President, had advised him to keep his distance and from his pulpit at Washington, unsullied by the bartering of European interests, to proclaim the purity of America's purposes. When Lansing gave this advice, Wilson's face grew harsh and obstinate. ("He said nothing, but looked volumes," Lansing recorded in his diary.) Herbert Hoover ventured to give the same counsel; and Tumulty suggested that domestic affairs would suffer and that the rising Republican tide would swirl into the vacuum in the capital. Masaryk, just elected president of the infant Czechoslovak Republic, came to say farewell and begged his American benefactor not to go to Paris, or at least not to remain there after the opening of the Peace Conference.

Most of the Cabinet, however, felt that the President should go; and Secretary Lane was applauded when he told a conference of state governors that the success of the Peace Conference depended on Wilson's presence at the head of the American delegation. General Bliss wrote to Newton D. Baker: "I wish to God that the President could be here for a week. I hear in all quarters a longing for this. The people who want to get a rational solution out of this awful mess look to him alone.

. . . In this dark storm of angry passion that has been let loose in all quarters I doubt if anyone but he can let in the light of reason."

Ray Stannard Baker reported to the State Department a division of opinion in Europe: the people, seeing the triumph of their cause in Wilson, were clamoring for him; and the "ruling class," knowing that he would upset their plans for making a nineteenth-century peace, hoped that he would stay away. Liberals whose confidence Wilson had won both by his New Freedom and by his championship of farsighted war aims, were advocating that the President go to Paris, the *Manchester Guardian* describing him as "the only statesman of the first rank who has concerned himself seriously to think out any policy at all." [5] He was looked upon by the Germans as the one man who could be depended upon to insist on considerations of abstract justice.

It was on Colonel House that the President leaned most confidently in making plans for the Peace Conference. After the master stroke that had committed the Allies to base the peace treaty on the Fourteen Points, House had remained in Europe, preparing for the negotiations. His success in the Armistice parleys had so inflated his confidence that he would have liked to continue as America's chief delegate, with associates of his own choosing. Though he had felt at one time that Wilson should be the sole American spokesman in the peacemaking, he had advised the President, in the summer of 1918, not to go to Europe. He wished to deal in a friendly, firm way with the statesmen of the Allies, threatening politely when necessary and referring back to his chief for orders.[6] Finding Clemenceau of the opinion that it was neither desirable nor possible for the President of the United States to take part in the conference as an equal of European premiers—the Tiger felt that Ger-

---

[5] Lloyd George had said that the President must attend the Peace Conference but, like Clemenceau, he opposed Wilson's presence at the executive sessions. "Clemenceau and I can quarrel as equals and say anything we like," the prime minister explained to Cobb, "but we cannot talk that way to the President, and it is sometimes necessary to talk that way to achieve results." Frank Glass, an old schoolmate, cabled to Wilson that Balfour said: "Great Britain has no single leader able to grapple with Clemenceau." According to Glass, Balfour asked whether Wilson was a fighting man and, when assured that he was, pounded the table and said: "Then by all means the President should go to Versailles."

"Nearly everyone in the Department [of State] wished that he would not go," William Phillips wrote in *Ventures in Diplomacy*, p. 93. For a summary of advice given to the President on the question of going to Paris, *see* J. Daniels, *The Wilson Era, Years of War*, pp. 351–52.

[6] "I wish in my soul the President had appointed me as Chairman of the peace delegation with McAdoo and Hoover as my associates. . . . If I could have had these two men as my associates and only these, I would have been willing to guarantee results." House Diary, Dec. 3, 1918. In "Memories," a paper written by House in 1929, he confessed that at times, when his advice had been disregarded, he would have liked to be President instead of the President's adviser. "I did not approve of President Wilson going to Paris. . . . It was . . . the kind of work for which he was not best fitted and the strain of it was too much for him." House to George W. Watt, Oct. 16, 1934. A statement, House to Seymour, Jan. 15, 1938, records that the disagreement over Wilson's going to Paris was the first flat and vital difference of opinion between the friends.

many might use Wilson to escape just retribution—House passed this view along to Wilson three days after the Armistice, and explained that protocol required that Clemenceau be made president of the conference if it was held at Paris. Moreover, at the same time House cabled that though "everyone" wanted the President to come over for preliminary talks, Americans whose opinions were of value were practically unanimous in the belief that it would be unwise for Wilson to sit in the Peace Conference.

Having set his own heart on entering the lists, Wilson was cast down by this report. That he should go to Paris but not sit as a commissioner seemed a way of "pocketing" him. Objecting very strongly to letting protocol interfere with obtaining the results that he had set his heart on, projecting his own will into the minds of other men, he asserted without reason that it was "universally expected and generally desired" at Washington that he should attend the conference. He could only infer, he said, that the French and British leaders feared that at Paris he might lead the weaker nations against them. "I hope you will be very shy of their advice," he wrote House, "and give me your own independent judgment after reconsideration."

The Colonel had need of all his finesse. Actually, he thought Wilson not an effective negotiator *inter pares,* believing that he did not know when to yield and when to be firm. The President was not accustomed to debate. House was convinced that he himself could better attain the high purposes that were dear to both men; and yet he knew that he could not flatly advise Wilson to stay at Washington without seeming to put himself forward as the chief American delegate. This might break their understanding irreparably. And so he could only cable, inconclusively: "My judgment is that you should . . . determine upon your arrival what share it is wise for you to take in the proceedings . . . When you are here you will be in a position to assess the situation properly. It is impossible to do so from Washington."

Appearing unexpectedly at Lansing's house during a dinner party on the evening of November 18, Wilson said that he had decided to go abroad; and the next day he cabled to House that he would sail for France immediately after addressing the opening session of the new Congress.

When the decision was made public, partisan opponents renewed their charges of dictatorship and grandstand playing, and questioned the legality of his departure from his responsibilities at Washington. There was no possibility, now, of extending to the peacemaking the political truce that had attended the war effort. To be sure, there were many Republicans among the technical experts whom House had recruited to advise the President; and unity in the councils of peace was furthered when Taft judiciously warned his party that they would be held by the people to a strict accountability for the way in which they used their power. At the same time advising Wilson to consult the foreign committees of both houses about the treaty, Taft issued this admonition: "Should he consult no one but his closest personal and partisan advisers, he will run the risk of arousing the closest scrutiny of what he presents to the Senate and of awakening a popular approval of a critical attitude of that body toward a treaty."[7]

In June of 1918 Stockton Axson had talked with brother Woodrow about the opposition to the President's peace plans. Sitting on the veranda of the White House and chatting in the same intimate way in which they used to converse on the porch at Princeton when old Joseph Wilson was with them, Axson had urged the President to call all the war leaders together—Republicans as well as Democrats—and, addressing them as a family, to talk frankly about the great battle to come after the war was over. If only they might be given "a warm sense" of their leader's "personal nature!"

Edith Wilson had assented when her opinion was asked; but the President had listened with his eyes upon the floor. It was so like good old Stock, who could see possibilities of redemption in even the Republican sinners! "Well, it might be wise to do that," he remarked at length. "It may be that would be a step that would help to suppress party opposition." He never did it, though. His contempt of senators, Democratic as well as Republican, was too deep-seated to permit him to woo their good will.[8] He could not bring himself to make peace in the American

[7] Republican opposition took shape in mid-December, when the dying Roosevelt called Lodge and Root to his hospital bedside and mapped out a strategic plan for amending whatever settlement the President might bring back from Paris. These Republicans conjured up all the provisos that could be conceived by minds ruled by jealous and fearsome regard for their own country's interests and for their own party's position.

"I am insisting upon Nationalism as against Internationalism," Roosevelt had written to Senator Beveridge on Oct. 31. "I am for saying with a bland smile whatever Nationalism demands. I will then adopt with that extra consideration any wise and feasible plan for limiting the possible area and likelihood of future wars. Mine is merely a platonic expression, designed to let Taft and his followers get over without too much trouble, and also to prevent any accusation that we are ourselves merely Prussian militarists." *Letters of T.R.,* VIII, 1385. (Eventually Taft did "get over." *See* p. 345 below.) Roosevelt cautioned his disciples against any revelations of their true feelings to the public. The political situation, he assured Cabot Lodge, was so good that he must not "make the mistake of overplaying" their hand and "causing a reaction of sympathy." Lodge, who in August had become minority leader in the Senate, carefully followed this advice, never wholly rejecting the idea of a league, but exuding pessimism as to its practicality.

[8] When House asked Wilson whether Senator Gilbert M. Hitchcock knew that the President had tried to remove him from the chairmanship of the Committee on Foreign Relations, Wilson replied that he had told Senator Martin and others that he would not consult Hitchcock about anything because he would not trust him with any information. Pinning his friend down, the Colonel found that there was no other Democrat on the Committee on Foreign Relations whom Wilson would have preferred, that he considered them all "a rum lot."

family, in spite of House's urging that he cooperate closely with the Senate's Committee on Foreign Relations. Though he once had advocated this course in academic lectures, he felt that it would be futile to attempt to get cooperation from Lodge, whose leadership in the Senate he anticipated, he said, "with genuine anxiety." He could only fall back on an alternate method that he had mentioned in a lecture—the presentation of a *fait accompli* to the Senate for approval.

Associates at Washington who knew the President well took it for granted that he would hold full responsibility for the peacemaking in his own hands and be accountable for the outcome. Quoting Euripides on the power of the people, Brandeis felt that the realization of progressive ideals at Paris was "an affair of the prophets and not of the priests." James Kerney, a New Jersey friend, returned from a publicity mission to Paris and, telling Wilson of the intrigue and cunning of European politicians, found him aware of what was ahead. "The terrible thing about war," the President said, "is that the young manhood of the world is sacrificed to the stupidity of the politicians. It's my business to see that that kind of thing is stopped."

The prophet's defiance was building up in reaction against the Philistines abroad. On November 20, two days after he had told Lansing of his decision to go to Paris, he was in a crusading mood. Professor Rappard of Geneva, calling at the White House, found him more gay and candid than he had been a year before.

Urged not to become *pratique,* Wilson replied: "I'm not going to relax in the least. I'm going over to Europe because the Allied governments don't want me to." He hoped, he said, to keep the talks from taking a vexatious course.

His visitor suggested that public opinion would endow him with a power that would enable him to go over the heads of the Allied governments. "I know it," he responded, "and I know how jealous they are. I'm stubborn but one has to be worldly wise." He had had their jealously in mind, he said, when he had finally told the Germans that they must address all the Western powers.

The Allies thought he wanted "to run it all," Wilson remarked.

"But you are, I hope," said Rappard.

"I hope so too," the President replied, "but it would be unwise to let them feel it too obviously."

He talked intimately with this fellow professor, explaining that he hoped to do at Paris what he had failed to accomplish in the Americas, to make of the Monroe Doctrine "not a big-brother affair, but a real partnership" for mutual protection. He wanted disarmament, but when asked whether, in the absence of an international police, it would run into mutual rivalries and suspicions, he answered: "I'm sure of it. France and Italy, for instance, have no use for each other. It will be a long rocky road." [9]

In choosing four American commissioners to guide and protect him along the precarious path ahead, Wilson held to a principle that he had observed through the war. He selected the men who promised to be the most helpful in doing the job. To be valuable to him, they must be men who, if they did not have his spiritual purpose in their hearts, at least would be faithful, patriotic servants of their chief. If one or two of the delegates were Republicans, that would be so much the better; but they must not be partisans who might betray his cause to Lodge. He could not appoint any senator, he explained, because in that case the man eventually would have to vote upon the treaty that he helped to negotiate. When House had recommended Taft and Root as peace delegates, Wilson responded that he considered them "impossible" and out of sympathy with his ideas. Considering Root "a hopeless reactionary" who had failed in his mission to Russia and who would "discourage every liberal element in the world," Wilson was not willing even to appoint him to the international court at The Hague, for he thought that, at seventy-three, his mind was narrowing and losing resiliency and he was "past his period of usefulness." On November 29, 1918, Wilson wrote to Richard Hooker of the Springfield *Republican* thus: "I . . . must say frankly that I would not dare take Mr. Taft. I have lost all confidence in his ability. And other prominent Republicans whom one would naturally choose are already committed to do everything possible to prevent the Peace Conference from acting upon the peace terms which they have already agreed to [in the pre-Armistice negotiations]. It is a distressing situation indeed, but one which they themselves have created."

When Masaryk suggested one day that it would be wise to take Republican advisers to Paris, Wilson confessed that he had no talent for compromising differences that might arise within the American delegation. "I tell you frankly," he said, "I am descended from Scottish Presbyterians and am therefore somewhat stubborn." He and House would speak for the United States. He would have to take the secretary of state, on whom he depended for legal advice but whom he thought "not big enough" to lead the delegation. He would like to take Newton D. Baker; but when he had spoken to House of this wish, the Colonel had advised against it, fearing jealousy on the part of other members of the Cabinet. The matter was settled when McAdoo resigned from office,

---

[9] Quotations from Rappard's journal printed in William E. Rappard, "W.W., La Suisse et Genève," in *Centenaire Woodrow Wilson: 1856–1956* (Geneva, 1956).

pleading poor health and financial necessity, and it became essential that Baker keep his hand on affairs at Washington while the President was at Paris. At the suggestion of the secretary of war, Wilson appointed General Tasker H. Bliss, who had won the confidence not only of his American colleagues but of the members of the Supreme War Council as well.

For the fifth place on the American Commission, the secretary of state was authorized to offer appointment to Justice Day of the Supreme Court, a Republican who had negotiated with Spain in 1898. Day consulted the chief justice and declined to serve, and Lansing then suggested Henry White. This veteran diplomat, whose daughter married a German, had been conspicuous for his judicial poise during the period of American neutrality, and he had served the President well by informing him of *gaucheries* of Ambassador Gerard at Berlin and by transmitting reports of British liberal opinion from his half brother, W. H. Buckler.[10] At Wilson's request Lansing sounded White's opinion of the Fourteen Points and, finding him sympathetic, appointed him.

Everyone liked Henry White. He was "above such trifles as war," Henry Adams wrote of him. Known as "the first professional American diplomatist," he could be depended on to grace the peace table with tact and fidelity. Theodore Roosevelt, who had called White "the most useful man in the entire diplomatic service," was moved to write to Lodge that he was "simply overjoyed," in spite of the fact that White was "not a Republican but an Independent." Root also was pleased.

To solve the most urgent problem of Europe, Wilson chose another agent who had proved his capacity to serve and who was more patriot and humanitarian than party man. He proposed that Herbert Hoover, who had been pleading for united, nonpartisan support for the President, be delegated to direct the relief and reconstruction of Europe. The war food administrator had served as chairman of the Allied Food Council and had just completed a survey of the world's food supplies and needs. "I have learned to value your judgment and have the greatest trust in all your moral reactions," Wilson wrote on November 4 to this tried and able servant of humanity. The President agreed that his food administrator should work with the Allies along the line of recommendations that had come from House, who was eager that an "International Relief Organization" be set up under Hoover, to serve needy peoples without interference by Allied blockade or by traders seeking profits.

Wilson made it clear to the men of his Shipping Board that they

[10] In writing to Wilson about Gerard on April 5, 1915, White had said: "I often wish that I could be of assistance to you in your heavy labors."

must give first consideration to Hoover's need for ships, rather than to any desire of businessmen to make good sales. Moreover, he instructed that surpluses of raw materials should be held for future use. The control of exports, he had told Wiseman three months before, would be a formidable weapon at the Peace Conference.

The war council was breaking up rapidly now, with McAdoo resigning and Hoover and Hurley going abroad. Indeed, it seemed that soon there might be little need in the United States for economic administrators of this type, for Wilson sensed a reaction in popular feeling toward governmental economic controls. On November 29 Baruch submitted his resignation and recommended that his War Industries Board be discontinued as of January 1, 1919. Members of the board's price-fixing committee soon resigned also, stating that "no new price regulations seem to be called for."

Wilson's political advisers were worried by the haste with which the transition was being made. Winter was coming on, and men were working on war contracts hundreds of miles from their homes. It was an impolitic hour to take away their jobs. But the prophet of peace had little time now to comfort politicians and extend controls over normal business. Though he approved a bill that had been designed by the Federal Trade Commission to regulate a favorite political target—the meat-packing industry—he drew back when urged to form a federal board to advise local public utilities.

The President and his advisers had learned much, since their first venture into economic legislation, about the headaches that come from conflicts of interests. The nation was now clamoring for a lower cost of living; and at the same time Herbert Hoover, though gradually removing controls over many commodities, was insisting on maintaining certain prices so that production would be stimulated and there would be surpluses with which to feed Europe. Moreover, while exporters demanded that world trade be allowed to flow freely, Hoover insisted that it was "positively necessary" to continue the embargo, or every foodstuff would be overdrawn and the American people faced with shortages.

In November the President had to face up to another conflict between efficiency and political expediency. With the authorization of Congress, he had announced in July that the telephone and telegraph systems of the country would function under Burleson's direction, as a war measure. Subsequently the postmaster general had learned that to assure continuous transmission of overseas messages without delays, the cables must be operated under the same authority as that governing the land wires. Moreover, it had been found necessary to keep a wire from France constantly available for the State Department, and another for the War

Department. On November 2, therefore, Wilson signed a proclamation that placed all marine cables under Burleson's direction. Putting the decree into effect ten days later, the postmaster general gave assurance that the news associations would be given every facility for handling press dispatches during the period of the Peace Conference.

Political advisers of the President sensed the danger that the public might confuse government control of the cables with censorship, which ended on November 15. However, when Wilson was advised to reconsider his decision, he wrote: "I have not the least fear that the misrepresentations . . . will do any harm. They are too contemptible to be worthy of notice, and it will presently become evident that what we did was done in the course of business . . ."

Only very rarely had the President suggested that government officials consider anything but efficiency in the management of the nation's business. Nevertheless, though he could do nothing for his family and little for old friends in the way of preferment,[11] he continued to give of himself to less fortunate relatives. When the daughter of his brother "Dode" planned to marry a clergyman, Uncle Woodrow insisted that the wedding be in the White House and acted as best man himself, his dress clothes wilting in the August heat as he rejoiced in the young couple's happiness. ("Do not be a chaplain," he said to the groom. "There are plenty of those. Be a missionary.")[12]

In mid-November, with daughter Margaret gone to France to entertain soldiers with her singing and the McAdoos soon to leave Washington, he felt bereft of his flesh and blood. Except for McAdoo, however, the men of the Cabinet stood by loyally. In the eyes of those closest to him, despite the errors that the politicians attributed to him, Woodrow Wilson was still a master among men and the hope of the party, the nation, and now even of the world. The philosophical House had left the White House in October with the feeling that never would he meet a more sympathetic mind. The dynamic McAdoo was to cherish afterward the years of their close association, to remember Wilson as a president with a deeper instinct for accomplishment than he had ever seen in any other man and a horror of fatuous ideas—"blank cartridges," Wilson called them. One day the President had stretched the mind of National Committeeman Cummings over a panorama of the world's affairs; and on another he had listened patiently while a Cabinet

[11] In August he had asked that a family friend of long standing not be removed as postmaster at Rome, Ga., unless it was "absolutely necessary to the service to do so." And a little later he had requested the reappointment of a Princeton classmate as warden of Sing Sing Prison, but only if he deserved it. Herbert Hoover told the writer that in the course of his association with Woodrow Wilson, the President had asked only once that Hoover try to find a job for a friend, though the pressures were constant and strong.

[12] Alice Wilson McElroy to the writer, April 30, 1950.

officer confessed his perplexities, and then, by a few deft questions, had helped the disciple to see his way to a solution. On one day he would seem all Scot, talking with "Dr. Facts" or make Hurley think him the keenest man of business that he had ever met, and on another he would give play to the Irish in his nature, swapping stories with his Cabinet, chuckling at Tumulty's absurdities and practical jokes. He had "recruited" Henry Ford. He had cajoled Carter Glass, who complained that his experience had been too much legislative and too little administrative to permit him to fill McAdoo's place in the Treasury Department. With twinkling eyes he said: "I rather think, Glass, that we'll be able to manage the job together."

On December 2, Woodrow Wilson delivered his parting charge to the elders in the Capitol, at a joint session of the Congress. Crowds milled about, outside and in; and in the chamber of the House, foreign diplomats joined the high functionaries of all branches of the American government.

The President began hoarsely and uncertainly, as in his address on Armistice Day. He spoke first of the victory and the sacrifices that had made it possible. Then he discussed economic readjustment and made it clear that the nation could not revert to prewar conditions. Finally he came to the great concern that possessed him. Speaking of the sacrifices made by America's fighting men, he said: "It is now my duty to play my full part in making good what they offered their life's blood to obtain. I can think of no call to service which could transcend this . . .

"I realize the magnitude and difficulty of the duty I am undertaking; I am poignantly aware of its grave responsibilities. I am the servant of the Nation. I can have no private thought or purpose of my own in performing such an errand. I go to give the best that is in me to the common settlements which I must now assist in arriving at in conference with the other working heads of the associated Goverments. I shall count upon your friendly countenance and encouragement. . . . I shall be happy in the thought that I am constantly in touch with the weighty matters of domestic policy with which we shall have to deal. I shall make my absence as brief as possible . . ."

Many of the senators sat sullen and stolid as Woodrow Wilson concluded his speech. He had not asked their advice, had not invited any of them to go to the Peace Conference. So far as most of them knew, he had done no careful planning of American policy. No one knew to what he might try to commit them. But the prophet found it easy to ignore the political reckoning that was being calculated by the priests of the national temple as moral impulse drove him toward the New Jerusalem to keep his personal covenant with the millions who had bled and died.

CHAPTER XII

THE NEW WORLD RETURNS TO REDEEM THE OLD

TWO DAYS AFTER his challenge to the Congress, Woodrow Wilson boarded the transport *George Washington,* the first President of the United States to sail for Europe while in office. He expected to be able to return within two months, though doubtful that the work of peace-making would be entirely finished then.

The prospect of a sea voyage and a constructive role in the peace-making made him relaxed and genial, and he talked freely and frankly with those near him. To a query about his health he replied: "Yes, I have a cold in my throat. Grayson says he will get rid of it for me by the time we get over there. I am going to have to do some plain talking when we get on the other side and I'll need my voice."

He said: "Upon the very first opportunity I have after meeting the premiers and finding out at first hand what sort of chaps they are, as well as letting them know what kind of fellow I am, I shall find out from them what their program is. I have just had a cable from Colonel House. Lloyd George and Clemenceau held a meeting the other day in London at which House was not able to be present, because an unusually robust germ had boarded him which he could not get rid of soon enough. House's cable was badly garbled, but I gather that these men have agreed on a definite program. Apparently they are determined to get everything out of Germany they can, now that she is helpless. They are evidently planning to take what they can get frankly as a matter of spoils, regardless of either the ethics or the practical aspect of the proceeding . . . If they insist upon this sort of program, I shall be compelled to withdraw my commissioners and return home and in due course take up the details of a separate peace. But, of course, I don't believe that that will come to pass. I think that, once we get together, they will learn that the American delegates have not come to bargain, but will stand firmly by the principles that we have set forth; and once they learn that that is our purpose I believe we shall come to an early agreement."

What would probably be the English program at the conference? he was asked.

"You know," he replied, "I was surprised at Colonel Roosevelt's statement that England won the war and should have anything she wants.[1]

[1] The irreconcilable ex-President had publicly denied Wilson's authority to speak for his countrymen, in view of the loss of Congress to the Republicans. He wrote: "Mr. Wilson and his

I don't believe our soldiers will be inclined to feel just that way about it. The question of who won the war is a relative one, but if they want to be specific about it, we have as good a claim as anyone else . . . England in agreeing to the Fourteen Principles written into the Armistice is in the parodoxical position of submitting to the principle of disarmament and simultaneously announcing through her spokesmen that she means to retain naval supremacy. I once said in fun, but with sufficient point, to M. Tardieu that, if England insisted upon maintaining naval dominance after the war, the United States could and would show her how to build a navy! If England holds to this course at the conference, it is tantamount to admitting that she does not desire permanent peace, and I will so tell Lloyd George. I'll do it with a smile, but it will carry its point. . . .

"Militarism is no different on sea than it is on land. The suggestion which has been made that the American and British navies act together as the sea patrol of the world is only another form of militaristic propaganda. No one power, no two powers, should be masters of the sea; the whole world must be in on it. It must be definitely set forth in the treaty that no one nation or group of nations can say what shall or shall not be done on the high seas. It should be left to a league of all the nations to declare a blockade or override international law for the purpose of retaliating upon a power which threatens the peace of the world. . . .

"The freedom of the seas is itself subject to a variable interpretation . . . This war has demonstrated that international law must be altered to meet the new conditions of marine warfare . . . By the arbitrary use of her blockade England very seriously infringed upon our rights as a neutral before we became a belligerent—and with no other excuse than necessity. I am frank to admit that if I had not been convinced that Germany was the scourge of the world I was ready then and there to have it out with Great Britain on that point.

"England will want the German colonies. Mr. Borden, the Canadian premier, has declared that Canada would be opposed to the mother country's acquiring any more colonies. He incidentally expressed the desire that the German colonies be turned over to the United States, if to anybody. Of course, we don't want them and wouldn't have them. . . .

Replying to a question as to his insistence upon a league of nations, he said:

Fourteen Points and his four supplementary points and his five complementary points and all his utterances every which way have ceased to have any shadow of right to be accepted as expressive of the will of the American people." "Of the terrible sacrifice which has enabled the Allies to win the victory, America has contributed just about two per cent." And so, Roosevelt asserted, the United States had no right to set herself above her allies in making the peace.

"I am going to insist that the league be brought out as part and parcel of the treaty itself. A league I believe will of necessity become an integral part of such a treaty as I trust we shall work out . . . The nucleus of the league will probably be Great Britain, France, Italy, the United States, and Japan. The other nations will enter to preserve their interests. Germany's present chaotic state will undoubtedly make it necessary to put her on probation until she can qualify in the estimation of the other powers for entrance. A similar policy will have to be followed in the case of the new states to be carved out of portions of the Austro-Hungarian Empire. . . .

"The principle of self-determination has given rise to an interesting problem to be worked out. As you know, German Austria has declared her desire to become affiliated with the original German Empire. Now, such an affiliation, if permitted, would mean that the new Germany would be the most powerful country on the Continent—and a great Roman Catholic power. I have no bias derogatory to the Roman Catholic Church, but I do not want to see that church or any church become a great political entity. The dangers are obvious. It is certainly a hard knot to unravel, if we are to apply the principle of self-determination literally, and I am just now thinking that it might be handled by requiring that Austria and Germany, although affiliated, act separately until they have proved themselves in the eyes of the world. . . . Poland is another knotty question. I am determined that the new Polish state should have an outlet to the sea . . . But all these things will have to be worked out carefully and deliberately." [2]

Aboard the *George Washington*, to aid in working out the settlements that the President outlined, were several hundred advisers and assistants, and cases of books, maps, and reports. Though a little distrustful of the enthusiasms of specialists, Wilson welcomed the counsel of The Inquiry—the body of competent scholars that House had assembled, at his request, more than a year before. He called these gentlemen to his cabin on December 10, as the vessel stood in toward the mist-shrouded Azores. Though he had taken it easy during his first days at sea—staying in his cabin until nearly noon and retiring early at night—he had been pondering further on the matters that he had discussed informally. As he recovered from his cold, he took up his burdens again, working even on Sunday; and on the 10th he gave the scholars his gospel—fervently, candidly, quite charmingly.

He committed them to a standard of justice that he hoped all the world would accept—the same sort of justice that the United States had

[2] These quotations are taken from the records of Charles Swem in the Princeton University Library.

championed in keeping an "open door" in China. It was his wish that by proving themselves "square" Americans would win the regard of the rest of the world and could act as trustworthy umpires. He gave the impression that he felt that absolute justice in specific cases would be actually unattainable. However, with an obtuseness to reality that he often showed when purposes that he held sacred were at stake, he remarked that the peoples of Europe were being betrayed by leaders who did not truly represent them and seemed to him "too weather-wise to see the weather." Unless the Peace Conference followed the will of the people rather than that of the European leaders, he predicted, there would soon be a breakup of the world that would be no mere war, but a cataclysm. The American people were to get the truth about the Peace Conference, for already he had arranged with some difficulty for the removal of British and French restrictions on political news. If they did not get the truth, he predicted, the peace treaty would not work; and if it did not work right, the world would "raise hell."

The new order, the prophet proclaimed, must be neither a repressive concert of great powers such as had emerged from the Congress of Vienna, nor the balancing of powers that had failed so dismally. His hope for both elasticity and security lay in the forming of a league of nations. Like the Monroe Doctrine, the international league would develop through experience. A council would be set up, and war-breeding issues referred to it and thereby given full publicity. When a nation was found guilty of evil designs against a neighbor, it might be cut off from trade and communication with the world. The President suggested that the German colonies become the property of the league, to be administered under trusteeship. The new organization would be given stability by assuming responsibility for material possessions, he foresaw.

In conclusion, the President said that, though he expected the experts to work through the other American commissioners, he wanted them to feel free to come straight to him with anything that affected a critical decision. "Tell me what's right and I'll fight for it," he covenanted with them. He spoke as a seeker of truth, an unassuming scholar among peers. His colleagues were charmed and went back to their quarters reassured of their opportunity to serve humanity and of their important role in a great historic event.[3]

Messages came to the *George Washington* that kept alive Wilson's

---

[3] The substance of Wilson's talk to the experts has been taken from contemporary notes made by Isaiah Bowman and printed in Miller's *The Drafting of the Covenant*, I, 41–44, from notes taken by Charles Seymour and read by him to the writer, from contemporary letters written by Raymond Fosdick, from the diary of George Louis Beer, at the Columbia University Library, and from James T. Shotwell's *At the Peace Negotiations*.

suspicions of the motives of the Allies. The Armenians sent a plea for
succor; the Jews asked favors for Palestine; the Koreans, defense against
Japan; the Swedes wanted the Aaland Islands; Vienna, the return of
stolen pictures. Little Albania lamented that she had found no advocate
in Europe to take her part. Along the Adriatic coast, Italians were
squatting on coveted land. Everyone wanted something; no one seemed
eager to help America to apply high principles to the peacemaking.

Approaching the dock to board the *George Washington* early on the
morning of sailing, Raymond Fosdick had asked a laborer coming off
the ferry how long he worked each day. The man had replied: "Fourteen hours"; and then, pointing to the *George Washington*, the workman had continued: "Do you see that boat? There's a man aboard her
that is going to Europe to change all that!"

When Fosdick brought this story to the President, with a recommendation that a bill of industrial rights be written into the peace treaty,
Wilson replied that it frightened him to think how much the people
expected, that it did not seem possible to take up such questions at the
Peace Conference, that he hoped an international conference of labor
would press for these things.

Among the messages of good will sent to the *George Washington*
was one that brought to Woodrow Wilson, over the years, the voice that
often held him true to his trust, that had kept him obedient to the ideals
of service that had ruled a little manse in Georgia. Stockton Axson,
now serving as an official of the Red Cross, had written movingly to his
brother-in-law: "I wonder if you fully understand how entirely you
carry overseas with you the hearts, and hopes and dreams, and desires
of millions of your fellow Americans. Your vision of the new world
that should spring from the ashes of the old, is all that had made the war
tolerable to many of us. That vision has removed the sting, has filled our
imaginations, and has made the war not a tragedy, but a sacrament.
For many of us your thoughts have been our daily thoughts, and we
have tried to 'catch your great accents,' not in vainglory, but in a desire
to assist even a little in driving the great truths home by reiteration.
Nothing but a new world is worth the purchase price of the war, and
the comfort of millions of us is that you have the vision to glimpse it
and the power to realize it in action."

Reading these words, the prophet could hear again the voice of Ellen
Axson Wilson. He found inspiring, also, an expression of confidence
from the wife of William Phillips, assistant secretary of state. In reply
he wrote:

It is not the people "in the game" whom I am seeking to serve, but the
people not in the game and with whom political motives count for nothing

except to excite suspicion. That you should judge me so encourages the hope that I am judging myself without self-deception, and makes the whole immense task easier. It transcends my comprehension, and the only thing I can hope to make sure of is my motive.

With the warmest regard,
Gratefully yours,
WOODROW WILSON

This is not dictated but written on my own typewriter.[4]

Out on the Atlantic, the Commander in Chief went often to the bridge of the ship, cloaked in a heavy coat with coonskin collar. Captain McCauley came to love him as a passenger who put on no "side" and contributed to the morale of the ship's company. To keep the spirit democratic, Wilson attended a Sunday service in the hall of the enlisted men and went below to the "Old Salt" theater that the troops attended. He liked to hear the boys sing war songs, and to join in. They sang "Old Nassau" for him, and eagerly accepted his invitation to shake his hand. When he walked on deck his quick, eager step matched that of his wife, who, vivacious and trimly dressed, held his attention with small talk. To those around him he seemed young for his sixty-three years.

Sometimes, though, he would stand alone at the rail, gazing over the bow, across the wintry sea—toward Europe. At such moments the hewn face seemed to be set against the political erosions of the era. Parting from Tumulty at New York, Wilson had predicted that his trip would be either "the greatest success or the supremest tragedy in all history." "I believe in a Divine Providence," he had said. "If I did not have faith, I should go crazy . . . it is my faith that no body of men . . . can defeat this great world enterprise." [5]

To the Scot who had thirteen letters in his own name and had often marked the close association of this number with his career, it was a good omen that the *George Washington* steamed into the harbor of Brest on Friday, the 13th of December. A thick mist was rising. From tiers of land batteries and the decks of warships salvos of welcome boomed as the presidential ship came on. Woodrow Wilson was on the

[4] William Phillips, *Adventures in Diplomacy,* p. 94.

[5] At the same time, Wilson had taken care to supplement prayer with vigilance. He would depend on Tumulty, he had told his secretary, for candid reports on the state of public opinion in America. "When you think I am putting my foot in it, please say so frankly," was his parting shot. And to Secretary Daniels he had written before sailing: "I know you and all my colleagues will keep your eyes skinned against anybody getting the better of us while I am on the other side of the water."

bridge, laughing and waving in appreciation of each tribute. The day was just cold enough to be invigorating.

In the outer harbor the great liner came to anchor just as the sun broke through. French and American dignitaries boarded her and went to the President's suite. There was a boisterous reunion of war heroes. John J. Pershing had come to meet the eye of the Commander in Chief whom he thought a good President to him; and Admiral Sims, seeing the general for the first time since the Armistice, hailed him with: "Hello, Jack, how the hell did you do it? I didn't know you had it in you." [6]

A side-wheeler ferried the President's party to the quay, where they were met by officials who wore sashes of tricolor. Words of mutual greeting were exchanged with Brest's Socialist mayor. And then, stepping on French soil with silk hat in hand, his face radiant, Wilson bowed right and left to acknowledge the cheers of peasants who were crowding close—women in quaint headdresses, fishermen standing with wooden shoes in the mud. Between lines of French soldiers, past generals in red hats and Bretons in vivid costumes, through streets thronged with children waving American flags, the President was conducted to a pavilion decorated with crimson silk. There he heard the mayor hail him as the apostle of liberty, come to release the people of Europe from their tortures. The trim, formally dressed gentleman from America looked grave as he listened to the extravagance of the greeter. He responded in the intimate, appealing way that he had when he reached out to pluck at men's heartstrings. But he laughed when he read a banner that saluted him as the founder of a league of nations. This, he said, was a bit premature.

Arriving at Paris at ten in the morning, the party left their rose-colored armchairs and stepped into the vestibule of the car. There were cheers, and Wilson responded with a thin, shy smile. Down on the platform was Raymond Poincaré, President of the Republic, correct and formal in morning coat, and beside him his lady. A few paces behind stood a squat man under a high hat, wearing a square-tailed dress coat of good broadcloth, very much in need of pressing. His long arms were folded across his breast and he was grinning impishly. "Now I am going to see him," he was mumbling. "This is where we first take each other's measure." Lunging forward to the side of the car, Georges Clemenceau, The Tiger of France, the soul of his nation's resistance, stretched his hand high toward the American about whom everyone was talking.

Stepping out into the pale sunshine, the Wilsons found themselves in

[6] Palmer, *Bliss, Peacemaker*, p. 358; Charles Seymour, who was present, to the writer.

a city gone mad. On both sides soldiers bordered the avenues, statuesque at present-arms, yielding only to let wheel chairs carry comrades to the edge of the line of march; and behind them stood myriads of people, waving flags and yelling. Parisians who for years had muttered *c'est la guerre* now shrieked *"Vive Wil-son! Vive l'Amérique! Vive la liberté!"* There were miles of them, some delirious in the contagion of excitement, some weeping for joy. They crowded the sidewalks and the buildings, even perched on creaking trees. From windows and roofs, flowers rained down on Edith Wilson's carriage. Planes zoomed and battle flags dipped.

The hero from the West stood up in his open victoria, bareheaded, his hands stretched out toward the people, on his flushed face a smile that was to the Parisians the dawn of a new day. *"Le grand Américain,"* they called him, *"le pur champion du droit et de la justice, le Christophe Colomb d'un nouveau monde."* The press gave him more space than they had devoted to visits of kings, the Socialist journals acclaiming him as their champion, the conservatives accepting him indulgently.

Suddenly the carriages turned, rolled between heavy doors through an ivy-draped wall, and swept around a drive to imposing steps. The Wilsons found themselves in the privacy of the Murat Palace, where the voices of the people penetrated only faintly. Here this American of simple tastes was to dwell for two months—his sensibilities chilled by the artificiality of the furnishings.

Buttoning himself tightly into an old-fashioned frock coat that his valet had providently brought along, Wilson was soon off for a formal luncheon in the palace of the French President. There he found a world remote from the men and women who had greeted him along the boulevards. In this salon of Old World diplomacy, after a feast of fine viands and choice wines, the first sniping shots in the warfare of the peace were fired in the toasts of the two Presidents.

The host, who had advocated a harsh reckoning with Germany, gave his guest a taste of bitter sentiments. "The French government will hand you documents," Poincaré promised, "in which you will yourself see how the German Command, with astounding cynicism, set forth its program of pillage and destruction. Whatever precautions we may take, nobody, alas! can assert that we shall save humanity forever from further wars!"

Wilson responded directly to the challenge in a speech that was translated. "From the first," he said, "the thought of the people of the United States turned toward something more than the mere winning of this war. It realized that . . . it must be won in such a way as to insure the future peace of the world . . ." Sympathizing with France's indigna-

tion against German wantonness, the American said: "I appreciate, as
you do, sir, the necessity of such action in the final settlement of the
issues of the war as will not only rebuke such acts of terror and spolia-
tion, but make men everywhere aware that they cannot be ventured
upon without the certainty of just punishment."

Labor leaders of Paris, hoping to use the American as a lever to pry
concessions from Clemenceau, proposed a "manifestation" at the Troca-
dero, where thousands of working women were to present a bas-relief
to the American as the "incarnation of the hope of the future." When
the French premier cannily referred this proposal to Wilson, the President just as shrewdly told the workers that their own government
should make the decision. When conditions were imposed that made
the women abandon their plan, they went instead in a small group to
the Murat Palace and gave their trophy to their hero.

Before the President had left America he had from House a timetable
of projected events and a warning that the Allies were tending to delay
discussions. Even when Wilson arrived at Paris, the French had not
appointed their commissioners; and Lloyd George, who had been occupied in securing a mandate from his constituency in a national election,
was waiting to see what would happen in Germany and was conferring
with representatives of the Dominions. The Colonel, loyally accepting
Wilson's decision to come to Paris, kept on working to create an atmosphere of understanding. He assured the President that his suspicions of
a reactionary conspiracy among European statesmen were groundless—
a journalistic dream—that in reality all the powers were trying to work
with the United States and not as a European bloc. Now, with Wilson
on the scene, the Colonel considered that the second House mission had
ended its duties and henceforth, though a peace commissioner of equal
rank with the President, he would not take responsibility for making
decisions, but would revert to his old role of informant, impresario, and
friend. When Wilson told him that a league of nations would be the
center of his program, that almost all the difficulties would vanish once
the league was set up, the Colonel faithfully curbed his fears of anarchy
in Central Europe and his own inclination to give priority to a military
and economic settlement.

Impatient at the lagging of the peacemaking, Wilson was irritated by
news that came by cable from Washington. Especially was he aroused
by a message from Frank I. Cobb of the New York *World,* saying that
that influential liberal had reached the opinion, in his talks with high
officials at London and Paris, that Clemenceau and Lloyd George had
been stacking the cards against the President. Wilson had depended on
Cobb to direct the publicity policy of the American delegation at the

conference. Consequently, when he arrived at Paris and found that House had allowed the editor to sail for home, the President expressed deep disappointment, even though the Colonel had established cordial relations with other journalists.[7] Moreover, Wilson was very angry when he heard of two appointments that had been made in the American secretariat by Lansing.

The President had not been at Paris long before Tumulty was cabling that news of the peacemaking was inadequate, that the President must cooperate more actively with the press. Specifically, he must visit hospitals, sit at the bedside of private soldiers, shake hands with the *poilus,* "put across" his wonderful smile, and always have reporters and photographers on the alert beforehand.

And so Wilson motored with his wife to the American hospital at Neuilly, where he went from cot to cot, missing not one of the eleven hundred patients, making a little speech, telling a private who gave his name as Thomas Wilson that he was glad to be the namesake of such a brave man. Later in the same day they went to a pathetic Christmas party in a shabby ward in a French hospital. On Christmas Eve they boarded a frigid train, to awake at Chaumont in a snowstorm and be driven with General Pershing to crude billets where green sprays and bits of red paper were the only reminders of the season. There was a review of troops that sloshed through deep mud, and then joking and storytelling over a turkey and pumpkin pie, and a drive to the general's château, where they sat before an open fire and steaming tea.

The President was disappointed because he had his Christmas dinner at an officers' mess rather than with the soldiers in their barracks. But out in the gray dampness he looked for a few moments into the faces of the men who had fought for him and for whom he now stood ready to fight. "You knew when you came over what you came over for," he said, "and you have done what it was appointed you to do. I know what you expect of me . . . It is difficult, very difficult, men, in a formal speech like this to show you my real heart . . . A thrill has gone through my heart . . . with almost every gun that was fired and every stroke that was struck in the gallant fighting that you have done . . . I feel a comradeship with you today which is delightful. . . ." The nearer he approached to the fields of death, the stronger he found the impulse of the people toward a league of nations.

During the days of waiting at Paris there were evenings when the President could sit quietly with his wife in a room dimly lit by a shaded

[7] Cobb, who had been urged by Auchincloss to print an editorial eulogistic of House, felt that the Colonel, wishing to keep the reins in his own hands, had kept essential information from Wilson. It seemed to Cobb that House had made an unnecessary capitulation to Lloyd George on the freedom of the seas in the pre-Armistice negotiations.

lamp and flickerings from an open fire. An old friend found them sitting up late. "Edith never wants to go to bed," Wilson explained, "but along about this time I begin to get drowsy. When we retire from the White House we are going into vaudeville as 'Dopey Dan and Midnight Mary.'" Spread before him was a sheet of paper, cross-ruled, and on it he was rating Bermuda, California, and five Eastern cities on the score of Freedom, Climate, Intellectual Advantages, Social Advantages, Recreation, and Amusements. Like millions of Americans, he was finding refuge from the tempestuous present in anticipation of a secure old age.

Forced to bow to the exigencies of both European and American politics, Wilson and House conceived ways in which their sacred cause could be furthered directly. The President said bluntly to journalists that he believed the formation of a league of nations to be indispensable to the maintenance of peace. The ideal could be kept alive in the headlines, he hoped, by personal conference with Clemenceau and Lloyd George and by public appeals to the Allied peoples.

When he asked House to be present at his first meeting with The Tiger, the Colonel was prepared to coach each of his friends for the occasion. During the pre-Armistice negotiations House had won the personal respect of Clemenceau and had secured from him a pledge to bring up no matter in the coming conference that he did not first discuss with Wilson.

The champion of French resistance, facing in his seventy-eighth year the greatest ordeal that he had met in a half-century of public life, came to the conference professionally skeptical but personally cordial. The skullcap that he wore perpetually was on his massive head. Gray gloves covered the diseased skin of his hands, giving a silky gloss to a squat body and a mind tense with the coiled springs of epigram. Half-concealed under heavy eyebrows and a brushy mustache, eyes and mouth did not betray the thoughts of this redoubtable pleader as he exchanged pleasantries. Having lived in the United States for four years—he had entered Richmond just after General Grant and had married a New York girl from whom he had been divorced—Clemenceau spoke the language of the Americans.

Wilson greeted him charmingly and showed himself the brilliant colleague whom House had been commending, not the intractable bigot that political enemies had been caricaturing. Afterward the Colonel gloated. "I have never seen an initial meeting a greater success," he wrote in his diary. "The President was perfect in the matter and manner of his conversation . . . neither said anything that was particularly misleading. They simply did not touch upon topics which would breed discussion. I saw to that in advance." House was coming to look upon the Peace Conference as his Grand Guignol.

The cordial interview fired Wilson's impatience to come to grips with the formidable Frenchman on the subject that was to him all-important —the league of nations. And so House was asked to set the stage for a more serious conversation. This time, arriving at the Murat Palace fifteen minutes before the French premier, the Colonel suggested to Wilson that Clemenceau could best be brought around to the league through mention of freedom of the seas, a topic on which American and French views might be expected to harmonize, in contrast with Britain's ideas. Again House's tactics were successful. The President talked at great length—and very well indeed. The Tiger began to see that the American could be counted on to be fair to France on questions on which Lloyd George had been opposing her; and soon he was hoping that Wilson would sit in the inner councils of peacemaking. Frankly doubting that a league would prove to be practical, Clemenceau nevertheless agreed that the experiment should be tried.

While committing their leader, the prophet from the West continued to woo the French people. At the Murat Palace the hours were filled with dinners, receptions, auto rides, calls from the great men of Europe. On a Sunday he went to the American Presbyterian Church, and then to Lafayette's tomb, insisting that he go himself with a wreath instead of commissioning a florist to deliver it. The next day an open carriage took him to the Hôtel de Ville to be acclaimed a citizen of Paris; and again there were crowds and troops in brilliant array, and a presentation of a gold pen with which to sign the peoples' peace, and toasts drunk in the best champagne.

The members of the French Academy—robed in yellow, blue, and scarlet—rose and cheered the American scholar when he appeared at a ceremony at which Marshal Joffre was made one of the Forty Immortals.[8] Invited to the Sorbonne to receive the degree of *Doctor Honoris Causa,* Woodrow Wilson felt himself back in the atmosphere that he most loved. Speaking without notes, as in all of his appearances at Paris, he extolled the university spirit for its intolerance of all things that put the human mind under restraint. He took the occasion to set forth his concept of a league of nations.

During these days of honeymoon with *La Belle France,* Wilson was disturbed by the tardiness of the British peace delegates. Northcliffe, whose cooperation House had been cultivating, noted the President's

---

[8] From Marshal Joffre's address on this occasion, Wilson jotted down this sentence: "Let her [France] never forget that the weak and the small cannot live free in the world if the strong and the great are not ever ready to place their strength and power at the disposal of right."

impatience and suggested to Balfour that Wilson be invited to visit England. As plans for the trip took shape, House thought it wise to use newspaper space that had been put at his disposal by Northcliffe. Accordingly, a report of an interview with the President was drafted by House's men, accepted by Wilson with slight changes, and published in the London *Times*. In this statement the President paid tribute to the British fleet and recognized "Britain's peculiar position as an Island Empire," but showed no sympathy for the imperialistic ambitions of some Englishmen.

The King was irritated because Wilson's arrival was set for Boxing Day—a bank holiday. Nevertheless, he and the Queen and the prime minister met the Wilsons on a crimson carpet at Charing Cross Station. The President's smile grew broadest when he greeted Lord Robert Cecil, English champion of a league of nations.

When Professor Woodrow Wilson had traveled in England some twenty years before, frequenting literary shrines and quiet, rural places, he had gone home feeling himself a better American for having been there. He still loved the traditions that had become familiar to him in his youthful studies of Gladstone and Bright; and yet he was amused by the fuss made over him as a statesman, and quite unawed. The next morning he exchanged familiar greetings with the servants—all except one, whose crust he could not pierce.

After a palace dinner His Majesty toasted the efficacy of American arms; but the President, standing in his black dress suit and flaunting no medals, responded by asserting the obligation of governments to obey "the great moral tide running in the hearts of men." He gave no brotherly pat on the back for a war well fought, no glorification of Anglo-Saxon victory in battle. He seemed to take England for granted. ("After all, in a certain sense, England is a success in the world," Walter Bagehot had written fifty years before.)

Lloyd George, sitting at the table, noted a coolness in the applause and remarked on it to Reading. Word was passed to the President; and the next day, speaking at the Guildhall, Wilson did lip service to the "prowess and achievements" of the British and the other Allies. Then the prophet went on to preach his gospel, hoping to align the dignitaries publicly with his own thinking. "There must now be," he proclaimed, "not a balance of power, not one powerful group of nations set off against another, but a single overwhelming group of nations who shall be the trustee of the peace of the world . . ." This was the "incomparably great object" that had brought him overseas, this "final political enterprise of humanity."

At luncheon in the Mansion House the next day, in a hall medieval in atmosphere, the lord bishop of London asked grace; and when wine was poured for toasts, it was tasted first by a functionary as a precaution against poison. After this demonstration of ancient ritual the American prophet assailed the fetters of old custom. It had seemed a normal thing for him to come to Europe, he said, because the necessity for intimate conferences took precedence over every other duty. "After all," he proclaimed, "breaking of precedents, though this may sound strange doctrine in England, is the most sensible thing to do. The harnessing of precedent is sometimes a very sad and harassing trammel." Determined not to be absorbed by British atmosphere, as he felt that Page and Sims had been, he preached an American gospel.

After the speechmaking there were complaints among the shipping interests that the American had not congratulated England on her incomparable fleet; and Lloyd George was far from satisfied by Wilson's preceptive attitude. It seemed to him poor taste, to say the least, for the American to preach on the ascendancy of right over might to men who for four years had been bleeding in support of his text.

In the Midlands, however, the President found auditors were congenial. Early on a rainy Sunday morning the King's train brought him into the town of Carlisle, near the Scottish border. The old kirk in which his grandfather had preached offered a restful contrast to the glitter of royalty. In deference to Thomas Woodrow's aversion to lay preaching, Wilson determined to remain silent, but less than an hour before the service the minister prevailed on him to change his mind. Invited to the pulpit, he preferred to stand in front of the communion rail. Harking back to his grandfather, he recalled "how much he required" and "the stern lessons of duty he gave." He could still hear that voice— flavored by a mild toddy and smoke from a clay pipe—asking, challenging: "Tommie, what is the chief end of man?" As he stood on boards that his mother's tiny feet had once trod, he was moved to recall her "sense of duty and dislike of ostentation." He spoke fervently of his twentieth century mission to the world: "I believe that as this war has drawn the nations temporarily together in a combination of physical force we shall now be drawn together in a combination of moral force that will be irresistible . . . It is from quiet places like this all over the world that the forces accumulate which presently will overbear any attempt to accomplish evil on a large scale."

Save for the compelling voice, there was no sound but the patter of rain on the roof. The bishop of Carlisle, closing the service, could hardly master his feelings to articulate the benediction: "God save you and guide you, sir!" The President was glad to step into the seclusion of the vestry to sign the book, for there he could get control of his emotion.

At Manchester the lord mayor hailed him as "foremost of all Americans who have ever visited England." He spoke twice, making the most of this chance to attack the old order and to steady the merry-go-round platform of Lloyd George. In the Free Trade Hall in which John Bright's voice once had thundered he said:

You know that heretofore the world has been governed, or at any rate an attempt has been made to govern it, by partnerships of interest, and they have broken down. Interest does not bind men together. Interest separates men, for the moment there is the slightest departure from the nice adjustment of interests, jealousies begin to spring up. There is only one thing that can bind people together and that is a common devotion to right. Ever since the history of liberty began men have talked about their rights, and it has taken several hundred years to make them perceive that the principal part of right is duty, and that unless a man performs his full duty he is entitled to no right.

Serving notice that the United States would "join no combination of power which is not the combination of us all," he ended with a devout wish that like his "very stern ancestors . . . who were known as the Covenanters," they might enter into a great league and covenant for all the world.

Here was the essence of Wilsonism—the same vague and generalized appeal to common counsel and dynamic morals that had transcended the interests of ingrown groups at Princeton and at Washington. It cut across national boundaries, soared above party concerns. It was working in the hearts of Europeans.

Going to the Midland Hotel for luncheon, he declared that it was not skill of hand, but elevation of spirit, that made worthy men; and stopping at the Royal Exchange, he reminded the traders that he knew something about their business, and hoped that they "would all make money out of it." They laughed when he added, with a sly wink: "I suspect that in the transactions at this place occasionally a little is lost." The bustling lord mayor found him comradely and jovial, as they sat on the captain's bridge on a tender in the ship canal and watched an American vessel unload cotton. The people of the Midlands discovered in their visitor a warmth and understanding that he had not revealed at London.

Wilson received assurance in England that not only the liberal citizens, but their leaders as well, were devoted to his ideal. Grey, Asquith, and the archbishop of Canterbury came to him to plead for a league of nations and found him utterly confident. He said proudly that his wife considered him the most obstinate man in America, and that nothing could induce him to yield. He told of an issue that had come before Lincoln's Cabinet: after a unanimous chorus of "noes," the President said "aye" and then "the ayes have it!" At this evidence of fanaticism Asquith's heart sank and filled with grave forebodings for the success of their ideal.[9]

Some British politicians with whom Wilson conferred gave more heed to the voters who had just re-elected them than to the American prophet who had been repudiated by his own electorate, by ex-President Roosevelt, and, in a speech in the Senate in mid-December that was intended chiefly to impress the Allies, by Henry Cabot Lodge. David Lloyd George, especially, seemed no man to take up a great cause and joust for it against all comers. He had a record of prewar liberalism, however, that matched that of the President. The "born politician" that Wilson fancied in himself could not but admire Lloyd George's adroitness, his accessibility to people with whom he did not agree. Wilson felt that if only he could trust the "little man" he could get along with him more easily than with the rather terrifying intellect of Foreign Secretary Balfour. If only he could set the veering Welsh weather vane steadfastly toward the league of nations!

The British leaders had been studying their man and as a result feared to cross the President unnecessarily. Both Lloyd George and Balfour inclined to agree that, once set up, a league could assist in working out specific settlements that seemed vital. The prime minister was relieved to get assurance that Wilson did not contemplate giving executive powers to a league, and to learn that the American's ideas resembled those of Lord Robert Cecil and General Smuts of South Africa.[10] But they disagreed on the question of indemnities; and when the President's

[9] Sir Gilbert Murray in *The Listener*, LIV, No. 1388 (Oct. 6, 1955). Grey wrote on Dec. 30 to assure House that if a league took "practical form," the undercurrent of opposition would be "completely snowed under by an overwhelming mass of public opinion." But Grey feared that a treaty creating a league might be wrecked by the United States Senate. "We are afraid that for us to force the pace here might contribute to that result," he wrote.

[10] House had not felt well enough to accompany Wilson to England and in his place had sent his son-in-law, Gordon Auchincloss. By telephone, the Colonel had advised that the President bear down on the league of nations but keep off the dangerous topic of "freedom of the seas."

Auchincloss, attempting to set up Wilson-Lloyd George conferences in the way in which House had guided Wilson's meetings with Clemenceau, offended the President and his official "family" by his officiousness. The presence at Paris of the Colonel's daughter and son-in-law and the latter's law partner, David Hunter Miller, as well as that of Mrs. Mezes, Mrs. House's sister, put a severe strain on the President's respect for his beloved Colonel. (American delegates were expected to leave their wives at home.) Moreover, Dr. Mezes did not include among the experts taken to Paris the President's own son-in-law, Francis B. Sayre, who had canceled other plans in order to work in New York for The Inquiry.

It was suggested to the President by those near him that the Colonel had presumed on his friendship. Later, when it was proposed that Auchincloss serve as Wilson's secretary in council meetings, the President resented this, as an attempt to "keep track" of him on the part of House and the other commissioners. Irwin H. Hoover's notes, Library of Congress.

views were reported by Lloyd George to the Imperial War Cabinet, they were received with skepticism and partisan feeling.

Wilson returned to Paris on the last day of 1918, surprised at Lloyd George's acquiescence in a league and doubting the steadfastness of the Welshman's support. He put greater faith in a plan published by General Smuts, and hoped that the South African's influence in British councils might be strong enough to bring the great cause to fruition.

Talking with his fellow commissioners in House's rooms, Wilson said that his trip to England had cleared the air, that Britain was closer than France to the American point of view. This feeling was confirmed in discussion of a speech that Clemenceau had made in the French Chamber three days before, favoring the balancing of power through international alliances, accepting a league of nations only as a supplementary guarantee of French security, and referring to the *"noble candeur"* of the American President—a phrase that was interpreted to imply that Wilson was a well-intentioned simpleton.[11]

With House, the President went through stacks of papers from Washington. He unhesitatingly signed documents that the Colonel vouched for, but remarked that he would veto any legislation sponsored solely by the Republicans. Together the friends disposed of a vast accumulation of business in a few hours. House was in deep gloom. But the President, holding to his faith in "the people," seemed confident that they would drive their statesmen to base the peace on a durable foundation.

On the first day of the new year, he left Paris for Italy, where, his ambassador had reported, English propagandists had been undermining American prestige.

All forebodings, however, seemed at first unwarranted. The Wilsons were given a triumph worthy of the Caesars, as the royal coach drove them from end to end of Rome's Via Nationale and the multitudes waved flags and shouted *"Viva Wilson!"* To Edith Wilson it was a day of thrills. They visited the war hospital to which most of the rooms of the palace were still devoted and, lunching informally with Their Majesties at a villa outside the city, they saw the royal family at home— genuine, lovely, talented. She appraised every detail and loved it all, while her husband chafed and bridled at delays that made it impossible to get on with his mission.

[11] Clemenceau explained to House that he had not intended to give offense and had used the phrase to applaud Wilson's frankness and loyalty, while giving warning that both he and the President were in a difficult situation and must necessarily view it from different standpoints. Bonsal, *Suitors and Suppliants*, p. 211.

The vote in the Chamber approving Clemenceau's policy was about in the ratio of four to one.

Honored by a request that he be the first nonmember to address the Italian Chamber of Deputies from the floor, Wilson found that the Socialists had protested by withdrawing in a body. Undaunted, he asked for sympathy for the Balkan States that "must now be independent." It was a bold stroke, this plea for tolerance toward Yugoslav aspirations that ran head-on into Italy's territorial ambitions along the Adriatic. Again the prophet warned Old World politicians that a new concept of government was dawning.

Whether the President should visit the Pope was a problem without precedent. Protestant clergymen in America had warned against it; but Cardinal Gibbons had urged that the President call on "the highest moral authority left in the world" and Tumulty had reminded Wilson of the influence that His Holiness could throw behind a league of nations. And so the President agreed to visit the Vatican, but insisted on attending a Protestant reception on the same day.

Pope Benedict greeted him warmly in English, commending his efforts toward a league of nations. While these spiritual leaders talked, sitting in gilded chairs before an open window, a multitude of Italians stood in a piazza for hours, waiting for a speech by the American that had been advertised. However, when the time came for him to go out and address them, they had been dispersed by officials. Foreign Minister Sonnino explained that the authorities feared that the crowd might get out of hand, that it was unnecessary for the President to speak.

Wilson was angered. He was not used to being denied the right to preach to a congregation, wherever he found it. But he was not surprised. House had directed his attention to the failure of the Italian ministers to urge him to go to North Italy, where he might expect to find liberal support in the industrial cities.

On the way back to Paris, however, he made brief stops. Leaving the train at Genoa, he paid lip service to Christopher Columbus, and stood with bared head before Mazzini's monument, deeply moved, he said, by a spirit of "veneration" and "emulation." There were six brief speeches at Milan, where placards announced: "Italy demands only the frontiers marked out for her by God." When his voice was drowned by a band playing a Sousa march he waved his arms and led the music until the last bar. The next day he made five short talks on a rainy day in Turin, one of them at the university, where Wilson delighted the students by wearing one of their blue caps. More than a thousand mayors came from surrounding towns to shake his hand—some to bend and kiss it. Here, in North Italy, he had his chance to appeal directly to the people for a new world order, and they swarmed about him and cheered themselves hoarse.

When the train stopped at Modena, a messenger brought in a tele-gram. As he glanced at it, his companions saw in his face, first, surprise, then pity, and finally relief. His political archenemy would throw no more stilettos into his back, would never again declare him politically bankrupt and without honor in his own land. The Scottish fiber in him had somehow outlasted a rival who was his junior by two years. Theodore Roosevelt, his lusty antagonist, was dead.

Sitting quiet for a moment, he dictated a message to Roosevelt's widow. The news had "deeply grieved" him, he said, but on second thought he changed "grieved" to "shocked." It was equally decorous and more honest.[12]

Woodrow Wilson returned to Paris with a confidence that was all-possessing. It was easy, at this point, to convince himself that the people of Europe had been cheering for Wilson the peace giver rather than for a living symbol of their own victory or a guarantee of security for themselves in the future. Moreover, he did not doubt that his Americans would repudiate the disciples of the fallen Republican leader, once he could go home and plead with them. However, his advisers were feeling the brute force of nationalistic ambitions. House had reported to the President in November that the whole world was vitally interested in America's plans for using her vast resources of credit and raw materials; and the Colonel had suggested that experts in these matters be brought to Paris. This had been done, and as the American specialists had wrestled with the immediate problems of reconstruction in a spirit of charity and forbearance, their apprehensions were being realized all too fully. Herbert Hoover, who had been made director general of relief and rehabilitation, was striving to give practical effect to the ideal of collective altruism. He worked day and night to break down economic barriers to a flow of food and fuel to Central Europe. Scores of thousands of civilians were stalked by famine; city populations were threatened by anarchy and by the unpredictable bolshevism that was seeping westward; more than a dozen little nations—many of them just liberated—were writing provisional constitutions, building armies, grabbing territories, setting up obstacles to trade. But, torn as the Continent was by political parturition, officials of the Allies were slow to yield to Hoover's appeals for civilian relief. As individuals, they thought idealistically; but as representatives of peoples who had been ruined and bled white, they naturally thought first of the welfare of their own constitu-

---

[12] Lloyd George reports that when he entered the President's room at Paris and expressed sorrow at Roosevelt's death, he was "aghast at the outburst of acrid detestation which flowed from Wilson's lips." Lloyd George, *Memoirs of the Peace Conference*, I, 147.

encies. They too expected succor from the United States—a nation that had gained much in credits and lost little in blood. Moreover, they were suspicious that Uncle Sam would use his bulging granaries to buy political influence in Central Europe. Wilson was shocked when Hoover denounced many of the Allies as "second-story workers" who thought Americans a foolish people, pliable to ingenious propaganda, and accepted the United States as a "golden-egged goose." [13]

When the President returned to Paris he learned of political machinations that aggravated his distrust of his allies. There were rumors that the French were holding back the rehabilitation of war-ravaged lands so they might exhibit them to him and make him "see red." Suspecting that there was some truth in this report, Wilson put off a French suggestion that he visit the devastated region, and explained to his staff that he already knew enough about the ravages of war: his own family's property had suffered when Sherman marched to the sea.

There was an even more ominous undercurrent in a secret meeting of the British delegation that was held early in January. Giving his colleagues a realistic picture of American politics, Lloyd George portrayed Wilson as a man whose political credit was insecure, whose drafts America might not honor, and yet a powerful leader whose thin skin must not be pricked by any reminder of the precariousness of his position.

[13] Hoover in the *Saturday Evening Post*, Nov. 1, 1941; and Hoover to the writer. Hoover's experience in economic relief led him to advise Wilson to give a league of nations no powers, but only the right to inquire and to state facts. The only solid foundation for a league was a spirit of cooperation, this enterprising executive felt, and such a spirit might be dampened by too legalistic a constitution.

Though Wilson thought him unduly pessimistic, Hoover did not despair of effective action. At a dinner party he told guests who were criticizing the President that he had seen Woodrow Wilson solve many difficult problems by sheer force of intellect.

CHAPTER XIII

MAKING A COVENANT FOR THE TWENTIETH CENTURY

WOODROW WILSON RETURNED to Paris on January 7 physically worn out. Dr. Grayson saw that before coming to grips with the premiers he must rest for a day or two. The physician himself, in an effort to shield his patient from strain, performed many of the duties of a staff officer, fending off importunate journalists and pleaders for divers causes.

In his struggle for a world political order Wilson would have to operate without the party machinery that he had used at Trenton and Washington. There would be no caucuses, no patronage, no party whips, no legislative committees to help to frame new measures. Even his most intimate and incisive weapon—The Word—would be blunted by translators. More than ever before, he was to need a well-disciplined, competent staff; but he had only his White House secretaries, who knew little about either the languages or the diplomacy of the Continent.

On the very day of his return from Italy, the President talked for a half hour over the private wire that ran directly from his study to the desk and bedside of Colonel House. The Colonel, established at the Hotel Crillon, was already performing many of the functions of diplomacy. Wilson was well pleased, he said, with his trip to Rome, and he listened eagerly to House's résumé of events at Paris during his absence. Late in the afternoon he met the American commissioners. He was received respectfully by the four appointees who were technically his equal in rank and who had been meeting together during his absence, unsure of their powers and responsibilities in relation to those of the diplomats, the military and naval staffs, and the special agents.

Lansing, to whom the President had paid little attention, was thinking of resigning. Sitting alone at his desk, hour after hour, the secretary of state recorded his dissents in a diary in a copybook hand.[1] He was

---

[1] Lansing's views were, in brief: "democracy was enough; no sanctions or legislative power were needed (by an international body); the peoples wanted justice and peace; expansion was legitimate against half-civilized people; rival territorial claims could be settled by diplomacy or court action." W. E. Rappard, *op. cit.*, p. 4.

Flatly opposing Wilson's positive plan for guaranteeing nations against aggression, Lansing complained in his diary that it was farcical to think that any foreign government would surrender a single right or aid any victim of aggression unless it appeared to be to its material advantage to do so. Moreover, he wrote in his diary that the right of self-determination—"government by consent of the governed"—was "simply loaded with dynamite" and "bound to be the basis of impossible demands on the Peace Congress and to create trouble in many lands." He felt that nations could be expected to do nothing more than sign a legalistic, negative

scornful of Wilson's deficiencies as an international lawyer and perturbed because the President had not even acknowledged a proposal for
guaranteeing security that he had taken pains to draft. He attributed
Wilson's rejection of his ideas to inordinate ambition to cut a heroic
figure in history.

Told by Henry White of Lansing's pique at the President's preference
for the counsel of House, Wilson said, "It never occurred to me," and
then, underestimating the Colonel's intelligence, "I am quite sure it
never did to House." Discussing the problem with Edith Wilson and
with the Colonel, he concluded that, as had been the case with Bryan,
this dissenting Presbyterian had better be in his bosom rather than on
his back. Not willing to risk shaking public confidence in his cause by
dismissing a servant unsympathetic to it, he patiently suffered Lansing's
repetitive dissents with courteous smiles and nods that were misinterpreted as signs of sympathy.

Like Lansing, General Bliss had strong views of his own. Gruff, very
shy of personal publicity, a man who always carried a Latin text in his
pocket, studied Oriental botany, and swore beautifully, Bliss craved
peace. He saw, perhaps more vividly than any of the military men at
Paris, the handwriting on the sky of the future. He was distressed by
the vagueness of the President's remarks on policy and by the casualness
of the meetings of the American Commission; and he put more emphasis than his chief on the necessity for disarmament.[2] Bliss was to
prove a valiant lieutenant, rarely volunteering advice, quickly supplying
information when it was called for. Wilson thought him "a real thinking man who takes the pains to think straight."

The President could depend, too, on the disciplined loyalty of Henry
White, a diplomat of fine old vintage with a bouquet of quality and
tradition, commanding both respect and affection as he limped into the
Crillon from his daily walk, his cheeks apple-red under thick white
hair, in one hand a proper cane and in the other a tall black hat with a

---

undertaking not to commit acts of aggression. Lansing criticized Wilson as "too deliberate" or
else "not just sure what he wants."

Lansing brought his misgivings to House and the Colonel did his best to excuse Wilson's
indifference toward the secretary of state by attributing it to ill-health and by telling white
lies. Lansing set down House's tactful approaches to the President as evidence of weakness.
Though the Colonel's method seemed to work, it was to him *infra dig.* "I must either keep
quiet or else speak frankly my views," he protested. And yet only a week before writing this
in his diary he had indulged, in talking with Wilson, in a diplomatic prevarication of his true
feeling about the positive guarantee that was so dear to the President.

[2] A letter from Baker to Bliss, dated Dec. 3, 1918, reported the invention of an aerial bomb
that could be produced in quantity and, carrying 200 pounds of high explosives, would deviate
less than one-eighth of 1 per cent at a range of 50 miles. It seemed to Bliss that such a weapon
would be a constant argument for a league of nations as well as for limiting armaments to
policing necessities.

broad band around it. Wilson became fond of the old gentleman. A master of French and of diplomatic protocol, gallant with the ladies, White did his best to create teamwork among his compatriots and liaison with Europeans. He hinted to Wilson that he be detailed to make the personal contacts that his experience had taught him were necessary. Not encouraged, he presumed no further, but sought the confidence and help of Edith Wilson. At first lukewarm toward the President's league ideal, he grew to appreciate Wilson's character and his purposes, and wrote appreciatively of them to his Republican friends at home— "affectionately" to "Dear Cabot." [3]

It was at the office of Colonel House—not at the President's residence —that the American commissioners first met formally with their chief. The Colonel soon excused himself from the meeting and went into another room to greet Clemenceau, just back from a soothing respite in the Vendée. In a heart-to-heart talk House pointed out that France no longer could count on Russia as an ally against Germany, nor could she be sure of the support of Britain and the United States except under a league of nations. "Wilson can force the league through," House asserted, because with all their "brag and bluster" the Senate would not dare to defeat a peace treaty and thereby continue alone at war.

The champion of France seemed to see it all clearly, and placing both hands on House's shoulders, he said: "You are right. I am for the League of Nations as you have it in mind and you may count upon me to work with you." [4]

[3] Before accepting a place on the peace commission, White had lunched with his friend Lodge and other Republicans of the Senate Foreign Relations Committee. Moreover, he had conferred with Root at the bedside of Roosevelt, and had taken notes on the ideas of these men on international organization. Just before sailing he had received from Lodge a long message, insisting that Germany be crushed, divided, and heavily loaded with indemnities, and warning that any attempt to weave a league of nations into the peace treaty would make the Senate's ratification of the treaty extremely doubtful.

Lodge asked that Henry White show this paper in strict confidence to Balfour and Clemenceau, hoping that it would help "in strengthening their position" at the expense of that of the President of the United States. White, however, disapproved his friend's views on Germany; and realizing that the senator's maneuver might subvert the President's dearest ideal, he kept the message discreetly to himself. White assured Lodge that Wilson was quite equal in argument and clearness of statement to the European statesmen. To William Phillips he wrote on Jan. 24: "The President is really a wonderful man . . . He has absolutely established the combination of President and prime minister to an extent that I should never have believed possible."

[4] Ever since the Armistice, Colonel House had been as busy in Wilson's interest as recurring disorders of his gall bladder had permitted. Under the carte blanche that the President had given to him, he had placed his large clerical staff at Wilson's disposal. He felt that the President was burdening himself needlessly by taking the care of documents on his own conscience and by getting along with the aid of only two permanent secretaries whom he had brought from Washington.

Journalists came to regard the Colonel as "the small knothole through which must pass many great events." Moreover, many of the pressures of cranks and promoters of sundry causes— exerted through hundreds of scouts and lobbyists—tried the unfathomable patience of the Texan. Then, too, spokesmen of nations large and small, born or reborn, flooded through House's hospitable door to whisper messages that they could not, or dared not, deliver to the

House then took Clemenceau into the room where the President was talking to the American commissioners. Immediately The Tiger leaped at Wilson with an old, sore question: When would the President go to see the devastated areas of France? Wilson put him off, and he did not like it. Nevertheless, he now agreed with the President's desire to begin the conferences at once, and seconded Wilson in urging Lloyd George to come to Paris.

Having given little thought to peace terms until the war was won, Clemenceau had hastened after the Armistice to have traditional procedures laid down for the peacemakers. His Foreign Office had drafted a precise and conventional plan: first, settlement of the war; secondly, organization of a society of nations; thirdly, study of territorial and political affairs and general international questions.

Wilson had been unimpressed by the exact, legalistic coldness of the proposition, when it had been sent to him by the State Department. It characterized his principles as "not sufficiently defined in their character to be taken as a basis for a concrete settlement of the war."

In the first week of January, when Wilson had expected that the Peace Conference would begin, there was still no agreement on a program. Indeed, the Anglo-Saxon leaders preferred to improvise a procedure from day to day rather than commit themselves to a plan dictated by Latin logic. As explosive fears and ambitions flew about in a vacuum of indecision, Wilson moved cautiously but persistently toward his Fourteenth Point, the league of nations that he thought vital to establishing many of the other points.

He thought that if he rightly interpreted the temper of the world's people, through the intuitive sense on which he prided himself, they would respond now, while the wounds of war were still open; but soon they might sink into a coma of complacency from which only a more terrible war could rouse them. To those who were near him he disclaimed credit for originating the idea of a league. "Along with thousands of my fellow countrymen," he once explained, "I got the idea twenty years ago, chiefly from Republican public men."

Wilson hoped that at least he might lay a durable foundation for a league before he had to return to the United States for the closing of Congress in February. But he made up his mind that, if the Allies made this impossible, he would surprise them by returning later to France.

President, remote in the Murat Palace. Bypassing the secretary of state, the British delegation kept liaison constantly with the Colonel through Sir William Wiseman.

House's position depended on holding the confidence that Wilson had extended to him as to no other man. He must make sure that he kept a finger on all vital pulses of opinion and action during the peacemaking. He must guard vigilantly against personal animosities and jealousies. His inmost thoughts were preserved for history in a diary to be opened thirty years later.

Moreover, he said that, if necessary, he could use financial pressure to bring them around.

Early in January he communicated his enthusiasm to his American colleagues; and they agreed with him in placing the league first among five topics to be proposed for discussion by the Supreme War Council.[5] In giving the American list to the premiers, he spoke of the folly of regarding it as a fixed agendum and suggested that each national delegation be asked to comment on it. He wished to avoid the appearance of dictating anything, but he insisted that all eyes be kept intent on the highest objectives. His own ideas about both the method of making peace and the terms were still in a formative stage, and he was as shy as ever about releasing the product of his political thinking until it was complete and ripe.

Still looking to the poets and philosophers for truth, he turned more readily to academic talk than he had under the pressures of the war. One night he spoke feelingly of the impossibility of peace on no moral foundation but hatred. The world's people wanted a just settlement, he thought, but the ruling classes did not. Justice did not require that the German people be punished, for they would suffer enough when the world shunned them for generations to come.

He spoke of the resentment of the people against their statesmen for delay in the parleys, a delay that some of the French newspapers had been unjustly attributing to him. It was so hard to get people together. Clemenceau had needed rest, but was now back. However, dear House was stricken severely by influenza. After the Colonel's fever subsided, the President went almost daily to his bedside to take counsel.[6]

Finally, the statesmen of Europe turned their thoughts in earnest toward the inevitable battle of peacemaking. Woodrow Wilson's sensibilities were shocked at the very first gathering of the Supreme Council on January 12. Giving up his Sabbath rest on that afternoon, he donned his frock coat and silk hat, tucked a large black portfolio under his arm, and motored with Dr. Grayson to the Quai d'Orsay. There he was met

[5] One topic on the agenda suggested by the American Commission—representation of the various nations at the conference—already had been discussed by the council. The other five were: league of nations; reparations; new states; territorial adjustments; colonial possessions.

[6] Colonel House shared his friend's political faith with a quiet sincerity that other Americans lacked. He did not forget that only the impulse of the people could give life to the league, that democratic spirit could be stirred by phrases that touched men's hearts, that the President had given his country mottoes that had sent men to their death with cheers. In his book, *Philip Dru,* he had envisioned a league of nations. The public of America and Europe demanded this, he felt, and he wrote in his diary that "the consensus of public opinion comes nearer being right than the opinions of the leaders of a country." The President's dependence on House's skill in negotiation was more complete than ever. When Wilson visited the Crillon, he passed swiftly by Lansing's office and went up to House's room. He was vexed if anyone but the Colonel took initiative.

with diplomatic flutter and bustle. The President found twenty-two men from the major powers sitting along three sides of a formal room—the premiers and foreign ministers in the forefront, and the secretaries, experts, and interpreters behind or to one side. Soon serious discussion was interrupted by retirement to a tea table, where all munched macaroons and brioches. It all reminded him of an old ladies' sewing circle: everyone talking and to no purpose.

Wilson had foreseen the ineffectiveness of such a group. He had said, while on the *George Washington*: "Twenty-five or thirty delegates in one room mulling and quarreling over the details of a treaty would be a criminal waste of time . . ." He favored a small council, composed of the premiers of England, France, and Italy, and himself, to meet secretly and prepare tentative proposals for presentation to a general gathering of delegates in the public view. It was obvious to him that the first of his Fourteen Points—"open covenants openly arrived at"—could not be applied literally to all the proceedings at Paris.

Wilson expected that arrangements for the first plenary session would be discussed at the meeting of January 12. Instead, with their military men present, the French insisted on taking up conditions for extending the Armistice agreement, which was to expire in five days. Perceiving what was in the wind, the President quickly summoned General Bliss to his side. Then, asking for a reading of the original terms, he made it clear that it would be unsportsmanlike to force more severe strictures upon Germany now if the military advisers had failed to think of them at the proper time. The question of renewing the Armistice was referred to General Bliss and the other military men. Nine days later, still resisting French pressure for further emasculation of Germany, Bliss wrote to his wife: "Peace seems to be worse than war."

Clemenceau retained the chair without challenge. He adroitly eliminated the military men from the Supreme War Council and transformed it into a Council of Ten in which the five major powers (Japan was the fifth) were to write the peace. The ministers of state who sat in this body were not, like the American President, secure in their positions for a definite term of years. They were doughty parliamentarians, accustomed to battle for their political lives; and they had magnetism that was hard to escape, when they turned the currents on.

The question of national representation came up, and Lloyd George stepped forward to plead for the British Dominions. Dressed in an unconventional gray suit and a bowler, the Welshman was accustomed to come to meetings a moment late, with a step that seemed to swagger a bit and greetings that were bluff and genial. When he claimed two peace delegates from each of the Dominions, Wilson took issue with him. Arguing that the question of representation was "largely one of sentiment and psychology," the prophet warned that if the empire were given so many delegates, it would appear that the large powers dominated the Peace Conference. To this the Welshman replied: "After all, they ran the war. Those who fought hardest should talk loudest."

The discussion turned then to the representation of small powers. Sitting bolt upright in his armchair, inclining his head at times toward his advisers, Wilson listened intently. Then, leaning forward and resting on the arms of his chair, he spoke like a college professor criticizing a thesis.

Everything affecting the world's peace was the world's business, he remarked. The dispatch of Serbian troops into little Montenegro distressed him, he said, for Montenegro had a handsome political history.

"Do you recognize the King?" quizzed Lloyd George.

"We do," Wilson replied.

"We pay for him," Balfour put in.

Clemenceau let himself go in a demand that small powers, though having moral rights equal to those of all, should not be allowed to share in decisions on matters that did not directly concern them. Wilson and Balfour had in mind some sort of preliminary conversations among the great powers, to be followed by consultation with the little countries when their interests were at stake. All were agreed, however, that enemy nations should not be represented until agreement had been reached among themselves.

They were trying each other out in this first session. The American scholar-prophet puzzled the others with his passion for academic justness, his desire to get the "sense of the meeting." British secretaries thought him very tiresome and "a quaint bird." It seemed so hard to bring him to a decision on details on which European negotiators were used to speaking quickly and firmly. When Clemenceau asked his opinion, he reviewed arguments that had been made on both sides of the case. And when The Tiger canvassed the other members of the council and came back to the President with "Well, what shall we do?" Wilson suggested referring the question to a committee of experts or asked whether anyone had prepared a resolution. Usually the British delegation had one ready and was quick to put it forward, though sometimes, if the President had expressed his own views, Clemenceau would ask him to draft a resolution. Then, writing in pencil and without revision, Wilson would phrase his thoughts with a clarity and conciseness that no colleague could match. They soon came to admire his control of his tongue, his utter fairness, his patient courtesy toward all shades of opinion, his eagerness that decisions, when finally made, be carried out.

The perfection of his discourse gave an air of finality to his words. Perhaps realizing this, and embarrassed by the thought that anyone should consider him an oracle, he sometimes interrupted the flow of language with a little nervous chuckle—a mannerism that his associates had noted seldom before. He wished to treat these able fellow statesmen as colleagues, bearing with their thought as long as possible, making no remark that would give offense, until his conscience was satisfied and a decision had to be made.

Face to face with what he called "conjectural journalism," Wilson saw that something must be done about relations with the American newsmen who swarmed about, standing in doorways, looking over shoulders, hungry for copy, many of them unfamiliar with the language and customs of Paris. There were five hundred of them, more or less. Some were more interested in the market value of sensational news than in aiding the President, and they looked forward with unholy glee to the "wig-pulling" that they expected when the great statesmen came to grips on the issue of the league of nations.

At Paris, Wilson's desire to avoid discrimination among newspapers or to influence their opinions obsessed him to the point of squeamishness. Realizing that he could not hope to talk with all the journalists, he decided to see none. But he gave the newsmen daily access to each of his colleagues on the American Commission; and he persuaded Ray Stannard Baker to direct the release of daily bulletins through an American Press Bureau. The President hoped that under this policy news might be handled with discretion, efficiency, and impartiality.

Wilson's disappointment over the lack of progress of the meeting on January 12 was slight, in comparison with the letdown that the public opinion of the world suffered when the people were given only an official four-line report of the session. The American journalists sent a formal protest to their President. Where, they asked, were the "open covenants openly arrived at"? Moreover, Tumulty cabled that the President should do anything—even bolt from the conference—rather than submit to a policy of secrecy.

In the absence of fact, rumors mushroomed overnight. Furthermore, facts somehow seeped into the French newspapers; and they seemed so well chosen, from France's point of view, that Wilson was moved to speak bitingly of "careful leakage." The French, however, explained that their journalists actually were at a disadvantage because they were censored and the Americans and British were not. Perhaps, if all could be restricted to one official communiqué a day . . . ? But Wilson felt that under such an arrangement he would lose the right to appeal directly to the idealism of humanity, over the heads of the national leaders.

Lloyd George said that the British press well understood that it was excluded from Cabinet meetings, and here at Paris the delegates were acting as a cabinet for the nations. He put in a compromise suggestion: that the public be educated in the danger of giving out information on negotiations before decisions were reached. And when Wilson proposed that such an explanation be made to all press representatives at Paris rather than directly to the public, his colleagues assented.

The journalists were brought together, but the national loyalties of the correspondents proved to be stronger than any common devotion to their profession. The American newsmen were not convinced of the good faith of these diplomats who promised frankness within the limits of discretion, and they continued to agitate. Tumulty cabled frantically to urge that Wilson talk personally with three correspondents representing the press associations. But the President replied that the rule of secrecy made it impossible to correct the imaginative accounts that were reaching America. Once, to be sure, he did address a group of newsmen; but after a reporter betrayed a confidence he had no stomach to try it again. And so he became the only important chief at Paris who refused to meet his nation's correspondents regularly and personally. Ray Stannard Baker implored him to use his magnetism on the journalists. When he urged the President to explain something to them, however, Wilson protested: "But I've already said that." It was true. He had said it in a speech; and he hated to repeat as much as he disliked to be told things twice.

The council gave their compromise explanation to the press, Baker went on issuing a daily bulletin to the American journalists, Dr. Grayson gave interviews and fended off the curious as best he could, American correspondents went listlessly to interview their commissioners, and the leaks continued. Bound by nothing but his own conscience and judgment, Wilson was free to adhere to the policy of Cabinet confidence or to use his favorite weapon in case of crisis—an appeal to the people.

When the Peace Conference met in plenary session, however, the press was invited and the people of the world were given fuller reports.[7] The first of six general assemblies met on January 18. To the Salle de la Paix came seventy-two delegates from twenty-six nations and four dominions. Most were dressed in sober black coats. At the end of the

---

[7] At first the policy of admitting the press to plenary sessions had been opposed by the Old World diplomats; but finally Wilson's view—buttressed by the demands of the press of America, England, Italy, and small nations—prevailed. Actually, the result was that vital discussions were excluded from the plenary sessions. The negotiating came to be done, the tentative decisions made, in "conversations" in small groups and behind closed doors, after study of masses of data supplied by expert advisers.

horseshoe sat the President of France, directly in front of a statue of Peace bearing the torch of Civilization.

After Poincaré had paid a gracious tribute to each country, Wilson stepped forward. Black and trim in his striped trousers, he wore a high collar, cravat with pink pin, and pince-nez. Playing the role ordained for him, he grasped the hand of the French President. Then he nominated Clemenceau as permanent chairman of the conference, lifting both the man and the occasion to the awesome heights on which he sensed that the hearts of mankind were placing them. He spoke appreciatively of the sufferings of France, of the historic importance of her capital in the making of peace.

Clemenceau rose from his great golden chair to respond to Wilson's declaration of confidence, and he pleaded for union among the peoples who had fought together. He spoke like one converted to the ideals of perpetual peace and a league of nations. Laying on the table the rules that had been prescribed for the conference by the council, he made it clear that the program of the President of the United States would be followed—the five-point procedure that Wilson had worked out with his American commissioners, placing the framing of a league Covenant first. Within two hours the meeting had adjourned without dissension and Wilson was free to indulge in philosophical talk with General Smuts, whose thoughts on the league he found agreeable and stimulating.

At the second general session, on January 25, The Tiger showed his claws and established a mastery over procedure that he was never to yield. Delegates from certain small nations protested against the council's ruling that they would be allowed representation in that body only when questions affecting their interests were to be discussed. The threat challenged Clemenceau's parliamentary skill. Rising slowly, he sprang into action and cuffed the irreverent cubs with a blow of eloquence. Then he snapped his jaw on an "adopté!"—thus clinching a point already set up by the caucus of major powers.

When his turn came to speak, Woodrow Wilson seized the occasion to give the people of the world another glimpse of his vision. From the eyes of the men of little faith—already in their speeches revealing the direction of their national interest—he swept the cobwebs of tradition. Taking them up to his high perspective, he made them see the largest issue of the day, the problem of human survival. He warned that mankind must break loose from worship of the juggernaut-nations that had been colliding with each other for generations. His own United States, he said, could not take part in guaranteeing European settlements "unless that guarantee involved the continuous superintendence of the peace of the world by the associated nations of the world."

A league of nations was essential, "a vital thing," with "a vital continuity." "It should be the eye of the nations to keep watch upon the common interest, an eye that does not slumber, an eye that is everywhere watchful and attentive." Science as well as armed men could be kept within the harness of civilization only by vigilant cooperation.

"I have only tried in what I have said," he explained, "to give you the fountains of the enthusiasm which is within us for this thing, for those fountains spring, it seems to me, from all the ancient wrongs and sympathies of mankind." Seizing his own pulse and holding up his hands, he came to a dramatic finale: "The very pulse of the world seems to beat to the surface in this enterprise."

Resolutions favoring the creating of a league of nations as part of the peace treaty were adopted by the delegates,[8] many of whom stepped forward to congratulate the speaker. The American had won the first skirmishes of his greatest battle. Elated, he jotted a sentence on a fragment of paper that he passed to House: "We have got them all very solemnly and satisfactorily committed." He had bound first his own commissioners, and then the delegates of the other powers, to the proposition that a league of nations was essential to the world's welfare and that it should be an integral, inseparable part of the treaty of peace.

The initial success stimulated the President to pursue his cause even more ardently. Throwing the full weight of his prestige into the fray, he decided to sit with the commission that was chosen to work out a constitution for a league of nations. As chairman of this body he must face up to problems that lay close to the nerves of national protagonists.

While avoiding commitments that might be attacked by enemies at Washington and Paris, Wilson had kept the problem constantly on his conscience since he and House had drafted their tentative Covenant at

---

[8] After informal talks in House's rooms at the Crillon, where Cecil and Smuts went to discuss the arguments that might best persuade the other statesmen to make the Covenant of a league an integral part of the treaty, Wilson had approved, with a few slight changes, a set of resolutions that had been drafted by the British. The resolutions, as presented to the plenary session on Jan. 25, were:

"1. It is essential to the maintenance of the world settlement, which the Associated Nations are now met to establish, that a League of Nations be created to promote international cooperation, to ensure the fulfillment of accepted international obligations, and to provide safeguards against war.

"2. This league should be created as an integral part of the general Treaty of Peace, and should be open to every civilized nation which can be relied on to promote its objects.

"3. The members of the league should periodically meet in international conference, and should have a permanent organization and secretariat to carry out the business of the League in the interval between the conferences."

Magnolia. In September he had felt that there must be a league of nations with force enough to bring any chauvinistic government to terms. If an economic boycott was not enough, the united forces of other nations must be called into use, and no country could withstand that. When he talked with Professor Rappard in November, after he had learned of House's difficulties in committing the Allies to his Fourteen Points, his opinion had changed somewhat. He felt that if an effort were made to set up an international police force, the question of command would break up the Peace Conference. Nor had he been ready to embrace a plan of Frederick J. Turner, the historian whose work on the American frontier he had admired and encouraged, for a world league with a legislature in which there might develop around the arc from left to right, international political parties that might hold the interests of groups and sections in equilibrium.

Immediately after reaching Paris, Wilson had talked with House about their tentative Covenant for a league that would operate through a council of diplomats at the capital of a small nation. He drafted new articles, and drew help from a pamphlet that was published by General Smuts on December 15. From this document, which like his own draft omitted plans for compulsory arbitration, he had taken a provision for a permanent council that would act as the executive committee of the league. He accepted much of Smuts' language on the matter of mandates and was captivated especially by that statesman's phrase: "Europe is being liquidated and the League of Nations must be heir to this great estate." [9]

On January 8, after House assured him that his second draft was a great improvement on the first, the President was ready to show the secret document to others. First taking his fellow commissioners into his confidence, he asked their advice. Already Lansing and his counselors had pressed their objection to the positive guarantee against aggression on which Wilson insisted. The secretary of state had been encouraged by Colonel House to put his ideas of a league of nations into a draft of a treaty; and the commissioners had approved a plan to have a tentative text prepared that would make use of the court at The Hague. On January 10, at a meeting of the American commissioners,

[9] Smuts' pamphlet, "The League of Nations—A Practical Suggestion," was given to Wilson by Lloyd George at London. It dealt with territories formerly belonging to Russia, Austria-Hungary, and Turkey. In the preface Smuts wrote: "To my mind the world is ripe for the greatest steps forward ever made in the government of men . . . If that advance is not made, this war will from the most essential point of view, have been fought in vain, and great calamities will follow."

The principle of trusteeship of undeveloped territories was not a new one. It had appealed to House as early as 1914 and was set forth in Wilson's Point Five. It was formulated, in the technical sense in which it was eventually used in the treaty, in a memorandum submitted to The Inquiry on Jan 1, 1918, by George Louis Beer. *See* House Papers, IV, 284.

Lansing mentioned a draft treaty that his experts had prepared and given to his colleagues so that they might reach an understanding.

"Who authorized them to do this?" Wilson asked sharply. "I don't want lawyers drafting this treaty." Why had they wasted their time on this, he wondered, when they knew that he himself was preparing a draft? In his fervor for immortal ideals he was forgetting the mortal men about him. (House could have answered the President's question but did not, preferring to confide later in private that he had encouraged the draft in order to keep the mind of the secretary of state harmlessly occupied.) The sharp challenge lodged in Lansing's mind and festered, until it loomed as an insult to him and to his profession. The next day, however—perhaps to compensate for his curtness—Wilson solicited and accepted advice from his commissioners.

In the daily meetings of the Council of Ten Woodrow Wilson found a more appreciative response than that from his own commissioners. This was a body larger and less familiar, and its members listened respectfully to the prophet from the New World, heeding him not merely because of his power and their fear that he would use it to bargain in their own manner, but because his moral and intellectual force impressed them. Balfour was astonished to see him "as good round a table as he was on paper." He was showing the qualities with which he had mastered his Cabinets in Washington—firmness, restraint, intelligence, eloquence.

For a few days he held his moral indignation in check, despite European attitudes that seemed sinful. Near the end of January, however, Wilson found himself engaged in combat with the British Empire over the disposal of Germany's colonies. Disregarding the approval that the council had just given to the President's plan to put the league of nations first and colonies last, Lloyd George began to plead that colonial problems be attacked at once. This, he argued, would be the best way to satisfy the public appetite for definite decisions promptly. When Wilson did not oppose this argument resolutely the council decided to ask that all powers having territorial claims should file them within ten days.

This gave Lloyd George an opening, and the next day he seized it with a flourish of drama. His claims had been ready for weeks. Now, after first committing Wilson and the others to agree that the German colonies should not be restored to Germany, he advocated a system of mandates that, he said, would not differ greatly from the colonial methods of the British Empire in the past. But the lands that had been captured by the Dominions were an exception, he explained. These territories were described as populated by uncivilized peoples who had suffered under German misgovernment; and therefore, the prime

minister contended, they should be administered as part of their cap-
tors' territory rather than by an organization in Europe. Invited by
Clemenceau to "bring the cannibals in," Lloyd George introduced the
delegates of the Dominions, who presented their demands. And other
nations revealed imperialistic ambitions.

Wilson said, frankly, the game was to use American principles as a
cloak to cover selfish designs. Sitting forward in his chair, fixing his
eye first on Lloyd George, then on Clemenceau, he told them what the
world would say. He warned that such acts would make a league of
nations impossible and would bring back the old system of competitive
armaments, with accumulating debts.

Some institution, he asserted to the council on January 27, must be
found to carry out the ideas that all had in mind, namely, the development of a country for the benefit of those already in it and those who
would live there later. A league of nations could perform this function,
laying down certain general principles and at the same time giving
mandates to safeguard the interests of both the inhabitants and all members of the league who might wish to trade freely with them. As for the
United States, he thought it her duty to accept mandates but felt that
the nation would not do so, for the people would feel that they were acquiring territory under false pretenses. (A month later he characterized
the attitude of his people on this question as "Pharisaical cleanliness.")

In general Lloyd George approved the principle of trusteeship, but
there were the Dominions to consider. Hughes of Australia and Massey
of New Zealand recognized the ideal but disputed its immediate application to the lands that they wished to annex.[10] The French, however,
were more blunt: they considered that they had a right to the territories
assigned to them in secret understandings made with England during
the war. They were prevented from reading letters substantiating their
claim only by Lloyd George's fear that Wilson's patience might be
strained beyond endurance. As for the Japanese, their spokesmen reminded the gathering of their claim, under the secret understanding
that had brought them into the war, to the German Pacific islands north
of the equator.

At this Wilson rose and, urging trusteeship rather than annexation,
told an appropriate story from Mr. Dooley. One of the American
experts laughed aloud and Lloyd George smiled. Clutching at the
one risible response, the President went out of his way, the next morning, to shake hands with the expert who had laughed. Obviously the

---

[10] Arthur Sweetser, assistant to Ray Stannard Baker, reported to Secretary Newton D. Baker
on Feb. 4, 1919, that "it was only by strong pressure, when the President took along his stenographer to give a speech out to the world, that he [Hughes] was temporarily calmed."

colonial question was too hot to be handled even in the comparative insulation of the council. Anglo-Saxon statesmen therefore undertook to reach an agreement in private talks.

The next day Wilson exerted pressure upon Lloyd George in the council. He said that, since the principle of mandatories had been denied in the discussions of the past days, it looked as if their roads diverged. He begged that the intensity of his own feeling should not be ascribed to personal antagonism. Really, the league would be a laughing-stock without the attribute of trusteeship. They must agree genuinely on this ideal and leave its application to the league. If the principle were not accepted, the United States would have to believe that her sacrifices during the war had been in vain, and in that case her people would feel that they had to maintain a large army and navy. That, he reminded his colleagues, would be intolerable to the thought of Europe. Old Testament iron could be detected in the voice of the prophet.

Lloyd George, convinced that the President was adamant, seized upon a plan drafted by General Smuts as a solution; but before presenting it to Hughes and Massey, he asked Smuts to ascertain whether Wilson would approve. Though this lofty, lonely South African had caught the imagination of Wilson the literary historian, and though House had commended his plan as "a fair compromise," the President was not ready to accede to it. "I could agree to this," he wrote on the document, "if the interpretation were to come in practice from General Smuts. My difficulty is with the demands of men like Hughes and the certain difficulties with Japan. The latter loom large. A line of islands in her possession would be very dangerous to the United States."

In the council on January 30 Wilson said that he could not accept a convenient theory of Lloyd George's that the league had been established by the plenary session and therefore those who made the league could immediately hand out colonies on terms to suit the recipients. Actually, the Covenant was still an undefined instrument; and if vital questions like this were settled without reference to it, it might never command enough attention to be adequately defined. The building of the league must precede the assignment of mandates.

At that point the tempers of the premiers gave way. Lloyd George, who had worked hard to get agreement, almost yielded to despair. Patiently, Wilson tried to cheer him. He would accept the Smuts resolution as "a precursor of agreement," he said, and subject to reconsideration when the full scheme of the league was completed; [11] and in turn

---

[11] The Smuts resolution, defining three classes of mandates, was later adopted, almost intact, as Article XXII of the Covenant. Wilson agreed orally to France's demand that she be permitted to raise volunteer troops in territory mandated to her, but would not consent to an explicit statement to this effect.

Lloyd George agreed to urge his colleagues to hasten the drafting of the Covenant.

When Hughes and Massey argued [12] that their people could not be expected to invest in the Pacific islands without the security of permanent possession, Wilson asked whether these representatives of only six million people were prepared to defy the will of "the whole civilized world."

"That's about it," Hughes retorted doggedly, resenting the tone.

In this crisis General Botha—a solid, generous man from South Africa, full of sense and humor but weakened by a fatal disease—made a long, conciliatory appeal. Wilson, all pins and needles from too much sitting, got up and paced back and forth on the soft carpet, kicking his black shoes. Immediately afterward he told Lloyd George that Botha's speech was the most impressive to which he had ever listened.

In the afternoon session on the 30th the British representatives agreed that the Smuts compromise resolution be taken as "a provisional decision." The prophet achieved what to disciples of slower zeal had seemed impossible. The framing of the league Covenant would take precedence over a division of spoils.

Despite his distaste for the philosophy of the Council of Ten, the President dared not be absent from the daily meetings for fear that something would be put over on Lansing. He was infinitely bored, sometimes roused to righteous scorn, and at least once was moved to make peace between quarreling colleagues.

Against Clemenceau's campaign for material protection for France, the President was kept on guard by his advisers on military and economic affairs. Marshal Foch, whom Wilson thought as able as he was narrow, was developing a grandiose scheme for an anti-Bolshevik army in Central Europe to which the United States was expected to contribute troops and financial support. When this was reported to him, the President backed General Bliss in opposing it—only to have the scheme crop up again and again. "In my opinion," Wilson said once, "to try to stop a revolutionary movement by armies in line is to use a broom to stop a spring tide." [13]

---

[12] Hughes released, for publication in London, an account of the discussions of Jan. 28 that portrayed Wilson as a doctrinaire schoolmaster to whom the British government was kowtowing. Quivering with indignation at this when he came into the council on the 30th, the President threatened to resort to publicity himself. So far, he reminded his colleagues, he had played the game and had released no statement of his views. Nevertheless, he warned, he might be compelled against his wishes to make a full public exposure of the situation and to break off negotiations and go home. *Lord Riddell's Intimate Diary,* p. 18. That night he said, at home, grimly, that he felt sure there would be no leakages from *that* meeting.

[13] Paul Mantoux, "Le Président Wilson au Conseil des Quatres," in *Centenaire Woodrow Wilson: 1856–1956* (Geneva, 1956), p. 21.

When French economists proposed military restrictions on German industries, Wilson denounced the scheme as a "panic program." He had hoped to hold regular meetings with his economic experts, like those of his war council at Washington; but he was diverted by other affairs. Finally, on January 30, House called a conference of economic advisers with General Bliss and Admiral Benson and it was agreed to protest against a food blockade of Germany. On February 7, buttressed by a strong letter from Hoover, Wilson introduced the matter in the council and his European colleagues gave assent to the American program; but the blockade was not relaxed. "I am surrounded by intrigue here," the President lamented, "and the only way I can succeed is by working silently, saying nothing in public unless it becomes necessary to bring about an open contest."

Emancipated nationalities of Europe for whom Wilson had sought self-determination were now coveting territory and power, raising armies, and begging the United States for troops, money, and arms. In several instances they had seized disputed territories and peoples of other nationalities. Wilson said that he would not stand for aggressive annexations, that he would rather be stoned in the streets than give in. The council finally had to issue a warning that nations that tried to establish themselves by force in disputed territory would harm rather than help their cause before the Peace Conference.

Rumblings of militarism were heard from Germany, too. To meet the threat of a resurgent enemy and Western demands for quick demobilization, a special commission under Foch recommended that naval and military terms of peace be drawn immediately and imposed— a proposal that Wilson approved with the additional suggestion that the Armistice be renewed without change and made terminable on a few days' notice. Clemenceau dissented at first, fearing that this would bring premature demobilization, which would make the Germans "ferocious" and leave the Allies impotent to enforce hard terms of peace. However, when Balfour pointed out that German disarmament could keep pace with Allied demobilization, and the military experts promised to draft final terms very rapidly, The Tiger assented and the council took formal action.[14]

As the French statesmen became unnerved by signs of truculence in Germany and at the same time came to see in Wilson the main obstacle to the guarantees of immediate security on which they had set their

[14] There was concern that the Germans might not accept a renewal of the Armstice on this basis. However, on Feb. 16 they agreed. Neither French nor German public opinion was satisfied, and both blamed Wilson for the arrangement.

hearts, criticism and innuendo came from the press of Paris.[15] Public morale was afflicted by a depression that journalists called *La Malaise*.

Thinking that he was disliked because he insisted on sympathizing with small nations as well as with France, Wilson burned with resentment. After nine years in public life, he was not yet callous to criticism. His sensitive skin was pierced when the French press lampooned him as a comic and irritating busybody and suggested that the United States, which had come into the war at the last moment, would rob France of the fruits of victory and would set up a league of nations, only to go home and shirk responsibility for its functioning. He became doubly secretive and suspicious. On February 10 he asked Dr. Grayson to drop a hint to the American newsmen that they let it be known that if the Parisian press continued its obstructive tactics it might be necessary to remove the conference to a neutral country.

As the full scope of the purposes of the Allies was revealed, Wilson grew dour. By the end of January he was totally possessed by his work, giving to it sometimes as much as eighteen hours a day. Life was becoming very tedious, he wrote to Newton D. Baker, and "the difficulty of weaving all the strands into a single pattern" bewildered him.

When it was suggested that a whole day be devoted to prayer for the world, the prophet was cool to the idea. He felt that the business of the Peace Conference was lagging and must be pushed forward. He gloated a little, once, when his pride of authorship was gratified by the acceptance of some of his phrasing by colleagues. But when Edith Benham, his wife's secretary, spoke of him as a Messiah, he protested. Religious teaching had never found a practical solution for the world's troubles, he asserted. Presbyterianism, like patriotism, was not enough. His intellect told him that God revealed himself to man in many ways, that some of the worst wars had been incited by religion. The hope of the world lay in a *man*, he said, a Carlylean hero. Like the Scottish seer of whom he had written in "Leaders of Men," Woodrow Wilson would be "the apostle of a vague sort of lay religion—a religion with sanction but without hierarchy." The prophetic vision that had outspanned the Princeton campus, New Jersey, and Washington was now transcending heights of Western Christianity. Standing on Ben Nevis, he was aspir-

---

[15] A French editor gave to Wilson a copy of an order issued through the government's *Maison de la Presse*, instructing newspapers—

1. To emphasize news of opposition to Wilson by Republicans and others in America.

2. To emphasize disorder and anarchy in Russia, in order to provoke Allied intervention.

3. To publish articles demonstrating Germany's ability to pay a large indemnity.

Baker, *American Chronicle*, p. 387. On Feb. 12, taking a paper from his pocket, Wilson read this order to Professor Rappard and said that France's press was not free and her government was as bureaucratic as Prussia's. Rappard, *op. cit.*, p. 56.

ing to Everest. Scottish instinct was urging him to the stature of individuality that the race had always demanded of its great men. Then he could give the people of the world relief from international anarchy.

Yes, Edith Wilson assured him, he could do it. Henry White had told her that the President was "the greatest statesman of the age," and her faith in her husband's powers was as great as his own.

He went on to say, mystically, that he thought he sensed in the minds of the American people certain ideals for the world, latent and unsuspected by them but nevertheless of high potential. When he phrased the ideals and presented them to his congregation, he felt sure that they would say, as they had always said before: "Why, yes, that's true." He was asked how he detected these budding ideals, if not from the press, which he felt to be controlled by venal interests and out of touch with the pulses of the people. And he explained that his insight came from various sources, from saturating himself in American political history, from wooing the spirit that seemed to him essentially American. His mind, he said, pieced together all the fragments supplied by sense and intuition, fitting them into a mosaic. He said this all very simply and humbly, but with a confidence founded upon the rocks of ages.

He did not respond now so quickly to his wife's loving solicitude, her cheery smile, her mimicry and anecdotes. He begrudged even the time that it took to walk to the Quai d'Orsay, preferring to take no exercises. He delegated little, and within the limits of his strength refused nothing that he thought politically constructive. In the evening, after a bath and a change and a good dinner, he would go to a conference at the Crillon, or into his study to bend over his typewriter.

By giving up a Sunday's rest he mitigated one of the annoyances that the French press had inflicted upon him. He had said, petulantly, that if all France were a shell hole, it wouldn't change the peace settlement. But finally on January 26—the day after Lloyd George had dealt Wilson a backhanded blow by reminding the conference that *he* had seen the devastated areas of France—the President and Edith Wilson went to the battlefields near Château-Thierry, where they saw meadows and orchards stark and shell-holed, and the landscape marred by trenches, barbed wire, and burial mounds. At Rheims, where 120,000 had once dwelt, they found some 5,000 living in cellars among the debris, and snow falling through the roof of the riddled cathedral.

Going through Soissons, they noted that the town was virtually deserted; but returning unexpectedly a few minutes later, they perceived that the place was suddenly teeming with French troops who clamored for a word from the President. Where had these soldiers been when they first passed through the village? the Wilsons asked. Ordered to stay in their billets, the Americans were told, while the President's car was going by. "So that is what is going on," he thought. To a friend who had asked him weeks before whether he would visit the devastated areas, he had replied: "I don't want to get mad over here because I think there ought to be one person at the peace table who isn't mad." But he had yielded, finally, and now he was angry, not at the Germans, as he had feared, but at French officialdom.

The visit had been made too late to silence the voices of criticism that had been rising against the prophet. "It might help if I could get to the people," he said to Creel, "but I am being shut off completely . . . Every day the Republicans tell Lloyd George, Orlando, and Clemenceau that I do not and cannot speak for America, and that my one function is to act as their rubber stamp." [16]

Wilson was standing alone, with no man on whose sympathy and discretion he could depend entirely. Lansing had annoyed and embarrassed him,[17] and he missed House, who was suffering from gallstones.

Fortunately House's health permitted him to resume his role before the Commission on the League of Nations held its first meeting. From his sickbed, through intermediaries, the Colonel already had been discussing the Covenant with Lord Robert Cecil. "He agrees with our views more than he dares admit," House recorded. "I am to get Orlando in line and he is to get the French, and when this is done we will have a general meeting."

When the Colonel brought the Italian premier to the Murat Palace on the evening of January 30 to discuss a league of nations, the question of Italy's eastern boundaries was considered. After Orlando showed sympathy for the league and offered suggestions that the President accepted, Wilson reciprocated by saying impulsively that as far as he was concerned the Trentino was as good as ceded to Italy. When the talk was over, the American, who had semed dog-tired and depressed at luncheon, was in high humor and generous in praise of the attitude

[16] Creel, *Rebel at Large*, p. 214.

[17] Lansing insisted, in a meeting of the American commissioners, on a resolution that would restore peace immediately and proclaim the general purpose of the league, leaving the details of the Covenant for later consideration. The President rejected the idea with a curtness that cut into Lansing's pride. The next day the blundering secretary went over his chief's head to repeat his proposal in a session of the Council of Ten, where the President could not oppose him frankly without weakening the American position before the world. When the council had received Lansing's views sympathetically, Wilson managed to conceal his annoyance and asked the secretary of state to put his ideas in the form of a resolution. Accordingly, a draft was sent to the President on Jan. 31, with little faith on Lansing's part that Wilson would "see the wisdom of it." The President did not acknowledge it, and the secretary of state found it hard to keep his temper. In his diary, Lansing recorded that Wilson was even a greater egotist than he had thought him to be.

House, constantly on guard against the jealousy of those over whom he was given precedence by his friend, persuaded the President to hold ensuing meetings of the American Commission in the rooms of Lansing and the others, instead of in the Colonel's suite.

of the charming Italian toward his great cause. In his elation, however, he sinned against his doctrine of self-determination. Agreeing to a commitment of the secret treaty of London that violated his Point IX, he delivered almost a quarter-million Germans in the Trentino to Italian rule, and thus sowed the seed of a grave crisis.

At House's suggestion, Wilson met the next day with Lord Robert Cecil and with Smuts, to whom the President had secretly dispatched Grayson with his latest draft of the Covenant.[18]

On February 2, the compromise text was explained to Wilson. But the President was not satisfied. Objecting that it lacked "warmth and color" to win the allegiance of the people of the world, he asked that his own draft be rewritten, with a few clauses taken from the joint version. This was done overnight, and Wilson awoke on February 3 fully intending to present this third American draft to the commission when it met in the afternoon.

House, however, foresaw friction. Wiseman warned him that Lord Robert had heard of the President's work on the new draft and was disturbed because this matter that he thought settled might be reopened. Telephoning to Wilson, House reminded him that Lord Robert was the Englishman who had the league most at heart and that they must maintain harmony with him. The Colonel managed to bring Wilson and Lord Robert together in his study fifteen minutes before the first session of the commission was to open. "The meeting bade fair to be stormy for the first seven or eight minutes," he recorded in his diary. "After that things went better and the President finally decided . . . to take the joint draft . . . and use it as a basis for discussion. After that everything went smoothly."

Woodrow Wilson had made a personal sacrifice that hurt; he had deferred to another in the drafting of the greatest creation of his life. From House's study he went into a salon in which the members of the Commission on the League of Nations were gathering, and he held their attention with a speech while an agent hurried to get a copy of the British-American draft of the Covenant to lay before them.

Between February 3 and 13 the Commission on the League met ten times,[19] often working late at night so that the Covenant might be com-

---

[18] Grayson was asked by Wilson on Jan. 18 to put his draft into Smuts' own hands. At the meeting with Smuts and Lord Robert on Jan. 31, apparently conscious of crosscurrents of feeling among his delegates, Wilson came back to a suggestion that he had made on the *George Washington*, remarking that it might be best for the nations to be represented in the league's assembly by their regular ambassadors. He had observed jealousy and contention about unimportant things, he said, when there were two representatives of a country in one place.

[19] The Commission on the League of Nations consisted at first of fifteen members—two from each of the major powers and five from small nations. Though Wilson felt that the proceedings would be unduly delayed by the enlargement of this commission, the little countries made such strong representations that four more delegates were chosen to speak for them.

pleted before February 14, the date set for the President's departure for home. In contrast with the meetings of the Council of Ten that Wilson attended in the mornings, the sessions of the League Commission were more delight than duty to a man whose lifelong hobby had been the study and the making of constitutions. He took a lively part in the discussions, opposing the keeping of minutes because he wanted to be free to shift his mental ground on this new political frontier. He explained that, like the body of men who had drawn up the Constitution of the United States, they should withhold their work from the public until it was finished. He desired complete fluidity of thought and frankness of expression.

Clemenceau, conceding that there must be a league created if for no other reason than to humor his American colleague, was bent upon making the new body of some practical value to France's security. And so Léon Bourgeois—the French spokesman on the commission and a man who had used the phrase "league of nations" as early as 1910—was instructed to advocate a strong military arm, with a general staff that would command an effective army, dictate its recruiting and training, and inspect the military establishments of the member nations.

Anglo-Saxon statesmen were traditionally apathetic to the principle put forward by Bourgeois. Conscript armies, which appealed to French democrats as protection against sneak attacks as well as against *coups d'état* by volunteer units, were anathema to peoples who were nurtured on tenets of individual self-restraint and freedom and whose territory was well enough protected by water barriers so that the threat of invasion had not driven them often to national regimentation.

When the British-American draft was presented, Bourgeois proposed amendments. Yielding to French objections to a general denunciation of conscription by the Covenant, Wilson consented that a clause on that point be eliminated. But this concession did not suffice. By February 11 the question became so acute that the commission met all day. The French spokesman threw Wilson's own words at him, reminding the President that he had once said that "force must be created, force so superior that no nation or combination of nations can challenge or resist it."

Wilson listened with an indulgent smile to the retranslation of his words and made a correction. At first not inclined to reply, he whispered with House and then spoke up. Courteously acknowledging the allusion to his own statement, he pointed out that it had been made "in the stress of desperate war." His attitude had not changed, he said. "The situation" was different, however. The construction of a unified military machine in time of peace merely would substitute international militarism for national. Moreover, coming down to hard reality, he pointed out that the Constitution of the United States made international control of its army and navy impossible. In fact, enemies of the league in the Senate were complaining that American troops might become liable to fight at any moment for the most remote causes.

With a despairing gesture the French delegate slumped back in his chair, to emerge later with a hint that France might not join a league of the kind that the Anglo-Saxons visualized. Bourgeois was building up bargaining power that Clemenceau would know well how to use later in his crusade for security for France. At one juncture the French gave notice that they would present reservations at a plenary session.

Wilson met the opposition with a fervent plea for mutual trust. In the meeting of February 11 he gave the French an expression of his own feeling of solidarity with them. "When the danger comes," Wilson said to Bourgeois, "we too will come, but you must trust us."

By the morning of February 13 all of the articles of the British-American draft of the Covenant had been passed tentatively and the commission was ready to begin a second reading, with Wilson in the chair. At one o'clock, however, when the President had to leave to attend a session of the Council of Ten, he was despondent because only six of the twenty-six articles had been agreed upon.

Into the breach at this critical juncture stepped Colonel House. Heretofore, in the meetings of the commission, he had expressed his thoughts only in discreet whispers to the President. But now the Colonel came into his own. Inviting Lord Robert Cecil to take the chair, he stiffened Lord Robert's backbone against a new French drive for an international general staff. Then by an understanding with the Japanese delegates, whose confidence he had won already, it was arranged tentatively to omit from the Covenant both a religious clause that Wilson had inserted and a guarantee of racial equality for which the Japanese had been clamoring and which Hughes of Australia had refused to accept even in a diluted form.

Lord Robert cut off fruitless discussion by calling for votes, and by seven o'clock House was able to tell Wilson over the telephone that the Covenant had been approved. Immensely relieved to learn that there would have to be no night session, as he had feared, the President gladly assented to the Colonel's sacrifice of his religious clause in the interest of harmony. Against Wilson's judgment, also, provisions for arbitration and for a world court were allowed to stand in the final draft.

Under the hand of Woodrow Wilson the League Commission had been driven harder than any other peacemaking body. He had both drawn out discussion when it was needed, and checked it when it ran too wide in speculation or too deep in technicalities. From the very first he had kept the delegates facing forward. As the days went by, the majesty of his faith in the reasonableness of free men sunned dark fears and cleansed sordid ambitions. The real sanction of the principles of the Covenant lay in public opinion, he said.

The public for whom he labored knew little of the details of the President's achievement, but Colonel House intended that it should not be forgotten. One day he recorded in his diary: "I have never known anyone to do such work so well." Resolving that the great feat of Wilson's commission be recorded for posterity, House arranged on the last day for a photograph of its members. But when flashlight pictures were proposed, Wilson objected. "Everybody looks as though he was laid out in a morgue," he said, "and besides the flashes hurt my eyes." When the Colonel insisted that history should not be cheated, the man who aspired to speak for a billion people stood shyly among the chattering statesmen and turned to his interpreter for support. "You mustn't leave me in this Tower of Babel," he said.

Under Wilson's presiding genius the Commission on the League not only had achieved agreement among the nations, but had done so with more consideration of the small powers than European peace conferences had been accustomed to show. Meeting in a milieu new to diplomacy, a salon of the Hotel Crillon, while the Council of Ten met in the gray, tradition-webbed Quai d'Orsay, "Wilson's commission" had taken in representatives of several countries that could not claim a seat in the council. And so the President regained some of the prestige that had been lost in the eyes of democratic peoples when he had failed to protest against Clemenceau's bullying of the small powers and when he favored only a minimum representation of little countries on the Executive Council of the League itself.[20]

On February 14—the greatest day in a life that had known many superlative occasions—the American President stood before the world as the victorious leader of a great and triumphant cause. He was to give a constitution to the twentieth-century world. When the hour came for him to present the Covenant to a plenary session—the hour for which Woodrow Wilson had been born into the world—he was recognized by

[20] In the second session of the Commission on the League, Wilson with Lord Robert Cecil's assent had said that, since the League was to guaranty the political independence and territorial integrity of large and small nations alike, he thought it no injustice to give the major powers five seats on the permanent council, and the small powers only two. The larger the membership, he pointed out, the slower would be the proceedings of the body. It was finally agreed that the small powers should have four seats in the League's council. "It is of course our purpose," Wilson said at the second session of the commission, "to call in the lesser powers and also the neutral powers as progress is made." Bonsal, *Unfinished Business*, p. 25.

the chairman. Conscious of his responsibility to the twelve hundred million mortals who were represented in the stately room, he read the document in even tones, without gestures, and then went on to speak of its significance. A ring of resolution came into his voice and his eyes shone when he declared: "A living thing is born, and we must see to it that the clothes we put upon it do not hamper it . . . I think I can say of this document that it is at one and the same time a practical and humane document. There is a pulse of sympathy in it. There is a compulsion of conscience throughout it. It is practical, and yet it is intended to purify, to rectify, to elevate. . . ."

For a moment it seemed as if the political morality of the world had been lifted into a new dimension by a major prophet. "Dear Governor," House jotted on a slip of paper, "your speech was as great as the occasion." The voice through which the Colonel hoped to secure a place in history had not failed him. Returning the chit, Wilson scribbled in the margin: "Bless your heart. Thank you from the bottom of my heart." [21] As the day outside faded into a misty dusk and the lights in the crystal chandeliers sparkled over the rococo scene in the Hall of Clocks, the listeners sensed that it was a great moment in history. Scores of newsmen, standing on chairs and tables, rose on tiptoes to see the President's face. When the calm, almost casual voice ceased, the hall was as silent as a church. Then, after Bourgeois and the Japanese presented the matters that they had reserved for the occasion and the draft of the Covenant was deposited with the secretariat of the conference, the delegates besieged the American to shake his hand and thank him for his leadership. Sophisticated statesmen walked out into a cold fog with warm confidence that the horrors of world war would not afflict humanity again.

Wilson smiled radiantly at the American soldiers who were saluting him as his car went through the gates of the Murat Palace. He got out and mounted the steps two at a time, in his elation that he was going home as a minister who had been true to his charge.

At the station in the evening all of official France was on hand to say *adieu*. From the gloomy drizzle in the streets the President walked from curb to train over a long red carpet, shaking hands punctiliously with diplomats who clicked heels and kissed Edith Wilson's hand.

Georges Clemenceau, leaving the railroad station, was asked how he liked the President. His reply was: "He is a nice fellow." And then, smiling at two Americans who were present, he added: "He may mean well, it is quite possible."

---

[21] According to Bonsal, House now felt that he had erred in feeling that the President should not come to Paris, for he saw that without Wilson's personal leadership the powers would have split into groups and would have made contradictory peace treaties that would have been worthless as guarantees against war. *See* Bonsal, *Unfinished Business*, p. 282.

CHAPTER XIV

THE NEW WORLD GROWS OLD

IT WAS A WEARY but jubilant prophet who set sail for his native land on February 15, as the guns of Brest reverberated in the wintry air and French Marines stood at salute along the old city walls. In a period of six weeks he had fought the greatest battle of his life, had built the house of his Lord and put the ark of the Covenant into it, that nation might not lift up sword against nation.

Wireless messages came to him on the *George Washington* from Colonel House. Wilson had asked that no one should know of this, and his secret code was used. The news received was disconcerting. Orlando, who had returned to Rome, had not been able to persuade his government to join the Yugoslavs in accepting the President's offer to arbitrate their territorial disputes. Lloyd George had returned to London to deal with domestic problems, boasting that, while Wilson had only a bundle of assignats, he had come home with a pocket full of sovereigns in the shape of German colonies. And on February 19, Fate in the guise of a demented fanatic struck down the only member of the Big Four who remained at Paris. As Clemenceau drove in his automobile to meet with House and Balfour, seven shots were fired at him point-blank, one of them lodging behind his shoulder blade and forcing him to bed for several days.

Before leaving for Washington for the closing of Congress, the President had thrown his mantle upon the shoulders of the Colonel, confident that his "alter ego" could somehow hold the line of law and order against greed, apathy, and panicky fears that were possessing the minds of Europeans. As he bade his friend *au revoir*, he had fervently clasped his hand and put an arm around his shoulder. "Heavy work before you, House," he said. It was the last time the Colonel felt "the Governor's" embrace.

Though Lansing would be the official chief of the American delegation, Wilson asked House to take his seat in the Council of Ten and to act for him. "I do not wish the questions of territorial adjustments or those of reparations to be held up," he said. But when House asserted that he could "button up everything within four weeks," Wilson showed alarm. The Colonel noted the shadow crossing his friend's countenance and quickly reassured him. He would not attempt to make decisions, but would try merely to prepare the way for a final settlement when the President returned. Four things should be done, he said, to facilitate a preliminary peace with Germany.[1]

Asked if this agenda would suffice, Wilson agreed that it would; and then House, wishing that his friend would put specific instructions in writing but realizing that that was not his way, reminded Wilson that to get action it might be necessary to compromise on details, as the President himself had done and as House hoped that he would do again when he returned to Washington. But there would be no compromise of principle, the Colonel asserted: particularly, he was resolved there be no concession to France's demand for a Rhenish Republic, for that, the Colonel realized, would invalidate the fundamental doctrine of self-determination. With this unwritten understanding, the Colonel remained at Paris to try to get constructive action toward settlements.

One of the grisly problems that was unsolved when Wilson left Paris and that fell upon the Colonel's shoulders on February 14 was that of relations with Russia. American policy in this sphere was embarrassingly entwined with British and Japanese ambitions; and on the very day of his departure Wilson had clashed with Winston Churchill, who had come over from London to plead for more vigorous military intervention.

As we have seen, the President had reluctantly consented, as an inevitable part of the struggle with Germany, to join with his allies in sending troops into Siberia and northern Russia. He had hoped thus to aid in restoring law and order under a responsible native government to which economic aid might later be given, and he had carefully qualified his assent to military action in such a way as to guard against a recrudescence of nineteenth-century imperialism. However, not many weeks passed before the expeditions in Russia were acting in ways that placed the President's political principles in jeopardy.[2]

[1] House had in mind a *general* preliminary peace, not a settlement merely of military matters such as the Council of Ten already had decided on. His four points were:

    1. A reduction of Germany's army and navy to a peace footing.
    2. A delineation of the boundaries of Germany. This to include the cession of the colonies.
    3. The amount of money to be paid for reparation and the length of time in which to pay it.
    4. An agreement on the economic treatment of Germany.

[2] Through a confusion of orders at Washington, the troops sent to northern Russia failed to report to Ambassador Francis, and instead put themselves under the British commander in that area and soon were involved in an offensive against Soviet forces. Learning of this, Wilson ordered General March to place the troops under the orders of Francis. Francis, *Russia from the American Embassy,* p. 271, confirmed by Breckinridge Long to the writer.

    During the autumn of 1918, moreover, the Japanese justified the misgivings that Wilson had held regarding their intentions. After the United States, through a misunderstanding, sent 8,500 men instead of the 7,000 agreed upon, Japan took advantage of this technical error and poured troops into Siberia by the tens of thousands.

Wilson had grounds for considering the Soviet government as an ally or as an enemy. He was not willing to consider them neutral, for that would imply recognition of the peace of Brest-Litovsk. The problem was further complicated when his diplomatic agents and those of the Allies were forced out of Russia and the terror sank into a mire of blood and billingsgate. Furthermore, on September 15, 1918, with Wilson's approval, Creel published certain controversial documents that were sent from Russia by his agent, Edgar Sisson. These papers purported to be facsimiles and copies of correspondence by which the German General Staff had secretly bought peace from the Council of People's Commissars.[3] House asked the President whether the release of these documents was not virtually a declaration of war on the Bolsheviki. Wilson admitted that it was.

The publication of the Sisson papers and the expedition to Siberia in collaboration with Japan—Russia's historic enemy—had evoked a blast of anti-American propaganda from Moscow. A scornful, taunting note, signed by Chicherin and dated October 24, had been addressed to the President of the United States, who was being classed by Soviet spokesmen with the "imperialist robbers" of the Allied nations. At about the time when Wilson read this provocative challenge, he learned that the leaders of the revolution were sending funds into Sweden and Switzerland to stir up unrest and that they hoped for a revolution of the proletariat in Germany and in Hungary. He feared that, with the Hohenzollerns out of the way, another absolute regime might be set up in Germany. His imagination even saw his own America menaced from within by the hammer and sickle. To allay fears at home, it was important to come to an understanding with Moscow.

All through the autumn of 1918 the President had waited vainly for the appearance of a reliable political core that could represent the Russian people. The use of force was provoking a need for more force. Yet when the Armistice with Germany was signed, the policy of intervention lost its main moral prop—the necessity of combating German influence in Russia. Consequently, Wilson had become more doubtful than ever of the wisdom of military action; and in his conference with Lloyd

[3] The Sisson documents, consisting of facsimiles and copies of secret correspondence that was alleged to have passed between the German General Staff and the Council of People's Commissars, had been placed in Wilson's hands on May 9, 1918. Creel had the documents checked by two scholars—Dr. J. Franklin Jameson, director of the Department of Research of the Carnegie Institution, and Professor Samuel Harper of the University of Chicago—who consulted other experts and concluded that there was no reason to doubt the authenticity of the papers. They were published in newspaper installments on Sept. 15 and were made available in October in a government bulletin entitled "The German-Bolshevik Conspiracy." Their authenticity was challenged immediately by the British Foreign Office and by the Department of State Lansing did not know of the papers in time to stop their publication.

George at London in December he had made it clear that he was very much opposed to armed intervention, indeed was inclined to withdraw American troops from North Russia, and was reconciled to the Siberian expedition only as a means of arresting Japanese aggression.

However, when the question of evacuation was raised at a meeting of the American peace commissioners in January, Wilson said that, since this matter would be one of the first considered at the Peace Conference, he wished to take no immediate independent action. He insisted that the Western powers should reach an immediate decision, and together go in effectively or get out of Russia. He felt that he knew too little about the Soviet government to make any public statement. "What I am at present keenly interested in," he wrote to Lansing on January 10, "is in finding the interior of their minds." What actually was the "chief end" of these rulers? What was their moral direction? If only he had firsthand knowledge!

A note addressed to him on December 24 by Maxim Litvinov had presented an opportunity to study the new regime more closely. The tone and substance of it impressed Wilson favorably. "The real thing with which to stop Bolshevism is food; . . . force will not stop it," he wrote to Lansing on January 10; and he urged haste in dispatching an agent to confer with Litvinov at Stockholm. Accordingly, W. H. Buckler was ordered to the Swedish capital and there on January 14 he received proposals that Wilson reported to the Council of Ten on January 21.[4]

The council had been discussing the Russian situation for several days, Lloyd George having introduced the subject with the assertion that it was "impossible to make peace for Europe without settling the Russian question." There was a certain latent force behind bolshevism, the President reminded the council, that attracted sympathy as much as its brutal aspects provoked disgust. Throughout the world there was an impulse of revolt against "large vested interests" that operated in both the economic and the political sphere.

[4] Litvinov told Buckler that the Russian people had been impressed by President Wilson's expression of friendship and sympathy for their revolution. But intervention in northern Russia had raised doubts of the sincerity of the President's belief in the right of a people to regulate its own affairs. And, moreover, Russians at Moscow resented the fact that Americans had been misled by such "forgeries" as the Sisson documents. Consequently, Litvinov said, the people of Russia were now asking whether the aim of the Western powers was peace or the total destruction of the Bolshevik government. He promised that if the fighting could be stopped, revolutionary propaganda, violence, and terror would cease. Realizing that for many years Russia would need to import technical advice and manufactured goods, his government was said to be ready to compromise on all points at issue, including that of assuming the czarist debt on practical terms to be worked out by experts. Skeptical of the power of an association of imperialistic nations to prevent war, Litvinov doubted that a league would materialize immediately. W. H. Buckler's manuscript recording a conversation with Litvinov at Stockholm, Jan. 14, 15, 16, 1919, House Collection.

Wilson was not at all sure that out of the Russian Revolution would grow a government that would give the guarantees to individual liberty that Americans demanded; but he felt that the old order, if it were restored, would be more disastrous than the present one. "We should be fighting against the current of the times if we tried to prevent Russia from finding her own path to freedom," he prophesied. He knew that the threat of foreign intervention had given to Bolshevik leaders a whip with which to lash their people into line.

Lloyd George, explaining that he had honored Britain's obligations to the remnants of Czarist armies that had fought on against the Germans after the peace of Brest-Litovsk, professed himself now ready to deal with the Soviets as the *de facto* government of Russia. He felt that Wilson would like to support him in this. These leaders, however, despaired of carrying with them either their fellow commissioners or electorates that had been thoroughly terrified by the violence that had been done in Russia to life, to property, and to religious faith. When Lloyd George proposed that all Russian factions be haled to Paris to state their cases, Clemenceau protested that his Chamber was unanimously opposed. He threatened to resign if they came.

Wilson acted to break the deadlock. Informed by a cable from Tumulty that Lloyd George's proposal produced a very unfavorable impression in the United States, the President suggested that the Russian factions come together at a place nearer to Moscow and be heard together, "all in one room" if possible. Wilson hoped that a reaction against extremism in Russia might be brought about.

At first Clemenceau would not consider such a proposal. Thinking the Bolsheviki not worthy of the notice of civilized peoples, he denounced the Litvinov overture that Wilson had read to the council. The Tiger's own preference had been to erect barriers to prevent the spread of bolshevism. But perceiving that the sense of the meeting was against him, he asked Wilson to draft a paper setting forth the views of the Allies, explaining that they had no wish to interfere in the internal affairs of Russia or to restore czardom, but wanted merely to hasten the creation of a dependable government. He urged that the manifesto be, above all, a humanitarian appeal.[5]

It was a great triumph for the prophet of the New World. Never before had an American taken the lead in a council of European powers on a matter that primarily concerned the Old World. Woodrow Wilson,

[5] Afterward in the antechamber, as he pulled on his big fur-lined coat, The Tiger was asked how the discussion had come out, and replied in one word, explosively, "Battu!" He was beaten, but he felt that Wilson's suggestion of an all-Russia conference had made it possible for him to yield gracefully. C. T. Thompson, *The Peace Conference Day by Day,* pp. 132–33.

having been "all the way round the clock," gave to the council a draft of an eloquent message of good will. He proposed that each Russian faction should cease military action and send delegates before February 15 to Prinkipo, a resort on the Sea of Marmara.

This invitation, however, elicited only curses from the most influential Russian conservatives at Paris, who knew that they could refuse without forfeiting French sympathy and aid. As for the Bolsheviki, they sent a belated acceptance of Wilson's invitation but failed to promise to stop the westward advance of their troops, which at the moment was rapid. Wilson thought their reply "studiously insulting." Behind a protestation of readiness to make concessions in economic and territorial matters he sensed an undertone that seemed to say: "We are dealing with perjured governments whose only interest is in striking a bargain, and if that is the price of European recognition and cooperation, we are ready to pay it."

Wilson was exasperated not only by the apparent disingenuousness of the Soviet leaders but by agitation among his conservative associates for military action. There was guerrilla fighting in North Russia, where the Allied expedition remained, icebound, and tried to protect a wobbly anti-Bolshevik government at Archangel.[6] Admiral Kolchak was mobilizing and terrorizing the peasants of Siberia by methods made familiar by the old regime. French generals, spurred on by the Russians at Paris and the conservative press, were training a Polish Army in France to act as nucleus of a force that was to include all the peoples that lived along the western fringe of Russia.

As Wilson was about to sail for America and Lloyd George prepared to return to London, the French militarists were reinforced in the councils at Paris by Winston Churchill, who had taken the opportunity to come from the War Office to put forth his views. On February 14 they collided with Wilson's. The President remarked that among all the uncertainties of the Russia situation it was quite clear to him that Allied troops in Russia were doing no sort of good, did not know for whom or for what they were fighting, and ought to be withdrawn. Churchill insisted, however, that withdrawal would lead to the destruction of all non-Bolshevik armies in Russia, numbering a half-million men: thus the "linchpin" would be pulled from "the whole machine" and Russia would be doomed to an interminable vista of violence and misery. To

---

[6] On Feb. 12, General Bliss reported to Wilson that the 5,100 American troops at Archangel would not be safe unless the railroad was kept open to Murmansk and the British headquarters. For security and to assure an easy withdrawal, Bliss approved a British request for two companies of American railroad troops, and Wilson assented. In the President's view, the United States was "irrevocably" committed to withdraw its troops as soon as the weather permitted, and this was the intention of the British also.

Wilson, withdrawal seemed inevitable. "Sooner or later we'll have to clear out," he predicted.[7]

But Churchill persisted. After Wilson's departure he proposed to the council at Paris that the Bolsheviki be given ten days in which to stop fighting or expose themselves to the consequences. He advocated that a staff be organized to consider military intervention on a larger scale and suggested that publicity be given to these measures. Colonel House, on whom both Wilson and Lloyd George[8] depended for resistance to Churchill, set aside his own views[9] and wirelessed a report of Churchill's proposals to the President.

Wilson replied immediately with a protest that checked the trend to which fear had driven the secondary men of the council. He would not favor any course, he said, that would not bring "the earliest practicable withdrawal of military forces." He made it clear that the United States was not at war with Russia and that it would be "fatal to be led further into the Russian chaos." He was relieved when, after sessions of the council in which House and Balfour argued with Churchill in words too acrimonious to be reported fully in the minutes, the Colonel cabled to him on February 23: "Churchill's proposal is dead."

As Wilson looked forward to the United States from his cabin on the *George Washington*, the prospect was more familiar and more pleasing. He was coming home to his own people. A generation of Americans that had produced vast wealth and escaped the ravages of war and famine were sharing their bounty with the people of impoverished lands that their ancestors had left. Now they were ready to prescribe a Chris-

---

[7] Wilson's feeling against military intervention had been reinforced by a cable sent by Secretary Baker on Feb. 12: "Public opinion at home has been restless about our troops in Russia on three grounds: (1) fear that the force is insufficient for our safety; (2) desire to have the soldiers all brought home; (3) fear that our forces may find themselves opposed to popular government and in alliance with reactionaries." Baker urged that the American forces be withdrawn "by the next boat."

[8] Wilson could not understand why Lloyd George had allowed Churchill to make these proposals, and the prime minister himself had been concerned about the independence of his young colleague. Willing to fulfill commitments already made to anti-German generals in Russia, but convinced that a full-scale war with the Bolsheviki would be "the direct road to bankruptcy and Bolshevism" in the British Isles, Lloyd George wired his views from London to Churchill at Paris and took the precaution of having his telegrams shown to Balfour and to House.

[9] House, who had been wondering "how to finesse the situation against the Bolsheviks," did not agree with Wilson's policy of trying to draw together the various factions. Russia, he thought, was "too big and homogeneous for the safety of the world." With Siberia separate and European Russia divided into three parts, however, he hoped that there would be no more danger than was posed by the British Empire. Balfour favored taking steps "to put the Bolsheviks in the wrong" in the eyes of those who held the view that bolshevism was democracy gone astray with large elements of good in it. DeWitt Poole reports: "High military leaders [of Britain and France] had definite plans for dividing Russia up, as they frankly told me in Paris in July, 1919. The top leadership did not." Poole MS, Oral Research History Project, Columbia University.

tian justice for all the world [10]—a *Pax Americana* that would confer liberty even upon individuals who had not learned how to exercise it and somehow would give to every people the right to self-determination that the American colonies had asserted in 1776.

But there were doubters and scoffers in America, and the seeds of opposition were sprouting. Philistines talked about their country's sacrifices in terms of net gain and loss, invoked the constitutional right of the Senate to make war and peace, spoke knowingly of the cussedness of human nature. A creed of isolationism developed that cut across the lines of political parties. A supreme preaching effort would be required to arrest a backsliding of the American congregation.

The President was advised to land at Boston, where a well-financed movement for the League of Nations was under way, with Taft, Lowell, and ex-Senator Crane participating. It was thought that Lodge's own state would give a welcome that would make the senator take notice and would, moreover, impress European opinion. Fearful of the bad impression that a Roman triumph would make upon Congress, Wilson stipulated that the reception at Boston should be informal and extemporaneous and should not appear to be a personal tribute.

The *George Washington* took a southerly route, and several times the President went to the top deck to cheer up soldiers who were convalescing in the sun. One evening he went to see a hilarious minstrel show that was put on by the male crew; and once the leading "lady" left the stage, threw hairy arms around him and, nuzzling a rope wig against the presidential brow, chucked him under the chin. To the prophet, this was an insult to his high office. His face turned to ice. Franklin D. Roosevelt was in the audience and never forgot that look.[11]

At the entrance to Boston harbor a freak current took the vessel off its course. An island loomed up directly ahead, and the captain had to reverse the engines at full speed, shaking the ship so that the passengers were alarmed. Wilson came out on deck, with the precious Covenant tucked securely in the breast pocket of his greatcoat. Just then a heavy snow squall blew down on the ship and it was necessary to anchor until the visibility improved. Noting the skill with which the emergency was met, the President sent for Captain McCauley and congratulated him.

The next day—the 24th of February—Governor Calvin Coolidge

---

[10] The St. Louis *Globe-Democrat* commented on Feb. 15: "It [the Covenant] is born, and no birth in history, save one, is of greater importance to mankind." On Feb. 25 the New York *Tribune* remarked: "The discussion . . . must be lifted above the plane of personalities. To do other than this is to degrade a theme almost as lofty as that contained in the *New Testament*." On March 29 the *Literary Digest* reported: "Not one member of the religious press, so far as we have observed, opposes the League *in toto*."

[11] F. D. Roosevelt to R. S. Baker, Oct. 3, 1939, Baker Papers, Princeton University Library. Eleanor Roosevelt to the writer, March 8, 1954.

came on board and escorted the Wilsons ashore and through thronged streets. Stores and schools had declared a holiday, and thousands lined the route. At Mechanics Hall eight thousand Americans—a curious mixture of Irish Democrats and liberal intellectuals—waited more than an hour for their hero. Governor Coolidge welcomed the President with a speech in which he characterized the reception as "even more marked than that accorded General George Washington, more united than any that could have been given at any time during his life to Abraham Lincoln"; and Mayor Andrew Peters hailed the Covenant as a document that would go down in history with Magna Carta and the Declaration of Independence.

Wilson knew, as he faced this reception from his own folk, that his opponents in the Senate had read the Covenant and had opened fire on it. He had expected nothing better. Condemning "narrow, selfish, provincial purposes," he broadcast a warning: "I have fighting blood in me and it is sometimes a delight to let it have scope, but if it is challenged on this occasion it will be an indulgence." He declared: "Speaking with perfect frankness in the name of the people of the United States I have uttered as the objects of this great war ideals, and nothing but ideals, and the war has been won by that inspiration."

And then he brought home his great challenge. "We set this nation up to make men free and we did not confine our conception and purpose to America, and now we will make men free. If we did not do that, all the fame of America would be gone and all her power would be dissipated. . . . Think of the picture, think of the utter blackness that would fall on the world." Asserting that peace could not be maintained for a single generation unless guaranteed by the united forces of the civilized world, he declared: "Any man who thinks that America will take part in giving the world any such rebuff and disappointment as that does not know America. I invite him to test the sentiments of the Nation."

"I have tried in all soberness and honesty," he told his people, "to speak your thought." At this point, a journalist wrote, the applause "leaped to thunder before the words were fairly out of his mouth."

The acclaim of audience and press struck a chill into the soul of the venerable senator from Massachusetts, whose sense of honor had moved him to respect the President's request from Paris that the League Covenant be not discussed until it could be explained by Wilson to members of Congress. Lodge suggested to his Republican colleagues that the President had taken an unfair advantage. Wilson had asked him to say nothing and then had gone to his home town and made a speech. "Very characteristic," the senator asserted.

On the floor of the Senate, on December 21, 1918, Lodge had served notice that that body could reject a treaty of peace or debate and amend it *ad infinitum*. Five days after the League Covenant was published in American newspapers, the senator described the document as "not only loose, ill-drawn, full of questions about which the signatories will be disputing within a twelfth-month, but . . . a breeder of misunderstandings if not of war."

The lines of partisan battle already had been drawn indelibly when the President arrived at Washington on February 25. His train was very late, but he was told that a huge crowd had waited hours in the streets to welcome him. He said, almost choking up: "I thought I had been entirely deserted."

Before leaving Paris, Wilson had thought that it would suffice to explain the Covenant in an address to the Congress; but House had feared that this method might seem dictatorial and had suggested that the President win the confidence of the legislators and satisfy their pride by consulting their committees.

Wilson, however, had little faith in his ability to convert senators who were already emotionally committed—in some cases publicly—against him and all his works. He had cabled home in January to ask that the House of Representatives pass a pro-League resolution, and nothing had happened. He felt that he could expect even less of the Senate, that he would have first to educate the people, and through them influence their representatives. But there were hopeful omens of popular support. Many Republican journals approved the Covenant and few Democratic papers of importance opposed it. More than half of the governors and state legislatures had indicated their support.

The President had yielded to House's urging and at Paris had signed a message asking that a dinner be arranged for the Congressional committees on foreign policy. On the evening of February 26, Wilson welcomed thirty-four curious members of Congress to the White House. Senators Borah and Fall had refused to come. The others found the state dining room made festive for the first time in two years. Edith Wilson, beautiful and gay, sat next to Henry Cabot Lodge and reminded him—"innocently," her husband later explained—of the magnificent reception that Boston had given to them. After dinner the guests went to the East Room; and the host, sitting in the open end of a horseshoe of chairs, put himself at their disposal.

As he sat down and leaned back in his chair, something fell out of his pocket and bounced loudly on the floor. It was the horse chestnut that he had treasured since Princeton days, for good fortune and because he liked to run his sensitive fingers over its velvety surface. When a congressman retrieved it and handed it to him, he reddened and looked sheepish. "It's my good-luck buckeye," he explained with a smile. "I keep it in my pocket to ward off the rheumatism." The roar of laughter that followed seemed to unify the group.[12] They listened respectfully as he told them what he had done at Paris. Senator Knox, who had been Taft's secretary of state, sat at first in sullen silence and then opened fire with questions. For more than two hours Wilson gave his best to these men, noting their honest anxieties, freely and frankly answering their queries, pleading with them to accept the document. But no conversions were made, and the legislators had gathered new grist for the mill of argument in the press[13] and on the floor of the Senate. The gentleman from Massachusetts listened with a stony face; his crony, Senator Brandegee, hectored the witness; and the two went home feeling only as wise as they came, complaining to friends about the personal appearance of their hostess, the paucity of cigars, and the temperateness of the drinks.

Only two days later, in a long polished speech, Lodge put the burden of proof on the proponents of the Covenant and suggested the first of what was to be an interminable barrage of amendments—"bad amendments as well as good amendments," Wilson called them when he learned of the speech, which he thought had been provoked, perhaps, by his wife's remarks to Lodge at the dinner table.

Lodge warned of threats to Washington's sacred doctrine of isolation, to the Monroe Doctrine, and to the right of the United States to control immigration. Coming to Article X, which Wilson had shown to be closest to his heart, he called its guaranty against aggression "a very grave, a very perilous promise." His eloquence dramatized an imaginary crusade by armed Americans in Europe's political jungles. Working on fears that had been aroused by the economic unrest that had resulted from demobilization and the reconversion of industry, he urged that the United States be not drawn "by any glittering delusions, through specious devices of supra-national government, within the toils of international socialism and anarchy." He asked for "consideration,

[12] Connally, *My Name Is Tom Connally*, p. 96.
[13] At the conference Wilson told his guests that they were free to discuss the affair afterward with newsmen. On Feb. 28, the unfriendly New York *Sun* reported that the President had "stated with finality" that "the United States must surrender vital points of sovereignty; Chinese and Japanese exclusion goes out of American control into the hands of League control; Ireland is to be left to the mercies of England." Hitchcock, McCumber, Brandegee, Knox, and Lodge were cited as witnesses that Wilson actually made these statements. Hitchcock immediately denied every part of the charge; McCumber soon made it clear that he had no part in thus falsely interpreting the President's remarks; but the others kept silent.

time, and thought." Peace should come first, and disarmament; and these things seemed to him to be delayed by discussion of the League of Nations.[14] Declaring that his opinion of the commission that had drafted the Covenant was not one of "veneration," Lodge said: "I do not think their intellect or position in the world are so overpowering that we cannot suggest amendments to this league."

Other senators joined the dissenting chorus. Going to Lodge's library early one morning, Brandegee suggested that it be made clear that a league of nations like that proposed could not win the approval of two-thirds of the senators. Hastening together to the home of Senator Knox, they drafted a resolution to that effect, and by the end of March 3 they had the names of thirty-seven senators signed to their "round robin"— enough to reject a treaty of peace. At two minutes after midnight, Lodge rose and read the document from the floor, knowing that he was out of order and depending on some Democrat to raise objections and thus prevent the resolution from being voted down. He had calculated well. Senator Swanson fell into the trap and objected; and so Lodge, immediately recognizing the objection, read the names of the signers into the *Record*. The resolution was circulated to the voters under government frank, the document was given to the press, and the whole world soon knew that the Covenant had been repudiated by an effective minority of the Senate of the United States.

At the same time the adversaries were asserting their will by another, and more familiar, method. They tightened the purse strings, hoping that the President would be compelled by impecuniousness to convoke the Senate by May and thus allow them to use the floor and the *Record* to publicize their criticisms of Woodrow Wilson. The Democrats lacked the strong leadership that was needed to secure the funds that Wilson and Hoover were requesting for European relief.[15]

At luncheon in the White House on the very day of Lodge's critical speech in the Senate, Wilson reminded Democratic leaders of the great

---

[14] This argument was used effectively and repeatedly by Wilson's opponents both at Washington and at Paris. Actually the framing of the Covenant, though leaving him time enough to attend the sessions of the Council of Ten, had diverted much of Wilson's energy from other urgent issues. On the other hand, however, the League had become a convenient repository for problems that could not be solved quickly and that threatened to delay the making of the treaty.

[15] Henry White had reinforced the plea for relief funds by cabling to Lodge to explain that Germany would pay cash for whatever food she got; but the senator had replied, incoherently, that there was a very strong feeling in America "against giving food or money to the Germans." A relief bill had passed the House; but in the Senate Lodge had amended the measure by excluding Germany, Austria, Bulgaria, and part of Turkey. At the urging of Hoover, Wilson had cabled to Congressional leaders on Jan. 10, 1919, and later to Glass, to urge the passage of the bill without amendment; but a conference report, accepting most of the Senate version with Lodge's amendment, finally had become law.

purposes to which he had committed them. Flicking the lash of discipline, he suggested that all the men of the party had not been as "cordial" in support of their leader's program as they might have been.

He insisted that the real issue of the day was the League of Nations, that they must not even appear to make a mere party issue of anything so sacred. "Believe me, gentlemen," he pleaded, "the civilized world cannot afford to have us lose this fight. I tried to state in Boston what it would mean to the people of the world if the United States did not support this great ideal with cordiality, but I was not able to speak. . . . I tell you, frankly, I choked up; I could not do it. The thing reaches the depth of tragedy."

Responding to Lodge's warning against involvement of the United States in "international socialism and anarchy," he said: "The only thing that that ugly, poisonous thing called bolshevism feeds on is the doubt of the man in the street of the essential integrity of the people he is depending on to do his governing." According to his reading of the Virginia Bill of Rights, any people is "entitled to any kind of government it damn pleases. Sometimes it will have a very riotous form of government, but that is none of our business. And I find that that is accepted, even with regard to Russia."

He explained that, though there was no real foundation for a League of Nations but the good faith of the subscribing parties, the Covenant was "a workable beginning of a thing that the world insists on." Though not a guaranty of peace, it came "as near being a guaranty of peace as you can get." The League was "the only solid basis of masonry" in the peace treaty.

"Now, if you put that case before the people of the United States," the prophet challenged, "and show them that without the League of Nations it is not worth while completing the treaty we are making in Paris, then you have got an argument which even an unidealistic people would respond to, and ours is not an unidealistic people but the most idealistic people in the world."

As for the adversaries—"I would reserve the right in private to say in unparliamentary language what I think of them, but in public I would try to stick to parliamentary language." And then, before the men of his own faith, he castigated the Philistines with a vehemence that revealed the chaos of his nerves.

It was a "very cheering thought," he said, that on the 5th of March, 1921—only two years away—he would "begin to be an historian again" and in that role "have the privilege of writing about these gentlemen without any restraints of propriety." Confessing that, if his own experience was a standard, the President of the United States was "liable some day to burst by merely containing restrained gases," he asserted:

Anybody in the Senate or House can say any abusive thing he pleases about the President, but it shocks the propriety of the whole country if the President says what he thinks about them. . . . But when the lid is off, I am going to resume my study of the dictionary to find adequate terms in which to describe the fatuity of these gentlemen with their poor little minds that never get anywhere but run round in a circle and think they are going somewhere. . . . My hope is that we will all put on our war paint, not as Democrats but as Americans, get the true American pattern of war paint and a real hatchet and go out on the war path and get a collection of scalps that has never been excelled in the history of American warfare.[16]

More patently than ever, Woodrow Wilson was the mind and soul of the Democratic party. Here was the hardened leader, following the *Realpolitik* that had been defined by Wilson the scholar in 1890: "A party likes to be led by very absolute opinions; it chills it to hear it admitted that there is some reason on the other side."

Wilson's complete devotion to the cause of the League left no enthusiasm for constructive domestic measures that Tumulty was urging upon him; but he was willing to review legislation proposed by men of the Cabinet to take care of problems raised by demobilization and reconversion. When he arrived at Washington he had gone to his desk as quickly and quietly as possible, to attack accumulated papers and to see the stream of callers who awaited him. However, when he addressed a meeting of governors and mayors on matters of reconstruction, his talk was brief and general and strayed inevitably to Europe.

He found his official family worrying about new problems. There was a streak of dependability in this group that contrasted agreeably with the opportunism of the men in the improvised councils at Paris. Carter Glass, who thought of public office as "human slavery" but whose elevation to the treasury secretaryship had not lessened his devotion to his herd of Jersey cattle, had been cabling often to Paris to seek the cooperation that the President had promised when he had appointed the Virginian. Glass faced the immediate job of selling a large Victory Loan to the American people. Realizing that Congress expected him to collect foreign debts to the United States, he nevertheless saw that further advances must be made to supply food in European areas that were threatened by anarchy. But it went against the grain of his integrity

---

[16] From quotations in Tumulty, *op. cit.*, pp. 332–34 and 367–79, that have been checked with Swem's transcription of his stenographic record, at the Princeton University Library. Cf. Blum, *Tumulty*, p. 305, no. 42.

to lend money abroad so that the Food Administration could sell American products, such as pork, at prices artificially pegged. The conflict of views between the Treasury Department and the Food Administration presented a puzzle that was not solved for some time. Nor did Wilson find a quick solution for a difference of opinion about the price of steel rails.

The other secretaries, too, had problems for the lap of their returning leader. Newton D. Baker, who amid public pressures for demobilization had needed more than ever the relaxing influence exerted by his favorite pipe, had held for Wilson's consideration an executive order to abolish censorship—a move to which General March objected. Josephus Daniels was advocating a government monopoly of international radio.

Burleson, fisherman for Potomac bass and Democratic votes, had turned businessman; and in administering the nation's communications systems he was incurring the wrath that accrues to those who set rates, hold down wages, and give less than perfect service. Franklin K. Lane was still arguing about the nation's oil reserves. Then there were Redfield and W. B. Wilson—men without hobbies, zealous in good works—the former despondent because the Industrial Board was meeting opposition to its efforts to fix prices,[17] the latter trying to carry out the President's charge to the War Labor Board that it "should use all means within its power to stabilize conditions and to prevent industrial dislocation and strife."

There were the philosophers and raconteurs, too: David F. Houston, with a new stock of epitaphs from rural tombs; and Thomas R. Marshall, telling ripe yarns of Newt Plum, Hoosier justice of the peace. Attorney General Gregory was resigning and going to Paris; and to replace him Wilson had appointed A. Mitchell Palmer of Pennsylvania, the aggressive custodian of alien property who was urged upon the President as a man who would strengthen the sagging Northern wing of the Democratic party.[18]

[17] An Industrial Board was set up in February, 1919, to extend such control as that exerted by the War Industries Board through the months of transition to a peacetime economy. Lacking strong support from public opinion as well as legal powers and including no officials immediate responsible to the President, this board was ineffective. Of the agencies set up to meet the war emergency, the only one of importance to endure was McAdoo's War Finance Corporation, under Eugene Meyer.

[18] It seemed clear that the preponderance of Southern influence had contributed to the party's defeat in the November election; and yet Wilson had found it hard to work this problem out in the "cold blood" of political advantage. The appointment of Palmer was much against the judgment of Gregory, who felt that his assistant, Todd of Virginia, merited the position. "This disturbs me," Wilson confessed to Tumulty. "It also disturbs me that, beginning at the bottom of the ladder in the Department of Justice, Todd worked his way to the top and earned every step."

However, the President had followed the wishes of Baruch, McCormick, and other party men. The experienced Todd resigned, and Palmer was placed in a post which he appeared to exploit to make political capital for himself.

"Everything looks so delightful and homelike to me over here," Wilson wrote to an old colleague at Princeton, "that it goes harder than I can say to pull up again and leave, but evidently the chief work is on the other side, at any rate for the present." Too rushed to confer with his aides individually, Wilson told them that they must carry on without him for another three months. He expected that he would be back again in June.

On the night of March 3 Lodge presented his Machiavellian "round robin" resolution, and the next day the Senate closed its session in a Republican filibuster, without acting on a vital deficiency bill or on the return of the nation's railways to their owners. While the obstructive talk went on, Wilson sat in his room at the Capitol and talked cheerfully with Democratic senators, preparing to denounce the infidels publicly. "A group of men in the Senate," he charged in a message to the people, "have deliberately chosen to embarrass the administration of the Government, to imperil the financial interests of the railway systems of the country, and to make arbitrary use of the powers intended to be employed in the interest of the people." Democratic Senator Martin already had seen through the Republican plot to force a special session during the President's absence. He had served notice, on February 26, that Congress would not be called until Wilson's final return from abroad. And now the President himself affirmed this in his statement to the press.

Soon after noon on March 4, the day on which this assertion was printed, Wilson took a train for New York. His indignation at his adversaries was boiling up dangerously. At Philadelphia there was a sweet, short interlude, when he went to a hospital to visit daughter Jessie and a new-born grandson and namesake. The infant could not be coaxed to open its eyes, but its red mouth gaped persistently. Observing this phenomenon, the President remarked gravely: "I think from appearances that he will make a United States senator."

The mood of the prophet was black when he reached New York and went to the Metropolitan Opera House to speak to five thousand people. He walked on the stage arm in arm with William Howard Taft, to whom he had appealed for support against Republican opponents of the League and who hoped that the President would continue to insist on including the Covenant in the peace treaty. Returning from a crusading tour across the country and appearing against the advice of his physician, Taft spoke first and refuted objections to the Covenant so convincingly that for a moment Wilson wondered what was left for him to say.

When the band played "Over There," the President took his cue from it. "I will not come back," he pledged, "till it's over, over there. . . . I pray God in the interests of peace of the world that that may be soon." His voice hardened as he laid down a public challenge:

Every man at the Paris conference knows that the treaty of peace will be inoperative, as Mr. Taft has said, without this constant support and energy of a great organization such as is supplied by the League of Nations. And men who, when I first went over there, were skeptical of the possibility of forming a league of nations, admitted that if we could but form it, it would be an invaluable instrumentality through which to secure the operation of the various parts of the treaty; and when that treaty comes back, gentlemen on this side will find the Covenant not only in it, but so many threads of the treaty tied to the Covenant that you cannot dissect the Covenant from the treaty without destroying the whole vital structure. The structure of peace will not be vital without the League of Nations, and no man is going to bring back a cadaver with him.

Advocates of a league were filled with misgivings. By bluntly defying the bloc of senators who had signed the "round robin" resolution, the President had alienated many citizens. He had failed to educate those whose minds were open. Overtired, overwrought, suffering from a cold, the prophet had unleashed his emotions too rashly. There was an edge upon his tone and menace in his manner as he threatened the vengeance of a wrathful God on his sinful adversaries. In his voice were echoes of lost causes—the South fighting for its concept of the right, the president of Princeton alienating alumni. The next morning the Indianapolis *Star* suggested that the President of the United States might be "riding for a fall."

Backstage, after the speech, the President found Tumulty ready to bring in a delegation of Irish-Americans who wished to plead for home rule for Ireland. Their leader was Daniel F. Cohalan, a man who had a record of disloyalty during the war and was beyond the pale of Wilson's morality. The President took out his watch and very decisively ordered that Cohalan be taken out of the building by a secret service man.[19]

After the ejection of its leader, the delegation gave its petition to an austere, steely-eyed chief executive, who thought the Irish Question a domestic concern of the British Empire in which no outsider should interfere—except, perhaps, someday, the League of Nations.

The Wilsons sailed the next morning, the President plagued by an aching tooth, indigestion, and a feverish cold that kept him in bed for two days. His sublime faith in his liaison with his constituency was

[19] Myles McCahill, the secret service man, to the writer.

still unshaken. "The people of the United States," he informed House, "are undoubtedly in favor of the League of Nations by an overwhelming majority . . . but there are many forces, particularly those prejudiced against Great Britain, which are exercising a considerable influence against it, and you ought to have that constantly in mind. . . ." The prophet did not see the newspapers the morning after his parting speech at New York and little criticism reached him now. When it did penetrate his sensitive mind, he showed irritation if it was unfavorable.

For a sweet interval, while the *George Washington* took the shortest route back to Brest, the President could cast off the net that was enmeshing his mind and be a whole human being, undivided by fears and pressures. He had his friends in for luncheon, said grace in a low, reverent voice, and indulged in familiar give-and-take, limericks and puns, and stories of golf. One day he signed the Prohibition Amendment, with a wry observation about the "personal deprivation" that it might cause. Occasionally, coming in from the damp, chilly air, he would himself take a very little Scotch.

Sometimes he would think of the precarious transatlantic tightrope on which he was walking, with head winds from France pressing him toward a guarantee against aggression stronger than that given in Article X and blasts from the Senate pushing him toward a less binding commitment.

Before leaving Paris he had let it be known that not one word, not even a period, of the Covenant could be revised. When House had quoted Burke to him—"to govern is to compromise"—the President quickly had seen the application and had laughed and shaken his finger. "For once," he said, "I do not agree with you or with Burke, if you have quoted him correctly. I have found that you get nothing in this world that is worth while without fighting for it." He saw that to reopen discussion of the Covenant at the conference would be to give France a chance to reassert her self-centered demands for security.

Nevertheless, Wilson's visit to America led him to wonder whether he should not make an effort at Paris to resolve the major doubts that were besetting his own people. While crossing the ocean he studied notes that he had made at the Congressional conference at the White House. "No matter what I do, they will continue their attack," he said disconsolately. But he had an encouraging letter that had been written at his request by Senator Hitchcock. This Democrat, who would be supplanted by Lodge as chairman of the Foreign Relations Committee in the next Congress, reported that some signers of the "round robin" actually would vote for the Covenant if it was a part of the peace treaty, and still more would support it if certain specified changes were made.

Though Wilson had little hope of appeasing the more implacable of the senators, he saw a possibility of taking some action to reassure those who sincerely accepted the basic principles of the League. Even mild reservations, however, might require compensating concessions to France when discussion was reopened at Paris. If only House had been able to stand firm in his absence, he felt, perhaps he would not have to concede so much as to make of the peace merely another "Holy Alliance." But if the Colonel had yielded a little to France and he himself now had to concede more to the French in order to get the changes in the Covenant that his people wanted, the outlook would be black indeed.

On March 13 House came to Brest to welcome his friend, eager to give a full account of his stewardship during the month of their separation. Left at Paris to conduct negotiations without specific instructions, he had maintained a good understanding with the leaders of the Allies and had tried to hasten decisions that would conform in general with his chief's principles.

Left alone among Europeans to whom he had made himself agreeable, the enterprising Texan had seemed to his colleagues to revert to the boy who had untiringly swapped jackknives, the businessman who had traded in such a way as to let the other fellow profit enough so that he would come back to trade again. Bliss and White had thought House too sympathetic to his French friends. Moreover, the Colonel himself had questioned his own ability to keep a hand on all the nerve centers at the conference. "When I fell sick in January," House wrote in his diary on February 26, "I lost the thread of affairs and I am not sure that I have ever gotten fully back."

The moral atmosphere that Wilson had cultivated had not long survived the absence of his own voice; and the specific provisions of his Fourteen Points on such matters as boundaries and reparations were proving inadequate as a basis for settlements. Colonel House, realizing the strength of Republican opposition at Washington, saw that the solidarity of Clemenceau and Lloyd George in their own constituencies "put the finishing touches to a situation already bad." In his chief's absence, House had assumed as much responsibility as the European premiers took. By cable and wireless he had faithfully reported the major moves and the trend of the thinking, though the exchanges of cables with the President had not been clear because of difficulty with a new code.

In reply he had had a sweet personal message from Edith Wilson, but only a few business notes and cables from the President. Wilson's messages had taken few exceptions to the Colonel's diplomacy. In fact, in replying to a report that Marshal Foch was urging an immediate imposition of severe terms upon Germany—territorial and economic as well as military—the President reaffirmed his faith in his agent. "I know," he said, "I can trust you and our colleagues to withstand such a programme immovably . . . we should not risk being hurried into a solution arrived at solely from the French official viewpoint . . ."

Believing that delay could be favorable only to Germany and thinking that the Germans would be more easily reconciled to severe military terms if they knew the whole reckoning, House wished to open Germany to a flow of food and trade by a preliminary treaty, set the League in operation, and leave the most thorny issues to be handled when order and confidence returned to Europe. He had initiated discussion of territorial and economic terms, in accordance with the procedure that he had laid before the President on February 14. Undertaking discussion of a settlement for the west bank of the Rhine, he reported to Wilson that Clemenceau was "insistent" on the creation of a disarmed Rhenish Republic, and then on March 7, that in a conference with Lloyd George and Clemenceau, no tentative agreement was reached "because of Clemenceau's very unreasonable attitude.[20]

The President, fearful of a breach of the principle of self-determination, had warned House specifically against determining the geographical boundaries of Germany. Now, on March 10, the President wirelessed that he was a "little uneasy" and hoped that House would not consent, even provisionally, to separation of the Rhenish provinces from Germany under any arrangement, but would reserve the whole matter.

Charles Swem, to whom Wilson's message of March 10 was dictated, thought that the President put it mildly when he described himself as "a little uneasy." Actually, he seemed deeply concerned.[21] Doubtless the President remembered that at their parting in mid-February, House had pleaded repeatedly for conciliation of the Senate and had warned that

[20] On March 2, House had convoked a conference in the apartment of Vance McCormick, who was serving at Paris as an economic adviser. The Colonel recorded in his diary: "I had a long talk with Tardieu and we got nearer together on the question of the Rhenish Republic . . ." McCormick, however, left the meeting with the understanding that a definite agreement was reached for the creation of a Rhenish Republic—an arrangement that he later learned was absolutely contrary to Wilson's wishes. McCormick's diary records that an agreement was reached also on a plan for the Saar Basin and on the transfer of Danzig to Poland and Luxembourg to Belgium, with reservations. No message reporting this meeting to the President has been found. It is not recorded whether McCormick's version reached Wilson, but this is not unlikely. *See* McCormick's Diary, March 2, 1919; also McCormick's statement to Ray Stannard Baker, July 16, 1928, Baker Papers. Lloyd George's *Memoirs of the Peace Conference,* I, 188, records that House told him and Clemenceau, on March 7, that they might reach agreement on Tardieu's plan "provided the principle of self-determination was postponed until the whole of the terms of peace had been fulfilled."

[21] Charles Swem to the writer.

he might have to compromise with the Europeans on minor matters in order to safeguard American principles. Moreover, news dispatches had given the impression that the Colonel had consented to—unpardonable heresy—the separation of the Covenant from the treaty.[22]

When the *George Washington* put into the harbor at Brest on a rainy afternoon Wilson was pale and anxious. He had to be polite to Jusserand, who came out to welcome him in the name of France; and he did not see House until he disembarked at a landing stage late in the evening, in full moonlight. After inspecting a French guard of honor, he went with the Colonel to a train. Before they reached Paris they went over the situation on both sides of the Atlantic. Wilson spoke fatalistically of the enemy in the Senate. Complaining of the sullen spirit of Knox and Lodge at the White House party that the Colonel had promoted, he said: "Your dinner was a failure as far as getting together was concerned."

The Colonel reminded his friend that at least the dinner had served to give evidence that the President was willing to listen to advice. It seemed to House that Wilson had been unduly irritated because true friends of the League criticized his New York speech as too contentious.

On the train to Paris the President did not reproach the old friend who had served him so long and so well. To his wife, however, he confessed the depth of his disappointment. He would have to start all over again, he felt, to restore the Covenant to pre-eminence in the peace settlement. By listening sympathetically to French demands for guarantees beyond those expected under the League of Nations, House had conceded that the protection given by the Covenant might not be adequate; and now, to meet the views of critics in the United States, Wilson would have to ask for revisions that would make the Covenant even less satisfactory to France as a guarantee of security. He saw his lonely task complicated because it must now be clear to foreign statesmen that even his own fellow commissioners did not cleave entirely to his ultimate principles.

He faced up to the challenge like the Covenanter that he was. "Well," he said to Edith Wilson, as he threw back his head and the light of controversy came into his eyes, "thank God I can still fight, and I'll win . . . or never look these boys I sent over here in the face again. They lost battles—but won the war, bless them."

---

[22] Actually, House merely had discussed with his secretary the possbility of making such a separation, to appease the Senate. Auchincloss told David Hunter Miller of this conversation, and possibly gave an inkling of it to others who were less discreet than Miller.

CHAPTER XV

Revelation and Revolution

WHEN WOODROW WILSON left his train at the Gare des Invalides on March 14—just three months after his first triumphal entry into Paris— he was no longer regarded by the French as a savior to be feted. They had expected that by this time their *poilus* would be sent home and Germany would begin paying for its depredations. But now their press was telling them that these essentials had been sidetracked in favor of an untested formula—President Wilson's League of Nations. The people of Paris plodded to their daily tasks muttering "So Wilson is back!"

Work was to take precedence over everything now, in the mansion at 11 Place des Etats-Unis that was placed at the disposal of the Wilsons. Lloyd George was waiting to talk business. In the afternoon Clemenceau joined them for a three-hour conference. The Colonel had arranged that The Three meet secretly in his wife's sitting room; for he was determined to spur these men to make peace with Germany at the earliest moment possible, and wanted to keep a hand on proceedings. He and Wilson perceived that, working in secrecy, The Three could rub along without deep wounds to personal vanity or political prestige.

The American emerged smiling from the first conference. The premiers, however, were solemn. They could not but contrast the session with those that they had had with Colonel House during Wilson's absence. The Texan had proved himself a gentleman who never preached, listened well. In Clemenceau's view, the Colonel was "really first-class" as a negotiator, a man whom he could frankly disagree with and yet respect—"a good American, very nearly as good a Frenchman." Both crack pistol shots, each thought the other's argument as straight as his aim. They had come to love each other like brothers. In this affection House saw opportunity of converting The Tiger to the President's views, while Wilson, for his part, envisioned the possibility that his Colonel would be subverted.

Sitting in his wheel chair, the wounded Tiger had done some deep thinking. Resisting the efforts of nursing sisters to give him bitter doses and make him say his prayers, he had been reviewing the Covenant with all the caution that he had warned Wilson he would exercise.

Actually, the more he studied it the more inadequate it seemed as protection against the outnumbering hordes from Central Europe that had swarmed upon France, twice within a half-century.

Lloyd George was fretful, too. In England his coalition had lost two seats in a bye-election. Northcliffe's press was flailing him because he did not support French demands along the Rhine. Traders who once had hoped to profit by a prolonged blockade of Germany were now complaining that they could not do business until peace was made; and the British command in Germany reported that food shortages raised a specter of anarchy.[1] The prime minister wished to get from the United States a promise not to build in competition with Britain's navy. He hoped also for support for England's claim for the payment of the costs of the war by Germany.

During Wilson's absence the statesmen had become indifferent toward the Covenant to which the American prophet had committed them and which he had kept constantly before them while he was at Paris. Even Colonel House, lacking eloquence, and driven by fear of anarchy to negotiate a quick settlement of issues in dispute, had not exerted himself greatly to keep the American vision of a league in the foreground. In the office of Arthur Sweetser, who was directing American publicity in the absence of Ray Stannard Baker, House conferred occasionally with a few favored journalists. He talked convincingly of his own deft diplomacy, of his efforts to reach compromises in private talks of secretaries and experts. "It slows up the preliminary work very much to have the big men here now," he had told them on February 27, "so we are glad to have them out of the way." On March 5 he so far forgot himself as to say that Wilson could have made his path very much easier by using newsmen at Paris as House had urged. "I have

[1] Herbert Hoover, who had gone abroad after the Armistice eager to use American surpluses to feed the hungry of Europe, soon had found that the idealistic professions of individuals at London and Paris did not square with their actions as officials of electorates that were swayed by war hatred and economic necessity. Shipments had been delivered to Allies and to neutrals, but British officials had refused to break their blockade to let cargoes go into Germany. Moreover, Germany had failed to act on an agreement to turn over merchant ships before receiving food, and showed no desire to pay for shipments in gold—a possibility that French financiers were thought to be opposing so that their nation might get what gold there was as indemnity.

Frustrated by apathy and obstruction, Hoover was brought on the carpet by Lloyd George, who was inclined to brush him off as "that Salvation Army man." The prime minister, distressed by reports of famine in Germany, wanted to know why Hoover had not done his job. At this the American let him have the bitter truth. Lloyd George, feeling that tact was not one of Hoover's great qualities, asked him to give the council an expurgated version of his remarks. This was done, and a stormy and wordy session ensued.

When Wilson returned to Paris, the long-dammed flow of food to Central Europe was beginning. On April 28, when Hoover complained that he was not getting enough American ships to carry food, the President wrote to Henry M. Robinson to urge that "the strongest representations" be made to the Shipping Board "to divert to carrying food ships that might make large profits on commercial routes."

never known a man," the Colonel said, "who has such a faculty for doing the right thing in the hardest way. He always makes the most conceivable trouble for himself . . ." [2] At last the disciple's tact had broken under the strain. When Wilson returned to Paris it was being gossiped not only that Auchincloss was singing the praises of his father-in-law immoderately, but that House himself had "swelled up like a poisoned pup."

There were many at Paris who were deliberately blurring the vision presented by the prophet. Irresponsible Americans were saying that the Republican party was the real friend of Europe, that the British and French ought to get together and compel the President to do what they willed. European observers had noted the outspoken opposition of American senators. Foreign Minister Pichon was proclaiming that the Covenant would not be in the treaty of peace; the French press was accepting this as a fact; and at London *The Times* assumed it. An able correspondent welcomed Ray Stannard Baker back to Paris with "Well, your league is dead." Even Lord Robert Cecil admitted that it had been sidetracked.

Believing that publicity was "the lifeblood of democracy," Ray Stannard Baker again urged the President to improve his public relations, advising him that the essential thing was not to convince the people of the world that a league was needed, but to persuade them that the Covenant drawn was the best obtainable. This was what Wilson had failed to do in his messages to his people in America.

But, though he could not bring himself to try to influence opinion by heart-to-heart talks with individuals, Wilson saw that in order to win in what he called the "deadly grapple" of Past and Present he must act emphatically. On the very morning of his arrival at Paris, he picked up his telephone and called Baker. "I want you to say," he directed, "that we stand exactly where we stood on January 25 when the Peace Conference adopted the resolution making the Covenant an integral part of the general treaty of peace." Baker phrased the manifesto and put it out that afternoon. On the same day David Hunter Miller was directed to confer with Sir Maurice Hankey, secretary of the British delegation, about the form that the Covenant should take in the final treaty.

In this hour of supreme trial Woodrow Wilson needed all the resources of his ancestors. He must husband his energy for bouts with the premiers. But when little men came to him with tales of woe and hopes of loot—patriots who were not satisfied to plead the cause of their nations to any ear less authoritative than that of the great champion of

[2] Arthur Sweetser's notes of news conferences, in his possession.

self-determination himself—he satisfied his conscience by seeing them. He signed his name hundreds of times to polite acknowledgments and reassurances written for him in French. Sometimes he would receive more than a score of petitioners in a day: Armenians, Albanians, Lithuanians, Irish, Egyptians, Jews, a Greek priest who impressed Wilson deeply, and Galician peasants who had walked scores of miles to a railroad station so that they might ask the great American to attach their little mountain pocket to Poland. And then there were special pleaders to be seen, representing world-wide associations of interest: women, labor, the farmers, the Negroes. He did not arrange to be briefed on the pleas of these visitors before he heard them; nor would he delegate the interviews to his staff. When they told their stories, however, he held his sympathy in reserve, not wishing to promise more than he could fulfill, and lacking energy for give-and-take. Often the pleaders thought his face stony as they talked, heard his formal greeting and dismissal, and went away to add their testimony to the legend of the inaccessible, schoolmastering prophet.

Sometimes Wilson gave fellow delegates the feeling that he was beating them down. He was advised to make more use of the arts of traditional diplomacy; but with the world on fire, he felt that there was no time for social chitchat, for palaver with journalists, or for nursing hurt egos among Americans whose total loyalty he wished to take for granted. "I fear being misquoted," he told Baker, "and if I talk freely I do not know how to be discreet."

Seeing in him America's "best instrument" to give her ideals to the world, resolving to feed his mind with useful facts, Baker went each afternoon at six to 11 Place des Etats-Unis. Usually the President was still in the study where The Three had met, picking up documents and putting them away in a steel box. There, or across the hall in a drawing room that was always bright with flowers, Wilson would go over the events of the day with Baker and decide what should be made public. Sometimes Edith Wilson joined them, and by her questions helped to clarify their thinking.

Baker gave a daily bulletin to the newsmen and listened to their grievances. The American commissioners continued to grant some interviews, but now knew less than ever about the actual negotiations in the inner council. Some journalists found that it paid to go to House for news. Even the Colonel, however, began to have difficulty in keeping his finger on the pulse of events, as The Three continued to meet at the President's house in secrecy, sometimes admitting Orlando and occasionally calling in expert advisers.

Having restored the Covenant to a place of honor, Wilson hoped that it would not now be necessary to bring up the amendments that fellow Americans were suggesting. When House and Lord Robert Cecil went to him on March 16, to urge amendment and clarification of certain articles of the Covenant, Wilson resisted—"with his usual stubbornness," the Colonel jotted in his diary. Any change at this time, the President felt, would be interpreted at home as a yielding to the Senate and would damage the chances for ratification of the peace treaty.

On the same day the President had a cable from Tumulty reporting that polls showed a strong drift of opinion toward the League and that Taft was urging slight changes of language to reassure "conscientious Americans" in whom unjustified fears had been aroused. Wilson replied that he appreciated Taft's advice and would welcome suggestions that the former President had offered to send. These came from Tumulty in a cable of March 18. The President had sanctioned an effort by House to get from Lodge, through Henry White, some definite and constructive suggestions; but the senator, faithfully pursuing the policy that had been outlined with Roosevelt and suspecting that White's request had been inspired by the President, replied that nothing short of redrafting would get the Senate's approval of the Covenant.

On March 18 Wilson invited House and Lord Robert Cecil to dinner to discuss possible revisions, one by one. When his guests approved an amendment on its merits, the President willingly accepted it; but let them so much as suggest that it would be expedient to yield to the Senate on any point, and he bristled ominously. He could not find the letter [3] in which Hitchcock had enumerated revisions that would please the Senate, but did his best to recall the contents.

Two days after his dinner with House and Lord Robert Cecil, the President welcomed a score of delegates from thirteen neutral nations to a hearing before members of the League Commission. This was their

[3] The disappearance of this important letter and the fact that the President did not cable to Washington for a duplicate of it are striking instances of the lack of organization and enterprise in Wilson's office of which House's men complained. Hitchcock had written to the President, on March 4, that the following revisions were "likely to influence votes in the order given:

"First, a reservation to each high contracting party of its exclusive control over domestic subjects.

"Second, a reservation of the Monroe Doctrine.

"Third, some provision by which a member of the league can, on proper notice, withdraw from membership.

"Fourth, the settlement of the ambiguity in Article 15.

"Fifth, the insertion on the next to the last line of first paragraph of Article 8, after the word 'adopted,' of the words, 'by the several governments.'

"Sixth, the definite assurance that it is optional with a nation to accept or reject the burdens of a mandatory."

opportunity, he told them, to make their views known as the Articles of the Covenant were laid before them. He answered their questions patiently and lucidly, explaining that members of the League assumed three obligations for action toward an aggressor: they must break commercial relations, allow the military forces of the League to pass over their territory, and consider whether they would join in military or naval action. They might make, among themselves, such alliances as the Executive Council decided were genuinely defensive; but offensive pacts would be strictly forbidden. The neutrals were encouraged to suggest changes in the text, and Wilson thanked them for participating and assured them that their suggestions would be examined by the council with great care. He was now showing what he meant by "open covenants openly arrived at."

When the Commission on the League of Nations met on March 22 to re-examine the text of the Covenant, the French brought out arguments that already had been worn threadbare but were still useful as a means of barter. Nothing short of international inspection of armament and an international general staff would make the French feel secure under the League, Léon Bourgeois insisted. The President had to remind the commission that it was their principle to reject the concept of a super-state.

He went home wearied by the staleness of the talk. He knew what these men were going to say before they opened their mouths; and their arguments made him wonder whether France wanted to renew the war, annex some of Germany, and stir up bad feeling generally. Nevertheless, he tried to conciliate French opinion by visiting devastated villages on a Sunday and by going with Clemenceau and Lloyd George to make peace with Foch, who was sulking because his plan for using Poland as a military base against Russia had not been accepted.

At an evening session of the commission Wilson tried to soothe Bourgeois, who felt that his life's work was wiped out because the world court at The Hague was not to be carried on under the Covenant. Out of respect for the feelings of the French jurist, he restrained his tongue, but later he said to House and Cecil: "The talkfest at The Hague in 1899 . . . ended in fog overhead and in bog underfoot. The whole business was wishy-washy—though well meant, of course . . . Now we are met here for hard-and-fast agreements, for binding stipulations, for commitments, and it's my task to see that no nation or group of men holds out on us—those silly pawns in the murderous game of power politics!" [4]

Wilson studied proposals for amending the Covenant that had come

4 Bonsal, *Unfinished Business*, p. 152.

from Lowell of Harvard,[5] and also Taft's constructive ideas. He found very useful, too, a poll of the world's newspapers that appeared in the Paris press.

On his typewriter he tapped out three amendments on a single sheet of paper.[6] That on the Monroe Doctrine, he told the commission at the meeting of March 24, would be introduced later. But two were presented to the commission that night. One of these, exempting from League action those disputes that might arise out of domestic matters, was approved in principle. The other provided for withdrawal of a nation from the League. Wilson sponsored this change with reluctance, having always been, he said, "an anti-secessionist." He told the commission that only moral compulsion could guarantee the historical continuity of the League. Yet the fact must be faced that his own nation might refuse to join the new body if definite provision was not made for withdrawal. For many public men, especially in the United States, sovereignty was "a sort of fetish." One had to make concessions to existing ideas in order to make new ideas viable. Some day, Wilson prophesied, "men will be as ardent partisans of humanity as they are today of national sovereignty." It was agreed, finally, that members of the League in good standing might withdraw on two years' notice.

By advocating this amendment to reassure the Senate, Wilson displeased Europeans who had counted on permanent American membership. The French, in particular, were distressed. If they must yield in this matter to American opinion, they hoped at least to get a concession in return. They had an amendment of their own to propose—a plan for an economic section in the League. But the President refused to barter. He warned that acceptance of the French proposal might result in "the flag following the dollar." Speaking of his own experience with commercial imperialists, he made it clear that there must be no economic exploitation by an international empire.

[5] The text of three amendments proposed by Lowell after his Boston debate with Lodge had been cabled to Lansing by the State Department on March 22. Moreover, Wilson had analyses of American press opinion and criticisms of the Covenant from William Phillips of the State Department, Dwight Morrow, and others, through Thomas W. Lamont. *See* Lamont, *Across World Frontiers*, pp. 186–91.

Furthermore, Polk cabled on the 20th that Charles Warren, assistant attorney general, had discussed the League with Root, and that they concluded that the paragraphs on the machinery of the new government were not clear enough. "Two or three friendly newspaper men have told me in the last few days," Polk reported, "that they feel the League is losing ground as no one seems to have authority here to explain the document or answer criticisms of Republican Senators. The opponents are carrying on a very active and cleverly planned campaign and something must be done . . . I find many friends of the President are becoming confused." A cable dated March 28, from Phillips to Lamont, concluded thus: "A very solid sentiment is appearing that it [the Covenant] should be amended in many vital particulars."

[6] For a discussion of the three amendments and a fourth, making the acceptance of colonial mandates optional, *see* Baker, *W.W. and World Settlement*, I, 329–31. The presentation of the amendment on the Monroe Doctrine is discussed on pp. 301–303 below.

Discussion in the commission's session of March 26 became heated; and as idealism ebbed and the conference gave the public no hint of progress toward peace, the spring mists of Paris thickened into thunderclouds. Rumblings of popular protest assailed the delays, the secrecy, the lack of decisive action against bolshevism in Central Europe. President Wilson and his League were blamed for it all—especially by those who saw no profit in the Covenant.

Wilson thought he knew the source of delay. From many of his experts came the same complaints: "The French are holding us back; the French are talking us to death." He himself would spend an hour in arguing Clemenceau around to a certain position, only to find when the subject was reopened that The Tiger had yielded again to the promptings of his instincts. One had to deal with him as one would play with a trout, Wilson thought, jerking him up suddenly, then letting him run a little, and all the while watching to see that he did not get away.

When American newsmen asked permission to be candid, the President told them that he would not object if they were "indiscreet enough to tell the truth." But Wilson could not bring himself to break openly with his French colleague in the little World Cabinet, run home, and tell Europe to save itself as best it could. He had declared himself responsible to all humanity. Convinced that the cause of peace could not be served by the public row that the headline-hunters hoped for, he resolved to curb his tongue a little longer.

However, he felt that he could speak in a general way to revitalize public morale. On March 27 he struck boldly and positively at subversive thought by giving out a reassuring word on the progress of the Commission on the League of Nations. He explained that the commission had met at hours that did not interfere with other discussions. Moreover, the revised Covenant, "practically finished," was in the hands of a drafting committee and would "almost immediately" be given to the public.

At the very moment when the prophet of the Western world was concentrating his powers on the revision of the League Covenant, the ogre of revolution was casting its darkest shadow from the east. On March 24 the republican government of Hungary was upset by a Communist coup. Soviet propaganda, originally devised in desperation as a defense, was being shaped by the new Comintern into an offensive weapon that was sapping Allied morale on several fronts.

The Bolshevik government had been in existence now for more than a year and had maintained itself in central Russia—an area comprising hardly a fourth of the Czarist Empire—against the pressures of a fringe of militarists of the old regime who had more or less support from the Western powers. What if men lacking respect for civil liberties and for sanctity of contract should seize control of all of Central Europe? What if Asiatic despotism should supplant German absolutism?

This denouement had been made less probable by Wilson's pre-Armistice dealings with Germany. The German revolution at the time of the Armistice had been liberal in purpose, peacefully executed, and Western in ideology. The problem now, in the spring of 1919, was to guide revolutionary forces in Eastern Europe, and particularly those in Russia, into paths equally sane.

During Wilson's absence from Paris it had seemed wise to House and Lansing, as well as to Balfour and Lloyd George, that an unofficial effort be made to bring about the understanding with Moscow that official overtures had failed to establish. It had long been the custom of the British Foreign Office to send daring young bloods on diplomatic adventures to the ends of the earth, under a gentlemen's agreement that they would be heroes if they succeeded but disowned if they caused embarrassment to their government. It happened now that there was a young liberal in the American peace delegation who was willing to take a chance.

William C. Bullitt, who had been briefing the American commissioners on incoming intelligence, responded to the challenge. Taking along the liberal journalist Lincoln Steffens, Bullitt reached Moscow two days after the Third International Congress closed its sessions. Talking with Litvinov, Chicherin, and Lenin, he found them resentful of the world's low opinion of their honor, but confident that President Wilson, whose Fourteen Points they praised, would understand that a dull, inexperienced people were trying conscientiously, but at cost of great suffering to themselves, to find a better way to live for the common interest. The ruling party seemed strong, politically and morally; but lack of food made the people an easy prey of anarchy. Their armies had been winning, and they feared that their enemies would use a truce to rally their forces.

In Nicolai Lenin, Bullitt saw "a straight-forward man of the quickest intelligence and a certain serenity, humor, and broad-mindedness." By exerting his persuasiveness against the will of Trotsky and the generals, Lenin said, he was able to persuade the Central Executive Council to give Bullitt a reasonable proposal to take to the statesmen at Paris.

The young emissary arrived with Lenin's written message on the evening of March 25, and went directly to House's bedroom. The

Colonel saw hope, at last, for solving the most baffling problem of the peacemaking. He telephoned immediately to Wilson, but found the President suffering from a headache and unwilling to see Bullitt that night.

Lenin, suspicious of France's military intentions, had set a deadline at April 10. Preferring to take up the question with the President first but given no opportunity to do so, House advised Bullitt to talk with Lloyd George. The prime minister, who had given unofficial encouragement to Bullitt's venture, seemed favorably disposed toward Lenin's proposition. If Wilson would take the lead in opening negotiations, he would follow along, Lloyd George said, though he feared that the Northcliffe press would tear him limb from limb.

In the American delegation Bullitt found the same skepticism that prevailed among other conservatives at London and Paris. All the while, however, Colonel House persisted in working for agreement. Realizing that Wilson was the only statesman of sufficient stature to build a bridge over the chasm, the Colonel sent Ray Stannard Baker to the President with Lenin's proposal. At the same time other liberals among Wilson's advisers were prodding him to act.

The President, however, did not see the picture in black and white. He could not believe that Lenin's proposals had been made in simple good faith; and even had he honored them he would have been restrained from action by reports that came from Washington.[7] Clearly, Americans did not want to fight the Bolsheviki; nor would they permit their statesmen to treat with them. Wilson perceived that the political temperature was too high in the democracies for any rational rapprochement. Lloyd George, summoned home to face questions in Parliament about alleged secret dealings with the dreaded "Reds," was forced to belittle the Bullitt mission and throw responsibility for ignoring it upon the President. And Wilson, meeting Bullitt at the Crillon after receiving a letter from the young man that seemed "insulting," cut him coldly. The prospect of solving what Wilson had called "the acid test" of the peacemaking grew very dim when news came that Admiral Kolchak's army was gaining rapidly in Siberia, for the reac-

---

[7] Before Bullitt's return from Moscow, American journalists got wind of his mission and cabled the news home. This disclosure aggravated the "anti-red" hysteria that had been stirred up at Washington by lurid hearings that were conducted by a subcommittee of the Senate's Committee on the Judiciary.

On April 2, when Bullitt was reminding House that only eight days remained for accepting the Russian offer, Tumulty sent this message to Paris: "The proposed recognition of Lenin has caused consternation over here."

Undersecretary Polk, who was about to "wind the Russians up financially," read Bullitt's report and cabled: "I do not think I would be prepared to act on any report framed by Bullitt and Steffens after a three days' stay in Russia."

tionaries at Paris then believed that military action might eliminate the
Soviet regime.[8]

While the time limit set by Lenin for action on his proposals was
expiring, the President was worn down by British and French efforts
to further their national interests by trading them against American
suggestions for revision of the Covenant.[9] On March 24 Wilson began
a series of intense sessions with Clemenceau and Lloyd George, in many
of which they were joined by Orlando or Makino of Japan or both.
At first there was no other man present but Paul Mantoux, the official
interpreter. "I never saw him lose his calm," Mantoux has testified. "The
relations of President Wilson with his associates were constantly the
most courteous, whatever the difference of opinion might have been at
certain moments and on certain points." Another interpreter noted that
the President depended on reason and never tried to exploit his rank as
the only chief of state among the peace commissioners.[10]

The Three argued over economic problems. British and French politicians had led their electorates to hope that the entire cost of the war
would be wrung out of Germany. There were suspicions that certain

[8] When House came on March 27 to plead for action on Lenin's proposal, Wilson asked
him to go to Hoover and to the Shipping Board to see whether ships and food could be sent to
Russia. The next day Hoover brought to him a proposal for "a second Belgian Relief Commission
for Russia," without political or economic advantage to the United States.

It seemed to the President that Hoover's plan made sense: it would convince liberals that
Russia's problems were not being overlooked, and at the same time it would forestall the
schemes of both militarists and economic exploiters. Consequently, a project was worked out
for sending food that the Russians would pay for. Though the plan was safeguarded against
perversion to political ends, it was regarded by French interests as tainted with American com-
mercialism. But Colonel House adroitly won Clemenceau's assent.

When the proposal for relief reached Moscow in May, the Bolsheviki expressed willingness
to talk about it and to pay for food; but they would not accept transportation controls that
might hamper their military movements. Their reply was a propagandist blast against the ways
of capitalism and the masking of political aggression by protestations of humanitarianism. The
vituperation of the Bolsheviki and the countercharges of their French foes could not be reconciled
by persistent efforts on the part of House and Hoover.

[9] Having agreed, on March 17, on military terms that set a time limit on the forcible control
of Germany and vested eventual jurisdiction over this matter in the League, the council soon
forgot its idea of concluding a quick preliminary peace. At one time Wilson gave Lansing reason
to think that he wanted to include the Covenant in a preliminary agreement, with an understanding that everything included in the tentative pact would go into the final treaty. The secretary of state advised plainly that any document that changed the situation from war to peace
had to be ratified by the Senate; and Wilson, who confessed that he felt compelled to free himself
from "the servitude which many of the senators seek to impose," expressed surprise that he
could not do it by this method.

[10] Paul Mantoux, "Le Président Wilson au Conseil des Quatre," Centénaire Woodrow
Wilson: 1856-1956 (Geneva, 1956); A. H. Frazier, ms., "Recollections of President Wilson at
the Peace Conference," p. 9.

The principal conclusions of the treaty with Germany were reached by the inner council of
heads of states. The foreign ministers met in a council of five, and occasionally the two groups
combined to meet, as they had in January, in a council of ten, which had been made ineffective
by leakage and by badgering from curious observers who asked whether this and that rumor
was true. The Supreme War Council of military men and the Supreme Economic Council, which
had been created on Feb. 8, continued to meet.

French militarists and industrialists sought to use their dominant position for economic exploitation of the people of Central Europe. When French peasants put in their claim for cows that the "Boches" had driven off, it was too much for Wilson's patience. Just how, he ventured to ask, could French farmers go into Germany and pick out their own cattle? It was difficult to separate France's pure passion for security from the lust that some of her citizens showed.

Bored by economic detail, as he had been all his life, Wilson felt at first that, since the United States claimed no share in reparations except a few ships, the settlement would have to be left to the political discretion of Clemenceau and Lloyd George. When he did join in the discussion, it was to suggest that the experts be cautioned against fixing a sum that would destroy Germany completely, keep her from accepting their proposals, or sow seeds of a war of revenge.

The political plight of Clemenceau and Lloyd George brought negotiations to a serious pass by the end of March; and the President came out of one of the intimate sessions to ask his advisers to try to meet the views of the premiers, else their ministries might fall. At the same time he reminded Lloyd George and Clemenceau that they must unite in submitting a definite bill to Germany.

A subcommittee of three experts was directed by the council to take up the question of defining "war costs," and Norman Davis, the American member, sought the advice of the President. Lloyd George was agitating for the inclusion of such indirect costs as soldiers' pensions and even separation allowances, under the heading of "war costs." (Was it fair, he asked, to repair damaged roofs in France at the expense of families that had lost a father?) Wilson's pre-Armistice agreement with Germany had made it clear that indirect costs were not to be assessed against the enemy, and the President deemed it unfair now to raise the reckoning against a prostrate debtor. Yet his experts told him that England would not get the share of reparations to which she thought herself entitled unless pensions were included among the damages. And in the suppliant position in which the Senate had placed him vis-à-vis revision of the Covenant, he must play ball with the prime minister.

In this quandary the President clutched at the sanctifying support of General Smuts. Wilson knew that this man wished to be fair to Germany; and so it was enough for him that Smuts had set down pensions as "damage to the civilian population." When the President's experts came to dissuade him and asserted that they could find no lawyer in the American delegation who could see logic in such a policy, Wilson's reply was: "Logic? I don't give a damn for logic! I am going to include pensions." And so the President sanctioned charging Germany with indirect war costs which a month before he had felt "bound in honor" to forgo. Those on whom he depended to tell him "what was right" thought this unwise and unnecessary, but he yielded to British interest and to a humane argument. At the time it seemed that actually no added burden would be thrown on the Germans, who would not be able to pay even the direct costs of the war; but the French, who would get a smaller share of what was paid, were unhappy. On March 29, after a session in which he had suggested that in the peace terms it would be best to repeat their pre-Armistice views on reparations, Wilson confessed that he did not know whether the conference could go on. "M. Clemenceau called me pro-German and left the room," he said.

French demands for a secure frontier also came to a head late in March. On the 17th Clemenceau had given notice that he must ask that the part of Germany west of the Rhine be detached from the Reich and shaped under the League of Nations into an independent state. He would have the new republic policed by French troops. However, France would assent to a limitation upon her military control of the Rhineland—thirty years was suggested—provided that Britain and the United States would bind themselves to give military aid to France in case Germany should commit an act of aggression.

To Wilson it seemed clear that the policing of more than five million Germans by French forces was inconsistent with the Fourteen Points and menaced the future peace of the world. He explained to Clemenceau that he sought to avoid a formula that, by substituting action by an alliance of states for action by the League, might suggest that the League's guarantee was inadequate. Asked whether the suggested guarantee could not be written in the League Covenant, Wilson replied that it would not do to put provisions applying to a particular nation in a covenant of general principles. He was willing that certain nations have a mandate to act without delay in a case of aggression, while waiting for an expected action on the part of the Executive Council of the League. But to the French plan of military occupation of the Rhineland he was unsympathetic. For days neither he nor Clemenceau yielded an inch, as House and Tardieu scurried back and forth with counter proposals. The ice that overlay this question was so thin that the President dared not venture upon it in direct conversation with Clemenceau. In the Polish settlement, when two of the Fourteen Points had been in conflict, the principle of self-determination was sacrificed to economic considerations; but to give in again and put Germans under French rule would compound a precedent that it would be hard to overcome later. On the other hand, he could not afford to break with Clemenceau, for then he might have to deal with a more vengeful

French premier who would not share The Tiger's determination to maintain unity among the Allies and who would be intolerant of the League of Nations.

Driven to the end of his wits by French intransigence on the Rhenish question and by a plan for military action against Russia that was sprung upon him on March 28, Wilson gave way to his impatience when Clemenceau introduced another claim of his nation. France, the premier said, thought herself entitled to annex the Saar Valley up to her old frontier of 1814 and, by way of indemnity, to seize coal mines beyond that border.[11]

Wilson, brushing aside the historical arguments, reminded his colleagues that the question of annexation of the Saar was one that the French had not brought up in the pre-Armistice negotiations. Delivering a little sermon about their responsibility to peoples who believed in a "just" peace, he told Clemenceau that it was "painful" to oppose him, but protested that he could not do otherwise without failing in his duty. The most that he would concede was the working of the mines by the French for a limited period. Annexation or political control did not seem a wise solution. "The only principle that I recognize is that of the consent of the governed," Wilson declared. France would like to own the mines, Clemenceau responded, but not on conditions that would set up perpetual conflict with the Germans for the future.[12]

Believing that the world's salvation depended on their going on with their talking, Wilson drove himself to continue. He had a feeling, confessed to House, that no one liked him. The time that he had long dreaded seemed to have come, the crisis in which he would have to break with those around him to fulfill what he thought to be his duty to humanity. Usually patient and calm in his own home, the prophet was in an irritable rage after luncheon on April 2. The French were delaying proceedings intentionally, he told his family, and they were throwing the blame on him, hoping to break him down. Their attitude, he thought, was "damnable."

Ray Stannard Baker saw the President every day and, though he did not love him, had come to believe and trust in Wilson beyond any other mortal and set him down as "the only great man here." Baker tempted

11 Here, again, two of Wilson's principles were brought into conflict. Self-determination forbade the political control of some 300,000 Germans in the Saar by the French. Yet the mines in France had been flooded by the invaders during the war, Point VIII promised reparation to France, and it seemed possible to give this in the Saar. The French statesmen not only insisted that as a practical matter they could not operate the mines under a German government, but they went so far as to adduce historical reasons to support their claim for outright annexation. Wilson opposed the historical argument of the French, explaining that Point VIII referred to the wrongs done in 1871, not 1815.

12 Mantoux, *Délibérations*, I, 74, 89. For the Saar Settlement, *see* pp. 299–300 below.

him now, as he had done a week before, to tell the truth to the people. American delegates were hoping that the President would notify the premiers that if they did not reach agreement he would go home and let Congress decide what to do.

"If I were to do that," the President replied, "it would immediately break up the Peace Conference—we cannot risk it yet. But we've got to make peace on the principles laid down and accepted, or not make it at all." If a decision could not be reached by the middle of the next week, he said, he might have to make a positive break.

For three weeks Woodrow Wilson had been under a crossfire such as no other man at Paris had sustained. He worked harder than any other major figure at the conference. Everyone wondered—even the redoubtable Lloyd George—how he survived from day to day. After an eight-o'clock breakfast, he did in two hours what in normal times might be thought a day's work at his desk. Then a conference or two before the morning meeting of the inner council; guests at lunch and sometimes at dinner; sessions all afternoon—sometimes two at once in adjoining rooms, with the President going back and forth and carrying in his mind the threads of argument. In the evening a daily talk with Baker, then dinner—for which he no longer took time to dress—and afterwards another conference, or study of maps and reports to prepare for the business of the morrow. Yet this man was being represented to the people of the world as the cause of delay in making peace.

Under the relentless strain the President had grown gaunt. His face was haggard and the muscles twitched alarmingly around his left eye—the one that had been impaired in 1906.

When Wilson questioned the wisdom of their arguments, the French began to insinuate that he was losing his powers. On March 23 Clemenceau had sent agents to House to suggest that too much activity had dulled Wilson's mental processes. "He seems quite *vide*, and then nothing is done," these men complained to the Colonel. "Clemenceau thinks that the President . . . is spending too much time in social matters which are also exacting . . . Clemenceau thought that you might suggest to the President that he cut out his jaunts with Mrs. Wilson." Yes, indeed, he might, House had replied, but most certainly he would not!

On April 2 Wilson had thought the skies as dark as dark could be. But on the 3rd there arose a cloud of jet. The advisers on reparations came early in the day to report that Britain's appetite for indemnities had not been sated. The President felt that Lloyd George had very nearly put something over on him; and he approved a plan drafted by his men to scotch the scheme. Later in the day, however, the Americans came back to their chief in deeper gloom. They reported that the Allies "were acting like the Devil." Discussing reparations in the council on that day, the Europeans reminded House of "a lot of children telling each other what they expected to do when they 'grew up.'"

When the American experts went to Wilson with their discouraging report, late in the afternoon of April 3, they found him in bed, suffering from what seemed to be a bad cold. It had come upon him very suddenly. As the night wore on, his condition took a sinister turn. Violent fits of coughing seized him, and profuse diarrhea. His temperature rose to 103 degrees. Dr. Grayson, suspecting at first that the President's food had been poisoned, brought the spasms of coughing under control; but his chest was congested and obstruction in his breathing prevented the deep sleep that he needed for restoration. For three days, too weak to leave his bed, he lay resting fitfully.[13]

While Dr. Grayson tiptoed in and out and Edith Wilson stood by, the sick man was at a loss to know how to solve the dilemmas that faced him. He felt powerless to use his favorite weapon—appeal to the people—for disclosure of discord would benefit only Germany and the subversive forces of Eastern Europe. Moreover, he could not afford to antagonize his European associates until he had finished the labor that Americans had saddled on him—the revision of the Covenant.

In his weakness his roused conscience pricked and goaded him to action. Not for a moment, after the first dreadful, feverish night, did he give up his trust. Grayson could see that anxiety about the handling of affairs for which he was responsible did more harm than actual participation. Therefore, the physician accepted his decision that the council should meet in the next room, with House sitting in his place and bringing to his bedside a report of each move. The day before he was

[13] Dr. Grayson wrote to Tumulty on April 10: "That night was one of the worst through which I have ever passed." Present-day experts on arteriosclerosis, with greater knowledge of this insidious affliction, have questioned Grayson's diagnosis of the illness at Paris as influenza and have concluded that it was caused by a slight vascular occlusion incident to the progress of arteriosclerosis and brought on, as the attack in 1906 had been, by prolonged high pressure on brain and nerves. *See* Dr. Walter C. Alvarez, "Cerebral Arteriosclerosis," in *Geriatrics*, I (May–June, 1946), 189–216.

In *Personal Recollections of Woodrow Wilson*, p. 52, A. W. Patterson reports that two distinguished doctors gave the opinion that Wilson was suffering from arteriosclerosis when he went to Paris and that while he was there the effects became quite manifest. Among those at Paris who have suggested that Wilson suffered a "stroke" are Herbert Hoover and John W. Davis.

"I never knew the President to be in such a difficult frame of mind as he is now," Gilbert Close, his secretary, wrote to his wife on April 7. "Even while lying in bed he manifested peculiarities . . ." The record of Head Usher Ike Hoover reports: "When he got back on the job, his peculiar ideas were even more pronounced. He now became obsessed with the idea that every French employee about the place was a spy for the French government. Nothing we could say could disabuse his mind of this thought. About this time he also acquired the peculiar notion he was personally responsible for all the property in the furnished place he was occupying. . . . Coming from the President, whom we all knew so well, these were very funny things, and we could but surmise that something queer was happening in his mind. One thing was certain: he was never the same after this little spell of sickness." I. H. Hoover, *Forty-Two Years in the White House*, p. 98.

stricken the President had talked for almost an hour over the telephone with the Colonel, who was confined by a cold, and had asked the Texan to do something to break the impasse with the French over the Saar and the Rhineland.[14]

Once more, now, House could serve. He could apply his talent for negotiation in the way that had proved effective before the Armistice and that he had hoped to extend to the peacemaking. He could explore solutions, discuss them tentatively, and refer the results to his chief for a final ruling. He was now in a position to make good his boast to newsmen that "peace could be made in an hour." Taking the President's seat in the council, the Colonel said little. In one long session he spoke only thrice—once to remark that he did not share Wilson's distaste for permanent commissions to inspect military conditions in Germany. From his sickbed Wilson tentatively approved a formula that House persuaded Clemenceau to put in writing as a basis for settlement of reparations.

On the afternoon of Sunday, April 6, the President was well enough to receive his commissioners and to discuss American strategy. Neither he nor House had seen the others for days. He said to them: "Gentlemen, this is not a meeting of the Peace Commission. It is more a council of war." The Colonel left the session with the impression that, if nothing happened within the next few days, Wilson would say in the council that he would have to go home or open the conferences to the public.[15]

Already he had given notice that his patience was near the breaking point. While Edith Wilson sat beside his bed, trembling for fear of a relapse, he asked her to call Grayson, and when the doctor came in, he ordered that word be sent to Washington that the *George Washington* should be put in shape for his return trip as soon as he was well enough to go.

Tumulty cabled from Washington that this was looked upon as an act of impatience and petulance, and not accepted in good grace by either friends or foes. Wilson should place responsibility for a break where it belonged, his secretary thought. A withdrawal would be interpreted in the United States as a desertion. That was the attitude taken

---

[14] However, when the Colonel reported to Mrs. Wilson two meetings in which the Saar and the Rhineland had been discussed with Tardieu, Wilson was alarmed, as he had been during his absence in February. He asked his wife to telephone to House to tell him not to commit himself on these questions.

The Colonel had sensed the suffering of his friend, his loneliness and frustration as he was denied both support from American colleagues and acclaim from the people whom he strove to serve. House was still sure that in the long verdict of history his hero would win out. He put aside a quotation from Gladstone to give to the President for comfort: "Men ought not to suffer from disenchantment; they ought to know that ideals in politics are never realized."

[15] Sweetser's summary of House's news conference of April 6, 1919.

by the French press, which jeered at the President as a spoiled child,
running home to mother; and Clemenceau, in private, likened him to
"a cook who keeps her trunk ready in the hallway" and threatens to
leave. But both officials and public got the point: the wrath of the
prophet was rising.

When Wilson struggled back into harness and met the premiers, he
found that negotiations were in the doldrums. House had tried to make
the most of his own last days in a seat of influence, advising his British
and French colleagues that they could get better terms from him immediately than from the President later. However, neither the Colonel's
hint nor the summoning of the *George Washington* brought progress.
French experts haggled over words and commas in the compromise on
reparations, and Clemenceau showed his age. To display his displeasure,
the Colonel had walked out of a meeting and reported to the President,
who commended his action.

The prophet's soul was torn apart, as his mind made him face realities. When Ray Stannard Baker resumed his evening calls to see how
he might give currency to the master's words, Wilson's eyes, protruding
from hollowed sockets, peered out at him. His hair had whitened and
his face was pale; and all the energy left in his haggard body seemed to
be burning in those large luminous orbs. Tell the newsmen, he directed,
to read again the Armistice agreements. He was unwilling to face up
to the fact that his Fourteen Points, conceived originally as propaganda, were a confusing and inadequate basis for a realistic settlement.
"The time has come to bring this thing to a head," he said. Negotiations
with Clemenceau had become to him "one mass of tergiversations."
Baker left the prophet's side utterly convinced that he had not been
bluffing when he had asked that the coming of the *George Washington*
be hastened. The statesmen at Paris felt the force of religious prophecy.
Their people recognized it; and here and there crystals of common
sense formed in the fog of military and financial hysteria. "Certainly
things are speeding up," the Colonel jotted in his diary.

Asserting that it was a great mistake to sacrifice a sound, constructive
economic plan to political expediency, Wilson nevertheless agreed that
experts on reparations should perfect a scheme that would suit the
statesmen of the Allies. He insisted, however, that the Reparations
Commission that was proposed should exact no more than Germany
could pay within one generation and should fix the sum as soon as
possible after ratification of the treaty.

As for the Saar, Wilson set his jaw hard against its political separation from Germany. He would concede the mines to France, but not
political control. He adopted a suggestion of the experts that for fifteen

years sovereignty rest in a commission under the League of Nations and thereafter be determined by a plebiscite. He feared that they might be imposing too many duties on the infant League, that they might not find enough worthy men to perform them. When Lloyd George tried to reassure him by referring to the civil servants of the British Empire as an example of what could be done, he replied: "Your functionaries have one of the strongest motives that act on men; they serve their country. That motive doesn't exist yet for the League of Nations." [16]

On April 14, he accepted, with a wry face, a plan that the Colonel brought from Clemenceau for making France secure along the Rhine; and a week later the text of an Anglo-American guaranty of French security was settled.[17]

While compromising with the French statesmen in order that he might secure their support for amendments to the Covenant that Americans were demanding, Wilson had to deal also with Lloyd George's determination to exact a *quid pro quo*. On April 7, just as he was struggling back to his feet, he had a letter from Secretary Daniels reporting Lloyd George to be very earnest in saying that he would not give "a snap of his fingers" for the League of Nations if the United States kept on building warships.

With further revision of the League Covenant in prospect, the issue of naval power was too incendiary to be left smoldering or to be entrusted to the contentious wills of navy men. Wilson therefore turned once again to the resourceful Colonel. Cautioning Daniels against making remarks in public on naval policy that might inflame British opinion, House tried to pin down Lloyd George. He got from Lord Robert Cecil a written statement of the British position, and with Wilson's approval sent a reply invoking the spirit of the League of Nations as a preventive against naval rivalry, pledging America's devotion to that spirit, and asserting that the President had no idea of building a fleet in competition with Britain.

However, on April 10 Wilson had to go to an evening meeting of the League Commission not knowing whether efforts to amend the Covenant would have British support. Already, at a session of the commission on March 24, he had signified his intention of proposing an amendment that would recognize the Monroe Doctrine. He had himself studied suggestions by Taft and Senator Hitchcock for the amendments

---

[16] Mantoux, *Délibérations*, I, 228.

[17] The treaty of guaranty was approved by Wilson and Clemenceau on April 20 and presented to the council on the 22nd. It included this clause: "The present treaty will continue in force until, on the application of one of the parties to it, the Council of the League of Nations—acting, if need be, by a majority—agrees that the League itself affords sufficient protection." It was in consideration of the treaty of guaranty, with this provision included, that Clemenceau accepted the House-Tardieu formula for the Rhineland.

that he had persuaded the commission to accept in March; but now he turned over belated proposals from Elihu Root to his legal counselors.

The text that was cabled to Paris did not elucidate the reasons for the revisions that the elder statesman proposed; and David Hunter Miller, to whom it was submitted for legal analysis, found most of the suggestions impractical. When he showed Root's proposals to Lord Robert Cecil, the British statesman said that he would prefer no covenant at all to one that followed these suggestions.

Root feared that in the long run the positive guaranty in Article X would make of the League "an independent alliance for the preservation of the *status quo*." In that event it would be futile, mischievous, and contrary to the laws of change and growth; and to prevent this he advocated that after a limited time—say five years—members might withdraw from the provisions of Article X.

Woodrow Wilson shared Root's dread of concerted enforcement of a *status quo* against legitimate change, and in his early drafts of the Covenant had taken pains to guard against it. One day at Paris a newsman told him, at luncheon, that his opponents were saying that Article X might compel the United States to support an old regime against a popular uprising; and Wilson jumped up, poked his informant in the chest with his forefinger, and exclaimed: "My boy, if I thought that, by direction or remote implication, any clause or phrase forbade to any peoples the sacred right of revolution, I would tear up the Covenant with my own hands." He was advised by Miller that the political aspirations of the world's people would not be strait-jacketed by Article X so long as the Covenant provided for its own revision and so long as member nations, under the amendment that had been adopted in March, could withdraw on two years' notice.

With some of Root's suggestions already cared for, and with his legal adviser questioning the practicality of others, Wilson was not inclined to act on the advice of this Republican statesman who was remote from the negotiations at Paris.

On March 28 William Howard Taft, who ten days before had advised that the "Monroe Doctrine reservation alone would probably carry the treaty through the Senate," suggested that without such a reservation the treaty would *not* be accepted in the United States. Heeding this dire warning, Wilson sat down to ponder over the text of a reservation that Taft suggested. Penciling a few changes on the cablegram that had brought Taft's advice, Wilson typed out a clause to be added to Article X, providing that "nothing in this covenant shall be deemed to affect or deny" the application of the Monroe Doctrine in both its positive and its negative aspects, which were explicitly stated.

This proposal, defining the doctrine but not naming it, was submitted through Colonel House to the British, who brought back a shorter statement that named the Monroe Doctrine without defining it. Revising the brief British draft slightly, Wilson and his advisers arrived at this formula:

Nothing in this Covenant shall be deemed to affect the validity of international engagements, such as treaties of arbitration or regional understandings like the Monroe Doctrine, for securing the maintenance of peace.

The President could put this generalized statement before the League Commission without appearing to ask special consideration for his own nation; and at the same time he hoped to reassure sincere friends of the League in the United States.

On the evening of April 10 he went into a session of the commission to plead his cause in a convincing speech that lasted only ten minutes. He was greatly cheered when Lord Robert Cecil, whose nation's position had been in doubt because of the controversy over naval building, supported him by explaining that the Monroe Doctrine was intended merely "to quiet doubts and to calm misunderstandings." Standing up against the British reactionaries in the trying days of April, this great liberal had threatened to resign if he were not given more authority; and now he answered the questions of the French with quiet sincerity. At eleven o'clock he was ready to call it an evening; but House and Wilson, willing to give their last breath in support of this all-important amendment, insisted that the session continue as long as anyone wished to talk.

It was near midnight when there was a pause and the President rose and gave the occasion its setting in the spiritual history of the race. A century before, he said, when the world was in the grip of tyranny, England had suggested to the United States that they take a step to keep this evil from the American continent. And so principles had been laid down that from that day to this had proved an effective barrier against absolutism. The Monroe Doctrine was the forerunner of the League of Nations. Absolutism had been ended by a world war that the United States had entered in accordance with principles that she always had honored. Now a document was being written that extended the Monroe Doctrine logically to the whole world. Was the United States to be refused recognition of her leadership in this glorious cause? Was there to be denied her, Wilson asked, the small gift of a few words which, after all, only state the undoubted fact that her policy for the past hundred years had been devoted to principles of liberty and independence? Indeed, were they not assembled at Paris to consecrate and extend the horizon of this document as a perpetual charter for all the world?

Americans who heard it thought this the most moving speech of the Peace Conference. It left the secretaries breathless, gasping with surprise and admiration, their pencils quiet in their hands and hardly a word set down. Afterward the President confessed to his colleagues that his effort should not be regarded as *ex tempore*. "To me at least," he said with a chuckle, "it had a very familiar ring. I was, or professed to be, a teacher of American history for twenty years, and rarely a month passed that I did not preach what the Monroe Doctrine meant to me, and now we are offering it to the world."

On the morning after the eloquent appeal to the commission, Wilson had his usual meeting with the council. It was a lovely spring day, and in the afternoon, above the city's park-lined avenues, a daredevil aviator was looping backward and forward under a clear blue sky. But the President had no time to get out of doors. Instead he breathed the fragrant air through an open window while Dr. Grayson stood foot to foot with him and, clasping his hands, pulled him to and fro. "Indoor golf," said Wilson whimsically when Baker interrupted the exercise.

In the evening, at the end of a full day, the President plunged into another stormy session with the League of Nations Commission. The winds of controversy whirled for hours around two Japanese proposals that were finally put aside. Then the delegates got down to the point on which Woodrow Wilson's political solvency seemed to hang in precarious balance. They had left the long meeting of the night before with the understanding that the reservation on the Monroe Doctrine should be attached not to the critical Article X but rather to Article XX, which dealt with obligations inconsistent with the terms of the Covenant. But now the French wanted to pile a nullifying reservation upon the reservation already agreed on.

Wilson protested immediately. If the French were to oppose the American amendment publicly, he warned, the effect on opinion in his country would be most unfortunate. He rejected the French redraft, and also a watered-down version that was so devoid of meaning that it seemed to confirm gossip that House had picked up during the day. The Colonel's network of intelligence had brought news that Bourgeois had confessed to an American friend that actually the French had cared nothing about the amendment on the Monroe Doctrine: they regarded it simply as a good thing to trade against. Therefore, when the President seemed momentarily disposed to yield, House suggested that the French could "go to Hell seven thousand feet deep." Finally Wilson declared their amendment defeated, and they gave notice that they would be heard from again at the plenary session.

When at last the meeting broke up, Wilson relieved the tension by saying that his mind refused to function after midnight and that whatever took the place of his mind was wholly unreliable. But this man who had just been ill held his own with the strenuous statesmen; and the strain put upon him was more than compensated by the feeling that at last they had found a formula that would make it possible for him to convert his own people and for Clemenceau to put the Covenant through the French Chamber. The reaction from the United States was quick and reassuring. "Monroe clause eminently satisfactory," Taft cabled; and Senator Hitchcock: "Congratulation on great success . . . You have done more than seemed possible. Sentiment for League has been much strengthened, opposition evidently diminished if not defeated."

The Monroe Doctrine reservation, House confided to his American colleagues, was "in the bag." Moreover, the President himself had quietly slipped into Article V a clause of far-reaching significance. Under this provision, the rule of unanimity that Wilson had found convenient in presiding over discussions in the commission was to be applied to all meetings of the League's Council and Assembly "except where otherwise expressly provided" in the Covenant. Thus each nation represented in the council was to have power to block action by a veto.

The public meeting on the 28th proved to be anticlimactic. Wilson rose to give explanations of changes that had been made in the Covenant, many of them against his best judgment and to reassure legalists. There seemed to be no fire, no grace, no lift left in him—simply grim, plodding devotion to The Word as it had been written. When he closed with "I now move the adoption of the Covenant," the applause merely rippled up to him.

Clemenceau then gave the floor to Bourgeois, and closed his eyes and masked his parchmentlike face. Wilson slumped in his chair, Balfour gazed at the ceiling; and the French delegate haltingly read a speech that they had heard a dozen times. After about ten minutes Bourgeois stopped for breath and probed into a pile of notes. Suddenly The Tiger pounced. Rapping sharply with his gavel, he announced loudly: "As I hear no objections, I declare that the conference has considered and adopted the revised Covenant."

House pooh-poohed the possibility that the League would be disowned in the United States; for in revising the Covenant they had taken care of most of the suggestions of Taft, Hughes, and Root. Moreover, a bulletin from the League to Enforce Peace reported sixty-four senators ready to ratify the Covenant, twenty doubtful, and only twelve opposed.

One of the twelve avowed enemies, however, was Henry Cabot Lodge, the man who had expressly warned Wilson not to do the thing that was now irrevocably done—tie the treaty into the Covenant with an umbilical cord. Fearing that his Republican colleagues might express pleasure at the revision of the Covenant, Lodge immediately sealed their lips with a telegram asking that opinion be reserved. He professed a desire to examine the Covenant carefully and said, ominously: "It is obvious that it will require further amendments if it is to promote peace and not endanger certain rights of the United States which should never be placed in jeopardy."

It was as the prophet had foreseen. Concessions to the Philistines at Washington, won from Europe with deep agony of soul and body, had begotten only demands for further change. Would the Congress, as Wilson had predicted in his speech to a joint session late in 1917, "feel the full strength of the tides that run now in the hearts and consciences of free men everywhere?" Would its conclusions "run with those tides"?

General Smuts put these questions in Olympian focus as he strode away from the plenary session at which the Covenant was adopted. Not the greatest man born of woman could have saved the Allies from their folly, in his opinion. Only the manliness and dogged will of a Woodrow Wilson could have carried through the Covenant of the League of Nations. The statesmen of Europe had thrown to the persistent prophet, as an innocent little sop, one of the greatest creative documents of the human race.

Colonel House, walking beside Smuts as they left the plenary session, looked into the noble face and sought out the steely eyes under the straight brows. The South African shrugged his shoulders, and then spoke: "The peace treaty may fade into oblivion—and that would be, I sometimes think, a merciful dispensation of a kind Providence—but the Covenant will stand—as sure as fate. It must and shall succeed because there is no other way to salvage the future of civilization."

CHAPTER XVI

The Peace Is Signed

THE ARK OF THE COVENANT was now built and dedicated. Woodrow Wilson had put into it American planks that were offered by Republicans and had set aside foreign timbers that seemed unsound. But the Ark was still high and dry. Before the League could be launched on the waters of strife that were inundating the earth, the treaty to which it was anchored must be firmly established.

Even while he had been fighting for revision of the Covenant in sessions of the League Commission, Wilson had been meeting almost daily with the inner council to consider many questions for which his Fourteen Points provided no adequate solution. In these sessions he had stayed both the grasping hands of aggrandizement and the raised fists of retribution, and he had softened the impact of the treaty on Germany's economy.[1]

On the advice of his counselors, he was "fighting shy" of economic involvement in Europe and was striving to keep his nation's purposes pure; but he took the risk of consenting to American representation on the commission that was to supervise German reparations, explaining that that body would "undoubtedly need an umpire."

On April 2, the day before he fell sick, he had spoken out against punishment of the Kaiser or any individual for starting the war. Heretofore, he explained, the responsibility for international crimes had been solely collective. It would be unfair, and contrary to judicial tradition, to place the responsibility now on an individual. One could not act on a principle before it was acknowledged as law. "I wish to doom Germany to the execration of history," he explained, "and to do nothing that would permit it to be said that we have gone beyond our right, in a just cause." Lansing had reminded him of strong sentiment among his own people for punishment of German leaders, and he had replied that he did not care what the people thought. His own sense of justice seemed adequate authority.

---

[1] It was decided that before May 1, 1921, Germany should pay—in cash, commodities, and bonds—fifteen billion dollars, of which bonds could make up at least two-thirds. The total amount that she might be required to pay was estimated at between thirty-two and forty-four billions. The Reparations Commission of the Peace Conference was to continue to supervise the settlement and could recommend abatements or require the issue of more bonds up to Germany's capacity.

When Lloyd George and Clemenceau insisted that history would condemn them if they did not punish crimes without precedent—such as those of Germany's submarines—Wilson rebelled against this obvious appeal to his personal experience. "As for myself," he observed, "every time I read documents about atrocities, I saw red and took care not to reach a decision in those moments, but always to be in a position to judge and act according to reason. . . . You think me unfeeling, but I struggle constantly against emotion, and I am obliged to bring pressure on myself to keep my judgment steady."

Clemenceau would not accept this. "Nothing is done except with emotion," he insisted. "Was not Jesus Christ moved by passion the day that he chased the merchants from the Temple?" And Lloyd George tried another line of argument to which he thought the American peculiarly vulnerable: "If we want the League of Nations to have, in the future, the power that we desire for it, it ought to show from the beginning that it is able to punish crime."

But the fibers of the prophet's morality would not ravel. "I think as you do about the crimes committed," he said, "but I wish that we ourselves might act in such a way as to satisfy our consciences." [2] Finally he drew up a formula that his own conscience could approve and his colleagues signed it.

His morality intruded also—quietly but forcefully—into arguments among his colleagues about territorial claims in Asia Minor that were based on three secret pacts that had been made in 1916 and 1917.[3] House thought that he talked too much on matters in which the United States had no immediate interest; but the prophet had declared himself responsible for everything that had to do with the peace of the world, and so he delivered another little sermon.

Asking whether the secret treaties provided a plan that would work, he suggested that the people concerned be consulted. He made it clear that, for his part, he was quite disinterested, since the United States did not want anything in Turkey. To be sure, it had been put to him by T. E. Lawrence and Emir Feisal that he should approach his own people on the question of taking a mandate for an independent Syrian state. He intended to try to persuade them, and felt that his nation must take

[2] Mantoux, *Délibérations*, I, 122–24. Also Swem notes taken on the *George Washington*, December, 1918.

[3] These were probably in Wilson's mind on Dec. 1, 1917, when he referred in a cable to House to "plans for division of territory such as have been contemplated in Asia Minor." The text of one of the three treaties (the Sykes-Picot Agreement) had been sent to Wilson by Balfour on May 18, 1917. Frank L. Polk's diary records under Oct. 11, 1918, that Barclay, British chargé at Washington, said that there had been three secret treaties made during the war regarding the disposal of Turkey and that it was a question how binding they would be. "Mr. Barclay explained the whole situation to the President," Polk wrote.

the responsibilities, as well as the benefits, of the League of Nations. Nevertheless, there was great antipathy in the United States to the assumption of the duties of trusteeship. Even the Philippines were regarded as something hot in the hand that should be dropped.

Having raised these questions, Wilson proposed an American method of solution. He suggested that the fittest men that could be obtained should form an inter-Allied commission to go to Syria, extending their inquiries, if led to do so, beyond the confines of that region. The body should be made up of an equal number of French, British, Italian, and American representatives. In his desire for objectivity, he proposed to send not experts on the region under consideration, but men without contact with Syria, educational or military. He would send them with carte blanche to tell the facts as they found them. This would convince the world that the conference had tried to do all it could to find the most scientific basis for a settlement. To make peace quickly, it was necessary now only to tell Turkey that she was to have nothing. The question of mandates could be settled later, under the League.

His plan accepted, the President told Ray Stannard Baker that he wished to appoint "the two ablest Americans now in Europe" to the proposed commission. Charles R. Crane and President Henry Churchill King of Oberlin College were chosen.

By April 14 both the revision of the Covenant and the discussion of the specific settlements had progressed far enough so that The Four felt that they should issue a public statement inviting Germany to send delegates to Versailles to receive the treaty of peace. Wilson was asked to compose this paper.[4] It announced that there would be no interruption in the discussion of pending matters, and priority would be given to consideration of questions affecting Italy. This promise was necessary to gain Orlando's consent to the summoning of the Germans; for the premier feared that the conference might rush to a close without satisfying Italian claims.

In fixing the boundaries of Italy the council was faced by two commitments that were based on irreconcilable principles. The Fourteen Points had promised Serbia—now merged with neighbors in Yugoslavia—"free and secure access" to the Adriatic Sea and had decreed that Italy's boundaries be readjusted "along clearly recognizable lines of nationality." On the other hand, the secret Treaty of London, signed in

---

[4] In protest against the refusal of the council to award the left bank of the Rhine to France, Marshal Foch at first refused to deliver this message to the Germans. When Wilson heard of this defiance of civil authority, he remarked: "If I were Clemenceau, he'd never have a chance to refuse again. I would know what to do with him."

1915 by Britain and France to bring Italy into the war, recognized the right of the Italians to a frontier that would include many alien people. This pact did not grant them the port of Fiume, however. Reminding Orlando of that fact in a session of The Four on April 3, Wilson suggested that it be made a free city, without customs link with any neighboring state.

Meanwhile the people of Italy, conceiving that they had fought to "liberate" their compatriots in Fiume, agitated for annexation of the city. But Wilson saw nothing but megalomania in the rising popular clamor. Already he had conceded to Orlando what the Treaty of London had given in the Trentino.[5] Now the Italians seemed to want the moon, and the planets likewise.

Confronted by divergent advice from his counselors,[6] Wilson gave hours of his time to the problem. He determined to grant to Italy all that his concept of justice would allow. But at the same time he instructed Norman Davis to hold up an advance of fifty million dollars to Italy for a few days, "until the air clears—if it does." Italy was particularly vulnerable to closure of the "financial tap," House said to newsmen who might be counted on to pass the word around.[7]

Commencing on April 19—the day on which Sir Maurice Hankey began to sit regularly with the inner council and to keep formal records that minimized emotional tensions [8]—The Three argued for hours with

[5] The Treaty of London is one of the secret treaties mentioned on p. 131 above. In the winter of 1918, Sir William Wiseman told Balfour that Wilson would like to know his thought on the treaty. On his first day at Paris, Wilson had asked for a copy of this troublesome document. When House had remarked that there might be substance to the Italian claim, Wilson replied: "Then let them plant their case in the full sun of publicity. If there is anything in it, then it will grow into a great cause. If there is nothing in it, then it will wither away."

Though Wilson had been told that the Trentino region that was promised to Italy by the Treaty of London included some 240,000 people who spoke German, he had agreed on Jan. 30, in order to get Orlando's approval of the Covenant, to the transfer of the district to Italian sovereignty. (See p. 255 above.)

In May, 1919, Wilson explained to Charles Seymour that the giving away of the Tyrol was "based on insufficient study." On May 28, Wilson told Ray Stannard Baker that he regretted the decision on the Tyrol, that he had been ignorant of the situation when he made it. Asked whether he could not change it, he said: "I am afraid not: but those Tyrolese Germans are sturdy people—and I have no doubt that they will soon be able themselves to change it." R. S. Baker's Journal, May 28, 1919.

[6] Wilson's conclusions, both then and later, followed closely the recommendation of his specialists on the Adriatic region. Sometimes he felt that he was not closely enough in touch with the specialists; but some of them felt that he did not consult them sufficiently. Mezes, Miller, and other American delegates gave more weight to Italy's need for security and considerations of general policy and sought by talking with Italian delegates to reach ground for compromise.

[7] Wilson wrote to Norman Davis on April 15 regarding credits other than those to Italy: "I think that it is perfectly legitimate that we should ask ourselves before each of these credits is extended, whether our colleagues are cooperating with us in a way that is satisfactory."

[8] House implored the President not to continue to meet with the clever premiers with no one of his own staff at hand to make a record; but Wilson was content when Sir Maurice Hankey, able secretary of the British delegation, began in mid-April to keep a procès-verbal.

the Italian statesmen. Orlando pleaded long and passionately, invoking
the principle of self-determination. Wilson could not resist the tempta-
tion to ask whether New York City was claimed because of its Italian
population.

Lloyd George made an eloquent effort to mollify Orlando, recalling
that Italy had carried out her part of the Treaty of London "in blood,
treasure and sacrifice" and reaffirming Britain's intention to fulfill her
bond. At this, Orlando began to gulp. Getting up from his chair, he
walked to a window and stood there and shook with great sobs. Woodrow Wilson rose and went to him, took his hand, assured him that he
had played his role well but that they were all responsible to consider
every claim and to be just to everyone. Then the President led the
premier back to his chair, feeling as if he were comforting a small boy
and ought to take out his handkerchief and dry the tears. The Three
assured Orlando of their affection for him; and he thought them all
generous, even Wilson, who promised him everything except what was
absolutely necessary to protect his position as premier. If they were fond
of him now, he said, they perhaps would be fonder still in a week, when
they might be confronted by the swashbuckling d'Annunzio.

Nevertheless, the President would not give Fiume to Italy; nor would
he shift his boundary eastward in Istria. He was ready to crack the
whip of public opinion over the heads of the Italian statesmen. On the
morning of Easter Sunday, April 20, he typed a manifesto that he
wanted Orlando to read to his parliament, and in the afternoon he sent
a copy to Balfour. His colleagues counseled delay, and the President
agreed not to publish immediately.

On the 23rd Lloyd George and Clemenceau, fearful that Wilson
might provoke an irreparable breach with Italy, introduced a draft of
a letter to Orlando that denied him Fiume, in accord with the Treaty
of London. Thus a way was open to the President to get from under and
shift the burden of opposing Italy to his allies. This would be smart
diplomacy, but it would give sanction to Italian possession of islands
and Dalmatian mainland that American experts assigned to Yugoslavia.

Wilson thought that the time had come to make a dramatic stand.
He feared that if the Yugoslavs felt that injustice was done them, a
path would be opened to Russian influence and the forming of a Slavic
bloc hostile to Western Europe. He reminded the council that the Slavic
people had behind them the immense reservoir of Asia's population—
eight hundred million people whose attitude and destiny would be the
great problem of the future.

To General Bliss, one of his Americans who had been pressing him to
act, the President explained that, though his colleagues in the council

thought it unwise for him to publish his manifesto, he was standing
out for his "constitutional rights." In a tense session of The Three on
April 22 he said: "Let me publish my paper. It could only clear the air."
And Lloyd George replied: "Yes, like a tempest." [9]

Wilson insisted on releasing the document. Appearing in the press in
the evening of April 23, it reminded the Italians that it had been agreed
that the peacemaking was to rest on well-defined principles of right and
justice. Wilson explained that under those ideals as well as under the
Treaty of London, Fiume must go to Yugoslavia; but he assured Italy
that adequate guarantees would be given, under international sanction,
"of equal and equitable treatment of all racial or national minorities,"
and that the eastern coast of Italy would be made secure by the reduction of armaments and fortifications. America, he reminded, was linked
in blood as well as in affection with the Italian people. "She trusts Italy,
and in her trust believes that Italy will ask nothing of her that cannot
be made unmistakably consistent with . . . sacred obligations."

The manifesto reverberated through the world and shook the apathy
of public opinion toward a conference that seemed to have burrowed
underground and disappeared from view. The conflict of the new
diplomacy against the old had never been highlighted more dramati-
cally. [10]

Orlando immediately struck back in justification of his position. He
characterized the President's message as an ill-timed precipitation of a
public crisis while diplomatic talks were still going on. Offended by

[9] Mantoux, *Délibérations*, I, 338. On May 2, Wilson recalled to Lloyd George and Clemenceau that it had been "agreed at first" that their letter would be published the day after his.
Ibid., I, 453. On this point Lord Hankey comments, after a review of the minutes and his
personal contemporary notes: "If there was any understanding, which I do not think there was,
it must have been reached informally outside of the formal conversations." Lord Hankey to the
writer, Dec. 24, 1953.

The British excused themselves to Wilson for not publishing the Anglo-French letter by
explaining that after reading the President's paper, Balfour had conferred with Clemenceau and
they had agreed that they could add nothing to Wilson's splendid exposition of the case.

Wilson resented a statement by Poincaré that added to the impression that the United States
was isolated. He was fearful that both House and Lloyd George would make efforts at reconciliation that would make him appear unreasonably hard. But House felt that the prime minister
had given the Italians "hope where there is none." Moreover, he thought that his wife's
brother-in-law, Sidney Mezes—the titular head of The Inquiry—had been too prone to compromise, that every time Mezes had dined with the Italians he was willing to give them another
island.

[10] The powerful labor federation of Paris sent a delegation to Wilson to express their
approval, and wired their views to their Italian brethren. Faithful Americans took courage from
the manifesto. "I have never been so proud of you," Tumulty cabled on April 24. The President's
stand was approved even by the Republicans, Polk reported. But Philistines made what capital
they could of the message. Henry Cabot Lodge wrote to the Italians of Boston to assure them
that, in his view, Fiume was as vital to Italy as New Orleans to the United States. The French
and British press, though publishing Wilson's appeal, found it so foreign to the thought of
the Old World that it was covered with a dust of ridicule and neglect. "Wild-west diplomacy,"
the London *Morning Post* asserted. "President Wilson has come among the allies like a rich
uncle. They have accepted his manners out of respect of his means."

Wilson's implication that his people could submit to a will other than its own, he felt that his self-respect demanded withdrawal from Paris, the calling of his parliament, and the re-establishment of his authority.

Wilson not only did not oppose Orlando's departure; he encouraged it. At the meeting of the council that both attended on the 24th, the President protested that he had never thought of going behind Orlando's back. He had merely wanted the premier to know the American position. He stood ready to discuss any aspect of the question, to go over the ground a hundred times if necessary. He suggested that the premier tell his constituents the truth, say simply that Britain and France were bound by the Treaty of London and the United States by certain principles, and then ask his parliament: "Have I the authority to go back to Paris and settle as I can?"

Before starting for the railroad station, on the 24th, the Italian premier was given a copy of the letter that had been signed by Lloyd George and Clemenceau, confirming Wilson's views on Fiume. Orlando therefore went away informed that The Three stood together; but before departing he persuaded Lloyd George not to have the Anglo-French letter published.

Time and again Wilson pleaded with his colleagues to extricate him from his apparent isolation by publishing their letter. He argued that by bolting from the conference, Italy had broken the Treaty of London and therefore was no longer entitled to the rewards promised by that pact. They debated for days and while they talked news came that Italy had sent a warship to Smyrna, had thirty thousand men in the Balkans, and was terrorizing the inhabitants of islands that wished to join with Greece. On May 3 Wilson was notified by his embassy at Rome that anything might happen, that no Italian government could yield Fiume and hope to stand.

Clemenceau, zealously guarding the unanimity of The Three, seconded Wilson's plea for the publication of the Anglo-French letter. But Lloyd George held back cannily, protecting the frail thread by which he hoped to mend the breach. If they did not stir public feeling any more than it already had been roused by Wilson's manifesto, perhaps the Italian premier would return in a mood for compromise. On the contrary, if they published the letter, against Orlando's wishes, Italy might send another man who would be not only more imperialistic, but pro-German as well.

Lloyd George's clever argument prevailed. Wilson tried to catch him in a contradiction, but the prime minister's wits were too nimble. When Wilson threatened to withdraw, the Welshman let him know that the feeling was growing among Europeans, and especially in London, that they were being bullied by the United States.[11] If this sentiment were not handled with care, Lloyd George warned, it might put an end to the League of Nations. Again and again he came back to a formula for compromise. When his policy was justified by the return of Orlando, the Adriatic question was driven into the background—a menacing cloud that constantly shadowed deliberations on other dark issues.[12]

On the morning of April 21, when the debate with Italy was approaching a crisis and the council could hardly afford to risk alienating Japan, Viscount Chinda went to the President's house and insisted that Japan's secret treaties with Britain and France be fulfilled to the letter, in respect both to Shantung Province and to the Pacific islands. After years of galling inferiority the island empire had emerged from the war as the most powerful nation of the Far East, and her ego was demanding recognition.

Wilson already was almost as unpopular in Japan as he had become in Italy. He had made enemies by supporting the British Empire in a minority veto of a "race equality" amendment to the Covenant that Makino had pressed. Moreover, odium fell upon him because the United States had forbidden the immigration of Japanese and also had denied them an outlet in Siberia for their dense population.

As Wilson's prophetic ardor had been dampened by unresponsiveness and misunderstanding, his wisdom in diplomacy had grown. He had begun to show awareness that the United States, like other nations, could not afford to be completely disinterested, that she would do well to think realistically of security and diplomatic rapport. He did not wish to interfere with treaties, he said. The war had been undertaken partly in order to establish the sanctity of treaties. Nevertheless, there were

[11] Lloyd George was told that some of his men at Paris were "fed up with Wilson" and "tired of playing second fiddle"; and he noted that America, which disclaimed self-interest, was to get from Germany twice as much merchant shipping as she lost. Geddes was complaining to him that the Americans were doing their best to appropriate the trade of the world "while Wilson was doing the big bow-wow." "Well, that is what they always say about Great Britain," the prime minister reminded his men. "I am one of the few people who think Wilson honest. . . . Occasionally he has to deviate for political reasons." Riddell, *Lord Riddell's Intimate Diary,* April 23 and 27, 1919.

[12] *See* p. 372 below. The Adriatic question remained undecided through the remaining weeks of the Peace Conference. Wilson told House that his mind was open to possible solutions as long as they did not give Fiume to the Italians; and the American experts worked diligently for agreement between Italians and Yugoslavs. The Colonel, feeling that the President was bungling the negotiations, very nearly succeeded in arranging a compromise, but his efforts broke down when the Italians demanded eastern Istria and the Yugoslavs and the President refused this. On May 18, Wilson threatened to send word to the Italians that he would make no further concession whatever.

Meanwhile Italy's passions ran unchecked. On June 17, Ambassador Page reported from Rome to the State Department: "A leaning toward German reaffiliation grows more apparent." By the treaty concluded with Yugoslavia at Rapallo on Nov. 12, 1920, Fiume was made an independent city and Italy got more in Istria than she had asked of Wilson.

cases, he felt, where treaties ought not to have been entered into. There was a lot of combustible material in China, he remarked, and if flames were put to it the fire could not be quenched, for China had a population of four hundred million people. As for Japan, he said that he knew from experience that her statesmen were "very ingenious in interpreting treaties."

Makino declared that Japan wanted an "open door" in China, that there had been precedent for Japan's twenty-one demands in an era of imperialism. The Japanese were not bluffing, Wilson knew, and would go home unless given what he thought they should not have. He could not break the legal bonds by which Britain, France, and China were bound. Moreover—hardest reality of all—the Japanese were in possession in Shantung; and who was going to use force to drive them out? But he made an eloquent appeal to Chinda and Makino, in the presence of the Chinese delegates. He warned that the peace of the Far East depended on mutual confidence between the two nations. He invited the Japanese to share the spirit of "his missionaries," and to carry out *all* of their obligations to China.

To the Chinese delegates, who were handicapped by political strife at home and among themselves, Wilson explained patiently that he had urged the Japanese, without avail, to put the leased property in Shantung under an international trusteeship.

The Chinese spokesmen were expert at winning the friendship of the American delegates. They accused the Japanese of behaving badly since they had taken over the German rights and of using dire threats to force China to keep their one-sided agreement secret. At the same time clever Chinese publicists were skillfully stimulating anti-Japanese feeling outside the council; and in this they were aided by Japan's brutality in suppressing a revolt in Korea.

Again Woodrow Wilson's heart tugged against his head. He was bombarded by emotional appeals from his own people. Tumulty tempted him to make political capital of the issue by publishing another manifesto like that to the Italian people. American colleagues whose advice he sought could see only the moral black and white of the question. "We shall be sowing dragon's teeth," General Bliss warned. Lansing felt that the Japanese threat to withdraw from Paris was a bluff and their claim to rights in Shantung quite bogus.

The question seemed the most baffling that the President had met at Paris. He recognized, he explained to Lloyd George on April 22, an apparent contradiction between his attitude toward Japan and that toward Italy. It stemmed from the fact that China still existed, and Austria-Hungary did not. But actually another difference between the

two cases was apparent to him; Italy had consented to the League Cove-
nant, and Japan was withholding hers and trading on it. "As for Japan,"
Wilson said, "one must do what is necessary so that she will enter the
League of Nations." [13]

On April 24 the Japanese presented a peremptory demand. The next
day, when Wilson tried "to take the chains off China" by suggesting
that all powers renounce their extraterritorial rights, Lloyd George
objected. Wilson told his family afterward that sometimes the statesmen
seemed no better than bandits.

On the 28th Ray Stannard Baker, after an evening of talk with
Chinese statesmen and their American friends, went to the President
to plead China's case. Wilson listened with an intensity that was disconcerting. Finally he said: "Baker, the difficulty is not with the facts
of the controversy, but with the politics of it." The easy way would be
to decide against the Japanese and go home. But there might be an
alliance of Russia, Germany,[14] Italy, and Japan, and a new balance of
power; and doubtless Japan would go more deeply into Shantung.
What, then, would become of the great cause of collective security
which, quite obviously now, included the security of the United States?

This question was put to the President by Colonel House, the only
fellow commissioner who had a divided mind. At the urging of Lloyd
George, House advised the President to accept a pledge of good behavior
that the Japanese gave orally to Balfour.[15] But the conscience of Woodrow Wilson would not subside. Was there not some way out, it kept
asking, some course that would be fair to Japan and China and true to
the Covenant? In the council on the 29th he lectured the Japanese.
Bearing down hard, he pressed them to make minor concessions.

In the evening, consulting no one, Wilson drew up a one-page statement about the settlement finally reached. He intended it for public use,
but not as a quotation from him. Permitting the release of the substance
of his decision, he asked Baker to explain his distressed thinking to the
Chinese. To keep Japan within the League of Nations and to prevent a

---

[13] Mantoux, *Délibérations*, I, 336.

[14] During the war Wilson had been aware of rumors of Japanese-German negotiations, but
he had never found any substantial foundation for them. However, his adviser, E. T. Williams,
felt that the Japanese were negotiating with the Germans behind the scenes and feared that
Japan might join Germany in an attempt to control Russia. Fifield, *op. cit.*, p. 221 n.

[15] On the 28th Lloyd George called House aside and asked him to put Wilson into a more
amenable frame of mind toward Japan's claims. Balfour recorded for the council, in writing,
conversations between himself and the Japanese in which they agreed to carry out the policy of
the open door "in the spirit as in the letter" and to give back the leased territory to China,
retaining only the economic rights held by Germany. Wilson explained to McCormick, on July 5,
1919, that this commitment was made to Balfour orally because the Japanese felt that to sign
a statement of this sort would be to admit that their good faith had been questioned. Japan
justified the confidence of the British statesmen by concluding a Sino-Japanese agreement in 1922
that resulted in more friendly relations and the return of Kiaochow to China.

separate alliance of that nation with the enemies of democracy, he was willing to risk denunciation by friends. Baker saw an heroic figure emerging. "He is the only Man here," he jotted in his journal.

"I find a general disposition," Wilson wrote in his statement for the public, "to look with favor upon the proposal that at an early date through the mediation of the League of Nations all extraordinary foreign rights in China and all spheres of influence should be abrogated by the common consent of all nations concerned."

It was the League that offered the best hope for eventual reconciliation with Russia, too. The menace of bolshevism was brought home to Wilson on May Day, when social disorders came almost to his own door. Wearing caps and little red boutonnières with sprigs of white lilies of the valley, workmen thronged the streets and shouted *"A bas Clemenceau," "Vive Wilson."* His message to the Italian people had made him once again their hope for deliverance from the scourge of war.

But liberal journals were criticizing him for yielding to Japanese imperialism as vehemently as they had applauded his opposition to Italian ambitions; and young Chinese agitators were denouncing him as a traitor. "Somehow or other," House mused, "the President is always put in a false light." Though distressed when ladies of his household rode through the streets on May Day, Wilson shrugged off physical danger, and his bodyguards were as hard put to protect his person as was the Colonel to safeguard his prestige.

The May Day riots kept alive the fear that had been roused by the March coup of Communists in Hungary. The possibility of intervention in Russia was still being discussed by The Three, as the pendulum swung between war and peace in Eastern Europe. By April 20 Lloyd George had veered toward use of force; but the President told him point-blank that he had lost patience, that every time Russian conservatives had been given a subsidy they had "backed away from their objective." The President directed that Ambassador Morris go from Tokyo to Omsk and see Kolchak and find out what sort of man he was and what motives controlled him.

Unable to get a report from Morris, Wilson went along with the policy of the Allies; for it was clear that The Three must stand together and avoid giving substance to Lenin's charge that they represented "imperialist powers" that devour each other. Nevertheless, he continued to work to get foreign forces out of northern Russia. "The withdrawal of our troops should be in no way interrupted or delayed," he wrote to Bliss on June 10. All of the American units were evacuated by autumn.

Thus Woodrow Wilson gave up hope of doing more for Russia than saving her from foreign invasion. The people should have economic aid without political interference, he told Hoover, but no foreign body could give help that the Bolsheviki would accept as disinterested. In the long run the world would be less distressed if the Russians solved their own political problems in their own way. "We cannot rescue Russia without having a united Europe," Wilson had said in February to his national committeemen at Washington. ". . . We may have to go home without composing these great territories [of Russia], but if we go home with a League of Nations, there will be some power to solve this most perplexing problem."

All rational paths seemed to lead in the end to the League. Problems of reparations, of boundaries, of colonies, of social revolution—all required a supranational code of justice evolving out of a parliament of mankind. It was not only the large nations that were offending against the common good. Even little Belgium—the very land in which martyred Nurse Cavell had proclaimed that "patriotism is not enough"— sought special favors. The pressures of national greed that assailed him would have seemed to Wilson to be crucifying human hopes for peace had not the Covenant been adopted by the plenary session on April 28 and given first place in the treaty that was to be presented to the Germans.

During the first week of May, many details had to be settled to make the treaty ready for presentation to the Germans. However, the Italian question took care of itself, temporarily. Orlando rejoined the council on the 7th, and the President said quite casually: "You will have the same chair as always." Wilson had yielded nothing, but, as Lloyd George had surmised, Italy could not afford to abstain from signing the treaty and forfeit her claims under the Treaty of London. The Belgians, too, after concessions to their demands, reluctantly agreed to sign. Only the Chinese were still standing aside.

As the clauses of the document were edited, Wilson was vigilant to scotch "jokers" that might creep into the official text. The Allies were suspected of tampering with the draft in order to bind the United States permanently to economic obligations in Europe.

Wilson was bedeviled also, during the first week of May, by responsibility under his pledge of "open" arrival at the covenant of peace. Lloyd George had been asserting stoutly that it would be foolish to let the small nations discuss, much less amend, the terms on which the council agreed. If the little fellows didn't like the treaty, they needn't sign, said the ministers of Britain and France. Prevailing against this view, however, Wilson effected the calling of a plenary session at the Quai d'Orsay on May 6, at which the terms of the treaty were read. It was a secret meeting, but at least the official spokesmen of the world's minorities were given a chance to comment.

Hours were spent, too, in setting up a plan for release of the huge document—the longest treaty ever framed. Clemenceau pointed out that if they did not give the entire text to the world, the Germans would; but Wilson supported Lloyd George's view that, since the document was not final, only a summary should be supplied to the press.

All of these perplexities took their toll. On May 3, when Baker went to the President for his news story, Wilson seemed "so beaten out that he could remember only with an effort what the council had done in the forenoon." A man due for a complete breakdown, he appeared to his associates; yet they knew it was no use to tell him to let go. More and more, he was demanding from those close to him an unquestioning loyalty that would build confidence in himself and his cause. Since his illness he had withdrawn further and further. Once, to be sure, Cary Grayson took him to Bernard Baruch's house at St. Cloud for luncheon. She persuaded him, too, to take an evening off and attend a musical show, and one day their afternoon drive took them past such idyllic fields as Millet had painted. But he preferred to stay at home with those whom he could trust, and pray over the great issues on which the peace of the twentieth century was poised. He had obtained a strongbox for his most vital papers, and held the secrets of state more closely than ever in his own head. Evenings, to rest his mind, he played cards, saying to the ladies: "I am afraid you will always think of me as an old man playing solitaire."

On May 7, the fourth anniversary of the sinking of the *Lusitania*, Wilson motored out to Versailles to meet the enemy whom he had been fighting but had never seen. He dreaded coming face to face with the men of Germany's new order, and had tried to think of some way of avoiding it. Their delegation, more than two hundred strong, included a manufacturer of poisoned gases; and it was headed by the foreign minister, Count Brockdorff-Rantzau—only recently a servant of the Kaiser's government.

The French had set the stage with traditional genius. This was their day of vengeance, just and sweet. Sunshine flooded the room in which the participants took their seats. Clemenceau sat grim-visaged at the center of the main table, Wilson at his right, Lloyd George at his left. At exactly three o'clock a functionary proclaimed: "Messieurs les Pléni-potentiaires Allemandes!" Everyone stood in funereal silence as the Germans entered and stalked to the places set apart.

Clemenceau rifled a few sentences at them, stern, almost harsh. "It is neither the time nor the place for superfluous words," he said. The observations of the German delegates were to be submitted in writing within fifteen days.

The squat old Tiger stood up as he spoke. But Brockdorff-Rantzau— tall, spare, black-clad, his face deathly pale and perspiring—merely leaned forward in his big leather chair, reached for some papers, then, still seated, began to talk. His bad manners accentuated the prejudice that his audience bore against him and his kind. Admitting his country's helplessness, he said defiantly: "It is demanded of us that we shall confess ourselves to be the only ones guilty of the war. Such a confession in my mouth will be a lie." The last sentence sizzled with bitterness.

When he alluded to the Allied blockade of Germany and ascribed to it the death of "hundred of thousands of noncombatants," Lloyd George fidgeted and broke an ivory paper knife in his hands. Clemenceau's face turned red with suppressed anger; he tapped the table, then turned to his British colleague and whispered biting comments. Wilson, toying with a pencil with which he seemed about to make notes, joined in the conversation *sotto voce*. However, when the German referred to his principles as binding upon the parties to the peace and promised to examine the treaty with these ideals in mind, Wilson leaned forward on his desk, gazed intently at the count, and shifted a little in his chair. He felt his blood rushing to his head. He knew that to get a League of Nations he had sacrificed many of his ideals.

Walking out of the historic meeting he said: "What abominable manners! . . . The Germans are really a stupid people. They always do the wrong thing. They always did the wrong thing during the war— that's why I am here. They don't understand human nature. This is the most tactless speech I have ever heard. It will set the whole world against them."

The treaty that was presented to the Germans at Versailles on May 7 seemed to Wilson to fall far short of his ideal concept of justice. "If I were a German," he said, "I think I should never sign it." Yet he hoped fervently that they would sign, if for no other reason than that he could be free then to go home.

He had shrewdly analyzed the plight of the enemy. He knew that their delegates, who represented a very unstable government, would have to consider each of the terms to decide whether it could be accepted without their being unseated. If they should be turned out, a weaker ministry doubtless would replace them. Hence the problem was one of dynamics. One must deal with the action of forces in a body that was in unstable equilibrium.

The treaty would hit the German economy hard, not only by depriving the people of property and of opportunities abroad, but by compelling them to open their own country to the enterprise of foreigners. The fact must be faced that Germany could not pay reparations unless she had a balance of trade in her favor. It would be ineffective to fine her unless she could pay the fine. "We ought to see that Germany could put herself in a position where she could be punished," Wilson said to the council.

The privilege of protest was exercised almost immediately by the Germans. It seemed to their spokesmen as if they were being committed to economic slavery for as long a time as the conquerors might set. "President Wilson is a hypocrite," Chancellor Scheidemann declared, "and the Versailles Treaty is the vilest crime in history." Their very first note of protest insisted that the terms were intolerable, impractical, and unfaithful to the "peace of right" that had been agreed on before the Armistice.

But Wilson was not moved. He felt that a submissive public opinion lurked beneath the official complaints. At the behest of the council, he drafted a retort. Asserting that the treaty had been drawn with constant thought of his principles, he wrote: "The Council can admit no discussion of their right to insist upon the terms of the peace substantially as drafted. They can consider only such practical suggestions as the German plenipotentiaries may have to submit."

More irritating than the expected dissents of the enemy were the criticisms of American delegates. The President was set upon by liberals whose disappointment in the shortcomings of the peace terms he himself shared. Ray Stannard Baker was in a quandary, and tempted to "go to the hills and nurse . . . happy plans for the human race." But Wilson held him true, and Baker concluded that the alternative to accepting the treaty was anarchy. There were others, though, whom the prophet could not persuade. "Apparently he wants no help," one complained. "He never does," echoed another. Bullitt resigned on May 17. Several young liberals in the American delegation wrote letters of protest and offered to go home; and in June two of these resigned. Lansing and General Bliss, who had not forgiven the President for his decision on Shantung, were giving comfort to the dissenters.

Herbert Hoover felt that the economic consequences of the treaty alone would pull down all Europe. When Hoover denounced many of the treaty's articles in words that he later characterized as "over-vigorous," Wilson took personal offense, flashed back angrily, and did not again invite this able adviser into his inner councils. It seemed to Hoover that the President's mind had lost resiliency during his severe illness.

On May 22 word reached the President that Smuts and another British commissioner would not sign the treaty and that Lansing and Bliss were thinking of withholding their signatures.[16] The draft of the document, read as a whole for the first time by many of the delegates, seemed to suffer from lack of coordination between various parts that had been composed separately. There were inconsistencies, and certain terms made it difficult for other terms to be carried out.

The President himself, however, was less perturbed than his advisers by the shortcomings of the settlement. He had faith in the League as a means of rectifying maladjustments. Moreover, his own people had not objected to the treaty's terms and Tumulty had cabled that they would not approve any softness toward the enemy. Wilson seemed very conscious now of his position at home; the new Republican-dominated Congress began its sessions on May 19.

House, deriving comfort from John Morley's saying that the world's turmoil was not due to the realists but to "the tireless and often thoughtless activities of . . . *perfectabilitarians*," went to the President during May with pleas for concessions to Italian sentiment. He was as distressed by his friend's intransigence as was Wilson by the Colonel's importunities. House's friends among the journalists were embarrassing the Colonel again by immoderate praise. Wickham Steed wrote, in an editorial published April 6: "During their [Wilson and Lloyd George's] absence Colonel House, who has never found a difficulty in working with his colleagues because he is a selfless man with no personal axe to grind, brought matters rapidly forward. The delay that has occurred since the return of President Wilson and Lloyd George has been due chiefly to the upsetting of the good work done in their absence."

Mrs. Wilson read this and discussed it with Dr. Grayson, who suggested that it was typical of publicity inspired by the Colonel's staff. When she confronted House with it, he was embarrassed and anxious that Wilson should not see it.[17] Edith Wilson, who was not slow to

---

[16] This rumor reached Wilson through Hoover and McCormick. The President tried to hold Lansing's loyalty by writing to welcome him back from a trip to London: "We have missed you very much," he said. He did not believe that his Americans would refuse to sign and asked McCormick to sound out Lansing. The latter was found to be ready to sign but "a bit sore at not being consulted more." In the end, Smuts signed the treaty and protested publicly against its terms.

[17] On April 23, 1924, House recorded in his diary that, though the President had never expressed resentment, the Steed article "was one of the real grievances of the Wilsons." "I knew nothing of the article until it was published, and had as little to do with it as the man in the moon," the Colonel wrote. By printing stories of differences between Wilson and House, the press poured oil on the fire that Steed had helped to start. Auchincloss recorded in his diary on March 28, 1919, that the editorials in the *Daily Mail* since Jan. 1 often were "part and parcel" of his discussions with Wickham Steed.

apprise her husband of presidential ambitions that she saw or imagined in the hearts of his staff, had done nothing to check the suspicions that had been aroused by the Colonel's personal attachment to Clemenceau, his overplaying of the role of stage manager, his bestowal of favor on relatives lacking in tact, his advocacy of concessions to the Allies that he thought necessary to hasten the making of peace, to prevent anarchy, and to save the League of Nations, and his assumption of responsibility for saving the President from an isolation that threatened to shut out political realities and to separate Wilson from press and people.

Now she told her husband of House's reaction to the objectionable editorial. She had previously said to him: "If Colonel House had only stood firm while you were away, none of this would have to be done over. I think he is a perfect jellyfish." And the President had replied: "Well, God made jellyfish, so, as Shakespeare said about a man, therefore let him pass, and don't be too hard on House. It takes a pretty stiff spinal column to stand against the elements centered here." Now the President's first thought was for the feelings of the Colonel. "I would as soon doubt your loyalty as his," he said to his wife. "All this is another attempt to misrepresent things at home." [18]

After the episode of the Steed editorial, House did not go to the Wilson home except for business meetings at which others were present. Without personal intimacy he could no longer insinuate realistic political advice that the President did not care to hear. As the prophet went into the last days of his fight for the ideals that both held dear, he did not avail himself often of the help of the faithful ruling elder who had established Wilson's Points as the basis of the Armistice, who often had reconciled the views of his chief with those of Allied statesmen, who had removed many a hurdle in the path of the League Covenant, and whom European statesmen looked upon as America's most effective diplomatic negotiator.[19] Yet on May 6, when House thought of going home, Wilson told him that he must wait until the treaty was signed and that he was to represent the United States on the Mandates Commission of the League of Nations.

The President himself was cut off from further constructive work on

[18] E. B. Wilson, *My Memoir*, p. 252.

[19] The President's increasing dependence on his doctor after the April illness had resulted in Grayson's giving political advice and acting as an intermediary in political contacts, and behind Grayson was his friend Baruch. On May 19 the doctor cabled to Tumulty that he had advised the President to allow his message to the new Congress to be given out "in Washington alone," and that "Colonel House confers with newspapermen daily and gives out information of which we have no knowledge." Lunching with the Wilsons on June 5, Lansing heard Grayson say that the little man on the third floor of the Crillon—"the great little agreer"—was to blame for much of the trouble. House's critics referred to his organization, deprecatingly, as "upstairs." McCormick recorded in his diary on April 4: "Baruch . . . sore at the Colonel's crowd, which he thought too free in criticizing the President to outsiders."

the League, during May and June, by the cross fire of protest against the terms of the treaty. His allies, as well as the enemy and his own men, were rebelling against certain of the provisions. Word came to the President that aggressive Frenchmen were plotting a sham revolution and a coup that would give them political control of the Rhineland; and Wilson appealed effectively to Clemenceau to foil this scheme. It was more difficult to detect and defeat French machinations looking toward economic control of the left bank of the Rhine and the breaking up of Germany into small, weak states. His colleagues in the council sometimes seemed "madmen," possessed by fear of the Germans and pitiful self-commiseration.

Wilson had to sit with them, day after day, and witness frantic efforts to partition Turkey in a way that would satisfy the demands of secret treaties and popular greed. By the end of May, suffering from a severe headache, he was laughing contemptuously at the bartering of foreign peoples. The aging President was now almost perpetually on the defensive against the tides of attrition that threatened to overwhelm him. He conceived that he was engaged in a holding action. "No more changes in the Treaty will be considered," he said. "Here I am. Here I have dug in."

The main German reply came to Paris on May 29. It threw Lloyd George into a panic. Early in May the prime minister had urged coercion of Germany. Now he was thoroughly alarmed by rumors that the enemy was preparing to renew resistance, as well as by fears that a crisis in his Cabinet would be precipitated by allegations that the treaty strengthened France unduly at the expense of Germany. He felt that he must ask for an alleviation of certain terms.

Clemenceau, however, intended to stand firm against any betterment of Germany's position, no matter what the consequences. He would be overthrown in his Chamber if he yielded anything more, he said to the council on June 2.

Faced by this rift of opinion, Wilson studied the counterproposals of the German message. On June 3, moreover, he undertook to canvass the sentiment of the entire United States delegation in a way that he had heretofore neglected.[20] He had been warned that, if he did not do this, some of the experts would be disgruntled and might make trouble; and so he had arranged through Lansing to talk with his Americans in the office of the secretary of state.

He had become very proud of the men in The Inquiry: to journalists

[20] In May, Wilson had invited memoranda, from the American commissioners only, on questions remaining to be settled after the German and Austrian treaties were disposed of. He had carefully annotated the suggestions received.

he praised their efficiency and, above all, the "complete disinterested-ness" that made their views usually prevail. Frankly inviting their advice in regard to the German reply, he explained that the French and Italians were having similar meetings and he suggested interna-tional talks among the experts so that they might learn each other's minds "without the usual roundabout expressions of diplomacy." Wilson held constantly before his men the paramount necessities of the moment: they must make peace; they must maintain the alliance with Great Britain and France; and they must do these things without undue sacrifice of justice to expediency. The argument of expediency ought not to prevail, he said, lest they have to fight again for what had been won.[21]

In the last minutes of the two-hour conference, the President gave play to the emotion that he had kept in check in the meetings of the council. He was "a little tired" and "very sick" at heart, he said. Asked whether he was blaming the French, he replied: "Not so much as the British . . . From the unreasonable to the reasonable, from Winston Churchill to Eustace Percy, from the pert to the priggish, they are unanimous, if you please, in their funk. They ought to have been ra-tional to begin with and then they would not have funked at the end . . . it is not very gracious for me to remind them—though I have done so with as much grace as I could command . . . If we had written the treaty the way they wanted it the Germans would have gone home the minute they read it. Well, the Lord be with us." [22]

The next day Wilson suffered from a headache that he ascribed to bottled-up wrath at Lloyd George. "I have never seen him more pug-nacious or bellicose," Lansing noted. Everyone was getting on edge. There was no strong executive hand upon the President's work save his own. In his official household there was homesickness and grumbling, and contention between civil and military members. Only three of the President's "family" had not been changed by the atmosphere at Paris, Wilson thought—his wife, daughter Margaret, and "Ike" Hoover.

As the Austrian treaty took shape, the President again had to grapple with specific cases in which his principles were in conflict with the stark realities of Europe. There were some fourteen petty wars in prog-ress on the Continent, many of them abetted by resources that had been contributed by the United States for the purpose of reconstruction. Im-

[21] Apparently the premonition of another world war grew upon Wilson during his last month at Paris. According to Sir William Wiseman, he said to Philip Kerr, Lloyd George's secretary, on the night before his last departure from France: "This is all a great pity. We shall have to do the same thing over again in twenty-five years at three times the cost!" Sir William Wiseman to the writer, May, 1954, and April 22, 1957.

[22] R. S. Baker, *W.W. and World Settlement*, III, 503–4, amended by reference to the notes of Charles Seymour, who was present.

poverished by armament and undermined by disaffected minorities, the states that had succeeded to the territories of the Central Empires showed little genius for democratic government. Their concept of "justice" seemed to depend upon what they were able to seize and to hold. They responded willingly to the propositions of foreign agents who were distributing arms and busily developing future allies.

The prophet was disappointed in the people for whose liberation he had pleaded, and wrote to Henry White that he was going to see what could be done about it. Actually, however, hope had to be abandoned of any effective action short of eventual regulation of all armaments under the League of Nations.[23]

Under pressure to dispense with armament that they thought essential to national pride and safety, the small states were in no mood to applaud the terms that were drawn for a treaty with their neighbor Austria. They assembled on May 31 in secret plenary session and objected belligerently. It was argued that a clause safeguarding religious and political minorities would lead to undue interference in their internal affairs by the large powers, acting through the League of Nations. The debate began to get out of hand. Even Clemenceau's gavel was inadequate.

The President, however, stepped into the breach with a speech admirably conceived and perfectly expressed. In his conversations with British statesmen he had given the impression that he felt that their empire and the Anglo-Saxons would give the essential leadership and force to the League of Nations; but he had heretofore refrained from impolitic expression of this feeling. Now, he said, he wished to call attention to a fundamentally important fact: "the chief burden of the war fell upon the greater powers . . . therefore . . . in the last analysis the military and naval strength of the great powers will be the final guarantee of the peace of the world." In these circumstances, he asked, was it unreasonable or unjust for the great powers to say to their associates, as friends and not as dictators: "We cannot afford to guarantee territorial settlements which we do not believe to be right, and we cannot agree to leave elements of disturbances unremoved, which we believe will disturb the peace of the world"?

His assertion of the paramount interest of the world—that of peace for all men—soothed the ruffled politicians of the nascent states. Clemenceau was able to dismiss the gathering without untoward incidents.

Other small states than those of Eastern Europe gave anxiety to the

[23] When Lloyd George proposed that limits of armament be set for Austria and adjoining states, Wilson saw an opportunity to try again for a general application of one of his Fourteen Points—reduction of arms to "the lowest point consistent with domestic safety." However, he found his allies far more willing to apply his standards to others than to themselves.

President at this time. The aggressiveness of one, in particular, vexed him because of the political strength of its sympathizers in the United States. Late in February, more than five thousand partisans of a free Ireland had met at Philadelphia and sent a delegation of three men to France, headed by Frank P. Walsh, former cochairman of the War Labor Board.

Wilson was as embarrassed as his adversaries in the Senate had hoped. If he took action, he would offend British opinion by seeming to interfere in the very sort of domestic matter in which his American enemies would not brook interference by the League. On the other hand, if he sidestepped, liberals might accuse him of deserting his principle of self-determination and Republican partisans would tell the Irish voters that the President was letting them down. "My first impulse," he confessed later, "was to tell the Irish to go to hell, but feeling that this would not be the act of a statesman, I denied myself this personal satisfaction." Instead he received the delegation of three Irish-Americans.

He pointed out to Lloyd George that, unless some satisfaction were given to Ireland, her sympathizers would surely attack the peace settlement; and the prime minister, seeing a possibility of laying a ghost that had haunted Anglo-American relations for a century, received the three delegates, found them "very high-class men," and gave them a ride to Ireland on a destroyer. When they landed on the old sod, however, they felt the worse for their voyage and welcomed a few nips of usquebaugh. They broke into Fenian speeches, ranted of "atrocities" by Britain.

When the Irish-Americans returned to France from this lark, Wilson was not glad to see them. He had learned from Tumulty that the Senate had passed a concurrent resolution asking that the American commissioners get a hearing for the Irish delegates; and now he replied that their utterances while in Ireland gave the deepest offense to those with whom they were seeking to deal and had "rendered it impossible for the commission to serve them any further." The delegates returned to the United States in a mood to urge their fellows to make common cause with the enemies of Woodrow Wilson.

The President heard also from another large minority in his own land—the Jews. After a huge demonstration in New York against Polish pogroms, Rabbi Wise cabled to express uneasiness over the absence of an antirace-discrimination clause in the Covenant and asked for a reassuring message similar to one that Wilson had sent to Taft a few days earlier.[24] Moreover, Felix Frankfurter wrote on May 16 that he was

---

[24] "Please say to Mr. Taft," the President cabled to Tumulty on May 8, 1919, "that the necessity of protecting the Jews is fully appreciated here and that we are endeavoring to take substantially the action that he suggests."

plunged into gloom by Wilson's failure to champion the Balfour Declaration favoring the establishment of a national home for the Jewish people in Palestine.

On his nation's Memorial Day, Wilson rallied popular morale by an address at the American cemetery near the top of Mont Valérien. Beyond the flower-decked white crosses and the acacia groves stretched the panorama of the valley of the Seine. The great men of the world came subdued and reverent to the scene. Thousands of American troops, with many a scar and empty sleeve among them, listened pensively. Honest Scottish sentiments could flow freely here from the soul that had been stifled by months of haggling.

No one with a heart in his breast, no American, no lover of humanity, can stand in the presence of these graves without the most profound emotion. These men who lie here are men of a unique breed. Their like had not been seen since the far days of the Crusades. Never before have men crossed the seas to a foreign land to fight for a cause which they did not pretend was peculiarly their own, but knew was the cause of humanity and of mankind. . . . The League of Nations is the covenant of governments that these men shall not have died in vain . . . I look for the time when every man who now puts his counsel against the united service of mankind under the League of Nations will be just as ashamed of it as if he now regretted the union of the States . . . if this is not the final battle for right, there will be another that will be final.

Then Wilson made a personal profession of consecration. "I sent these lads over here to die. Shall I—can I—ever speak a word of counsel which is inconsistent with the assurances I gave them when they came over?" Only by summoning all his grit could he hold to the end the restraint that distinguished his effort. People were sobbing as he finished. He and Edith Wilson could not trust themselves to speak and drove home in silence. Told of the overwhelming impact of his words on both disciples and critics, the President responded humbly. "When I speak extemporaneously," he said, "I am as uncertain and nervous just after it is over as I usually am just before." To guide him, he had only a brief outline on two slips of paper.

Meanwhile, the terms of the treaty with Austria assumed final form in the Council of Foreign Ministers. On June 2 the document was delivered, at St. Germain, to delegates whose bearing was in contrast to the defiance of Brockdorff-Rantzau. They were given fifteen days to reply. Release of the text of this treaty did not relieve the anxieties that were felt about the economy of Central Europe. Austria did not sign until September 10, 1919.

With the signing of the peace still a matter of speculation, in the first week of June, social distempers broke out anew. Several thousand strikers paraded with red flags, and Foch and his generals were alarmed. In many ways this was the most critical moment of the entire conference. "I think if I could have a really good piece of news, I should fall dead," Wilson said. It seemed imperative that the statesmen quickly form a common front and move rapidly to agree on a response to the Germans.

But first Lloyd George's demands for revision had to be dealt with. To Wilson it seemed too late for major changes. He had covenanted with the French, and Clemenceau was learning to appreciate his dependability. Together the two advocates of consistency tried to hold the Welshman to the line that they had laid down. Lloyd George seemed to heed only expediency and to come to each meeting, like a chameleon, "bright with the color" of the last man he had talked with. One day the President thought the Welshman "very offensive." In fact, he told House, he took occasion to be ugly himself.

In the conference with his Americans, Wilson had decided to urge once more the fixing of a definite sum that Germany could pay. But to no avail. Clemenceau argued that Germany must be forced to sign the treaty as it stood; and Lloyd George feared to face his electorate with any set figure that the Germans would think possible. The Welshman was now at least definite on this point.[25]

Wilson felt that his colleagues erred in trying to make a treaty that would suit their parliaments. He was haunted by a mystical, irrational faith that there was, deep down, a fine, intelligent strain of public opinion that the leaders were failing to cultivate. But the President could not take issue with them at this juncture, publicly, without giving undue comfort to the Germans; and, moreover, their peoples were more deeply involved than the Americans. Consequently the reparations clauses remained to the end potential threats to the peace of Europe.

On other points raised by Lloyd George concessions were made by

[25] Helm Diary, June 9, 1919. One of Lloyd George's own economic advisers had quit. John Maynard Keynes, the ingenious juggler of words and credits whom the prime minister had called his "Puck of Economics," left Paris in disgust, covering his withdrawal with a brilliant sputter of criticism, asserting that Wilson, who had declined to accept Keynes's plan to have the United States guarantee German bonds, was "the greatest fraud on earth." Harrod, *Keynes*, p. 250.

Keynes's plan had been presented to Wilson in a letter from Lloyd George of April 23, 1919. Replying on May 5, Wilson had stated that Congress could not authorize a guarantee of bonds of European origin and that the Treasury wished to retire from the banking business and preferred that loans be made through private channels. "How," the President asked, "can anyone expect America to turn over to Germany in any considerable measure new working capital to take the place of that which the European nations have determined to take from her?" Any action that the United States might take, Wilson said, should be "along independent lines," though "in close and cordial cooperation with European governments."

the council. Wilson agreed to a plebiscite in Upper Silesia and promised Poland military protection during the voting and time enough to eliminate unfair German influences. Moreover, a compromise was reached on the terms of the occupation of the Rhineland, and two agreements on this matter were signed in June with Germany separately from the treaty. Furthermore, Wilson wrote into the treaty a weak statement looking toward the admission of Germany to the League "in the early future." So, very slowly, The Three progressed by a path that seemed to the prophet to "spiral" toward decisions.

By the 13th of June, Lloyd George's "funk" had passed and he again showed the agility that made General Bliss set him down as "a greased marble spinning on a glass table-top." The prime minister was ready to threaten reimposition of the blockade to supplement military measures that Foch was taking to make the enemy see the futility of resistance. Baruch had suggested preparation of "the fullest possible pressure of blockade upon Germany," to be applied in case of a German refusal to sign the treaty. But Wilson preferred military occupation to starvation, and grew angry when Lloyd George insinuated that the President's antipathy to a blockade reflected America's desire to sell surplus food at high prices.[26]

On June 16 Clemenceau, giving the last word of the Allies to the enemy, bore down hard. After the delivery of his manifesto, which gave Germany seven days to decide whether to sign or let the Armistice lapse, there was a lull in the work of the Peace Conference. The Wilsons took advantage of it to accept an invitation to visit Brussels that the Belgians had been extending for weeks.

Back at Paris, the President appeared refreshed and smiling, and wore a new straw hat jauntily. In the air around him, though, was a tenseness that had been created by sharp exchanges of notes with the enemy, and The Three met with their military men to prepare steps to be taken if the Germans failed to form a government that would capitulate promptly. The Cabinet at Weimar had lost its majority and resigned and a new government had not yet been formed.

Before seven on the morning of June 23, secretaries of the British and French delegations went to Wilson's residence to deliver a German note asking delay. Waking the armed detective who lay on the mat outside his suite, they were admitted to the President's chamber and taken by him into the bathroom. Perched on the tub, he read the dispatch. Its

---

26 Baruch was urging that the economic settlement in general should be fair to American foreign trade and that where commercial credits were granted, they should be used in the country making the advance. It was obvious that the United States, the nation best able to grant credits, would be favored by such an arrangement. *See* Margaret L. Coit, *Mr. Baruch,* pp. 231, 234, 264, and sources cited.

substance was laid before the council later in the day, and the Allied statesmen, angered by news of the sinking of interned German warships by their crews,[27] refused to grant another extension of their time limit. Finally, late in the afternoon, a meeting of the council was interrupted by an announcement that the Germans would yield to overwhelming force and sign unconditionally.

For three days no German officials could be found who would bear the shame of putting their signatures on the treaty. Nevertheless, Paris was celebrating the signing as a *fait accompli*. The President's automobile, driving him to the Crillon through back streets to dodge trouble, was almost hemmed in by boisterous, yelling crowds. On the evening of June 26, Wilson was dragooned to the Elysée Palace to a dinner in honor of President Poincaré, whose attempts to interfere and to hold Clemenceau to narrow views had made him loathsome to the American prophet. The two chief executives exchanged decorous toasts; but during the evening, with Poincaré almost at his elbow, Wilson spoke of his boredom at stuffy dinners such as the one that he had just attended.

On the morning of June 27 two Germans arrived at Versailles, prepared to sign the treaty. That afternoon, looking forward to the final session on the morrow—the event that would release him at last to go home—the President shook off his fatigue and talked for a full hour with newsmen, answering questions and commenting openly on many phases of the conference and of his plans for the future. Making the best of the situation, the prophet asserted that the peace was closer to his principles than he "had any right to expect." As for the archaggressor of 1914—Germany—it was "a pretty tough peace" for her; but after all, she had done a great wrong. In conclusion he said to the journalists: "All things considered, I think a wonderful success has been achieved . . . It's a long job that I'm glad to see finished, and it is a good job." Lincoln Steffens, one of the correspondents present, recorded that the President was "humble, mater-of-fact and yet very positive, and, of course, informed," that if he talked to the public in the same vein, he would win his fight for ratification in the United States.

Only one knot was still unraveled: he had not been able to persuade the Chinese to sign without reservations, nor would the French permit them to make exceptions. As a result, the Chinese delegates drew away

[27] It seemed to Wilson that the sinking had relieved the council of an embarrassing request by France for many of the ships that the British and Americans were inclined to scrap. On June 24, Wilson discouraged the raising of the question of the renewal of the blockade of Germany. He was having trouble enough, he said, in keeping Clemenceau from renewing the war on account of the sinking of the ships and the burning of battle flags that the Germans were to have returned to France. Finally the council merely sent a note of protest against the sinkings.

in tears and a fifth of the world's people were excluded from the peace settlement.

Otherwise everything was ready, on the afternoon of the 28th, for the sealing of the pact that would order the twentieth-century world. The air was bright and clear and Woodrow Wilson's spirit rose in the gay atmosphere of fiesta. Early in the afternoon, with Edith Wilson, he called formally upon the Poincarés, and later in the day the French President returned the courtesy. Wilson bought for his wife a blue and gray bag that matched her gown, and a single crimson rosebud. It was the nearest that he could come to red, white, and blue, he said. He bought orchids for her, too, and put on his own frock coat and high hat for the pageant at Versailles.

The ceremony was an impressive staging of history in the spirit of Louis XIV. In the *Galeries des Glaces*, at a horseshoe table in the middle, hedged about by great mirrors on one side and by rows and rows of tabourets, under a scroll proclaiming *Le roi gouverne par lui-même*, sat the squat Tiger of France, his short legs scarcely touching the floor. He remembered the birth of the Hohenzollern Empire here, and now he was to witness its death.

Wilson and Lloyd George are among the last to come in. They take their seats to the right and the left of Clemenceau, who makes a sign to the ushers. "Ssh! Ssh!" The chatter ceases. The bustle of secretaries and autograph hunters subsides. A quilt of hush descends. Then a sharp order cuts, and the swords of the guards at the doorway click into their scabbards. *"Faites entrer les Allemands,"* in the voice of Clemenceau, distant and harsh. Isolated and pitiful, announced by bugles and escorted by ushers, more ghosts than men, come the two victims, erect under their high collars, their feet clacking on the parquet when they step between carpets—one of them tall and thin, the other short and peering through thick lenses like a lost owl. Recalling the discourtesy of Brockdorff-Rantzau, the statesmen of the Allies do not rise to greet them. The silence is complete. Until the Tiger raps out: *"Messieurs, la séance est ouverte."*

The Germans are escorted to the table where the big seal-bound volume lies. They are to sign first, for Clemenceau is taking no chances on a last-minute balk by the enemy, after the Allies have signed. Wilson and his Americans follow. Hands reach out to congratulate the President as he walks, smiling broadly, to the table where the treaty lies. His seal already has been affixed to the document by use of a signet ring bearing the shorthand characters for his name. Beside this imprint he signs "Woodrow" firmly, the full significance of the moment striking him and his hand almost failing as he completes "Wilson." In less than an hour all the signatures are affixed.

Outside, guns boom, airplanes dip low, and the fountains on the terrace spurt for the first time since the war began. The Three walk out together. Crowds burst through cordons of troops and swarm upon them, shouting *"Vive Clemenceau!" "Vive Wilson!" "Vive Lloyd George!"* For a moment the three top hats are lost sight of. The statesmen stand stanchly together, as they did when the peoples of the world pressed divisive arguments upon them and they resolved to preserve unanimity at all costs. They are swept along the terrace—still together, arms locked—and finally rescued by a platoon coming up on the double.

With Sonnino and Makino, they went to the foyer of *l'Opéra de la Cour* for a final session. Wilson insisted that the minutes of their intimate sessions should not be published—indeed, not even cited. He said that he would not have permitted a recording of their sessions, filled as they were with plain speaking and changes of opinion, had he thought the question of publication would be raised. It was agreed that the intimate records would not be released to anyone, save to their successors. Wilson would not concede even that his successors had a right to the documents.

At the station there was more enthusiasm for the departing American than had been manifest at his leave-taking in February. He was cheered by a crowd that included most of the notable men at Paris except the British. Clemenceau was on hand, more than an hour after his bedtime, to walk to the train with the prophet who had almost, but not quite, converted him. At the steps of the car they clasped hands. A little teary, The Tiger purred: "I feel as though I were losing one of the best friends I ever had." France had her redeemed territories, her reparations, her treaty of guarantee. And America had, for her taking, her League, her Monroe Doctrine of the whole world.

But would she take it?

The train moved out. The lights of the Old World capital grew dim. Woodrow Wilson stood with his wife at an open window, happy at last to be on the way home. "Well," he said, "it is finished, and, as no one is satisfied, it makes me hope we have made a just peace; but it is all on the lap of the gods."

CHAPTER XVII

CHALLENGE TO AMERICA

ON JUNE 29, AT BREST, Woodrow Wilson boarded the *George Washington* for the last time. The social turmoil of Europe had pursued him to the water's edge; a Socialist demonstration was surging in the old French seaport even as the President's train moved between lines of American soldiers and took him alongside a quay.

Descending a steep flight of stone steps, he was ferried out to his vessel. A flicker of cheer shone through his haggard face. Here was the America for which he had been yearning. Safe on the big ship, escorted by the Navy, he felt again the thrill of the constructive genius of his countrymen. At last he was home among his own people, sailing under his own flag. His mind fell back into a native vale, to thoughts familiar and comfortable.

Looking back over the months of contention with the shrewdest politicians in Europe, he could feel that—as he had once said of John Hay—he had "promoted that concert of nations which is the best security for the peace of the world." He had exalted political ideals before the peoples of the world as cogently as he had once expounded them in Princeton classrooms. He had awakened faith in the power of man's reason to lift him out of political jungles; and his very presence at the peace table had been construed as assurance of moderation. Vast strides had been taken toward codification of political usages that might end international anarchy. Many peoples had been liberated from repressive rule, had been ministered unto with a generosity unprecedented in human history, and had been given a chance to develop political responsibility and to join as equals in the family of nations. Moreover, states that governed alien peoples were to be held accountable to world opinion through mandates. Then, too, by provisions of plebiscites and by a labor charter, recognition had been given to the rights of minorities to resist exploitation, both political and economic. Under the new order, mankind would have a chance to think and talk before fighting, to balance the cost of war against that of compromise. Public registration of treaties would be required, and disarmament encouraged. Small nations would have a hearing before the world. Germany would be given a chance for redemption.

Most significant of all, the centuries-old dream of idealists had at last come true: a League of Nations had been created to serve as a forum for the voices of morality and intelligence. In this respect the treaty of

1919 had set up a milestone in the progress of the race. Even statesmen who were unenthusiastic about the League had found it a convenient catchall for problems that seemed insoluble and disruptive.

Yet Woodrow Wilson confessed disquietude because he had fallen so far short of the aspiration of idealists. He said to Baruch that some people seemed to expect of him what only God could perform. Actually, patriots in the free states still thought in nationalistic patterns, so that the world seemed to revolve around them, rather than they and their sister states round a world-wide logos. Statesmen of the Allies went home muttering that, though the peace was perhaps the best that could have been salvaged from the cross fire of purposes under which they had negotiated, it was after all a bad job. The document seemed too strong to some, too weak to others; too vague in certain respects, too specific in others. Many critics thought its economic clauses hopelessly contradictory, its territorial changes provocative of strife.

The bitter plaints did not spare the statesman whom Europeans held chiefly responsible for its terms, and many of the voices that had hailed the American prophet as a savior were now the most vociferous in condemning the obvious lag between his promises and the product. Moreover, the very covenanting zeal that ran in his blood and gave his challenge its force had led him to project his convictions with a fervor that repelled responsible men who felt the awful shadow of Presbyterian sin cast over them.

But Woodrow Wilson, out on the Atlantic and homeward bound, was in no mood to join the voices of disillusion and despair. He did not lose faith in the people. The cause was so sacred to him, so vital to humanity, so dependent, for success, upon unanimity of opinion among those who had worked with him at Paris! He could forgive the ignorant—those who knew not what they did: but he had only frigid scorn for the "perfectabilitarians"—the men of little faith. Disappointed though he was in many of the provisions of the treaty, he was ready to uphold the document to which he had sworn fealty, with trust that the League of Nations eventually would correct maladjustments and injustices. No one knew better than he on how precarious a base the treaty rested. And no one felt more keenly the necessity for protecting this fragile handiwork in the jungle-era to which European politics seemed to be reverting.

Great as was Wilson's contribution toward a cosmic political order, however, he and his economic advisers had not lifted the world's trade and industry out of the old channels that had led persistently to war. The President usually had followed the counsel of the businessmen who advised him. He himself had had little time to ponder deeply on the economic causes of war. He had been urged to try to set up world-wide controls of trade similar to those in force in the United States. But the President had not acknowledged this proposal. From the beginning of the Peace Conference he had relegated economic matters to a subordinate place until they had thrust themselves upon him in connection with the reparation settlement. Woodrow Wilson's first love was politics, not economics. Nevertheless, he saw that the processes of history were making isolation impossible for the United States—economically as well as politically. He had reminded the new Congress that "America has a great and honorable service to perform in bringing the commercial and industrial undertakings of the world back to their old scope and swing again, and putting a solid structure of credit under them." [1]

Many of Wilson's own people, however, were no more willing to pool their economic resources with Europe than to put their military power at the disposal of foreigners. As the stimulus of a war emergency expired, Americans had become as impatient of political control of their foreign trade as of regulation of interstate commerce. The President saw no way in which he could carry out his desire to have his country put "a solid structure of credit" under the world's trade and industry. With the disbanding of the Supreme Economic Council, the tenuous economic bonds that had held the victorious nations together through the stress of war would be ruptured. To relieve Europe's financial burden, there seemed to be no feasible course but to issue still more credits from the United States to fund the existing indebtedness of the Allied governments. [2]

[1] In his message to Congress, on May 19, Wilson had hedged his assertion of idealism by recommendation of a tariff that would protect American industries that were essential to military defense and that would enable the nation to retaliate effectively against any foreign legislation that might militate or discriminate against American interests.

[2] Wilson had permitted Hoover to notify the Supreme Economic Council, on June 27, that that body should cease to function after the ratification of the treaty "lest it should give the impression to the world of an economic block of the governments who have been aligned in war." In a session of the inner council, on his last day in Paris, Wilson explained his unwillingness to prolong the Supreme Economic Council. "I shall have to take up this question on my return to America," he said, "and if need be, I shall call for appropriate legislative measures. I have a mind to authorize the Supreme Economic Council to present a plan to us. I ask only that this plan be drawn in a way to avoid the criticisms that I have indicated." In the one important instance in which the United States was committed to joint economic action in Europe after the war—representation on the Reparations Commission—Wilson had made the same reservation that he had quietly worked into the Covenant. Under this safeguard the commission, like the Council of the League, must act unanimously; and thus the United States retained a power of veto against any issue of bonds that might upset the money market in New York.

On June 4 a committee of economists of the four Western powers had made a confidential report that was never seriously considered by the council, recommending that steps be taken to reorganize currencies, that international trade be re-established ultimately on private rather than government credit, but that governments should set up immediately a fund to supply raw materials and producer's goods for the new states of Europe.

So far as the United States was concerned, Wilson felt that the question of further interna-

On the *George Washington*, the President kept more to his cabin
than during his earlier crossings. Now and then he called in advisers
for conferences. He walked the deck each day, hating it and doing it
only because his wife insisted.

He lunched with Baruch and McCormick, and almost every day he
met them on deck and chatted about economic matters. These veterans
of his little War Cabinet were devoted disciples who gave advice
straight from the shoulder, respectfully and without the arts of sales-
manship.[3] They saw no feet of clay in their leader, and their admiration
for his wisdom had grown.

Uppermost in the President's mind was ratification of the peace
treaty by Congress. Within the new political order, he hoped, economic
adjustments could be worked out in peaceful cooperation. At Paris his
hero, General Smuts, had challenged him directly. "*Can* you carry the
treaty? *Can* you get your two-thirds majority?" the South African had
asked. And Wilson had responded solemnly: "I absolutely can." Com-
muning still with the poets and the seers, he was depending on his
intuition, what he called his "independent mind," unprejudiced by fact
and logic. With no security but good intentions, he had given his word
to men whom he honored. He must now redeem his pledge.

He had been assured by messages from Washington that his political
lieutenants were looking to him for leadership. "There is a great depression in our ranks here," Tumulty had reported on June 16, "but
with a definite thing presented by you to the people in the League of
Nations . . . our enemies will be left in a most pitiable plight."[4]

---

tional conference on economic matters must rest for decision with the officials of the permanent departments of the government at Washington.

Though he hesitated to use his economic power brazenly, for political advantage, Wilson
had wielded it in emergencies of the peacemaking to enforce his concepts of justice. Under moral
and spiritual pressures, the prophet had turned ruling elder, conscious of his power to withhold
the beneficence of a welfare fund from unworthy brethren; and Hoover's men were exercising
this power in distributing grants for relief. Thus the United States had been tightening to some
extent the financial grip that Wilson had foreseen two years earlier. How much the President
might have made of his economic power, had he been willing to make full use of the methods
of Old World diplomacy, has been suggested by Herbert Hoover in his *Memoirs*, I, 451.

[3] Baruch had displayed genuine concern for the common good by willingness to share his
personal fortune through taxation and charity, and he had shown devotion to Wilson by declining
to serve as secretary of the treasury for fear that a taint of "Wall Street" might embarrass the
President.

[4] The "great depression" in the party ranks to which Tumulty referred is described vividly
in a letter from R. W. Woolley to House, dated June 17, 1919. "There isn't any Democratic
Party in this country," Woolley wrote. "He is with you in Paris. You and I know what will
happen when he returns. Meanwhile the pigmies are having a wonderful time. Every fellow
with a grouch is romping over the landscape . . . Senator Hitchcock, who has put his grievances
on ice for the time being, is doing his best to represent the Administration in the Senate, while
other so-called Democratic leaders,—Senator Walsh of Montana excepted,—let everything go by
default and the Republicans get away with pretty much all they undertake . . . Outside of
officeholders—and a goodly number of them are none too loyal—the aggregation championing
the Administration is fast assuming the aspects of Falstaff's army."

Political interest coincided with Woodrow Wilson's personal devotion to the cause of the League. But it was to be understood that his own political fortunes were to be subordinated to the great cause. From now on, the Covenant was to be The Word. During the transatlantic voyage, which was extended at Dr. Grayson's insistence to give the President a longer rest, Wilson worked hard on a message that would present the treaty to Congress. He read his draft to his associates and asked for advice. Baruch counseled aggressiveness. It seemed to him that the President should explain just what the League of Nations was and what it would do, that if Wilson delayed long in doing this he would find himself on the defensive. But the President heeded only his inner voices. He was obsessed by his dream of unity with the plain people, and by intuitive confidence that he expressed their latent aspirations. His doctrine and his motives seemed to him so transparent that souls of good faith would understand and sympathize. There were sincere isolationists, he knew, but he thought that his people would perceive that many of the criticisms of the League were captious. He had placed the same prophetic faith, once, in Princeton's alumni, and they had disappointed him grievously.

On the morning of July 8 the *George Washington* neared New York. Escorted by battleships, destroyers, and planes, saluted thunderously, she steamed majestically up the harbor. Sailors clad in white lined the deck. The sun was bright, the sea calm, and the ship's company happy and expectant.

The great city that had so often cold-shouldered the prophet now put on its best manners. He had first visited its canyons of wealth as Miss Ellie Lou's fiancé, ashamed of his plain clothes; and it was here that the Philistines had laughed and raged at him most irritatingly. But Manhattan now blared its recognition of the returning President. Members of his Cabinet and Governor Alfred E. Smith met him in the harbor, and Frank L. Polk, who had taken the new title of undersecretary of state. He was so glad to be home that even the docks of Hoboken looked pretty, he said with a twinkling eye. Citizens crowded the route across Twenty-third Street and up Fifth Avenue, to lavish cheers and tears upon their leader. Their enthusiasm drew him to his feet and kept him standing in his automobile.

But behind those who cheered and shook his hand in welcome there were men who blamed him for misfortunes personal and national. Politicians whom he had offended were spewing poison, souring public opinion, making it curdle around nodes of anti-League sentiment. George Harvey was spreading vitriol through his weekly journal. Neurotic William F. McCombs, ill in a suite at the Waldorf-Astoria, went to his window and leaned far out over the street to put a curse upon the prophet whom the crowds applauded.

The Covenanter entered the hotel and closed the door of his suite. His daughter Margaret, ecstatic with pride, threw her arms around him and rejoiced in the plaudits of the multitude. But he regarded her with a look that she knew she could never forget. "Wait till they turn," he said quietly, remembering the cooling of the peoples of Europe.

At midnight he reached the White House. The quiet dignity of the old mansion offered sanctuary. It was sweet to be home once more, sheltered from the summer heat and from distasteful persons, in the care of servants whom he knew as friends and trusted. There were flowers everywhere, the summer linen was on the chairs, and everything was spick and span, and simple. And there came a reminder that his old friends—the class of '79 at Princeton—still loved him. "The class drank your health in the usual liquid," one of them wrote. "I exhort you never again to miss a reunion. You really count on Great Occasions."

Two days later, dressed immaculately and carrying a bulky copy of the treaty, he went before the Senate to seek their approval of it. He had thought of calling a joint session of the Congress, but Tumulty had advised that this would be adding insult to the upper house.

He had written out his speech painstakingly; the occasion was so solemn that he did not trust himself to speak extemporaneously. As he stood before the Senate, his emotions threatened his forensic perfection. Now and again he stumbled over a word. Sometimes it seemed that he was not addressing the senators, but rather projecting his spirit to the galleries and to the people whom they represented. "Senators do not know what the people are thinking," he had remarked at Paris. "They are as far from the people, the great mass of the people, as I am from Mars."

He told the senators and the people above them that the forming of a League of Nations was no academic concern, but a matter of life and death to human civilization. Actually, what had once seemed a counsel of perfection had come to seem a plain counsel of necessity. The League was "not merely an instrument to adjust and remedy old wrongs under a new treaty of peace; it was the only hope for mankind . . . Dare we reject it and break the heart of the world?"

"America may be said to have just reached her majority as a world power," he asserted. Then, laying aside his manuscript, he gave these elders his charge. "The stage is set, the destiny disclosed . . . We cannot turn back. We can only go forward, with lifted eyes and freshened spirit, to follow the vision. It was of this that we dreamed at our birth. America shall in truth show the way. The light streams upon the path ahead, and nowhere else."

He did not need to ask, as in his sesquicentennial challenge to the men of Princeton: "Who shall lead us to this place?" It was obvious that the establishment of the League of Nations under American leadership was now the "chief end" of this Presbyterian. He could not rest except in pursuing this single track to a logical, ethical, destination. Putting on a mien of complete confidence, he said to newsmen on the day of his address at the Capitol: "The Senate is going to ratify the treaty."

Earlier in the year 1919, while the memory of the horror of war was fresh and poignant, many associations of citizens had been advocating a league of nations. The churches had declared themselves in favor, the women of the country were for it, the American Federation of Labor supported it, and the American Bar Association voted unanimously for participation by the United States. A poll of the press taken early in April had shown opinion leaning heavily toward ratification of the treaty.

Nevertheless, as the shock of carnage passed and the wounds of war healed, subversive emotions of race and religion had asserted themselves. Citizens of Italian blood responded warmly to a denunciation by Lodge of Wilson's stand on Fiume; Chinese intellectuals and their American friends could not forgive the Shantung settlement; communities on the West Coast dreaded that the League might forbid barriers against the immigration of Orientals.

Americans of older lineage were turned against the Covenant by impulses that they thought "patriotic." Some felt that the League would prove to be merely a device for the aggrandizement of the British Empire. Others feared that the United States would give more than she got, that her tariff laws might fall under control of the League, and above all, that the positive guarantee against aggression that appeared in Article X would involve the nation in war against its will.

Independent efforts had been made by anti-League zealots of both parties to organize those who preached "America First" into a League for the Preservation of American Independence. This association argued that an appeal to force as a means of preserving peace was "at best futile and at worst dangerous," that the United States should be assured "freedom to defend right, to refuse to fight, to mind our own business." [5] Conferring with irreconcilable senators at the Washington home of Lodge on the evening of April 28, the day the revised Covenant of the

5 G. W. Pepper, *Philadelphia Lawyer*, pp. 124–29.

League was adopted, the leaders of this crusade had found Lodge "cautious and resourceful." Moreover, at subsequent sessions of Wilson-haters at the homes of Brandegee and Alice Roosevelt Longworth, plans were laid for spreading propaganda through mass meetings and the press.

While Wilson was still at Paris, Lodge had begun to marshal his forces in the Senate for relentless warfare. Observing that the Democratic party would stake its position in the 1920 election on Wilson's peace treaty and the League, Republican leaders saw that their own party—divided as it was by a vast range of personal views toward the Covenant—must be united on defensible ground if they were to retain the power given them by the previous Congressional election. Lodge discussed strategy with Senator Borah of Idaho, who thought the peace treaty a breeder of future wars and the League a bar to America's freedom of action. Lodge, according to his own record, explained to this archisolationist that any immediate attempt to defeat the treaty by a straight vote in the Senate would be hopeless, even if it were desirable, that there was only one thing to do and that was to proceed in the discussion of the treaty by way of amendment and reservation. The senator from Massachusetts felt that the public, unaware of dangerous implications of the Covenant to which their President would commit them, could best be enlightened by debate on specific ways of improving the instrument.

With a Republican majority of two in the Senate and thirty-nine in the House, Lodge was ready to draw the lines of battle. Making the most of his prerogative as chairman of the Foreign Relations Committee, he appointed new members on whom he could count [6]; and he looked for aid on the floor of the Senate from a few dissenting Democrats, especially Reed of Missouri.

Turning Wilson's own phrase against him, Lodge served notice that the peace treaty was not to be debated in closed session but was to be given "pitiless publicity." Already, on June 6, the Senate had passed a resolution calling on the secretary of state to give the tentative treaty to the Senate. And on June 9, Borah, too impulsive to await the constitutional process by which treaties are customarily submitted to Congress, got a copy from a newsman and had it read into the *Congressional Record*. Lodge and Borah stirred the jealousy of their colleagues by talk

---

[6] When Lodge appointed irreconcilable Hiram Johnson instead of moderate Frank B. Kellogg, several wavering Republicans were in a mood in which they might have been won by Democratic diplomacy. Dissertation of James E. Hewes, Jr., Yale University Library, pp. 223–26. The packing of the Foreign Relations Committee with senators opposing Wilson's League gave Lodge control of nine of the seventeen votes. His tactics were assailed by Taft publicly, and on the floor of the Senate by the Democratic minority leader, Hitchcock, who had charged that the purpose of the Republican was "to kill the League of Nations, if possible, and to kill it by indirection."

of a "leak" that had permitted "special interests" in New York to get the treaty while the august representatives of the American people were kept in darkness.

This was partisan, political nonsense, Wilson had perceived at once. The President had nothing to conceal, had curbed his own inclination to publish the tentative treaty merely out of a desire to cooperate with Lloyd George, who had hoped for changes before the final signing. When Senator Hitchcock put through a resolution calling for a full investigation of the alleged "leak" and the American press published the treaty, Wilson was relieved.

During the last month at Paris, Wilson had been plagued by other heckling moves in the Senate. Long debates spun out the campaign of delay and questioning on which the cabal was well embarked. Knox attacked Article X and tore the Covenant to shreds.[7] When Fall proposed that the war be ended by decree and a separate peace made with Germany, the President felt that the senators' assertion of their right to advise had gone too far. He then reminded the newsmen that the Senate was empowered by the Constitution only to advise and consent, or refuse to consent, to treaties brought before it by the executive. "If they go beyond that, and undertake to change the treaty," he warned, "then the executive can reject such action as exceeding the Senate's prerogative, and entering upon that of the executive."

The scholar who had written forty years before about the "treaty-marring power" of the Senate did not propose to be put upon. He had insisted to Lansing that the attacks were all part of a general plan to make as much mischief as possible. "The only way to handle them," he wrote at Paris, "is by making a direct frontal attack in reply. Article X is the king pin of the whole structure . . . without it, the Covenant would mean nothing. If the Senate will not accept that, it will have to reject the whole treaty. It is manifestly too late now to effect changes in the Covenant, and I hope that Polk will urge Hitchcock and all our friends to take a most militant and aggressive course, such as I mean to take the minute I get back."[8]

[7] Knox's name was scarcely less distasteful to Wilson than that of Lodge. Attending a baseball game on Labor Day, 1919, he turned to a friend and taking off his straw hat and pointing at the "Knox" label on the band, said: "Isn't that a hell of a name to wear near one's brain?" Louis Brownlow, *Lectures and Seminar at the University of Chicago in Celebration of the Centennial of W.W.,* p. 143.

[8] In his autobiography, *Across the Busy Years,* II, 201, Nicholas Murray Butler reports (without complete dating or documentation) that Ambassador Jusserand, having secured the assent of the British and French Foreign Offices to a set of reservations to which Butler had committed several wavering senators, took these reservations to Wilson at Paris and assured the President that if the Democrats in the Senate would support them, enough Republicans would join them to ratify the treaty. "To Jusserand's horror," Butler reports, "the President in a stern voice replied: 'Mr. Ambassador, I shall consent to nothing. The Senate must take its medicine!'"

He felt that he had acted on Republican proposals for reservations to the best of his judgment and ability. Yet, during his last month at Paris, the Republicans had continued to formulate reservations. The essence of their objections appeared in a public letter written on June 21 by Elihu Root to Lodge, who committed forty-seven of the forty-nine Republican senators to support the reservation on Article X that Root proposed, and all forty-nine in favor of two other reservations suggested by Root—one safeguarding the right of withdrawal from the League, the other asserting positively the two aspects of the Monroe Doctrine. The Republican elder statesman believed that his reservations could be included in a nation's instrument of ratification without requiring a reopening of negotiations with other signatories. He thought that the reservations could be approved effectively by silence on the part of the other contracting parties, that if there should be any doubt on this point it could be dispelled by asking the four largest signing powers to state their positions.[9]

Sensitive to the danger of reopening and again probing the festering matters that he had treated so painfully at the Peace Conference, Wilson was in no mood to act on Root's suggestion that the opinions of the four largest Allied governments be sounded. Never a man to probe deeply into legalism, the President, in the fatigued condition to which work and worry had reduced him, had no will to take steps that might seem obedient to an opposition that he had resolved to fight. His patience had worn thin at advice that had become repetitive and was, he suspected, insincere. He explained to newsmen, on the day of submitting the treaty to the Senate, that reservations "presented a grave difficulty in that every nation joining the League would have to assent to them, and while this slow process was going on the United States would

[9] Chandler P. Anderson, a lawyer who undertook to fabricate reservations for the Republicans, wrote to his friend Root on July 10 that, though he had little doubt that the other signatories would accept the United States on its own terms, strict legality required that each sign a *procès-verbal* definitely accepting the reservations.

The solicitor of the State Department advised the President that the United States had a right to deposit interpretive resolutions with the ratified treaty, but that these would not bind other governments unless adopted by them. In giving his opinion, the solicitor confessed that he found no authoritative statements concerning the effect of reservations on the obligations of the United States to the other signatories or theirs to the United States. The solicitor adduced further advice on this debatable point that had been given by Solicitor J. E. Clark of the State Department on Aug. 5, 1911. Clark wrote: "The uniform practice of the Executive is now and seems always to have been that where the Senate proposed an amendment to a treaty submitted to it by the President for its advice and consent, the President, upon receiving the treaty with such proposed amendment, renews negotiations with the other Power to learn whether or not such an amendment is acceptable to such Power. If the amendment is not acceptable, either an entirely new treaty must be negotiated or the treaty falls." On this opinion David Hunter Miller commented, on Sept. 13, 1919: "Submission to the various Powers . . . means, in most cases, submission to their legislatures . . ." *See* two memoranda forwarded from the solicitor to Adee of the State Department and printed in Miller Diary, XX, 494–501.

be at war with Germany." On the same day he told a newspaper publisher who had friends in both camps that he was "open-minded as to every proposition of reasonable interpretation," but would not "consent to any proposition that we scuttle."

This statesmanlike position, however, availed nothing. McAdoo wrote the next day to suggest that the noble address to Congress was "like casting pearls before swine, so far as the Senatorial cabal is concerned." To Senator Brandegee the speech was "soap bubbles of oratory and soufflé of phrases"; and to Senator Warren G. Harding it was "utterly lacking in ringing Americanism."

Having failed to make conversions from the pulpit in the Senate chamber, the prophet called a few of the wavering brethren to the White House and pleaded with them.[10] He talked for hours, patiently and persuasively, as he had talked so many times before with legislators who seemed to need educating. He refused to risk a controversy by discussing the merits of the reservations that they proposed. He chose rather to explain that to attach amendments to the treaty would be to jar the delicate balance into which conflicting national interests had been brought at Paris. It was distasteful, this business of begging men to do what seemed so patently their duty; but when Senator Hitchcock had said that it must be done, there had been no course but to comply.

Unfortunately, however, the press dramatized the talks at the White House. Senators sensed that the public was watching them, ready to interpret any yielding on their part as surrender or acknowledgment of sins for which they had received pastoral reproof. Thus their pride was stirred and they became the more receptive to partisan arguments that they should assert their right to a share in the authorship of the treaty.

"I am pondering very carefully," Wilson wrote to McAdoo on July 15, "the method of action best calculated to bring about the right results in these difficult days." And to Senator John Sharp Williams: "Your advice about using gentleness and tact in our present task . . . is good advice." Undersecretary Frank L. Polk, conferring with Wilson near the end of the month, found him changed and more conciliatory.

On the 18th Sir William Wiseman came for luncheon, and Wilson talked frankly with him. The President was eager to go before the people, he said, and explain the treaty to them; but the State Department had advised against it, fearing that wavering senators might construe the move as an appeal over their heads and take offense. He pre-

[10] On July 16, Wilson wrote as follows to Senators Capper, Colt, Jones, Kellogg, Kenyon, McCumber, McNary, and Nelson: "Matters of so grave a consequence are now under consideration that I would very much appreciate an opportunity to have a talk with you about the treaty and all that it involves."

ferred to try to win the legislators personally; in fact, he had talked with three Republicans that very morning. If he were able to gain enough votes in this way, he would not have to carry his case to the people.

He confessed to Wiseman, most confidentially, that to hasten action and to avoid foolish reservations that might lead the world to believe that the United States gave only half its heart to the League, he might have to approve "interpretations" of the language of certain articles of the Covenant. After all, he had traded his ideals against selfish interests at Paris, and if absolutely necessary, he would do the same at Washington; but he was resolved to drive a hard bargain in the name of humanity's common good, to concede nothing until it became inescapable. In public he would maintain an adamant front as long as possible; for he felt that any sign of weakness would be taken by the opposition as a signal for inflated demands. Actually, there was only one criticism of the Covenant that seemed to him to be very persistent outside of the Senate chamber. That was the objection that the United States might not be able to withdraw at will from the League.

It seemed to the British visitor that anxiety had gnawed deeply into the President. His face was gray and drawn, and twitching as it had after the illness at Paris. Heeding a warning from Edith Wilson, Wiseman sheered away from controversial topics that might excite his host.

The President did not go often now to the executive offices, but instead made appointments at the White House. He would retire to his chamber during the day from time to time. Immediately after lunching with Wiseman he went downriver on the *Mayflower*, hoping to relax; but even on his voyages on the Potomac he took his typewriter and papers, and after dinner went below and worked late into the night, while Edith Wilson sat on deck and entertained those in their party.

During the summer he spent an occasional evening at vaudeville. But when a friend invited him to the theater, he wrote: "Not on your life! I would not go to a serious play, no matter how fine, which dealt with the critical matters now daily pressing upon my judgment as matters of policy, for anything in the world. The weight of this weary unintelligible world is great enough anyhow on those of us poor devils who have to take some part in straightening things out, and when I go to the theatre I must, for psychological reasons, see something that does not extend the strain of the day. You will understand."

As the President's health failed, the ravening wolves of the Senate raised the pitch of their cries. To Hiram Johnson the League seemed a "gigantic War Trust." Wilson was smeared by Borah as "Britain's tool

—a dodger and a cheater," and by Penrose and Reed as a man who preached sacrifice but took extravagant presents from crowned heads. Moreover, these old warriors were joined by the voice of one who had thus far held aloof—William Howard Taft.

When Wilson had acted on his proposals at Paris, Taft had continued to give ardent support to the League. In June he had advised the President not to attack the Republican senators personally but to concentrate on pleading his cause, and Wilson had followed this counsel. When the President returned to Washington in July, however, he had given to Taft no recognition of his generous aid.[11] Under pressure from Chairman Hays, who was trying to draw all elements of the Republican party into unanimity, the ex-President finally heeded the call of the political pack. On July 21 he sent a draft of five interpretations and one "reservation" to Hitchcock. Stating that there was no objection to showing the letter to the President, Taft expressed the hope that Wilson would continue to confer with the mild reservationists and would make more converts among Republicans. Though he said emphatically that were he a senator he would vote for the treaty as it was, he suggested that it would be good statesmanship to recognize the personal and political exigencies of the day. Taft's temporizing proposals were released for publication on July 23 by Will Hays.

Root and Lodge had put forward objections that, Wilson felt, France and Britain might not accept. And now it seemed to him that Taft was muddying the rapidly fading vision of international understanding by suggesting that a time limit be placed on the efficacy of Article X. As Roosevelt had foreseen before his death, the Republican policy of giving lip service to a league of nations was paying out: it had indeed enabled Taft to "get over" from his independent position to the party line. If Wilson had "dug in" before he left Paris, he was now completely mired in emotional revulsion toward men whom he could think of only as devils. "I have been talking to some more senators about the treaty," he told Hurley on July 31, and then he added: "They are endeavoring to humiliate me." The sad tone of his voice suggested that he realized now that he had been thrown back into a defensive position.

The seed of doubt had been sowed so well that the public was begin-

---

11 House had tried to foster the Wilson-Taft understanding by suggesting that David Hunter Miller, an expert on the Covenant, go to the United States in June to talk with Taft; but Wilson had not encouraged this.

Men in the State Department felt that Taft might have been held loyal to the Covenant as drawn if the President's pastoral ardor had been greater. "Taft would not have flopped," wrote William Phillips to Polk on July 26, "if the President had sent for him as soon as he had returned and patted him gently on the shoulder. How much easier it would make everything if the President would only put his arm on a few other shoulders."

ning to believe that reservations would do no harm and would be a wise safeguard of American rights. Lodge had reason to feel that, though the moderate men of his party might not support "amendments," he could get the majority vote that was needed to approve "reservations." The wily senator "had very much at heart," as he explained in a book six years later, the creation of "a situation where, if the acceptance of the treaty was defeated, the Democratic Party, and especially Mr. Wilson's friends, should be responsible for its defeat, and not the opponents of the treaty who were trying to pass it in a form safe for the United States." And so the articles that had been put together with such pain at Paris were hacked apart.

Debate raged back and forth on the floor of the Senate. The wolves nagged and snarled. Why did the President insist, they wanted to know, that the absurd language of Article XXI protected the Monroe Doctrine? Why was the British Empire given six votes in the League's Assembly, and four-fifths of the mandated territories? Soon it became clear to Wilson that no desire of his could command the votes of a majority of the Committee on Foreign Relations.

Rebuffed in one instance in which he had been led to expect cooperation—a request for the Committee's assent to American representation on the Reparations Commission—and incensed by the unfair attacks of his enemies, the President was in no mood to live up to an offer that he had made to the Senate on July 10. He had declared himself willing, then, to put all his information at the disposal of Lodge's committee at any time. But it was not until July 29 that, responding to a Lodge resolution, he formally transmitted to the Senate the treaty of guarantee with France that already had been published in full in the American press. And the protocol with Germany was not formally submitted until a day or two later. When the Senate went so far as to ask by what legal authority Wilson had acted at Paris and to demand the minutes that the members of the inner council had pledged not to reveal, the President drew back.[12]

Once more Woodrow Wilson was thrown into confusion as practical difficulties impinged upon his ideal. Asked for the successive drafts of the Covenant, for a full record of all discussion on the League, and for the text of an agreement on reparations signed by The Three, Wilson's faulty memory betrayed him, his moral indignation got the better of

[12] The spirit of the Committee on Foreign Relations did not encourage the President to cooperate. Having badgered him for the text of the treaty of guarantee, the senators lost interest once they had it, and pigeonholed it. As for the Treaty of Versailles, Lodge gave it a deliberate official "reading," intoning all 268 pages in his cultured accent, sometimes with several members of his committee as audience, often with only a clerk present, and, on the last day, in a roomful of empty chairs.

his reason, and he gave equivocal answers, as he had done under the cross-examination of Princeton trustees.[13]

The wolves took up other scents for a time. On July 31 Chandler P. Anderson, Root's protégé, had a revealing interview with the secretary of state. Lansing confessed his objections to the League, his preference for arbitration, but said as long as he was in office he could do nothing publicly in support of the opposition. Anderson sensed that he had considerable satisfaction because the result of their failure to follow his advice had gotten the Administration into its present difficulties.

Within a week the Foreign Relations Committee gave Lansing an opportunity to speak publicly. Getting little satisfaction from him, the committee questioned a series of witnesses in open hearings that extended from August into the autumn, hoping for evidence that might be turned against the President in press propaganda. Baruch, who was trying to make contact between the moderate senators in the two camps, was asked to testify on the economic clauses of the treaty. But Lodge, told of Baruch's efforts, said that no compromise was possible, that if the Democrats did not agree with the reservations that the Republicans had power to make, they ran the risk of having the whole Covenant thrown out of the treaty. Lodge was confident now that public feeling was growing rapidly against the Covenant.

In the Senate, on August 12, Lodge delivered a speech that was both learned and impassioned. From his knowledge of history he conjured up ill-fated efforts for an international concert of power. He criticized, one by one, the articles of the Covenant that seemed to him "most dangerous," showing how some of them, instead of preventing war, might induce it. He appealed again to George Washington's wisdom. "Let us beware how we palter with our independence," he warned. Alluding to "those who have tried to establish a monopoly of idealism" through "a murky Covenant," he proclaimed: "Our first ideal is our country, and we see her in the future, as in the past, giving service to all her people and to the world. Our ideal of the future is that she should continue to render that service of her own free will." It was one of the

---

13 It was obvious that publication of the minutes of acrimonious debates in the councils at Paris would not aid the cause of peace. Moreover, Wilson could not honorably release the records of the Peace Conference without permission from the other participants, the more so because on his last day at Paris he had pledged his colleagues to secrecy and because he already had refused to permit Clemenceau to submit to his Chamber of Deputies the minutes of the League of Nations Commission.

In replying to the Senate's demand for drafts of the Covenant, Wilson at first intended to say that he had withheld certain papers, such as the minutes of the League of Nations Commission, because they were in the hands of colleagues at Paris. But when Lansing suggested that the Foreign Relations Committee might ask him to send for copies and that it would be better to tell the whole truth—namely, that it was the policy of the Peace Conference to hold the papers in confidence—Wilson wrote to Lodge accordingly.

great orations of American history: veteran Marines who sat in the gallery were carried away by its eloquence and applause reverberated for several minutes.

Woodrow Wilson, standing in the west wing of the White House with Stockton Axson, put his hands in his coat pockets, spread his feet, and brought them together precisely. "Stock," he declared, "if I said what I thought about those fellows in Congress, it would take a piece of asbestos two inches thick to hold it." [14]

On July 30 four Republican moderates had told him frankly that the treaty could be ratified quickly, but only with reservations, and that if he did not approve them now, the Senate would force them through eventually. Senator Kellogg assured him that thirty-seven Republicans would support the treaty with moderate reservations; but Wilson did not seize this opportunity. On August 1 Republican Senator Watson, to whom Lodge had revealed his basic, long-range strategy, had come to the White House and told the President that there was only one way by which the United States could be taken into the League, and that was by acceptance of the Lodge reservations.

"The *Lodge* reservations!" the prophet fairly snorted. "Never! Never! I'll never consent to adopt any policy with which that impossible name is so prominently identified." The black fury on which Lodge depended was mounting.[15] Wilson's temper flared up, too, when Lansing appealed to him to lose no time in reaching agreement with Republican moderates. He felt that such a course would raise the very questions in other nations that he had determined to avoid. He would have his America go into the League boldly, intent upon serving, not counting only the cost and the gain.[16]

Finally Lodge closed in upon the President himself. Two days after his oration, he gave notice that the Foreign Relations Committee would take advantage of Wilson's offer to confer with them in a public session. The President accepted the challenge immediately, setting August 19 as the date.

Somehow Woodrow Wilson managed to overcome his fervent indignation and to welcome the Foreign Relations Committee on the morning of August 19 with a display of courtesy that seemed to the head usher almost obsequious in its extravagance. This was the first time in history when this body had come to the White House to interrogate the Presi-

---

[14] James Woodrow, who was present, to the writer.
[15] Watson, *As I Knew Them*, pp. 201–2.
[16] Wilson's position at this juncture was weakened by an ill-considered statement given by Senator Hitchcock to the press after a conference at the White House on Aug. 15. Even mild reservations would be "tremendously embarrassing" to the President, Hitchcock said, and therefore it was necessary "to remove absolutely any probability of the dotting of an 'i' or the crossing of a 't.' "

dent. It was an occasion of great moment, the press sensed, when the big iron gates were unlocked and the senators began to arrive, some in limousines, some on foot, Senator Borah walking and carrying a copy of the treaty under his arm. Reporters waited at desks that Tumulty had arranged in the corridors, poised to transmit every word to the American people. It had been agreed that nothing said should be treated as confidential. The senators brought their own stenographer, and the President had his.

In the East Room, with Lodge and Knox sitting almost within arm's length, Wilson presented a strong case for prompt action. Reading a message that he had prepared after receiving reports from Cabinet members on the necessity for peace, he cited certain examples of American industries that were being hurt by the halt in foreign trade. The United States could not compete for the markets of Central Europe, he said, if they did not act presently. "Every element of normal life amongst us depends upon and awaits the ratification of the treaty of peace."

Nothing stood in the way, he asserted, except doubts about the meaning and implication of certain articles of the Covenant. "I must frankly say," he confessed, "that I am unable to understand why such doubts should be entertained." Nevertheless, he respected the sincerity of some of the doubters. Summarizing the objections that had been raised at his previous conference with the committee in February, he said: "On my return to Paris all these matters were taken up again by the Commission on the League of Nations and every suggestion of the United States was accepted." He then commented on each of the articles in question, concentrating on Article X. Explaining carefully that the United States would be doubly protected against dictation by the League Council under Article X—once through the clause that he himself had cannily inserted to give veto power to each member of the council in disputes to which it was not a party, and again through the constitutional right of Congress to exercise independent judgment on matters of peace and war—he set forth his own views on reservations very clearly:

There can be no reasonable objection, to . . . interpretations accompanying the act of ratification provided they do not form a part of the formal ratification itself. Most of the interpretations which have been suggested to me embody what seems to me the plain meaning of the instrument itself. But if such interpretations should constitute a part of the formal resolution of ratification, long delays would be the inevitable consequence, inasmuch as all the many governments concerned would have to accept, in effect, the language of the Senate as the language of the treaty before ratification would be complete. . . . If the United States were to qualify the document in any way, more-

over, I am confident from what I know of the many conferences and debates
which accompanied the formulation of the treaty that our example would
immediately be followed in many quarters, in some instances with very
serious reservations, and that the meaning and operative force of the treaty
would presently be clouded from one end of its clauses to the other.

After the President had read his formal message, his adversaries
aimed the darts that had proved most piercing. When the prosecutors
delved for weaknesses in his position on reparations, on mandatories,
on Shantung, they got nothing but the truth, so far as Wilson remembered it and could tell it without betraying diplomatic confidences. He
admitted frankly that the Shantung settlement had not pleased him [17]
—an admission that was used by his enemies to make him appear the
victim of Japanese blackmail.

Unable to prove that the Covenant would bind its members too
strongly, the adversaries then took the opposite course and criticized the
document as "a rope of sand and not an effective tribunal which would
result in promoting peace." Senator Warren G. Harding asked timidly
what permanent value there was in the Covenant if the United States
had veto power, what would happen if nations shrugged off their
obligations as "only moral."

"Why, senator, it is surprising that that question should be asked.
There would be a repudiation of good conscience," the prophet replied
in mild reproof. ". . . I should think that was one of the most serious
things that could possibly happen . . . a moral obligation is of course
superior to a legal obligation and, if I may say so, has a greater binding
force . . . In every moral obligation there is an element of judgment.
In a legal obligation there is no element of judgment." He conceded
that it would be quite as moral for the United States to determine its
own obligations as for the Council of the League to do so. Actually, it
seemed to him that generally his people would concur in the moral
judgment of the world; and without specific assurance of concerted
action by all the responsible governments of the world, he warned, "you
have reached the situation which produced the German war." By joining in a "concert of judgment," he insisted, the United States "steadied
the whole world."

---

[17] Wilson had made strenuous efforts to hold Japan to her promises. On July 25, Lansing
had told the Japanese chargé that, unless Japan published her promises regarding Shantung
within four days, the President himself would do so. A day later Wilson asked his secretary of
state to tell the chargé that negotiations with China on the basis of the treaties of 1915 and 1918
would not be tolerated.
  The requested Japanese statement on Shantung was received by the State Department on
Aug. 1 and was forwarded by Lansing with a report that it was unsatisfactory and a recommendation that the President state his own version of the understanding at Paris. This Wilson
did; and Lansing released the statement to the press on Aug. 6.

Many observers felt that a "concert of judgment" was hard to attain and offered an unstable basis for peace. His adversaries were giving him, according to the New York *Tribune*, "probably the most searching inquiry ever directed, for a public record, at any President of the United States or any other head of a great power." Wilson had never been a strong witness under cross-examination; and now when they asked him specific questions about his knowledge of the European secret treaties, he made the mistake of trying to pluck answers from a nebula of vague memories.

Under the blunt questioning of William E. Borah, Wilson's sensitive mental processes broke down. When this opponent asked when the Administration had first learned of the secret agreements regarding Shantung, the President replied candidly: "I thought that Secretary Lansing had looked that up and told you . . . I heard of them only after reaching Paris."

Assuring the witness that Lansing had indeed agreed on this point, Borah asked about the secret agreements concerning Europe. Did these also first come to his knowledge at Paris?

"Yes," answered the President. Encouraged by the fact that his recollection as to Shantung had agreed with Lansing's record and had satisfied his doughty inquisitor, he ventured to depend further on his faulty memory.[18] "The whole series of understandings," he asserted, "was disclosed to me for the first time there."

Was the United States government informed before the Armistice of pacts like the Treaty of London? asked Hiram Johnson of California.

"No, sir." He had had no knowledge of the secret agreements, he declared, when he had proclaimed the Fourteen Points in January of 1918.

This testimony was incredible to senators who did not know Woodrow Wilson well, and it was amazing to the public. How could their president have been ignorant of vital international understandings that had been exposed by the Bolshevik government and published in newspapers? Wilson's lapse of memory now put him in a position as awkward as that into which he had fallen before the trustees of Princeton. Actually, he had had at least an awareness of the existence of many of the secret treaties before he went to Paris.[19]

[18] Apparently Wilson never came to realize the imperfection of his memory. In the autumn of 1920, filling out a self-evaluating questionnaire, he characterized his memory as "rather good."

[19] *See* pp. 130–31, 146, 307, 309, and Mary Reno Frear, "Did President Wilson Contradict Himself on the Secret Treaties?" *Current History*, June, 1929. Wilson's fragmentary and inaccurate recollections remained in his mind at least as late as Feb. 28, 1920, when he wrote to Polk: "They [the Allies] do not even attempt to justify the fact that they did not let even their associates, e.g., the United States, know anything about it [the Treaty of London], and that we discovered it, so to say, after we reached Paris."

But the inquisitors were not done with him yet. They read from the testimony that they had wrung from Lansing a few days before. The secretary of state had confessed that he had yielded at Paris, in deference to the President, his opinion that the Japanese would have joined the League even if the decision on Shantung had gone against them. Wilson's face reddened as if it had been slapped. But he responded suavely: "Well, my conclusion is different from his, sir." He had been "notified" at Paris to the contrary, he explained.

There was a volley of other queries to be parried; and finally Senator Fall tried twice to introduce a list of twenty questions. At this the President ventured at last to speak in self-defense. "I have no objection to sitting here all day," he said mildly. "Indeed, I have taken the liberty of having lunch prepared. But since your questions are written, perhaps you would leave them." The next day he wrote out replies to the queries, one by one.

A half hour after the usual lunch time, having sat continuously for three and a half hours, the conference was ready to break up. "You have been very considerate in putting your questions," Wilson said to them. "Will you gentlemen not come to lunch with me? It will be very delightful to have you." They went to the dining room, were well entertained, and emerged in good humor, declining to accept their host's offer to continue the quizzing into the afternoon.

And so the inquisition ended, and the committee recessed and subsequently adjourned. No votes were changed, but the pro-League minority was inspired by the patient elucidation to which they had listened. The independent press commended the tone and substance of Wilson's replies, an editorial in the *New York Times* declaring: ". . . the President has exhausted the resources of reasoning and exposition."

It seemed possible at this juncture that Lodge might overplay his hand. Root, impressed by accusations of obstructionism, cautioned the senator against overdoing the policy of reservation, and urged him to get into final form a proposition on which all Republicans could agree. There was no yielding, however, on the part of the enemy. Feeling that they had the President on the run, they nagged at his heels, making the most of Wilson's lapse of memory in regard to the secret treaties, asserting that under the Covenant the United States would have to guarantee the terms of pacts that her allies might conceal from her. A few days after the August conference at the White House, Brandegee was threatening to separate the League from the treaty. Knox invited the other irreconcilables to luncheon to lay plans for a speaking tour of the West to oppose ratification. Senators who wished only mild reservations swung to Borah's view that the reservations must be made a part of the treaty and be approved by other signatory nations.

On August 26 the Foreign Relations Committee adopted some fifty amendments that would keep Americans from membership on almost all of the international committees that were to carry out the treaty. At the end of the month, representatives of small nations who had not been invited to Paris or were dissatisfied with the treaty were given their "day in court"; and thus the divisive prejudices of hyphenated Americans were stimulated. Lodge read to his Republican brethren a list of British subjects who would hold influential positions in the League, citing this as evidence that the body would be a tool of the empire. Moreover, he wrote to the President to ask for the text of various collateral treaties and agreements that had been concluded in Europe. And he put through the Foreign Relations Committee, by a vote of 9 to 8, a motion that would reverse the decision of the Peace Conference on Shantung.

At the end of August Wilson wanted to rally his faltering Democrats, to get them to concentrate on a policy of keeping all reservations out of the formal act of ratification. On the President's behalf, Senator Pittman offered reservations similar to those proposed by Kellogg and other Republican moderates, but these were to be put in a separate instrument expressing America's understanding of the treaty. Forty-six Democrats were said to be ready to accept this proposal, but Lodge held the moderates of his party to the principle that reservations must be included in the resolution of ratification.

Though this effort failed, Wilson took one more step of great significance. Calling Hitchcock to him privately, the President gave him four interpretive reservations and told the Democratic leader to accept them if compelled to, to save the treaty. If Lodge knew that he was making this concession, he thought, that infidel would demand four times four reservations. Hence he swore Hitchcock to keep the authorship of his proposals secret. As a result other senators never knew whether they were "official," whether they might be used effectively as a rallying-point for true friends of the League.

The pattern of action that had brought about Woodrow Wilson's administrative failure at Princeton was taking shape again. He had once more allowed a difference of opinion to become a personal feud. The resources of political leadership that had served him so well when he had a Democratic Congress to whip, or a Peace Conference to master by moral prestige and economic power, were inadequate now. He was justifying House's estimate of him as a man with little talent for negotiating with adversaries whose power equaled his own. He had made it easy for sincere Republican advocates of the League to believe the charges of intransigence that his enemies were casting at him. By the end of August he regarded the Republican senators as a body of wicked men who wished to humiliate him and who could be driven to the Truth only by denunciation before their masters, the American people. In this state of mind, he was ready to court temporal failure as surely as when he had denounced Andrew West and appealed his case to the alumni of Princeton. He seldom laughed heartily now; but a note from Charles Hamlin of the Treasury amused him hugely. "Sometimes I wonder if Senator Lodge has any sense of humor," wrote this Massachusetts Democrat. "His frantic wailing about the danger of petty war and his willingness to reject the treaty and to plunge the nations into incessant strife reminds me of an ode of Martial:

> 'Poor Fannius who greatly feared to die
> Embraced the enemy he fain would fly.

> 'Strange contradiction, weary of strife
> He ceased to live for very love of live!

> 'With his own hand, he stops his vital breath:
> Madness extreme! To die for fear of death!' "

"It is most apposite. I shall be tempted to quote it to Mr. Lodge himself," was the response of the embattled President.

CHAPTER XVIII

LAST APPEAL TO THE PEOPLE

WHILE LODGE'S COMMITTEE was working its will upon the treaty of peace, Woodrow Wilson persisted in thinking about consolidating and extending the New Freedom. On the 8th of August—the same day on which young Franklin D. Roosevelt proposed half-holidays for federal departments and better coordination of their labor policies—the President delivered before Congress a challenging message that he had drafted in shorthand. In this Wilson suggested that the food control act be extended to years of peace and that its provisions against hoarding be applied to other essential commodities. He asked, too, for licensing legislation that would "secure competitive selling and prevent unconscionable profits," and he favored the passage of laws to control the issue of securities. He advocated, once again, full publicity as a cure for profiteering and made a moral appeal to producers and merchants to deal fairly with the people.

Voices had been challenging the weary prophet to take the lead in further advances toward social ideals. George Record, who more than any other man had stimulated him toward progressivism in New Jersey, had written a strong letter to him on March 25: "As conditions are now, your political fortunes are at a low ebb, your prestige impaired, and your party demoralized." The one big reason for this, Record's argument went on, was that Wilson had "ignored the one great issue" that was slowly coming to the front—"the question of economic democracy, abolition of privilege, and securing to men the full fruits of their labor or service." These questions seemed as essential to Record as slavery had been in the middle of the nineteenth century. These were the issues that caused wars; and the League of Nations, valuable as it was, would assure peace only to the extent that economic justice was established in the nations that were parties to it.

Record had proposed a definite program that the President might lay before the Congress to divert public attention from the investigations that the Republican majority seemed sure to undertake into the war record of their opponents. Tumulty had encouraged Record to send his advice to Wilson while the President was at Paris; and on June 4, after American radicals had put bombs in the mails of prominent officials and an unsuccessful attempt had been made on the life of Attorney General

Palmer, Tumulty himself drew up a comprehensive program for economic action and challenged Wilson, as leader of the liberal forces of the world, "to speak the truth about the whole situation and to propose a remedy." It was not until August 15, however, that the President wrote to Record to say that he had read his letter with "genuine interest and appreciation," that he realized "the gravity and pressing importance" of the things that were urged.

To get essential appropriations, Wilson had been forced to do what he had hoped to avoid—call the new Republican-controlled Congress into special session on May 19. In his message to them he had suggested that transportation and communication revert to private agencies, with governmental regulation to assure coordination. He gave primary attention to issues that had been raised by the unrest of American labor.[1]

On the homeward voyage from Europe, Wilson had had time to ponder on the ever-present problem of adjusting the shifting line between the "necessary functions" and "optional functions" of government. With violent action on the extreme left and clamor for *laissez faire* on the right, he was unwilling to yield to either. Chatting with Baruch, he said that the time soon would be ripe to apply a well-planned program for government control of such necessities as water, electricity, and rail transportation—things which seemed almost as vital to the national life as air for the lungs. Under the stress of bad feeling between capital and labor, the President was inclined to bring more of the nation's economy under a strong hand that would protect the public interest against sabotage from left or right.

In August the President was forced to act in a crisis precipitated by a strike of railway workers. On the 7th he told Walker D. Hines, McAdoo's successor as director-general, that the men must return to their jobs before their demands could be considered. On August 25 he

---

[1] As a sop to laborers who were agitating so strenuously for alcoholic beverages that Tumulty feared that Wilson might find himself "whipped into action," the secretary persuaded the President to allow him to insert in the May message to Congress a paragraph recommending that provision be made for the sale of light wines and beer until July 1, when the Prohibition Amendment, which had become part of the Constitution on Jan. 16, 1919, took effect. The question of what liquor should be deemed intoxicating was finally settled when the Volstead Act was passed over the President's veto on Oct. 28, 1919. Wilson vetoed the Act because he felt that it invaded the police power of the states and, being impossible to enforce, would lead to nefarious practices. Baruch, "The Democracy of W.W.," an address at Brown University, Oct. 25, 1950.

Legislation in the field of labor was chiefly the function of the states, Wilson told Congress, and at best could "go only a very little way in commanding what should be done." For solutions he looked to "common counsel and voluntary cooperation of capitalist, manager, and workman." However, he believed that some federal legislation was practical. Referring to the achievement of the eight-hour day and the improvement of conditions of work, he expressed faith in the ability of Congress to find a way of preventing child labor and to help in coordinating existing agencies for arbitration and in setting up new sources of information and advice. Though the League would provide international agencies, he put his trust in national action to get immediate results.

addressed an appeal directly to the representatives of the railway shop-men, who had called a strike to take effect on September 2. He went on to make it plain that he was in no mood to throw off the responsibility for economic justice that the federal government had been assuming under the compulsions of war. His pleas were effective. The leaders of the shopmen postponed their strike, and inflationary increases in wages were avoided.

Having called a truce in labor-management strife until settlements could be made "by peaceful and effective common counsel," Wilson hastened to act. At a meeting with his Cabinet September 2—the last in which the aging leader was to bring his full powers to bear upon the problems that his men put before him—a plan was discussed for airing the vexing issues of industrial relations. In a Labor Day message, the President already had announced that a conference would be called in which "authoritative representatives of labor and of those who direct labor will discuss fundamental means of bettering the whole relationship of capital and labor and putting the whole question of wages upon another footing."

The call for an industrial conference went out on September 3. It followed almost exactly the plan that had been proposed by Tumulty on June 4. Wilson asked that the proposed gathering be attended by fifteen representatives of labor, fifteen of management, and fifteen men to uphold the public interest.

The meeting of these minds, Wilson prophesied, would result in the devising of "methods by which we can speedily . . . obviate the wastefulness caused by the continued interruption of many of our important industrial enterprises by strikes and lockouts." The delegates were asked to gather in Washington on October 6.[2]

Lansing, who equated labor unrest with bolshevism, had been recommending blunderbuss tactics. He was alarmed when the President suggested that the tendency of labor to revolt against the economic order

[2] Before Oct. 6 arrived, the antipathy between labor and management was intensified by a steel strike and by a threat of a walkout of miners of bituminous coal. On Oct. 19, Secretary of the Interior Lane, representing the public at the Industrial Conference, notified the President that constructive action was impossible. "The elements have come to an impasse." Lane informed Wilson. "They cannot agree as to collective bargaining. The labor people say that unless we can recognize this right we can get nowhere. The employers say that they are not yet ready to give up dealing with their men as individuals. The public group is most liberal, siding strongly in this matter with the labor group . . . some of the delegates are angry and pretty nearly everyone disgusted . . . and so I turn to you for a word that will help."

By the time this plea reached him, the President's health had failed and he could give no leadership. He was barely able, on Oct. 22, to send to the Industrial Conference a letter of appeal that Lane had proposed. When this failed to bring about an understanding, Wilson, leaning upon advice from representatives of the public, called together a new group of men to continue the conference that, he hoped, would find a way of orderly negotiation within industries. The second National Industrial Conference, however, came to an end without fulfilling his hopes, although significant patterns of federal action were shaped.

sprang from an awakening consciousness of a right to share profits that was essentially just, that "industrial democracy" was fundamental to political democracy. There would be "violence and bloodshed," Lansing foresaw, "because the demands of labor will be beyond reason. Then the reformers who started the movement will too late attempt to check it . . . The President . . . will issue appeals but they will not be as effective as they were in the past."

A crisis that threatened law and order right at the President's gates gave point to Lansing's fears. Disturbed when the American Federation of Labor granted a charter to a policemen's union in the District of Columbia, Wilson advised the commissioners of the district to forbid affiliation with any national labor body. On Labor Day Wilson courageously appeared at a baseball game between the police and a Home Defense League and threw out the first ball; and the next day, with his approval, an ultimatum went out threatening the discharge of anyone who remained after September 7 in any organization affiliated with a labor union. A few weeks later, after the Boston police had struck, he reaffirmed his advice to the commissioners in the face of hostile senators.[3]

In the summer of 1919 messages from abroad reported disintegration and despair. The tensions of a state of war were wearing on the nerves of the peoples of the world and undermining the institutions that held them in political and economic balance. The emancipation that had been achieved in Central Europe would result only in chaos if the steadying hand of the League did not take hold soon.

He had an urgent cable from House who, working at London for the League, was embarrassed because senators were blocking the appoint-

[3] On Sept. 5 the District of Columbia police union secured an injunction against the commissioners. Wilson was attacked by Republican senators, who offered to back Commissioner Brownlow against the President. On Sept. 17 Brownlow received this wire from Wilson, who was then in California: "I am quite willing that you should tell the Senate Committee that my position in my conversation with you was exactly the same as I have expressed recently in my speeches here in the West, and, of course, I am as desirous as you are of dealing with the police force in the most just and generous way, but I think any association of the police force of the capital city, or any other great city, whose object is to bring pressure upon the public or the community, such as will endanger the public peace or embarrass the maintenance of good order, should in no case be countenanced or permitted." Eventually Congress raised the pay of the district police and forbade unionization.

Wilson held a Washington newspaper responsible for inciting riots on June 21 in order to embarrass the police commissioner. He hoped to see the owner indicted for this, and sent word to the district attorney to this effect. The President was determined that employers as well as labor organizations should not influence police action.

This issue was as black and white to Woodrow Wilson as to Governor Calvin Coolidge, who was making an equally strong—and more dramatic—stand against police unionization in Massachusetts. It was embarrassing to the prophet of world peace that there were threats of violence among his own flock. He was hurt, one evening at Keith's, to hear a stage joke that linked his name with an organization that had resorted to illegal use of force—the Industrial Workers of the World.

ment of Americans to commissions that had been set up under the treaty. The Colonel asked when the Senate might be expected to come to a vote. Would it help, he inquired, if the treaty were ratified soon by Britain, France, and Italy? And what about the meeting of the International Economic Council that was to convene on September 15?

On August 21 Wilson replied that he could not prophesy what would happen at Washington, that it would be a distinct advantage if the Allies would ratify the treaty as soon as possible. He asked Congress for funds to keep the American peace commission operating at Paris for another four months. He thought that the Council of the League ought not to organize until at least four powers and a majority of the minor nations had approved the treaty; otherwise the organization would lack moral authority and would resemble the Old World alliance that its opponents accused it of being.

All the domestic problems besetting the President were overshadowed by the categorical imperative of the moment. Above everything, international order must be restored. If the United States did not take the lead in adapting political forms to new conditions, she might have to defer to those who were more enterprising. It was imperative, Wilson felt, that his own people should not fulfill the cynical prophecy that had been made in the French press. They must not, after giving birth to the League of Nations, go home and shirk responsibility for its nurture.

It was inconceivable, to a mind disciplined by Presbyterianism, that responsible men could try to stop the process of inexorable universal law. And to a mind steeped in British tradition it was equally unbelievable that an Anglo-Saxon nation would not put aside considerations of party and, acting as a principal, ratify the Covenant to which its accredited agent had committed it.

At the end of August it seemed time to take direct action. He would "appeal to Caesar," he said. On the 25th, enraged by the effort of Lodge's committee to reverse the treaty's ruling on Shantung, he told Lansing that he would go to the people at once, that if the senators wanted war he'd "give them a bellyful." Instead of remaining at Washington and encouraging the compromise settlement to which Senators Kellogg and Pittman were close, he chose to risk everything on his power to sway his national congregation.

Wilson had long contemplated a speaking trip to educate his people.[4] He had been advised by the State Department that an appeal to the

[4] A letter written by Gilbert Close to his wife on March 22, 1919, records that the President was then thinking of making a trip to the Pacific coast very soon after he reached home. Tumulty had made out a tentative itinerary in June, an outline had been drawn up at Paris, in consultation with House on May 17, of what should be said in the speeches, and Wilson had spoken of his plans to newsmen just before leaving France.

country over the head of the Senate would offend and alienate senators who held moderate views about revising the Covenant. Lansing felt that industrial unrest made it unwise to go among the people. Moreover, some observers noted that most senators, having four to six years to serve, would not be swayed easily by sentiment stirred up among the voters. At the end of July he had deferred his trip until he could make more efforts to convert wavering legislators.

During August, voices came to the prophet from beyond the stuffy rooms of the capital. Leaders of his party who had toured the West had found the people eager for an oracle who would guide them to an honorable place in the world community. Moreover, House reported that there was "a noticeable sag" in popular interest in the League in Europe as well as in America and that the President's voice was eagerly awaited to remind the whole world how the new institution could serve it.

It was as inevitable that the prophet embark on this last educational crusade as it had been that his Uncle James Woodrow seize the challenge of his adversaries in order to educate his denomination in the truths of natural science. There was still a Woodrow down in old Columbia who understood this as none of the President's household could. "You have my deepest sympathy," wrote James Woodrow's daughter, "in your struggle with those wicked men in the Capitol. God grant you strength to stand firm, to refuse to consent to the slightest change, reservation, or interpretation of the Treaty . . . If you should yield finally and consent to the change of the obscurest jot or more obscure tittle a shout of triumph would go up from their ranks; for they would use their consent as a lever with which to overturn the whole beautiful fabric, and lay all the blame on you. Thank God, you see this more clearly than anyone else can, and I am sure He will give you strength to stand firm, and guard . . . your precious treasures." [5]

It was this niece of his proud little mother who had once reminded him of the Woodrow motto: *Audaci favet fortuna.* She was the historian of the clan, and now perhaps he could give her another great controversy to add to the annals. If only he could beat the enemy—"horse, foot, and dragoon"—as his father had vanquished the Kentucky theologians when he had "come down from the stilts of study." Maybe, after all, he could be worthy of his greatest heroes—his father and his Uncle James. To Tumulty he seemed an old man intent on dying with his face to the enemy. He said to a journalist who suggested that he was

---

[5] To W.W., Aug. 30, 1919. In acknowledgment of this advice from Marion Woodrow, Wilson wrote, on Sept. 11, 1919: "I want to express my deep appreciation of your generous attitude towards what I have been trying to do."

not well enough to undertake a speaking trip: "I don't care if I die the next minute after the treaty is ratified." He was not ready, yet, to pay the price that even moderate Republicans were asking. He would not allow reservations to be included in the resolution of ratification, and thus perhaps reopen the peace settlement to further attrition by Europeans. He would give his life, if necessary, to avoid this and to keep the faith that he had pledged in behalf of his country.

His Cabinet and his physician begged him not to toss his life away in what seemed to many a mad gesture. No doctor could be responsible for the outcome, Grayson warned.

Wilson listened attentively, then walked to a window and looked out pensively at the monument of George Washington. "I promised our soldiers," he said, "that it was a war to end wars; and if I do not do all in my power to put the treaty in effect, I will be a slacker and never able to look those boys in the eye. I must go." It was a last desperate resort. "If the treaty is not ratified by the Senate," he explained, "the war will have been fought in vain and the world will be thrown into chaos."

And so the prophet went forth to castigate his adversaries and preach in the clear, crisp air of the West. Perhaps there came back to him the lines that he and Miss Ellie Lou had quoted often:

> In front, the sun climbs slow, how slowly,
> But westward, look, the land is bright.

To meet the economic ills for which the timorous Lansing prescribed repression, the racial passions that had erupted in violence, the religious prejudices that were perverting the political thinking of citizens, he would boldly proclaim a living, cosmic gospel to which all Americans might constructively turn their emotions. Moreover, by regenerative preaching he might make whole again his own split self, might redeem his pledges and escape the political bankruptcy that had haunted him ever since the Congressional election of 1918. He could not forget that in 1912 his one-man evangelical crusade through the West had paid off in votes.

On September 3, then, after directing that all communications about the treaty from legislators should be forwarded to him in cipher, and after charging Senator Hitchcock to present four interpretive resolutions only if necessary—Wilson put on his straw hat, a blue coat, and white trousers, and went with his wife to the special train that was to take him west. He was in the high humor that always came to him under the stimulus of a campaign.

Every minute of the journey had been mapped out. One itinerary after another had been drawn up and discarded. All had provided for a few days of rest at the Grand Canyon; but when the President heard of this he would have none of it. It was to be a "business trip, pure and simple." He had brought along his indispensable typewriter but, he confessed to Tumulty as they boarded the train, he was "in a nice fix." He had not had time to prepare speeches and did not know when he would get time. "For the past weeks I have been suffering from daily headaches," he said, "but perhaps tonight's rest will make me fit for the work of tomorrow." He could but exist from one day to the next—hoping, praying, working late and early on his speeches, enduring the nagging headaches.

The next day, however, at Columbus—in Senator Harding's state of Ohio—he delivered an address that reassured those who wondered whether he still had his power to work magic with words. His heart was so full that he needed no script. He talked now as a teacher among friends. "I have for a long time chafed at the confinement of Washington," he confessed quite ingenuously. "I have for a long time wished to fulfill the purpose with which my heart was full when I returned to our beloved country, namely, to go out and report to my fellow countrymen concerning those affairs of the world which now need to be settled . . ."

Expressing astonishment at misinterpretations of the peace treaty, he explained its historical importance. The peacemakers had done a huge job, he insisted. So far as the scope of their authority permitted, they had rectified wrongs that had been a fertile source of wars. They had made advances in the history of the race that were of far more consequence than the temporary task of punishing Germany.

The next war, the prophet warned, would have to be paid for by American blood and American money. As the wealth and power of the United States grew, her interest in preventing war would exceed that of any other power. Hence it seemed inevitable that she be "trustee for the peace of the world." The people must decide whether they would be "ostriches or eagles," whether they would play their part in history "as members of the board of directors or as outside speculators." "It is acceptance of great world duties or scuttle now and come back afterwards," he prophesied.

To more than a thousand businessmen, at a Chamber of Commerce luncheon at St. Louis, he posed a practical question: "Who can say that our interests are separate from the interests of the rest of the world, commercially, industrially, financially?" But he did not like to argue on this level, he said, for "America was not founded to make money; it was founded to lead the world on the way to liberty."

In speech after speech, some from the rear platform of his car, some before vast assemblages, he proclaimed the contributions that had been made at Paris. He warmed to the challenge that his scholar's conscience had put upon him thirty years before. And yet, against the scholarly tradition that bade him keep pace with the latent thinking of his people and refrain from attempting, by what he had once called "the foolishness of preaching," to revolutionize the whole thought of a nation and of an epoch, against this monitoring force the prophetic impulses of his ancestors surged. The spiritual fires deep within him were fanned as he spoke to twelve thousand in St. Louis's Coliseum and was hailed as "Woodrow Wilson, Father of World Democracy." He challenged "some gentlemen" to show him how they would prove that, having gone into an enterprise, they were not "absolute, contemptible quitters" if they did not see the game through. He threatened that such men would be "gibbeted" in the annals of mankind. He remarked, too, that he sometimes wished that "both parties might be smothered in their own gas."

This "peacemaker" was talking like Andrew Johnson who, according to Wilson the historian, uttered "violent speeches which swelled the number of his radical opponents as rapidly as the leaders of the Congressional majority could have desired." By setting himself up in a righteous pulpit above the folks of the West, Wilson opened himself to suspicions of his motives. *Harvey's Weekly* portrayed him as a "whirling dervish" taking a "hippodroming excursion" at the expense of the taxpayers. It was whispered that he was beginning to campaign for a third term in the Presidency.

Thoughtful proponents of the League saw the danger and from Washington advised the President that he was stiffening the opposition, that he must not allow political controversy to divert him from direct, positive explanation of the peace treaty. Accepting the warning, Wilson typed on a single sheet a list of topics to be interpreted. As he progressed westward he spoke on matters that he had previously brushed aside as "hypothetical questions" in which the people were not interested. He dealt now more explicitly with the controversial clauses of the Covenant. Moreover, he paid heed to the special concerns of the various audiences.

As he went into the Northwest, where labor agitation had been violent, he departed from his main theme to speak of industrial conciliation and to hold up the example of "pitiful Russia." A "lovable people," he explained, had "come under the terror of the power of men whom nobody knows how to find . . ." The President paused for a moment in his pleas for the peace treaty and spoke out to strengthen the arm of the law in American cities. The principles that he held dearest, indeed his very faith in America's ability to give order to the world, were shaken by the Boston strike. The next day, in Idaho, he came back to this "intolerable crime against civilization."

The prophet was making converts in all walks of life. The constituencies of irreconcilable senators turned out to honor him in the stimulating air of the Northwest.

At Seattle, however, a sinister plot was hatching. There had been serious strikes in the city, and representatives of the I.W.W. had prepared to call on Wilson and petition for the release of political prisoners; but the city government announced that the radical leaders would not be allowed to "annoy" the President. The presidential party drove through dense crowds of citizens whose fanatical cheers drowned out the music of the bands. Then, suddenly, there were five long blocks of awesome silence and sidewalks packed with thousands of men in grimy overalls, the sleeves of their work-shirts rolled up above muscles that bulged from arms folded across their chests. Among these demonstrators were ex-soldiers wearing overseas caps and others displaying hatbands that read: "Release Political Prisoners!" With their women beside them, they stood still and silent. Not a sound, not a move. Not even a glance at the President, for they had been instructed to look past him. It seemed, suddenly, as if the light of the sun had gone out.

Woodrow Wilson had been standing in his automobile, bowing and smiling. Suddenly his face went white. His jaw sagged and the lines in his countenance deepened. He looked limp and hunched up, and the hand holding his tall hat hung at his side. But he remained standing in his swaying car, and after the five awful blocks had been passed and people began to cheer again he waved his hand and smiled wanly.

Here was a patent distemper in the body politic, to be faced with sympathy and courage. The next morning, though it was Sunday, Wilson requested a delegation of labor leaders to make the call upon him that the fearsome city fathers had forbidden. He received these outcasts while naval officers were kept waiting in the lobby of the hotel. He was determined that all citizens should have access to their president. He could not forget that he had said in a speech only a few days before: "Revolutions come from the long suppression of the human spirit. Revolutions come because men know that they have rights and that they are disregarded."

The labor delegates found him at his rooms in the afternoon, standing by a long, heavy table, holding on to its edge, looking very old. The hand that he gave to them felt dry. There were two ex-soldiers in the group and he could scarcely summon courage to meet their eyes. The leader of the delegation cleared his throat but could not get a word out, so he merely offered the petition to the President.

Wilson took it with a hand that shook until he steadied it by gripping the lapel of his coat. In a voice that sounded strained he said that he would read their plea immediately, that he had been displeased by the decision of the local authorities to keep them away from him and deny their right of petition.

The spokesman managed to mutter a few words. He had planned to refer to some of his comrades as "ex-soldiers and ex-sailors who have served in the war to make the world safe for democracy." But he had forgotten this line, and later he was glad that he had. The breaking man before him might not have been able to bear it. During the interview Wilson's eyes closed and he looked even more ghastly. His face twitched. When the men left, he followed them for a few steps, then stopped in the middle of the high-ceiling room, with bowed head.[6]

Only those close to him knew that in Montana the hot, dry air had brought on an asthmatic affliction. Headaches clamped down upon him and made the faces of his audiences blur and multiply. Tobacco smoke in halls in which he spoke made him suffer. Dr. Grayson sat up at night to spray his throat, fed him liquids and predigested foods. At Seattle, worn as he was, he spoke three times in one day. When he reviewed the Pacific fleet, his launch collided with another boat, listed badly, and shipped a little water. A secret service man leaped to his side; but the President dismissed the danger with a smile. That night he sat with Edith Wilson in a little roof garden of their hotel and gazed in awe at the lights of the Pacific fleet, stretching out to sight's end. When he retired he did not sleep, and the next day a headache beset him, so that when he tried to dictate he sat with his head resting on the back of a chair.

A day later, as the presidential party sought relaxation in motoring, one of the automobiles crashed and a popular newsman was killed and another injured. As soon as Wilson heard of this he went to the bedside of the surviving victim and arranged that he be given a drawing room on the party's train. Ever since leaving Washington he had shown concern for the comfort and morale of his comrades of the road, sharing the vicissitudes of travel with many a good story and never a complaint. But when the journalists urged him to speak flatteringly, in each city, of local units that had served conspicuously in the war, he would have none of it. When they spoke of the effectiveness of "sob stuff," the phrase sank into the Covenanter like a knife and there was a freezing silence. And when a newsman watched him composing on his typewriter, he remarked pointedly that he could do much better work when no one was looking on.

[6] Louis Adamic, "The 'Assassin' of Wilson," *American Mercury*, XXI (October 1930), 82.

Tumulty was standing by valiantly, working up little memoranda that would focus the Chief's efforts upon salient, nonpartisan arguments, and adducing quotations from Republican statesmen that acknowledged that the age of isolation was past and advocated the idea of a League of Nations. The ebullient secretary, who through the years had plagued the President with many a "dose" of advice, had so well mastered the trend of affairs, during Wilson's absence at Paris, that his political sense was rising toward the level of statesmanship.

At Portland, on September 15, journalists brought word that William Bullitt, whose plan for peace with Russia had not been accepted by Wilson at Paris, had given damaging testimony before the Committee on Foreign Relations. At a session at which no Democratic senators were present to check him, this frustrated young man had asserted that he had been urged to publish a report on his Moscow venture by Lloyd George and by some of the American commissioners, that "it was only Mr. Wilson" who stood in the way. The Senate committee had struck pay dirt. When the testimony was concluded, Lodge expressed his thanks warmly.

The *Nation,* for which Wilson had privately expressed "utter contempt," now reopened its fire on the President. The *New Republic* also took the "perfectabilitarian" view. In articles that were made a part of the Senate's record, the treaty was denounced as wicked and its acceptance by Americans as "a violation of faith." The ideal concept that Wilson had set forth in the first of the Fourteen Points and later had found impractical—"diplomacy shall proceed always frankly and in the public view"—was thrown back in his teeth.

The worst shock came, however, when Bullitt exposed the full measure of the infidelity of the secretary of state. He asserted that Lansing had said privately at Paris, on May 19, that the League was useless, that the great powers had simply arranged the world to suit themselves, that if only the senators could understand what the treaty meant and if the American people could really understand it, it would unquestionably be defeated.

At this exposure of his defection from the faith, the secretary of state took alarm and hastened to telegraph a palliating version of the May interview with Bullitt. Lansing resorted to pious denunciation of his accuser, whom he called "a disloyal young man who is seeking notoriety at the expense of all honorable men."

Ah, yes, Brutus was an "honorable man." The pastoral insight that had been able to perceive House's essential loyalty in spite of the Colonel's indiscretions saw clearly where the truth of this matter lay. Wilson had surmised that Lansing was undermining and upsetting morale.

And now here was verification of everything that he had suspected. "Think of it!" he exploded to Tumulty. "This from a man whom I raised from the level of a subordinate to the great office of secretary of state of the United States."

Woodrow Wilson went down into California, then, in a mood approaching despair; and yet there was hope in the increasing ardor of the people for his message. It sometimes seemed, as he gave four addresses in the bay cities within two days, that they would smother him with flowers, glut him with feasts, suffocate him with tobacco smoke, wear him down with their long parades and blaring bands, talk him to insanity in conferences and interviews, badger him to death with questions and protests directed against the British Empire and the Japanese. When he began to speak at the civic auditorium, his voice was drowned by heckling from little hostile groups, and at the end there was only a polite patter of palms; but another audience, composed of women, cheered him heartily. Coming to his rooms from the din of admirers who milled around him, he dropped into a chair and groaned: "They mean so well—but they are killing me!"

Yet in public he yielded not at all to weariness of the flesh, nor to inner voices of discouragement that were rending his soul. An ominous message from Washington reported that the "mild reservationists" had worked out a program of changes in the treaty that had Lodge's approval.[7] Nevertheless, the President said to a San Francisco audience: "I am arguing the matter only because I am a very patient man. I have not the slightest doubt as to what the result is going to be."

Popular excitement reached its highest pitch at San Diego, where Wilson spoke through an amplifier to an audience of fifty thousand in a stadium. The next day he talked at Los Angeles, and many of the effervescent, progressive people of the region were converted. The toll of the effort was so severe, however, that the President was in need more than ever of a restful Sabbath. On Sunday morning, taking a few hours from "business" for the first time on the trip, he drove out to a humble bungalow on an unfrequented street to call on a girlhood friend of Miss Ellie Lou—a woman whose lot in life had been hard and to whom Ellen Wilson had ministered until her own death. Joe Tumulty loved him that day for the purity and simplicity of his motives, though the secretary was vexed because the act of kindness was not capitalized by a "tip-off" to reporters and photographers.

[7] The day after the speech at San Francisco, Vance McCormick wired that the reservations on which the moderates were working with Lodge would make United States action under Article X or United States acceptance of a mandate dependent "in any particular case" upon action by Congress. Wilson wired to Lansing that McCormick's information should be conveyed to Senator Hitchcock with advice that the President would regard any such reservations "as a practical rejection of the Covenant."

Having performed this mission for Miss Ellie Lou, Woodrow Wilson returned to his hotel. He had asked his old friend Mary Allen Hulbert to lunch with him and to meet his second wife. Edith Wilson and Dr. Grayson received the guest warmly; and soon the President came in, animated at the prospect of a visit with one who had often brought him release from his cares. He looked less worn than Mary Hulbert had expected, and she commented on his appearance. "Oddly enough," he replied, "I do not feel well. I feel as if all those things which I have succeeded in escaping have fallen upon me." After luncheon they went into another room, where they were interrupted now and then by the calls of delegations whom the President felt he must see—"Converts, sir," Grayson whispered as he announced them.

From each interruption Wilson came back to chat with his old playmate. The material world had dealt as harshly with his vision of feminine charm as with his dreams of human security. The blooming, vivacious Mary Peck was still sweet-faced, but faded and careworn. She had been slightly lamed by an accident. To earn bread and butter, she and her son had tried their hands at many things: ranching, writing stories, selling books, movie acting. And all the while she had been persecuted by enemies of Woodrow Wilson who hoped to find immorality in her relationship with the President. They had shadowed her, insinuated, threatened, cajoled, ransacked her rooms. At his pastoral urging, every detail of her story came out. When she told him of traducers who had claimed to have support from members of his Cabinet, he murmured: "So-and-so did that? Why did So-and-so do that?" More dirt, more disloyalty!

He laughed over the ludicrous tales of their iniquity that gossips had been circulating for years. In his overwrought condition, however, he blamed himself for her plight. "God," he cried out at last, "to think that you should have suffered because of me!" As they were about to part he laid his hand on his wife's shoulder and said: "Isn't there something we can do?" Edith Wilson went out of the room for a moment, and they were alone. He repeated the practical question that he had asked his wife; but, chin up, Mary Hulbert replied that she would take care of herself, but perhaps he might help her son. As they paced slowly down the hall, she recited lines that were familiar to them:

> "With all my will, but much against my heart,
>   We two now part."

From Los Angeles the prophet turned eastward. In the Sierras he suffered from gas fumes in the tunnels, the acrid smoke of forest fires, and sudden changes of altitude. Crossing the desert, he met suffocating heat and dust; and the nervous twitching in his face that had been so marked at Paris became continuous. At this juncture Congress was adding insult by introducing a resolution for an inquiry into an alleged "shower of gifts" received by the Wilsons in Europe.

Speaking in the tabernacle of the Mormons, at Salt Lake City, he read the reservation to Article X that had been proposed by "mild reservationists" and approved by Lodge. This, he asserted, would be a refusal on the part of the United States to carry the same responsibility that other League members assumed. Hence it would be a rejection of the treaty.

The auditorium was packed, and the air grew stale and oppressive. Edith Wilson gave him a handkerchief soaked in lavender salts, and somehow he got through an ordeal that lasted for two hours. Once he lost control of his nerves and replied tartly to a heckler. Tumulty told him afterward that in his speech he failed to land a "punch." He left the hall soaked with perspiration; and when he changed to dry clothes, they were soon wet through. The next day, at Cheyenne, he was too exhausted to deny that he was ill.

Yet he could not be persuaded to undergo a week's rest. There were still eight speeches left on the schedule, and he refused the continuing pleas of wife and doctor for a brief respite. "No," he said. "I have caught the imagination of the people." Sensing his wife's deep concern, he tried to cheer her. "This will soon be over, and when we get back to Washington I promise you I will take a holiday."

The sympathy and admiration of the newsmen on his train had increased almost to the point of veneration. Whether he would be able to complete the tour was a sporting question among them. But he assured them that he could finish. "My constitution may be exhausted," he jested, "but I ought to get along for a good while on my bylaws."

He reached Denver late at night and was greeted by a lady whom he had loved in idyllic days—his Cousin Harriet Woodrow, now Mrs. Welles. They chatted at his hotel until after midnight. He was up early, though, and at nine o'clock began a parade between lines of cheering school children to the state capitol, where he spoke outdoors to a huge gathering. Then on to the auditorium in which he had made his great address on the English Bible. Here the aging prophet faced a sympathetic audience, but had to contend with faulty acoustics.

He went on for an afternoon program at Pueblo, where in 1911 he had walked from the station to the hotel carrying his own bag. He wished now that he might be let alone as he had been then. He objected petulantly when told that he was expected to appear at the fair grounds before going to the city hall to speak; but since citizens had bought tickets with the understanding that they would see him, he agreed to compromise by riding in his car past the grandstand.

"This will have to be a short speech," he said in a new auditorium that he took a part in dedicating. And in an aside to the newsmen: "Aren't you fellows getting pretty sick of this?" But soon his spirit transcended the bonds of his protesting body, and the emotional taps that Tumulty had opened for him were allowed to run freely. He harked back to the moving scene at the cemetery outside Paris where he had spoken over the graves of American soldiers on Memorial Day. If only the opponents of the treaty could visit such a spot! Tears came into his own eyes, and his voice seemed to lose its sonority. "I wish," he said, "that they could feel the moral obligation that rests upon us not to go back on those boys, but to see the thing through . . . to the end and make good the redemption of the world. For nothing less depends upon this decision, nothing less than the liberation and salvation of the world." [8]

There was moisture even in the eyes of newsmen who had heard him many times. To Tumulty he seemed a great organist playing expertly upon a keyboard of emotions. Finally he came to his valedictory, the last words that he was ever to speak face to face with a large assemblage of his people. "Now that the mists of this great question have cleared away, I believe that men will see the truth, eye to eye and face to face. There is one thing that the American people always rise to and extend their hand to, and that is the truth of justice and of liberty and of peace. We have accepted that truth and we are going to be led by it, and it is going to lead us, and through us the world, out into pastures of quietness and peace such as the world never dreamed of before."

The hurrahs of the audience at Pueblo were still ringing in his ears when the racking pains that had pursued him for ten days settled upon his head. He had asked several times whether he could not get some exercise, and now Dr. Grayson prescribed a walk in the crisp mountain air. When the train stopped for a change of locomotives, the Wilsons strolled on a white, dusty road, stopping on a wooden bridge and looking pensively into the stream beneath. Urged by the doctor to exert himself, the ailing man ran until he was winded, and color came into his face.

---

[8] Wilson never fully exploited a line of argument that General Bliss had suggested to him before he left Paris: that in his speeches he dramatize the horrors of future wars. According to Bliss, Wilson believed that the next war, if it came, would be no worse than that just concluded, for he thought that noxious gases and other barbarities would be effectively outlawed. At Denver, however, Wilson alluded to this theme in a paragraph in which he said: "What the Germans used were toys compared to what would be used in the next war."

He returned to the train to eat some dinner, and remarked that his head bothered him less than it had for days. But late in the evening he knocked at his wife's door and said that he was in great distress.

She found him sitting on the edge of his bed, his tortured head resting on the back of a chair. Dr. Grayson was summoned but could do nothing to give relief. He observed a curious drooping at the left side of the President's mouth, and a trace of saliva trickled out. The patient's nervous controls were shattered. He could not recline comfortably on the pillows that were provided, felt that he must move about, got up and dressed. Then followed long hours of agony, and a harrowing vigil for Grayson like that of the April night at Paris. It was another acute episode in the relentless progress of arteriosclerosis.

At five in the morning, while he sat upright on a hard seat, the tortured head drooped and sleep came. His wife sat opposite; and his ghastly face told her that she now, alone, would have to bear responsibilities that she had shared with him. She felt that henceforth she must protect him from the public. Moreover, she must shield him from himself; she must never let him know how ill he really was.

Soon after seven he appeared, shaved and dressed but piteously sick. Immediately they began to urge him to end the speaking trip then and there. It might be fatal to continue, Grayson warned. His wife and doctor decided that it was their duty to be firm, no matter what anguish of soul their decision might cause. He accepted their verdict as a decree of fate and took up a cross that he was to bear for four years without a murmur of self-pity. But he was to feel, in future years, that it would have benefited his great cause if only he could have died that night.

When the train slowed down near Wichita, and Tumulty went out to tell a welcoming committee that the President was unable to meet them, Wilson realized the finality of the decision that had been made for him. He sent messages to his daughters so that they would not be unduly alarmed by press reports of his condition; and he dictated a statement to the people of Wichita, telling them of his regret at disappointing them.

With shades drawn against the stares of the curious, the train roared on to Washington. For two days and two uncomfortable nights the Wilsons sat in the confinement of their car, he sitting disconsolate and contemplating the ruins of his ambitions, brooding upon the disloyalty of Lansing and the others, she knitting and trying to divert him with small talk.

He mulled over reports from Europe that had been distressing him for several days. Racked by pain and unable to digest anything but liquids, he approved Polk's intention to send strong American naval reinforcements to the Adriatic as quickly as possible, as an expression of disapproval of Italian demands for more concessions.[9]

In his last mission to the American people, the spirit of the old Covenanter had defied the bounds of his mortality, had driven him through thirty-four addresses and scores of interviews, parades, and rear-platform talks within twenty-two days. Bands had waked him up and bands had played him to bed, and the crowds had been vociferous enough to encourage him to plan to extend his tour to New England. He had told the people what he thought they ought to know. He had given a picture of the whole Covenant of the League, to prevent the basing of a national decision on a line, a clause, or only on one or two of the twenty-six articles. He had preached a gospel of arbitration as opposed to armament, of playing-the-game against sulking-on-the-bench. He had explained the veto power that the Senate would hold against illegitimate drafts upon America's strength to settle controversies beyond the scope of her interests; and as for involvement in a dispute to which the United States was a party from the beginning, he reminded his people that in such a case they would be "in the scrap anyway." His life-long scorn of special privileges, unequal opportunities, and secret arrangements had been burned into the minds of his Western audiences.

Finally, he had delivered to his age the warning that was to establish his place securely among the major prophets of his century: "I can predict with absolute certainty that within another generation there will be another world war if the nations of the world do not concert the method by which to prevent it." And in that struggle, he prophesied, "not a few hundred thousand fine men from America will have to die, but as many millions as are necessary to accomplish the final freedom of the world."

However, the effect of his efforts upon the voting of the senators was insignificant, perhaps even negative. His eloquence had intensified the hatred of his enemies and roused resentment among some who, by a laying on of hands, might have been persuaded to accept the interpretative amendments that he had given secretly to Hitchcock. Against the venom of personal hate that had been spewed out against him, Wilson

---

[9] Frank Polk, now head of the American Commission at Paris, had been conferring with Lloyd George and Clemenceau about a solution of the Adriatic question, which had become acute once more in September when swashbuckling Italians squatted in Fiume. Polk had worked out a solution that the President had accepted. But Lloyd George and Clemenceau, who wanted quick ratification of the treaty by Italy because the League Council could not act on certain questions vital to France and Great Britain until the treaty was ratified by three powers, were now supporting an Italian demand for more concessions.

At news of this yielding, Wilson had grown indignant. It seemed to him that d'Annunzio was "behaving like an ass," that everyone was failing him—Lloyd George, Clemenceau, Orlando —all of them!

knew that he was helpless. "If I had nothing to do with the League of Nations it would go through . . ." he had confessed to Mary Hulbert.

The broken man returned to Washington on a Sunday morning. At the station his daughter Margaret ran down the platform to greet him. He insisted on walking to his automobile, and smiled and nodded to a group of soldiers who cheered him. For four days he made spasmodic efforts at a normal life. He saw movies in the White House, and went out motoring huddled in an overcoat. But the servants remarked that the President was not the same jaunty man whom they had known. He was more peaked and florid and he kept much to his own apartment.

He was encouraged by a report that Clemenceau, speaking in the Chamber of Deputies, had referred to him with respect and had urged the American Senate to ratify the Covenant. Moreover, on the second day after his return to Washington, Tumulty cheered the Chief with news that sentiment on Capitol Hill was improving.

On October 1, after evening movies and before retiring, the President felt well enough to read a chapter from the Bible as he had been wont to do during the war. His voice was strong. But after he wound his watch he forgot to take it to his bedroom, and this aberration worried him.

When he awoke in the morning his left hand had no feeling in it, and he had to ask for help in getting to the bathroom. He moved with spasms of pain. Edith Wilson, alarmed, went to the telephone to call Dr. Grayson. Returning, she found her husband on the floor. The voice that had commanded the thought of millions was barely able to whisper to ask for a drink of water. He stirred a little and his wife managed to slip a pillow under his head. His faithful doctor came hurrying, and together they lifted him to the big bed that once had been Abraham Lincoln's. There he lay, looking as if he were dead, while his family rallied to give him comfort and hope, and specialists came to consult. The verdict was that a thrombosis—a clot in a blood vessel—had impaired the control of the brain over a side of the body that already had been weakened by neuritis. The President's left arm and leg were helpless. Though there had been no lesion, there was danger of one. If the clot was not absorbed by nature, it might impair the heart's action and cause death.

CHAPTER XIX

Pulling Down the Temple

For days it was touch and go, and for weeks it seemed possible that a Wilson prophecy might be fulfilled straightway—the prediction that he had made eight years before, that if ever he entered the White House he would not come out alive.

The old mansion became a hospital, as a procession of doctors and nurses visited the sickroom, bringing medical apparatus of many kinds. Cary Grayson stayed constantly at his patient's side through six nights of vigil. After two weeks of precarious progress, a stricture of the bladder set back recovery. Consulting specialists recommended surgery; but the two old Virginians who knew him better—Dr. Grayson and Edith Wilson—felt that an operation would kill him and that nature could cure the abnormality if given a chance. Their faith in rest and quiet was justified, and with the aid of external treatment the crisis passed. For the next six months, however, the sick man was pitifully dependent, and his wife and daughter Margaret kept alternate watches over him.

Four years had gone by since this mortal had had an adequate vacation. Now he must pay the price for the pace at which he had driven himself through the years of crisis. His nerves were raw, and any excitement was torture to them. On the second day after the thrombosis he was able to take a little nourishment; after a week he even had some appetite, took an interest in pending affairs of state, and listened to his wife's reading.

The sick man himself never doubted that he would recover. He was eager to know nature's methods of healing and to cooperate as best he could. He was considerate of those near his bedside, tried to cheer them with jests. When a doctor tapped him he asked: "Why are you knocking? I am at home." And when they took a sample of his blood he said, "That's what the Senate has been trying to do to me." He seemed, to Grayson, as game a patient as the doctor had ever known.

His thought still burned clearly, but feebly as a flickering candle. By the end of October he was able to read papers that were brought to him when his powers rallied a little. Charles Swem, the brilliant young stenographer who had served him since the 1912 campaign and who was trusted to send off dictated statements without checking by the

President, came now to his bedside to take dictation—at first once a week, then more frequently. The invalid would start a letter; then, articulating more and more indistinctly and finally losing the thread of his thought, he would stare into space. Minutes later, reminded that he had been dictating, he would pick up the thread and go on as if there had been no lapse. When they brought a letter to him for signing, they put a pencil in his hand and steadied and pointed it so that he could scrawl out a poor imitation of his copper-plate signature. By November he was dictating as many as three or four letters a day with characteristic perfection.

The psychological ravages of arteriosclerosis were evident as his emotions swung in an arc that was wide and eccentric. There were vast expansions of charity, and contractions that shut his heart implacably against the sinners in the Senate. He wept too easily, and was no longer able to probe a subject deeply or to go "round the clock" in the judicial way that had once been habitual. This man who always had prided himself on earning his pay by being "first-rate" now was unable to grapple rationally with the problems raised by his own disability. His acute creative impulses remained and, thwarted by lack of strength, threw him into moods of frustration. He could not face up squarely to the fact that he, a great moral leader, was not doing his own job from day to day. He even made those around him promise not to reveal his condition to the public. Indeed, he connived with them to conceal his infirmities.

From the secluded sickroom little news of the President's condition seeped out to the people. To ensure absolute quiet, it was necessary to bar all casual visitors from the White House and its grounds. Those nearest to the invalid felt that it would be a betrayal of trust to reveal the truth about the prophet of Truth. To Edith Wilson the suffering man was first of all her husband and her hero; to Admiral Grayson he was a commander in chief whose orders must be obeyed, and also a patient whose health was of prime importance. It was clear to them that any effort to remove the incapacitated President from the White House would disturb his emotions to a degree that might be fatal. The passing weeks brought gradual improvement, and it seemed quite possible that he would again be able to perform the routine of office. The bulletins of Grayson and Tumulty were written in vague generalities and at every opportunity stressed the patient's progress.

This secretive policy had an unfortunate effect on public opinion. Once again—this time, mercifully, without his knowledge—Woodrow Wilson was the victim of a spate of rumors. It was gossiped that he had venereal disease, even that he was insane. Most cutting of the canards, however, was the insinuation that the President was not really ill, but merely sulking in his chamber because he had learned on the western trip that his people did not agree with him about the peace treaty. He himself had become a ruler whom "nobody knew how to find." Loyal friends noted the vicious gossip and wished that it might be stopped by a recital of the truth.

For a while the executive arm of the government seemed to share the paralysis of its chief. Letters sent to the sickroom for the President's signature did not come back; even emergency communications vanished. No pardons were signed, no proclamations issued, and bills were allowed to become law without the President's signature.

As the invalid's interest in affairs of state returned, Tumulty could refer important matters to him through Edith Wilson, who with Dr. Grayson worked out a policy intended to conserve both the strength of their patient and the interests of the nation. Problems for the President were to be presented in writing, and as succinctly as possible. The documents that came were to be screened by Edith Wilson, whose work on "The Drawer" during the last four years had given her insight into the processes of the executive office. The invalid was to be consulted only on those matters that seemed to his wife likely to interest him and unlikely to irritate him.

Under this regimen, the mind that Woodrow Wilson had "discovered" at college and that had been applied to the greatest problems of the age now worked feebly and without adequate knowledge. The failure of resiliency and sensibility that advisers had noted after the severe illness at Paris was now patent. His thoughts ran like a shrunken brook in autumn, clear as ever, but trickling only in the deepest channels. The "single tracks" had become deep ruts, and though he could still perceive their direction he could scarcely see over the sides.

All through October, Joe Tumulty parried questions about his chief's health, and officials of the government had no direct evidence of the President's competence except a few notes bearing a scraggly signature. The secretary, however, conceived it his duty to give an inkling of the truth to the vice-president and to members of the Cabinet of whose discretion he felt sure.

Most of these men acquiesced in the policy that had been laid down by the consulting doctors. However, Lansing felt that, if the work of the Administration was to go on at all, it might be necessary for Vice-President Marshall to act as chief executive. When it was learned that the Republican majority in the House of Representatives was proposing a resolution for an investigation of Wilson's condition with a view to enabling Vice-President Marshall to act for him, Grayson was informed that the Cabinet should be convened to block such a move. Consulting with Tumulty, therefore, the physician and the secretary of state arranged for a meeting on October 6, only four days after the thrombosis.

When the men assembled, Lansing quoted from the Constitution: "In case of the removal of the President from office, or of his death, resignation, or inability to discharge the powers and duties of the said office, the same shall devolve on the Vice-President." Tumulty, who was summoned to the meeting, repeated what he had told Lansing previously, that he would take no part in certifying to the President's disability. The Irish in him flared up, and other stanch supporters of Wilson were hardly able to suppress their indignation at Lansing's suggestion.

The Cabinet called in Grayson for advice, and he told them that Wilson's mind was clear, that he was suffering from nervous breakdown, indigestion, and a depleted system. The scales might tip either way, the doctor said, and excitement by matters of business would press them the wrong way; in fact, he reported, the President already had been irritated by a rumor that his associates were to convene without a call from him. "The President asked me what the Cabinet wanted with me and by what authority it was meeting," said Grayson, with a gleam in his eye that suggested the displeasure of the stricken, egocentric prophet. As for himself, the doctor would have no part in a verdict of disability.

Secretary Baker asked Grayson to say to the President that they had met primarily to extend sympathy, to get information about him, and to consider departmental business that had been held up since the last meeting, a month earlier. The doctor took this message to his patient and, with Wilson's knowledge, the Cabinet held other informal meetings through the autumn. They studied the critical labor problems of the coal mines and railroads, and maintained contact with their chief through Secretary Houston, Grayson, and Tumulty. There was no more serious talk within the official household of disability and retirement.

However, allegations of boudoir government were not easily countered. The adversaries in the Senate seized upon all rumors of disability and magnified them. Bills to oust the President were introduced. Some of Lansing's friends among the Republicans were remarking that only foreigners were allowed to call on the President of the United States. Foreign embassies, they complained, were better informed than his own people about Wilson's condition, through visits to the sickroom by Belgium's monarch and the Prince of Wales.

The members of the Committee on Foreign Relations took a particularly keen interest in the President's health; and it happened that in November a diplomatic crisis arose that provided an excuse for an inquisitorial expedition to his sickroom. When Senator Fall cast doubt on Wilson's ability to cope with a crisis in relations with Mexico that had arisen out of the alleged kidnaping of Consular Agent William O. Jenkins,[1] Hitchcock suggested that his colleague go himself to call at the White House and drew his own conclusions; and finally Fall and Hitchcock were delegated to do this.

By December 4, two days after Congress had heard the reading of an annual presidential message that had been composed by Charles Swem under the direction of Tumulty,[2] the curiosity of the legislators about Wilson's health could be withstood no longer.

Henry Cabot Lodge, who was now complaining to Root that "a regency of Tumulty and Barney Baruch . . . was not contemplated by the constitution," was instructed by his committee to telephone for an appointment. When he did so, on December 5, he was invited to send delegates to the White House that very afternoon.

Before receiving Fall and Hitchcock, the President was briefed by letters from Lansing and from Senator Pittman. The latter suggested that the jingoism of irresponsible senators could be stopped, and the interview cut short, if Wilson would merely ask for a copy of a report that Fall was to file with the Foreign Relations Committee, and promise to study the matter.

The President and those around him, however, set the stage for a more elaborate denouement. Propping him up with pillows, covering him with bedclothes to the chin, and allowing only his sound right arm to protrude, Dr. Grayson and Mrs. Wilson bade the senators enter the

---

[1] The Jenkins case was brought up by Lansing at a Cabinet meeting. Secretary Daniels suspected that there was some truth in the Mexican allegation that Jenkins was the tool of oil prospectors who wanted armed protection from the United States government. When it became clear that Lansing had no facts to disprove this suspicion, and the secretary of state remarked that the Mexican embassy at Washington spawned "red" propaganda and that by intervening in Mexico it might be possible to settle social problems in the United States, a majority of the Cabinet reacted strongly against such a policy. The Jenkins case must be settled on its legal merits, they insisted, regardless of the opinion of interested parties.

Lansing hoped to make use of the Jenkins affair to put an end to the violations of civic rights that American citizens had been suffering in Mexico. He went before Lodge's committee and urged delay. When Mexico replied equivocally to his note of protest, the secretary of state called in the Mexican ambassador and insulted him. Though Tumulty telephoned to urge that the policy toward Mexico be discussed with the President before the State Department went too far, Lansing held to his independent course. He sent another note to the Mexican government, this one so sharp that the editor of the *New York Times* found it hard to discover in history "a severer indictment of bad faith, a more scathing condemnation of unfriendly behavior."

[2] Tumulty collected reports from the Cabinet members and, tossing them on Swem's desk, said: "You know how the Chief writes. You can put them together." Swem to the writer. The draft of the message shows corrections in Mrs. Wilson's hand, presumably dictated by the President. A word was changed here and there (for example, a sarcastic reference to Russia as "a fine object lesson" was changed to "a painful object lesson"). A plea for ratification of the peace treaty was struck out, and also paragraphs contributed by the director-general of railways on problems that Wilson chose to cover in a message of Dec. 24. At the urging of advisers who feared that Republican legislation pending in Congress would take the initiative away from the President, and in the face of a plea from labor leaders that government ownership be extended for two years, Wilson proclaimed the return of the railroads to their owners on March 1, 1920.

sickroom. To guard against misquoting of her husband's words, Edith Wilson sat across from the visitors, ready with notebook and pencil to record the conversation.

Fall approached the bed with a smile that seemed to ooze oil. Woodrow Wilson seldom had been so moved to hit a man. For some time he had thought of this senator as a man who did not even try to tell the truth. He put all his strength, however, into a handshake. The senator presented his views on Mexico and promised to send a memorandum, and the President thanked him for his statement and commended its fullness. The caller noted that his host articulated clearly, though somewhat thickly, and that he could freely turn his head and move his right arm about. The talk was lively, and the sick man proved his wit still sharp by repeating his favorite remark of Mr. Dooley's Hennessy: "Sure, with Mexico so contagious, we'll be takin' it soon whether we want it or not."

Hardly had Fall presented his case for intervention and asserted that four-fifths of the Mexican people would welcome it, when Grayson came in to report the release from jail of Consular Agent Jenkins. Fall could hope only to escape from the sickroom quickly. But in his confusion he opened himself to one more body blow. "I hope you will consider me sincere," the senator said, unctuously leaning over the bed and pressing the sick man's hand between his own. "I have been praying for you, sir."

Again Wilson's temper threatened to get the better of him. Why did this unconscionable meddler want to queer him with the Almighty? he wondered. But he restricted himself to three words: "Which way, senator?"

At the next meeting of the Committee on Foreign Relations the question of the President's mental disability was laughed off and dropped; and soon a message came from Wilson reminding the committee that "the advice of the Senate is provided for only when sought by the Executive in regard to explicit agreements with foreign governments." The passage of such a meddling resolution as Fall had proposed, the President asserted, "would constitute a reversal of our constitutional practice which might lead to very grave confusion in the guidance of our foreign policy." Thus the immediate danger of armed intervention in Mexico was averted.

The ordeal took a toll on the President's limited energy. And yet it gave him confidence and cheer to know that he could still smite the Philistines. He was able to derive some pleasure from the festivities of a family Christmas and from a deluge of birthday greetings three days afterward. He was able to dress himself each morning and to sit up for several hours; and on the day after Christmas, bowed forward in a wheel chair, he was taken to the East Room of the White House to see a moving picture. A horse race was portrayed and it exhausted him, but the cinema became a regular diversion every morning except Sundays. Edith Wilson was constantly at his side; and when his head fell forward, she raised it and caressed it, oblivious of the presence of guests. At first the cinema was merely a means of killing time, but soon he became a "fan," with a weakness for western and detective films and an aversion to those that scoffed at marriage. Before the daily show they sometimes wheeled him through the downstairs rooms on a sightseeing excursion, with Grayson's infant son perched on the foot rest, or, wrapping him in blankets, out to the south portico to take the sun and talk with Tumulty through a window.

Very gradually, but persistently, the invalid gained a measure of control over his paralyzed arm and leg. He found that he could take a few steps—totteringly, at first, with someone supporting him on each side; then more confidently, leaning on a blackthorn stick. As the winter wore on, he found strength to hook his cane around a pillar of the portico and triumphantly swing his wheel chair about on the flagging.

At the same time the President was regaining some power of decision and action. During the winter Secretaries Lansing and Lane, who had dissented from the view of the majority of the Cabinet toward oil interests and intervention in Mexico, became embarrassingly aware of their chief's recovery.

The President's impulsive opinions on matters affecting Europe and the Far East yielded usually to the advice of Polk or Phillips or Long— men in the State Department whom he trusted; but anything that Secretary Lansing proposed was almost certain to meet rebuff at the White House. It seemed as if the Wilsons were acting with the intent of provoking Lansing to resign, so that they would be spared the unpleasantness of dismissing him. When the secretary pleaded with Mrs. Wilson for action on pressing matters of state, she informed him— curtly, it seemed to him—that the President did not like to be told a thing twice.

The breach between the President and the secretary of state was bringing the diplomacy of the nation to a standstill. European statesmen were refusing to accept messages from the State Department as authoritative, and awaited definitive verdicts from the sick President. Indecision and delay were nurturing seeds of dissension in the Balkans, in Asia Minor, and especially at Fiume. Italy, smarting under moral rebuke, tended toward the policy that was to bring her into World War

II as an ally of Germany. And Russia received no response to a public offer to negotiate a settlement of all questions making for hostilities.

It was impossible, even, for the State Department to establish normal relations with Britain. Pending the appointment of a permanent ambassador to succeed Lord Reading, Grey had come to Washington in September to deal with questions left unsettled at the Peace Conference. Disinclined to do business outside official channels, he waited patiently for Wilson's health to improve, marveling the while at the awkwardness of the government.

Unfortunately there was on Grey's staff an officer whom the Wilsons did not like. When they became aware of the presence of this undesirable, they wrote to Lansing to ask that the man be sent home. Grey, however, was as loyal as Wilson himself to men who served him well, and contended that it was unfair to condemn anyone unless charges were brought and proved. As a result the British statesman was not invited to the White House, not even to accompany the Prince of Wales.

After listening to Republican amenders of the League Covenant and sympathizing with their views, the envoy returned to England and sent to the London *Times* a letter intimating that in practice the Lodge reservations probably would prove to be harmless and that Britain would accept the conditional cooperation of the United States. This statement, which was supported almost unanimously by the press of Britain and France and was quoted in American journals, brought biting comment from Mrs. Wilson,[3] who thus introduced another obstacle to an understanding that might have resulted in the Senate's approval of the peace treaty.

A well-intentioned effort that Lansing made in Grey's behalf proved to be merely another plank in the coffin that the secretary of state had been building for himself for a year. At last, under the succession of insults that had come from the White House, the man sensed that the Wilsons not only distrusted him, but thoroughly disliked him. His thoughts again turned longingly toward retirement, as his chief had intended. Journalistic predictions of his resignation became more insistent.

Another and stronger nudge was required, however, to push the secretary of state to the point of action. Whether or not the President's own mind went "around the clock" on this question is uncertain.[4] But on

---

[3] Mrs. Wilson's written statement said: "It may be safely assumed that had Lord Grey ventured upon any such utterance while he was in Washington as an ambassador . . . his government would have been promptly asked to withdraw him."

[4] According to Mrs. Wilson's *My Memoir*, p. 301, the "precipitating incident" was "the last and almost the least" of many disloyalties on Lansing's part. When she asked her husband why he opened himself to allegations of meanness and injured vanity by resting his case on this single basis, he replied: "Well, if I am as big as you think me I can well afford to do a

February 7, 1920, he struck directly at Lansing by reminding him by letter that no one but the President had a right to summon the Cabinet, that only the President and Congress could legally ask for the views of the secretaries on public questions.

The edge of this letter was sharp enough to draw blood. The secretary of state thought the language "brutal and offensive" and the argument like that of "a spoiled child crying out in rage at an imaginary wrong." The absurd charge that Wilson cited put the secretary in a position to resign with honor. The President had delivered himself unwittingly into his hands, the obtuse secretary thought. "And of course I took advantage of his stupidity," Lansing recorded. When the resignation reached the White House, the President gladly accepted it, to take effect "at once."

In the opinion of the press and of his good friends, the President performed a necessary operation on the body politic, but used the bluntest of instruments. The egocentric prophet was showing himself hopelessly out of touch with political realities, and incapable of taking good advice even from those nearest and dearest to him. Lansing was now free to consort as much as he chose with his Republican friends and to tell all he knew and all he felt. He was received enthusiastically by Wilson's enemies and by those who had lost confidence in the President. Lodge assured him that his final note to Wilson was "extremely good." Two days later the secretary of state drafted a reply in pencil: "It is a satisfaction to receive your praise. The friendly good will which you have constantly shown me will always be one of the pleasantest memories of my public service."

The resignation of Lansing was but one of the withdrawals from the Cabinet early in 1920. In the opinion of Franklin K. Lane, who had spoken often in support of Lansing's views, the President seemed to have given way to petty impulses. Lane had sent to the White House certain leases of government oil lands, assuring Mrs. Wilson that they were legitimate. But when the agreements were put before the President, Wilson drew back. He suspected the motives of Lane, who wrote to Grayson on January 5 that he was contemplating resigning from the Cabinet in order to make money. Too ill to study the matter, Wilson thought it better to wait than to take a step that might be questioned.

When this word went back to the secretary of the interior through Edith Wilson, he was deeply hurt, and on February 5 he made the

---

generous thing. If not I must take the blame." Professing a liking for Mrs. Lansing and respect for her father, former Secretary of State John W. Foster, he explained: "The disloyalty is a personal act; the calling of meetings of the Cabinet is official insubordination; it is my duty to put a stop to that."

move that he had been considering for four months; he wrote to Wilson to offer his resignation, to take effect on March 1.

At about the same time another Cabinet seat became vacant when the governor of Virginia appointed Secretary Carter Glass to fill the unexpired term of Thomas S. Martin, the deceased Democratic leader in the Senate. Encouraged by the Virginians close to him, Wilson had come to depend much on the secretary of the treasury. Glass's resignation took effect on February 2, 1920, and on the next day he took his oath as a senator. Secretary Houston replaced him at the Treasury.

Colonel House noted, in December, that never in his political experience had he seen "such a desertion of the ship in times of stress." The infirm President no longer had genius for binding men to him. Emotional instability precluded rational transaction of the business of government. He gave reality to the character in which caluminators had cast him: the spoiled child who would have his own way at any cost, the vain preacher who pointed the only path to redemption, the proud author who refused to submit his masterpiece to revision, the dictatorial executive who would not take counsel from Congress, the politician who was not serving a great cause but using the cause to keep himself in office. People forgot the gallantry of the European and western trips as under the influence of arteriosclerosis the prophet revealed more and more the streak of pettifogging that ran in his Scottish ancestry. Shorn of his powers, he was an easy prey to the tortures that his adversaries were inflicting upon his soul. The people saw the President in the austere light in which he had put himself—an implacable opponent of any reservations that might require assent or provoke objections by other signatories of the treaty.

The counselor who had been most helpful in political crises of the past could not help now. Colonel House had remained in Europe and had tried to keep alive the prophet's vision of world democracy by giving substance to the League of Nations. The Colonel's appeal for concessions to British opinion confirmed the impression that had lodged in Wilson's mind and that was strengthened by those closest to him. House still seemed too sympathetic to foreign points of view, too much the good fellow. But the President did not reproach the Colonel, nor let anyone speak ill of his old friend. When the press again printed stories of a "break" between them, Wilson had been incensed. He wished to spare House's feelings, and he did not want the ending of this political partnership, like his separation from Hibben and Harvey, to provoke the charges of personal disloyalty that political foes would know so well how to exploit.

It had seemed unwise, however, to risk the return of the Colonel to

Washington, for doubtless he would seek compromise with the foes of the treaty and perhaps undermine the solid front that the prophet had resolved to present.

However, when it became apparent that the treaty might fail in the Senate if reservations were not accepted, the Colonel decided to take matters into his own hands and do what he could for the cause that his friend could no longer further effectively. On the 5th of October, two days after the French Chamber ratified the peace treaty, he embarked for home.

At this juncture the Colonel's health, which had been precarious, failed badly. An attack of renal colic grew worse as he neared the United States; and at New York he was taken from the ship on a stretcher. His vitality was so low that the doctors feared to perform an operation that was long overdue. His first impulse was to go to Washington to bare his heart to his friend. Immediately he sent off a letter to Senator Lodge, expressing his willingness to testify before the Committee on Foreign Relations as soon as his physician would permit.

Receiving a noncommittal reply from Lodge, the resourceful Colonel made a more devious effort. He asked Stephen Bonsal, Wilson's interpreter at Paris and a personal friend of Lodge, to go to the senator and tell him frankly that House could explain everything as soon as he was able to travel. The mediator quoted to Lodge what Smuts had said at Paris of his article dealing with mandates: "I warn you that if even a word is changed or perhaps even a comma, the whole edifice will collapse." Bonsal was able to report to House that there was some prospect of concessions by the senator; but if this information ever reached the President, it did not move him to seek compromise.[5]

Senator Lodge seemed to Wilson's friends to be determined to cut out what the President regarded as "the heart of the Covenant." On November 6 his majority in the Committee on Foreign Relations presented fourteen reservations to the Senate. The next day another reservation was added that was particularly offensive to Wilson—a change in the preamble of the Covenant that would require acceptance of all the reservations by at least three of the four major cosigners of the treaty.

[5] Bonsal recorded that Lodge wrote on a printed copy of the Covenant about forty words of altered phrasing and about fifty inserts that would make the treaty acceptable to him and, he felt sure, to the Senate, and that this document was mailed to House and that the Colonel mailed it to the White House.

This document is not in the Wilson Collection in the Library of Congress, and the only evidence of its existence is Bonsal's testimony in *Unfinished Business*, pp. 277 and 285–86, in his letters to Charles Seymour, May 27, 1944, and April 9, 1944, and in his conversations with Robert W. Woolley and James F. Reynolds. When Charles Seymour asked Colonel House and his secretary, Miss Denton, about this incident several years later, neither had a definite recollection of it. Charles Seymour to the writer, Dec. 8, 1953. There is no reference to the episode in House's diary.

On the same day on which this culminating indignity was proposed, Hitchcock was admitted to the President's bedside for their first consultation since the thrombosis. As acting minority leader in the Senate and a member of the Committee on Foreign Relations, Hitchcock had taken no effective initiative on the basis of the interpretive reservations that Wilson had left with him in August. He had been so accustomed to depend upon the White House for leadership that he was at a loss without it. He had, however, observed Republican tactics closely and he concluded, in mid-November, that Lodge's reservations were intended to defeat the treaty. The Democratic leader was willing to compromise with the mild reservationists on almost any revisions that would command enough votes to frustrate Lodge's intentions.[6]

When Hitchcock went to Wilson's chamber to suggest concession, he was shocked by the emaciation of the white-bearded figure that had been propped up in bed to receive him. With Edith Wilson and Grayson standing by to protect their patient, Hitchcock dared not attempt rational argument. He could merely convey the black truth: the Democrats could not raise even a bare majority for ratification without reservations, to say nothing of the two-thirds needed.

"Is it possible! Is it possible!" the tortured prophet groaned.

"Mr. President," Hitchcock ventured, "it might be wise to compromise . . ."

"Let Lodge compromise!" Wilson shot back.

"Well, of course, he must compromise also," the senator conceded, "but we might well hold out the olive branch."

"Let Lodge hold out the olive branch," the President retorted.

Hitchcock came again to the President's bedside on November 17, as the hour of voting drew near. In this second conference Wilson did not refuse all of Lodge's measures, but gave ground to meet the views of the mild reservationists. He threatened, however, to give the treaty a pocket veto if it were passed without a change in the reservation on Article X and if senators did not omit the preamble that required three of the major signatory powers to assent in writing to the American reservations. In Wilson's view, Article XII of the Covenant, which provided for compulsory arbitration, was a second line of defense to which he was unwilling to retreat. That method had been tried before, and found inadequate to preserve peace. Rather than assume the responsibility of vetoing the treaty, however, and thus play out the role that Lodge had

---

[6] On Nov. 13, Hitchcock prepared to introduce the four reservations that Wilson had given him secretly before setting out for the West, and a fifth that he had added himself. These interpretive reservations dealt with withdrawal from the League, Article X, domestic questions, the Monroe Doctrine, and the votes of the British Dominions in the Assembly. The reservation on Article X was almost identical with the one sponsored by moderate Republicans.

assigned to him, the President supported the plan of his men in the Senate to vote against ratification with Lodge reservations. "I would like," he said, "to have some of the senators go home to their constituents while the treaty is still pending." If there was a deadlock, he felt that public opinion would break it in his favor. He put faith still in the cheers that he had stirred in the West, in the tears that he had seen in the eyes of American mothers when he had talked of another war.

McAdoo advised concessions, and the prophet answered: "Mac, I am willing to compromise on anything but the Ten Commandments." Baruch went to the sickroom to press the Chief to yield: and the master, thinking this friend "true to the bone" for giving advice known to be unpalatable, said, "And Baruch too!" Finally, after a talk with Hitchcock, Mrs. Wilson came to her husband and asked whether for her sake he would not "accept these reservations and get this awful thing settled."

Turning his head on the pillow, he responded with a challenge to her fealty. "Little girl, don't desert me, that I cannot stand. Can't you see that I have no moral right to accept any change in a paper I have signed without giving to every other signatory, even the Germans, the right to do the same thing? It is not *I* that will not accept; it is the nation's honor that is at stake." His eyes were afire as he dramatized his cause— the grandest that he had ever fought for, the greatest of his century. "Better a thousand times to go down fighting than to dip your colors to dishonorable compromise," he told his wife.

His mind set, he dictated a letter to Hitchcock, adapting a text supplied by Hitchcock but replacing the word "defeat" by "nullification." The Senate Resolution, he wrote, did not "provide for ratification but rather for the nullification of the treaty." "I sincerely hope," he advised, "that the friends and supporters of the treaty will vote against the Lodge resolution of ratification. I understand that the door will probably then be open for a genuine resolution of ratification. I trust that all true friends of the treaty will refuse to support the Lodge reservations."

Wilson's letter was given to the newspapers and was read to the Democratic senators in caucus and later on the floor of the Senate. Reservationists who were fundamentally friendly to the League saw in the message an imputation of bad faith, and they resented it.

On November 19 a vote was taken. The party men stood, with four exceptions, against the revised treaty. Their ballots, added to those of thirteen Republican irreconcilables, were enough to block the two-thirds vote needed for ratification. Afterward, Republican moderates joined the irreconcilables to defeat a Democratic motion for approval of the treaty without reservations; and a similar alignment defeated a motion to consider the treaty with the President's interpretive reservations.[7] Then a resolution declaring the war with Germany at an end was introduced by Senator Knox and referred to the Committee on Foreign Relations.

Many of the Democratic leaders, favoring compromise, continued to try to work through House and Tumulty to put political realities of the day before the cloistered prophet. Indeed, their pressure was so insistent that House overcame his reluctance to impose advice on his friend. In November the Colonel was well enough to operate in his characteristic way. He established contact with Lord Grey and with Republican policy makers, and on November 24 he wrote to Mrs. Wilson to suggest that her husband's place in history was "in the balance," that otherwise he would not disturb the President while he was ill. At the same time House composed an accompanying letter to the President himself, recommending that the treaty be turned back to the Senate for action, for thus the Republicans could be saddled with responsibility for passing the measure in a form that would be acceptable to the other signatory nations. Three days later the Colonel pressed his argument home in another letter. There was no reply from the White House to either. It seemed to Edith Wilson that her husband's place in history was already assured.[8]

Margaret Wilson did her best to restore the old relationship. Going to New York, she talked with House about the things that had offended her father and found that the Colonel thought himself justified in what he had done out of concern for the League and his friend's political welfare. But when his explanations were brought back to the White House, Wilson gave a sigh of disappointment. In the old days, he said, when he conversed with House it seemed as if he were talking with himself. Now his clear concept of his friend was overlaid and blurred by a picture of a man different from the one that he had known. It would be awkward to bare his mind in the presence of a stranger. Unless he could talk without shyness, he would not really be talking with the friend that he remembered. And so it seemed best not to see the Colonel. Moreover, if House was the man Wilson thought him, he

[7] Hitchcock hoped that enough Republicans would support his motion to keep the matter before the Senate for possible compromise. He had proposed this course in a conference with Lodge, who said that he could not accept this procedure unless he knew in advance what compromise the Democrats could offer. Hitchcock reported this to Mrs. Wilson by letter on Nov. 18; but since no definite proposals for compromise came from the White House, Lodge blocked Hitchcock's motion for consideration of the treaty with interpretive reservations.

[8] Unlike letters written to Wilson by House in September of 1919, which were not opened until they reached the Library of Congress in 1952, the Colonel's letters of Nov. 24 and 27 were opened before they reached the Library. But it is not known whether Wilson ever knew of them. By Dec. 2 House himself had changed his mind, and thought that the treaty should not be returned to the Senate until sixty-six senators were committed to vote for it with reservations agreed on in advance.

too would be embarrassed by a meeting that would remind them both
of the failure of their exalted mission. Maybe the fault was his own, he
said. Perhaps he had expected too much in thinking that the good
Colonel could stand against strong pressures. The President loved the
Texan still, but considered him of a caliber too light to bear the cross
that the prophet was prepared to carry to the grave, alone. And so
Colonel House's independent effort to save the treaty came to naught;
and this disciple, loyal to his friend and his great cause, and feeling that
only illness prevented their continuing collaboration, grew bitter toward
what he called "the shortsighted coterie" that surrounded the President.

On one point, the wisdom of throwing responsibility on the Republican senators—Wilson's mind ran along with that of House. The President had contemplated this strategy after the Congressional election of
1918 and now his thought harked back and seized on it again. When
Lodge stated that nothing further could be done until the President
withdrew the treaty from the Senate and resubmitted it, Wilson countered in mid-December with a public assertion that the Republican
leaders who controlled the Senate's vote should continue to bear "the
undivided responsibility."

A year earlier, after the adverse vote in the Congressional election, he
had been sensitive about his political insolvency; and now he was on the
brink of bankruptcy. His nerves could endure no more palaver with the
Philistines in the Senate. He had said to them, directly and through
Hitchcock, everything that he had to say. On some days he would sit
glum and unresponsive to all ideas of constructive action, fearful that
any move might be construed as a yielding to an enemy and an exposure
of his feebleness. In his determination to die facing forward he was
possessed by the very fear of seeming fearsome.

Yet in January of 1920 he explored two ways to bring the sinners to
the truth. His first scheme was fantastic. Consulting the attorney general, he hoped to work out a plan whereby opposing senators would be
challenged to resign and stand for re-election on the issue of the treaty;
and if his opponents won, he himself was prepared to resign from the
Presidency. His advisers, however, were able to persuade him that his
plan was impractical under the election laws of the nation.

Balked in this venture, the prophet next resolved to use the occasion
of Jackson Day to give the infidels a public flailing. On January 8
Chairman Homer Cummings read his message to Democrats who
crowded into the dining rooms of two Washington hotels. It asserted
that the United States had "enjoyed the spiritual leadership of the world
until the Senate failed to ratify the treaty." The party men were reminded that they were still at war with Germany, that the old stage was

"reset for a repetition of the old plot," complete with alliances, secret treaties, and intrigues. "Five of the leading belligerents," the message explained, "have accepted the treaty and formal ratifications will soon be exchanged. The question is whether this country will enter and enter whole-heartedly . . ." The President's impression that ratification was the wish of an "overwhelming majority of the people" had been "confirmed by the unmistakable evidences of public opinion" during his visit to seventeen of the states. If there was any doubt on this matter, he asserted, "the clear and single way out" was to submit it to the voters at the next election.

The President had commented on the iniquity of delay in making peace. So when he suggested postponing ratification for almost a year, until he and Lodge could submit their differences to the voters, it appeared that he was trying to give himself and his party a strong issue for the 1920 presidential campaign. Sincere friends of the League were forced to conclude that, in the three months that had passed since his last public utterance on the treaty, their President had shrunk deplorably in mental and moral stature. As in the 1918 election, it would be impossible to draw the issue so clearly that the popular vote could be regarded as a mandate; and, moreover, even if the Democrats won all the Senate seats that would be open in 1920, it still would be mathematically impossible for them to gain the two-thirds vote that was necessary for ratification.

Members of the Cabinet had recognized the folly of Wilson's tactics and had done their best to tone down the Jackson Day message. Experts on whom Wilson had depended at Paris signed an appeal of the League of Free Nations Association, urging acceptance of reservations necessary for ratification. Moreover, leaders in education and finance were giving similar advice. Pressures for concessions by both parties reached their peak soon after the opening of the new year.

The prophet in the White House, however, would admit no share of guilt for the failure of the treaty. In his view, it had been butchered to death by the Foreign Relations Committee. Feeling that public opinion would force one side or the other to capitulate, he resolved that it would not be his side.

In January this policy seemed to bear fruit: for toward the middle of this month, Republican mild reservationists, who on December 26 had served an "ultimatum" on Lodge demanding compromise, induced him to arrange a bipartisan conference, in which four Democrats and five Republicans were to meet informally to discuss revision of the fourteen reservations that the Senate had voted down in November. This move was welcomed by Senator Hitchcock, since proposals from

Republicans obviously would command fairer treatment from Lodge than would those from Democrats. Moreover, Hitchcock dared to hope that Wilson might accept a definite bipartisan suggestion for compromise even though he would not initiate or encourage such a proposal. Tumulty, in collaboration with members of the Cabinet, tried to persuade the President to sign and send to Hitchcock a letter accepting the core of Lodge's reservations but safeguarding the rights of the Executive. This proposal went to Edith Wilson on January 15—the day before the Council of the League convened at Paris at Wilson's call, but without a representative from the United States.

The Wilsons, however, felt that Lodge's profession of open-mindedness was not sincere. Hitchcock had reported on January 5 that this adversary was "a cold-blooded, calculating politician" who was merely dallying with and trifling with the moderate Republicans to keep them quiet.[9] It seemed to the Democratic leader that a "deadlock of opinion" existed that might be broken by careful negotiation and by winning recruits to the bloc of moderate Republicans. But there was no response from the sickroom to Tumulty's proposal.

On January 22 Hitchcock reported that the conferees were seriously considering a revision of Lodge's reservation for Article X. The new draft, which the senator enclosed with his letter, was sponsored by Democratic Senator Simmons. Replying in a letter dated January 26, Wilson expressed his views on Article X, clearly and frankly. To the substance of the Simmons reservation, he said, he adhered. He was bound to, having sworn to obey and maintain the Constitution of the United States. But he went on to say: "I think the form of it very unfortunate. Any reservation or resolution stating that 'the United States assumes no obligation under such and such an article unless or except' would, I am sure, chill our relationships with the nations with which we expect to be associated in the great enterprise of maintaining the world's peace. That association must in any case, my dear senator, involve very serious and far-reaching implications of honor and duty, which I am sure we shall never in fact be desirous of ignoring. It is the more important not to create the impression that we are trying to escape obligations."

---

[9] Hitchcock to Mrs. Wilson, Jan. 5, 1920, in Garraty, *Lodge,* p. 385. Hitchcock's diagnosis of Lodge's motive is confirmed by a note written by the senator to his friend Beveridge on Jan. 3, 1920, and printed in Garraty, *op. cit.,* p. 384. "It would have been a mistake," Lodge wrote, "for me to have taken the attitude . . . that we would not even consider modifications. We could not afford to say that . . ."

Insight into Lodge's thinking at this time is given by Alice Roosevelt Longworth in *Crowded Hours,* pp. 294–95. Her conclusion after talking with the senator on Sunday before Christmas, 1919, was: "In his heart he was really as opposed to it [the League] in any shape as any irreconcilable but his job was to see that the reservations were on and to deal with and harmonize the mild and strong reservationists to that end."

Realizing finally that negative criticism was not all that was called for in so serious a matter, he gladly reaffirmed his approval of the four interpretative reservations that he had given to Hitchcock in August and that the senator had returned to him at his request, with one addition, on January 5. Included among the five interpretations was one on Article X that reserved the rights of Congress without denying the obligation of the United States to exercise its conscience and judgment on each appeal from the League's council.

In forwarding the letter of January 26 to Hitchcock, Mrs. Wilson indicated that he might make it public at his discretion. The senator did not do so, however, until February 9, when the Senate again considered the treaty. It was already too late for the conciliatory note to be effective. For on January 23, after the bipartisan conference had agreed on many compromises and just as Lodge seemed to be leaning toward the views of the moderates of his party, he was summoned out of the session by his friend Brandegee and haled before a powwow of the irreconcilables that was meeting in Senator Johnson's office. The bitter-enders threatened the Republican leader with a public scalping if he bated a jot on Article X and drew from him a promise to stand firm on all but matters of phrasing. Consequently, the bipartisan conference was unable to reach agreement on Article X and two other clauses, and at the end of the month it finally broke up.

Early in February Wilson was plunged into a cloud of fatalism. Perceiving that dismal thoughts wore on his nerves when he was alone, Edith Wilson stayed at his side almost constantly and tried to divert and rest him. Late in each day a massage soothed his distress, and early in the evening he was enveloped by a comforter that had seldom failed him—sleep.

During February the morale of the Democratic senators, like that of the President, reached a low ebb. Realizing that they were fighting for a lost cause, they were disposed to abandon their struggle to soften the Lodge reservations. In fact, Hitchcock warned the President on February 24 that only another command from Wilson would hold his men in line.

From the President's chambers, however, came no guidance. The Lodge reservations, Wilson said dolefully to Ray Baker, represented "a dishonorable attempt, on the part of the leaders who do not speak for the people, to escape any real responsibility, so far as the United States is concerned, for world peace in future years." They were essentially partisan political devices, the President went on. "If I accept them, these senators will merely offer new ones, even more humiliating." And then, after a long pause: "These evil men intend to destroy the League."

The senators moved swiftly, once the treaty was called up for action in February.[10] On March 4 Lodge complained that the Democrats had not been satisfied with the compromises evolved. For the first time he confessed, with pious solemnity, that the treaty had "fallen by the wayside." Actually, either the Senate would pass the treaty as he had revised it, and he would get credit for establishing peace with security for his country, or else the Democrats would oppose the treaty and Wilson would be blamed for killing it and would be repudiated by the voters. Either denouement would be satisfactory to Henry Cabot Lodge. The Republican party would be drawn together and Woodrow Wilson discredited.

Wilson acted on his own initiative in a way that played into the hands of this archenemy. He snuffed out all lingering hope for ratification by the tone of a letter that he sent to Hitchcock on March 8. In this message his emotions surged militantly. Somehow he drew echoes of his pristine vigor from his shattered physique and showed himself once more the rough-and-tumble fighter of a political frontier, cudgeling scribes and pharisees with whacks of spiritual truth. He begged everyone "to consider the matter in the light of what it is possible to accomplish for humanity, rather than in the light of special national interests." Practically every so-called reservation—those still under discussion as well as those already accepted by a majority vote of the Senate—was denounced as "a rather sweeping nullification" of the terms of the treaty. Declaring that he could not understand the difference between "a nullifier" and "a mild nullifier," Wilson killed any impulse that might linger in the mild reservationists to break from Lodge's control. Even the efforts of his own men to establish interpretative reservations were dismissed as a work of "supererogation." Opponents were branded as men of little faith—secessionists, militarists, imperialists.

Thus the prophet, isolated in the White House, his mental diet carefully controlled, his body made comfortable by an ingenious chair-back for his bed, a wheel chair, and a fur muff for his feet, completed the process of alienating independent citizens that had begun with his appeal for a Democratic Congress in 1918. Partisans of the League who after the thrombosis had envisioned a martyr's halo above their stricken President now saw him as an egocentric zealot or a scheming politician. Yet even now Elihu Root was disturbed when Lodge, reacting against Wilson's glorification of Article X as "the essence of Americanism," added two phrases to his reservation that made it a still stronger negation of the gospel that the President preached. Root cau-

---

[10] On Feb. 9, the Senate voted to reconsider the treaty and referred it to the Committee on Foreign Relations. It was reported back the next day with the Lodge reservations, and debate was resumed on Feb. 16. By March 7 eight of the fourteen reservations had been passed again, either unchanged or revised as agreed in the bipartisan conference.

tioned the senators of his party against action that might be interpreted by the voters as nullification. But Lodge explained in reply that he had not acted with his eyes shut, that he was making sure that the treaty would not be killed by Republicans alone.

Fantastic as some of the reservations were, it was doubtful whether the Democratic senators could be held in line to deliver the negative votes that the President was requesting. The alternative was more clear-cut than ever, between a Republicanized treaty and no treaty at all. Now, fearing an extension of the state of war in which the nation still lived, independent journals of Democratic leanings were urging the party's senators to vote for ratification; and they were joined by the voices of two ex-secretaries of state, Bryan and Lansing.

The outcome was in doubt, therefore, when the Senate prepared to vote on March 19. Would the senators approve a resolution to ratify the treaty with the Lodge reservations included? The clerk began to call the roll. Of the first four Democrats to respond, three turned against Wilson and voted for the treaty. The next was venerable Senator Culberson, House's old comrade of Texas campaigns. A "yea" from him might have stampeded the party. Not sure what he should say, he looked perplexed and hesitated. But finally his habit of party loyalty prevailed and he uttered a "nay."

While twenty-one Democrats—mostly from the North and candidates for re-election that autumn—voted with the opposition, twenty-three others—all from the South—adhered to their losing cause as fatalistically and steadfastly as their grandfathers had clung to Robert E. Lee. This time, however, the diehards were standing not for secession but for a union far more challenging, more venturesome, than that championed by Abraham Lincoln.

There was a majority of the Senate in favor of the treaty—forty-nine to thirty-five—but not the two-thirds vote that was needed for ratification. Hoping that some of Wilson's men might come over, Lodge proposed unanimous consent for a motion to reconsider the matter; but Hitchcock, holding firm to the last, blocked this move.

Thus, after more than eight months of fruitless conference and oratory, Woodrow Wilson had pulled down the temple that the Philistines had set up in place of the Ark of the Covenant. Taking refuge in a pettifogging subterfuge, he indignantly denied a charge that he had refused to sign the treaty. But everyone knew that he had obstructed participation in world affairs by his nation in any spirit but that of the Covenant. Moreover, as Europeans pursued their centuries-old habit of doing diplomatic business by conference, Wilson was shying away; for now he felt that America's few ventures in international cooperation had not been successful.

He became, in the eyes of European statesmen, a man who would not practice what he preached. Germans felt that he had laid a peace trap for them by declaring Fourteen Points that had not been fully honored. French statesmen lamented America's crippling blow to the effectiveness of the League as a protection against aggressors. Georges Clemenceau, thinking that France would accept a version of the treaty that the Senate would ratify, regarded Wilson and Lodge as "two stubborn old mules kicking each other around." To Lloyd George it seemed that when the American Senate walked out of the League and slammed the door behind them, 50 per cent of its power and influence vanished.

The reproaches of Europe made Wilson's conscience cringe under the weight of the sin that he felt resting upon the nation and on himself as its responsible leader. His first impulse was to shift the burden of guilt to those senators who, he had convinced himself, had maliciously scuttled the peace.

Righteous fury possessed him when Congress passed Knox's joint resolution declaring the war at an end. Without consulting his men in the Senate, he vetoed the measure and wrung from his tortured nerves a brilliant arraignment of its inadequacy. It represented, he said, a shameful shirking of moral responsibility and a repudiation of pledges that the nation had made when it entered the war. "Nothing is said in this resolution," he pointed out very specifically, "about the freedom of navigation upon the seas, or the reduction of armaments, or the vindication of the rights of Belgium, or the rectification of wrongs done to France, or the release of the Christian populations of the Ottoman Empire from the intolerable subjugation which they have had for so many centuries to endure, or the establishment of an independent Polish state, or the continued maintenance of any kind of understanding among the great powers of the world which would be calculated to prevent in the future such outrages as Germany attempted, and in part consummated. We have now in effect declared that we do not care to take any further risks or to assume any further responsibilities with regard to the freedom of nations or the sacredness of international obligations or the safety of independent peoples."

The Knox resolution was not passed over this veto. The American nation, which had entered the war in order to end war became the last of the contestants to make peace.[11] Mankind's inexorable search for a cosmic political godhead was set back a quarter-century.

[11] The United States remained at war until July of 1921, when a resolution similar to Knox's was passed and signed by President Harding.

CHAPTER XX

LATTER DAYS

ON APRIL 14, 1920, for the first time in more than six months, Wilson was able to meet his Cabinet.[1] The members were ushered into the President's study and found him seated behind a desk at the end of the room. Each man was announced as he entered, so that the invalid would be sure to recognize him. His old friends almost wept as they looked at his drooping arm, saw his jaw sag to one side as he struggled to articulate, and heard him repeat himself in a voice curiously weak and strained. He tried to rally them with a volley of jokes and did his best to soothe wounded feelings that had been festering during his absence. Turning to the attorney general, who had alarmed the nation by ordering dramatic raids on New Year's Day and had been feuding with the secretary of labor over methods of handling subversive workers, he cautioned: "Palmer, do not let this country see red!"

His mind was clear about things that had happened before the thrombosis; but when the men began a discussion of new developments in the railroad situation,[2] he seemed unable to follow. The talk went on for an hour or so, while Dr. Grayson anxiously observed his patient's condition from the door; and when Mrs. Wilson came in and suggested that the session break up, the President explained that the meeting was an experiment and he could not stay long. It was so successful, however, that others followed. Before the spring was over, Wilson was able again to stimulate his men to work for the large objectives that had caught the imagination of his people in 1913 but now were thought secondary to immediate peace and prosperity.

Though unable to reach common ground with Republicans and Europeans, the President reasserted his influence over his party. For the

[1] On Feb. 10, 1920, Lansing had had the Cabinet notified that there would be no more meetings unless called by the President. From April 14 to Dec. 14 the Cabinet met with Wilson on many Tuesdays.

[2] The President had referred the matter of railroad regulation to Congress in December of 1918, without recommendations on his part; and when the Esch-Cummins Transportation Act came to his desk on Feb. 28, he signed it in spite of opposition from the brotherhoods and four members of his Cabinet. At the suggestion of Director General Hines, Wilson himself talked on Feb. 13 with a delegation of railway workers and asked them to cooperate with him by withdrawing their strike orders. The roads reverted to private ownership on March 1. Soon after the situation was discussed at the Cabinet meeting of April 14, a nine-man rail labor board was functioning in a way that was to make it a model of conciliation machinery.

senators who had stood with him in a losing cause he had no reproaches. "You did everything that it was possible to do," he assured Hitchcock four days after the final vote on the treaty; but he had only lashes for the deserters. He felt that he could confide in Bainbridge Colby, a progressive lawyer whom he had appointed to succeed Lansing because he would write and speak effectively.[3] He became impatient with the censorship that had been placed on his communications; and by August he was directing Secretaries Colby and Daniels to send messages directly to him, and not "through third persons." He explained that this would save "a great deal of time and roundabout traveling of papers."

As he became able once again to give spiritual backing to his ruling elders, they rallied even more closely to him in defense of executive prerogatives against Congressional encroachment.[4] With his little band of disciples once more functioning, Wilson continued to denounce and defy his adversaries in the Capitol.

Grayson did his utmost to persuade his patient to go away to a cool, quiet resort for the summer; but, although one such arrangement was made, it was canceled by Wilson. Even to attempt to motor into Maryland to join his old Princeton chums seemed to him "folly." He clung to the familiar, comfortable things that he and his wife had come to enjoy—the movies, the sunning on the south portico. He went often to vaudeville, refusing free tickets, and unaware that friends bought a block of seats adjacent to his box, to protect him against the fate of Lincoln. He refused to be photographed for the movies, saying that he would not make an exhibition of himself by displaying his affliction to the country.

Wearing a cape because he could not easily put his limp arm into an overcoat, he went automobiling when warm days came. They lifted him into the front seat where he was braced so that he would not slide down nor topple over. He took comfort, on his rides, in following regular routes and making roadside acquaintances. Little vignettes from

[3] To succeed Lane as secretary of the interior, Wilson appointed Judge John Barton Payne, chairman of the Shipping Board, after failing to persuade McCormick and H. M. Robinson to take this post. Lansing suggested to the opposition that Payne was untrustworthy and that Colby, whose lack of experience made him seem pathetic in the eyes of career men, would be embarrassed by his identification with oil interests that were still being pleaded before the department. J. W. Alexander, appointed to succeed Redfield as secretary of commerce, became the second Missourian in the Cabinet. These appointments reflect the sick President's inability to comprehend political and economic realities.

[4] Wilson leaned on Houston, now secretary of the treasury and still ready to "dig stumps" for his chief, for a veto of a faulty bill that provided a federal budget system of unified estimates and independent audit. This was a reform long overdue; but the Republicans inserted an objectionable clause that provided that the comptroller general—an officer appointed by the President —could be removed by a concurrent resolution of Congress.

In his annual message of Dec. 7, 1920, Wilson advocated a modified form of the budget bill and it was passed soon after Harding took office.

real life were balm to the nerves; and the invalid took comfort, too, in watching the sheep that grazed placidly on the White House lawn. But he was easily irritated by small matters. It grieved him that live trees had been felled in Rock Creek Park and that the wood had been allowed to go to waste.

In the spring of 1920, long-simmering problems of labor and industry were brought before the recuperating President for settlement. During his illness the men of his Cabinet had been debating delicate, incendiary issues of law. Now, when Palmer suggested the use of an injunction to suppress a strike in New York Harbor, the President turned to him quietly and said: "Every lawyer knows that is an abuse of the writ." Labor could never be forced back into the conditions under which it had worked before the war, Wilson thought. He wished to deal with labor through processes of discussion and arbitration. He appointed commissions to adjudicate disputes in the coal mines, insisted on enforcement of the verdicts, and sought to terminate the work of the commissions when miners and operators came to an agreement.

In June of 1920 two laws were passed to guide and aid the development of economic enterprises in ways that were compatible with the national interest. Under a merchant marine act, the Shipping Board was to sell the nation's wartime merchant vessels to private operators and to operate ships that it would not sell. And under a water-power act, a Federal Power Commission that included the secretaries of war, agriculture, and the interior was given authority over all navigable streams and all waterways on public lands—a responsibility that was to be lightly held for many years until economic emergency made it suddenly vital.

Wilson wrote letters to hasten ratification of the Woman Suffrage Amendment by the states; and he had opposed Volstead's National Prohibition Act, which Congress had passed over his veto. These moves had endeared him to large masses of voters. But at the same time he showed a courageous concern for the general welfare that made him unpopular with many groups. He backed Senator Glass and Secretary Baker in opposing raids on the Treasury by war veterans. He supported Secretary Houston in his contention that the government had no obligation to maintain the market price of its bonds in spite of the selling operations of thriftless or overextended citizens. Moreover, he offended starry-eyed voters by refusing even to listen to petitions for the pardon of Eugene Debs, the Socialist, whom he considered a "traitor."

At the beginning of 1920 the question of his role in the coming election was prominent in the mind of the convalescent President. On

January 8 he had released his Jackson Day plea for a "great and solemn referendum" on the League of Nations; and on February 29 the leaders of his party, dining at the Chevy Chase Club, had received a chit from him on which was written in his hand: "What part shall I play in politics this Fall?" The politicians had concluded that it would be unwise for their stricken leader to seek a third term; but their answer to the White House was equivocal. They could not bring themselves to tell their revered master that he was not the man that he had been.

William G. McAdoo, who had no desire to oppose his father-in-law, was in a strong position politically. New York's Democrats pledged their support to him. Though fellow executives had been offended because he seemed constantly to reach out for power and to encroach on their prerogatives, though he was vulnerable to insinuations that he was a nepotist—a "crown prince"—McAdoo appealed to the rank and file of the party as a strong man of action.

Wilson thought his son-in-law deficient in the qualities essential to a president of the United States. "The next President must be not only a man of action," he had remarked to Stockton Axson in 1918, "but he must also have great powers of reflection. Now nobody can do things better than Mac, but if Mac ever reflects, I never caught him at it." This being his measured opinion, Woodrow Wilson could not indulge his little daughter by giving professional endorsement to her husband. Actually, he felt that Newton D. Baker was best fitted for the Presidency and that Houston or Glass would make a good chief executive, but he doubted that these able servants had the fire and presence needed to win election.

As the spring wore on and the Senate worked its will with the treaty, the wretched prophet had no spiritual comfort but his faith in the verdict of the people at the polls. His wife and sycophantic friends encouraged him in this delusion. Mrs. Bainbridge Colby, lunching at the White House, noted the completeness of his dependence upon Edith Wilson, the lack of a vitality to stretch across the table and identify himself. Putting her hand over his and uttering a "darling," she seemed to speak for both.

In April, Wilson summoned energy to sound a keynote for the coming political battle. He wrote out a challenge to the voters and sent it to a national committeeman, Jouett Shouse.

Calling Homer Cummings of the National Committee to him on May 31, Wilson asked this lieutenant to represent him at the forthcoming Democratic convention at San Francisco.

Cummings found the Chief on the portico in his wheel chair, with his wife standing by. He appeared too weary to talk as much as of old, but when he spoke, it was with limpidity; and he hit the bull's-eye with every remark. The fingers of his left hand did not move, and he picked at them occasionally, as if they were numb or prickly.

They talked of a keynote speech that Cummings had prepared, and the President objected to an allusion to the possibility of defeat in the election. Furthermore, noting that the script referred to him as one who had been on the point of death, Wilson looked at his caller pathetically and said that that was not true. He still did not fully comprehend the seriousness of his affliction.

He recalled that past presidents, by seeking to choose their successors, frequently had provoked factional disputes that had split their parties. But he spoke a word of caution. "It is dangerous to stand still," he said. "The government must move, and be responsive to the needs and wishes of the people. Revolution is everywhere in the world and any body of men who think they could drive down stakes and pull the world up . . . are the most dangerous enemies that our country has."

Presenting a code book to Cummings for secret communications from San Francisco, he said: "This was Colonel House's code book. He won't need it any more." [5]

It was not in the tradition of the Woodrows and Wilsons to abdicate responsibility by leaving a pulpit; and their scion, weak as he was, still felt an urge to remain in the thick of the fight for the cause that he thought the greatest of his century. The impulse grew when an article in the New York *World* gave a rosy picture of his health and vigor and presented him as a man able to bear the strain of another term. This story, based on an interview that Tumulty had arranged with Louis Seibold, brought offers of financial support and made Wilson the favorite candidate of Wall Street betting. [6]

Just as the Seibold article appeared, McAdoo was telling his men that he wished to withdraw from the race and that he wanted his adherents to support Carter Glass. To Glass, however, who ascertained that McAdoo's managers had not accepted their candidate's disavowal as final, this was "amiable nonsense." Impressed by the obvious fact that

[5] Cummings Diary, May 31, 1920; and Cummings to the writer, Feb. 15, 1951. Like a John Bunyan, the President gave allegorical names to some of the Democratic candidates: "Bryan—Dove; Palmer—Pilgrim." And on the names of others, he could not resist punning: "Hoke Smith—Pokus; Glass—Crystal; Cox—Swain."

[6] Tumulty's plan had been to have the President give his views on the large issues of the day and deny any desire for renomination. However, to his distress, Mrs. Wilson let him know that nothing but exaltation of her husband would be countenanced. Seibold's article urged that the election be a solemn referendum, despite Republican efforts to becloud the issue of ratification of the treaty.

the party had no man big enough to follow Woodrow Wilson, Glass went to the White House to get final instructions.[7]

Sipping noonday tea on the portico with the senator, the President asked for an opinion of McAdoo's intentions.

"He says nowhere that he would not accept a nomination," Glass observed.

"No, he does not," Wilson responded with quick emphasis.

Discussing other candidates, the President remarked that the choice of Palmer would be "futile"; and when the name of the governor of Ohio was mentioned, the President broke in with: "Oh, you know Cox's nomination would be a joke!" The possibility of victory seemed to him to depend on the choice of his son-in-law or himself; and "dear Mac" lacked qualities that the Presidency demanded.

While the politicians were plying their trade, those who cared for Wilson undertook to save their patient from the consequences of his erring judgment. On Sunday, June 13, Dr. Grayson went to see Robert W. Woolley, who was to attend the San Francisco convention. The physician insisted that the President "just must not be nominated." Grayson said: "He still believes that it is possible to persuade the country to join the League without the Lodge reservations and he says that he would gladly resign when that has beeen accomplished. He couldn't survive the campaign. He is permanently incapacitated and gradually weakening mentally. At times by sheer grit he pulls himself together, keeps himself in good spirits for a week or ten days, transacts business through Tumulty, and even seems to improve. Then he slumps and turns so morose that it distresses me to be near him. We must take no chances at San Francisco."[8]

Woolley and Grayson agreed that Glass could be trusted to block any effort that might be made to prolong Wilson's suffering in public office; and the doctor put his case before Glass and got assurance that the convention would not nominate a man so disabled. But the old party

[7] Wilson had urged Glass to accept the chairmanship of the resolutions committee at the nominating convention, and had approved a platform that had been drafted by Glass for Virginia. "I have perfect confidence in Homer Cummings and Glass," Wilson wrote to Secretary Baker on June 11, 1920. Wilson asked Glass his opinion about the advisability of modifying the Volstead Act (he already had given to Cummings a platform plank that would permit the sale of light wines and beer), and the senator suggested that any effort in this direction would be interpreted as an attempt to modify the Prohibition Amendment in the interest of the brewers. "Maybe that is so," Wilson replied, dismissing the subject. Then he gave Glass an initialed paper advocating the assumption by the United States of a mandate for Armenia, and he asked the senator to get it into the platform. Glass Diary, June 1920, Glass Papers (Alderman Library, University of Virginia). "I have set my heart on seeing this Government accept the mandate for Armenia," Wilson had written on April 19 to Cleveland Dodge, who had missionary interests in that country.

[8] Woolley Papers, and Woolley to the writer.

regulars distrusted Secretary of State Colby, who had been made a delegate from the District of Columbia and whom Wilson favored for the permanent chairmanship of the convention.

Arriving at San Francisco, Glass found the city bowing down before pictures of Woodrow Wilson. Hucksters waved Wilson souvenirs in his face. The President's name flared in electric lights. Clubs paraded and yelled for the Chief. In the auditorium a huge American flag was lifted to reveal a portrait of Woodrow Wilson, and marching delegates stampeded in acclamation. Only the New York standard remained in its place—until a handsome young man leapt from his seat with a yell and, after a scuffle, seized the banner and carried it into the parade with the same precipitancy that he was to show as the next Democratic President of the United States.

The demonstration was one of admiration, however, rather than a stampede for a third term; for the nucleus of leaders who were loyal to their chief felt that they could best serve him by denying him the nomination.

When coded dispatches began to come from Cummings at San Francisco, Wilson showed them to no one. Sitting on the veranda, he deciphered them himself in his own shorthand. When Colby wired on July 2 that, "unless otherwise definitely instructed," he would move Wilson's nomination by acclamation, word was conveyed to Colby by telephone from the White House that his plan was not unacceptable to the President.

Wilson's friends at the convention were thrown into dismay by Colby's intention.[9] Called together by Cummings, they conferred for hours. They were indignant at Colby and told him that he was being cruel to their beloved chief. Glass, swearing that he would rather vote for Woodrow Wilson than for any other man alive, felt that his nomination would ruin both the man and his party; and the others agreed that the idea was fantastic. Therefore they forced Colby to explain in a telegram sent to the White House on July 4, that it was the belief of all their friends that the lines of existing candidacies were drawn very tight and that were Wilson's name put before the convention it

[9] Burleson, who at first had not considered renomination impossible, had been sounding out the delegates and had found nine-tenths of them in sympathy with Wilson and desirous of choosing him were it not for a fear that the stress of a campaign would kill him; and when he learned of the call to Colby, he wired the President that his friends were watching events closely and would act in his behalf if an opportune moment came. He was not given that opportunity, however; for Wilson, resenting the fact that Burleson had telephoned to the White House from San Francisco to try to get the President's support for McAdoo, directed Cummings to exclude the postmaster general from the inner councils at the convention. Wilson's wrath led him to consider dismissing Burleson, but Tumulty dissuaded him from thus chastising so loyal and devoted a servant. Burleson to W.W., June 3, 1920; W.W. to Cummings, June 4, 1920; Kerney, op. cit., pp. 456–57. Woolley and Swem to the writer.

would not command the votes sufficient to nominate and might draw a response that would be disappointing and injuriously affect the party's position in the coming campaign. Colby concluded his message with a request for a statement from Wilson to Cummings, that would ask for a course that the conferees might agree upon as "practicable and judicious." On the next day the President did as requested, using some of the very phrases that had been suggested to him.

When the ballots were cast at the convention, Woodrow Wilson was recognized on only one—by two complimentary votes. Governor James M. Cox of Ohio finally was nominated, and the vice-presidential nomination went to the young warrior who had flung out the banner of New York State—Franklin D. Roosevelt.

The decision of the party did not please its proud leader. He found it hard to understand the motives of his lieutenants, for no one had told him of the precariousness of his hold upon life. He felt, however, that Cummings and Glass were loyal to him and devoted to his cause, for these men had seen to it that the party platform advocated Wilson's treaty. Therefore he accepted their judgment.

The President was sympathetic when Cummings came to him and complained that by appointing a national chairman from Ohio, Cox was "yielding to pressure" and bringing ward politics into national affairs. "It is a terrible mistake," replied Wilson. "If Governor Cox ever gets to be President and continues that course of conduct, temporizing with situations, his administration will be a failure and will end in a guffaw very much like the administration of Mr. Taft." As for himself, he confessed: "I would rather be hated than be the object of derision." So long as he could convince himself that, in the view of his God and of human history, he was right, so long as he had disciples who would share his vision of politics as a crusade rather than a means of livelihood, he could sustain his self-respect against the attacks of those who derided him.

At the end of July his health was the best since the thrombosis. One day he swapped golf yarns with Cummings, and then, commenting on the election, asserted that Harding could be easily destroyed. Still able to turn an inspiriting phrase, he said: "We must fight with lightning and not with thunder."

The prophet was still too ill, however, to campaign actively. He showed no heart for the fray and gave little help.[10] He excused himself,

---

[10] Wilson wrote to Tumulty late in September: "No answers to Harding of any kind will proceed from the White House with my consent." Undated note reproduced in Tumulty, *op. cit.,* p. 497. "Of course I will help," Wilson replied to one of Tumulty's pleas. "I was under the impression that I was helping. But I will do it at my own time and in my own way." Facsimile in *ibid.,* p. 503.

in a letter to Edward Bok, by explaining that he had "no intention whatever of qualifying as a Mr. Butt-in-sky." And yet he continued to hope that his people would perceive, better than their shortsighted senators, the inevitability of a world order and the opportunity of the United States to lead in establishing it. He acceded to arrangements for a visit from Cox, and sent the nominee away inspired to crusade for the League of Nations.[11]

Henry Cabot Lodge, however, had made it clear to the Republican nominating convention that in his view Wilson was whipped and his League beaten. After a battle between the isolationists and the internationalists of the party, a compromise plank was adopted. An agile straddle was maintained by the Republican candidate, Warren G. Harding, who had endeared himself to reactionaries by saying at Boston in May: "America's present need is not heroics but healing; not nostrums but normalcy; not revolution but restoration . . . not surgery but serenity." The Republicans made the most of the offenses that the President had given to partisan interests in his concern for the common welfare.

The pattern of political failure that had been unfolding since November of 1918 was in full view. As Wilsonian ideals went into eclipse in that tragic autumn, few believers dared to move boldly against the tide.

In October, Wilson broke his own silence. On the third of the month he released a paper asserting that the election was to be a genuine national referendum. A week before election day he roused himself to make the first formal talk that he had delivered for more than a year. Sitting in his wheel chair, he addressed fifteen pro-League Republicans. "The Nation was never called upon to make a more solemn determination than it must now make," he insisted. "The whole future moral force of right in the world depends upon the United States rather than upon any other nation, and it would be pitiful, indeed, if, after so many great free peoples had entered the League, we should hold aloof. I suggest that the candidacy of every candidate for whatever office be tested by this question: 'Shall we, or shall we not, redeem the great moral obligation of the United States?' "

Right up until the votes were counted, the prophet did not lose faith. "You need not worry," he said to his Cabinet on election day. "The American people will not turn Cox down and elect Harding. A great

---

11 Cox and F. D. Roosevelt went to the White House and found the "old man" very weak, and wearing a shawl over his left shoulder. They spoke of the extreme heat of the day, but Wilson assured Cox that the White House would be a comfortable place to live. With tears welling up, Cox said: "We are going to be a million percent with you and with your administration, and that means the League of Nations." And the invalid replied in a voice scarcely audible: "I am very grateful." Going directly to Tumulty's office, the nominee sat down, asked for paper, and drafted a statement that made the League the paramount issue of his campaign. Cox, *Journey through the Years,* p. 24.

moral issue is involved. The people can and will see it. In the long run, they do the right thing." He would not listen when Houston and Daniels tried to prepare him for the defeat of Cox.

While many Democrats were too apathetic to go to the polls, a landslide of hostile votes completed the burial of their party that had begun two years earlier. The leader who prided himself on mutual understanding with his people now knew the whole devastating truth. It was not only his partisan adversaries who were blocking the purposes that he held sacred. The people themselves had failed him. The ministerial bonds that he had woven were broken, and he was isolated. Driving through the streets of Washington, he saw in the faces of staring bystanders not faith but mere curiosity. His eyes showed his anguish and he groaned: "If only I were not helpless." Sitting almost alone in the middle of the great ballroom of the White House, he watched a moving picture of his triumph in France: the *George Washington* sailing majestically into Brest, and he on the bridge, erect, radiant, waving his hat; the Arc de Triomphe and Napoleon's Tomb, and the Presidents of France and the United States riding through a sea of idolizing mortals. Woodrow Wilson took in the re-creation of his past glory, sitting in the darkness of the big room, his head bowed, motionless and silent. He was no longer a hero who rode on winged steeds and magic carpets, but an old man who shuffled along floors from which rugs were removed for fear that he might slip on them, a cripple who tried daily to climb three or four low steps—and failed.

Stockton Axson went to the White House expecting to find the President prostrated by disappointment. But when he saw him, on the portico, Wilson's color was good and his face serene, save for pathetic little spasms at the corner of his mouth, as if he were pressing back grief. The day had come that he had foreseen in the heyday of reform, when he had prophesied to Axson that, once his step slipped, the Philistines would run over his prostrate form like cattle over a fallen steer. Indomitable spirit still shone in his large eyes and animated his handshake and his wit. Stifling his disappointment at being denied the privilege of leading his people across the River Jordan, he spoke compassionately of a nation temporarily misled in "a period of very great trial." The people's search for what is right could be depended upon, ultimately, to find the truth; and that was more than he could say for "so-called intellectuals" who were activated by prejudices and selfishness.

The day after the election he was able to laugh and tell stories. He took comfort in an anecdote about a man who had lost a donkey and was heard to repeat "Thank the Lord! Thank the Lord!" Asked why he was showing gratitude, the man replied: "I thank the Lord that I was not on him because I would have been lost too."

Never before had loyal and generous friends meant so much to Woodrow Wilson. Now that he was going out of office, his true disciples could open their hearts to him without rousing suspicions of sycophancy. They deluged him with messages of consolation, and assurance that, because of the equivocal position of the Republicans on the League, the voters truly knew not what they did. Actually the election had proved to be not the great national referendum on League membership that the President had desired, but merely a vote for a change.

Wilson responded in good spirit and wrote to Cox in appreciation of the fight that he had waged. Perhaps he had gone too fast, had given the people more than they could digest in eight years. Possibly they would have to have an awakening more horrible than that given to them by World War I.

A week after the election, and a few days before the Assembly of the League of Nations held its first meeting at Geneva without the participation of the United States, Wilson seemed stronger; but he looked worried and expressed grave concern for the future of the nation and the world.

During his last weeks in office his concern was to further as many constructive measures as a hostile Congress would permit, and not to embarrass his successor. Immediately after the election, Wilson summoned up courage to come to grips with the ticklish problem of European debts to the United States. Lloyd George had written on August 5 to urge that the United States be represented at conferences on European affairs by men of real authority and that America take part if a conference could be arranged with Russia. Specifically, the prime minister pointed out that France would not consent to fixing a definite and reasonable reparations burden on Germany unless she in turn could be granted relief from her heavy indebtedness to Great Britain; and furthermore, Britain could not afford to remit any of France's debt "except as part and parcel of all-around settlement of inter-Allied indebtedness."

Consulting Secretary Houston and getting from him a draft of an answer, Wilson replied on November 3 at great length. "It is not easy to understand," he wrote, "why wars, which arouse such high aspirations and require such willing and great sacrifices, should be followed by a lowering of ideals . . . As to Russia, I cannot but feel that Bolshevism would have burned out long ago if let alone, and that no practicable and permanent settlement involving Russian territory and rights can be arrived at until the great Russian people can express themselves through a recognized government of their own choice. . . ."

The President pointed out that the United States Treasury had been authorized to arrange a long-term funding of the demand obligations of the British government and to grant a postponement of interest payments. No one had been empowered by Congress, however, to remit or cancel any part of the demand obligations of the Allied governments to the United States. It was "highly improbable," he wrote, that either Congress or popular opinion would permit this.

Nevertheless, the President was willing to draw on the surplus wealth of his people to aid the weak and needy of the world. On February 28, 1921, he sent to Glass an eloquent appeal for an appropriation of funds for relief. To prevent "moral and material chaos," he wanted to have a small part of the nation's exportable surplus of food made available on credit. He still wished that the United States might serve as elder brother to peoples needing guidance in democratic government, as she had served in the Philippines.

The President urged Colby to go to South America to create ties of friendship, and in December the secretary of state undertook this mission. Moreover, the question of the recognition of Mexico was discussed with the Cabinet often and again. It seemed to Wilson "a matter full of doubts and 'ifs.' " [12] Though his policy of patience and faith was soon to be vindicated by the growth of a stable, indigenous government, the *de facto* regime of Obregón was not yet willing to negotiate a treaty that the Senate would approve; and so in this matter, as in many others, Woodrow Wilson was not able to share in the fruition of good seed that he had sown.

In preserving the purity of motive of his administration in its last days, the prophet sometimes had to contend with men who, too honest to take illegitimate fees while in government offices, had left his Cabinet to represent special interests. Thomas Gregory, ex-attorney general, wrote to him in behalf of oil men; and McAdoo was persistent in advancing the interests of clients. But Wilson now drew the line more

[12] W.W. to Colby, June 26, 1920. Pressed on the one hand by American and British financial interests and, on the other by George Creel, who claimed to have won Obregón's confidence and who in turn pleaded for Mexican rights and sensibilities, Wilson hesitated to follow the recommendation of the State Department that the embargo on shipments of arms into Mexico be lifted, and explained his views to Norman Davis in a letter of Nov. 23:

"Men like Doheny and others who are deeply involved in the oil intrigues have shown more and more recently their somewhat desperate anxiety to have this embargo lifted . . . We cannot be too careful not to serve these predatory interests, because they intend the demoralization of our own policies and the control of Mexican politics."

"Never was he more the master of his mental processes," Creel wrote in *Rebel at Large*, p. 228, of his talk with Wilson about Mexico in October of 1920.

finely than ever between the men who served the common good for love of serving and those who served a private interest for gain. He was more particular than ever about appointments, and more partisan. He continued to resist people who wished to pay personal debts by persuading him to sign certain executive orders. ("They would make the Government an eleemosynary institution," he once said of such tempters.) [13] He investigated recommendations for appointments to make sure that the candidates were untainted by legalism or by association with a political enemy.

In his final charges to Congress, also, Woodrow Wilson held true to his principles of earlier years. In the last annual message, which he dictated to Swem, the President pointed out that the government's expenditures for 1920 were less than the receipts and were at about one-third the wartime level of 1919. He pleaded for economy, for simplification of the tax laws, for adequate care of sick and disabled veterans of the armed forces, and for a grant of independence to the peoples of the Philippines. In the last days he vetoed a measure that would further postpone the effective date of an important provision of the Clayton Antitrust Act; and he refused to sign an emergency tariff bill that would set up barriers against the payment of European debts by a flow of goods.

As the winter wore on and the annual message to Congress and other responsibilities of state were put behind him, his prayers for greater vigor seemed to be answered. Giving up the invalid's chair, he came down for luncheon every day. He still used a cane—his "third leg," he called it—and found it a convenient excuse for not shaking hands with Senator Lodge when that antagonist came with a committee to notify him formally that Congress was in session.

He was thrilled to be recognized as a peacemaker by the award to him of the Nobel Peace Prize; and when his fellow prophet, General Smuts, published an article on "Woodrow Wilson's Place in History" and attributed the failure at Paris to "humanity" rather than to any man, the President wrote to the South African of his deep gratification: "I know of no one I have met whose good opinion I value more than I value yours."

The emotional bonds with the true disciples became taut in the last weeks of their association. Baker and Houston, in particular, marveled at the working of the invalid's mind in the meetings of the Cabinet. Though his speech was sometimes slow, and his left side almost immobile, he seemed to them to have a depth of perception beyond that of any of the little band of public servants. "The President finished strong,"

[13] Swem MS, p. 162, in the Princeton University Library.

Baker reported on March 17, 1921. "At the last Cabinet meeting he still showed that he saw more clearly and decided more impersonally than any of us or indeed all of us." And yet, when the business of the last meeting was over, Woodrow Wilson broke down and sobbed.

It was suggested that Secretary Colby call the Cabinet together so that they could discuss a suitable tribute; but Colby declined, reminding them that one secretary of state had been "bounced" for taking such a liberty. They decided therefore to sign a letter of appreciation:

March 3, 1921.

Mr. President:

The final moments of the Cabinet on Tuesday found us quite unable to express the poignant feelings with which we realized that the hour of leave-taking and official dispersal had arrived.

Will you permit us to say to you now, and as simply as we can, how great a place you occupy in our honor, love, and esteem?

We have seen you in times of momentous crisis. We have seen your uncomplaining toil under the heavy and unremitting burdens of the Presidency. We have had the inestimable privilege of sharing some of your labors. At all times you have been to us our ideal of a courageous, high-minded, modest gentleman, a patriotic public servant, an intense and passionate lover of your country.

You have displayed toward us a trust and confidence that has touched us all, supporting and defending us, when under partisan attack, with staunch and untiring loyalty, and placing at our command, always in the most considerate way, the wisdom of your counsel. History will acclaim your great qualities. We who have known you so intimately bear witness to them now.

We fervently wish you, dear Mr. President, long life and the happiness that you so richly deserve and have so abundantly earned.

On the morning after the final meeting of the Cabinet, Woodrow Wilson prepared to discharge the only public duty that lay between him and the freedom he had so long coveted. Putting on his cutaway and gray trousers, taking up his gloves and his high hat, he drank a stimulant to help him overcome his pain, grasped the blackthorn stick without which he could not walk, and went down to the Blue Room, where he exchanged courtesies with his successor. At the door of the White House he was helped into an automobile seat next to Harding and behind Senator Knox.

He had rejected suggestions that he use his infirmity as an excuse to escape the inauguration ceremonies. As the day had approached, his love of his country's institutions had triumphed over his distrust of his successor. When he had been urged to act in a way that would put Harding and the Republican party "in a hole" he had replied: "I do not wish to put Mr. Harding in a hole. The situation of the nation and the world is too serious . . . I should like to help Mr. Harding and I hope every good citizen will try to help him."

On Inauguration Day the presidential car moved slowly through crowds that disregarded the crumpled prophet and cheered the incarnation of "normalcy." At the Capitol, Harding mounted the long flight of steps in full view of the crowds, smiling and waving his hat, taking all the cheers. His crippled predecessor walked slowly to an elevator, his left shoulder drooping and his left arm hanging limp. When a friend extended a hand to him, Wilson was able to stand for a moment without other support. Reaching the President's room, he was relieved of his overcoat and sank into a chair. For just an instant he was nervous and fidgety; but grasping a pen firmly, he went about the business of signing bills passed during the last hours of Congress.

Finally, noting that the clock in the corner of the room was moving toward the hour of noon, he said, "Well, I think I had better scoot now." But before he could make good his escape he had one unpalatable duty to perform. A committee from the Houses of Congress appeared before him to give formal notice that their sessions were over. In the front row he recognized Henry Cabot Lodge—to him the personification of the forces of privilege and selfish interest that he had fought for two decades.

Woodrow Wilson's face froze in a way that suggested that he was struggling hard to control a demon within him. Looking his victorious archenemy straight in the eye, he said very clearly and frigidly: "I have no further communication. I would be glad if you would inform both houses and thank them for their courtesy—good morning, sir."

It was a distant "sir," uttered by one who seemed to be holding himself aloof from contamination.

After everyone but Wilson's immediate party had left the room, the old clock struck twelve and he ceased to be president. He struggled into his overcoat. Then, as the strains of "Hail to the Chief" came faintly from the inaugural ceremony, he walked to the elevator, his cane tapping the stone floor, his head downcast, his eyes steadfastly ahead.

He motored with Edith Wilson out Massachusetts Avenue to a house on S Street. When they passed the White House the prophet looked away and gazed inscrutably over the heads of strollers in Lafayette Park, self-control apparent in every gray feature. Told of this years later, one of his daughters remarked: "That was just like father; he never looked back."

CHAPTER XXI

Reconciliation

Had woodrow wilson been a man to look back upon his eight years in the White House, he might well have regarded his achievements with some complacency. Entering the Presidency with the same mental vigor that he had applied to the problems of Princeton and the state of New Jersey, he had pioneered a path around the pitfalls of plutocracy and mob rule and had effectively led a groping people toward political salvation. He had laid down a basic pattern for solving, without violence, those social and economic problems of the age that grew out of new ways of life. He had honored the principle that men's labor was not to be regarded as a commodity, had given impetus to collective bargaining, and had established the supremacy of the public interest above the advantage of any special combination of labor or capital or industrial management. His Federal Reserve policy gave promise of meeting the danger of recurring panic, and his tariff measures had helped to wean the nation from the pap of privilege. His administration had laid a foundation for a "welfare state" by providing for the matching of federal funds with those of the states to equalize certain facilities through the nation; new taxes had been levied to make this possible.

Moreover, Wilson had met, with firmness and patience, the threats to democracy and peace that had risen from Central Europe. He had restrained jingoes from resorting to war to further selfish purposes and satisfy partisan emotions, and he had restrained his people from fighting until the justness of their cause was clear enough to raise moral indignation to a crusading pitch. And in the great culminating ordeal of making a righteous peace he had advocated consistency with the philosophy that had sustained the war effort. To him, democracy had never ceased to be "a stage of development." He had succeeded in rallying free minds in many lands to support his moral purposes for humanity, until evangelical overconfidence and the psychological ravages of arteriosclerosis combined, as they had at Princeton, to bring him to temporal failure.

As he rode toward his new home on Inauguration Day of 1921, however, Woodrow Wilson was not given to casting up credits in the ledger of criticism. Asked at the last Cabinet meeting what he would do in retirement, he replied: "I am going to try to teach ex-presidents how to behave." He hoped that now, for the first time since the old days at Princeton, he could enjoy a home that satisfied his Scottish instincts.

In his years of devotion to public duty he had not adequately provided for himself. While he was at Paris, it had been necessary to borrow money to pay his income tax; and he had been generous to the White House staff. Four months before leaving the Presidency of the nation, however, Wilson had given way to a yearning for a dream house. Consulting an architect about plans for building on a site overlooking the Potomac, he wrote: "There are a good many 'ifs' in the case, the chief 'if' being if I have money enough." [1]

For several weeks the invalid had diverted himself by studying the plans, his instinct for architecture still as keen as it had been at Princeton. He read architectural journals and clipped pictures of lovely doorways and windows; and he considered practical details as well, even those having to do with the convenience of the servants. It became apparent, however, that funds were not available for building. When his wife expressed interest in a house on S Street, however, Wilson bought it with financial help from ten loyal friends, and surprised her by presenting the deed to her. A little later he performed the old Scottish ceremony of giving her a key and a piece of sod from the grounds.

Arriving at their new house on the morning of March 4, the Wilsons found the street below their front door crowded with cheering friends. Inside, everything had been done to make the transition smooth. An elevator was ready to take him to his third-floor bedroom, and he found there a duplicate of the Lincoln bed on which he had slept at the White House, and his old mahogany desk with secret drawers. He leaned on his cane at the threshold to marvel at the familiarity of the furnishings. He did not linger there long, however, for hundreds of citizens thronged the street in anticipation of a word from him. Twice he went to a window to greet them, but he choked up and could only wave and point apologetically to his throat.

In the days that followed, letters came in stacks from Americans who felt that, now that the bars of officialdom were let down, they could communicate directly with their hero. Some wanted only to help and to cheer him, others claimed a share of his time or sympathy or money. Hundreds of ex-soldiers asked for autographs from their old commander in chief, and they got them though other petitioners did not.

Though tears came too easily, Wilson could still smile at himself. In

[1] W.W. to P. M. Day, Oct. 11, 1920. Though Washington ranked lowest among five cities that the Wilsons carefully rated as possible residences, they decided not to go away from their physician, even in the summer.

his correspondence, as in his conversation, there were glimpses of the old-time force and brilliance. But for the most part his expression was perfunctory, and at times it was embittered and soured by disease.

Most of all he needed mental work that would be systematic but not too arduous. Mrs. Wilson had hoped that this would be supplied by a law practice that had been arranged before he left the White House. Bainbridge Colby had agreed to be his partner; and luxurious offices were opened in New York and Washington. His temperament was as ill suited to commercial practice, however, as it had been in his youth. He could not and would not seek private business, and went to the office only once. When dazzling fees were offered by corporations that hoped to use the former President's name to influence government action in ways that many officials thought legitimate, Wilson would not allow his partner to accept them. At the end of a year, he saw that he was a liability to Colby and agreed to end the venture.

He received proposals, also, that he exploit his literary talents for profit. While in office he had refused to allow his *History of the American People* to be used by the moving pictures, and he had declined an offer of thousands of dollars for a revision of this work.[2] And now he still shrank from using his public fame to swell his personal income. He was cold to proposals that he write reviews, prefaces, a column, a biography of Edmund Burke, and a life of Jesus.

"What I have done and stood for is of record," he wrote to Norman Davis in explanation of his reluctance to justify his deeds in print, "and any consequent interpretation or explanation that I might make would not affect the event, and would not be a contribution to history. So far as I am concerned, I have done the best I know how. My conscience is clear and clean. I am confident that what I have fought for and stood for is for the benefit of this nation and of mankind. If this is so, I believe that it ultimately will prevail, and if it is not, I don't want it to prevail." He was particularly determined that he should write nothing like Jefferson's *Anas*, that he should refrain from derogatory personal remarks in public prints.

Actually, Wilson explained to an editor, he had literary plans of his own that he had quite set his heart upon. He wanted absolute freedom to do his writing at the time and in the form that he chose. The one work for which he still had real enthusiasm was the colossal "Philosophy of Politics" that he had projected at Princeton. Just before leaving the White House he had told his wife that he soon would have leisure

[2] The offer was "not acceptable to the people of the country," he wrote to his publisher on Oct. 1, 1918. Nor did it excite him to be told that an autobiography might be made to "yield half a million." "As to my personal memoirs," he wrote to an inquiring agent, " 'there ain't going to be none,' if I may use the vernacular."

to carry through this venture. But here again he overestimated his powers. He wrote a brief, beautiful dedication of the book to his wife—and that was all. Even when he had been well he had confessed that he wrote "with difficulty," that the effort took "everything" out of him.

Though Wilson gave no heed to a publisher's offer of $150,000 for a record of his work at Paris, he was so impressed by a little book entitled *What Wilson Did at Paris* that he encouraged Ray Stannard Baker, its author, to undertake a longer work on the Peace Conference. In 1918 he had written to Professor Corwin of Princeton: "I have always had the feeling that an official 'Remembrancer' never could do the same work that a historian could do at a later time." But now he put trunkfuls of papers at the disposal of Baker and invited him to work in the new house. For this work Wilson released the minutes of the inner council at Paris, which he had been insistent upon keeping secret even from his successors in office; and thus he made it the more difficult for his European colleagues to understand him.

Baker found him propped up in bed by a pile of pillows, looking inconceivably old and brittle, his skin thin and parchment-yellow, drawn over his cheekbones in such a way as to thrust his nose into prominence. His eyes burned like glowing coals amid ashes. Flashlights were on the stand near him, and a book of detective stories and some chocolate; and near the head of his bed was a Bible that he read every day. There was a dignity of reconciliation about him as he shared his knowledge. Scholarly habit restrained him from surrendering to Baker's ardor, but one day he characterized the project as "the biggest work any American writer ever attempted."

By summer he was able to help Baker by deciphering notes that he had written in shorthand on the margins of the documents of the Peace Conference. Wearing a purple velvet jacket and keeping his helpless hand curled down and hidden by his side, he showed a more wholesome color and his voice was stronger. He had been told by Dr. Mayo that he might again use his crippled limbs if he would take certain exercises, and he went at them persistently every day.[3]

Though his daughters and Stockton Axson came often to the house on S Street, and Miss Ellie Lou's painting of the Madonna hung in the front room of the new residence, the glowing domesticity of the old days could not be re-created.

Woodrow Wilson wanted to be himself. He refused honorary memberships in fraternal organizations in which he had no genuine interest. It was his old, tried friends that he wanted to see. From his intimates

[3] F. W. McM. Woodrow to Mrs. James Woodrow, Dec. 20, 1921, letter in the possession of Mrs. Katharine Woodrow Kirkland.

came gifts large and small; and his acknowledgment of a brace of partridges or a book was as warm and gracious as that of a case of boot-leg whisky from a journalist or a Rolls-Royce that several men combined to present to him. Even strangers sent tokens of esteem of various and strange sorts.

Refusing to concede that there was such a thing as mental fatigue, he told his family that the more one used one's mind the more one *could* use it. But hard as he strove to master his misery with his mind, he found that mental exertion tired him easily. Most of his flagging mental strength was expended lightly—in playing games of solitaire of which he kept a running count, hearing readings of detective stories and the novels of Scott and Dickens, writing place cards for his wife's luncheons, enjoying vaudeville on Saturday nights at Keith's.

Off and on, however, the prophet brandished his old political torches. With Franklin D. Roosevelt he discussed plans for the use of a Wood-row Wilson Fund that friends were raising. He didn't want a "memo-rial," he said, because that would suggest that he was "a dead one." The development of the Woodrow Wilson Foundation, however, gave him satisfaction.

His worst fears seemed to be justified as his successor showed a will-ingness to put pleasure before duty. He denounced Harding to his friends as a miserable kind of politician and "a fool of a President," and his administration as stupid, faithless, and ill-principled—a dull regime that did not know "how to make anything happen." When a relative asked him what he thought of his successor, he made a noise far up his nose. He thanked God and took courage, he said, when the Democrats captured seventy-five seats in the House in the election of 1922.

Solicitous old friends kept in touch with him to prevent undignified utterances that might discredit the prophet and his party. Democracy had not yet been made an instrument of justice, the prophet told Homer Cummings. But of Karl Marx he said: "I know of no man who has more perverted the thinking of the world." Continuing to feel respon-sibility for the social and economic welfare of his people, Wilson wrote to Brandeis, Baruch, and others to solicit ideas for a party creed. He still feared revolution, and felt that the country looked to him for a constructive program that would avert violence.

Correlating the advice that he received, Wilson framed a platform. On April 9, 1922, he sent it to Brandeis—whom he still thought intel-lectually the most stimulating man that he knew—and a week later he invited the justice and several others to his home "to help round the matter out." He conceived that he was engaged, he wrote to Norman

Davis, "in concerting the measures and perfecting the means for emancipating the world by leadership on the part of this country and our party." During 1922 he was encouraged constantly to assume leadership in the next presidential campaign. On December 3 Carter Glass, reminded by Dr. Grayson that the excitement of a campaign would kill their friend, wrote in his diary: "Only the good sense of Mrs. Wilson saves the situation."

When Tumulty asked for a message that he might read at a Jefferson Day banquet in New York in April, 1922, the Chief replied that the time was not appropriate for the breaking of his silence. Nevertheless, Tumulty called at S Street and drew out some of Wilson's ideas without reference to the impending banquet; and the next day he gave out a brief statement over Wilson's name to the diners. A major address by James M. Cox followed, and the enthusiasm of the audience led the press to interpret the spurious message as an endorsement of Cox.

Actually Wilson thought the movement for Cox fatuous, even suicidal. Discovering Tumulty's equivocation, he flatly repudiated the words that his ex-secretary had put in his mouth, refusing a plea from Tumulty for mercy. He expected that his secretary would sulk for a few days, then come like a spanked child to ask forgiveness. But he did not come; and "the Governor," shortly before his death, gave to his devoted follower the solace of a recommendation for one of New Jersey's seats in the Senate.

In 1922, gaining in health, Wilson was stimulated by visits from men who had been his most intimate colleagues at Paris. Like himself, Clemenceau and Lloyd George had been thrust aside by their proud peoples after the crisis of war had passed; and the French leader had been pilloried for permitting the "autocratic Wilson" to bully him. When he came to the Wilson house, however, in December, the old Tiger was merry and genial. Scorning the elevator, he dashed upstairs to embrace the prophet whose gospel he had ridiculed at the Peace Conference. They forgave each other for their quarrels at Paris, tried to recapture the good moments of the past.

Lord Robert Cecil also was received at S Street, and it gave comfort to the old prophet to talk with this colleague, whom he regarded as the ablest Englishman of his acquaintance. They spoke of the ideals for humanity that were closest to his heart; and more than once he said, to encourage this idealist and the others who were keeping the faith alive through the dark days: "Remember we are winning: make no concessions." [4]

[4] Lord Cecil's speech to the Woodrow Wilson Foundation, Dec. 28, 1924; and Lord Cecil to the writer, Nov. 4, 1954.

Mercifully, there was no transatlantic radio to bring the voice of George Harvey, who, speaking as his country's ambassador at London less than three months after Wilson's retirement, asserted that the United States had gone to war solely to save itself and would never have anything to do with the League or its commissions, directly or indirectly, openly or furtively. Wilson was unaware that the German press was cursing his "poison fangs." He did not know that, because actual conditions had fallen far short of the hopes that he had encouraged, he was the most unpopular individual in the countries of Central Europe that he had saved from a peace of vengeance.

His faith in the inevitability of an association of nations never grew dim, and every step in that direction heartened him. A disarmament conference called by his successor cheered him somewhat. "The Conference seems to be doing some good at last," he wrote to Baruch, "though it is amazing to see the Republicans lead us into a group alliance after the European fashion."

He insisted that, had he not been stricken, he could have carried through the treaty. At times he derived comfort from the thought that American participation in the League should be complete to be effective, that if the nation had joined in 1920, it would have been only a personal victory for him and the misrepresentation of opponents would have prevented full allegiance on the part of the American people. Moreover, he philosophized, the aloofness of the United States had made Europeans more keenly aware of the need for a system of international cooperation. But philosophy was not enough. "If I had nothing but philosophy to comfort me, I should go mad," he said to Homer Cummings one day.

Once the boy Tommie Wilson had remarked that it was dreadful that Moses had not been permitted to enter the promised land; and his father's answer had been: "It was God's will and his work was done." Religion now gave secure refuge to the rejected American prophet. It taught him that statesmen were merely the very humblest instruments of a greater power. He thought that wells of popular thinking had been so poisoned that it might be thirty years before the people would see the truth; but he was sure that eventually it would be made clear to them, and when that day came it would be altogether right that they should enter an international organization. To hasten the day of revelation, he corresponded with private associations in England and the United States that were devoted to the cause of the League.

As the year 1923 wore on, it became clear to those about the old prophet that his days were numbered. To "Ike" Hoover, who was disconsolate because he had not been allowed to leave the White House and serve at the Wilson home, he said: "I am tired swimming upstream." When Lloyd George called, he found him badly warped in body and spirit.

He received callers slumped in a high-backed chair by the fireplace, his head set a little toward one side, a shawl over his shoulders. His face and body seemed heavier, and his wisps of hair were brushed straight back over a scalp almost bald. He did not move his head. Only his eyes followed his visitors. Sometimes he sat with his hands in his lap; and then as he talked in a feeble voice he would swing his right hand back and forth and occasionally strike the arm of the chair to emphasize an idea. One moment he would be the welcoming host—"You must excuse me for not rising; I'm really quite lame." And then he would turn crusader and say: "I've got to get well, and then I'm going out to get a few scalps." [5]

Not content to have had the whole world for a classroom, his thoughts went back to Princeton, and the old longing came again to realize his dream of the ideal university. He confided his vision to Raymond Fosdick. Higher education in the United States was at a crossroads, he said, and with strong progressive leadership might yet attain the standards of Oxford and Cambridge. He had made a start in Princeton, and now he wished to find an institution at which he might continue the reformation. In his view, beloved Princeton had been bought once, was probably "for sale again." "The sands are running fast," he said. "You must get your friends to provide me the opportunity." Tears rolled down his face as he begged for another chance to serve.

Begged by Mrs. Wilson to humor her husband, Fosdick discussed the matter with his colleagues of the General Education Board and they concluded that they had no power to appoint a president of any university. When he returned to S Street with this verdict, Wilson would not accept it as final.

There were other channels through which the failing prophet could leave a last testimony to posterity. His friends were reminding him that his people had not had a message from him for more than two years. Finally he brought his disordered thoughts to a focus. Neuritis prevented him from writing down his ideas, even on the typewriter; but as the sentences came to him, lying in bed, he rang for his wife and dictated them to her. Sometimes, at night, he could not sleep until he unburdened himself of a thought. Bringing the sentences and paragraphs into a semblance of order, he gave the paper to an agent, but then refused to permit publication in a magazine that he thought not appropriate. Actually, the article did not do justice to its author, and Edith

[5] F. L. Allen, *Only Yesterday*, p. 39; Wm. Phillips, *op. cit.*, p. 97.

Wilson gave him this critical verdict as they rode through the park with Professor Stockton Axson one afternoon.

"They kept after me to do this thing, and I did it," the invalid replied petulantly. "I have done all I can. I don't want these people bothering me any more."

When they reached home, Edith Wilson's fortitude gave way. Sobbing, she said to Axson: "I just want to help and I don't know how."

Asking for the script, Axson took out two or three paragraphs, made a transition, and gave the paper to Wilson with the remark that it was a challenge rather than an argument and should be allowed to stand as such.

"You see exactly the point," the invalid told his old comrade.

Sent to the *Atlantic Monthly*, the paper was published in August, 1923, under the title "The Road Away from Revolution." Warning against the sort of social system that had given rise to the Russian Revolution, Wilson wrote:

. . . We should not entertain a narrow or technical conception of justice. By justice the lawyer generally means the prompt, fair, and open application of impartial rules; but we call ours a Christian civilization, and a Christian conception of justice must be much higher . . .

The sum of the whole matter is this, that our civilization cannot survive materially unless it be redeemed spiritually. It can be saved only by becoming permeated with the spirit of Christ and being made free and happy by the practices which spring out of that spirit. Only thus can discontent be driven out and all the shadows lifted from the road ahead.

The prophet's people, ignorant of the pains that had gone into the composition of this article, welcomed it as a sign of recovery. But those who were closest to him knew better. Edith Wilson, returning in September from a visit to Cape Cod, saw a distinct change for the worse. Her dear one seemed to have slumped into an abyss of depression. To cheer him, Baruch's daughter Belle arranged that he speak over the radio. He agreed to do this, but the writing of a talk on "The High Significance of Armistice Day" was agony. Somehow his will wrenched a few paragraphs out of his ebbing reservoir of vitality, and on the evening of the appointed day he left his bedroom in dressing gown and slippers and went down to the library to confront a microphone.

It was too late now to employ the new invention to save the League, but the prophet did his best. Even though denied the direct intercourse with an audience that was the breath of life to him, he resolved to put his whole self into his effort. He insisted on standing up before the microphone, though one hand grasped his cane and he had trouble in handling the manuscript, which he was determined to hold himself. A blinding headache made the words blur, and his wife stood behind him with a copy of the script, ready to prompt him. When it was over he was sure that he had failed in his first public audition; and he went to bed depressed and spent a restless night.

The next morning, however, he learned that the public had heard him and had listened, that he had spoken to the largest audience ever reached at one time by a human voice. Buoyed by this news, he summoned his forces to make his way on swollen feet to the front porch, where an Armistice Day crowd of thousands had gathered. Casualties of the war—the armless, the legless, and the sightless—faced their crippled leader and drew his tears. His voice was husky and broken when it was his turn to speak. He was barely able to tell of his pride in being commander in chief "of the most ideal army that was ever thrown together," and to pass the laurels of victory to General Pershing.

Halting for breath, he whispered, "I can't go on." He started to hobble into the house, leaning on a servant, and the band broke into "How Firm a Foundation." Then, just inside the door, the old prophet turned and whispered to a Princeton disciple who put an ear close to his mouth: "Stop the band. I have something to say."

Struggling back to the steps, he began falteringly upon his last public challenge: "I am not one of those who have the least anxiety about the triumph of the principles I have stood for. I have seen fools resist Providence before, and I have seen their destruction, as will come upon these again, utter destruction and contempt." The fire came back to his eyes and the resonance to his voice as he concluded: "That we shall prevail is as sure as that God reigns."

The response to his Armistice Day efforts lifted the ego of the failing prophet. With the rise in his spirits his health improved. Wrapped in a blanket, he could sit out on an upper sun porch and chat with visitors. His mind was flashing brightly upon the hates and loves that were deeply ingrained. "His master's voice has spoken," he said of President Coolidge's message to Congress. He insisted that, in a desire to get their income taxes reduced, the Democrats must not surrender to the "pocketbook brigade."

He still fancied himself the leader who must set the moral tone of his party. When it was suggested to him late in 1923 that he might champion his ideals effectively by running for a New Jersey seat in the Senate, his thought seemed to veer rather toward a return to the Presidency. His intimates knew that he persisted in hoping that the nominating convention of 1924 might seek his leadership. In January he was collaborating with Newton D. Baker on a platform; and on the 16th

he asked Chairman Cordell Hull to bring the members of the Democratic National Committee to call on him. His feeble body was crumpled
in an armchair but his haggard face smiled recognition as he shook
hands with each.

When the McAdoos visited, he asked his wife not to leave him alone
with his son-in-law, for fear that he might be asked for an endorsement
for the presidential nomination in 1924. He had thought of declaring
publicly that McAdoo was not the man to lead the party, but memories
of Miss Ellie Lou restrained him. He could not bear to wound the husband of their daughter Nell. It comforted him to have this girl of his at
his bedside, to share recollections of the good days of family life—the
picnics, and Ellen Wilson painting, or reading poetry under the pines.
"I owe everything to your mother," he said tenderly one day.

He sensed that the end was not far distant; but he was still keen in
mind. When a guest asked about his health, he quoted a predecessor in
the Presidency: "John Quincy Adams is all right, but the house he lives
in is dilapidated, and it looks as if he would soon have to move out."
His thoughts ran back to 1914, and to the utter stupidity and waste of
international war as a way of settling anything. "It must never happen
again," he said. "There is a way of escape if only men will use it." Indignant at those who objected to the "idealism" of the League of Nations,
he exclaimed: "The world is *run* by ideals. Only the fool thinks otherwise." The new organization was America's great contribution to the
race, and already it had proved its worth, he said. It had handled various
disputes, had established itself as a clearinghouse of information, and
had worked for humanitarian causes. "They are learning teamwork at
Geneva," he said. "If only they will give the seed a fair chance, and let
it grow!" His guest went out haunted by a tear-stained face, an indomitable jaw, and a faintly whispered "God bless you!"

During this last month Wilson gave his blessing to a biographer—
Ray Stannard Baker—and granted access to his papers. In discussing the
work he stressed the importance of emphasizing principles and shrank
from the idea of "making too much of a single man." He was solicitous
chiefly for the immortality of his ideals. Mere men did not matter.

As his strength ebbed, the prophet drew nearer to the God of his
youth. His father and uncle still commanded his veneration. However,
the twentieth-century leader of the clan harbored none of the Presbyterian prejudices that his father had once denounced as asinine. He could
jest about peculiarities of form and ritual: with an arm around his
Episcopalian wife he loved to repeat a Negro's criticism of the Episcopalian service: "Dey spends too much time in de readin' ob de minutes
ob de las' meetin'." Talking one day with Bishop Freeman, he said:

"The old enmities and antagonisms are rapidly disappearing, and we lay less emphasis upon denominational labels than we once did." He conceived that a national cathedral that the bishop was planning might become "the greatest spiritual force in the country."

His belief in the goodness of God and the essential nobility of man had weathered all his vicissitudes, and asserted itself as the end drew near. Sacred love and holy rage resigned themselves to the force by which they had been inspired. Listening to a reading of Thompson's *Hound of Heaven* on a Sunday evening, he took comfort in assurance of the omnipresence of God and the futility of human efforts at escape.

Toward the end of January, Edith Wilson was kept from his room for five days by a high fever, and he made his way to her door to express his devotion. But when Dr. Grayson went on vacation, his concern for himself got the better of him for just a moment. When his wife started to cancel the doctor's vacation, however, he caught himself and reasserted the creed that he had preached all his life. "No," he said to her, "that would be a selfish thing on my part. He is not well himself and needs the change." And then slowly: "It won't be very much longer, and I had hoped he would not desert me; but that I should not say, even to you."

He failed alarmingly on January 28, and they telegraphed Grayson to return. The physician took up a desperate bedside vigil that lasted for three days, while the street outside was closed to traffic, so that members of his national congregation could gather and pray for the departing spirit. They remained there through the winter days and chilly nights, some of them kneeling, while the tortured body suffered its last agonies.

On the last day of the month he was better, and they expected him to recover. But on Sunday, February 3, he moved his lips and whispered: "I am ready." His suffering ended, as church bells summoned the people to worship.

Five minutes after he had drawn his last breath, Dr. Grayson appeared on the steps before the crowd of mourners. He read a bulletin in a voice that trembled but did not break. Many could not hear him, but when he wiped tears from his face they understood. Soon reporters were racing down the street to telegraph the news and church services were interrupted by announcements of the prophet's passing. A little boy climbed the steps, rang the bell, and gave a red rose to the servant who answered. A young woman, humbly dressed, handed in a single white lily as her tribute to a force that defied death. A big black limousine rolled up, and President Coolidge left a card that testified to the respect of the nation. Old friends and colleagues flocked to the scene, and Grayson greeted them with downcast eyes.

Those who were invited came again three days later to the funeral service in the house on S Street, where Wilson's body lay in front of the fireplace in the drawing room; but two who had served him most intimately were not present. Tumulty plodded in the cortege on foot; and House, informed that no reservation had been made for him and thinking that it might be embarrassing if he were to go to Washington uninvited, stood in the rain in New York and heard the memorial service broadcast through a loud-speaker.

At the service in the house, the bishop of the cathedral intoned the last verses that the prophet had read from a book that he kept by his bed: "The eternal God is thy refuge, and underneath are the everlasting arms: and he shall thrust out the enemy from before thee; and shall say, Destroy them."

Feeling that the growth of the national cemetery at Arlington had offended the dignity of the estate of the Lees of Virginia, Wilson had asked not to be interred there. And they did not lay him to rest beside Ellen Wilson deep in the Old South, in the plot on Myrtle Hill that he had once asked to have prepared for him. Instead, they carried his body to an elevation above the capital city, and buried him in a crypt beneath a chapel small and exquisite. Above him, the walls of a National Cathedral were rising. Woodrow Wilson was to serve to support, even in death, the realization of sublime visions.

Great universities are acting on Woodrow Wilson's concept of preceptorial teaching and democratic living in residential colleges, citizens intent on good government pursue his ideals, timbers of law with which he bulwarked American society against eroding currents are still sound after dire stresses, and the nations of the world have come closer to his envisioned parliament of man.

Jan Christian Smuts thought that at Paris the people had failed their prophets. But Woodrow Wilson took a more compassionate view. The people were not ready, he said, and perhaps they were right in thinking that the hour had not come.

Yet he never doubted that it would come. On a fragment of paper, unsigned and undated, the biographer finds written in the firm, familiar hand this favorite verse from Habakkuk:

The vision is yet for an appointed time, but at the end it shall speak, and not lie: though it tarry, wait for it; because it will surely come, it will not tarry.

It is upon the validity of this faith that the measure of Woodrow Wilson's greatness depends.

A NOTE ON SOURCES

The research on which this work is based, extending over a period of ten years, has taken account of all important sources that have been opened up to the moment of going to press. The Wilson and Baker collections in the Library of Congress have been studied with care, and also the papers relating to Wilson in the libraries of Princeton, Yale, and other universities.

In general, sources familiar to earlier biographers have not been cited in the footnotes. But reference has been made to important fresh sources.

Particular attention has been given to the documents that have come to light since Baker published the last volume of his incomplete work in 1939. New material has been found principally in the following repositories:

The Library of Congress. Some 18,000 pieces have been added to the Wilson Collection itself, and there have been many acquisitions of collateral papers. These, as well as the earlier accessions, have been described by Katharine E. Brand in the leading article in the *L. C. Quarterly Journal of Current Acquisitions* for February, 1956. In addition, certain papers of Edith Bolling Wilson have been acquired in 1957.

The Princeton University Library. Acquisitions pertaining to Wilson that have been made since 1945 have been described by their curator, Alexander P. Clark, in *The Princeton University Library Chronicle* (Spring, 1956), pp. 173-84. Attention has been given also to the earlier Wilson materials reviewed by Henry W. Bragdon in the *Chronicle* for November, 1945. The records of Charles L. Swem were used, and also transcripts from letters written at the Paris Peace Conference by Gilbert F. Close. Most of these important documents from Wilson's personal stenographer and secretary came to the Princeton library in the spring of 1957.

The Yale University Library. In the House Collection: the diary of Edward M. House, filling some 3,000 pages of typescript; also the correspondence of House, notably that with Wilson, Walter Hines Page, James W. Gerard, W. H. Buckler, and the principal political leaders of the United States and Europe; also the papers of Gordon Auchincloss, Sir William Wiseman, Frank L. Polk, William C. Bullitt, and George W. Watt.

The Harvard College Library. In the Houghton Library: Wilson's correspondence with Frederick J. Turner, and the papers of Joseph C. Grew, David F. Houston, Walter Hines Page, and Oswald Garrison Villard.

The Columbia University Library. Several manuscript records deposited in the Oral History Project by important men of the Wilson period.

The New Jersey State Library. Twelve boxes of Wilson's correspondence of the period of the New Jersey governorship.

Pertinent new material has been found also in the libraries of the University of Virginia, The Johns Hopkins University, The Massachusetts Historical Society, and The Woodrow Wilson Foundation, and in the Roosevelt Library at Hyde Park.

Certain letters of Wilson to Ellen Axson Wilson that are not otherwise available have been read or shown to the author by Eleanor Wilson McAdoo. His letters to Edith Bolling Wilson are not accessible.

Many of the witnesses who have been interviewed by the author (*see* Acknowledgments, Vol. I) have contributed valuable documents. In some cases these papers are still in their own hands and have been examined with their generous permission. Notable examples are a manuscript by Arthur Hugh Frazier, entitled "Recollections of President Wilson at the Peace Conference"; letters written by Raymond B. Fosdick from the *George Washington* and from Paris in December of 1919; notes by Arthur Sweetser of news interviews at the Paris Peace Conference (February–March, 1919); the diary of Thomas W. Brahany, clerk in the executive offices, covering days in the months of March and April, 1917; the diary of Mrs. C. S. Hamlin, in the possession of Mrs. Hamlin; a manuscript by Benjamin Chambers, Princeton 1909, which was based on contemporary notes and is in the possession of Cleveland E. Dodge; and letters in the possession of Margaret Callaway Axson, Katharine Woodrow Kirkland, Philena Fine Locke, and Edith Gittings Reid.

Extensive collections of printed sources are available at the Princeton University Library and the Woodrow Wilson Foundation. They include many of the voluminous writings of Wilson himself, which have been catalogued by Laura S. Turnbull in *Woodrow Wilson Bibliography* (Princeton, 1948); and also the "Books in the Wilson Field" that are listed by Miss Brand on pages 144 ff. of that volume.

Books and articles of the last decade that have contributed much to an understanding of certain aspects of Wilson are:

Em Bowles Alsop (ed.). *The Greatness of Woodrow Wilson.* N. Y., 1956.
Bernard M. Baruch. *Baruch, My Own Story.* New York, 1957.
Louis Brownlow. *A Passion for Politics,* Chicago, 1955.
——. *A Passion for Anonymity.* In press.
Edward H. Buehrig. *Woodrow Wilson and the Balance of Power.* Bloomington, Ind., 1955.
—— (ed.). *Woodrow Wilson's Foreign Policy in Today's Perspective.* Bloomington, Ind., 1957.
John M. Blum. *Joe Tumulty and the Wilson Era.* Boston, 1951.
Centenaire Woodrow Wilson. Geneva, 1956.
Margaret L. Coit. *Mr. Baruch.* Boston, 1957.

Jonathan Daniels. *The End of Innocence*. Philadelphia, 1954.

Josephus Daniels. *The Wilson Era* (2 vols.). New York, 1946.

John W. Davidson, Jr. *A Crossroads of Freedom*. New Haven, 1956.

Vincent L. Eaton. "Books and Memorabilia of Woodrow Wilson," *L. C. Quarterly Journal of Current Acquisitions*, November, 1946.

Russell H. Fifield. *Woodrow Wilson and the Far East*. New York, 1952.

Alexander L. George and Juliette L. George. *Woodrow Wilson and Colonel House*. New York, 1956.

John A. Garraty. *Henry Cabot Lodge, a Biography*. New York, 1953.

Louis L. Gerson. *Woodrow Wilson and the Rebirth of Poland*. New Haven, 1952.

Herbert Hoover. *Memoirs*. Vol. I. New York, 1951.

Edith Benham Helm. *The Captains and the Kings*. New York, 1954.

George F. Kennan. *Russia Leaves the War*. Princeton, 1956.

———. *The Decision to Intervene*. In press.

Lectures and Seminar at the University of Chicago January 30–February 3, 1956 in Celebration of the Centennial of Woodrow Wilson. Chicago, 1956.

McMillan Lewis. *Woodrow Wilson of Princeton*. Narberth, Pa., 1952.

Tien-yi Li. *Woodrow Wilson's China Policy, 1913–1917*. New York, 1952.

Arthur S. Link. *Wilson, The Road to the White House*. Princeton, 1947.

———. *Wilson, The New Freedom*. Princeton, 1956.

———. *Woodrow Wilson and the Progressive Era, 1910–1917*. N. Y.

Walter Lippmann. "Woodrow Wilson's Approach to Politics." *New Republic*, Dec. 5, 1955.

Paul Mantoux. *Les Délibérations du Conseil des Quatre*. 2 vols. Paris, 1955.

Alpheus T. Mason. *Brandeis, A Free Man's Life*. New York, 1946.

T. H. Vail Motter (ed.). *Leaders of Men* by Woodrow Wilson, with a preface. Princeton, 1952.

———. "Woodrow Wilson and the Power of Words," *The Princeton University Library Chronicle*, XVII, 3 (Spring, 1956), 163–72.

William S. Myers (ed.). *Woodrow Wilson, Some Princeton Memories*. Princeton, 1946.

George C. Osborn. "The Influence of Joseph Ruggles Wilson on His Son, Woodrow Wilson," *North Carolina Historical Review*, October, 1955.

Charles G. Osgood. "Woodrow Wilson," in *The Lives of Eighteen from Princeton*. Princeton, 1946.

Francis B. Sayre. *Glad Adventure*. New York, 1957.

The Virginia Quarterly Review, Wilson Centennial Number, Autumn, 1956.

Louis B. Wehle. *Hidden Threads of History*. New York, 1953.

Arthur Willert. *The Road to Safety*. New York, 1953.

The vast store of journalistic and monographic literature concerning Wilson and his times has been greatly enlarged by numerous articles and speeches that appeared in the centennial year of 1956. A collection of these is available in the library of the Woodrow Wilson Foundation.

INDEX